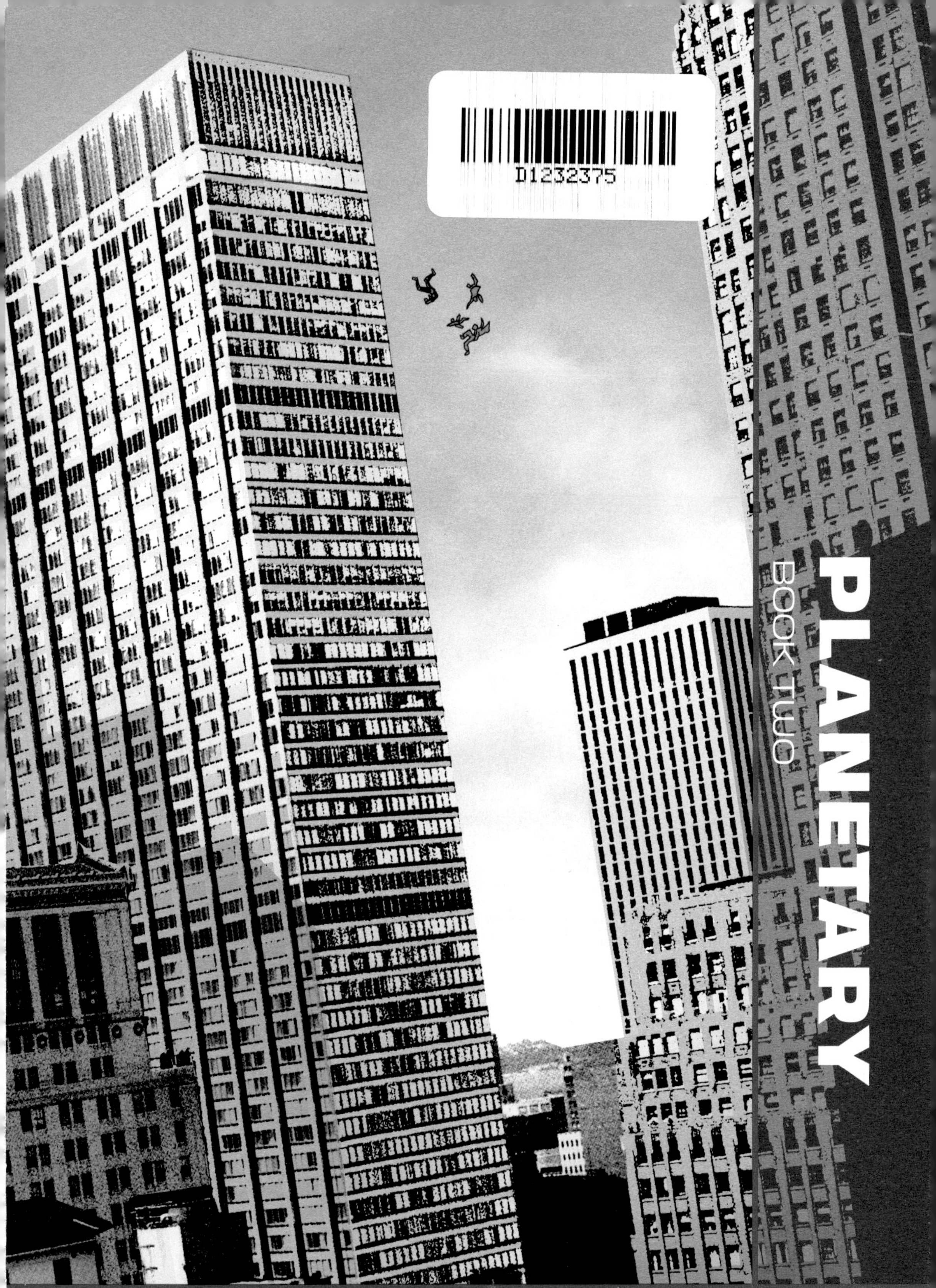
PLANETARY
BOOK TWO

WILDSTORM CLASSIC

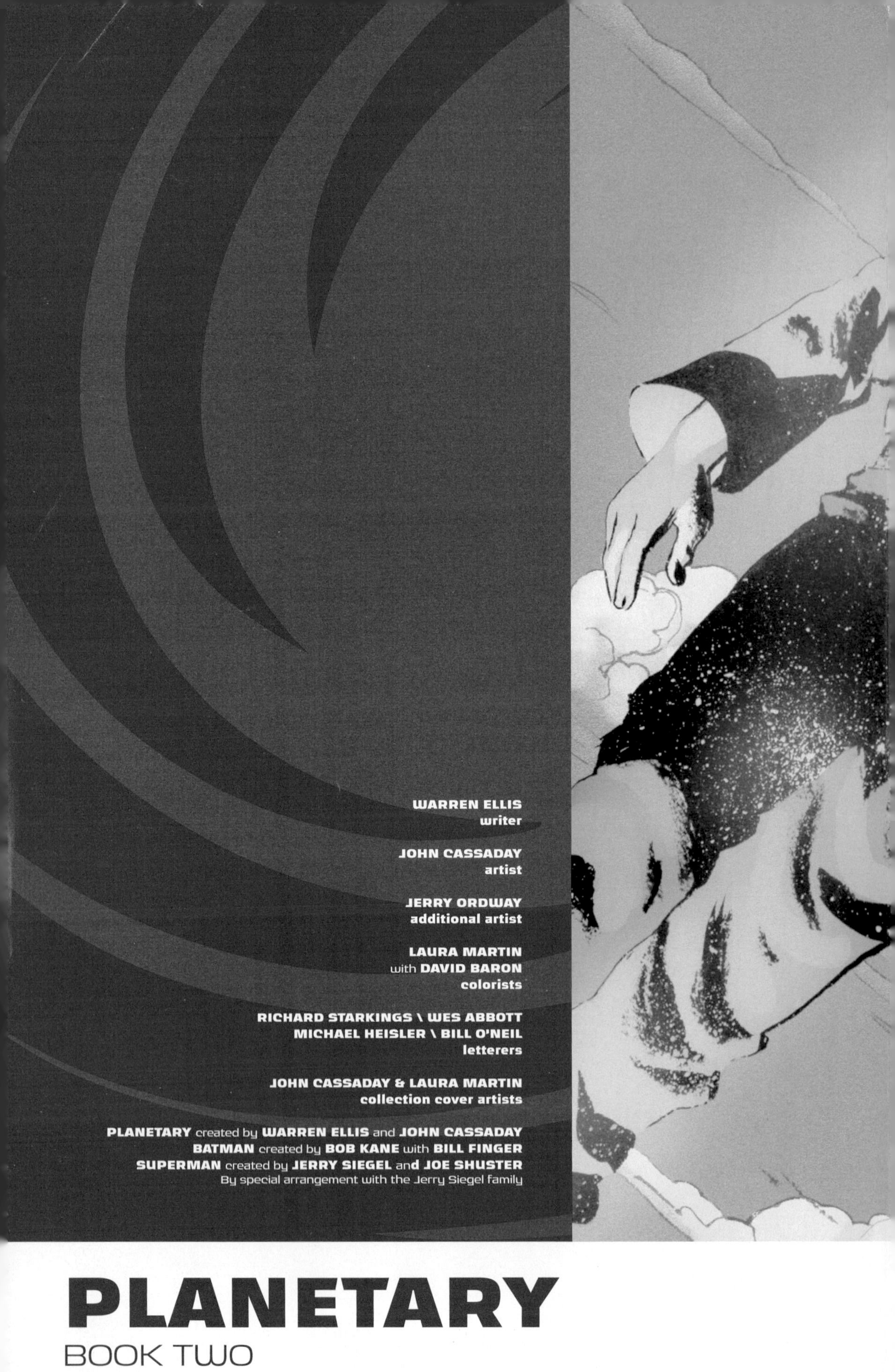

WARREN ELLIS
writer

JOHN CASSADAY
artist

JERRY ORDWAY
additional artist

LAURA MARTIN
with **DAVID BARON**
colorists

RICHARD STARKINGS \ WES ABBOTT
MICHAEL HEISLER \ BILL O'NEIL
letterers

JOHN CASSADAY & LAURA MARTIN
collection cover artists

PLANETARY created by **WARREN ELLIS** and **JOHN CASSADAY**
BATMAN created by **BOB KANE** with **BILL FINGER**
SUPERMAN created by **JERRY SIEGEL** and **JOE SHUSTER**
By special arrangement with the Jerry Siegel family

PLANETARY

BOOK TWO

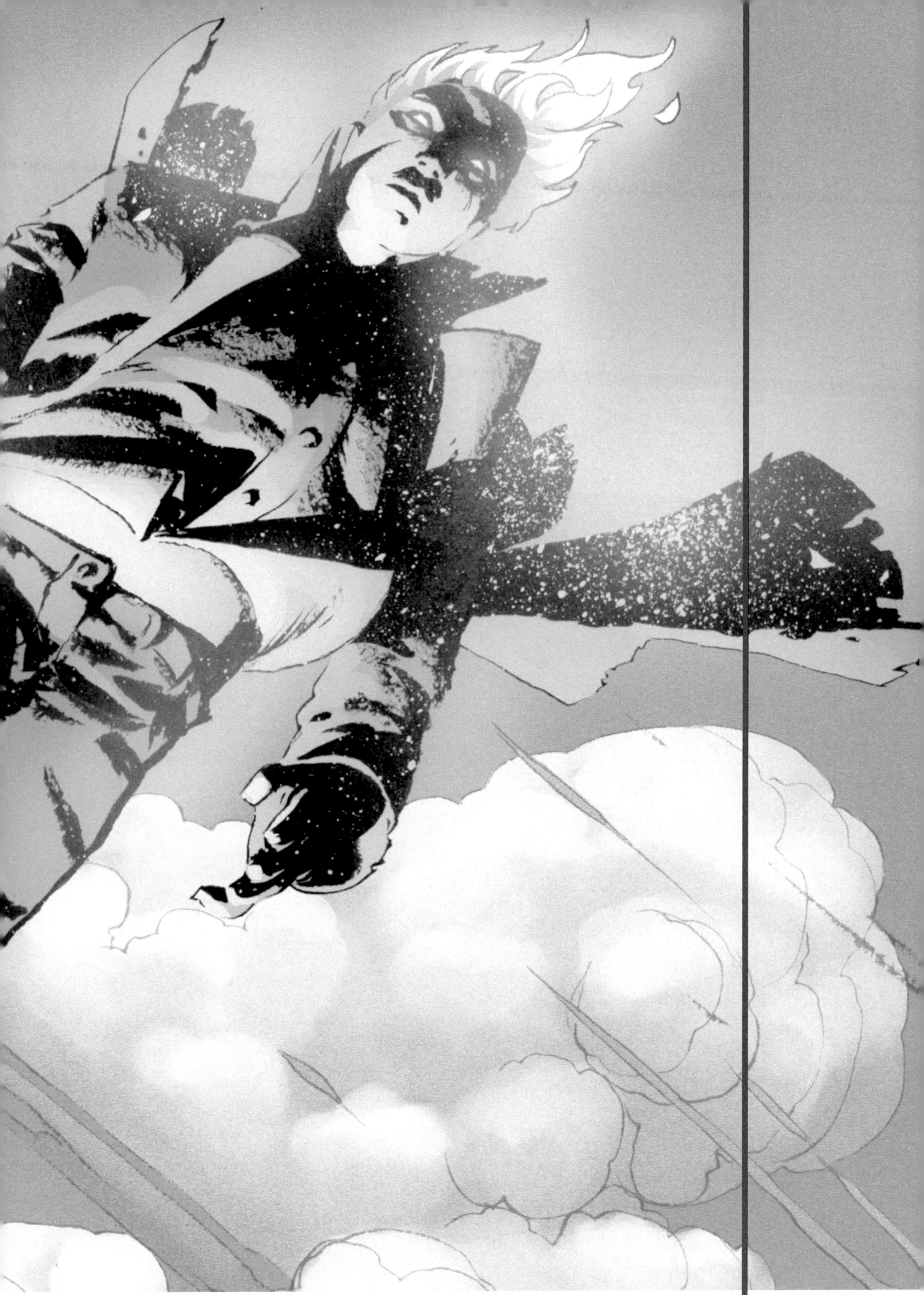

SCOTT DUNBIER \ BEN ABERNATHY \ JOHN LAYMAN EDITORS - ORIGINAL SERIES
KRISTY QUINN ASSISTANT EDITOR - ORIGINAL SERIES
JEB WOODARD GROUP EDITOR - COLLECTED EDITIONS
STEVE COOK DESIGN DIRECTOR - BOOKS
MONIQUE NARBONETA PUBLICATION DESIGN

BOB HARRAS SENIOR VP - EDITOR-IN-CHIEF, DC COMICS
PAT McCALLUM EXECUTIVE EDITOR, DC COMICS

DIANE NELSON PRESIDENT
DAN DiDIO PUBLISHER
JIM LEE PUBLISHER
GEOFF JOHNS PRESIDENT & CHIEF CREATIVE OFFICER
AMIT DESAI EXECUTIVE VP - BUSINESS & MARKETING STRATEGY,
              DIRECT TO CONSUMER & GLOBAL FRANCHISE MANAGEMENT
SAM ADES SENIOR VP & GENERAL MANAGER, DIGITAL SERVICES
BOBBIE CHASE VP & EXECUTIVE EDITOR, YOUNG READER & TALENT DEVELOPMENT
MARK CHIARELLO SENIOR VP - ART, DESIGN & COLLECTED EDITIONS
JOHN CUNNINGHAM SENIOR VP - SALES & TRADE MARKETING
ANNE DePIES SENIOR VP - BUSINESS STRATEGY, FINANCE & ADMINISTRATION
DON FALLETTI VP - MANUFACTURING OPERATIONS
LAWRENCE GANEM VP - EDITORIAL ADMINISTRATION & TALENT RELATIONS
ALISON GILL SENIOR VP - MANUFACTURING & OPERATIONS
HANK KANALZ SENIOR VP - EDITORIAL STRATEGY & ADMINISTRATION
JAY KOGAN VP - LEGAL AFFAIRS
JACK MAHAN VP - BUSINESS AFFAIRS
NICK J. NAPOLITANO VP - MANUFACTURING ADMINISTRATION
EDDIE SCANNELL VP - CONSUMER MARKETING
COURTNEY SIMMONS SENIOR VP - PUBLICITY & COMMUNICATIONS
JIM (SKI) SOKOLOWSKI VP - COMIC BOOK SPECIALTY SALES & TRADE MARKETING
NANCY SPEARS VP - MASS, BOOK, DIGITAL SALES & TRADE MARKETING
MICHELE R. WELLS VP - CONTENT STRATEGY

PLANETARY BOOK TWO

DC Comics, 2900 West Alameda Ave., Burbank, CA 91505
Printed by LSC Communications, Kendallville, IN, USA. 2/16/18. First Printing.
ISBN: 978-1-4012-7799-4

Library of Congress Cataloging-in-Publication Data is available.

Introduction

PLANETARY haunts me.

It haunts me like a dark, low-budget science fiction movie from the fifties, seen on a black-and-white TV when I was still too young to deal with it. It haunts me like a visionary short story from those pocket-sized magazines with words like Amazing, Astounding or Asimov on the cover. Like a history class that's so good that for a moment you realize people actually lived that stuff, and you're right there with them. Like a Leone western. Like James Bond, if he were actually as cool as we remember him.

Look at the covers. The logo. No two alike. Every issue its own short, dazzling tale that would bind the reader even if they had no idea it was part of a larger whole. I first picked up PLANETARY at issue #8, the second chapter of this volume. I was stunned by the imagination, the darkness, the scope of the thing. Plus, hey, giant ants. Going back and buying the first seven issues was an instant necessity, as was waiting droolingly for every issue since. What kept blowing me away was how different each piece was. There was more imagination and originality in every issue of PLANETARY than in practically any movie you're gonna see this year. Warren Ellis draws inspiration from so many cultural wellsprings that his work truly does become a sort of history of the twentieth century as it exists in popular fiction. But this is no mere pastiche—Ellis both subverts and elevates the elements he takes, making them fit perfectly in his own epic vision. No one who loves comics can get through issue #10, "Magic and Loss," without a true thrill of childlike dread.

Ellis' love of literature and history, filtered through his own strange vision, puts him alongside contemporary Alan Moore in more than just quality. One could easily see their universes entwined—Tom Strong and perhaps Miss Mina Murray bumping into Elijah Snow and Jenny Sparks of the Authority. While so many comics are rebooting, Ultimating and Year One-ing themselves into a masturbatory frenzy, these two are creating universes as rich and strange as any we could hope to encounter; eerily familiar and totally new. The two stand right now as the pillars of modern comics. (Or possibly the "intimidating British guys with intense facial hair of modern comics," but "pillars" is easier to say.) What separates them is that while Moore's pages overflow with visual information, his panels crammed with explosions of life and lore, Ellis gives us a sparer, more cinematic frame. He takes his time. He waits.

Then the giant ants.

Or the rocket, the well of ghosts, the pattern of ice in a grassy park. His sense of pace, of space, is truly epic. He is aided in this by the extraordinary John Cassaday. Capable of extreme detail but never giving more information than needed for the moment, Cassaday is the perfect match for Ellis' vision. Ellis clearly wants to let the visuals tell his story (another nearly lost art in comics), and Cassaday rewards us with breathtaking vistas alternating with quiet, wry moments of humanity. He puts us in giant alien chambers, and we are there, puts us up close in moments of appalling violence, and we are there. He captures. Plus, Jakita Wagner: wicked hot.

Jakita's hotness aside, it's really Elijah Snow that this book belongs to. It's in this second volume that pieces of the puzzle begin to come together, that Elijah does more than just excavate. The whole begins to take shape, and what would have been perfectly fine as an unrelated series of short stories begins to reveal itself as something much more complex and rewarding. Snow is a great character to walk this world with. The "creepy old goat," as one bystander calls him, is a man who's done too little, seen too much, and finally had enough. He's terminally cranky, and I admire that in a hero.

So go with him. Go back for a second trip through the warped scape Ellis and Cassaday have woven, and see if it doesn't haunt you a little bit. The game's afoot. Enjoy.

Joss Whedon, 1.1.01
Joss Whedon is the acclaimed creator of *Buffy the Vampire Slayer* and director of the *Avengers* motion picture.

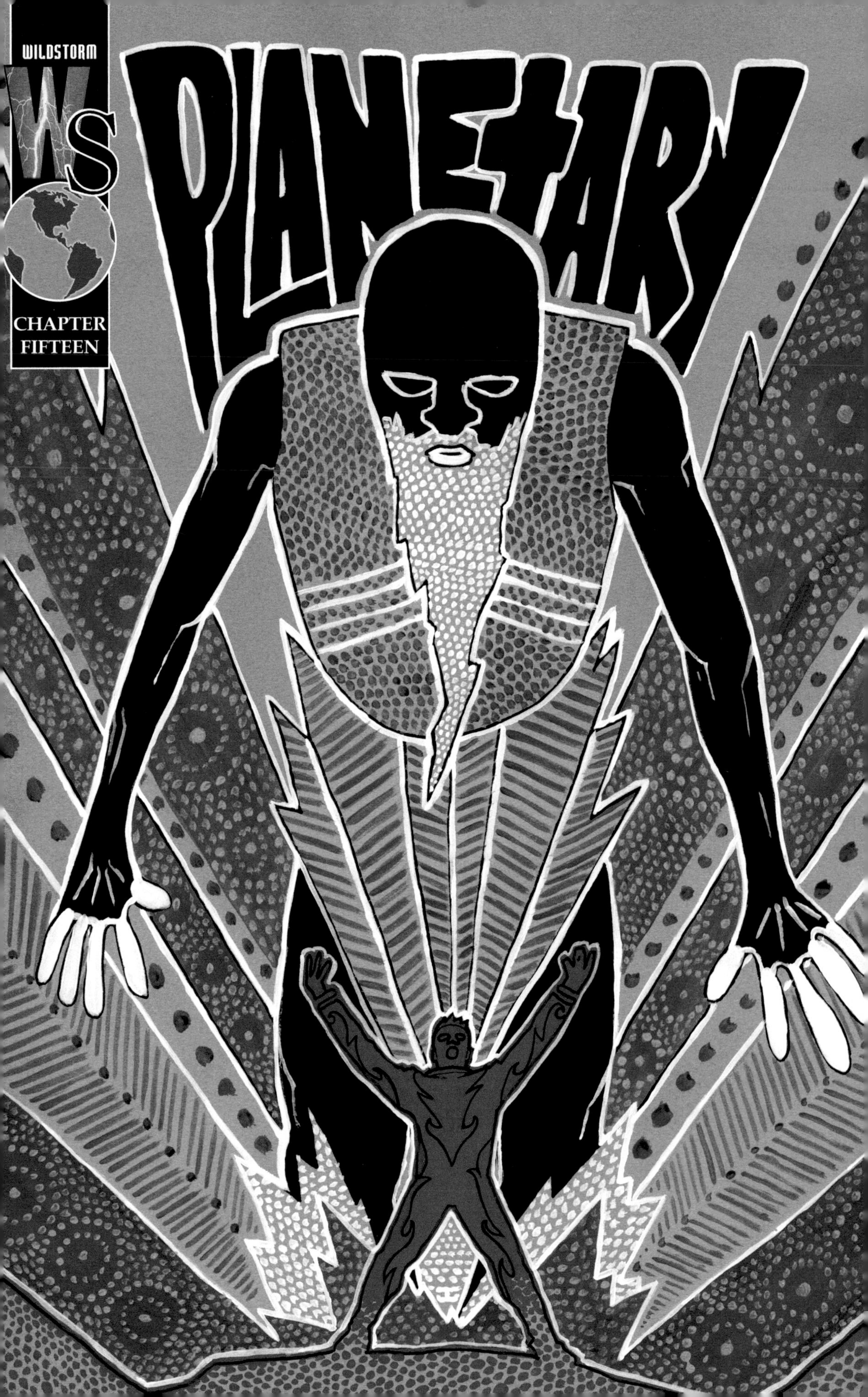
WILDSTORM
WS
PLANETARY
CHAPTER FIFTEEN

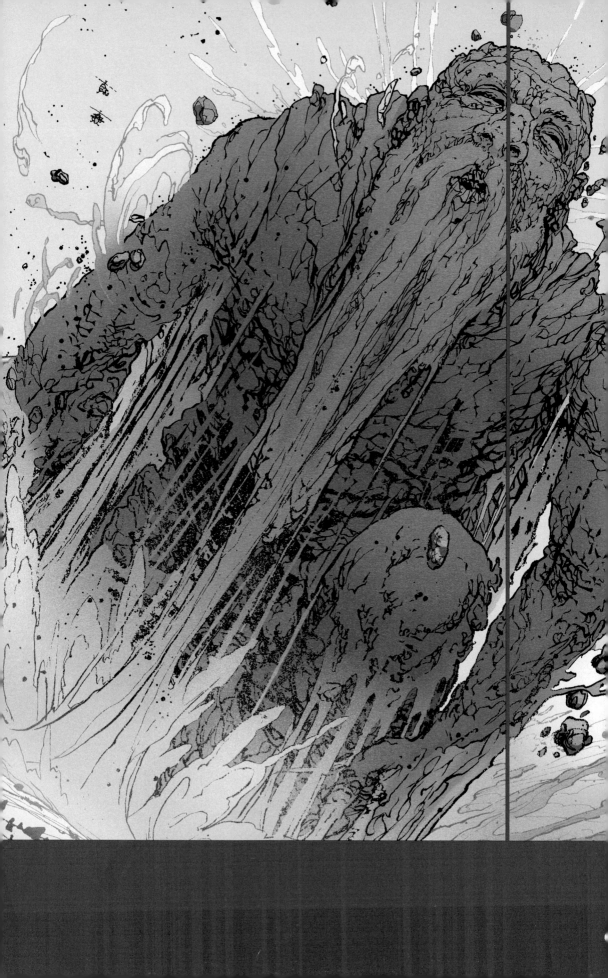

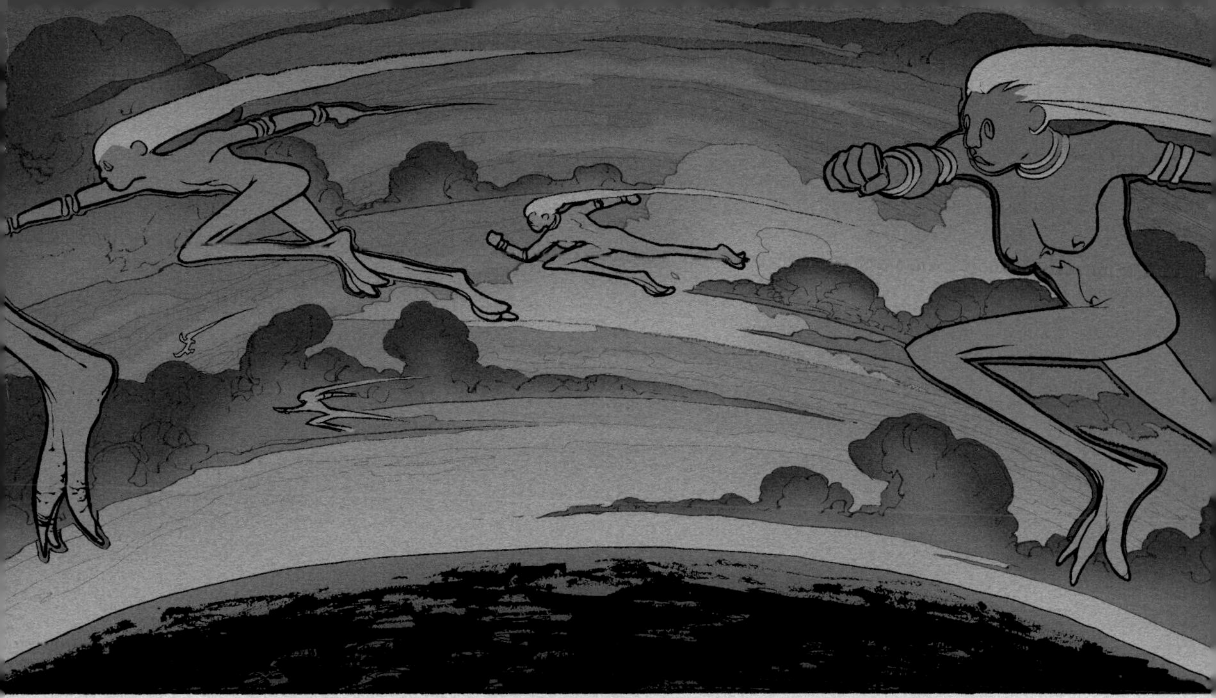

In the Beginning

The Earth was an infinite dark plain, separated from the sky and from the murky sea and enveloped in shadowy twilight.

There were no stars, no sun or moon.

In the sky, there were Sky-dwellers, running beyond the Western Clouds, ageless and sparkling.

On the earth, under the shallow ditches that in the future would become waterholes, laid The Ancients, so old they could do nothing but sleep. Like the ditches, they were pregnant with potential, for each contained the merest breath of aspirational life.

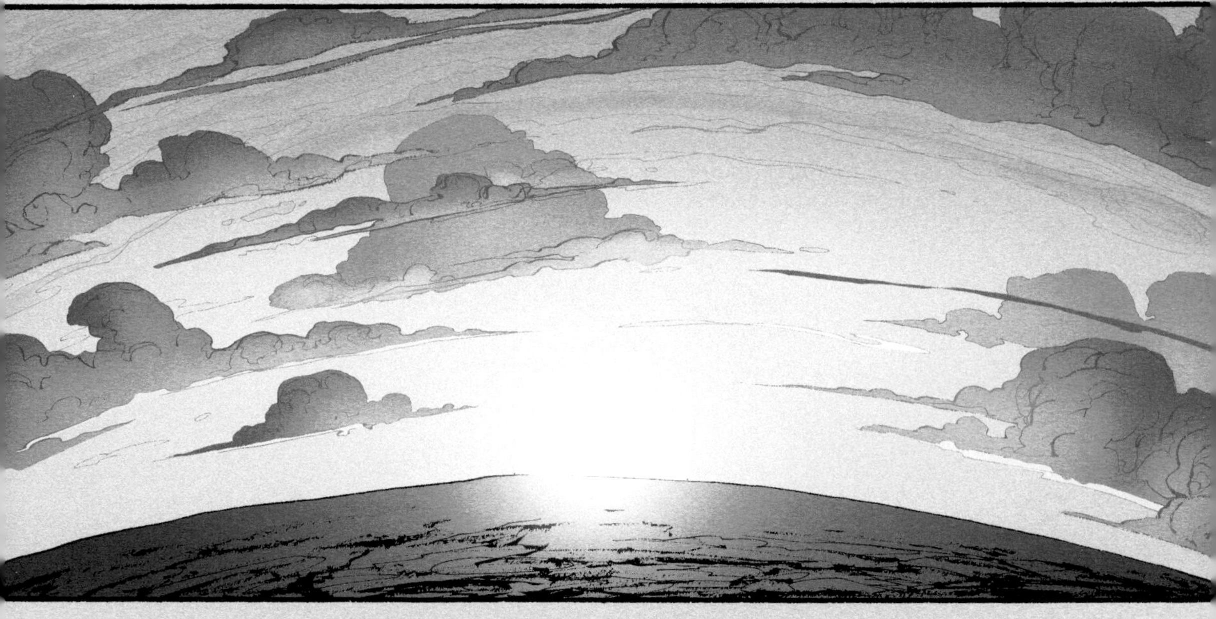

Under the plain were all the constellations, the burning sun, the shining moon. Waiting.

On the morning of the First Day, the Sun finally wanted to be born. It exploded through the surface and up into the sky, casting light and heat all about.

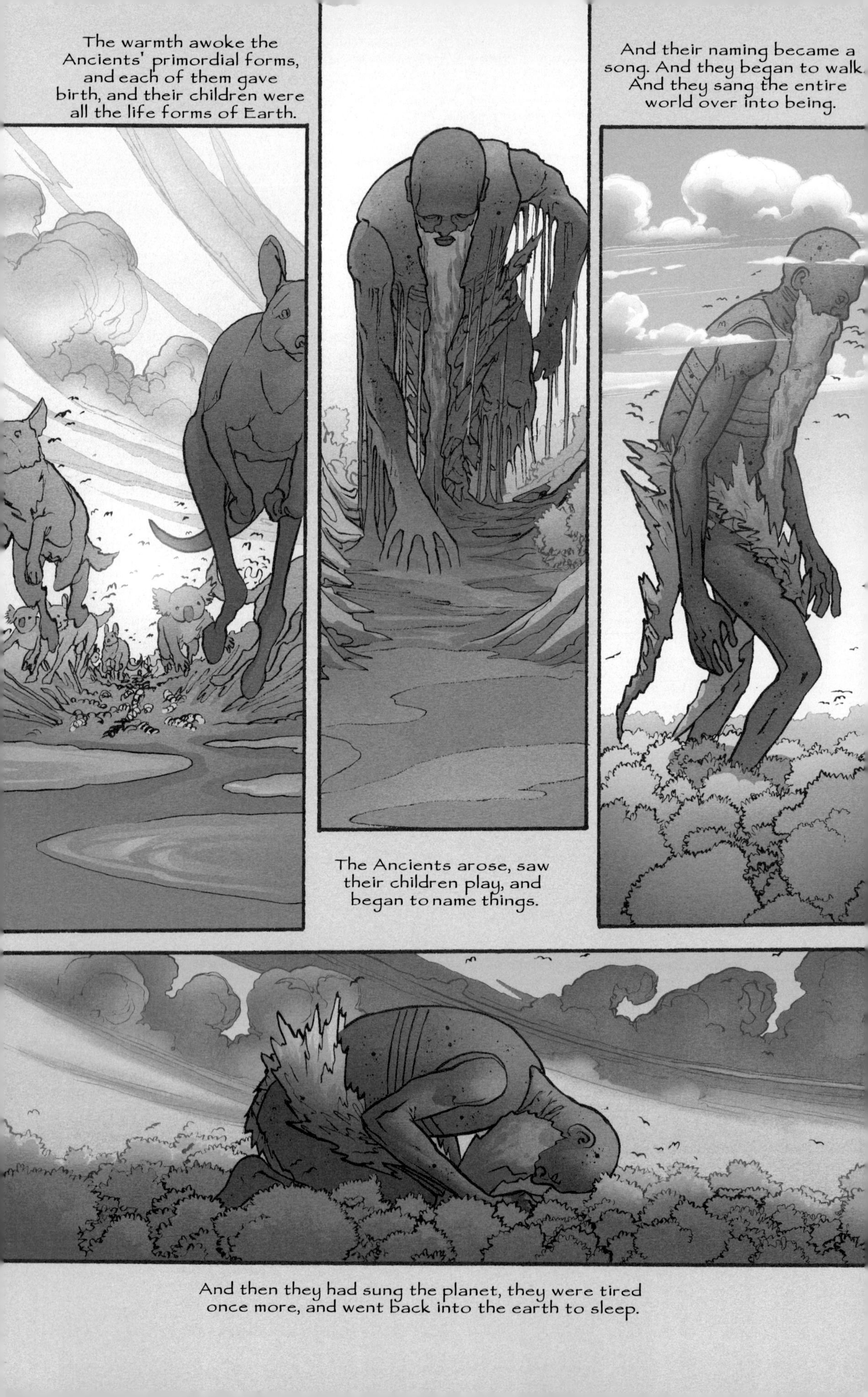
The warmth awoke the Ancients' primordial forms, and each of them gave birth, and their children were all the life forms of Earth.
The Ancients arose, saw their children play, and began to name things.
And their naming became a song. And they began to walk. And they sang the entire world over into being.
And then they had sung the planet, they were tired once more, and went back into the earth to sleep.

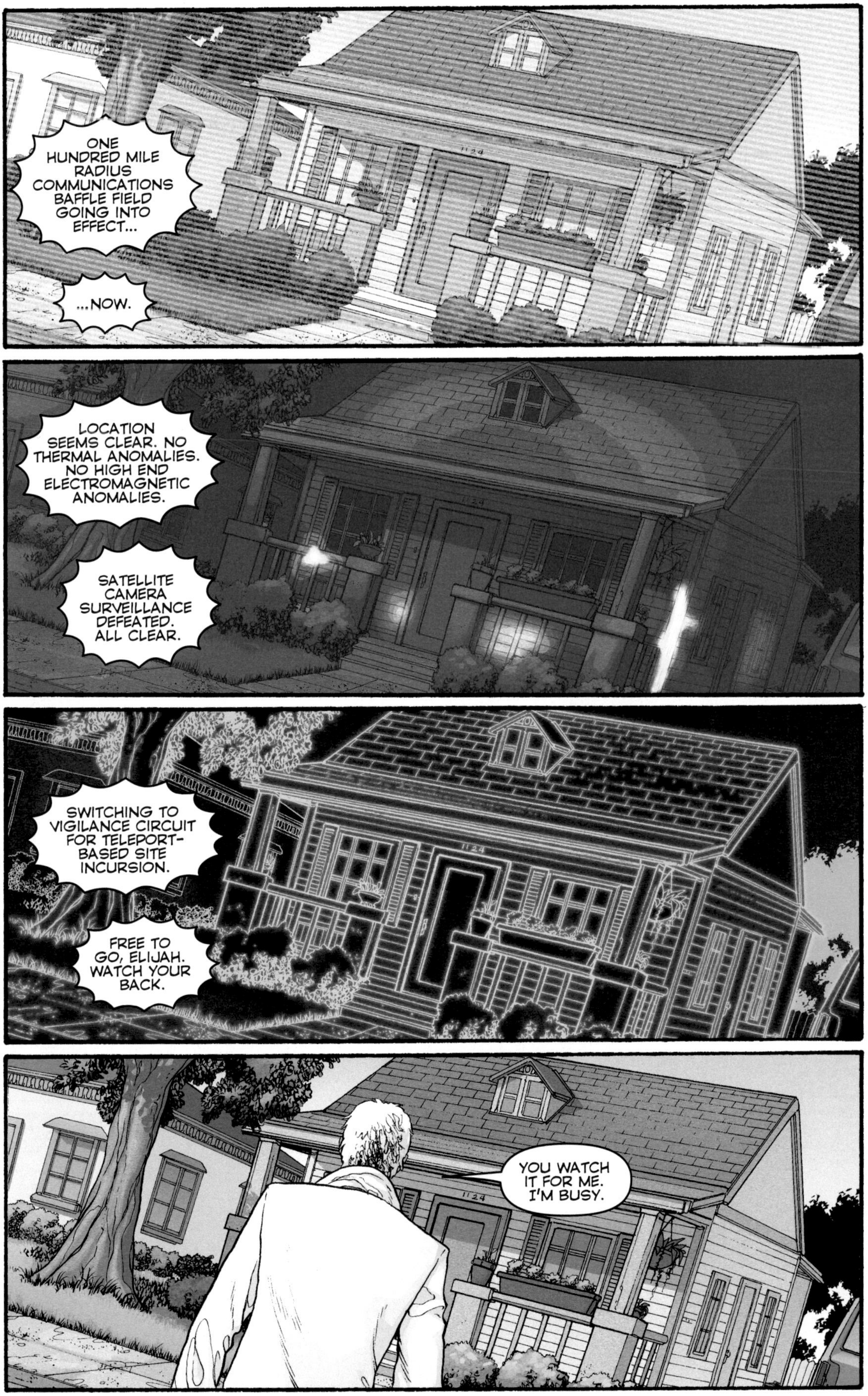
ONE HUNDRED MILE RADIUS COMMUNICATIONS BAFFLE FIELD GOING INTO EFFECT...
...NOW.
LOCATION SEEMS CLEAR. NO THERMAL ANOMALIES. NO HIGH END ELECTROMAGNETIC ANOMALIES.
SATELLITE CAMERA SURVEILLANCE DEFEATED. ALL CLEAR.
SWITCHING TO VIGILANCE CIRCUIT FOR TELEPORT-BASED SITE INCURSION.
FREE TO GO, ELIJAH. WATCH YOUR BACK.
YOU WATCH IT FOR ME. I'M BUSY.

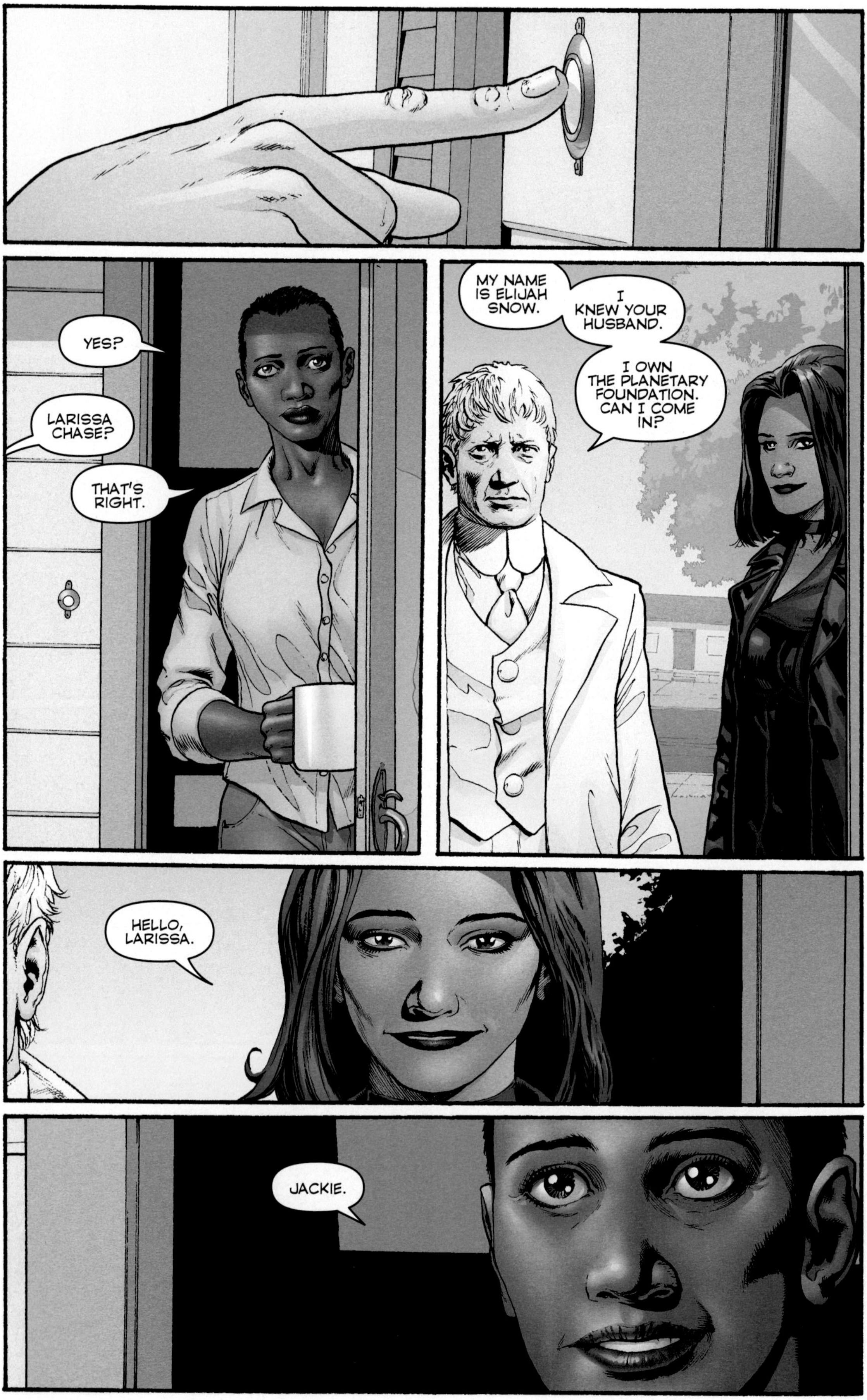
YES?
LARISSA CHASE?
THAT'S RIGHT.
MY NAME IS ELIJAH SNOW.
I KNEW YOUR HUSBAND.
I OWN THE PLANETARY FOUNDATION. CAN I COME IN?
HELLO, LARISSA.
JACKIE.

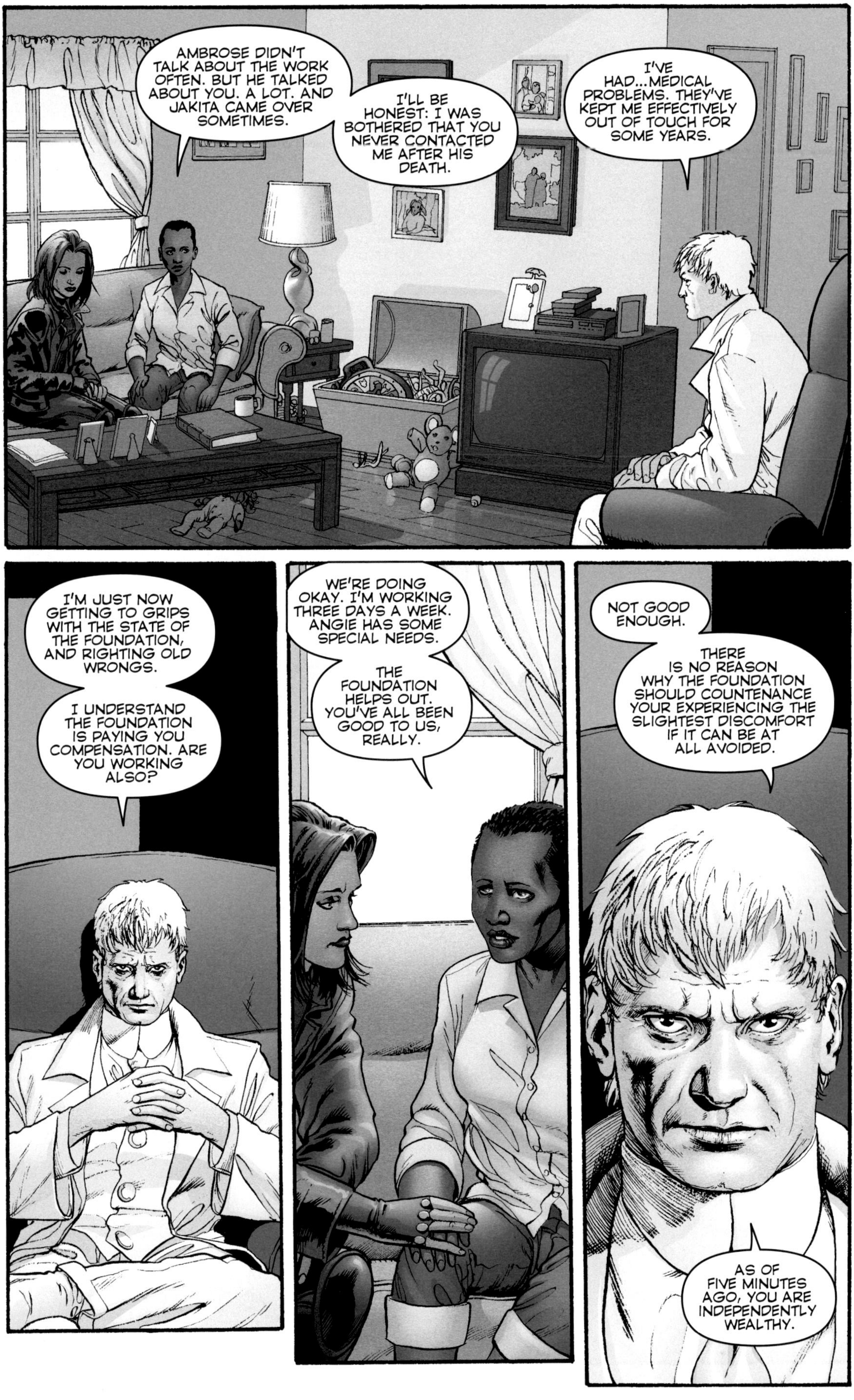
AMBROSE DIDN'T TALK ABOUT THE WORK OFTEN. BUT HE TALKED ABOUT YOU. A LOT. AND JAKITA CAME OVER SOMETIMES.
I'LL BE HONEST: I WAS BOTHERED THAT YOU NEVER CONTACTED ME AFTER HIS DEATH.
I'VE HAD...MEDICAL PROBLEMS. THEY'VE KEPT ME EFFECTIVELY OUT OF TOUCH FOR SOME YEARS.
I'M JUST NOW GETTING TO GRIPS WITH THE STATE OF THE FOUNDATION, AND RIGHTING OLD WRONGS.
I UNDERSTAND THE FOUNDATION IS PAYING YOU COMPENSATION. ARE YOU WORKING ALSO?
WE'RE DOING OKAY. I'M WORKING THREE DAYS A WEEK. ANGIE HAS SOME SPECIAL NEEDS.
THE FOUNDATION HELPS OUT. YOU'VE ALL BEEN GOOD TO US, REALLY.
NOT GOOD ENOUGH.
THERE IS NO REASON WHY THE FOUNDATION SHOULD COUNTENANCE YOUR EXPERIENCING THE SLIGHTEST DISCOMFORT IF IT CAN BE AT ALL AVOIDED.
AS OF FIVE MINUTES AGO, YOU ARE INDEPENDENTLY WEALTHY.

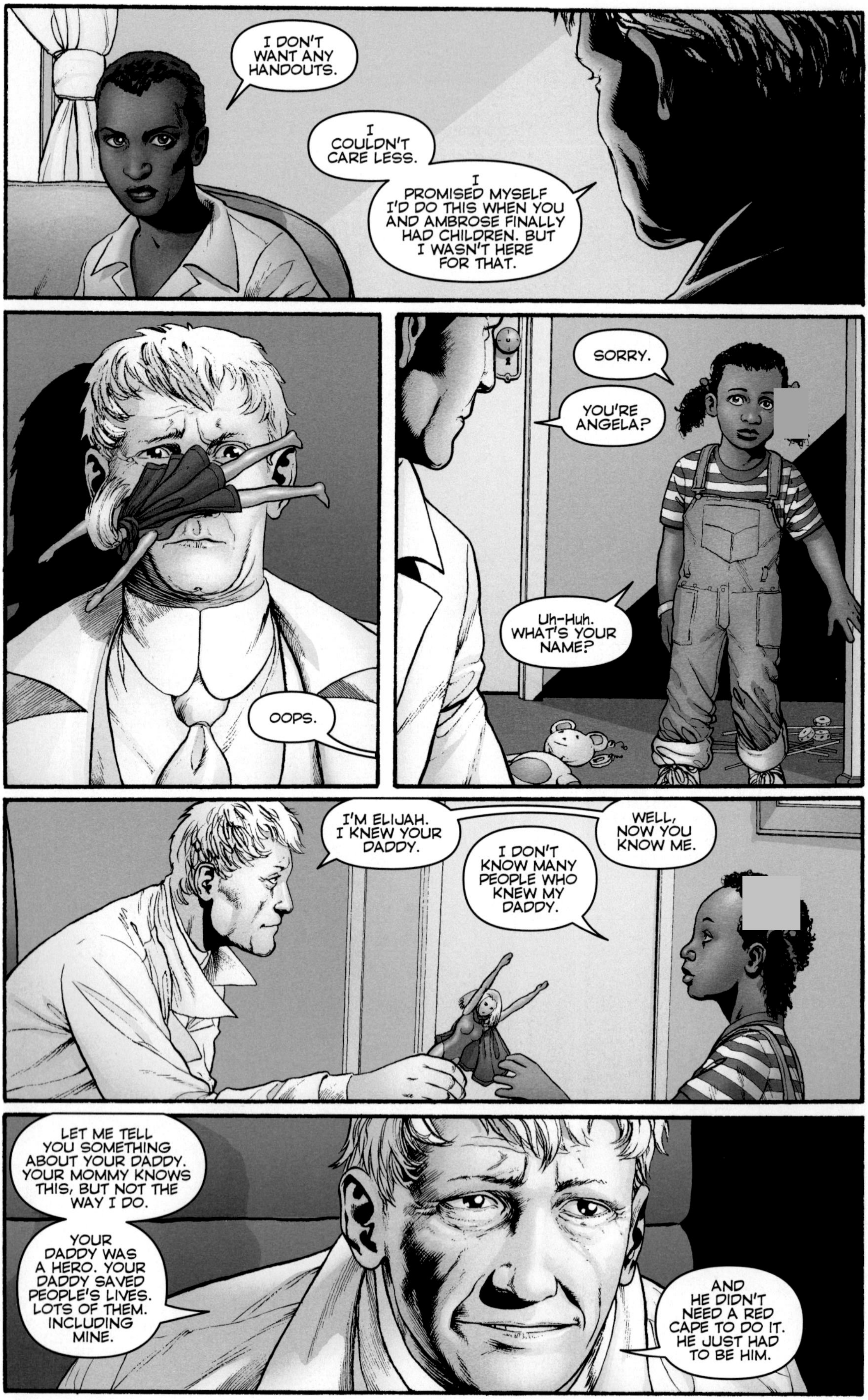

I DON'T WANT ANY HANDOUTS.
I COULDN'T CARE LESS.
I PROMISED MYSELF I'D DO THIS WHEN YOU AND AMBROSE FINALLY HAD CHILDREN. BUT I WASN'T HERE FOR THAT.
OOPS.
SORRY.
YOU'RE ANGELA?
Uh-Huh. WHAT'S YOUR NAME?
I'M ELIJAH. I KNEW YOUR DADDY.
I DON'T KNOW MANY PEOPLE WHO KNEW MY DADDY.
WELL, NOW YOU KNOW ME.
LET ME TELL YOU SOMETHING ABOUT YOUR DADDY. YOUR MOMMY KNOWS THIS, BUT NOT THE WAY I DO.
YOUR DADDY WAS A HERO. YOUR DADDY SAVED PEOPLE'S LIVES. LOTS OF THEM. INCLUDING MINE.
AND HE DIDN'T NEED A RED CAPE TO DO IT. HE JUST HAD TO BE HIM.

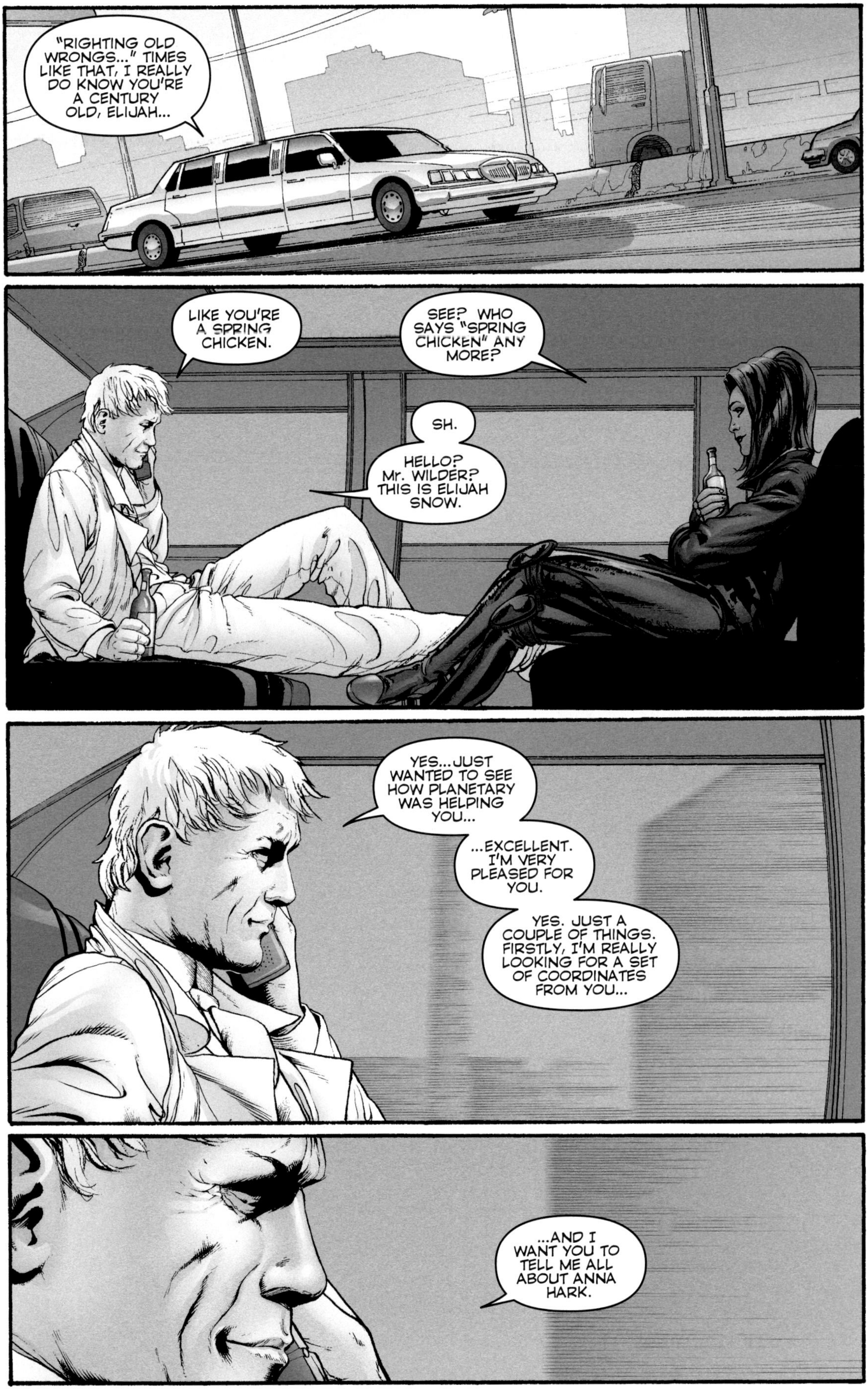
"RIGHTING OLD WRONGS..." TIMES LIKE THAT, I REALLY DO KNOW YOU'RE A CENTURY OLD, ELIJAH...
LIKE YOU'RE A SPRING CHICKEN.
SEE? WHO SAYS "SPRING CHICKEN" ANY MORE?
SH.
HELLO? Mr. WILDER? THIS IS ELIJAH SNOW.
YES...JUST WANTED TO SEE HOW PLANETARY WAS HELPING YOU...
...EXCELLENT. I'M VERY PLEASED FOR YOU.
YES. JUST A COUPLE OF THINGS. FIRSTLY, I'M REALLY LOOKING FOR A SET OF COORDINATES FROM YOU...
...AND I WANT YOU TO TELL ME ALL ABOUT ANNA HARK.

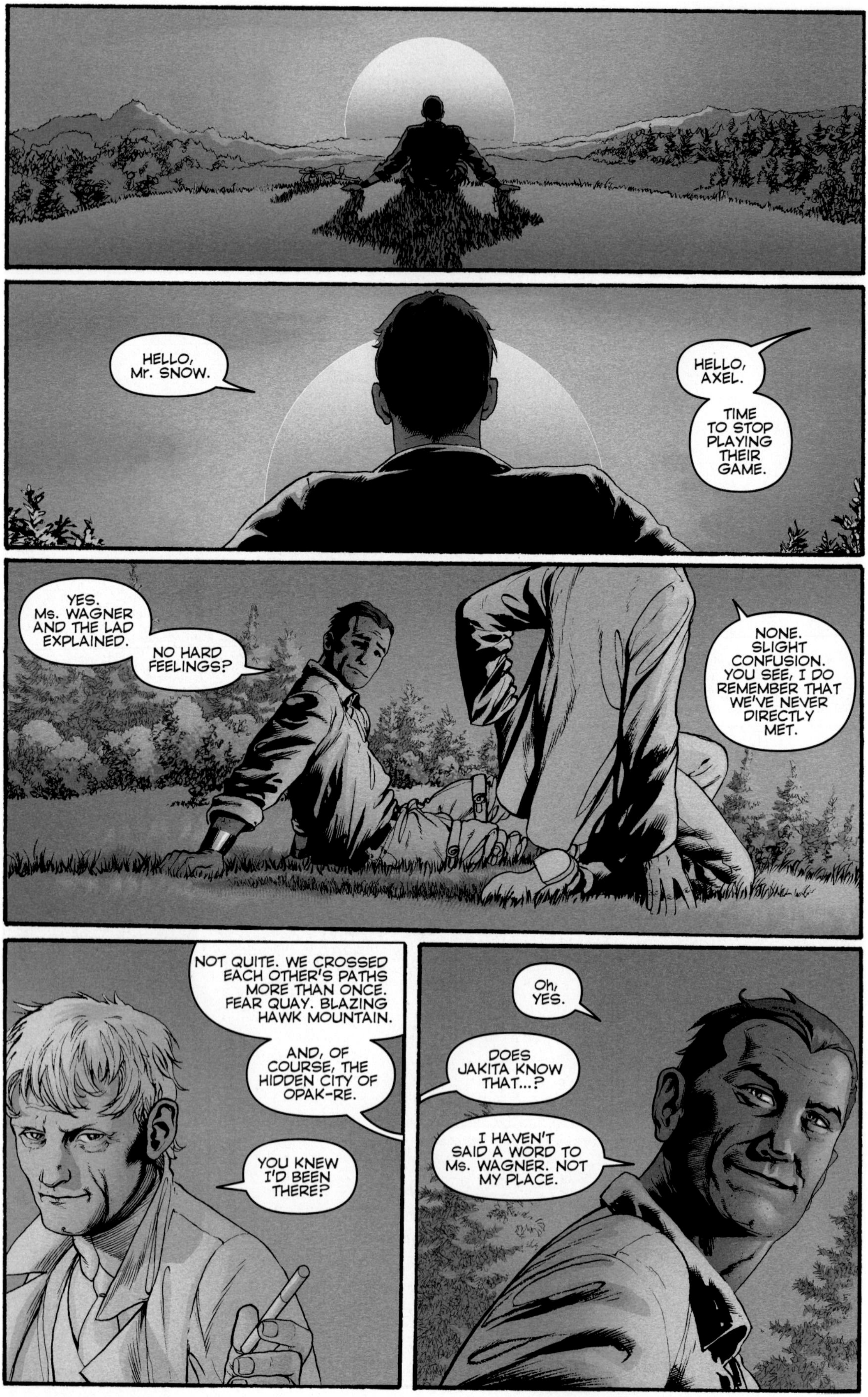
HELLO, Mr. SNOW.
HELLO, AXEL.
TIME TO STOP PLAYING THEIR GAME.
YES. Ms. WAGNER AND THE LAD EXPLAINED.
NO HARD FEELINGS?
NONE. SLIGHT CONFUSION. YOU SEE, I DO REMEMBER THAT WE'VE NEVER DIRECTLY MET.
NOT QUITE. WE CROSSED EACH OTHER'S PATHS MORE THAN ONCE. FEAR QUAY. BLAZING HAWK MOUNTAIN.
AND, OF COURSE, THE HIDDEN CITY OF OPAK-RE.
YOU KNEW I'D BEEN THERE?
Oh, YES.
DOES JAKITA KNOW THAT...?
I HAVEN'T SAID A WORD TO Ms. WAGNER. NOT MY PLACE.

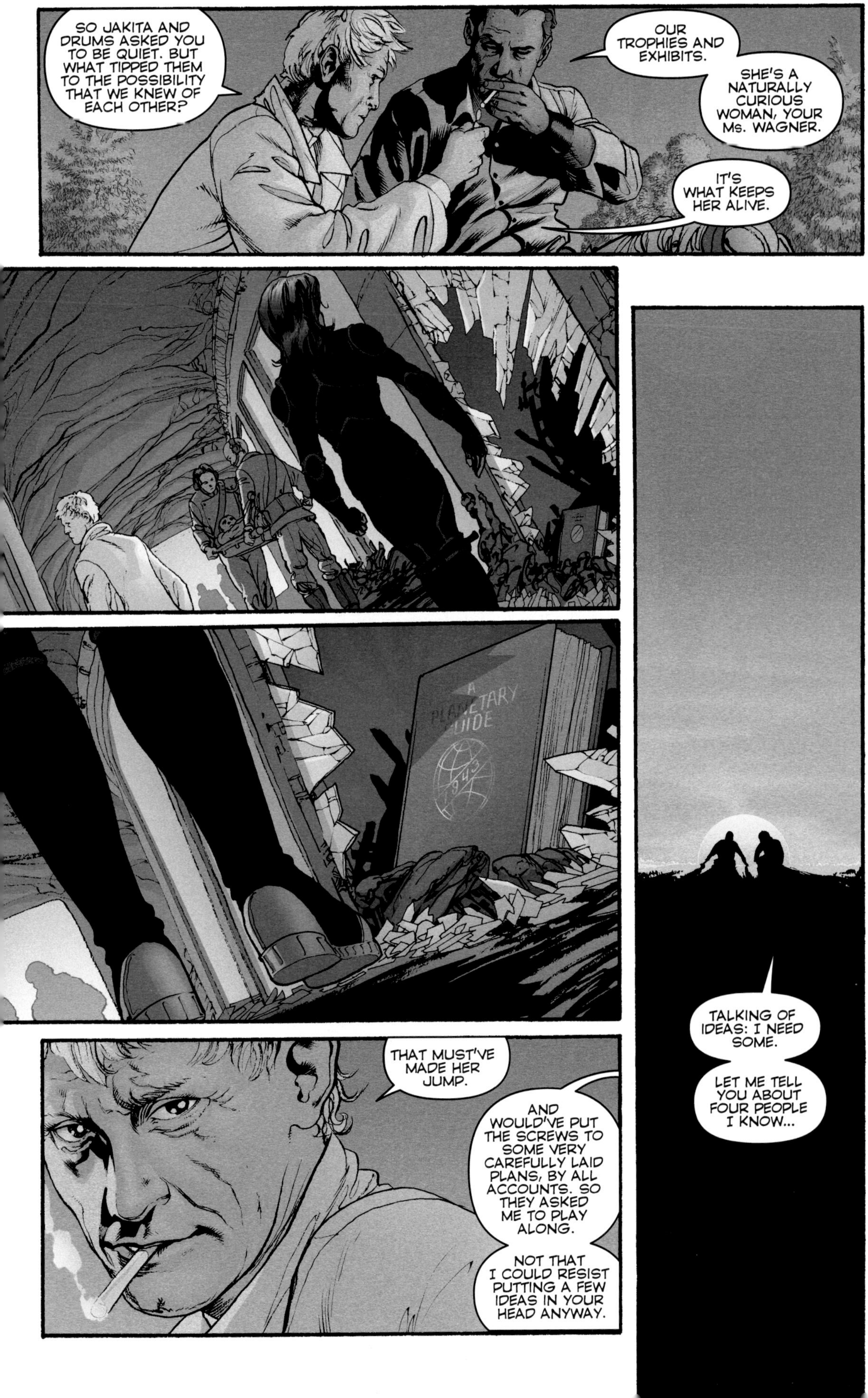
SO JAKITA AND DRUMS ASKED YOU TO BE QUIET. BUT WHAT TIPPED THEM TO THE POSSIBILITY THAT WE KNEW OF EACH OTHER?
OUR TROPHIES AND EXHIBITS.
SHE'S A NATURALLY CURIOUS WOMAN, YOUR Ms. WAGNER.
IT'S WHAT KEEPS HER ALIVE.
A PLANETARY GUIDE
1943
THAT MUST'VE MADE HER JUMP.
AND WOULD'VE PUT THE SCREWS TO SOME VERY CAREFULLY LAID PLANS, BY ALL ACCOUNTS. SO THEY ASKED ME TO PLAY ALONG.
NOT THAT I COULD RESIST PUTTING A FEW IDEAS IN YOUR HEAD ANYWAY.
TALKING OF IDEAS: I NEED SOME.
LET ME TELL YOU ABOUT FOUR PEOPLE I KNOW...

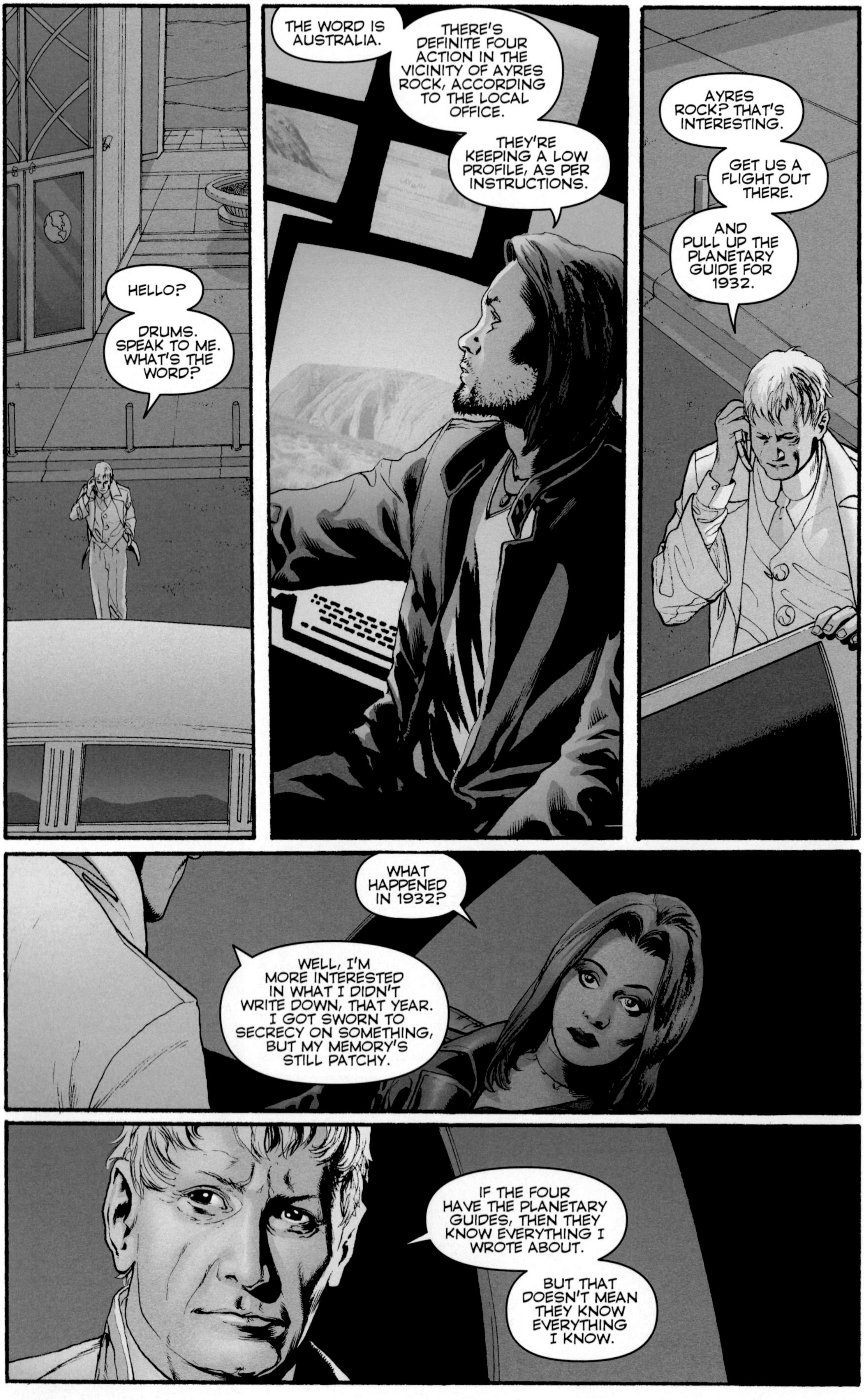
HELLO?
DRUMS. SPEAK TO ME. WHAT'S THE WORD?
THE WORD IS AUSTRALIA.
THERE'S DEFINITE FOUR ACTION IN THE VICINITY OF AYRES ROCK, ACCORDING TO THE LOCAL OFFICE.
THEY'RE KEEPING A LOW PROFILE, AS PER INSTRUCTIONS.
AYRES ROCK? THAT'S INTERESTING.
GET US A FLIGHT OUT THERE.
AND PULL UP THE PLANETARY GUIDE FOR 1932.
WHAT HAPPENED IN 1932?
WELL, I'M MORE INTERESTED IN WHAT I DIDN'T WRITE DOWN, THAT YEAR. I GOT SWORN TO SECRECY ON SOMETHING, BUT MY MEMORY'S STILL PATCHY.
IF THE FOUR HAVE THE PLANETARY GUIDES, THEN THEY KNOW EVERYTHING I WROTE ABOUT.
BUT THAT DOESN'T MEAN THEY KNOW EVERYTHING I KNOW.

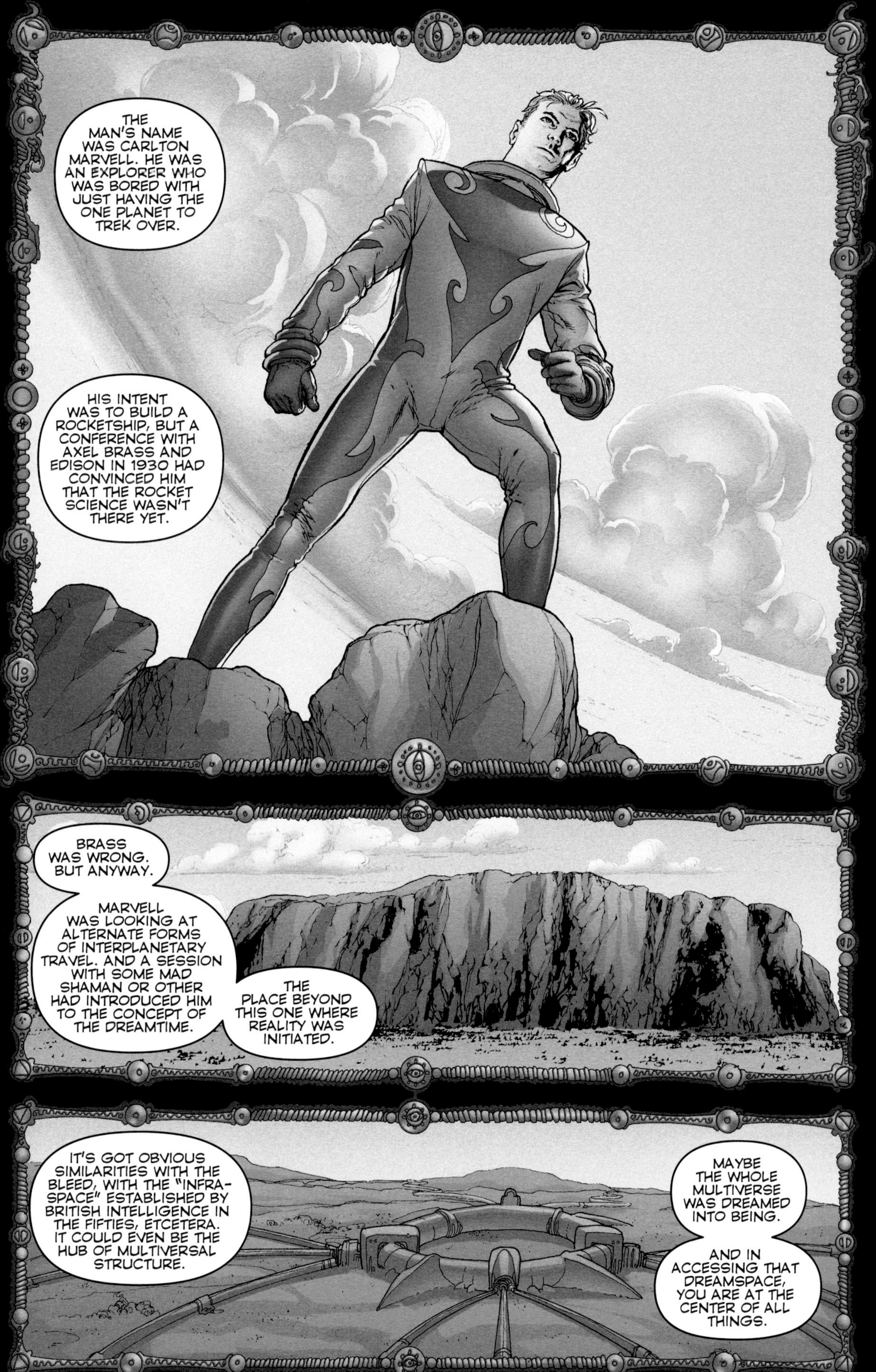

THE MAN'S NAME WAS CARLTON MARVELL. HE WAS AN EXPLORER WHO WAS BORED WITH JUST HAVING THE ONE PLANET TO TREK OVER.
HIS INTENT WAS TO BUILD A ROCKETSHIP, BUT A CONFERENCE WITH AXEL BRASS AND EDISON IN 1930 HAD CONVINCED HIM THAT THE ROCKET SCIENCE WASN'T THERE YET.
BRASS WAS WRONG. BUT ANYWAY.
MARVELL WAS LOOKING AT ALTERNATE FORMS OF INTERPLANETARY TRAVEL. AND A SESSION WITH SOME MAD SHAMAN OR OTHER HAD INTRODUCED HIM TO THE CONCEPT OF THE DREAMTIME.
THE PLACE BEYOND THIS ONE WHERE REALITY WAS INITIATED.
IT'S GOT OBVIOUS SIMILARITIES WITH THE BLEED, WITH THE "INFRA-SPACE" ESTABLISHED BY BRITISH INTELLIGENCE IN THE FIFTIES, ETCETERA. IT COULD EVEN BE THE HUB OF MULTIVERSAL STRUCTURE.
MAYBE THE WHOLE MULTIVERSE WAS DREAMED INTO BEING.
AND IN ACCESSING THAT DREAMSPACE, YOU ARE AT THE CENTER OF ALL THINGS.

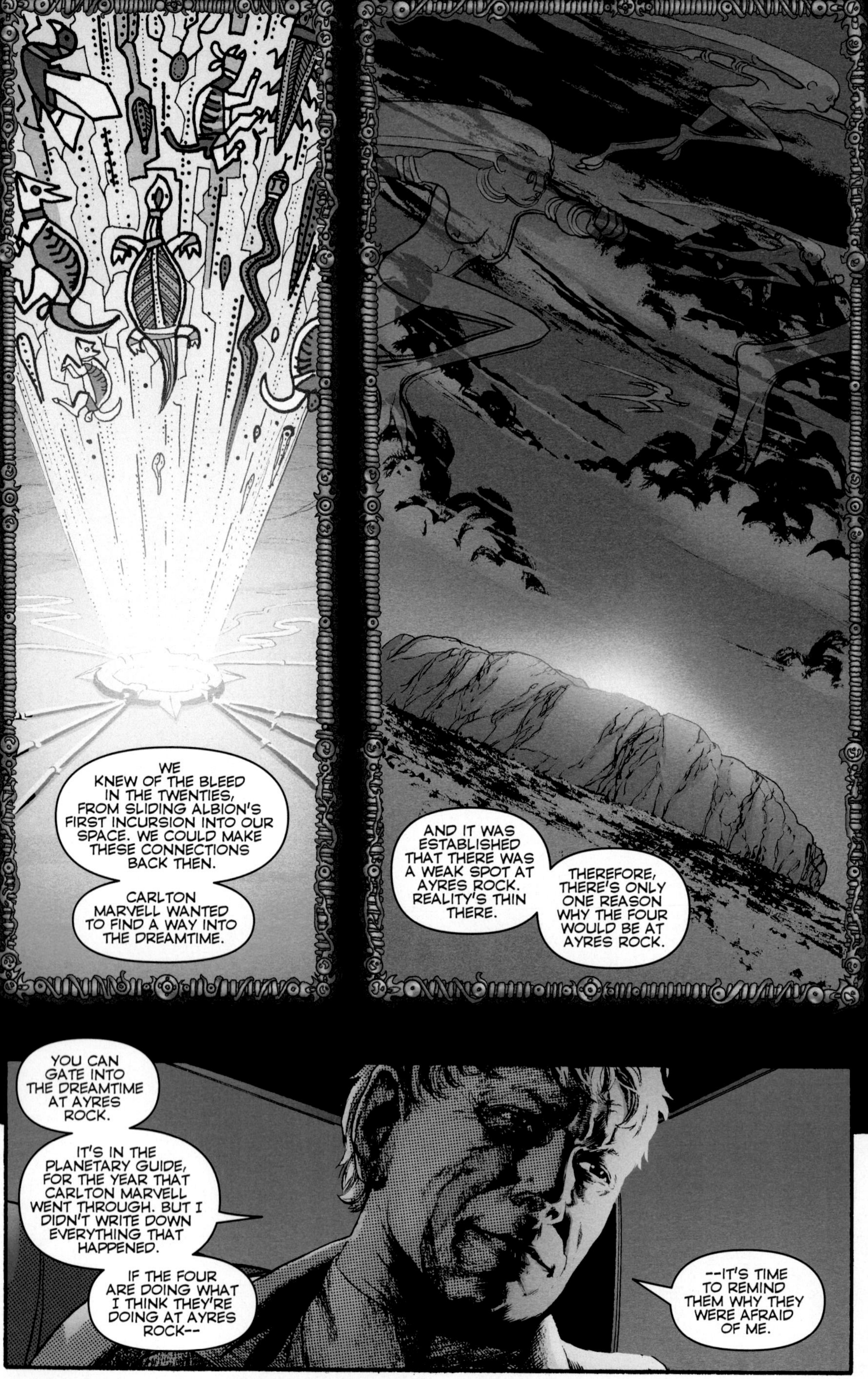
WE KNEW OF THE BLEED IN THE TWENTIES, FROM SLIDING ALBION'S FIRST INCURSION INTO OUR SPACE. WE COULD MAKE THESE CONNECTIONS BACK THEN.
CARLTON MARVELL WANTED TO FIND A WAY INTO THE DREAMTIME.
AND IT WAS ESTABLISHED THAT THERE WAS A WEAK SPOT AT AYRES ROCK. REALITY'S THIN THERE.
THEREFORE, THERE'S ONLY ONE REASON WHY THE FOUR WOULD BE AT AYRES ROCK.
YOU CAN GATE INTO THE DREAMTIME AT AYRES ROCK.
IT'S IN THE PLANETARY GUIDE, FOR THE YEAR THAT CARLTON MARVELL WENT THROUGH. BUT I DIDN'T WRITE DOWN EVERYTHING THAT HAPPENED.
IF THE FOUR ARE DOING WHAT I THINK THEY'RE DOING AT AYRES ROCK--
--IT'S TIME TO REMIND THEM WHY THEY WERE AFRAID OF ME.

CREATION SONGS

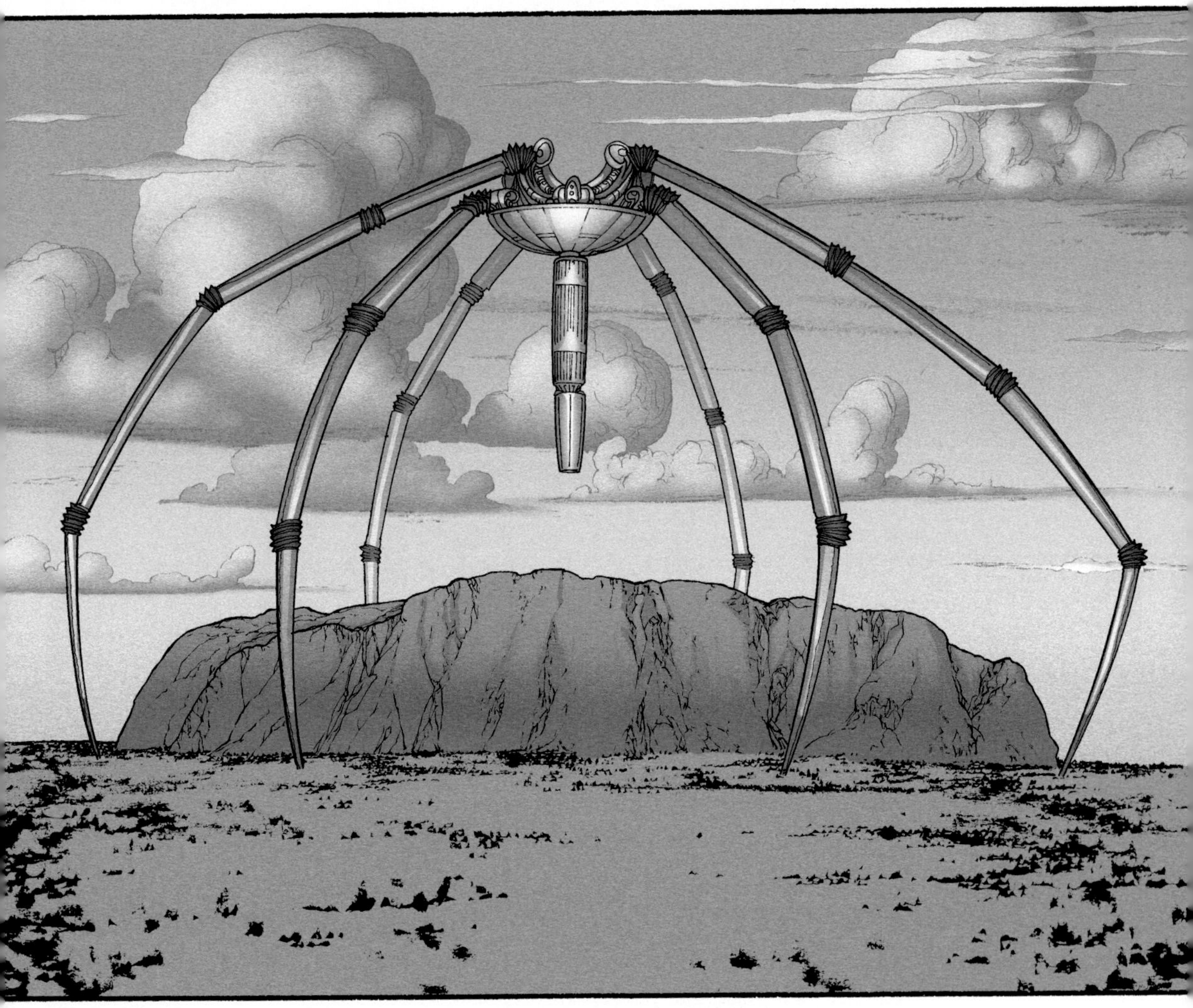

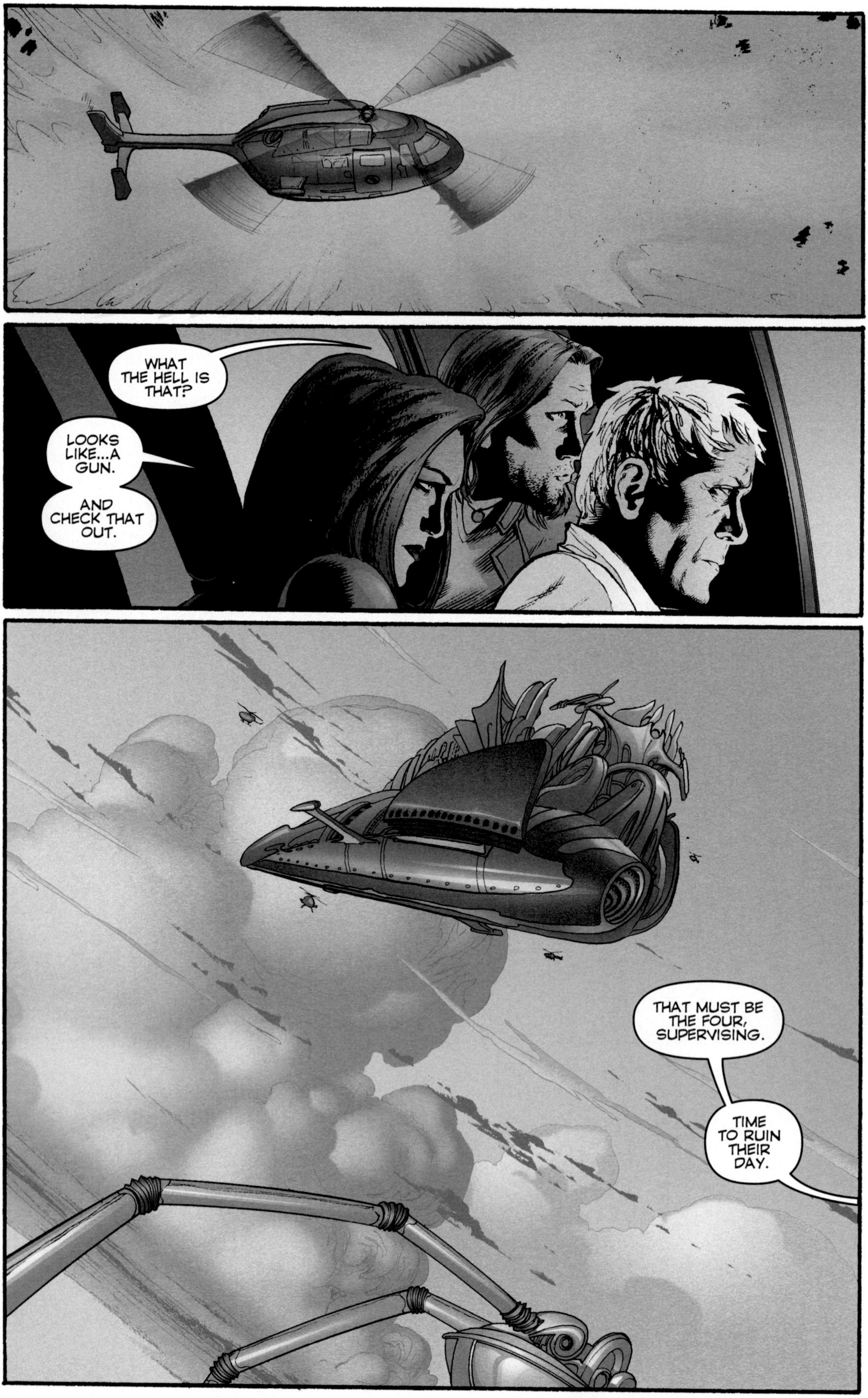
WHAT THE HELL IS THAT?
LOOKS LIKE...A GUN.
AND CHECK THAT OUT.
THAT MUST BE THE FOUR, SUPERVISING.
TIME TO RUIN THEIR DAY.

YOUR BRAIN'S GONE DRY. IT MUST BE CURLING LIKE AN OLD SANDWICH IN THERE.

IT'S THE PLAN, DRUMS. GET YOUR KIT.

CARLTON MARVELL SWORE ME TO SECRECY ABOUT WHAT WE REALLY SAW UP THERE BECAUSE HE DIDN'T WANT ANYONE TO FOLLOW HIM.

WHAT DO YOU THINK THEY'RE TRYING TO DO? SHOOT OPEN THE GATE THAT MARVELL WENT THROUGH IN 1932?

IT'S A VERY FOUR THING TO DO.

I DON'T KNOW, JAKITA. IT TAKES A SONG TO OPEN THE GATE.

THE OLD ABORIGINAL DREAMTIME STORIES SAY THAT THEIR ANCIENT ANCESTORS SANG THE WORLD INTO BEING. THE GATE SEEMED TO BE ON THE SAME OPERATING SYSTEM.

IT'S ALL OPERATING SYSTEMS. BUT YOU DON'T JUST SHOOT WILD INFORMATION INTO OPERATING SYSTEMS THAT BIG JUST TO SEE WHAT HAPPENS.

SURE YOU DO. I'VE READ ALL ABOUT IT. IT'S CALLED A "VIRUS."

THAT'S WHAT THIS IS.

YOU WANT ME TO SHOOT A COMPUTER VIRUS ANALOG INTO THE DREAMTIME?

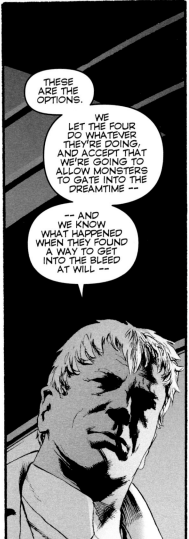

THESE ARE THE OPTIONS.

WE LET THE FOUR DO WHATEVER THEY'RE DOING, AND ACCEPT THAT WE'RE GOING TO ALLOW MONSTERS TO GATE INTO THE DREAMTIME --

-- AND WE KNOW WHAT HAPPENED WHEN THEY FOUND A WAY TO GET INTO THE BLEED AT WILL --

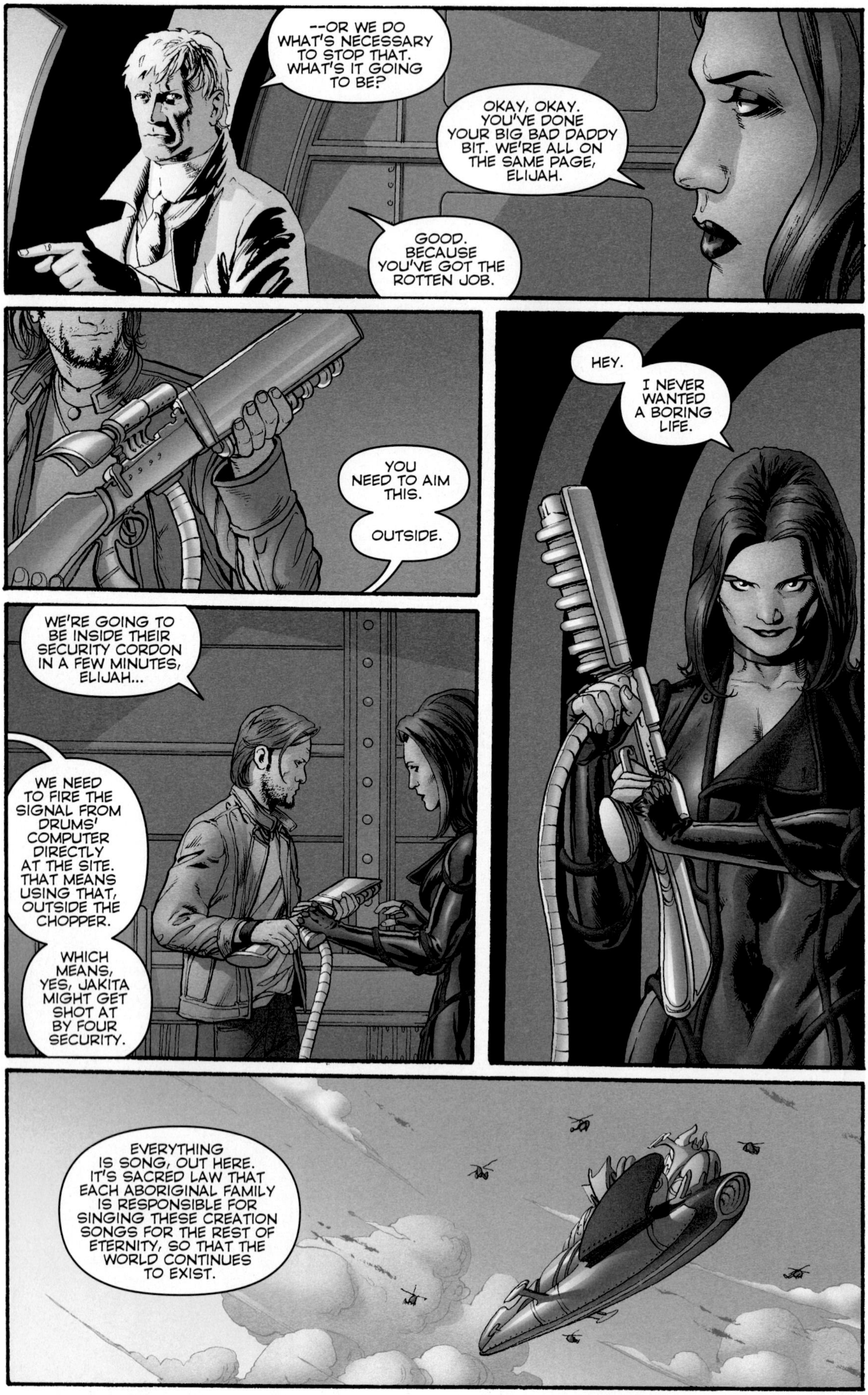
--OR WE DO WHAT'S NECESSARY TO STOP THAT. WHAT'S IT GOING TO BE?
OKAY, OKAY. YOU'VE DONE YOUR BIG BAD DADDY BIT. WE'RE ALL ON THE SAME PAGE, ELIJAH.
GOOD. BECAUSE YOU'VE GOT THE ROTTEN JOB.
YOU NEED TO AIM THIS.
OUTSIDE.
WE'RE GOING TO BE INSIDE THEIR SECURITY CORDON IN A FEW MINUTES, ELIJAH...
WE NEED TO FIRE THE SIGNAL FROM DRUMS' COMPUTER DIRECTLY AT THE SITE. THAT MEANS USING THAT, OUTSIDE THE CHOPPER.
WHICH MEANS, YES, JAKITA MIGHT GET SHOT AT BY FOUR SECURITY.
HEY.
I NEVER WANTED A BORING LIFE.
EVERYTHING IS SONG, OUT HERE. IT'S SACRED LAW THAT EACH ABORIGINAL FAMILY IS RESPONSIBLE FOR SINGING THESE CREATION SONGS FOR THE REST OF ETERNITY, SO THAT THE WORLD CONTINUES TO EXIST.

IF THE SONG IS NOT PASSED DOWN TO THE NEXT GENERATION, OR IF IT IS NOT SUNG, THAT ASPECT OF THE WORLD THAT THEY'RE RESPONSIBLE FOR CEASES TO EXIST.

FASCINATING, REALLY.

DROP THE UNDERCARRIAGE.

IS THIS GOING TO WORK?

CARLTON MARVELL DIDN'T WANT ANYONE FOLLOWING HIM BECAUSE IT WAS TOO DAMN DANGEROUS. WE BARELY GOT OUT WITH OUR LIVES.

SO I ONLY PUBLISHED HALF THE SONG IN THE GUIDE. AND THAT WOULD HAVE TO BE A COMPONENT IN WHATEVER THAT GUN'S PAYLOAD IS.

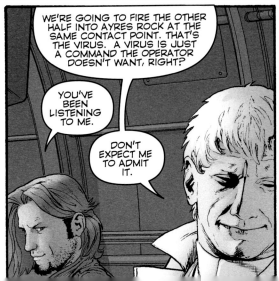

WE'RE GOING TO FIRE THE OTHER HALF INTO AYRES ROCK AT THE SAME CONTACT POINT. THAT'S THE VIRUS. A VIRUS IS JUST A COMMAND THE OPERATOR DOESN'T WANT, RIGHT?

YOU'VE BEEN LISTENING TO ME.

DON'T EXPECT ME TO ADMIT IT.

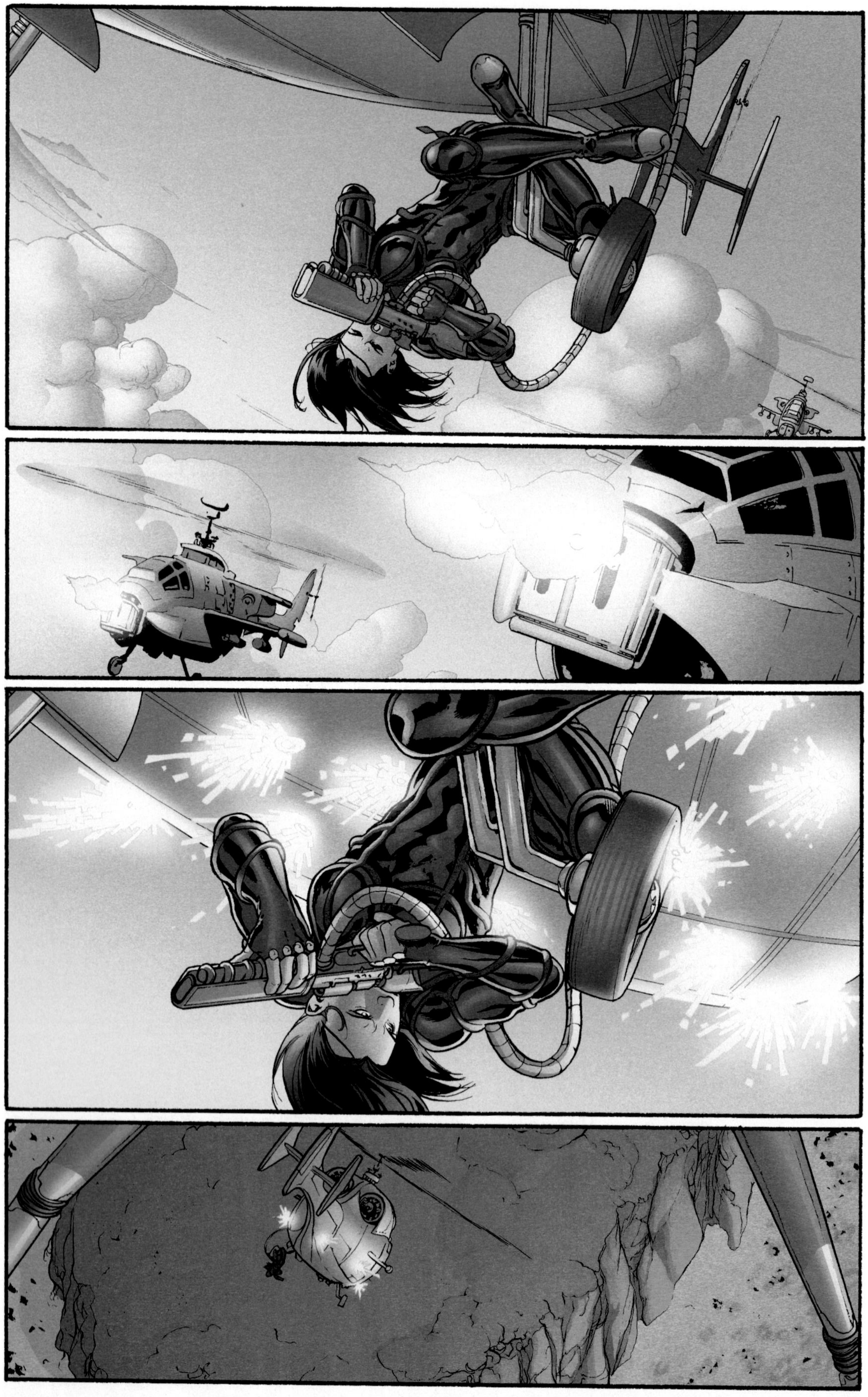

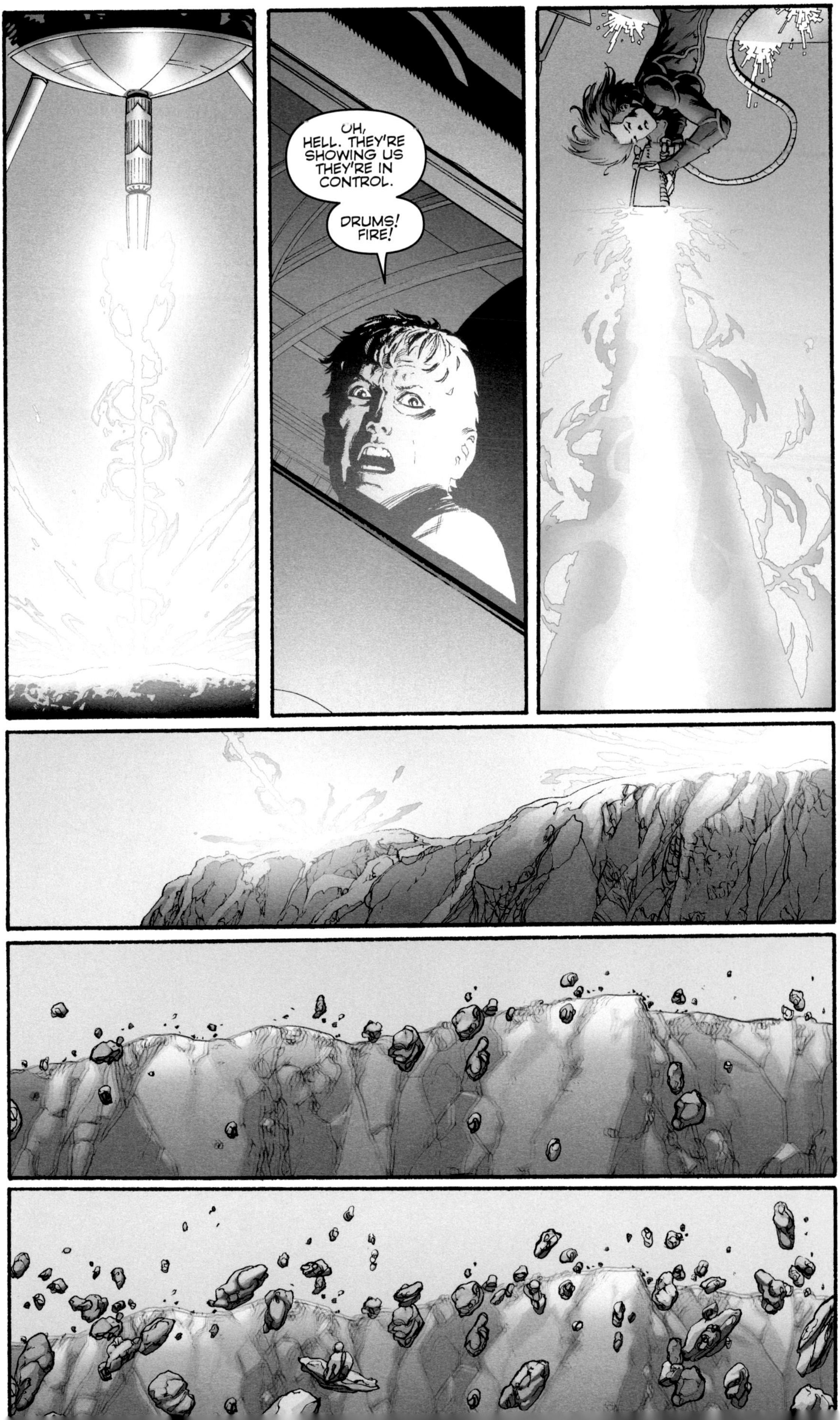
OH, HELL. THEY'RE SHOWING US THEY'RE IN CONTROL.
DRUMS! FIRE!

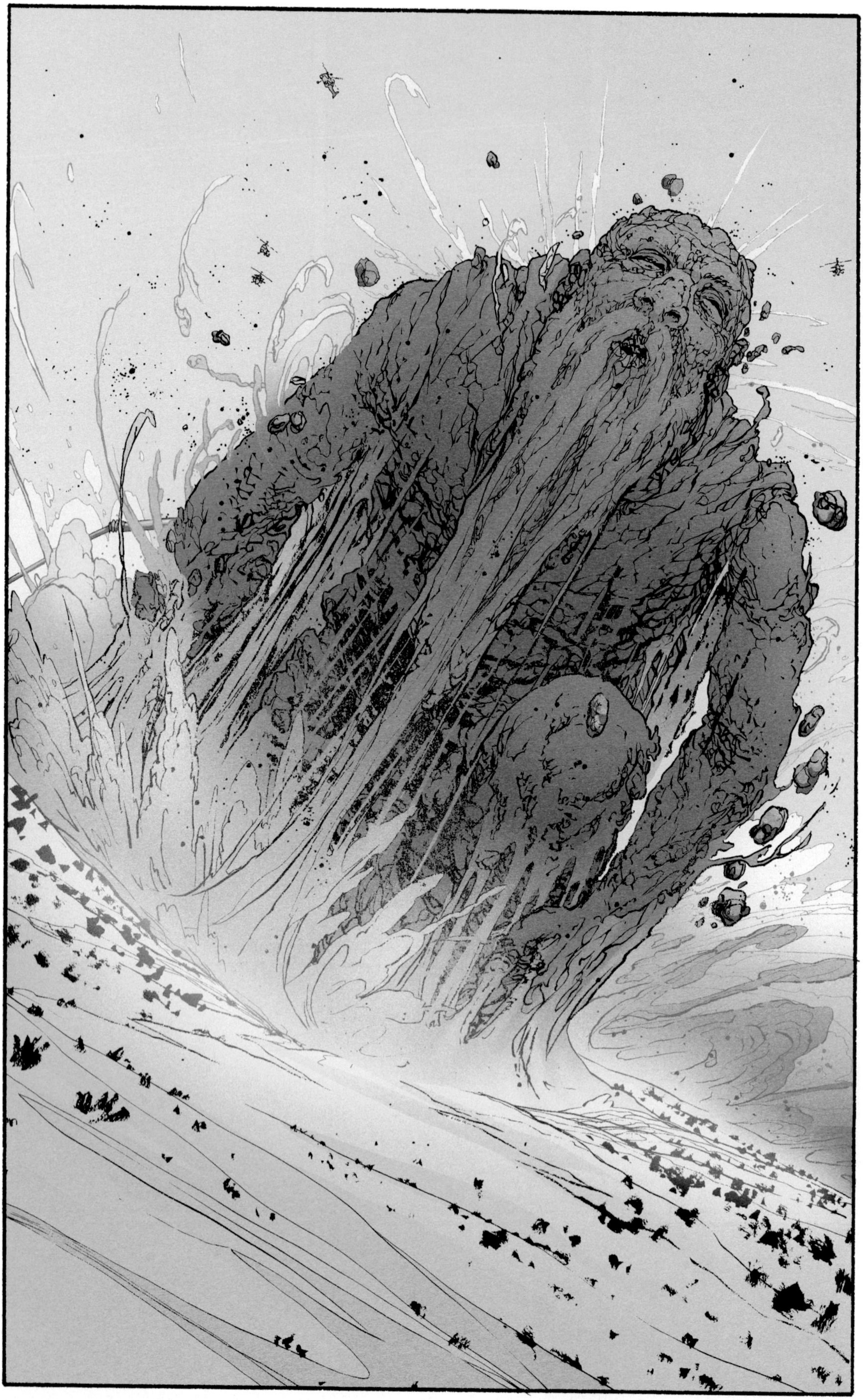

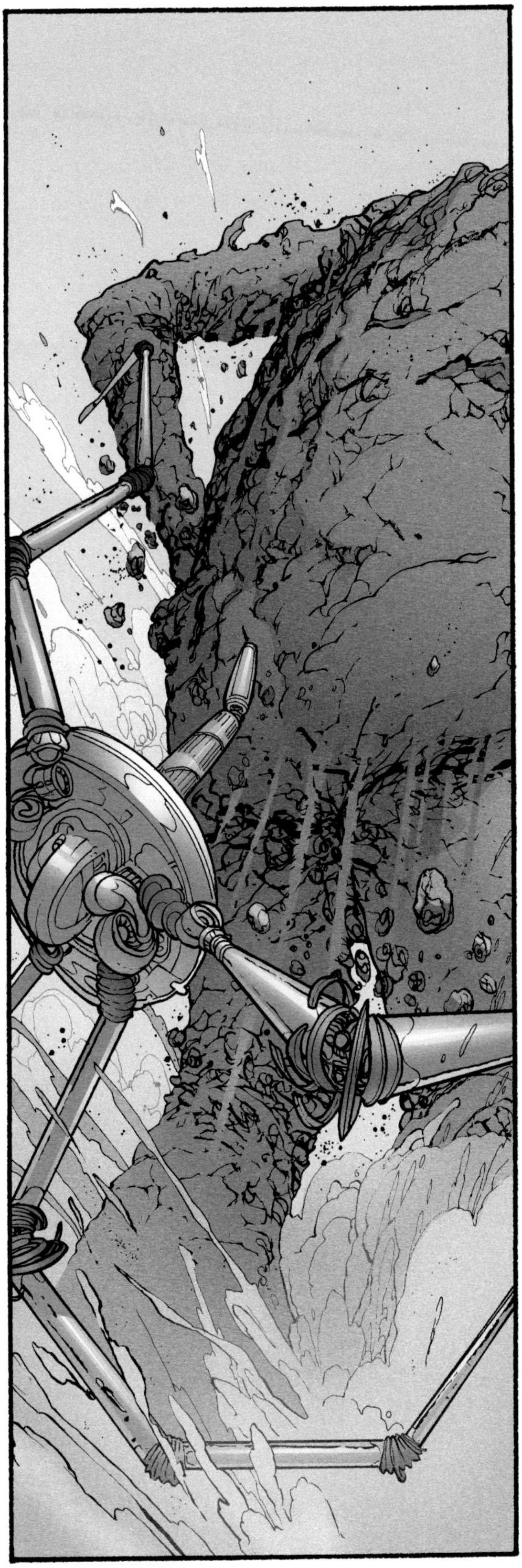

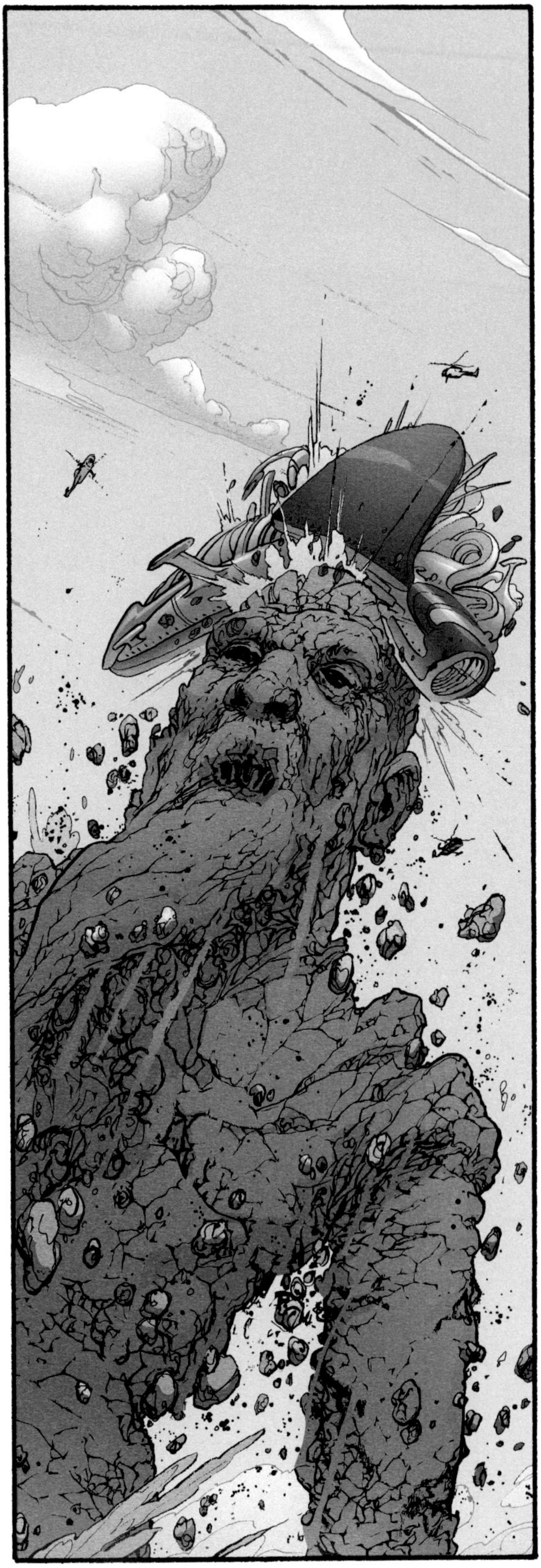

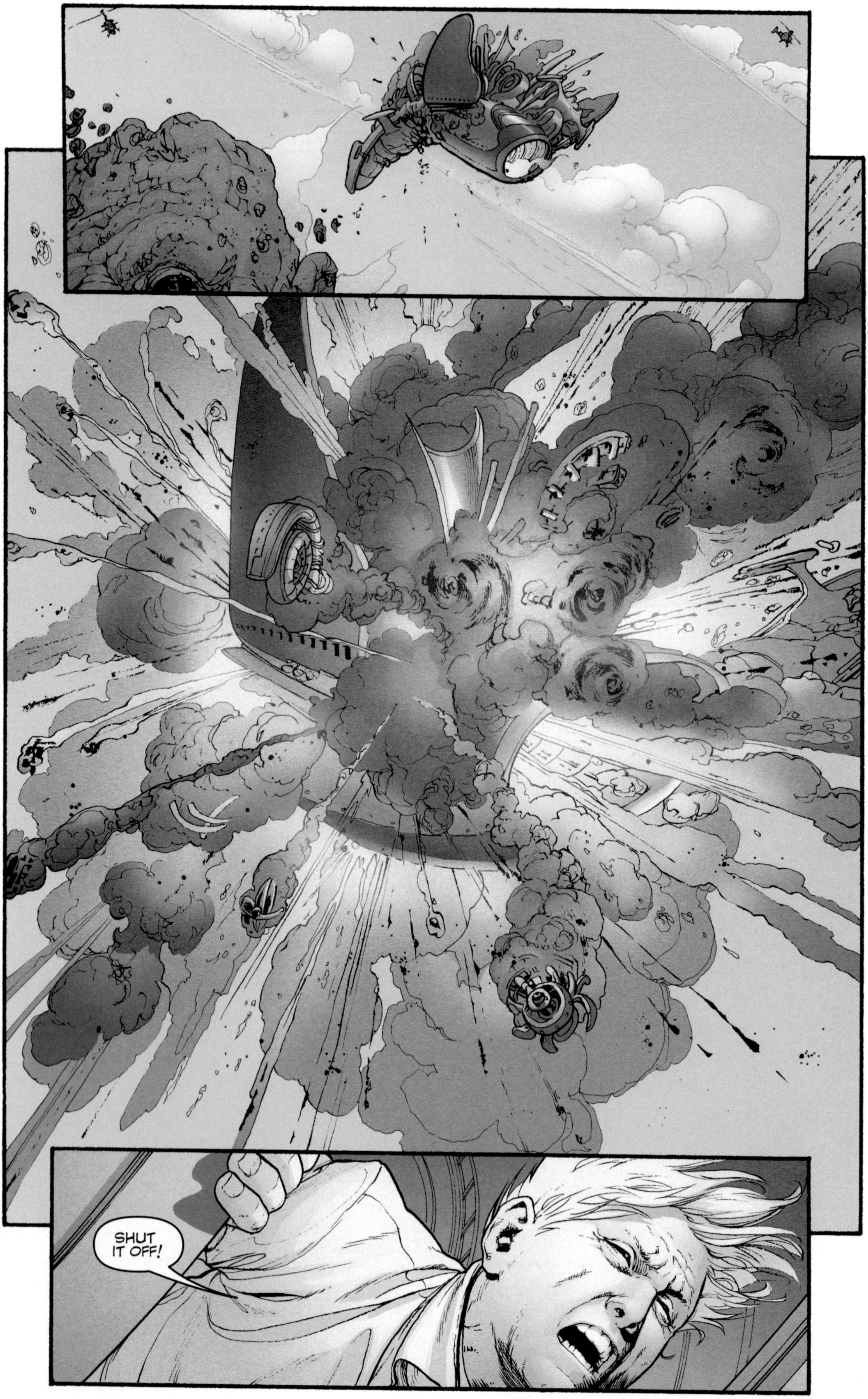
SHUT IT OFF!

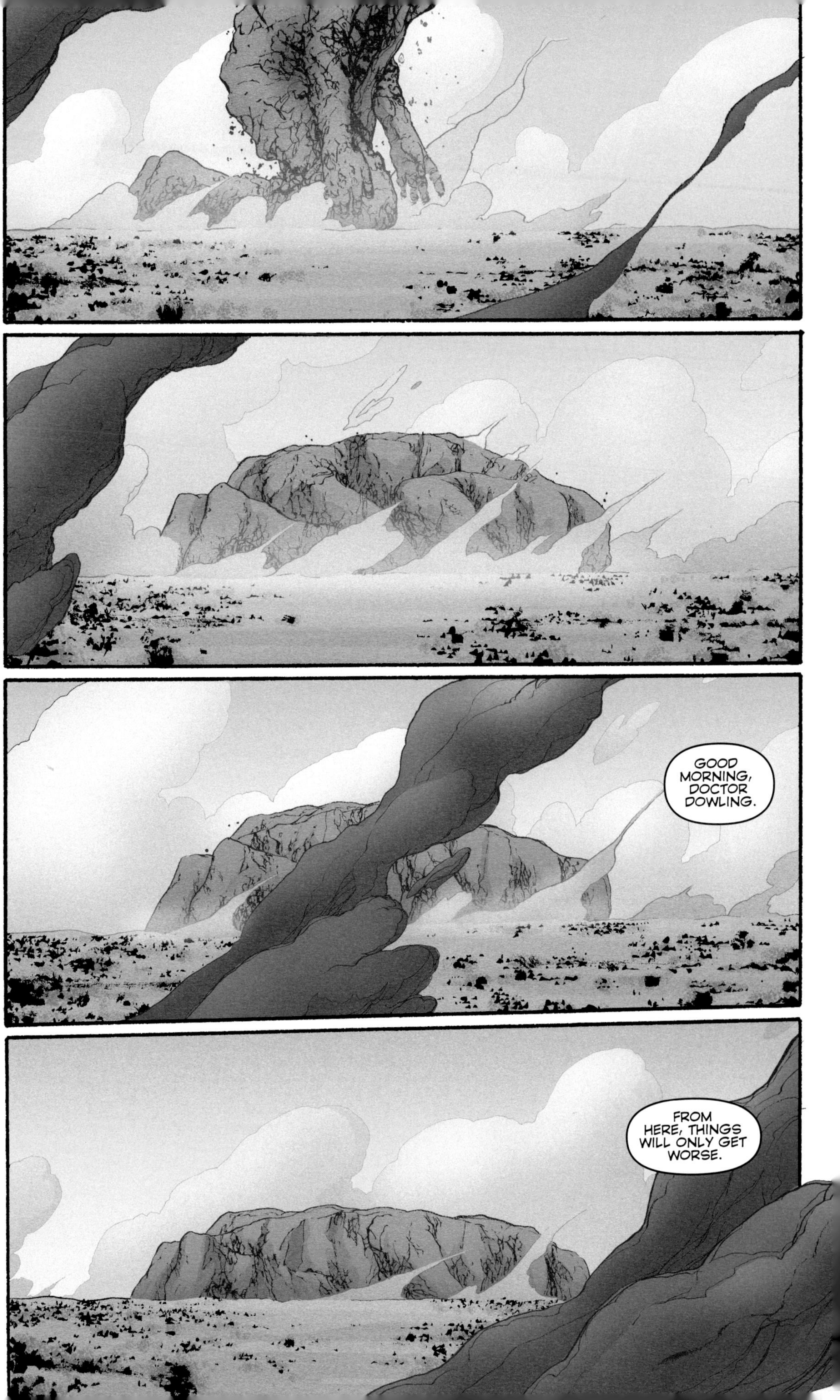
GOOD MORNING, DOCTOR DOWLING.
FROM HERE, THINGS WILL ONLY GET WORSE.

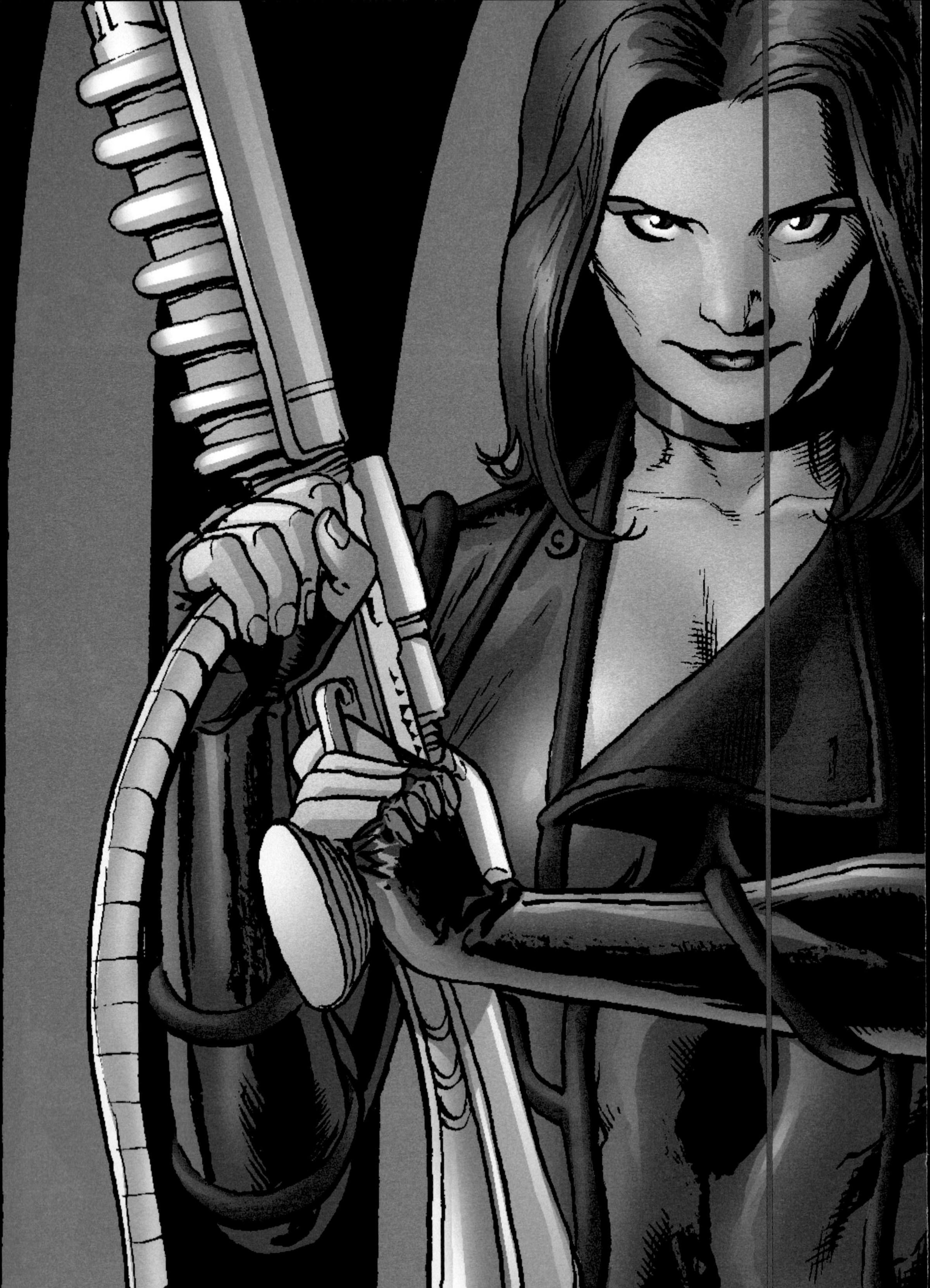

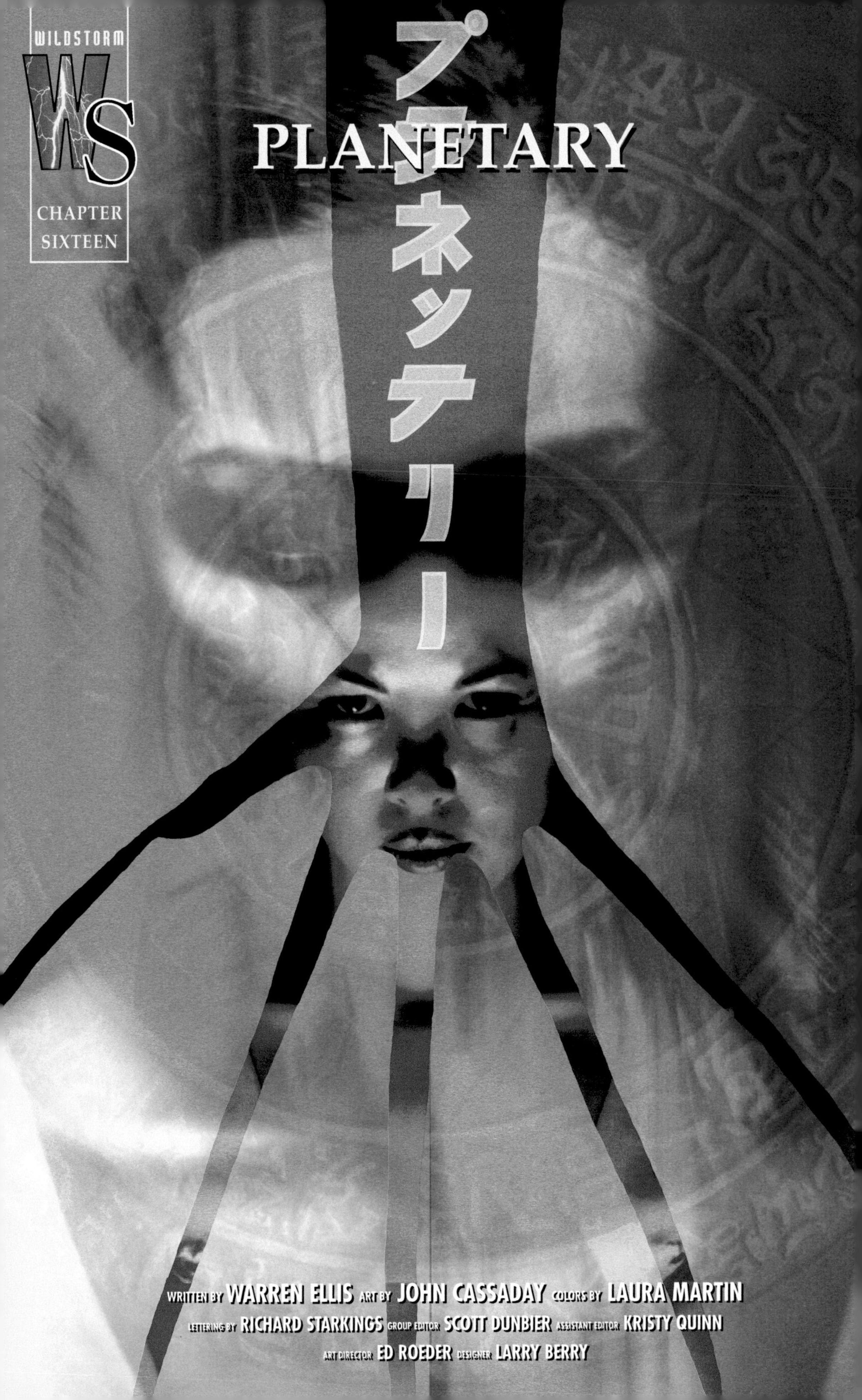

WILDSTORM
WS
CHAPTER SIXTEEN
プラネッテリー
PLANETARY
WRITTEN BY WARREN ELLIS ART BY JOHN CASSADAY COLORS BY LAURA MARTIN
LETTERING BY RICHARD STARKINGS GROUP EDITOR SCOTT DUNBIER ASSISTANT EDITOR KRISTY QUINN
ART DIRECTOR ED ROEDER DESIGNER LARRY BERRY

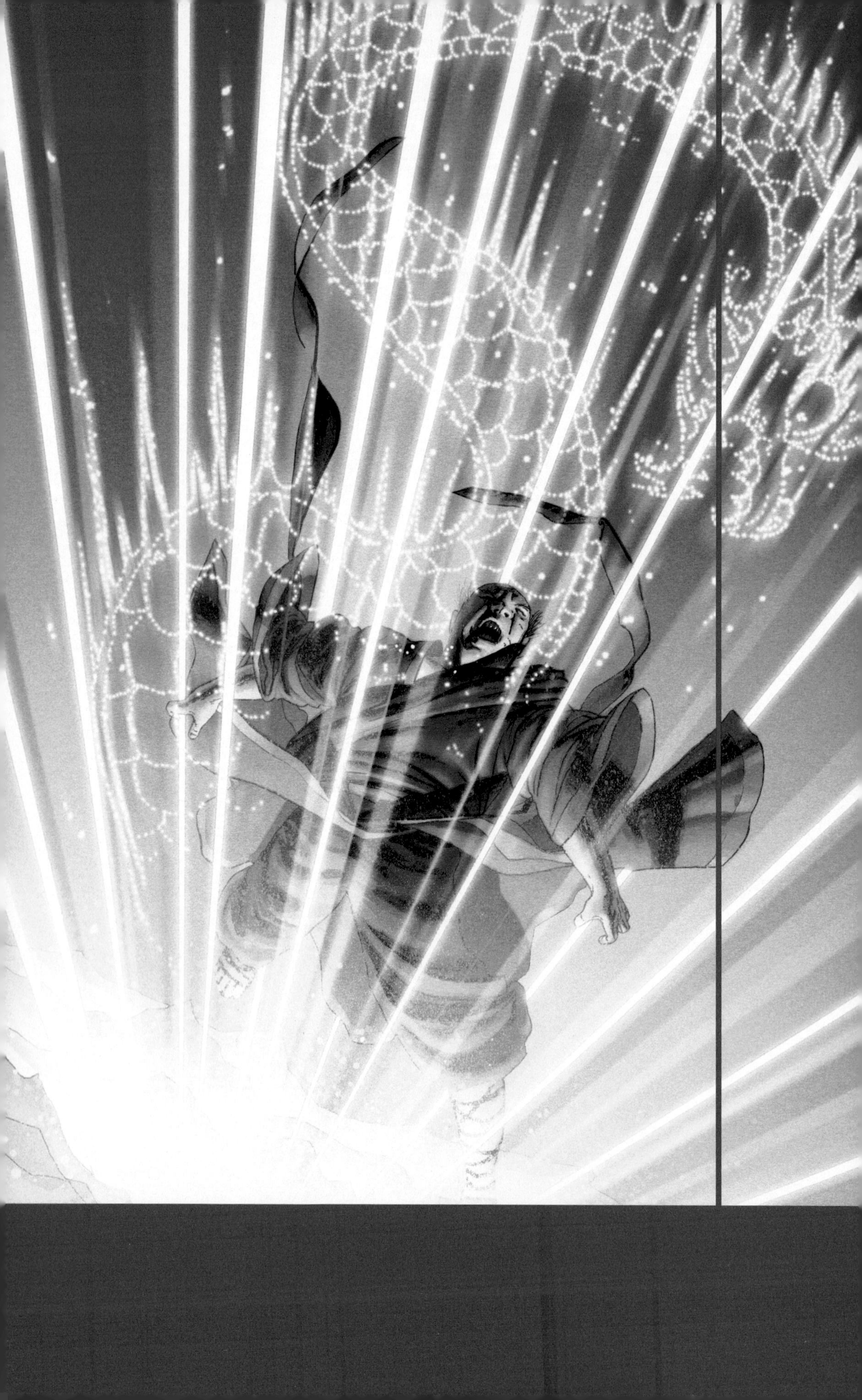

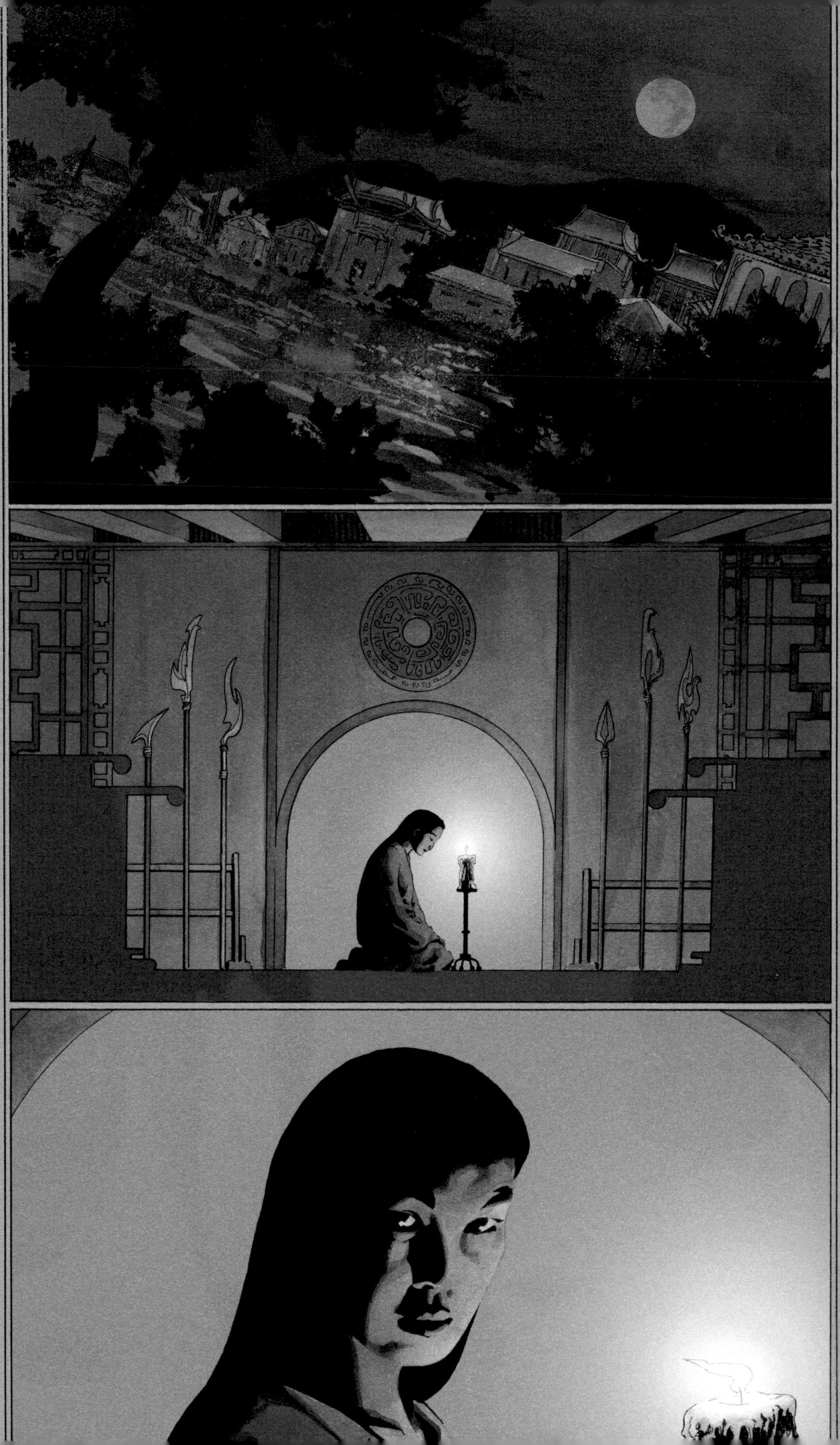

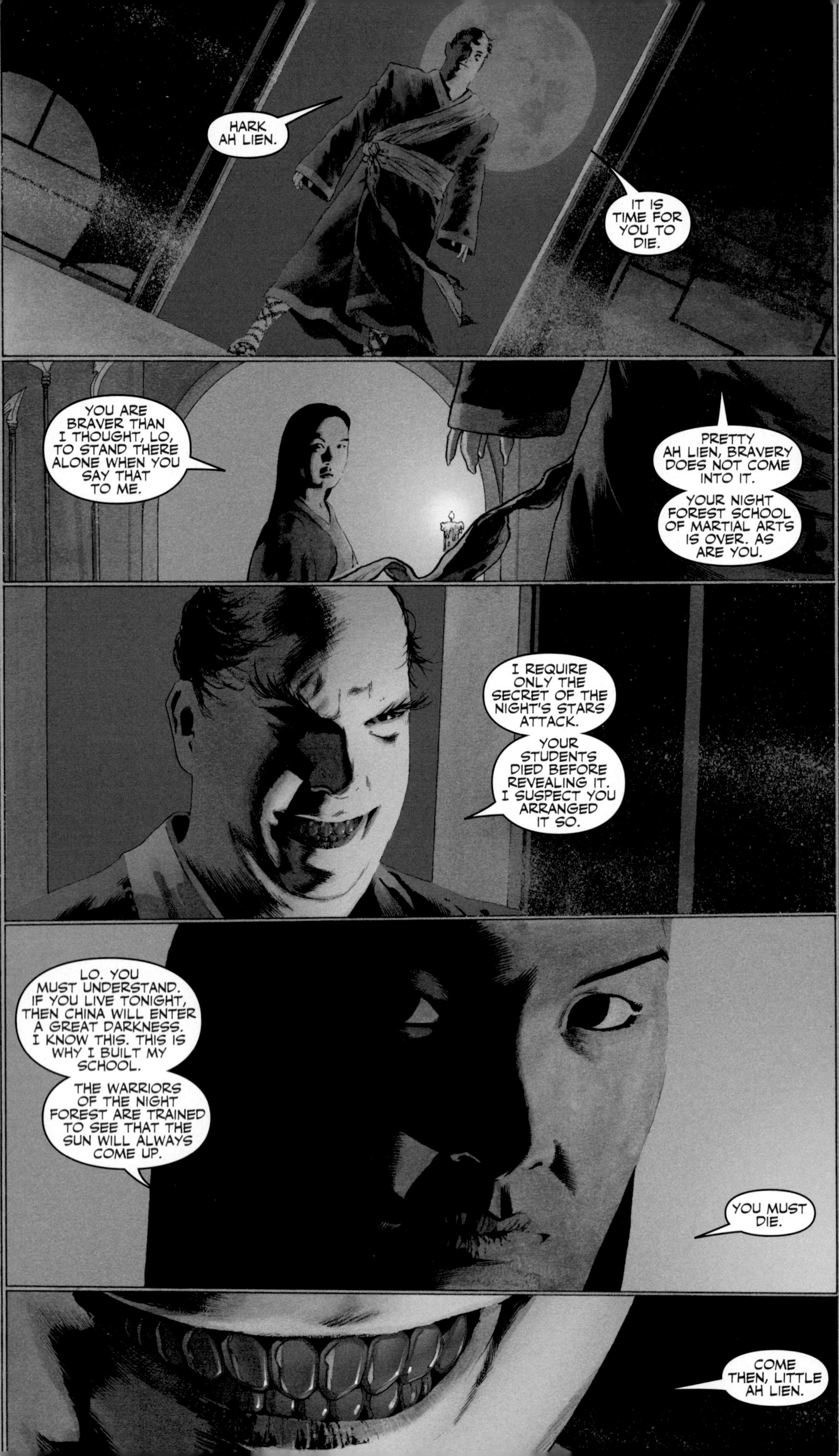
HARK AH LIEN.
IT IS TIME FOR YOU TO DIE.
YOU ARE BRAVER THAN I THOUGHT, LO, TO STAND THERE ALONE WHEN YOU SAY THAT TO ME.
PRETTY AH LIEN, BRAVERY DOES NOT COME INTO IT.
YOUR NIGHT FOREST SCHOOL OF MARTIAL ARTS IS OVER. AS ARE YOU.
I REQUIRE ONLY THE SECRET OF THE NIGHT'S STARS ATTACK.
YOUR STUDENTS DIED BEFORE REVEALING IT. I SUSPECT YOU ARRANGED IT SO.
LO. YOU MUST UNDERSTAND. IF YOU LIVE TONIGHT, THEN CHINA WILL ENTER A GREAT DARKNESS. I KNOW THIS. THIS IS WHY I BUILT MY SCHOOL.
THE WARRIORS OF THE NIGHT FOREST ARE TRAINED TO SEE THAT THE SUN WILL ALWAYS COME UP.
YOU MUST DIE.
COME THEN, LITTLE AH LIEN.

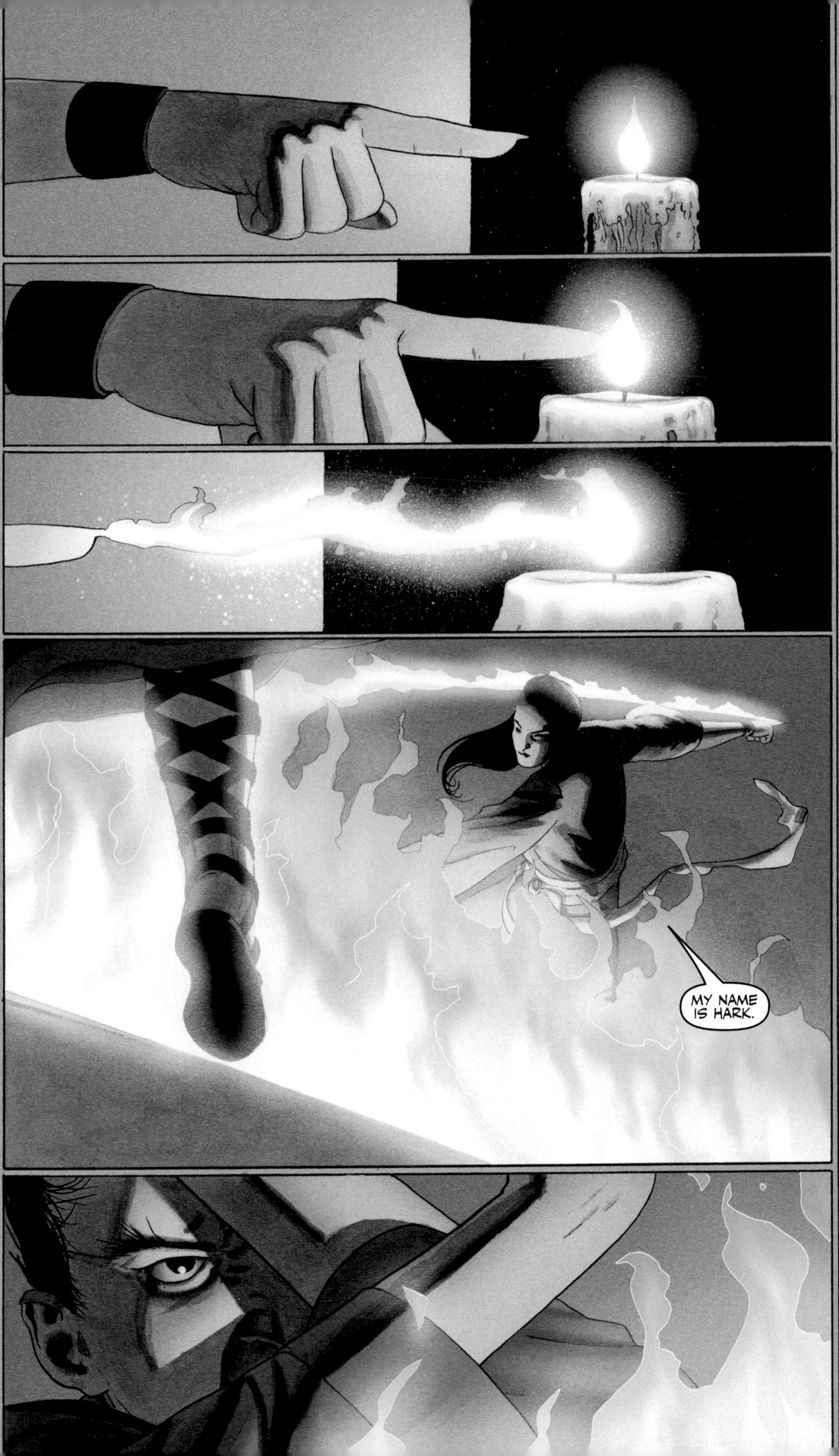
MY NAME IS HARK.

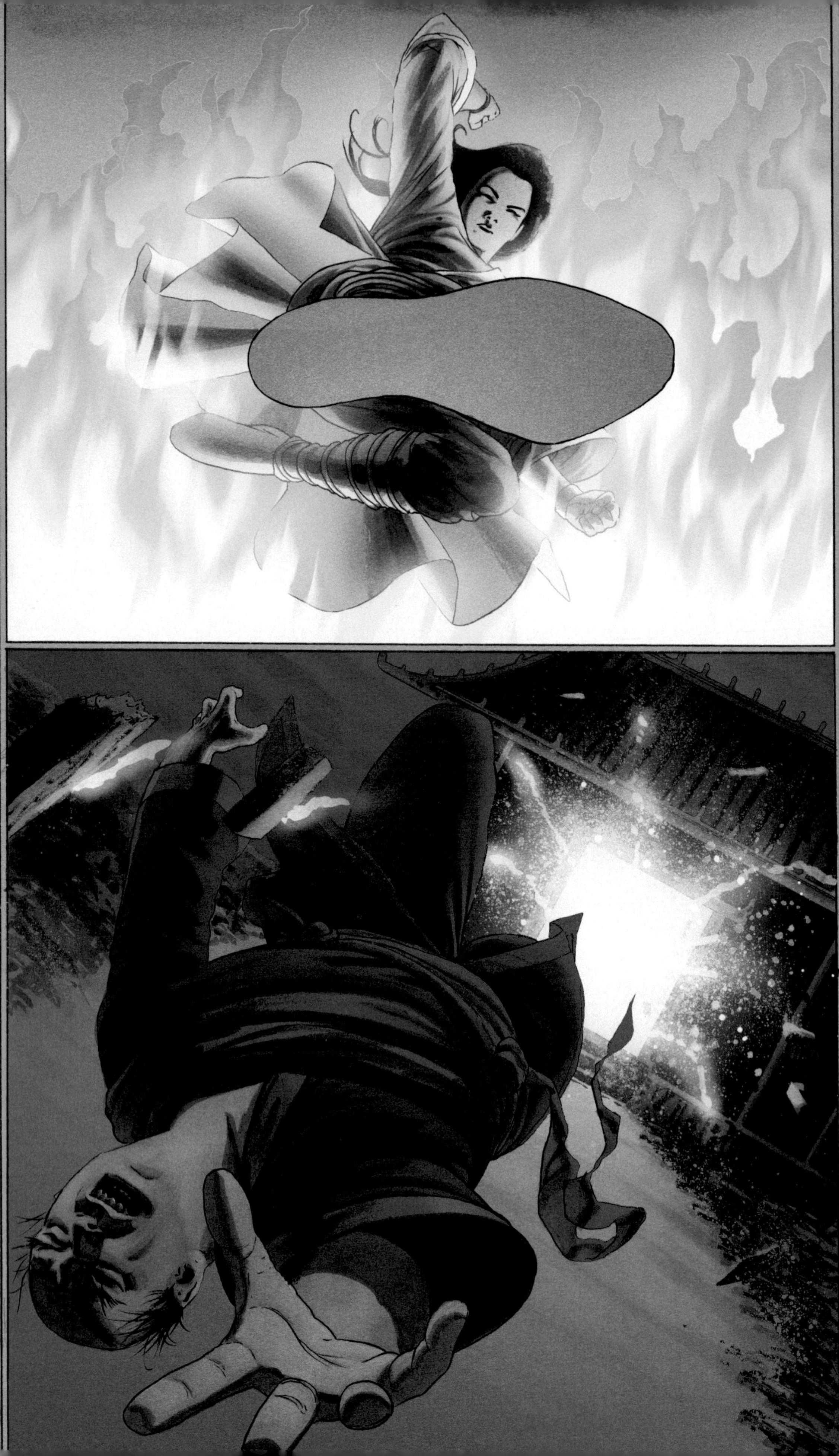

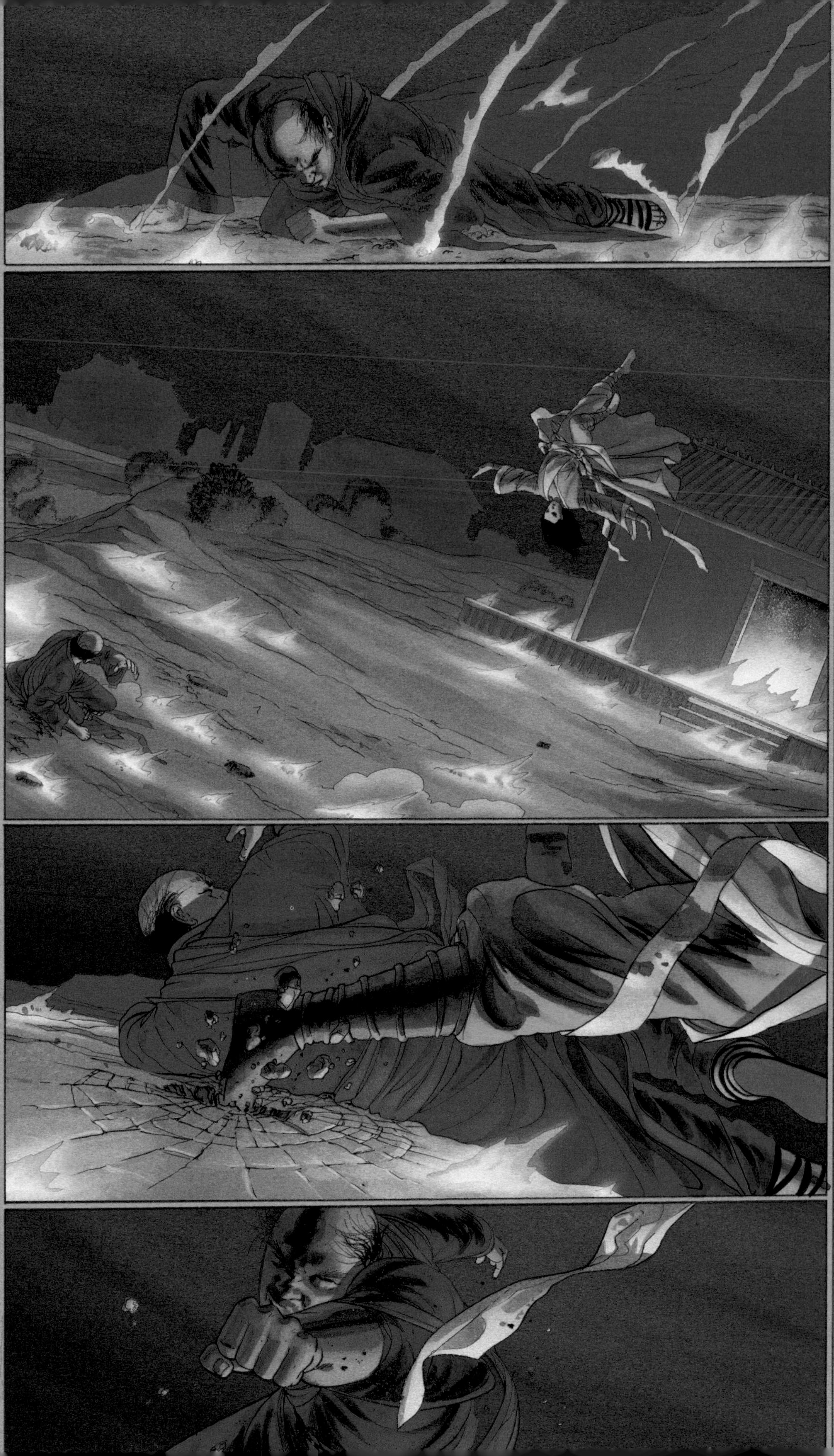

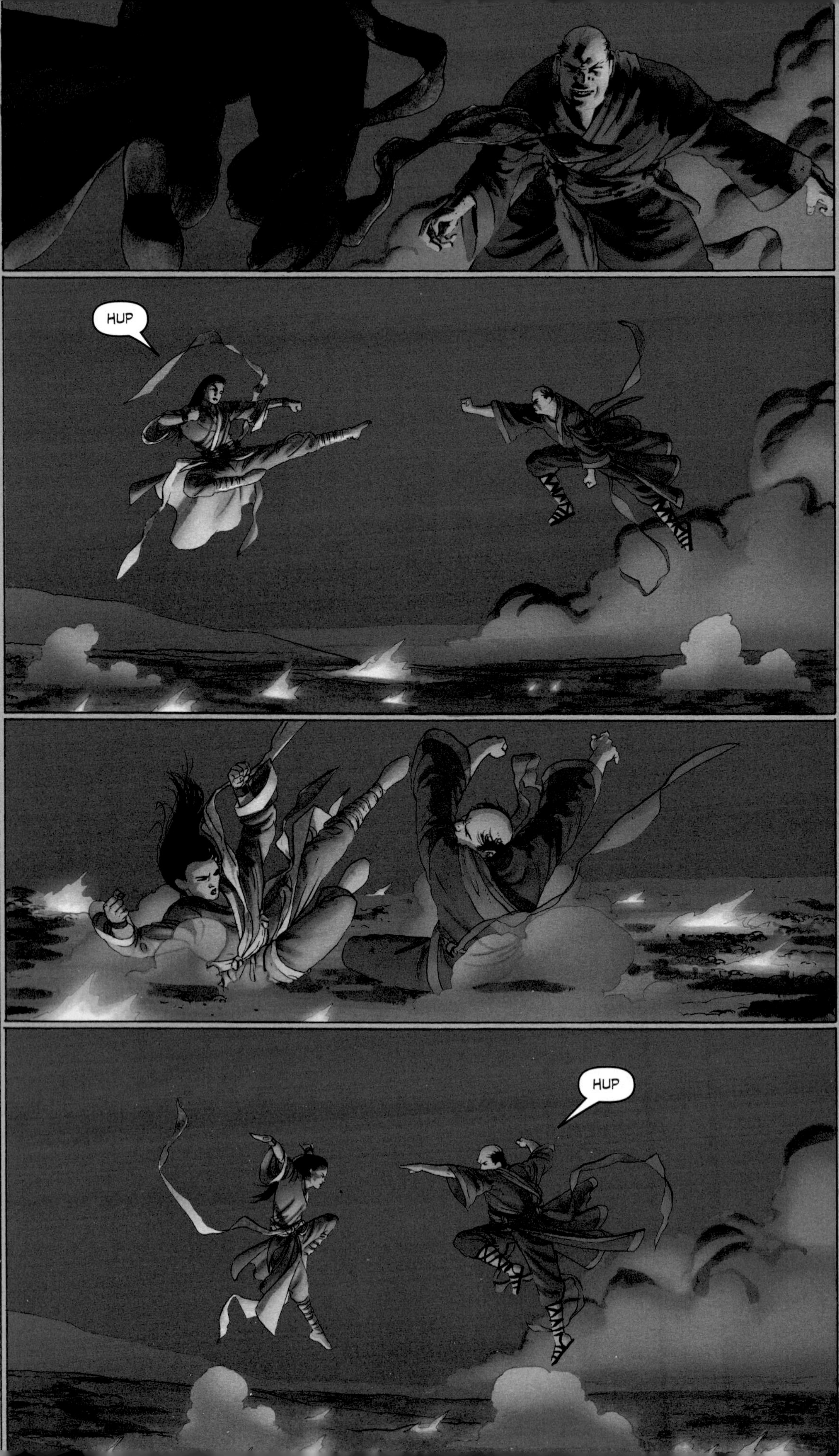
HUP
HUP

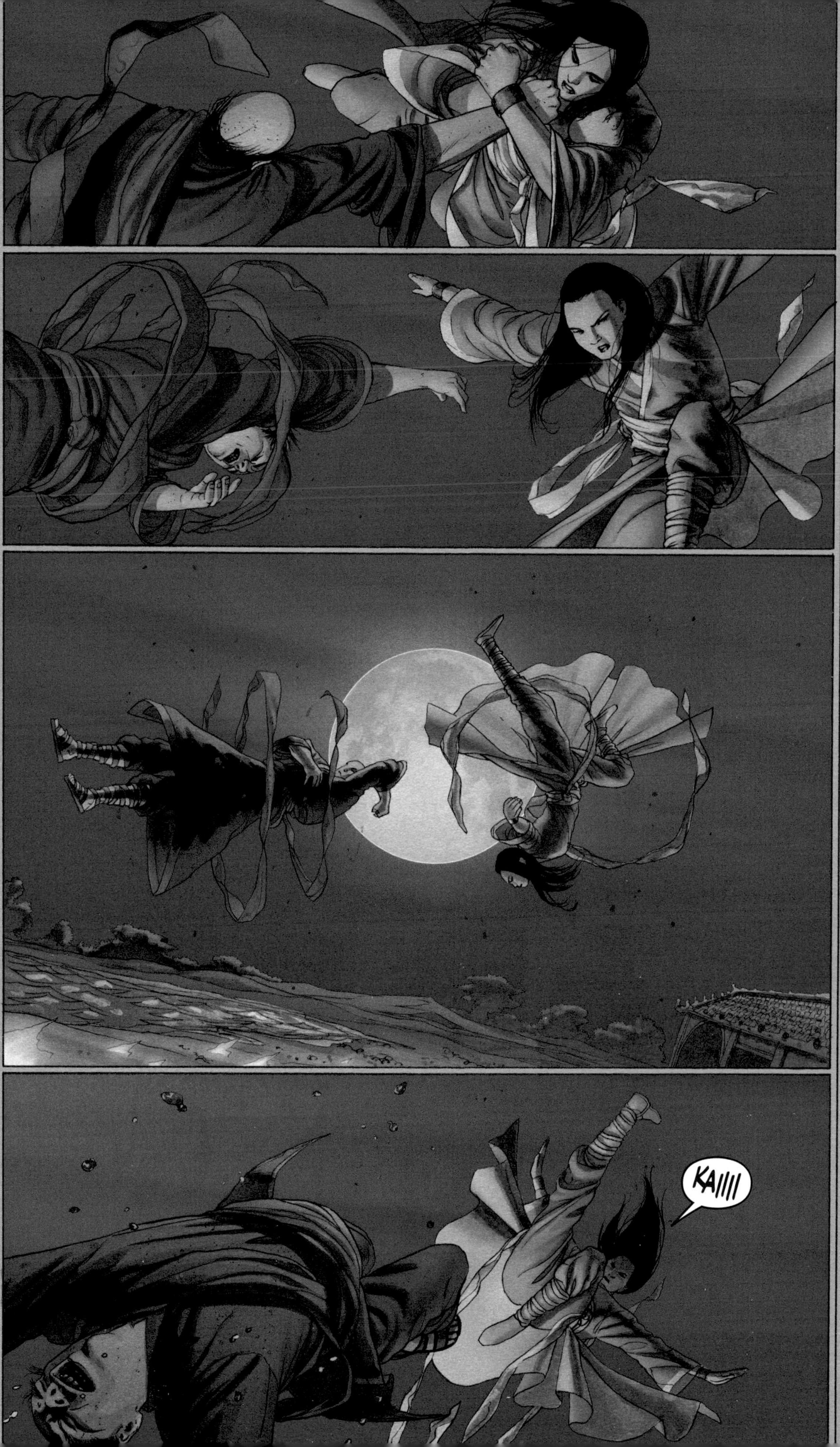
KAIIII

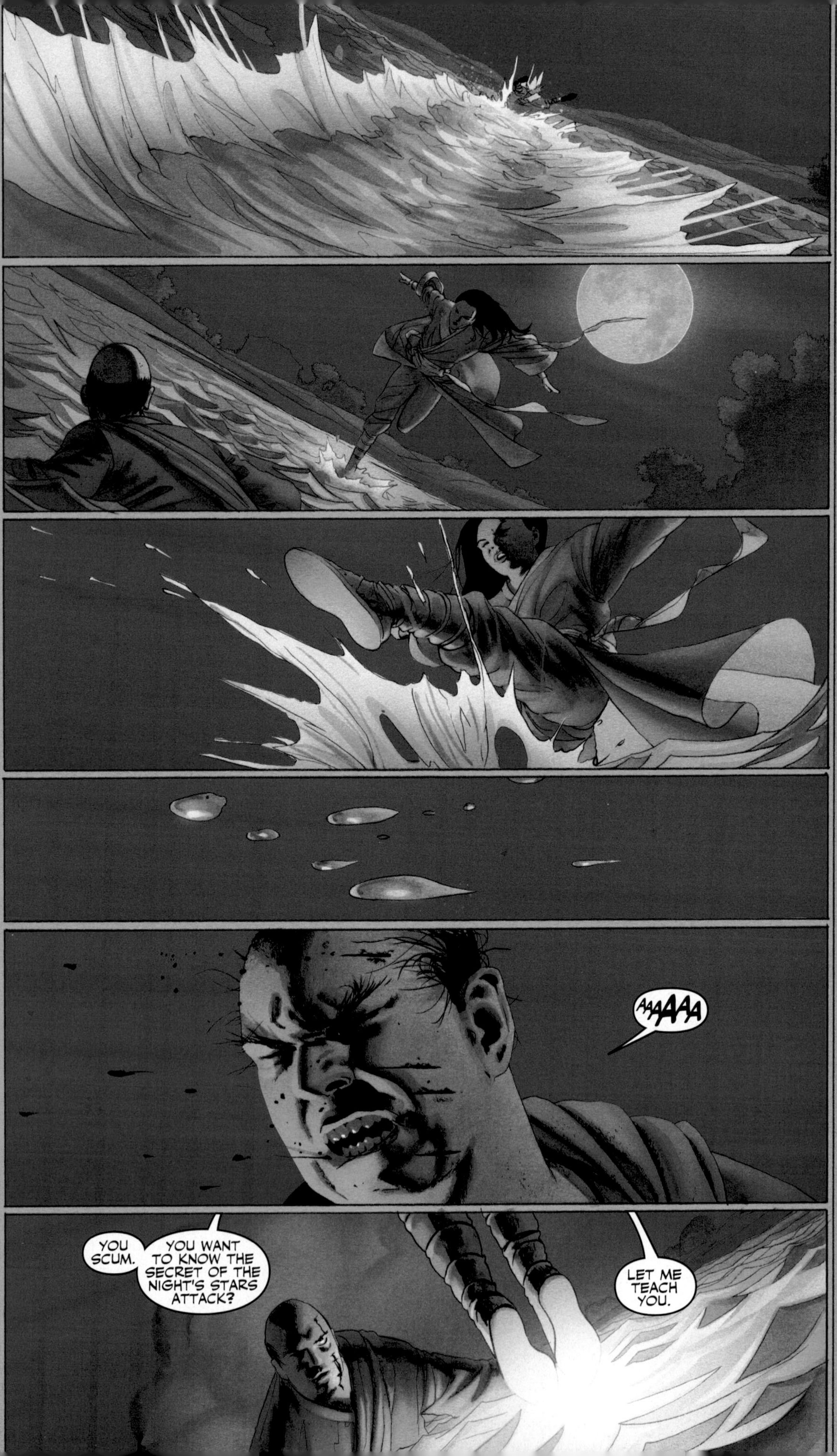
AAAAAA
YOU SCUM.
YOU WANT TO KNOW THE SECRET OF THE NIGHT'S STARS ATTACK?
LET ME TEACH YOU.

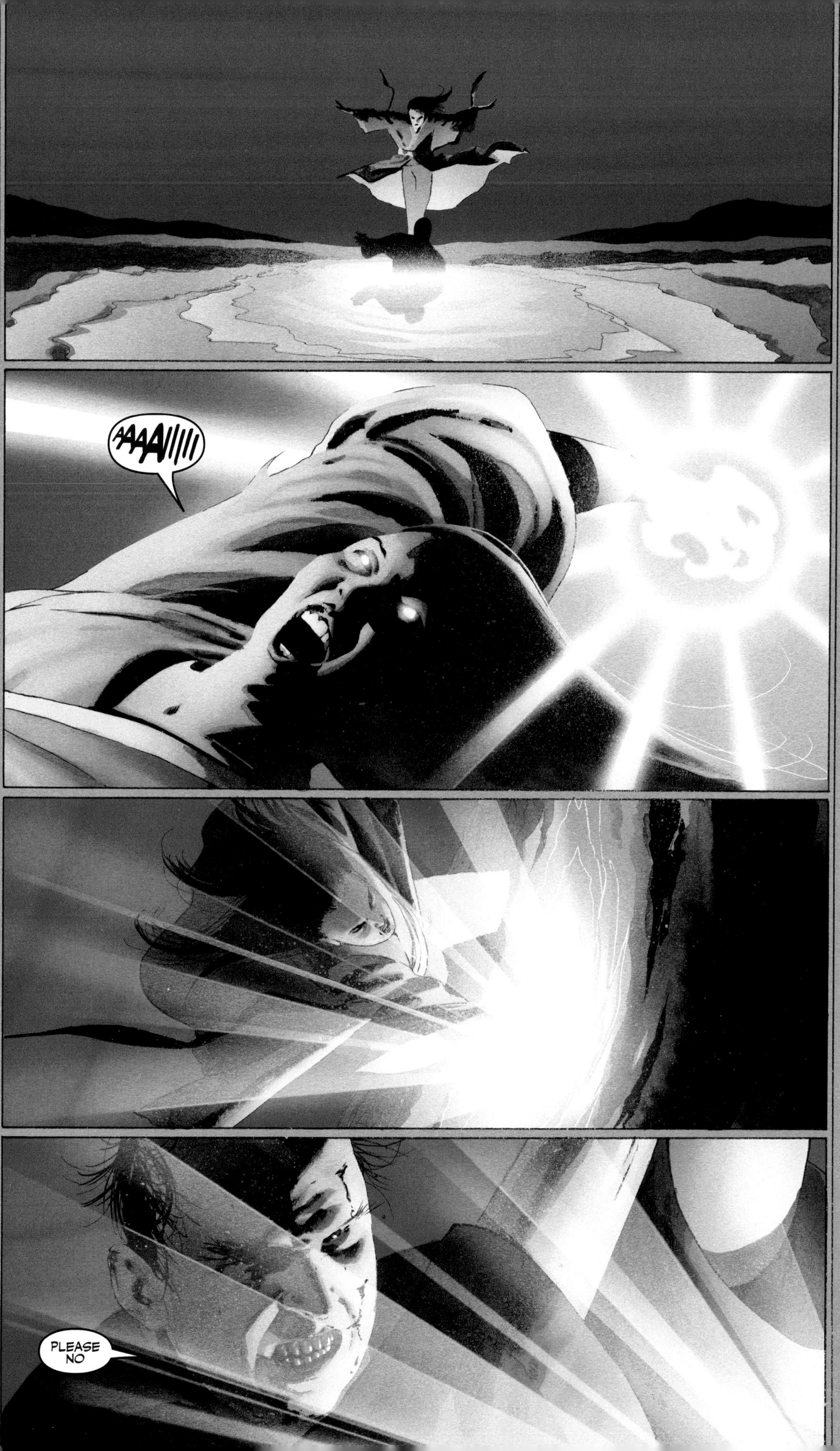
AAAAIIIII
PLEASE NO

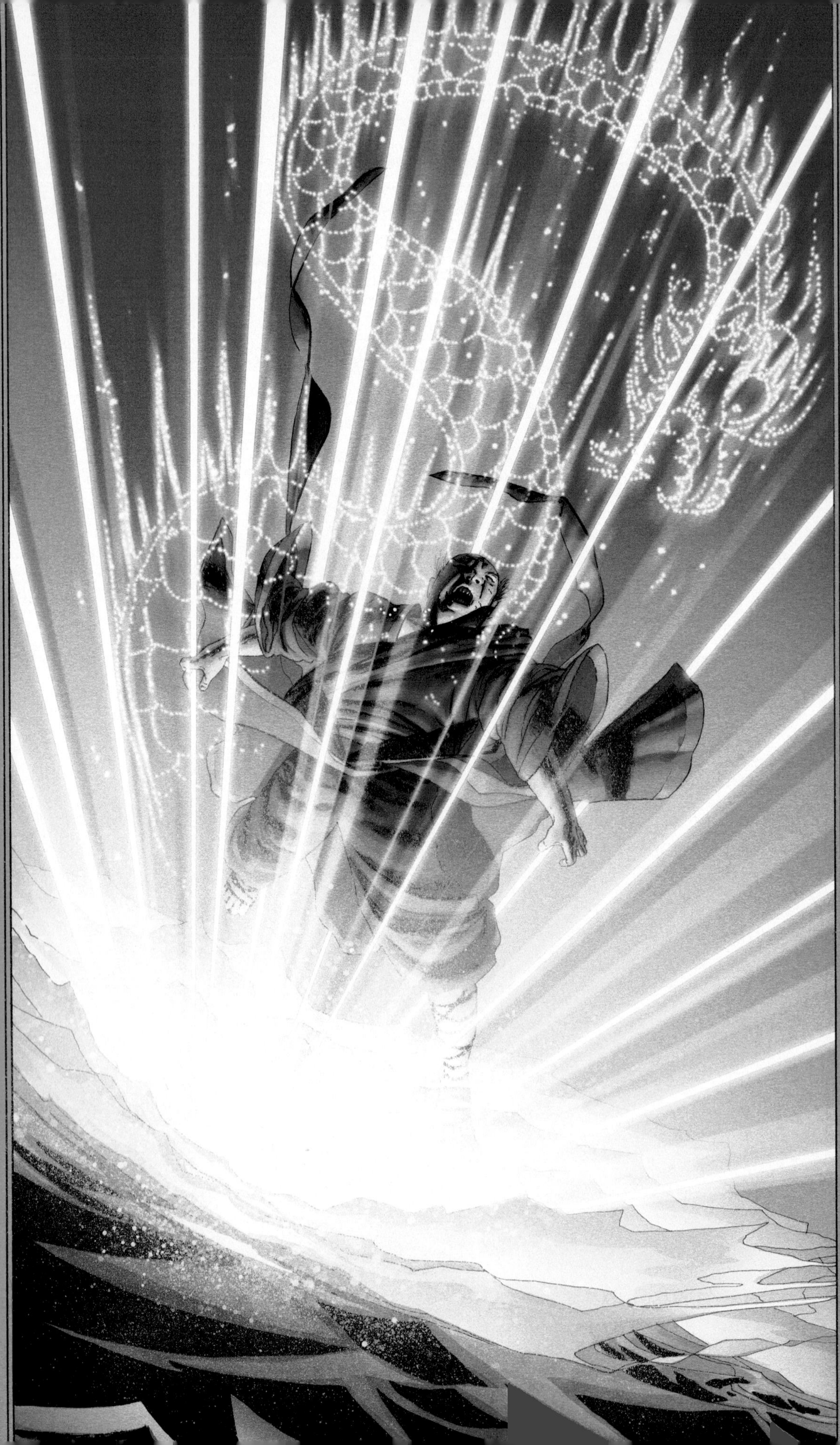

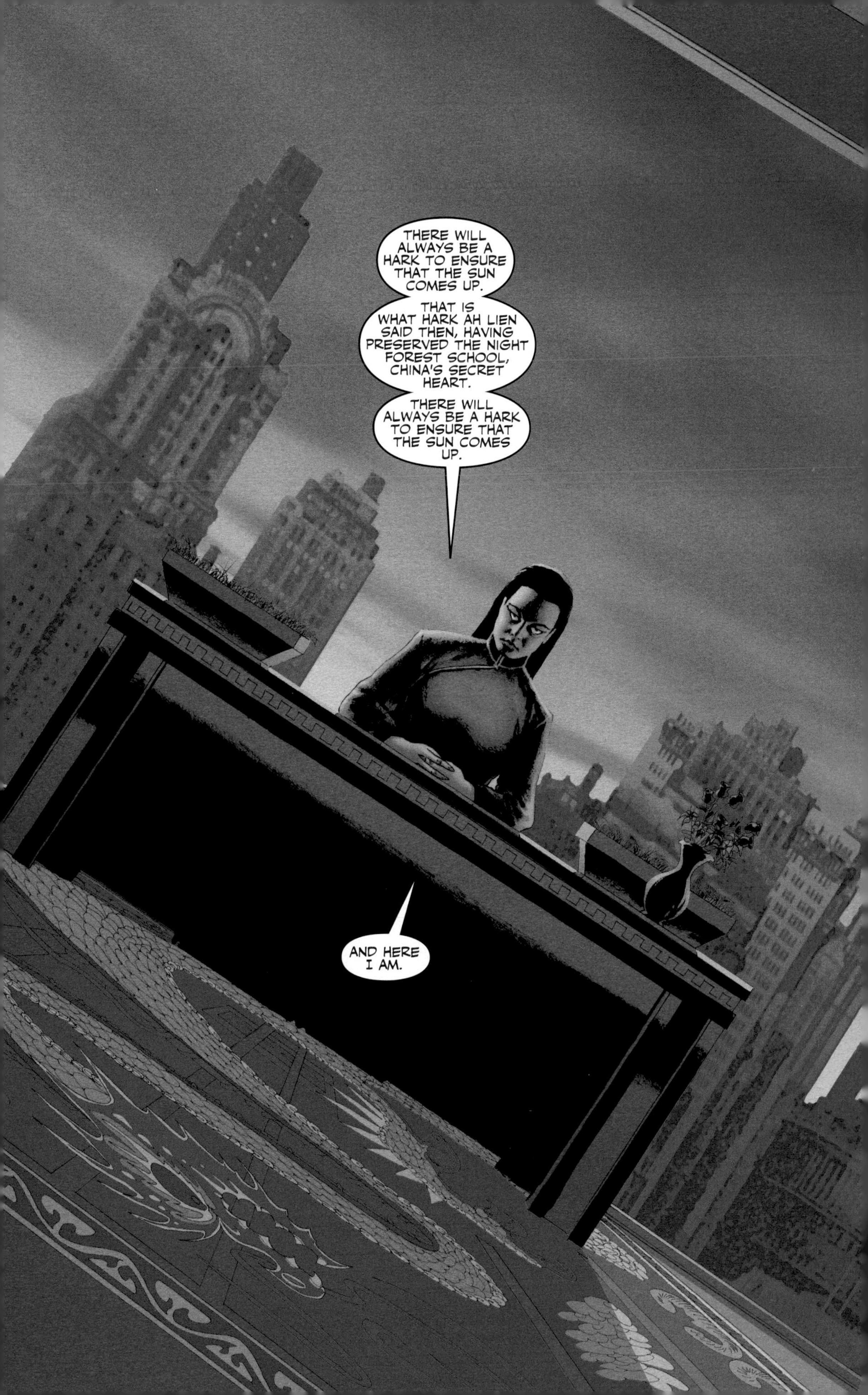
THERE WILL ALWAYS BE A HARK TO ENSURE THAT THE SUN COMES UP.
THAT IS WHAT HARK AH LIEN SAID THEN, HAVING PRESERVED THE NIGHT FOREST SCHOOL, CHINA'S SECRET HEART.
THERE WILL ALWAYS BE A HARK TO ENSURE THAT THE SUN COMES UP.
AND HERE I AM.

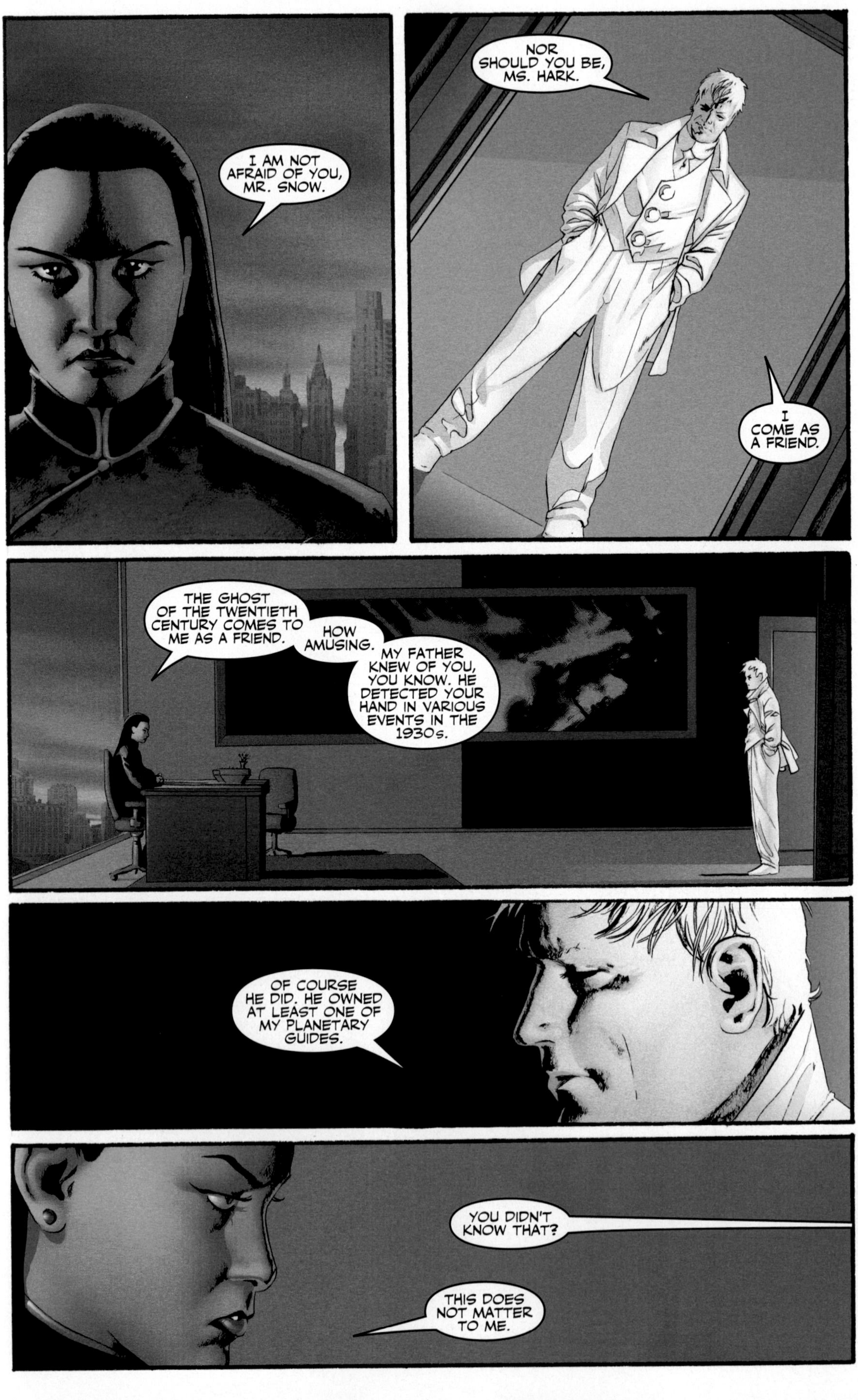
I AM NOT AFRAID OF YOU, MR. SNOW.
NOR SHOULD YOU BE, MS. HARK.
I COME AS A FRIEND.
THE GHOST OF THE TWENTIETH CENTURY COMES TO ME AS A FRIEND.
HOW AMUSING.
MY FATHER KNEW OF YOU, YOU KNOW. HE DETECTED YOUR HAND IN VARIOUS EVENTS IN THE 1930s.
OF COURSE HE DID. HE OWNED AT LEAST ONE OF MY PLANETARY GUIDES.
YOU DIDN'T KNOW THAT?
THIS DOES NOT MATTER TO ME.

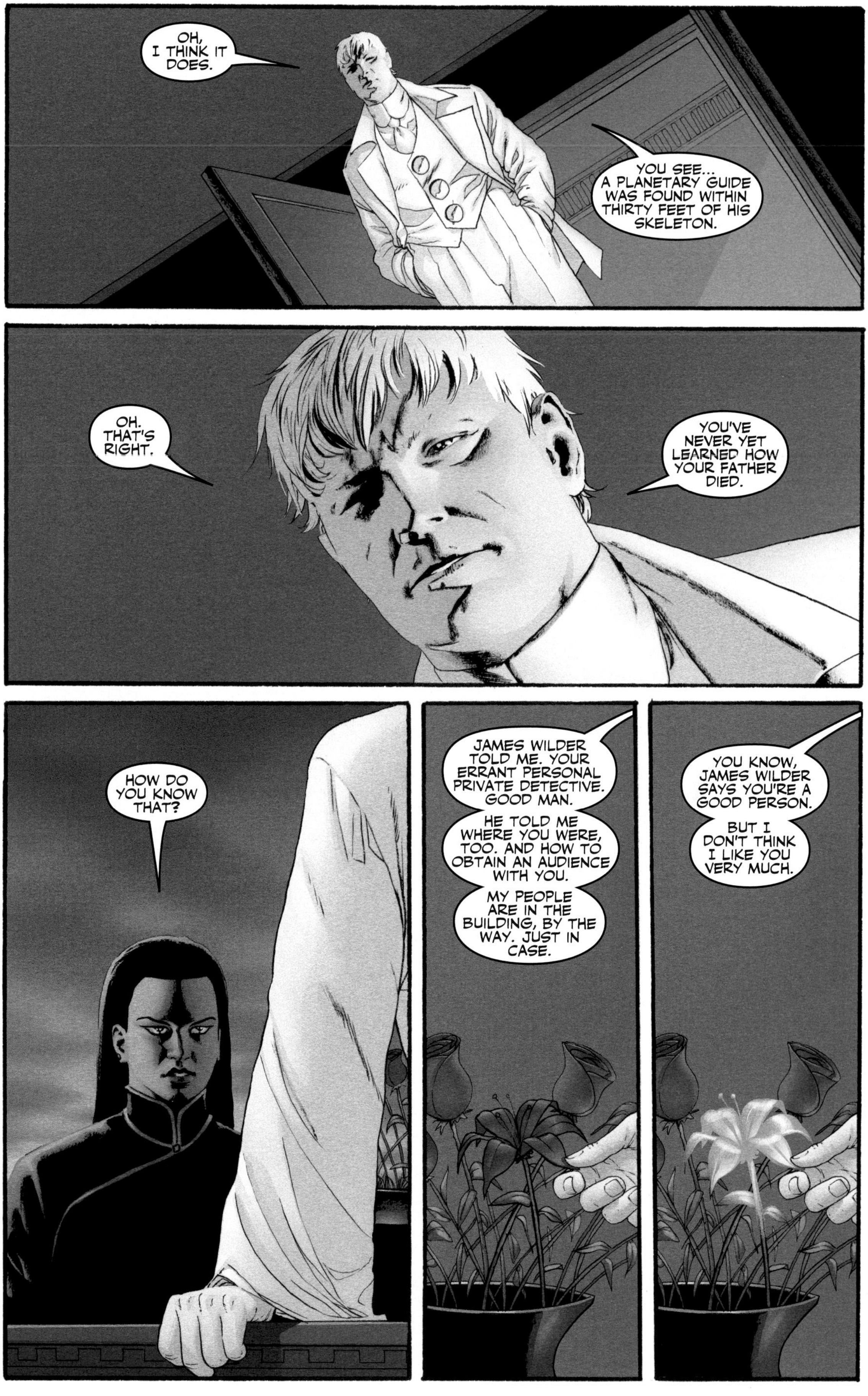
OH, I THINK IT DOES.
YOU SEE... A PLANETARY GUIDE WAS FOUND WITHIN THIRTY FEET OF HIS SKELETON.
OH. THAT'S RIGHT.
YOU'VE NEVER YET LEARNED HOW YOUR FATHER DIED.
HOW DO YOU KNOW THAT?
JAMES WILDER TOLD ME. YOUR ERRANT PERSONAL PRIVATE DETECTIVE. GOOD MAN.
HE TOLD ME WHERE YOU WERE, TOO. AND HOW TO OBTAIN AN AUDIENCE WITH YOU.
MY PEOPLE ARE IN THE BUILDING, BY THE WAY. JUST IN CASE.
YOU KNOW, JAMES WILDER SAYS YOU'RE A GOOD PERSON.
BUT I DON'T THINK I LIKE YOU VERY MUCH.

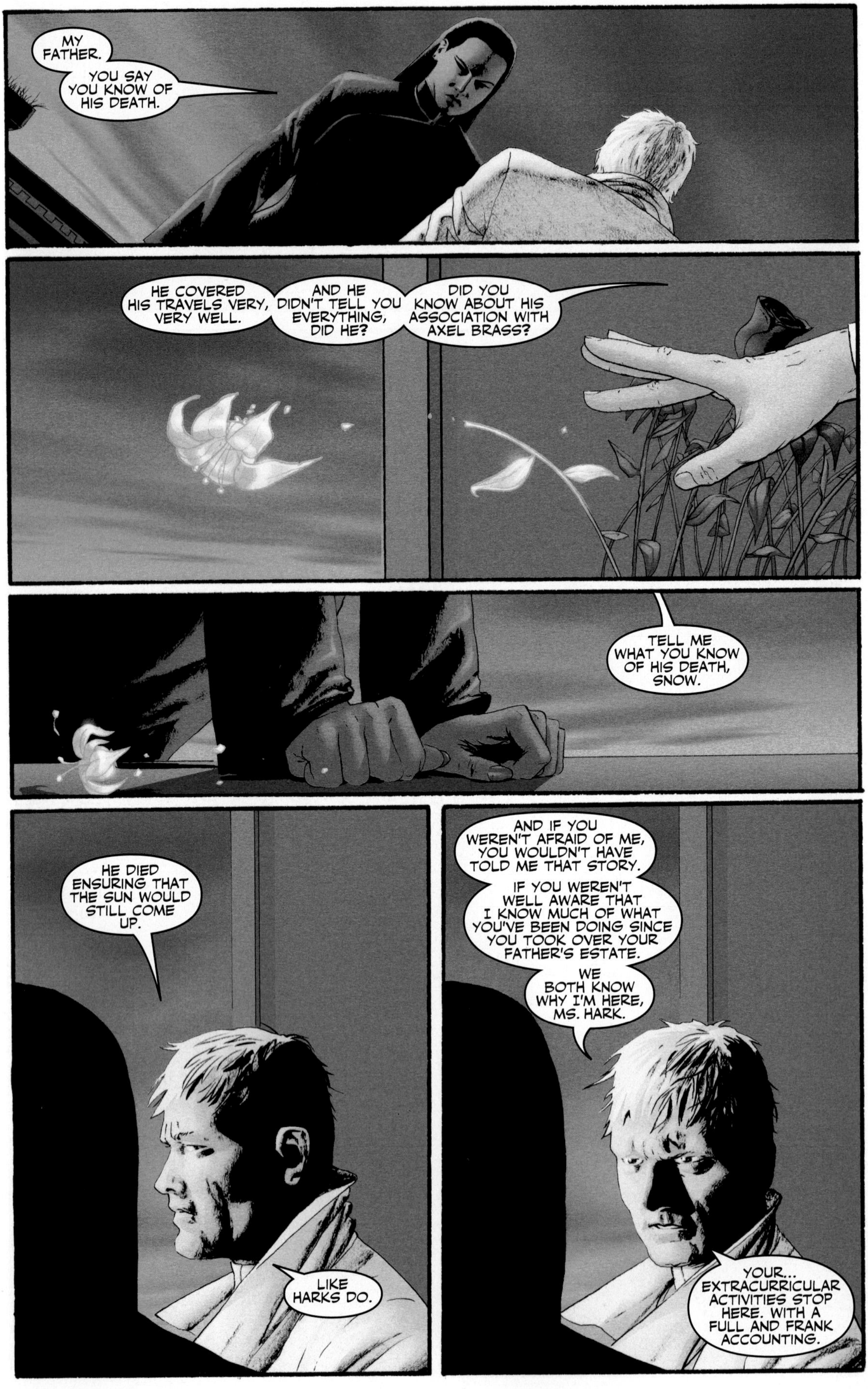
MY FATHER.
YOU SAY YOU KNOW OF HIS DEATH.
HE COVERED HIS TRAVELS VERY, VERY WELL.
AND HE DIDN'T TELL YOU EVERYTHING, DID HE?
DID YOU KNOW ABOUT HIS ASSOCIATION WITH AXEL BRASS?
TELL ME WHAT YOU KNOW OF HIS DEATH, SNOW.
HE DIED ENSURING THAT THE SUN WOULD STILL COME UP.
LIKE HARKS DO.
AND IF YOU WEREN'T AFRAID OF ME, YOU WOULDN'T HAVE TOLD ME THAT STORY.
IF YOU WEREN'T WELL AWARE THAT I KNOW MUCH OF WHAT YOU'VE BEEN DOING SINCE YOU TOOK OVER YOUR FATHER'S ESTATE.
WE BOTH KNOW WHY I'M HERE, MS. HARK.
YOUR... EXTRACURRICULAR ACTIVITIES STOP HERE. WITH A FULL AND FRANK ACCOUNTING.

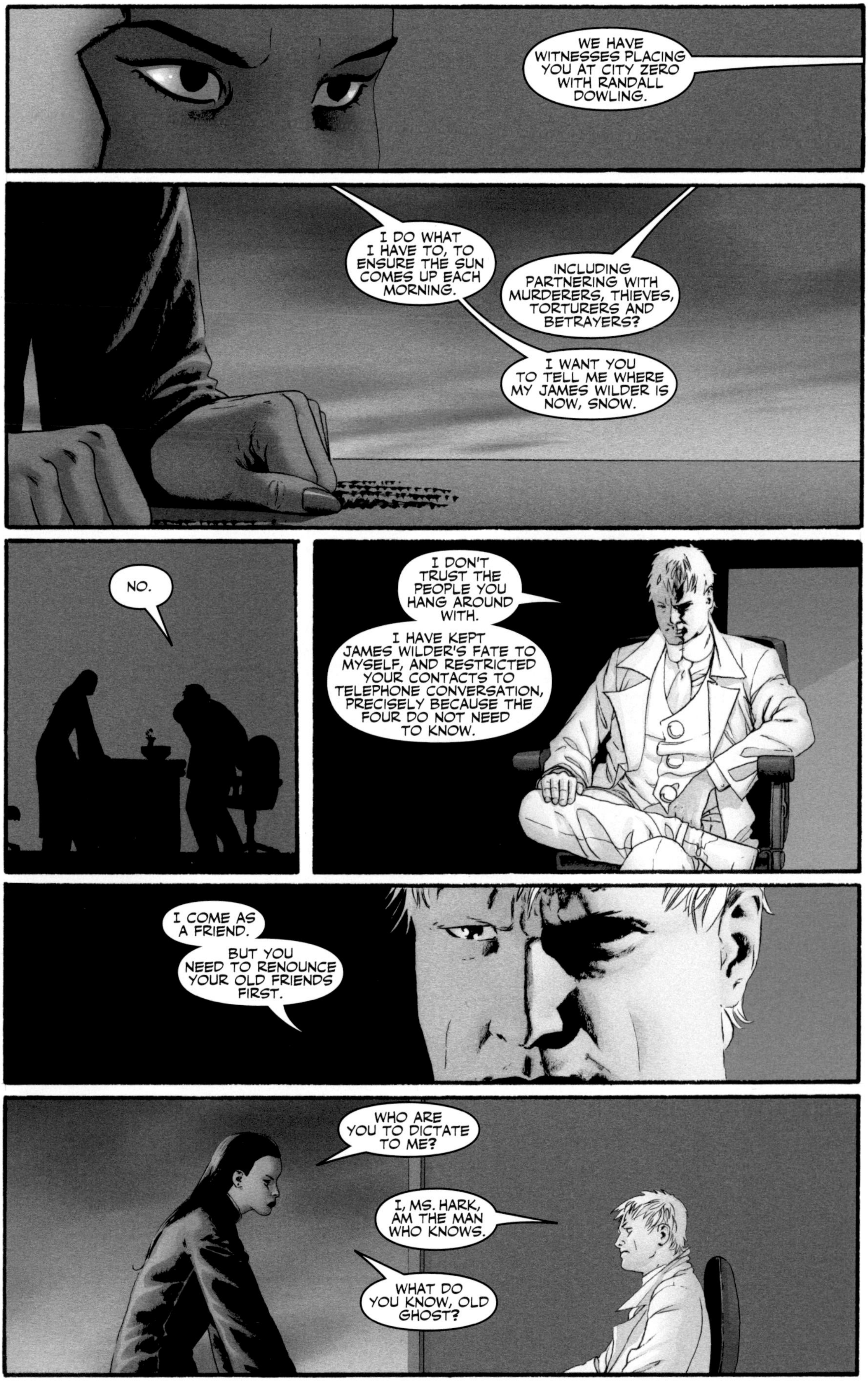
WE HAVE WITNESSES PLACING YOU AT CITY ZERO WITH RANDALL DOWLING.
I DO WHAT I HAVE TO, TO ENSURE THE SUN COMES UP EACH MORNING.
INCLUDING PARTNERING WITH MURDERERS, THIEVES, TORTURERS AND BETRAYERS?
I WANT YOU TO TELL ME WHERE MY JAMES WILDER IS NOW, SNOW.
NO.
I DON'T TRUST THE PEOPLE YOU HANG AROUND WITH.
I HAVE KEPT JAMES WILDER'S FATE TO MYSELF, AND RESTRICTED YOUR CONTACTS TO TELEPHONE CONVERSATION, PRECISELY BECAUSE THE FOUR DO NOT NEED TO KNOW.
I COME AS A FRIEND.
BUT YOU NEED TO RENOUNCE YOUR OLD FRIENDS FIRST.
WHO ARE YOU TO DICTATE TO ME?
I, MS. HARK, AM THE MAN WHO KNOWS.
WHAT DO YOU KNOW, OLD GHOST?

TWO THINGS.

I KNOW THAT I CAN AND WILL REMOVE THE FOUR FROM THIS PLANET, AND PUT THEIR KNOWLEDGE, AS WELL AS MY OWN, IN THE SERVICE OF THE PEOPLE OF THIS WORLD.

I'M ON THIS PLANET WITH YOU. IT IS IN MY BEST INTERESTS THAT THE SUN CONTINUE TO RISE EACH MORNING.

THIS PLACE IS A LAUNCHPAD FOR THE FOUR. ONE OF MANY. EARTH IS NO MORE THAN THAT TO THEM.

JOIN WITH ME, AND YOU CAN DO A HARK'S WORK WITH GREAT EFFECTIVENESS.

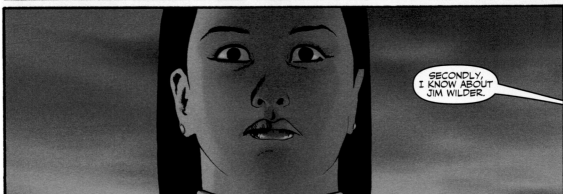

SECONDLY, I KNOW ABOUT JIM WILDER.

A HARK BUILDING BOMBED DOWN TO ITS FOUNDATIONS?

A STAGED MUGGING WHOSE PERPETRATOR LED WILDER RIGHT INTO THE BOMB SITE, AND LITERALLY RIGHT ACROSS THE TRAVELSTONE EXPOSED BY THE EXPLOSION?

YOUR FILES ARE VERY WELL DEFENDED. IT TOOK THE DRUMMER ALMOST A DAY TO HACK THE HARK CORPORATION SYSTEM.

YOU DIDN'T KNOW EXACTLY WHAT WAS DOWN THERE, BUT YOU HAD HEARD STORIES, AND MADE INTELLIGENT SUPPOSITIONS.

THIS WAS A CLEAR ATTEMPT TO CREATE A SUPERHUMAN.

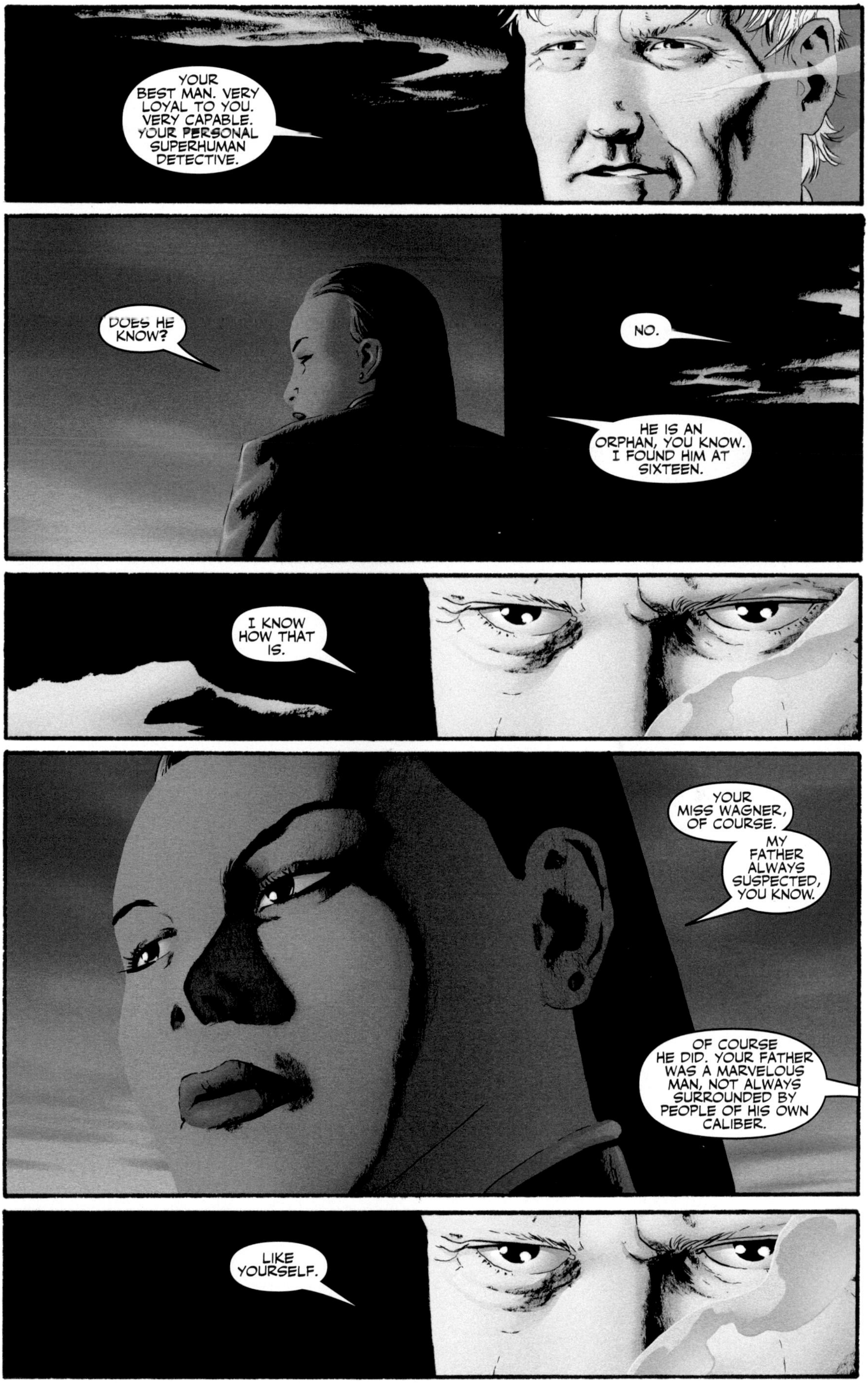
YOUR BEST MAN. VERY LOYAL TO YOU. VERY CAPABLE. YOUR PERSONAL SUPERHUMAN DETECTIVE.
DOES HE KNOW?
NO.
HE IS AN ORPHAN, YOU KNOW. I FOUND HIM AT SIXTEEN.
I KNOW HOW THAT IS.
YOUR MISS WAGNER, OF COURSE.
MY FATHER ALWAYS SUSPECTED, YOU KNOW.
OF COURSE HE DID. YOUR FATHER WAS A MARVELOUS MAN, NOT ALWAYS SURROUNDED BY PEOPLE OF HIS OWN CALIBER.
LIKE YOURSELF.

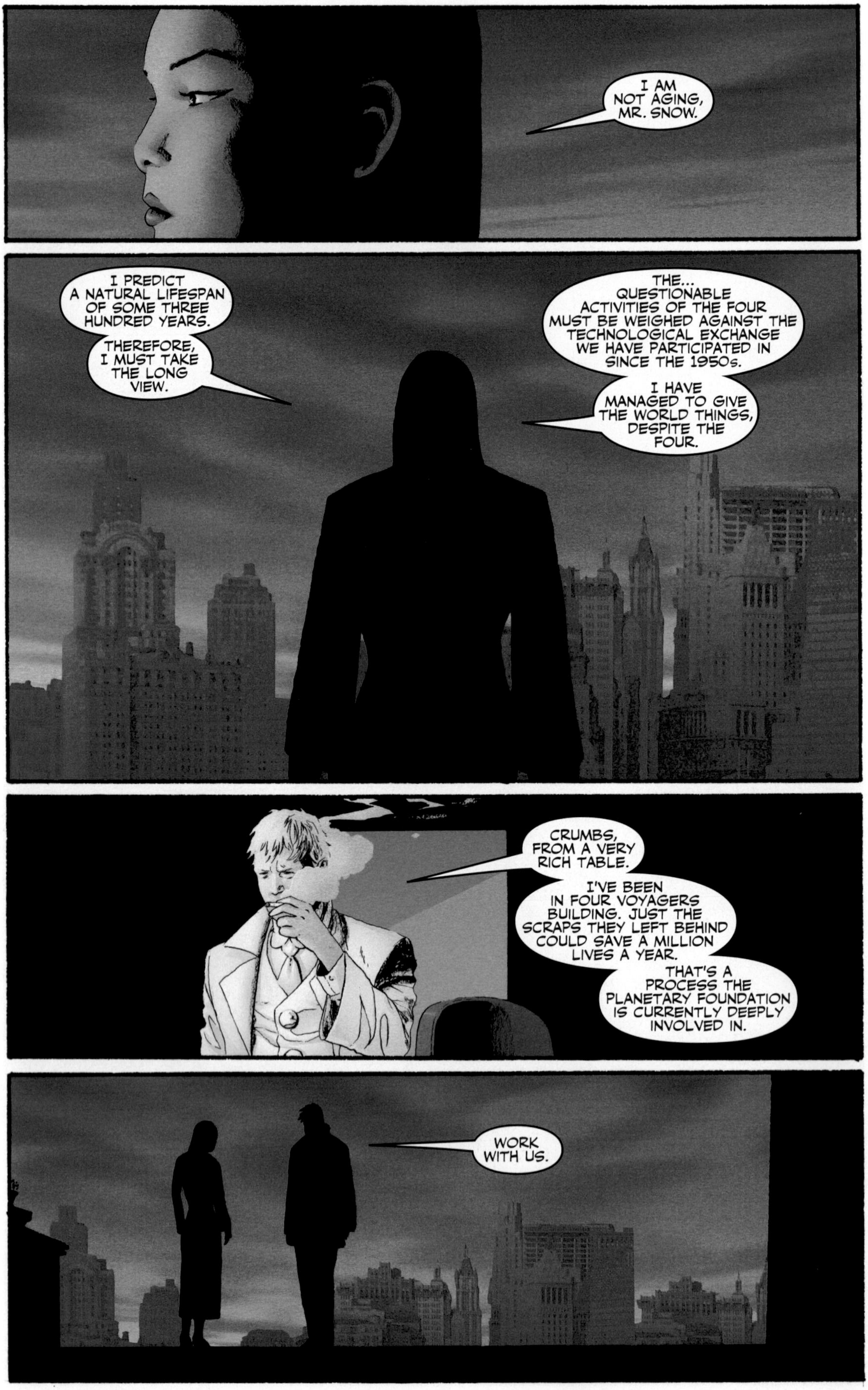
I AM NOT AGING, MR. SNOW.
I PREDICT A NATURAL LIFESPAN OF SOME THREE HUNDRED YEARS.
THEREFORE, I MUST TAKE THE LONG VIEW.
THE... QUESTIONABLE ACTIVITIES OF THE FOUR MUST BE WEIGHED AGAINST THE TECHNOLOGICAL EXCHANGE WE HAVE PARTICIPATED IN SINCE THE 1950s.
I HAVE MANAGED TO GIVE THE WORLD THINGS, DESPITE THE FOUR.
CRUMBS, FROM A VERY RICH TABLE.
I'VE BEEN IN FOUR VOYAGERS BUILDING. JUST THE SCRAPS THEY LEFT BEHIND COULD SAVE A MILLION LIVES A YEAR.
THAT'S A PROCESS THE PLANETARY FOUNDATION IS CURRENTLY DEEPLY INVOLVED IN.
WORK WITH US.

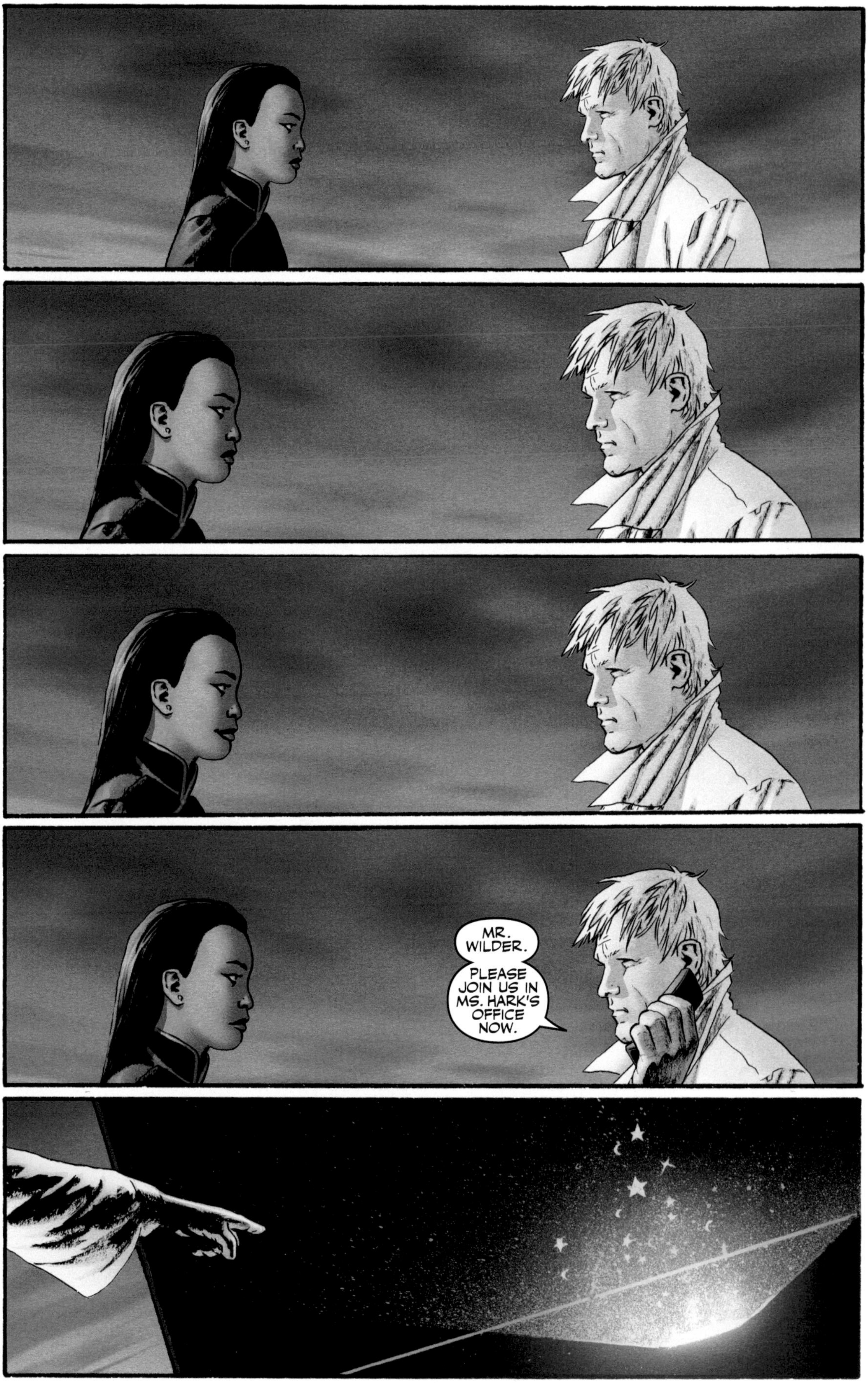
MR. WILDER.
PLEASE JOIN US IN MS. HARK'S OFFICE NOW.

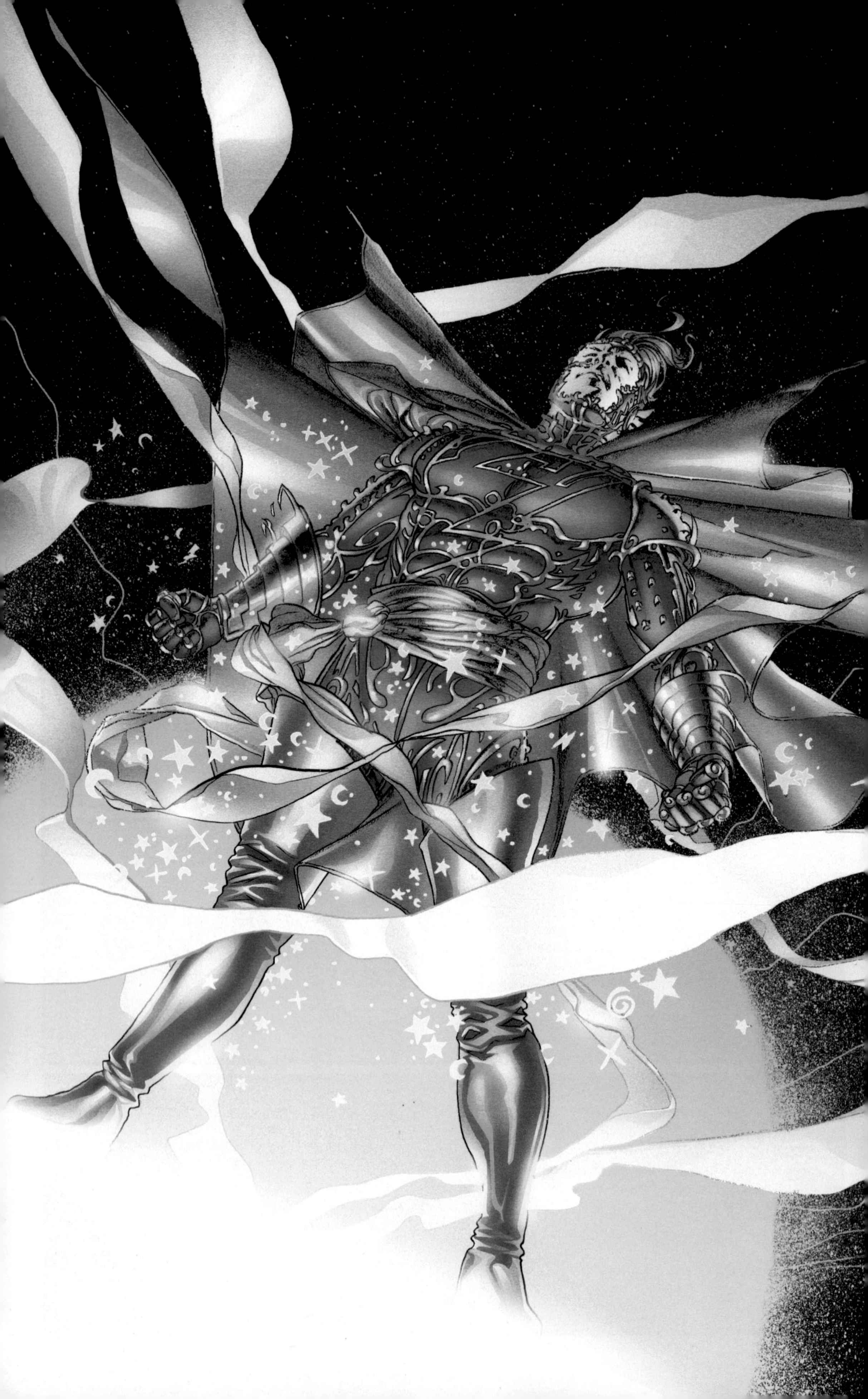

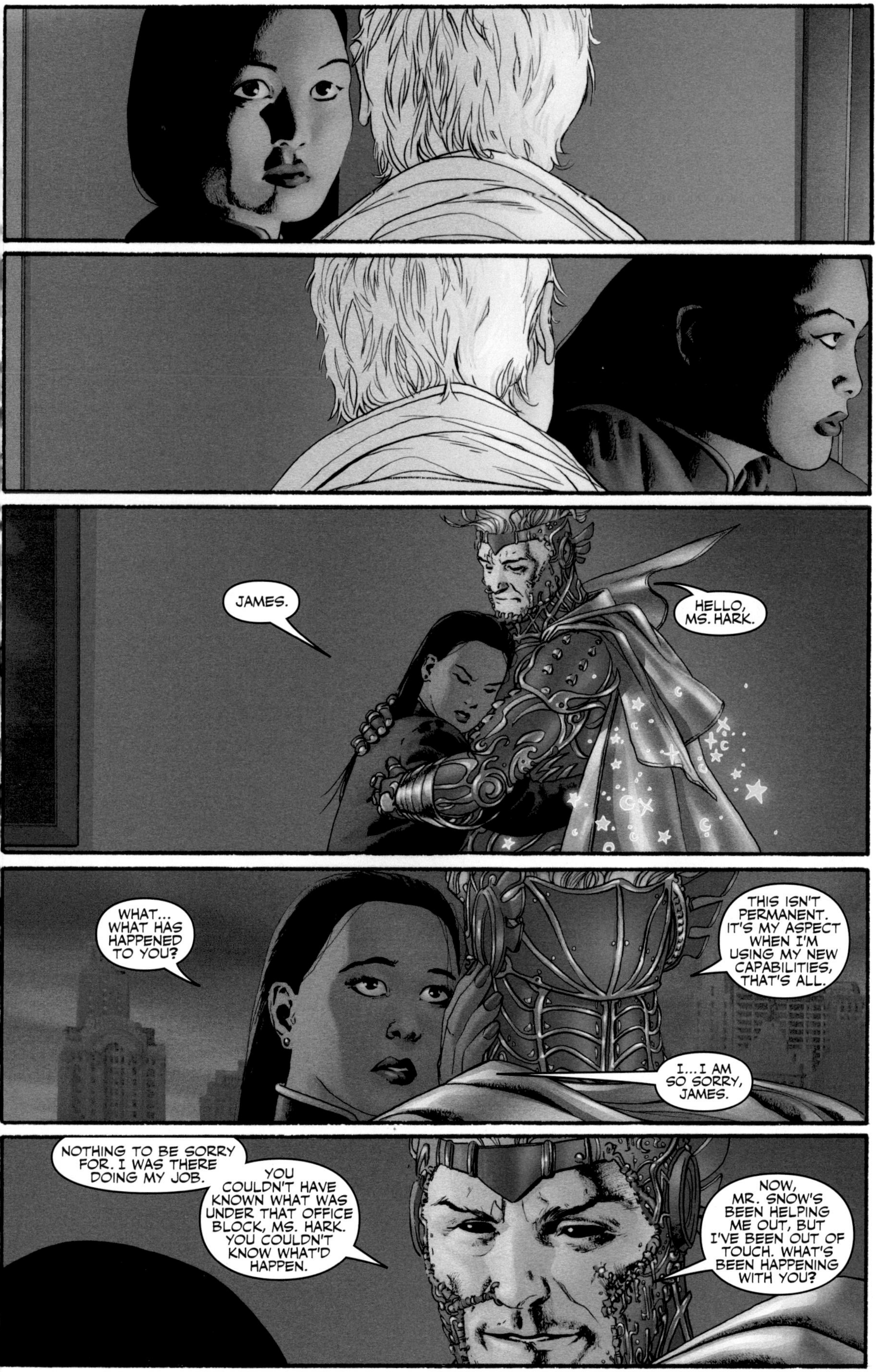
JAMES.
HELLO, MS. HARK.
WHAT... WHAT HAS HAPPENED TO YOU?
THIS ISN'T PERMANENT. IT'S MY ASPECT WHEN I'M USING MY NEW CAPABILITIES, THAT'S ALL.
I...I AM SO SORRY, JAMES.
NOTHING TO BE SORRY FOR. I WAS THERE DOING MY JOB.
YOU COULDN'T HAVE KNOWN WHAT WAS UNDER THAT OFFICE BLOCK, MS. HARK. YOU COULDN'T KNOW WHAT'D HAPPEN.
NOW, MR. SNOW'S BEEN HELPING ME OUT, BUT I'VE BEEN OUT OF TOUCH. WHAT'S BEEN HAPPENING WITH YOU?

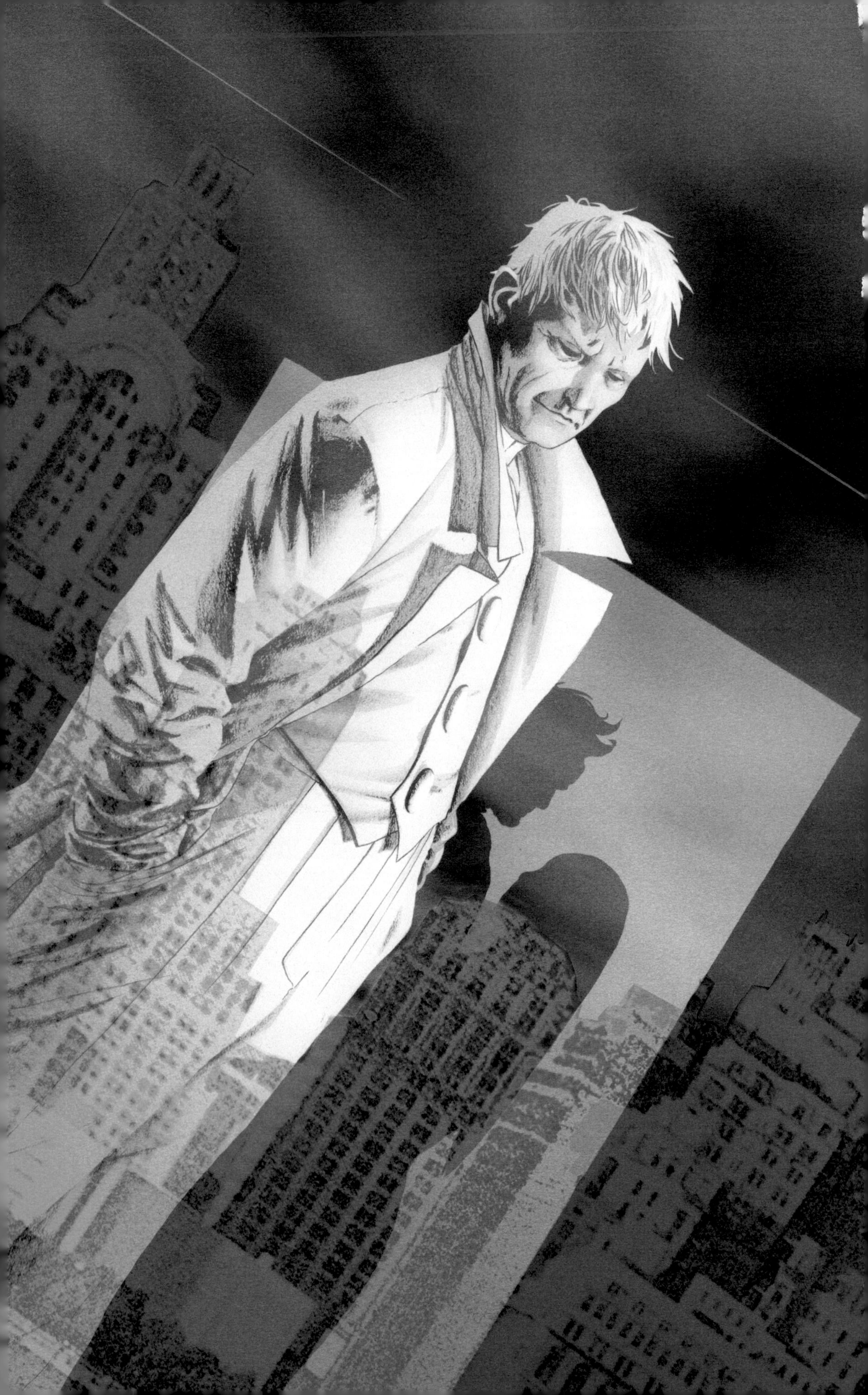

A WildStorm Magazine
Chapter Seventeen
PLANETARY
ELLIS • CASSADAY • MARTIN
In the lost city of
Opak-Re

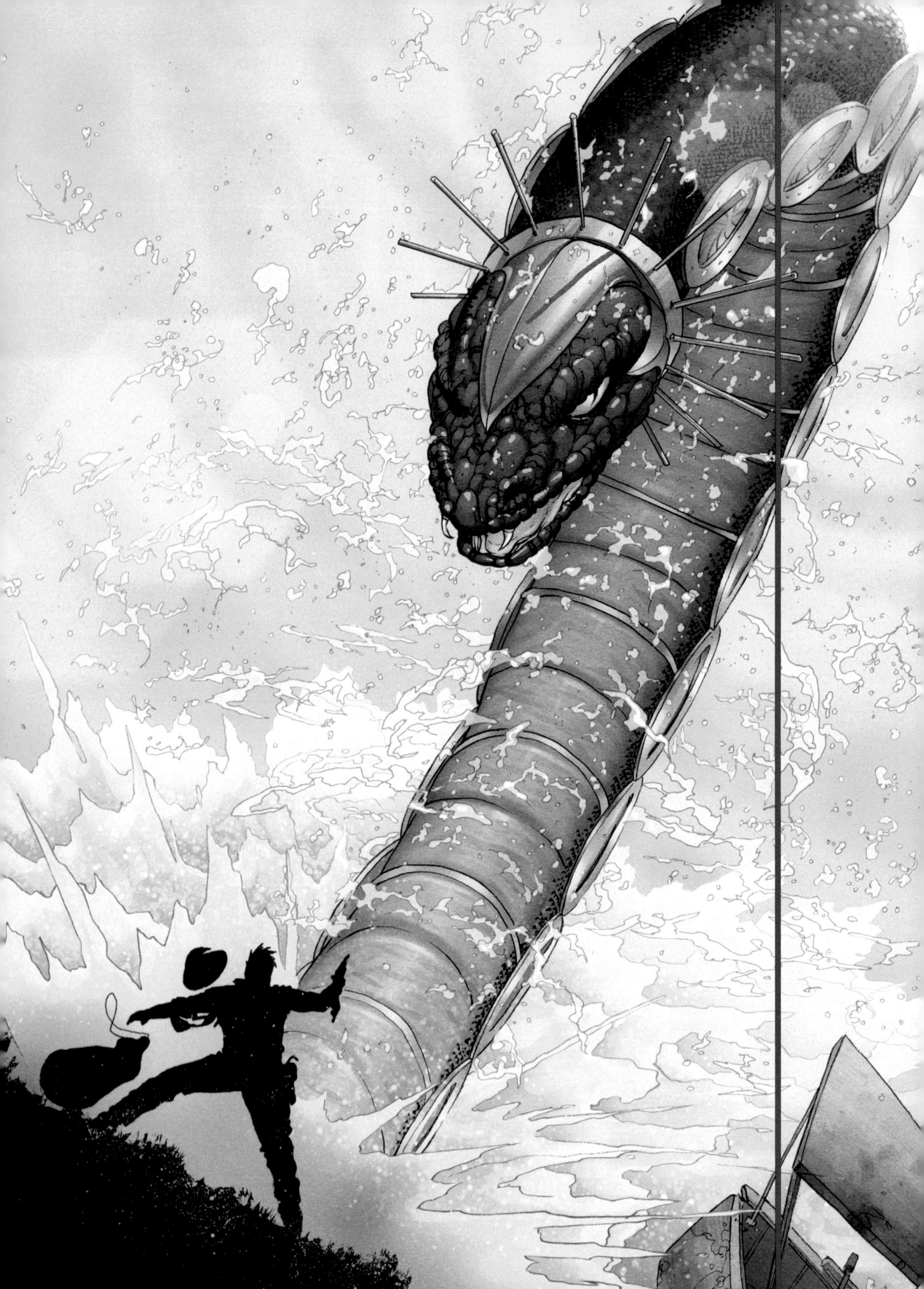

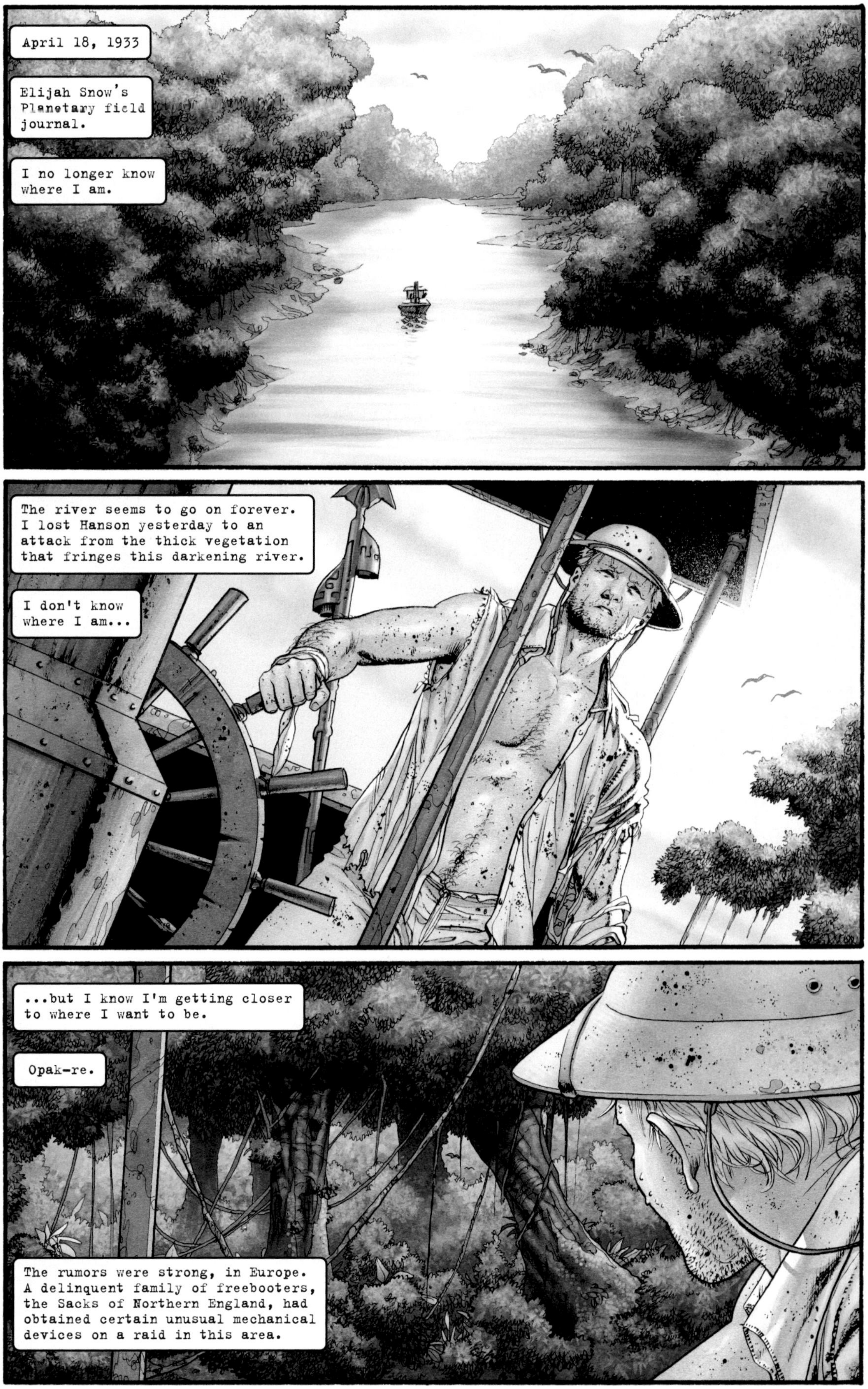
April 18, 1933
Elijah Snow's Planetary field journal.
I no longer know where I am.
The river seems to go on forever. I lost Hanson yesterday to an attack from the thick vegetation that fringes this darkening river.
I don't know where I am...
...but I know I'm getting closer to where I want to be.
Opak-re.
The rumors were strong, in Europe. A delinquent family of freebooters, the Sacks of Northern England, had obtained certain unusual mechanical devices on a raid in this area.

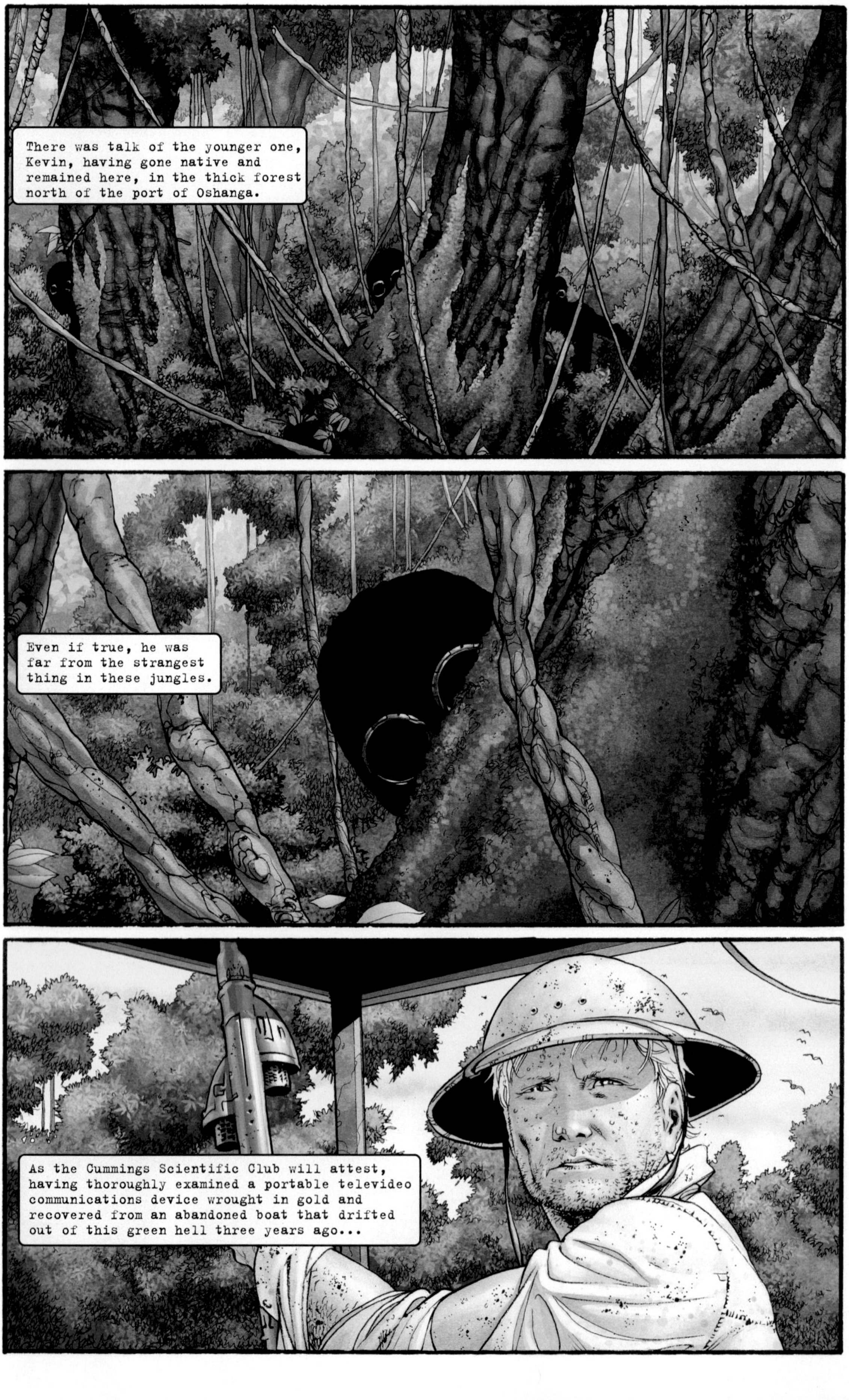
There was talk of the younger one, Kevin, having gone native and remained here, in the thick forest north of the port of Oshanga.
Even if true, he was far from the strangest thing in these jungles.
As the Cummings Scientific Club will attest, having thoroughly examined a portable televideo communications device wrought in gold and recovered from an abandoned boat that drifted out of this green hell three years ago...

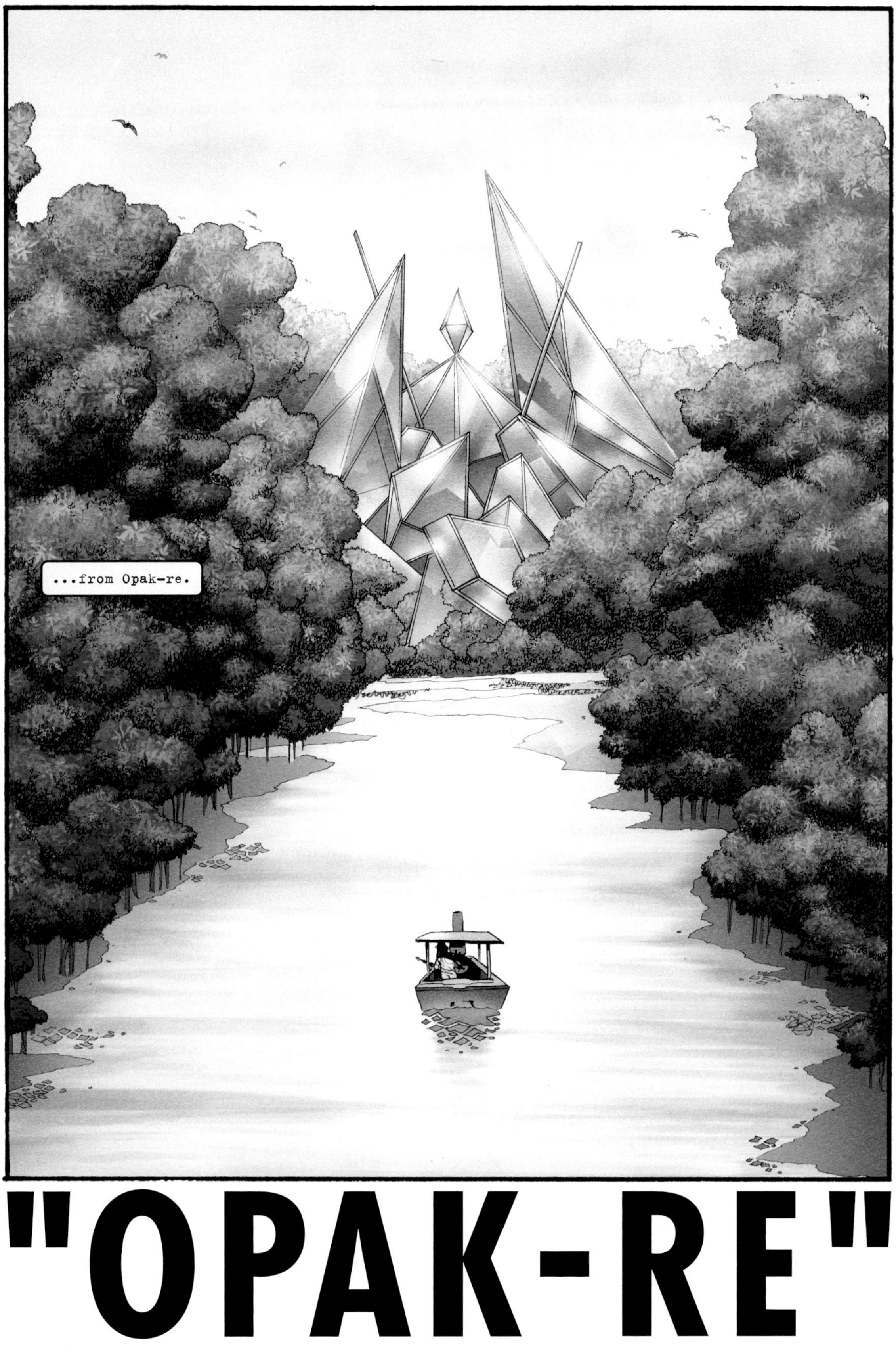
...from Opak-re.

"OPAK-RE"

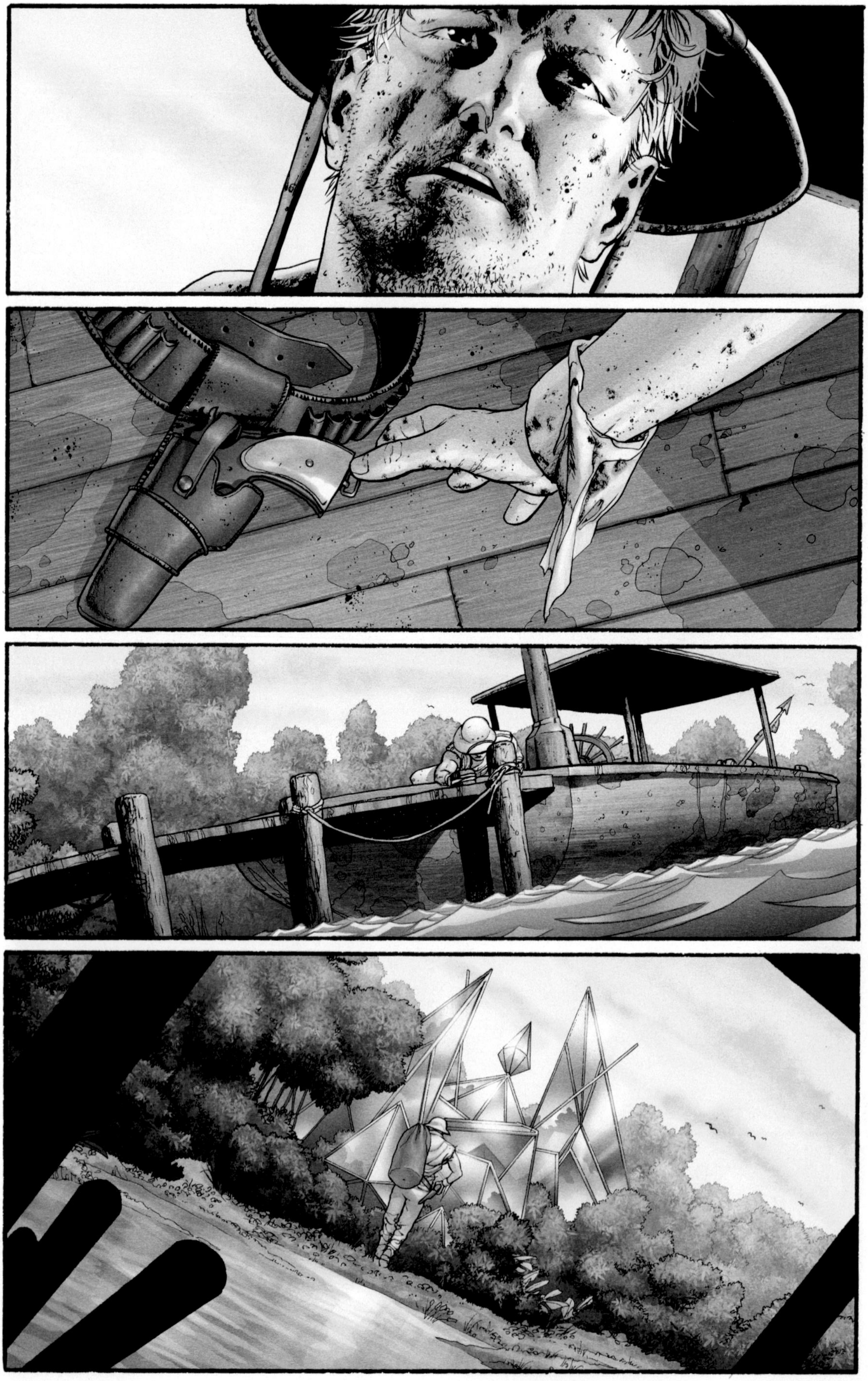

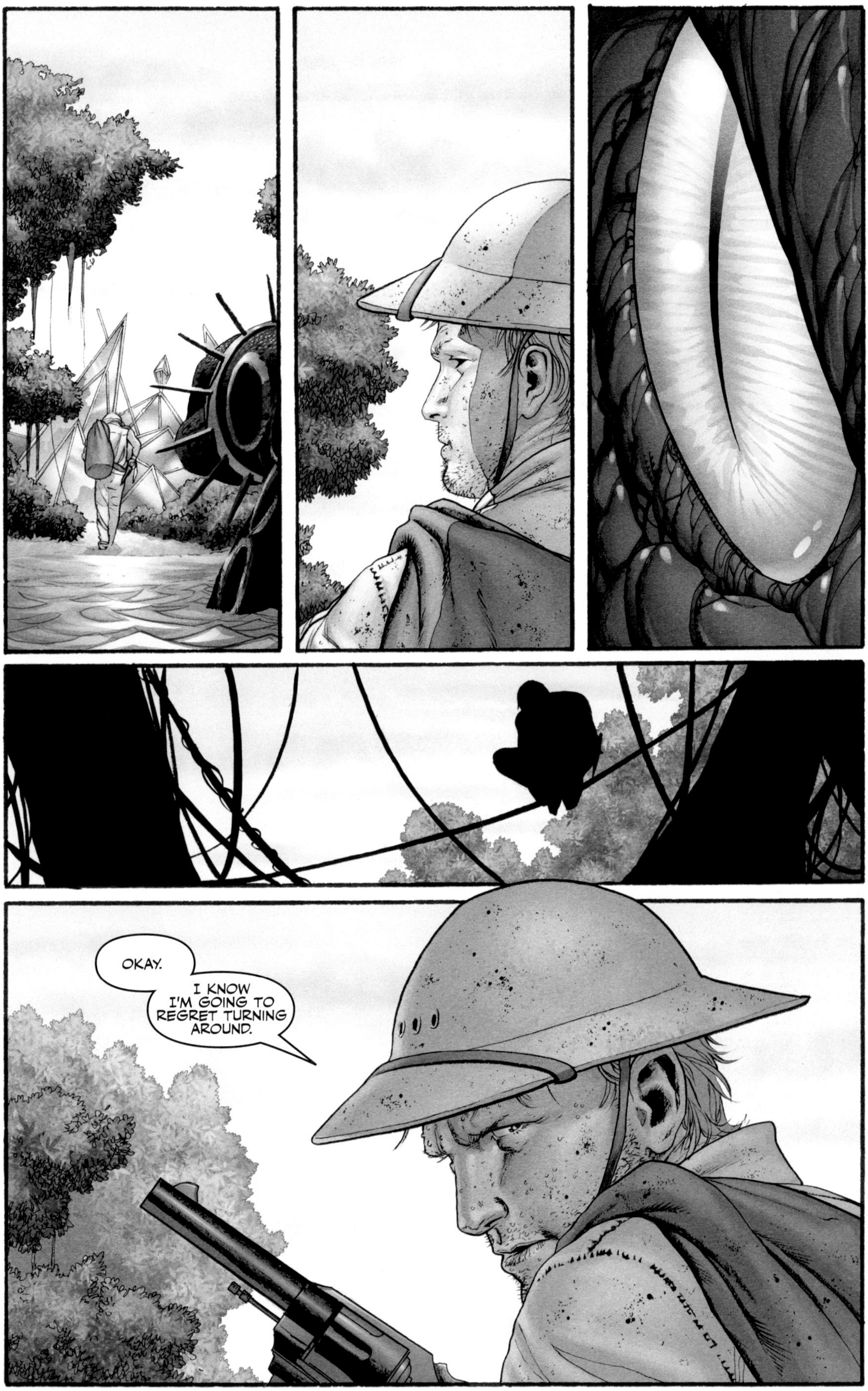
OKAY.
I KNOW I'M GOING TO REGRET TURNING AROUND.

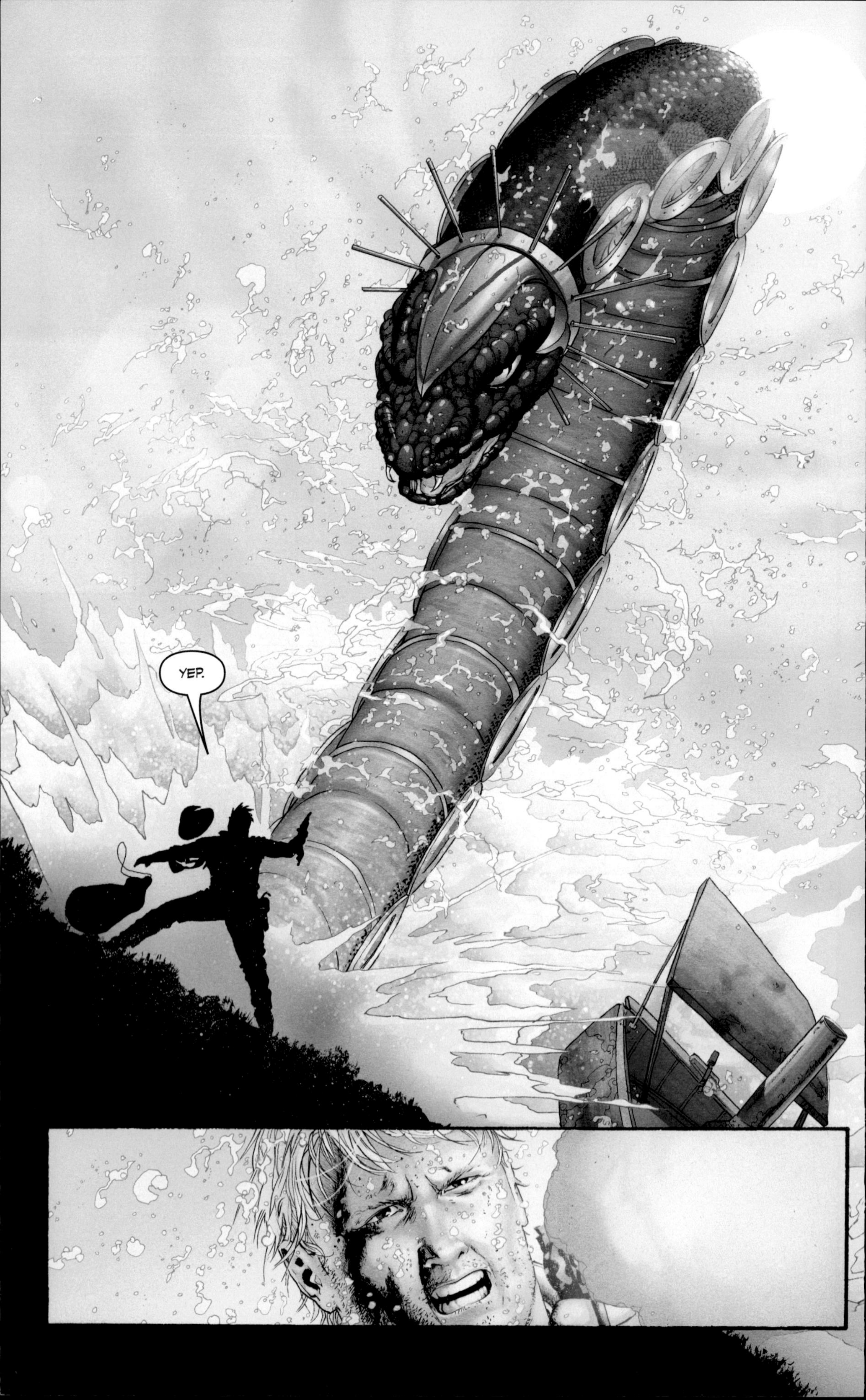
YEP.

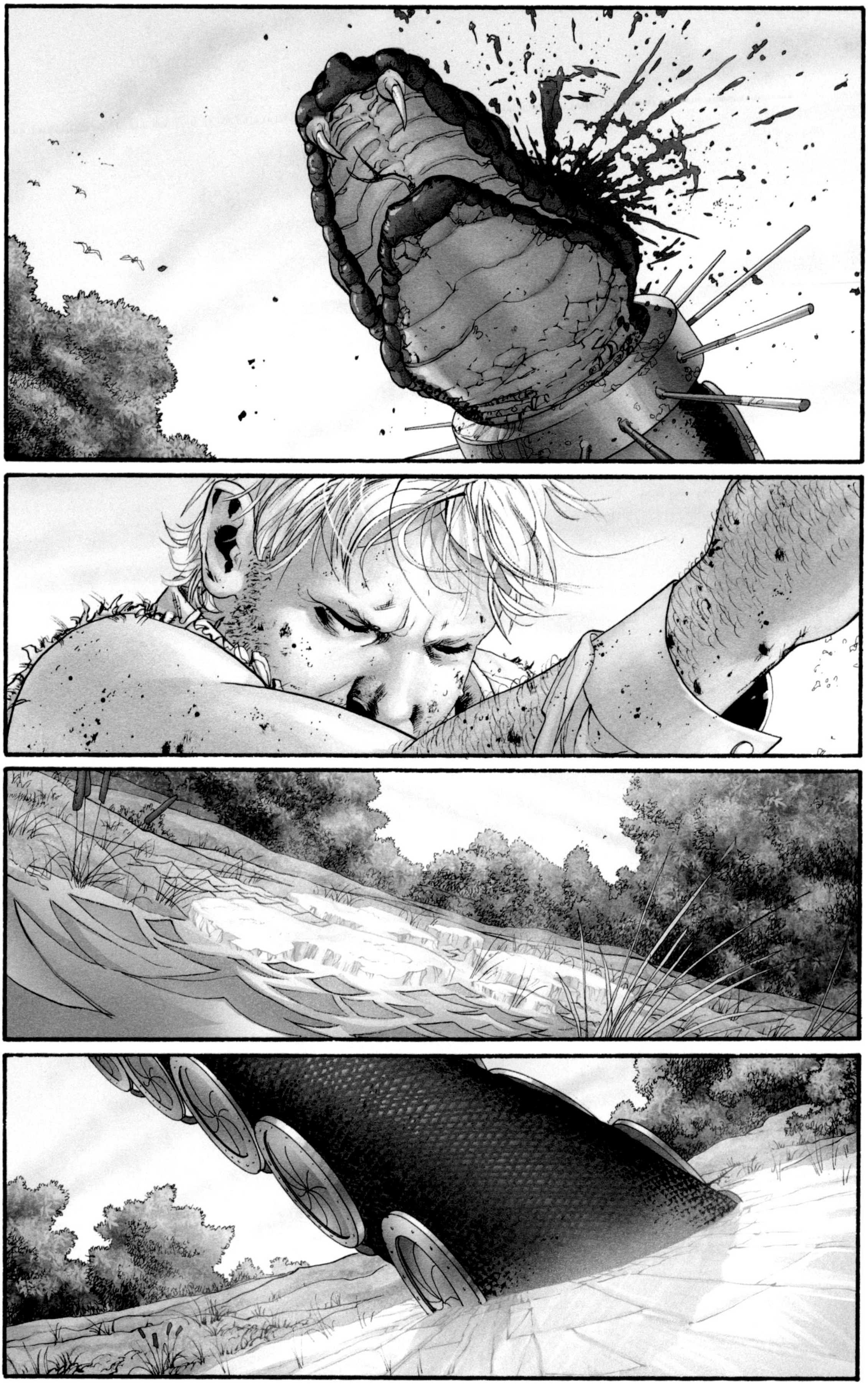

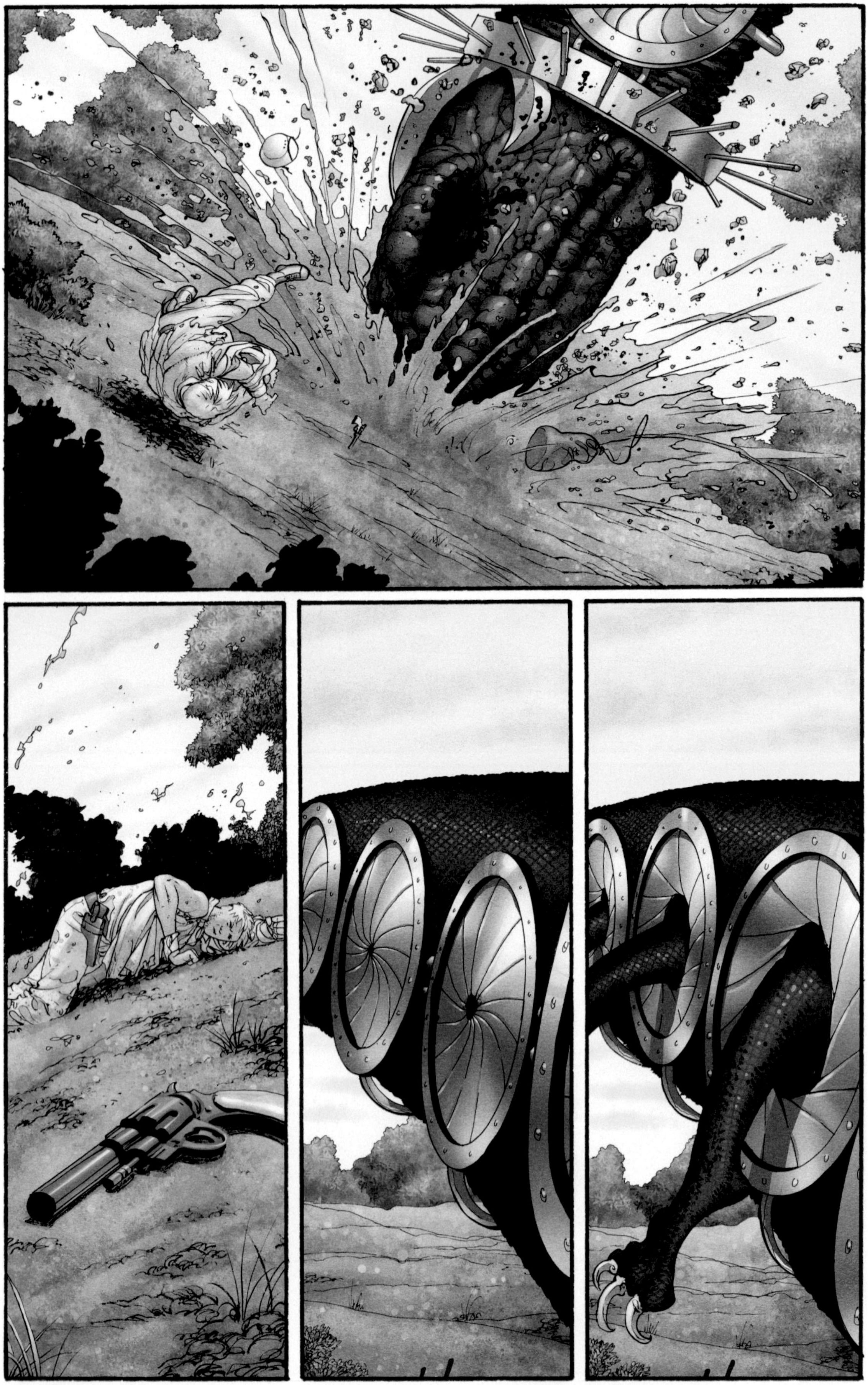

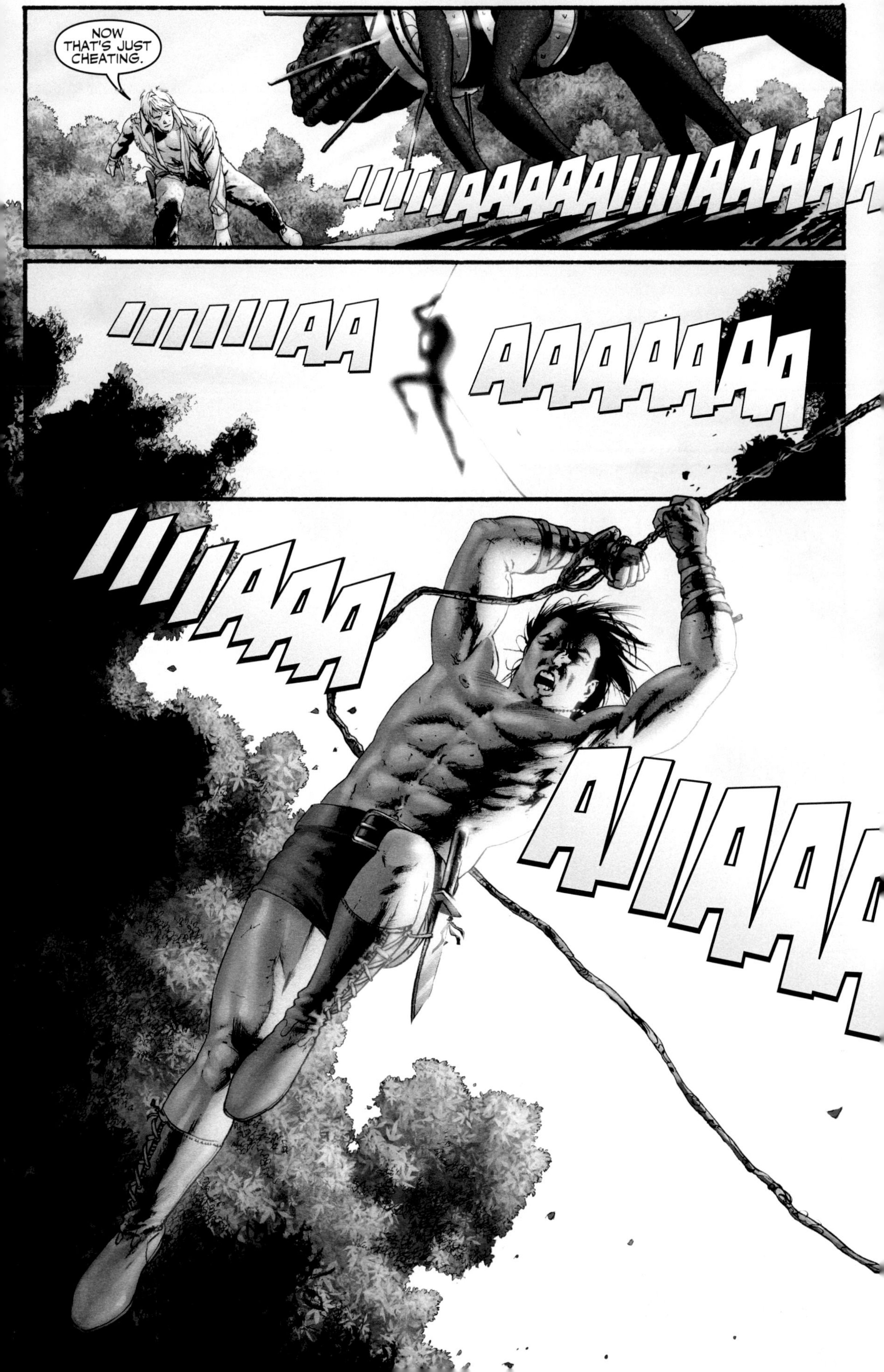
NOW THAT'S JUST CHEATING.
!!!!!AAAAAII!!!AAAAA
!!!!!!!AA
AAAAAAA
!!!!AAA
AIIAAA

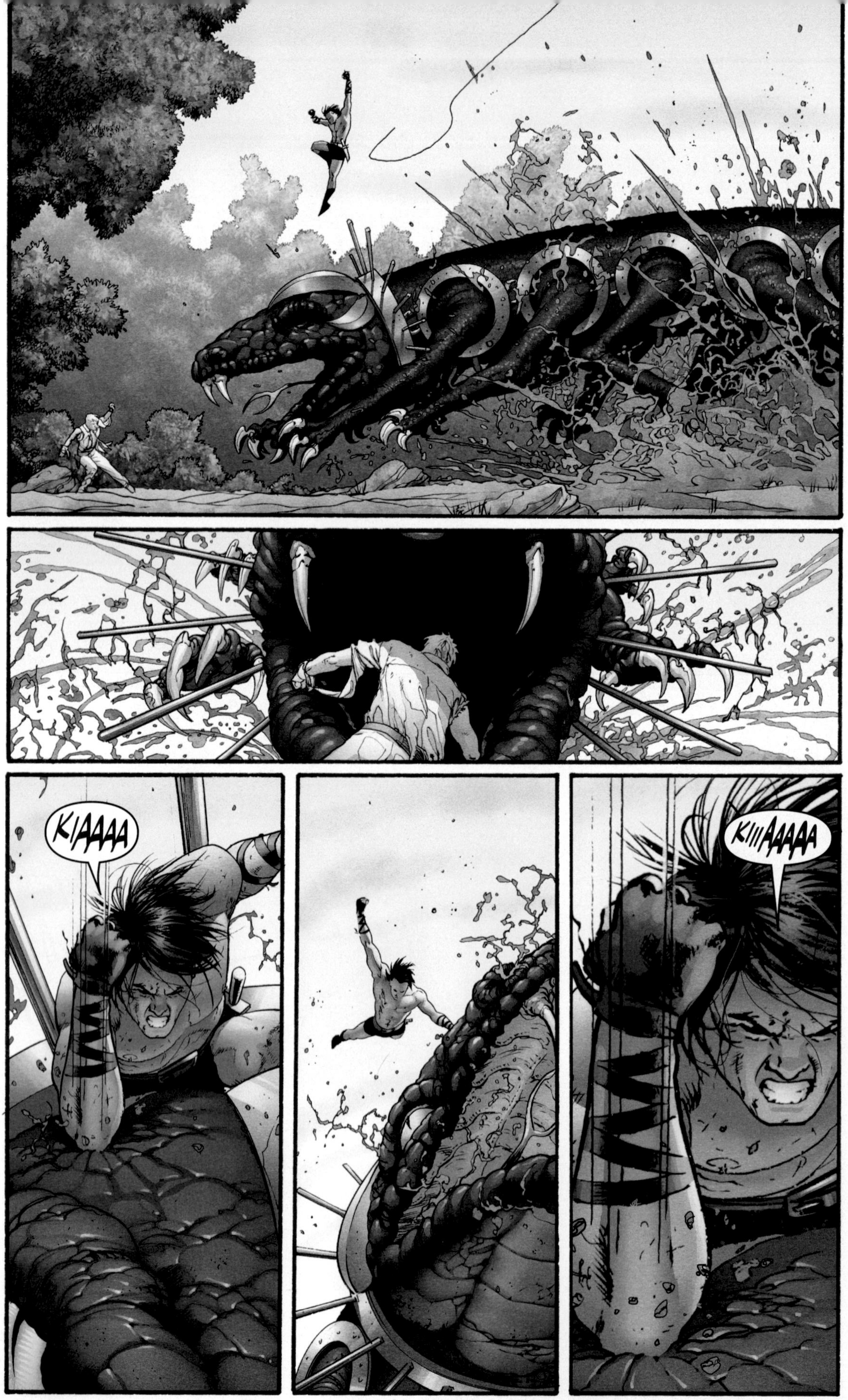
KIAAAA
KIIIAAAAA

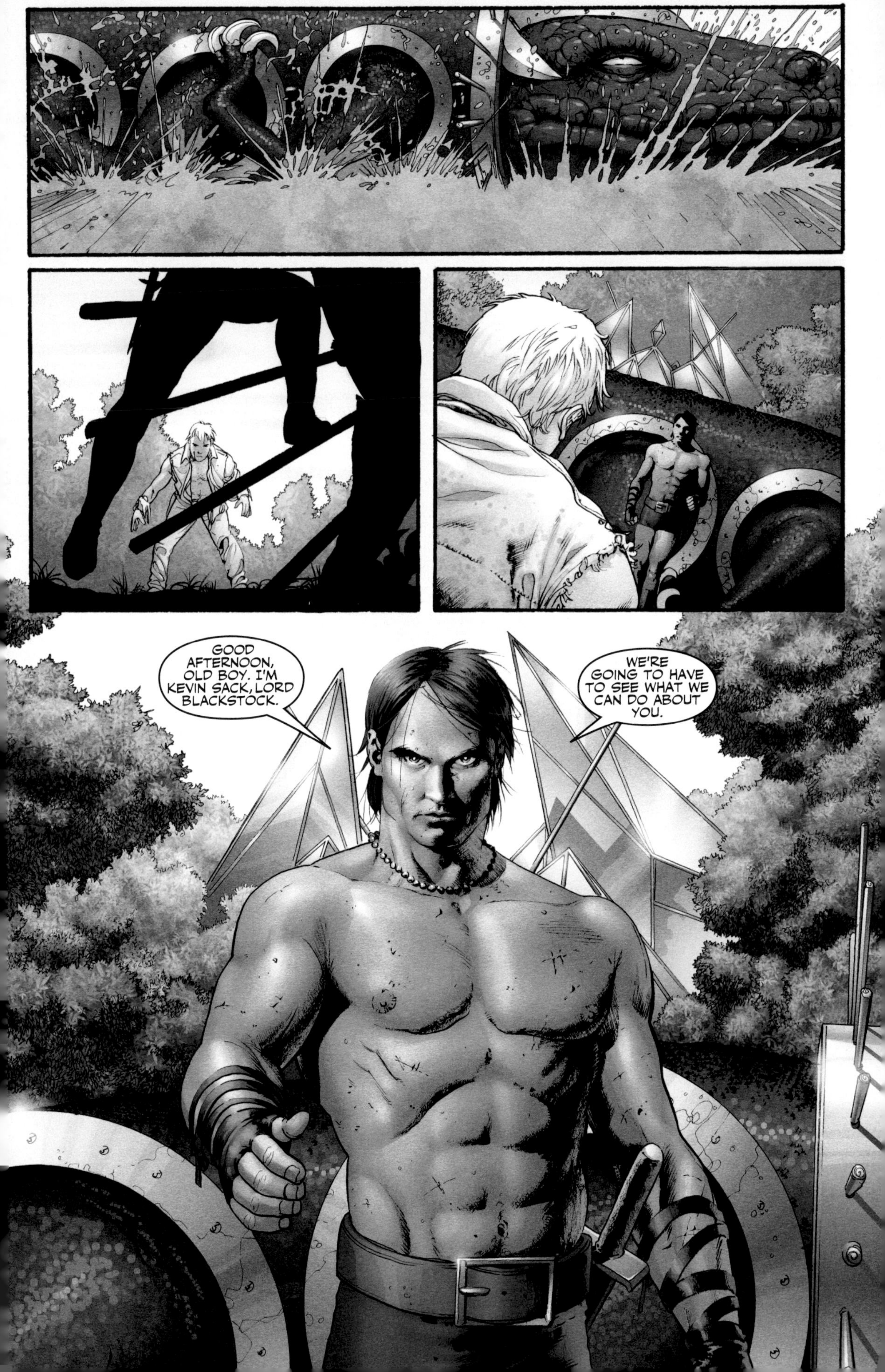
GOOD AFTERNOON, OLD BOY. I'M KEVIN SACK, LORD BLACKSTOCK.
WE'RE GOING TO HAVE TO SEE WHAT WE CAN DO ABOUT YOU.

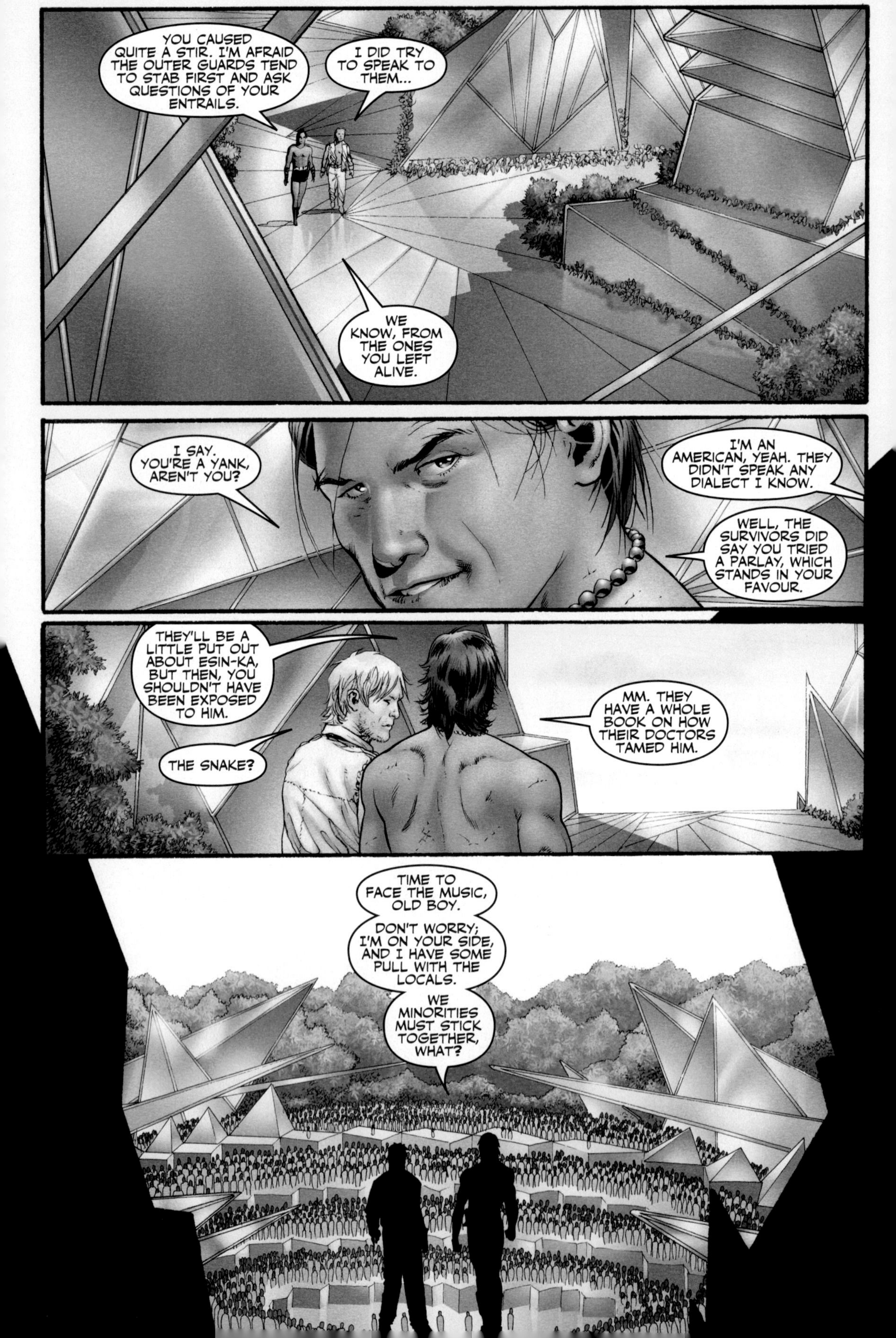
YOU CAUSED QUITE A STIR. I'M AFRAID THE OUTER GUARDS TEND TO STAB FIRST AND ASK QUESTIONS OF YOUR ENTRAILS.
I DID TRY TO SPEAK TO THEM...
WE KNOW, FROM THE ONES YOU LEFT ALIVE.
I SAY. YOU'RE A YANK, AREN'T YOU?
I'M AN AMERICAN, YEAH. THEY DIDN'T SPEAK ANY DIALECT I KNOW.
WELL, THE SURVIVORS DID SAY YOU TRIED A PARLAY, WHICH STANDS IN YOUR FAVOUR.
THEY'LL BE A LITTLE PUT OUT ABOUT ESIN-KA, BUT THEN, YOU SHOULDN'T HAVE BEEN EXPOSED TO HIM.
THE SNAKE?
MM. THEY HAVE A WHOLE BOOK ON HOW THEIR DOCTORS TAMED HIM.
TIME TO FACE THE MUSIC, OLD BOY.
DON'T WORRY; I'M ON YOUR SIDE, AND I HAVE SOME PULL WITH THE LOCALS.
WE MINORITIES MUST STICK TOGETHER, WHAT?

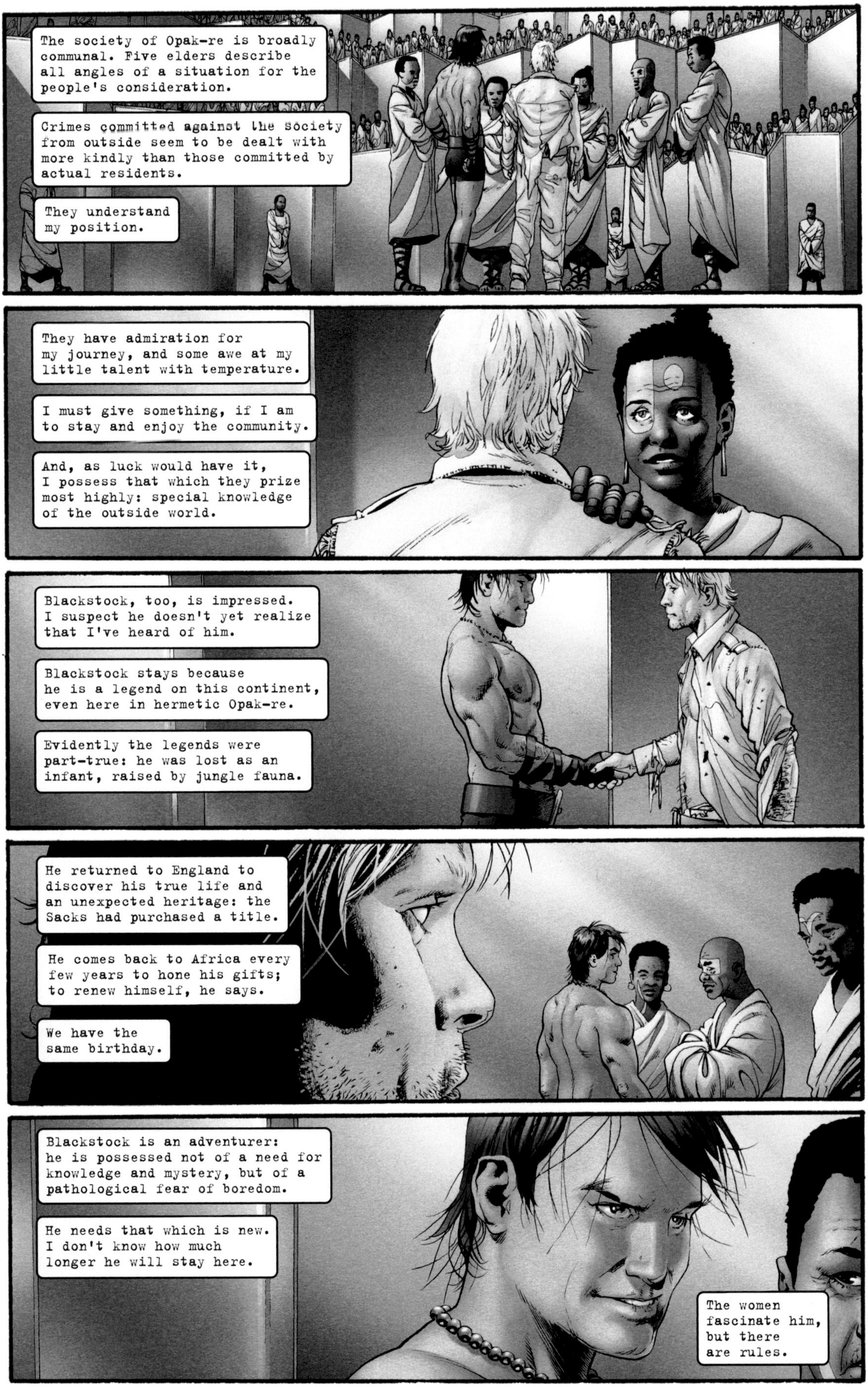
The society of Opak-re is broadly communal. Five elders describe all angles of a situation for the people's consideration.
Crimes committed against the society from outside seem to be dealt with more kindly than those committed by actual residents.
They understand my position.
They have admiration for my journey, and some awe at my little talent with temperature.
I must give something, if I am to stay and enjoy the community.
And, as luck would have it, I possess that which they prize most highly: special knowledge of the outside world.
Blackstock, too, is impressed. I suspect he doesn't yet realize that I've heard of him.
Blackstock stays because he is a legend on this continent, even here in hermetic Opak-re.
Evidently the legends were part-true: he was lost as an infant, raised by jungle fauna.
He returned to England to discover his true life and an unexpected heritage: the Sacks had purchased a title.
He comes back to Africa every few years to hone his gifts; to renew himself, he says.
We have the same birthday.
Blackstock is an adventurer: he is possessed not of a need for knowledge and mystery, but of a pathological fear of boredom.
He needs that which is new. I don't know how much longer he will stay here.
The women fascinate him, but there are rules.

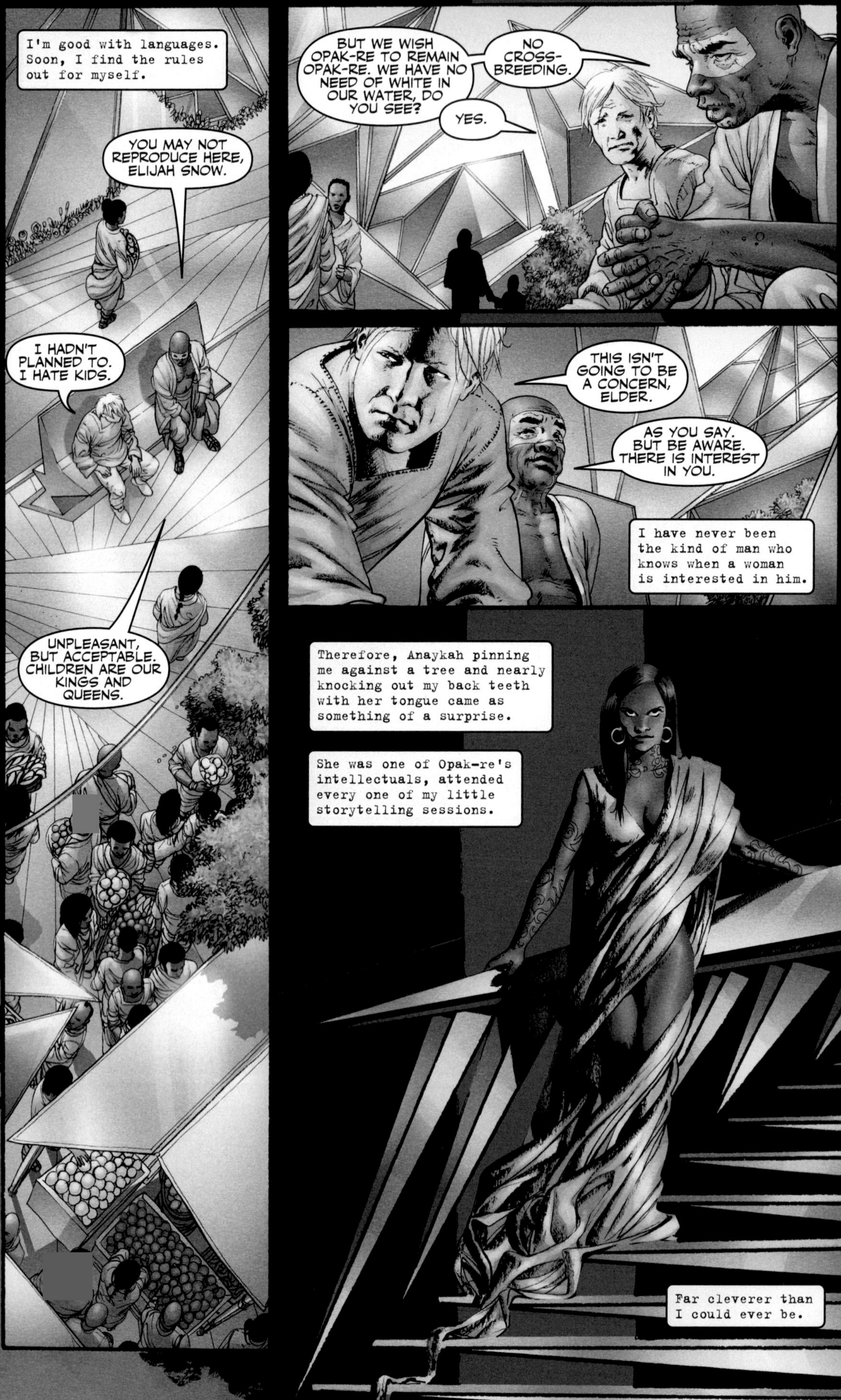
I'm good with languages. Soon, I find the rules out for myself.
YOU MAY NOT REPRODUCE HERE, ELIJAH SNOW.
I HADN'T PLANNED TO. I HATE KIDS.
UNPLEASANT, BUT ACCEPTABLE. CHILDREN ARE OUR KINGS AND QUEENS.
BUT WE WISH OPAK-RE TO REMAIN OPAK-RE. WE HAVE NO NEED OF WHITE IN OUR WATER, DO YOU SEE?
NO CROSS-BREEDING.
YES.
THIS ISN'T GOING TO BE A CONCERN, ELDER.
AS YOU SAY. BUT BE AWARE. THERE IS INTEREST IN YOU.
I have never been the kind of man who knows when a woman is interested in him.
Therefore, Anaykah pinning me against a tree and nearly knocking out my back teeth with her tongue came as something of a surprise.
She was one of Opak-re's intellectuals, attended every one of my little storytelling sessions.
Far cleverer than I could ever be.

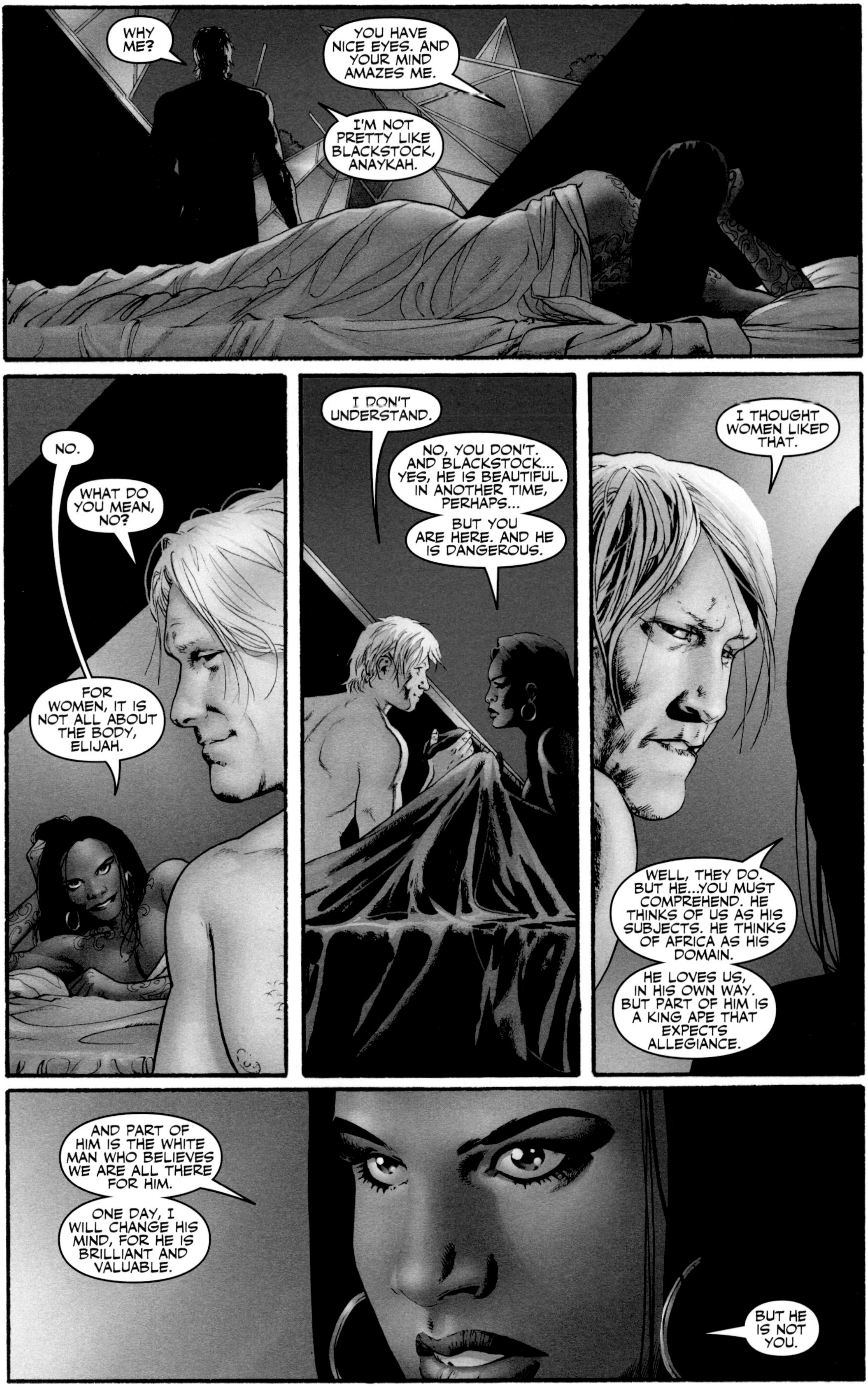
WHY ME?
YOU HAVE NICE EYES. AND YOUR MIND AMAZES ME.
I'M NOT PRETTY LIKE BLACKSTOCK, ANAYKAH.
NO.
WHAT DO YOU MEAN, NO?
FOR WOMEN, IT IS NOT ALL ABOUT THE BODY, ELIJAH.
I DON'T UNDERSTAND.
NO, YOU DON'T. AND BLACKSTOCK... YES, HE IS BEAUTIFUL. IN ANOTHER TIME, PERHAPS...
BUT YOU ARE HERE. AND HE IS DANGEROUS.
I THOUGHT WOMEN LIKED THAT.
WELL, THEY DO. BUT HE...YOU MUST COMPREHEND. HE THINKS OF US AS HIS SUBJECTS. HE THINKS OF AFRICA AS HIS DOMAIN.
HE LOVES US, IN HIS OWN WAY. BUT PART OF HIM IS A KING APE THAT EXPECTS ALLEGIANCE.
AND PART OF HIM IS THE WHITE MAN WHO BELIEVES WE ARE ALL THERE FOR HIM.
ONE DAY, I WILL CHANGE HIS MIND, FOR HE IS BRILLIANT AND VALUABLE.
BUT HE IS NOT YOU.

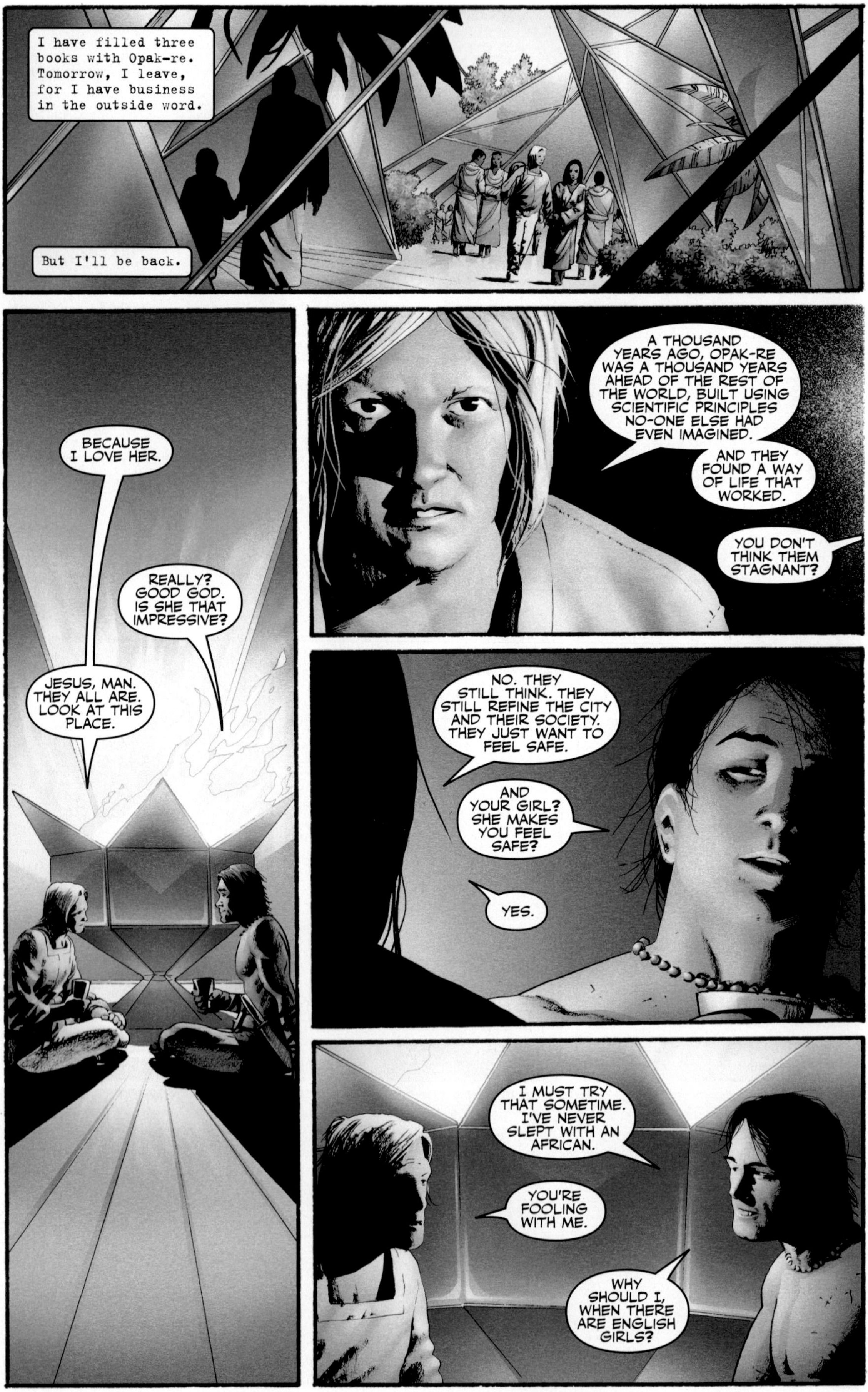
I have filled three books with Opak-re. Tomorrow, I leave, for I have business in the outside word.
But I'll be back.
BECAUSE I LOVE HER.
REALLY? GOOD GOD. IS SHE THAT IMPRESSIVE?
JESUS, MAN. THEY ALL ARE. LOOK AT THIS PLACE.
A THOUSAND YEARS AGO, OPAK-RE WAS A THOUSAND YEARS AHEAD OF THE REST OF THE WORLD, BUILT USING SCIENTIFIC PRINCIPLES NO-ONE ELSE HAD EVEN IMAGINED.
AND THEY FOUND A WAY OF LIFE THAT WORKED.
YOU DON'T THINK THEM STAGNANT?
NO. THEY STILL THINK. THEY STILL REFINE THE CITY AND THEIR SOCIETY. THEY JUST WANT TO FEEL SAFE.
AND YOUR GIRL? SHE MAKES YOU FEEL SAFE?
YES.
I MUST TRY THAT SOMETIME. I'VE NEVER SLEPT WITH AN AFRICAN.
YOU'RE FOOLING WITH ME.
WHY SHOULD I, WHEN THERE ARE ENGLISH GIRLS?

BUT YOU SPENT MORE THAN TWENTY YEARS HERE. WITHOUT BRITISH MORALS AFFECTING YOU. SURELY YOU--

OH, I HAD SEXUAL EXPERIENCES HERE, YES. BUT NOT WITH...

WELL.

WHEN WILL YOU BE BACK?

EIGHTEEN MONTHS OR SO. WILL YOU BE HERE?

NOT SURE. LOOK ME UP AT THE MANOR IN A FEW YEARS, OLD BOY. WE'LL HAVE MORE STORIES TO TRADE.

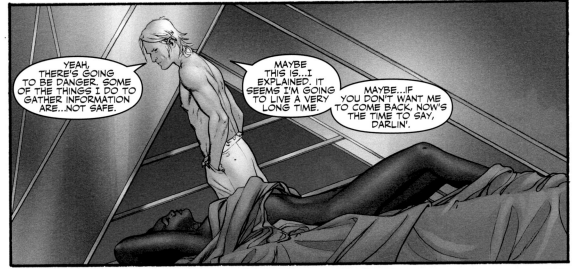

YEAH, THERE'S GOING TO BE DANGER. SOME OF THE THINGS I DO TO GATHER INFORMATION ARE...NOT SAFE.

MAYBE THIS IS...I EXPLAINED. IT SEEMS I'M GOING TO LIVE A VERY LONG TIME.

MAYBE...IF YOU DON'T WANT ME TO COME BACK, NOW'S THE TIME TO SAY, DARLIN'.

I DON'T CARE WHAT HAPPENS, I DON'T CARE HOW LONG YOU LIVE.

JUST NEVER FORGET THAT I LOVED YOU, ELIJAH.

And so I left the first great love of my life.

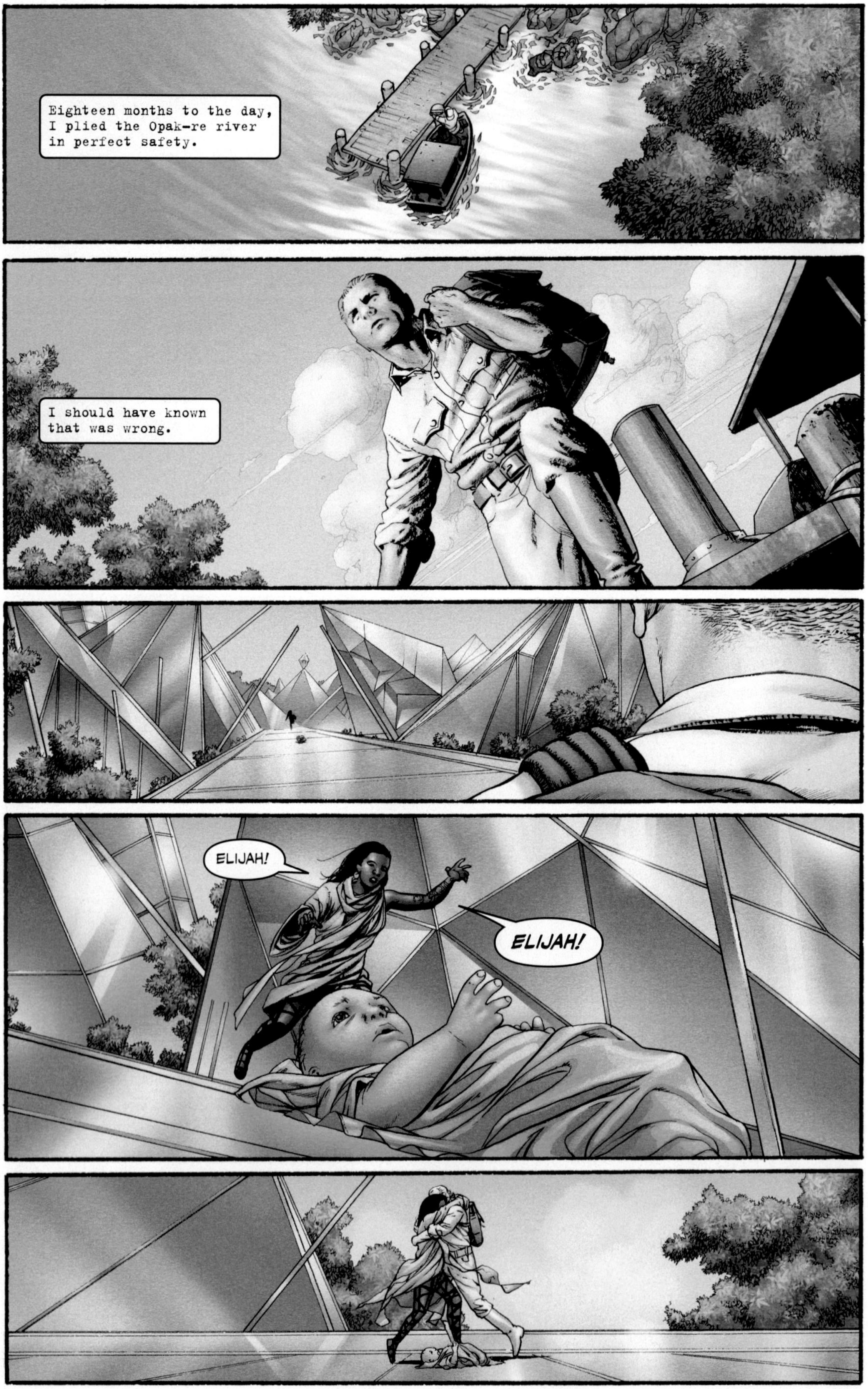
Eighteen months to the day, I plied the Opak-re river in perfect safety.
I should have known that was wrong.
ELIJAH!
ELIJAH!

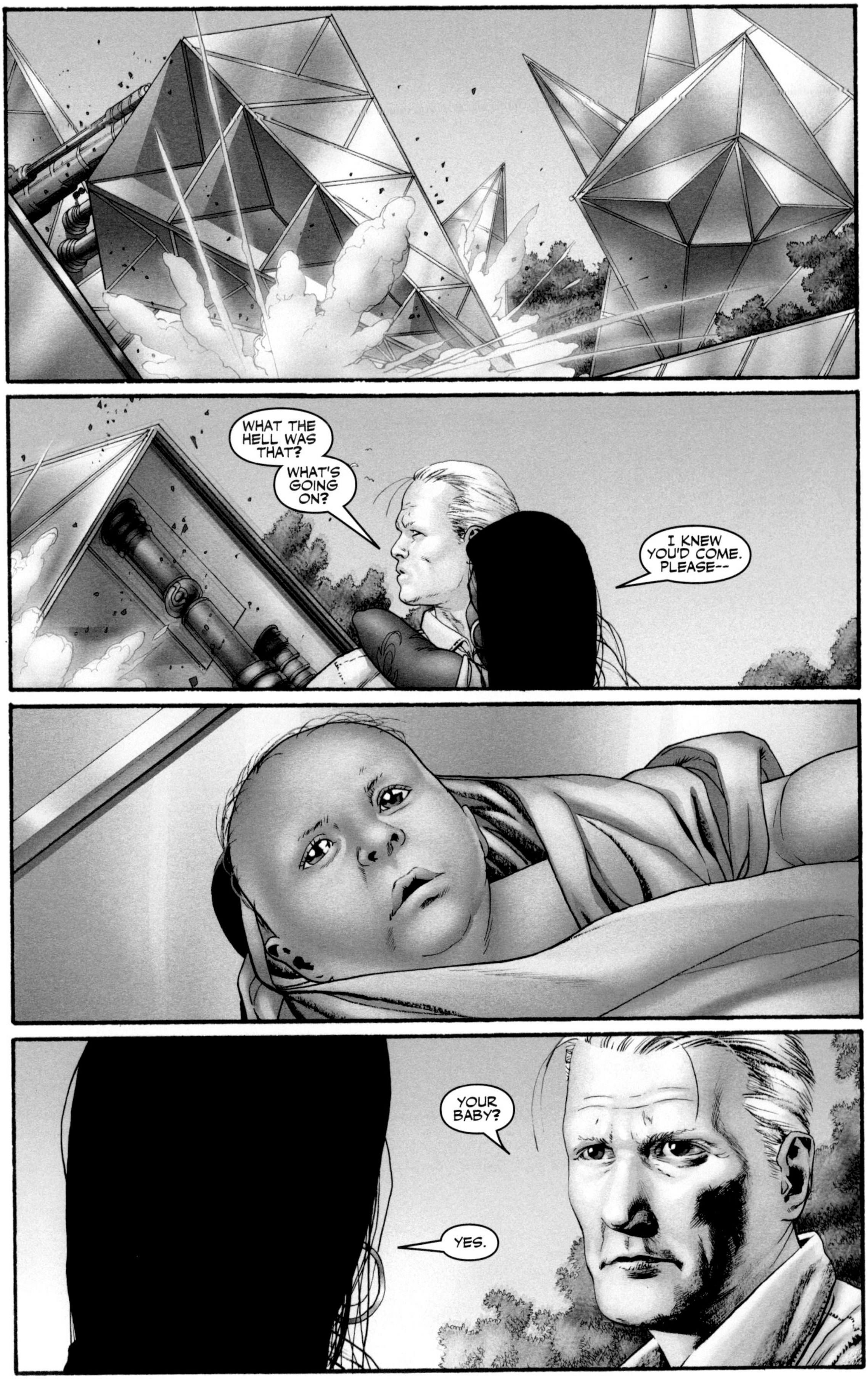
WHAT THE HELL WAS THAT?
WHAT'S GOING ON?
I KNEW YOU'D COME. PLEASE--
YOUR BABY?
YES.

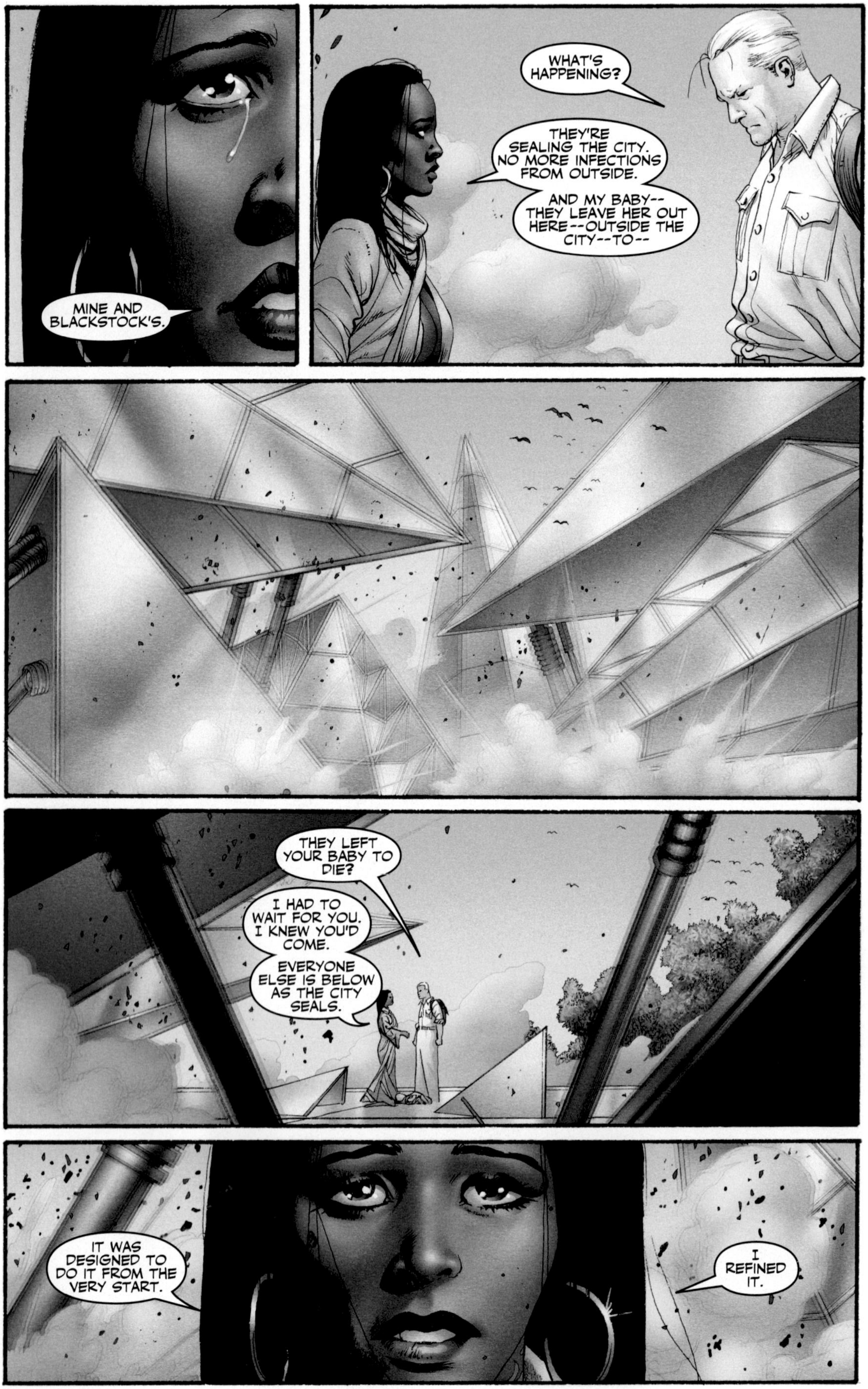
MINE AND BLACKSTOCK'S.
WHAT'S HAPPENING?
THEY'RE SEALING THE CITY. NO MORE INFECTIONS FROM OUTSIDE.
AND MY BABY-- THEY LEAVE HER OUT HERE--OUTSIDE THE CITY--TO--
THEY LEFT YOUR BABY TO DIE?
I HAD TO WAIT FOR YOU. I KNEW YOU'D COME.
EVERYONE ELSE IS BELOW AS THE CITY SEALS.
IT WAS DESIGNED TO DO IT FROM THE VERY START.
I REFINED IT.

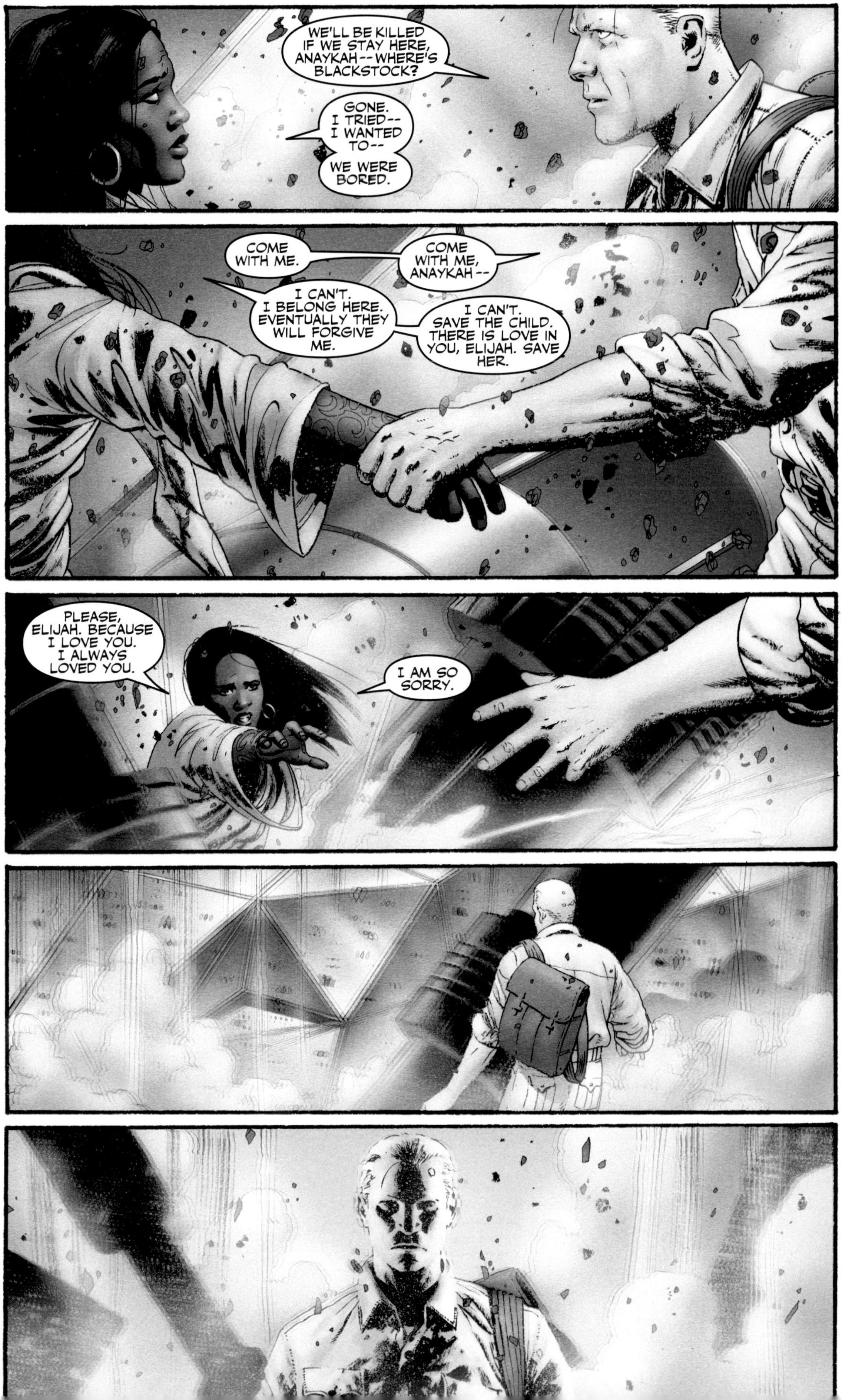
WE'LL BE KILLED IF WE STAY HERE, ANAYKAH--WHERE'S BLACKSTOCK?
GONE. I TRIED-- I WANTED TO--
WE WERE BORED.
COME WITH ME.
COME WITH ME, ANAYKAH--
I CAN'T. I BELONG HERE. EVENTUALLY THEY WILL FORGIVE ME.
I CAN'T. SAVE THE CHILD. THERE IS LOVE IN YOU, ELIJAH. SAVE HER.
PLEASE, ELIJAH. BECAUSE I LOVE YOU. I ALWAYS LOVED YOU.
I AM SO SORRY.

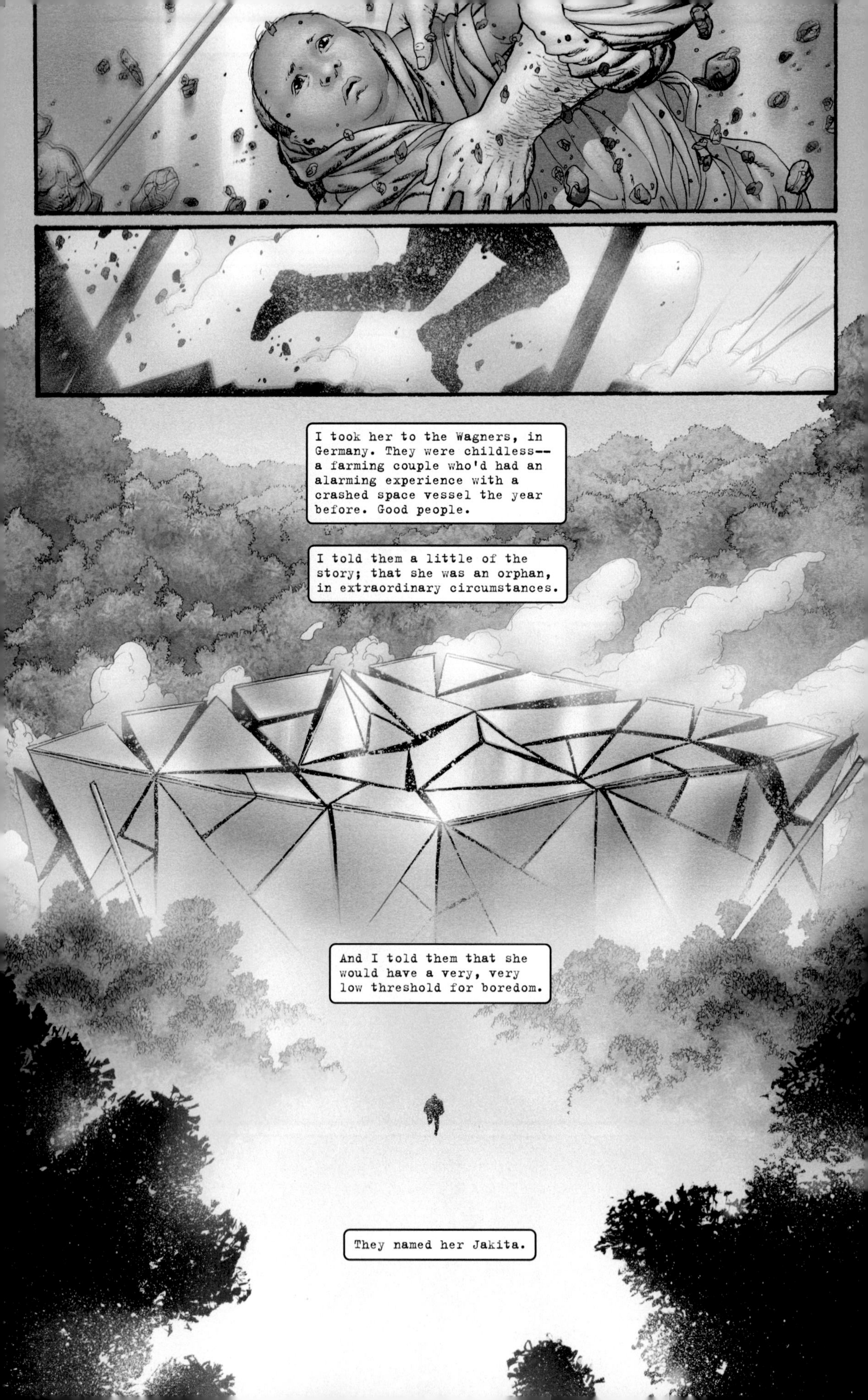

I took her to the Wagners, in Germany. They were childless--a farming couple who'd had an alarming experience with a crashed space vessel the year before. Good people.
I told them a little of the story; that she was an orphan, in extraordinary circumstances.
And I told them that she would have a very, very low threshold for boredom.
They named her Jakita.

CHAPTER

PLANETARY 18

CHAPTER 18

THE GUN CLUB

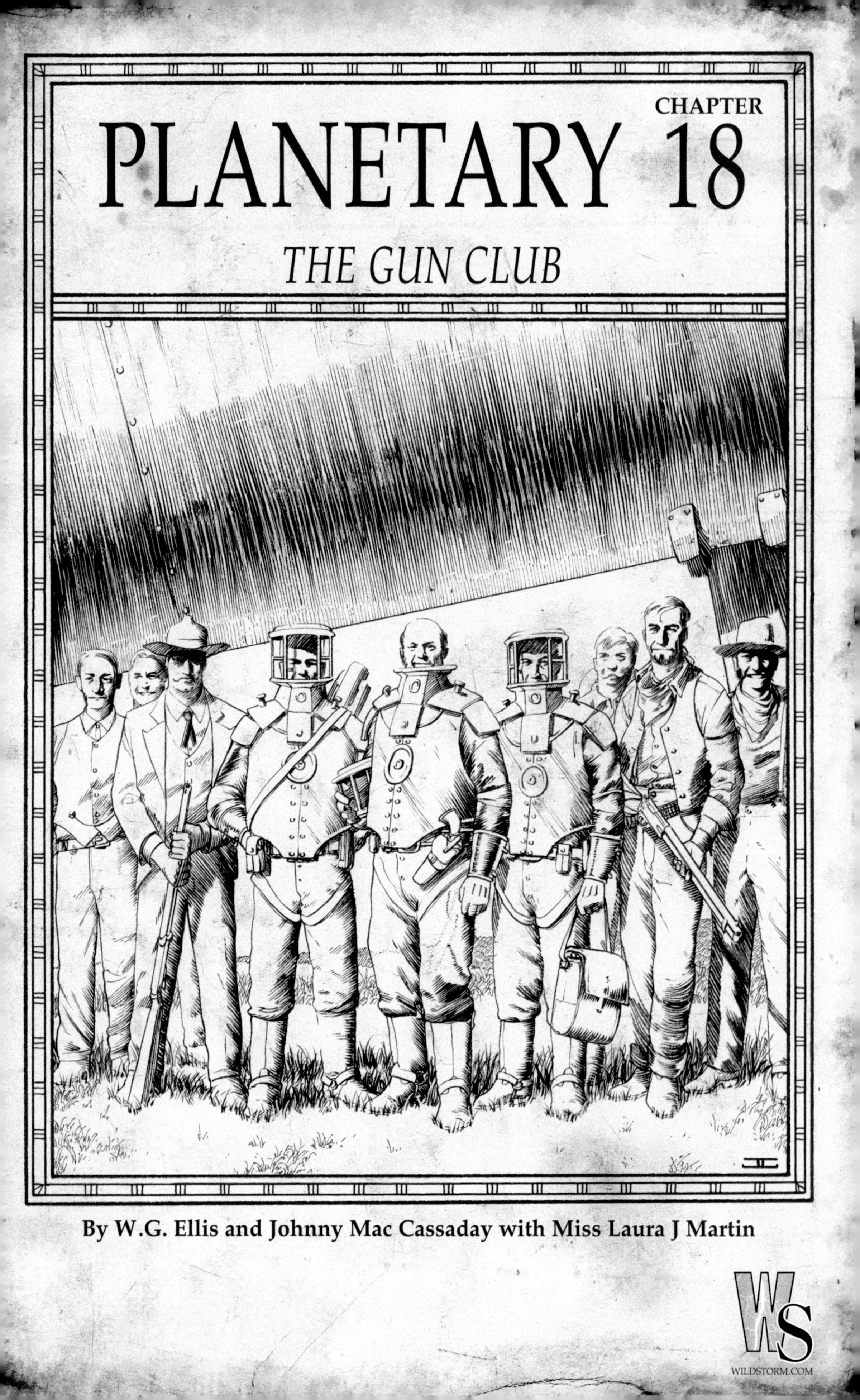

By W.G. Ellis and Johnny Mac Cassaday with Miss Laura J Martin

WILDSTORM.COM

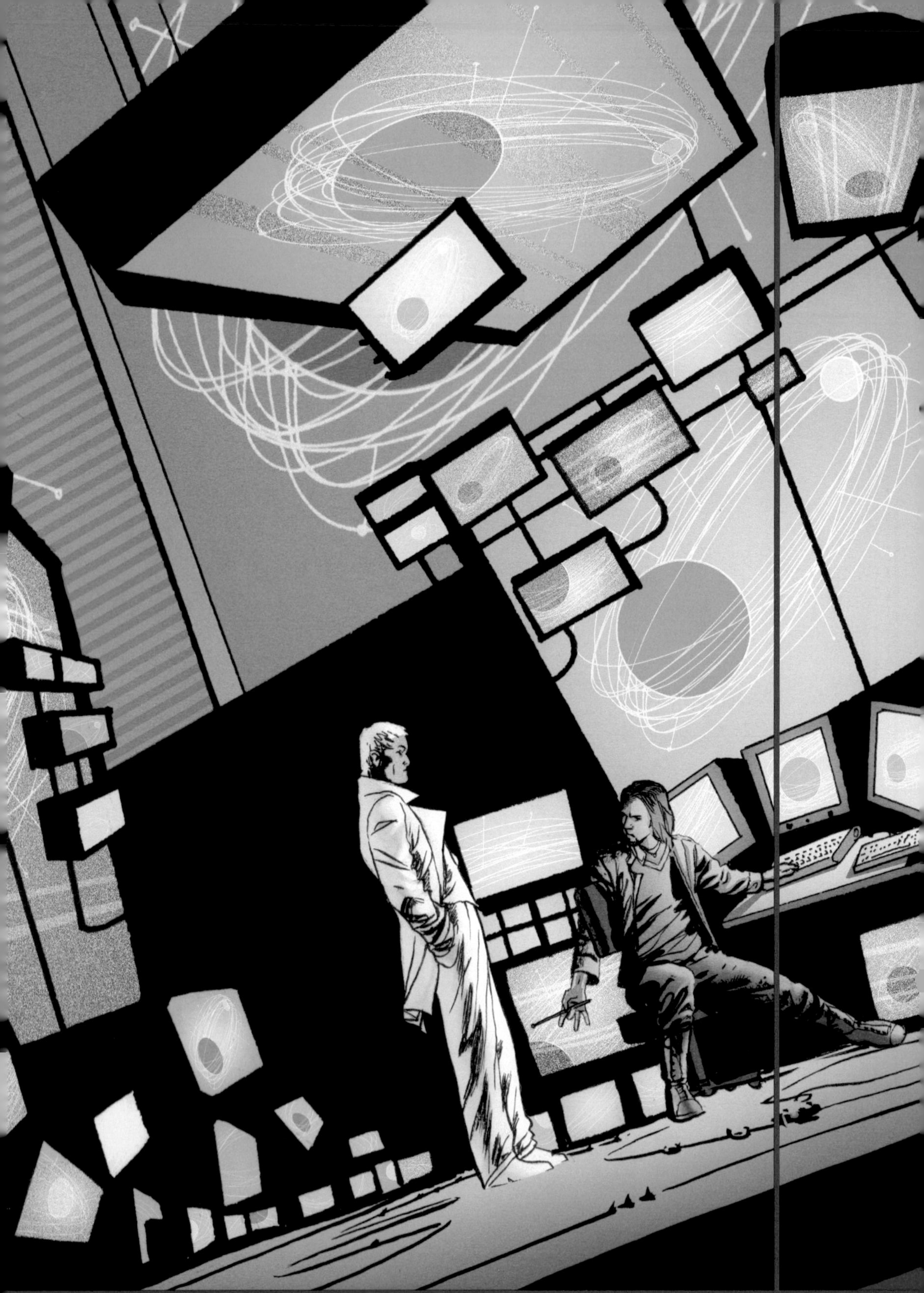

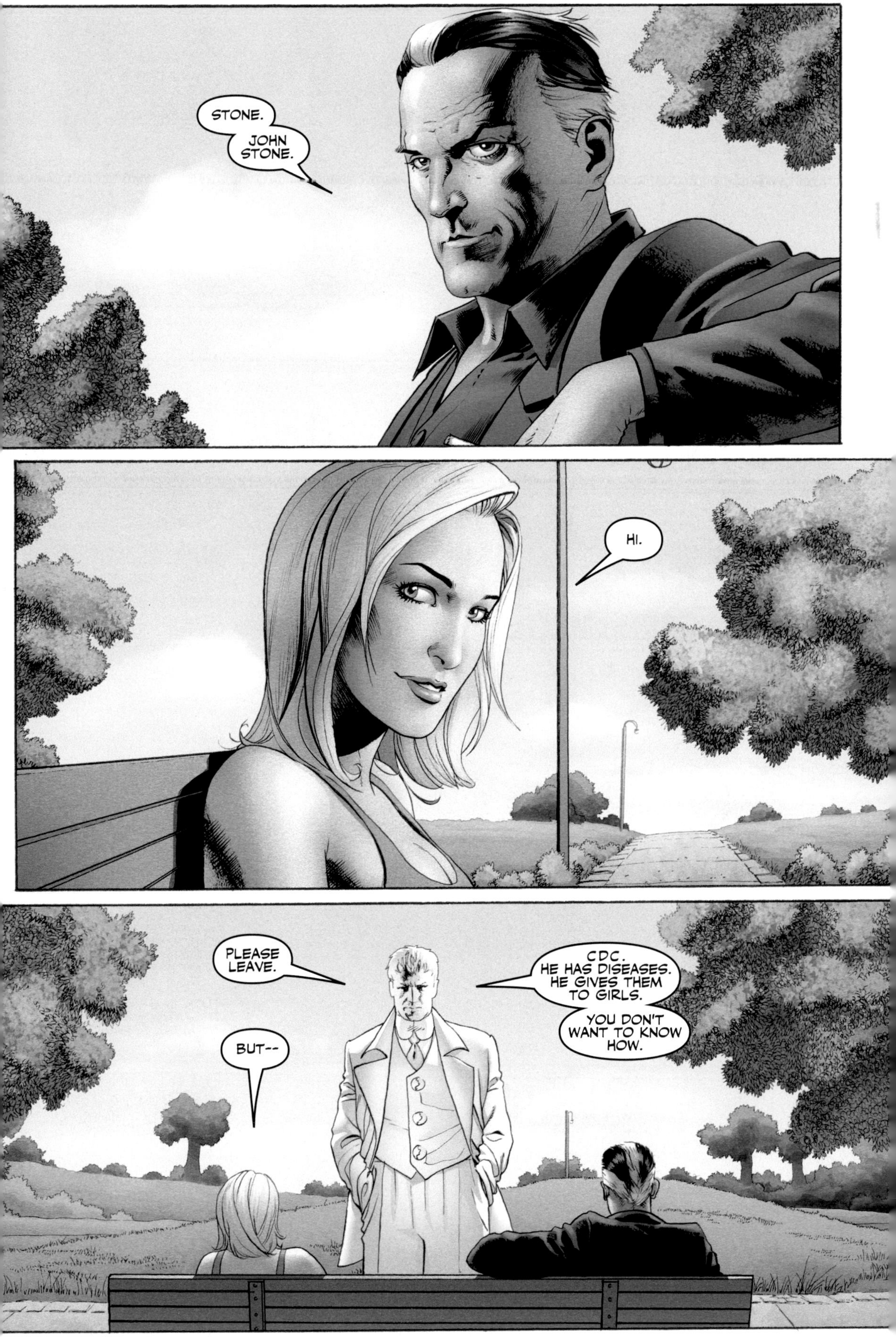
STONE.
JOHN STONE.
HI.
PLEASE LEAVE.
BUT--
CDC. HE HAS DISEASES. HE GIVES THEM TO GIRLS.
YOU DON'T WANT TO KNOW HOW.

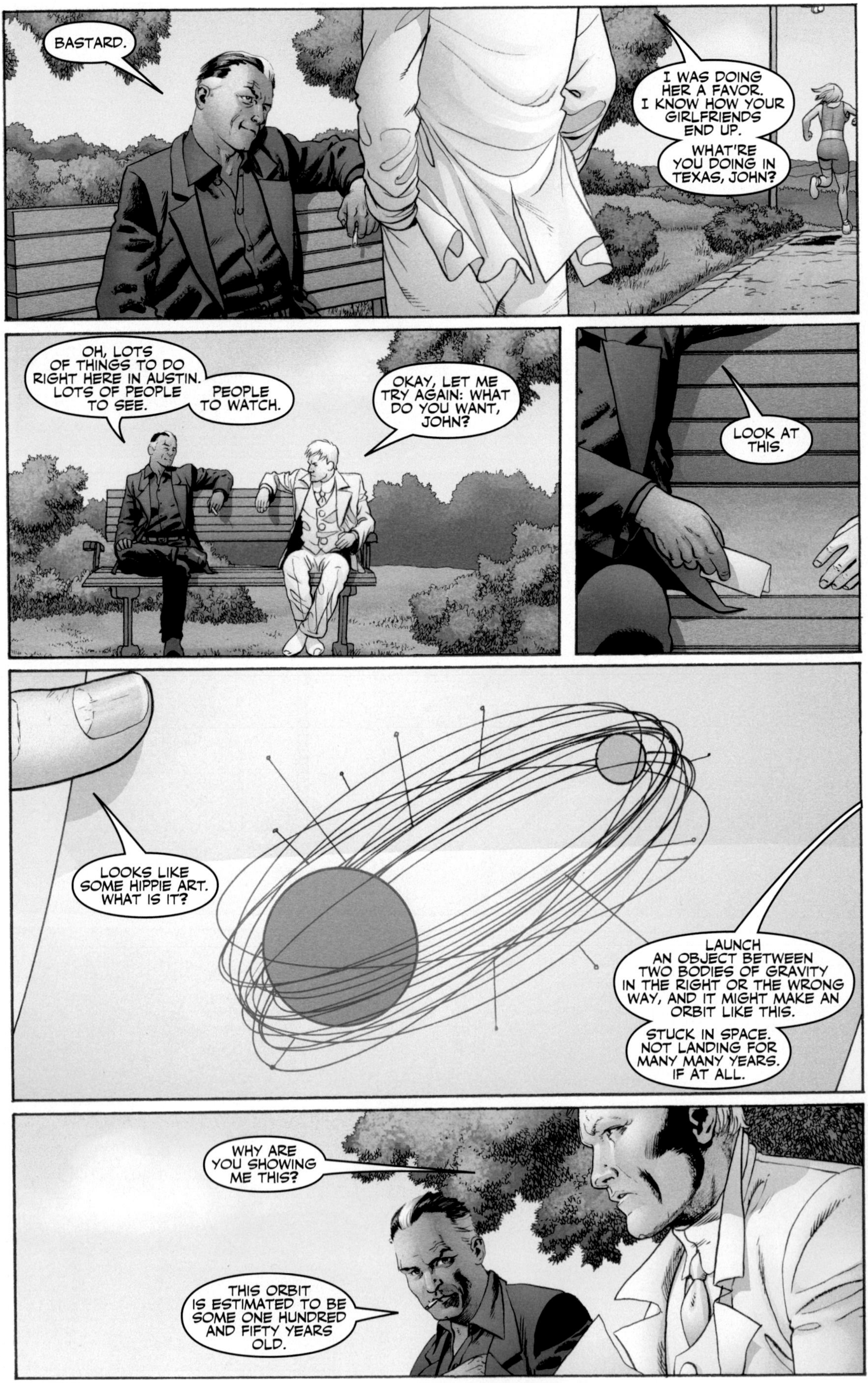
BASTARD.
I WAS DOING HER A FAVOR. I KNOW HOW YOUR GIRLFRIENDS END UP.
WHAT'RE YOU DOING IN TEXAS, JOHN?
OH, LOTS OF THINGS TO DO RIGHT HERE IN AUSTIN. LOTS OF PEOPLE TO SEE.
PEOPLE TO WATCH.
OKAY, LET ME TRY AGAIN: WHAT DO YOU WANT, JOHN?
LOOK AT THIS.
LOOKS LIKE SOME HIPPIE ART. WHAT IS IT?
LAUNCH AN OBJECT BETWEEN TWO BODIES OF GRAVITY IN THE RIGHT OR THE WRONG WAY, AND IT MIGHT MAKE AN ORBIT LIKE THIS.
STUCK IN SPACE. NOT LANDING FOR MANY MANY YEARS. IF AT ALL.
WHY ARE YOU SHOWING ME THIS?
THIS ORBIT IS ESTIMATED TO BE SOME ONE HUNDRED AND FIFTY YEARS OLD.

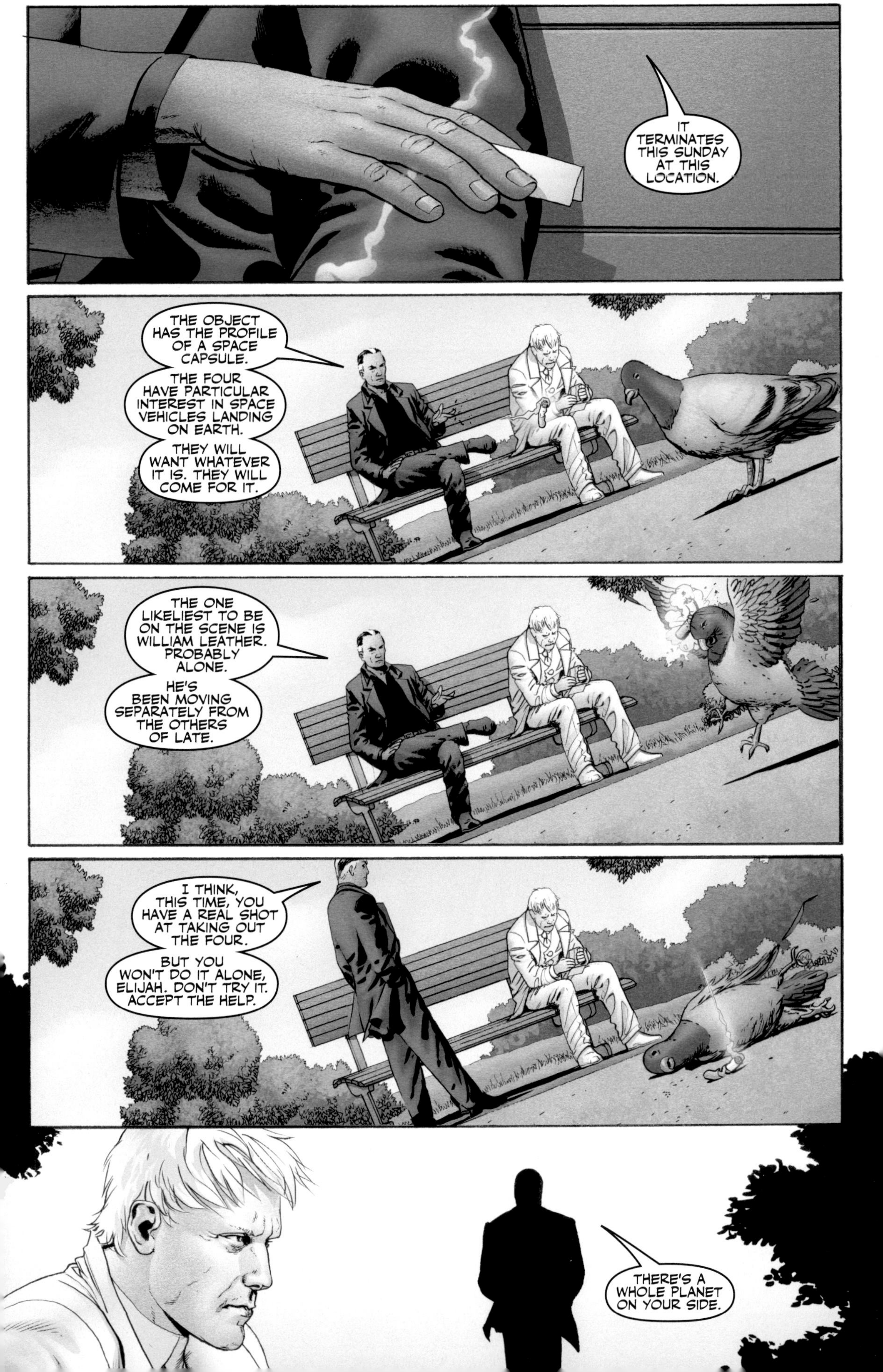
IT TERMINATES THIS SUNDAY AT THIS LOCATION.
THE OBJECT HAS THE PROFILE OF A SPACE CAPSULE.
THE FOUR HAVE PARTICULAR INTEREST IN SPACE VEHICLES LANDING ON EARTH.
THEY WILL WANT WHATEVER IT IS. THEY WILL COME FOR IT.
THE ONE LIKELIEST TO BE ON THE SCENE IS WILLIAM LEATHER. PROBABLY ALONE.
HE'S BEEN MOVING SEPARATELY FROM THE OTHERS OF LATE.
I THINK, THIS TIME, YOU HAVE A REAL SHOT AT TAKING OUT THE FOUR.
BUT YOU WON'T DO IT ALONE, ELIJAH. DON'T TRY IT. ACCEPT THE HELP.
THERE'S A WHOLE PLANET ON YOUR SIDE.

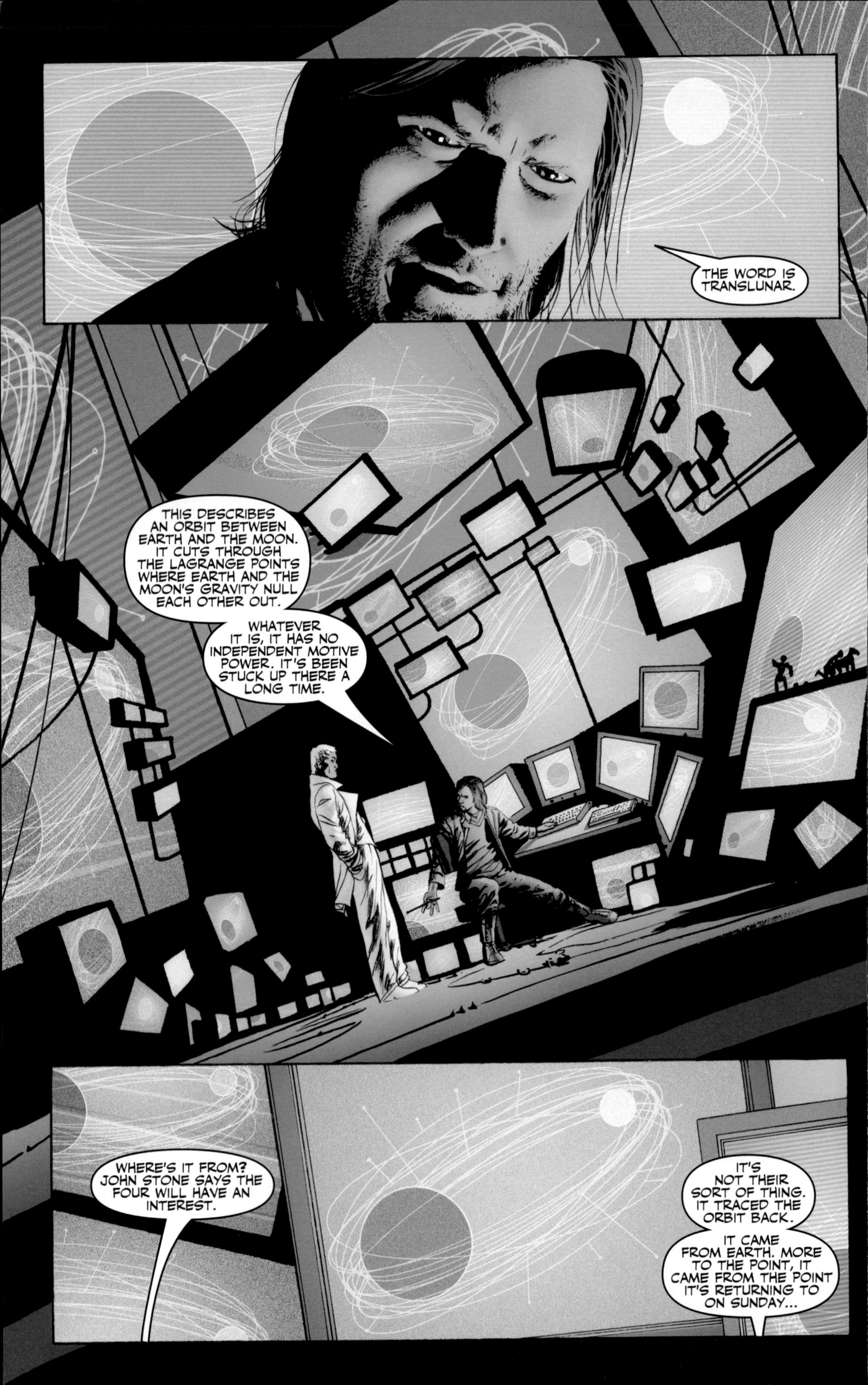
THE WORD IS TRANSLUNAR.
THIS DESCRIBES AN ORBIT BETWEEN EARTH AND THE MOON. IT CUTS THROUGH THE LAGRANGE POINTS WHERE EARTH AND THE MOON'S GRAVITY NULL EACH OTHER OUT.
WHATEVER IT IS, IT HAS NO INDEPENDENT MOTIVE POWER. IT'S BEEN STUCK UP THERE A LONG TIME.
WHERE'S IT FROM? JOHN STONE SAYS THE FOUR WILL HAVE AN INTEREST.
IT'S NOT THEIR SORT OF THING. IT TRACED THE ORBIT BACK.
IT CAME FROM EARTH. MORE TO THE POINT, IT CAME FROM THE POINT IT'S RETURNING TO ON SUNDAY...

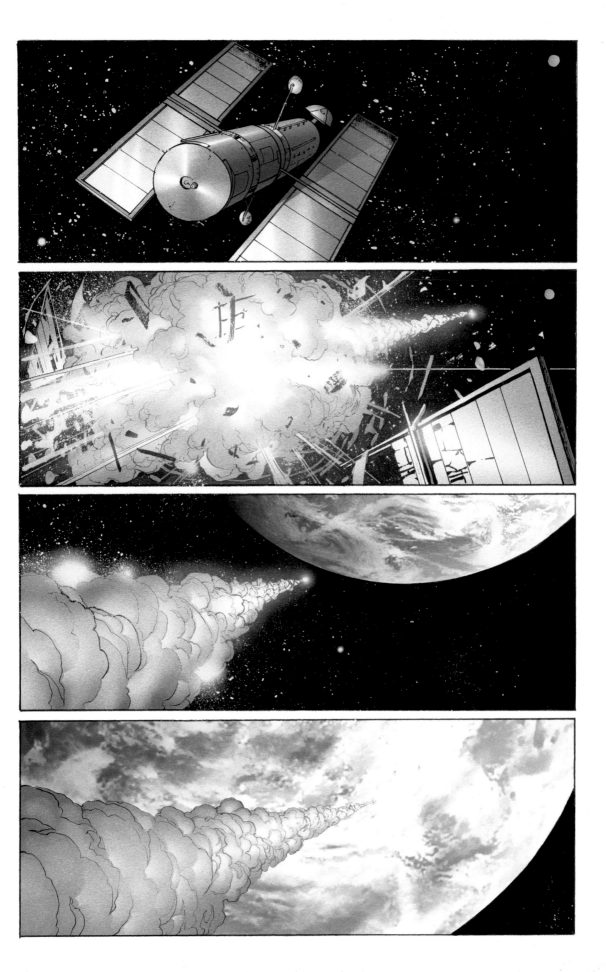

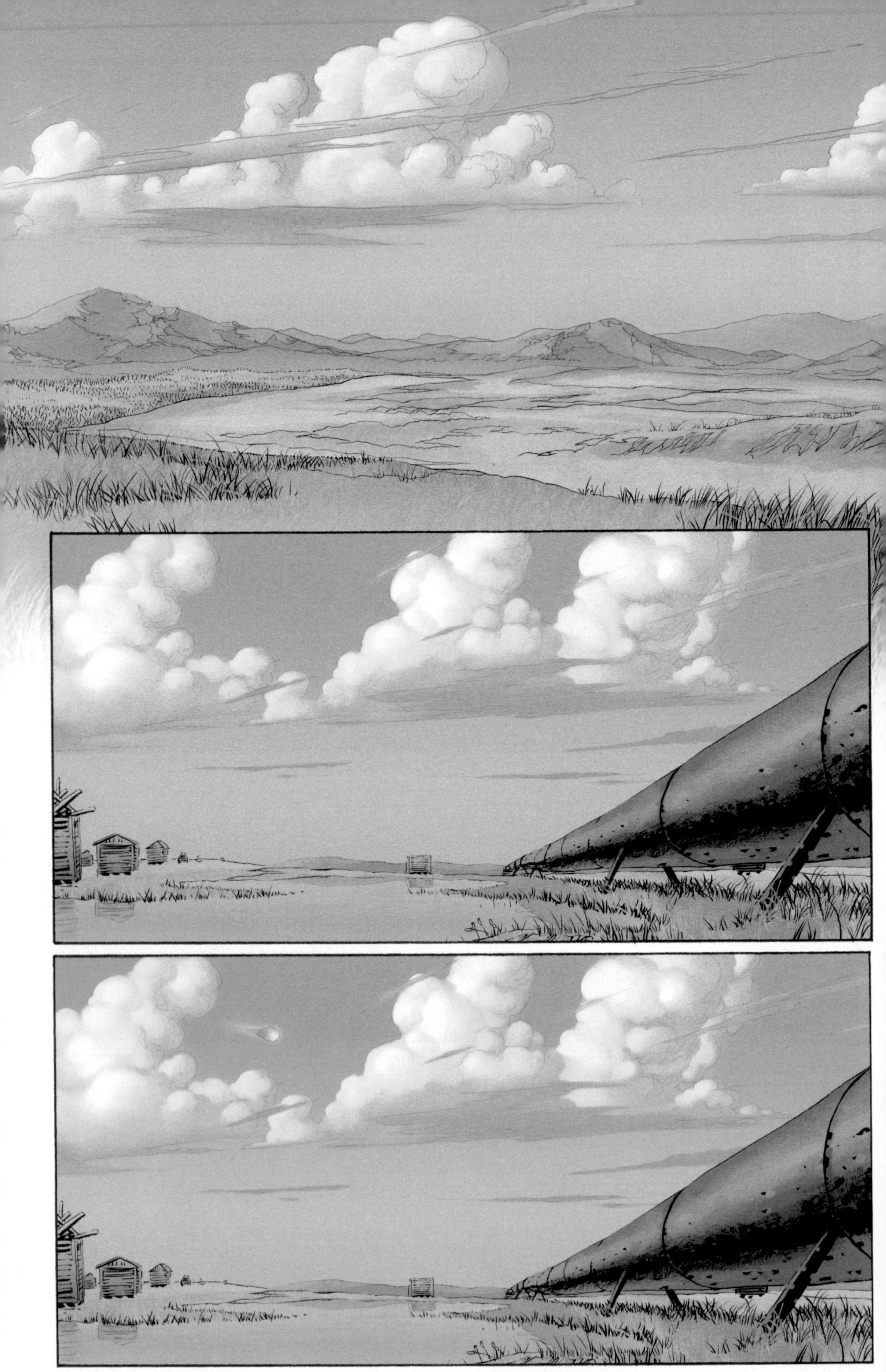

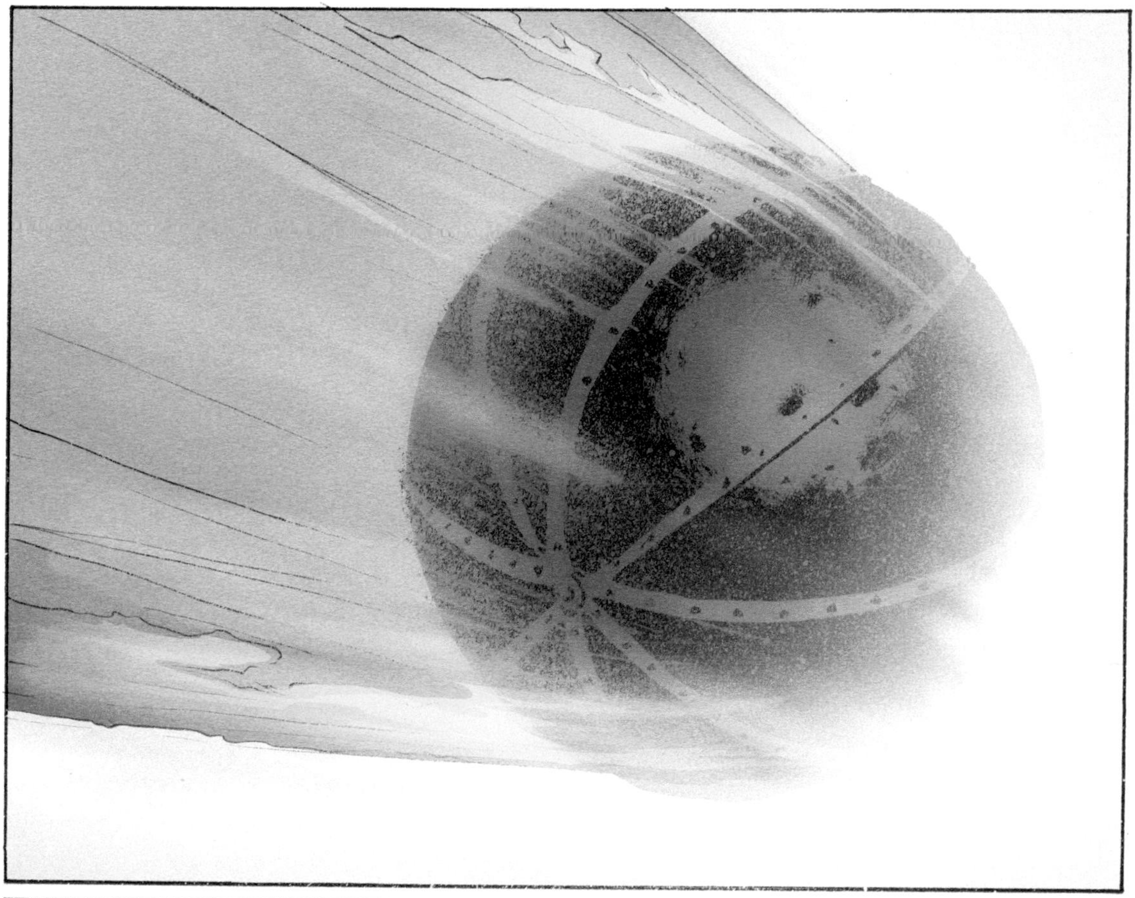

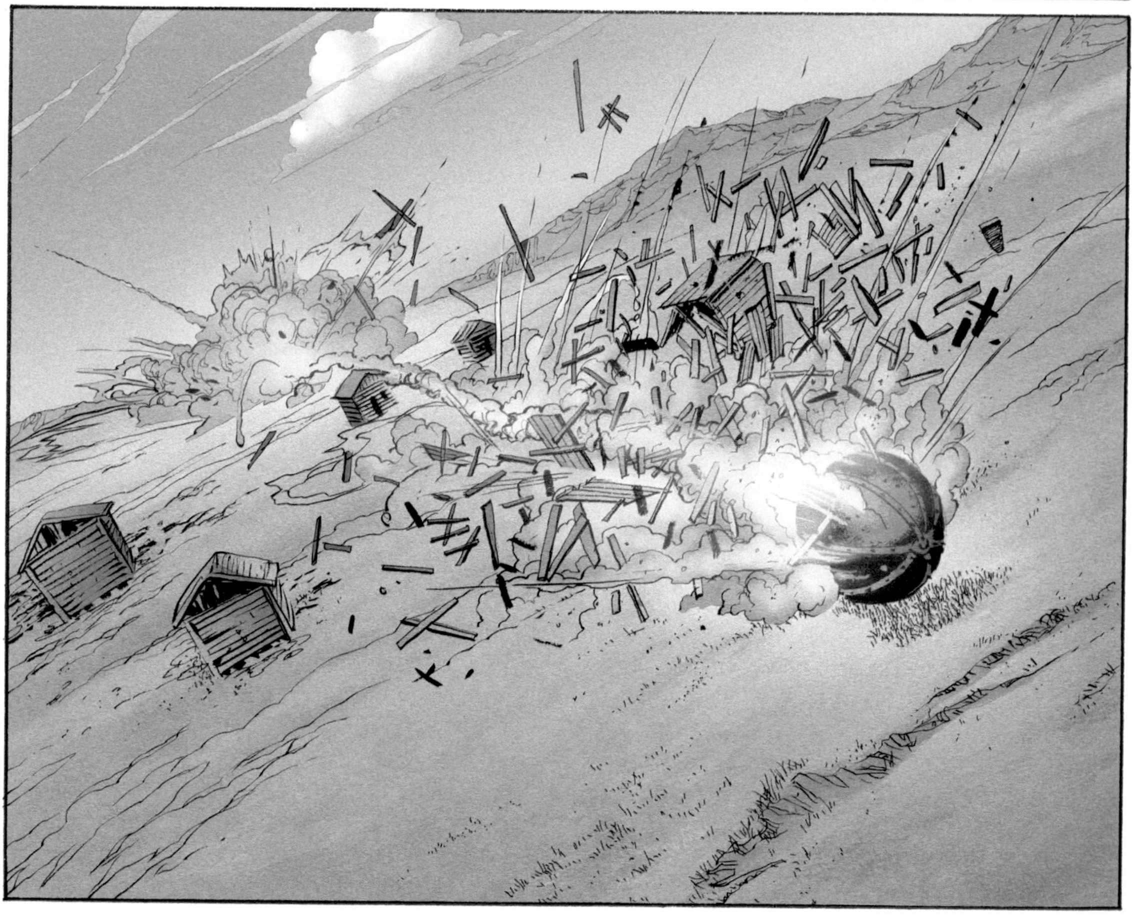

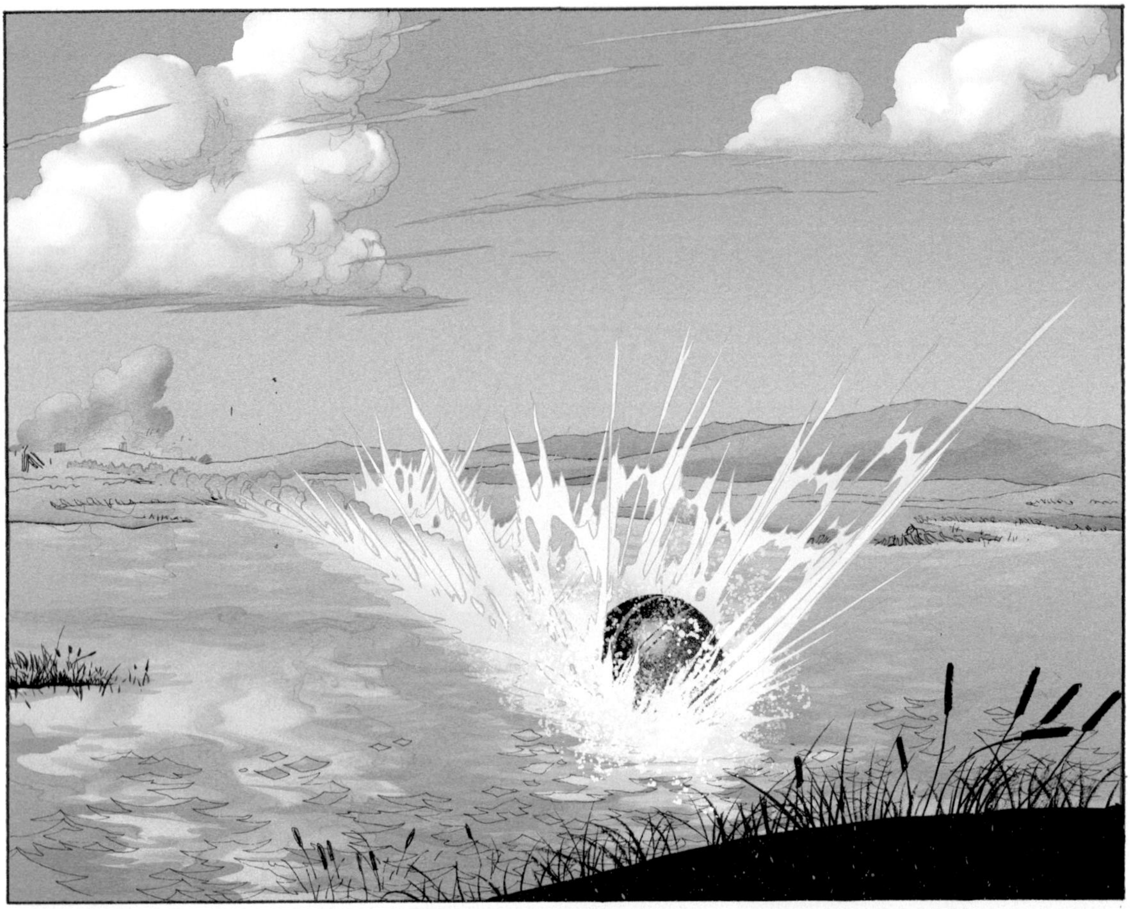

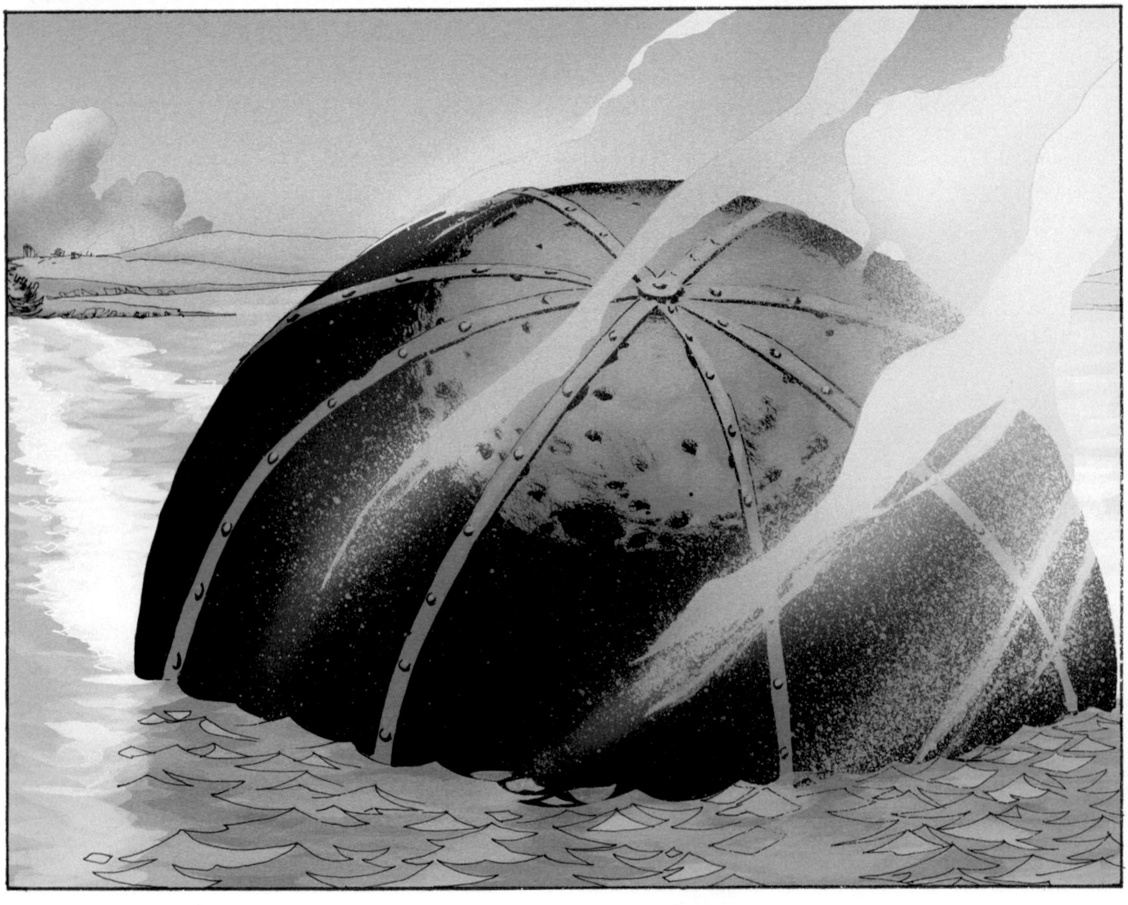

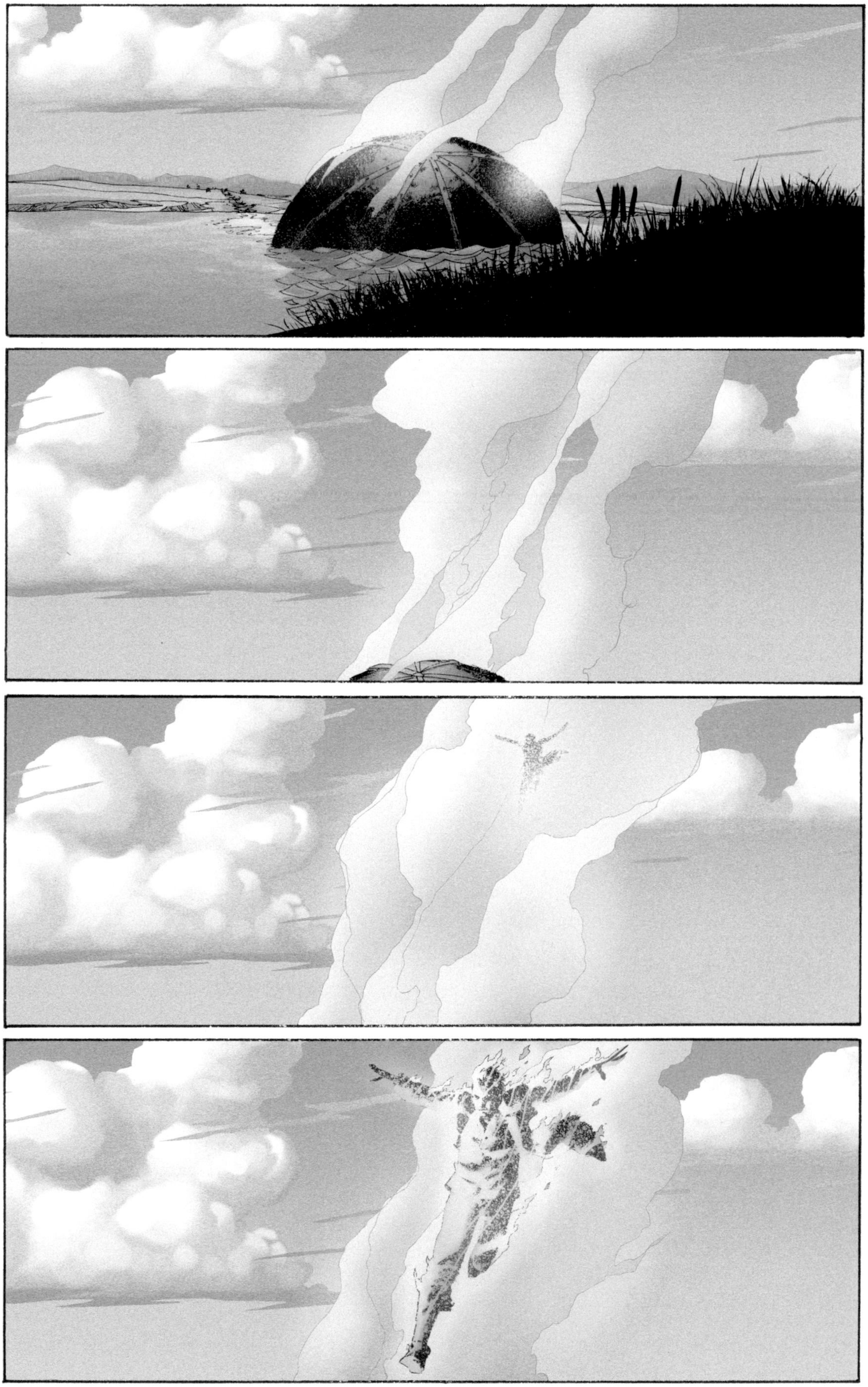

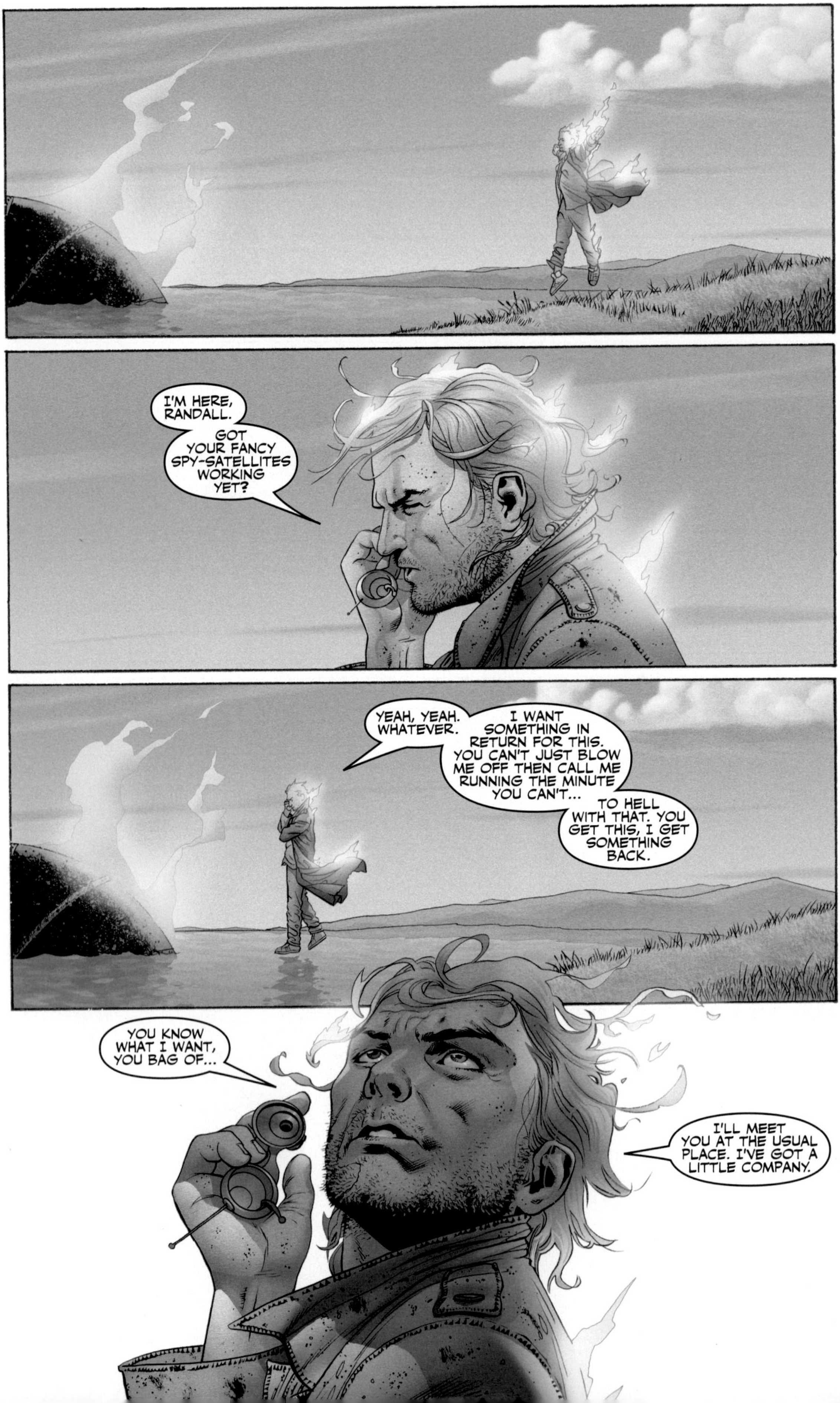
I'M HERE, RANDALL.
GOT YOUR FANCY SPY-SATELLITES WORKING YET?
YEAH, YEAH. WHATEVER.
I WANT SOMETHING IN RETURN FOR THIS. YOU CAN'T JUST BLOW ME OFF THEN CALL ME RUNNING THE MINUTE YOU CAN'T...
TO HELL WITH THAT. YOU GET THIS, I GET SOMETHING BACK.
YOU KNOW WHAT I WANT, YOU BAG OF...
I'LL MEET YOU AT THE USUAL PLACE. I'VE GOT A LITTLE COMPANY.

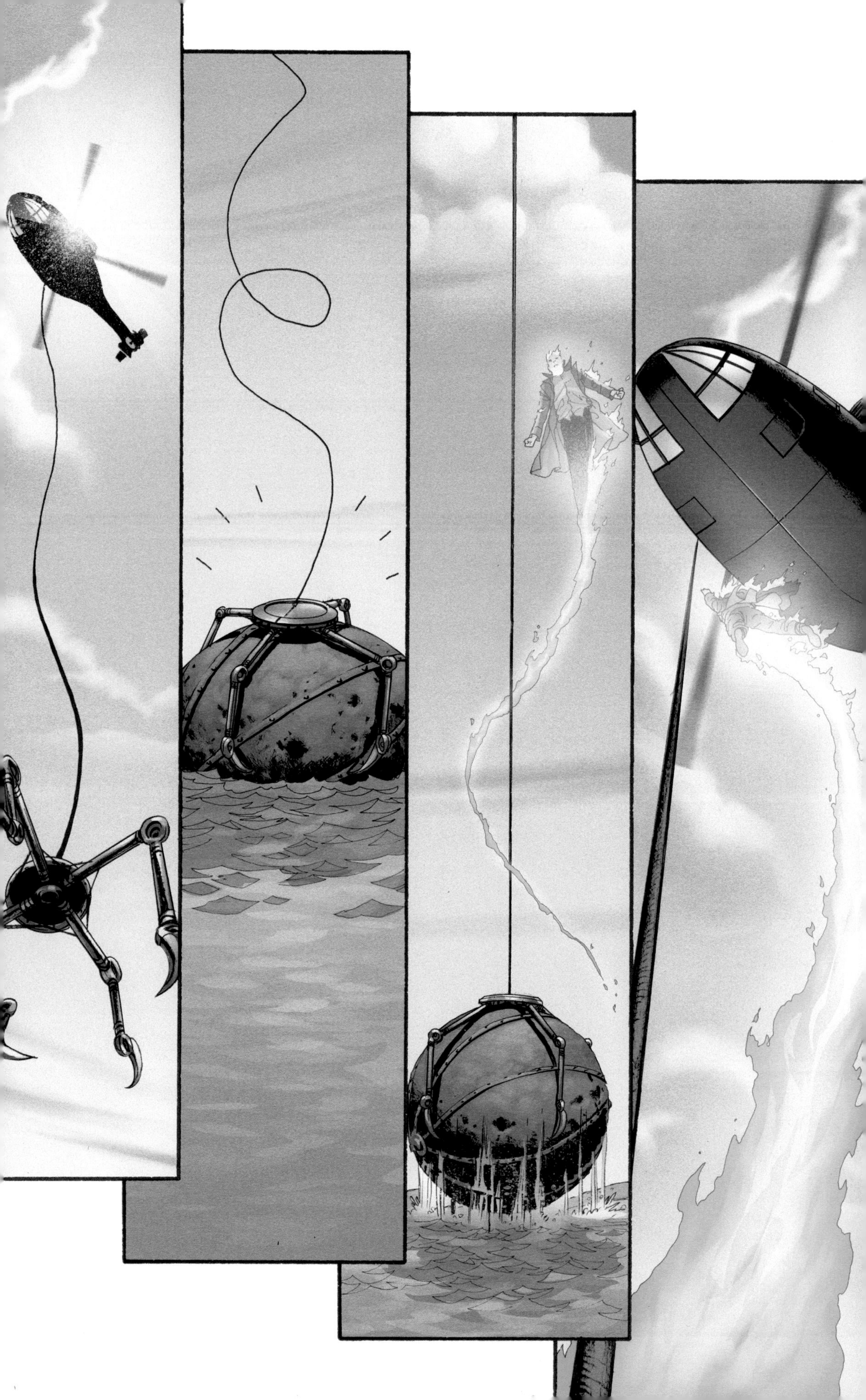

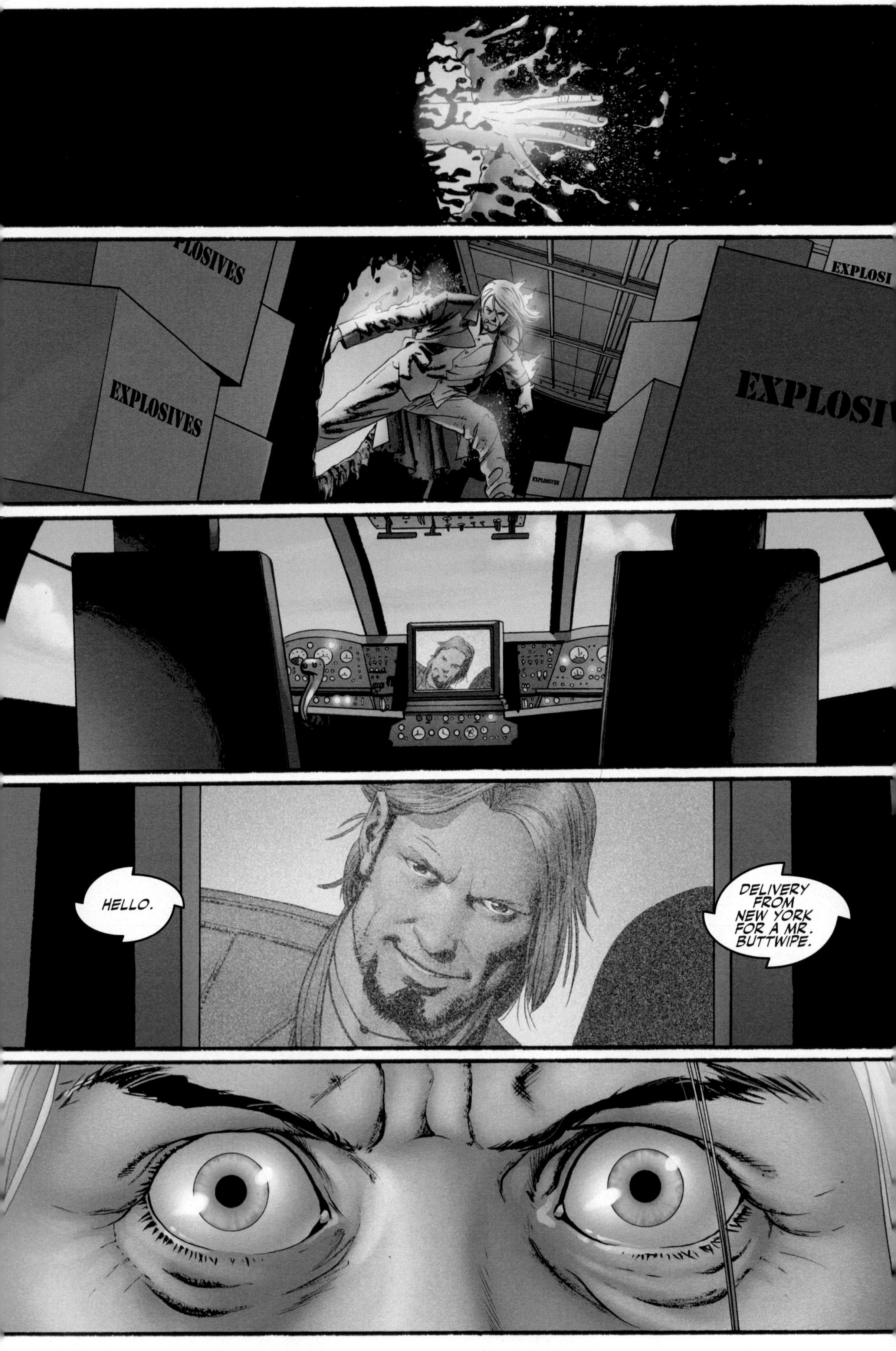
EXPLOSIVES
EXPLOSIVES
EXPLOSIVES
EXPLOSI
EXPLOSIV
HELLO.
DELIVERY FROM NEW YORK FOR A MR. BUTTWIPE.

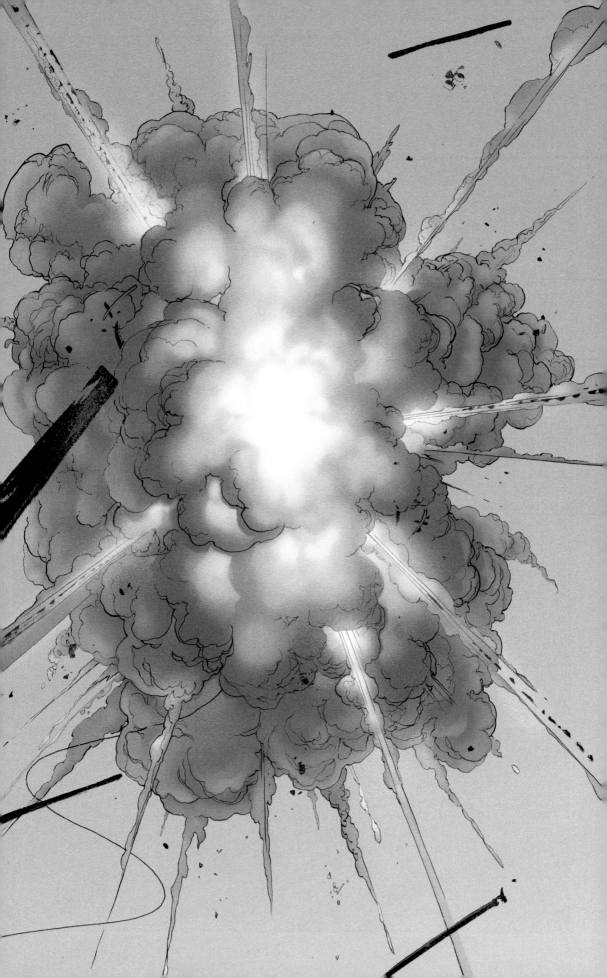

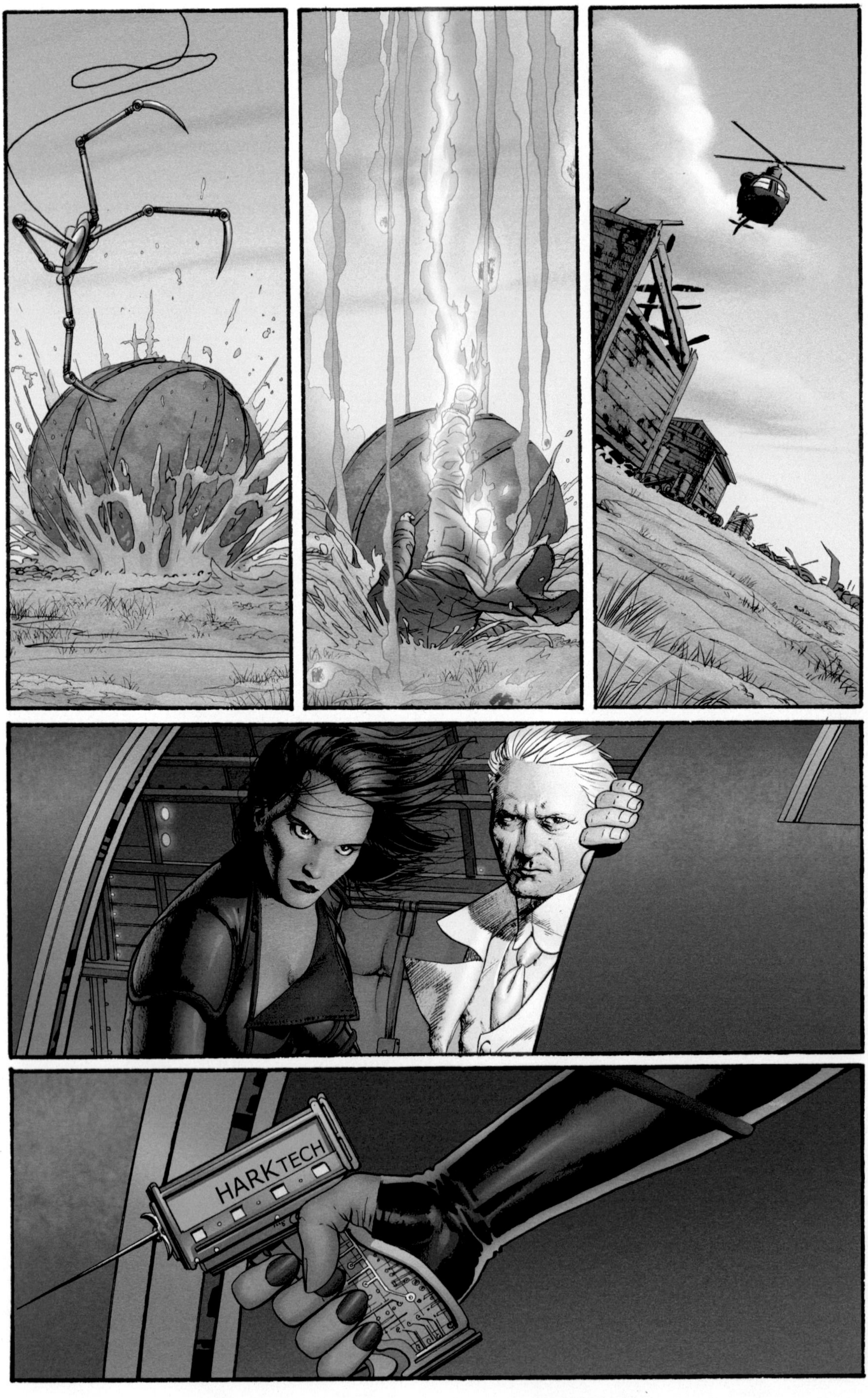
HARKTECH

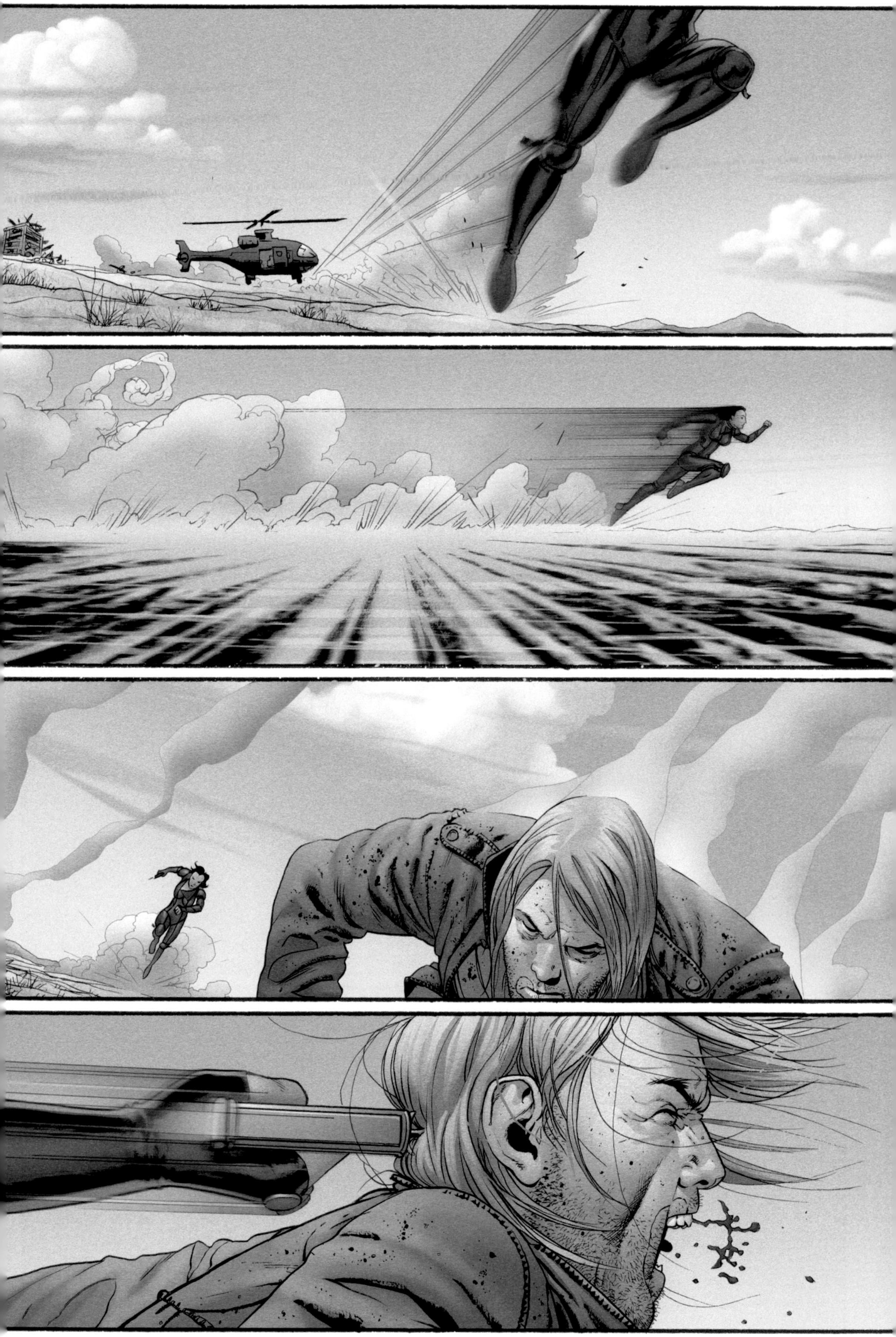

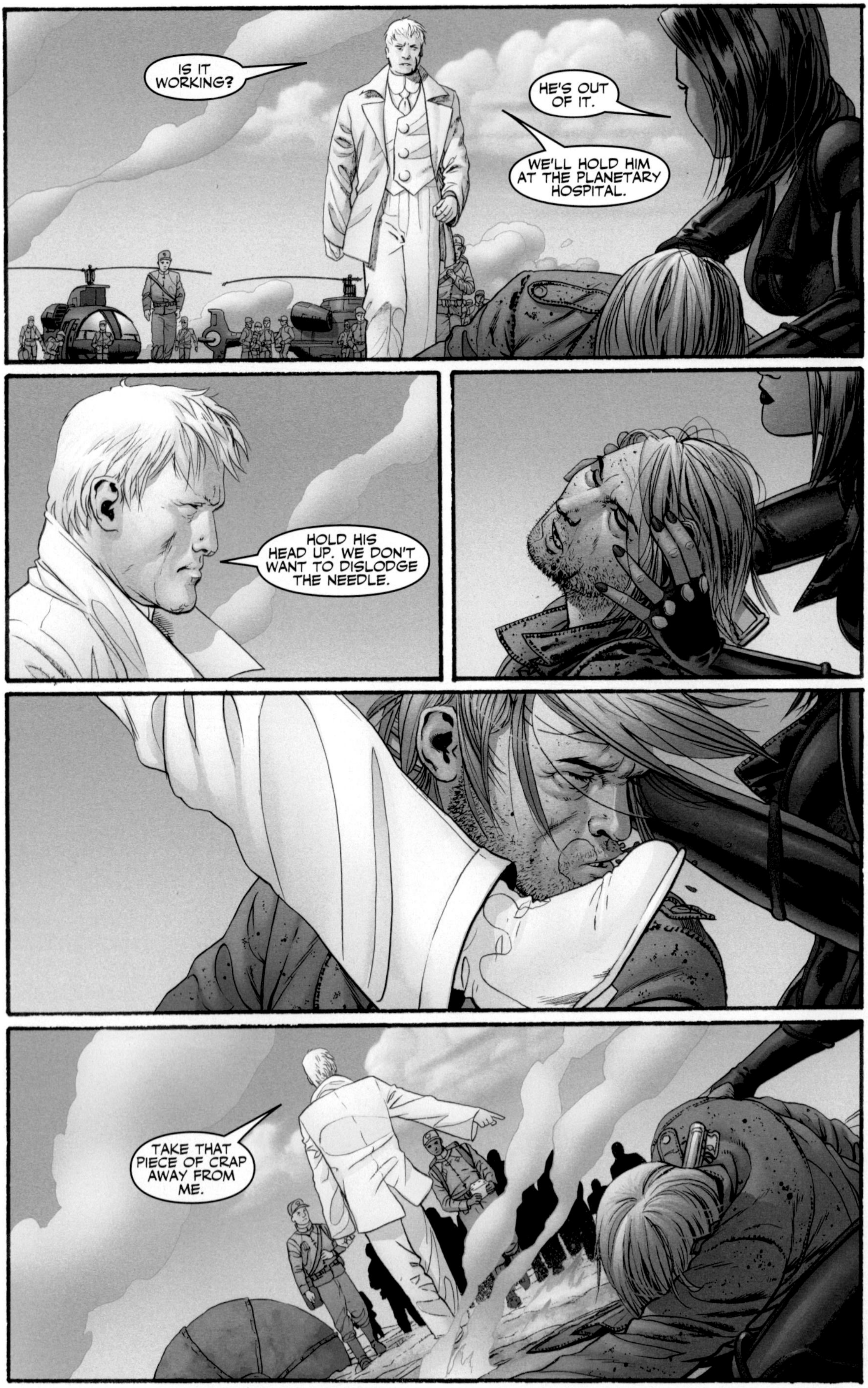
IS IT WORKING?
HE'S OUT OF IT.
WE'LL HOLD HIM AT THE PLANETARY HOSPITAL.
HOLD HIS HEAD UP. WE DON'T WANT TO DISLODGE THE NEEDLE.
TAKE THAT PIECE OF CRAP AWAY FROM ME.

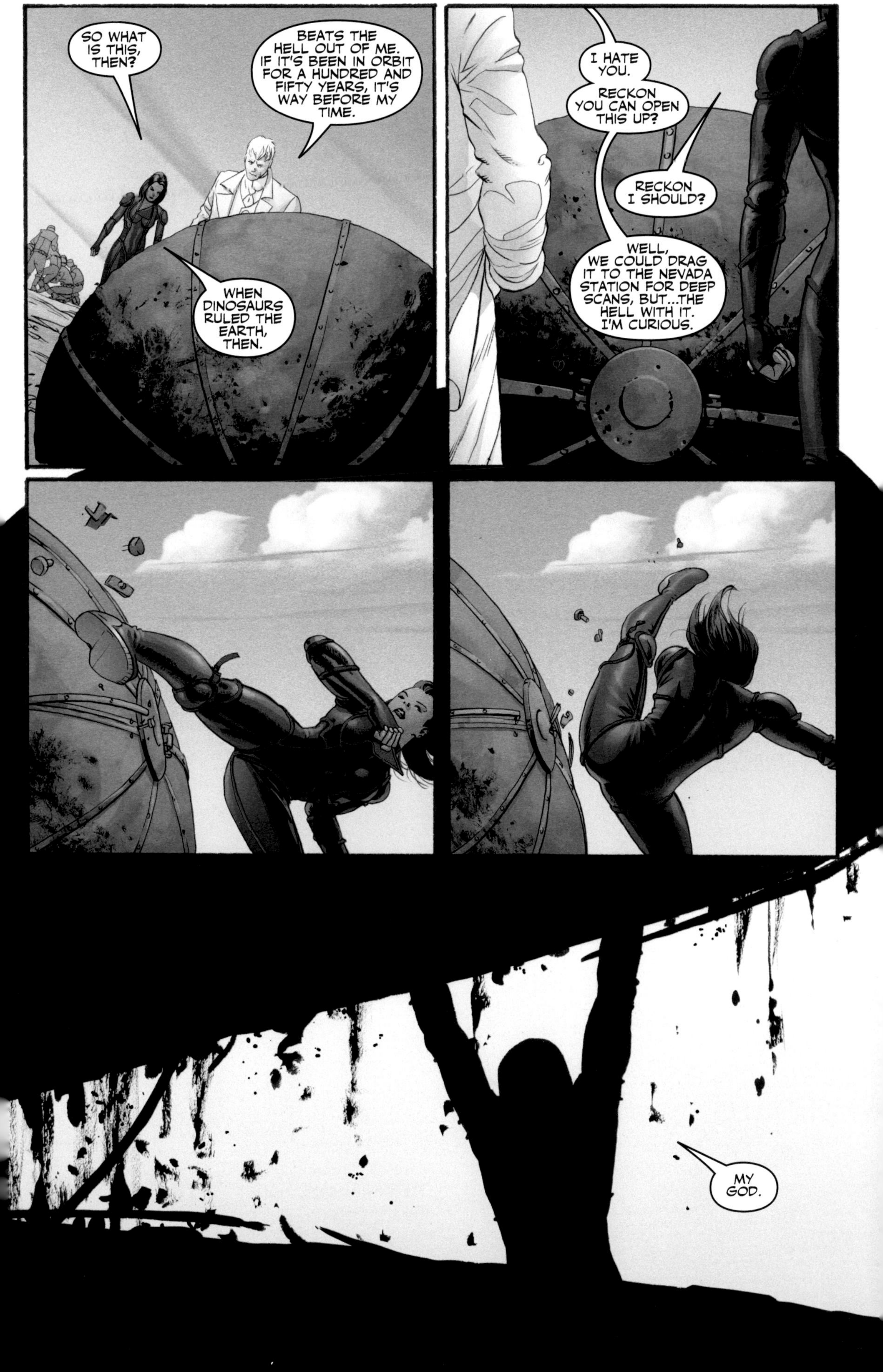
SO WHAT IS THIS, THEN?
BEATS THE HELL OUT OF ME. IF IT'S BEEN IN ORBIT FOR A HUNDRED AND FIFTY YEARS, IT'S WAY BEFORE MY TIME.
WHEN DINOSAURS RULED THE EARTH, THEN.
I HATE YOU.
RECKON YOU CAN OPEN THIS UP?
RECKON I SHOULD?
WELL, WE COULD DRAG IT TO THE NEVADA STATION FOR DEEP SCANS, BUT...THE HELL WITH IT. I'M CURIOUS.
MY GOD.

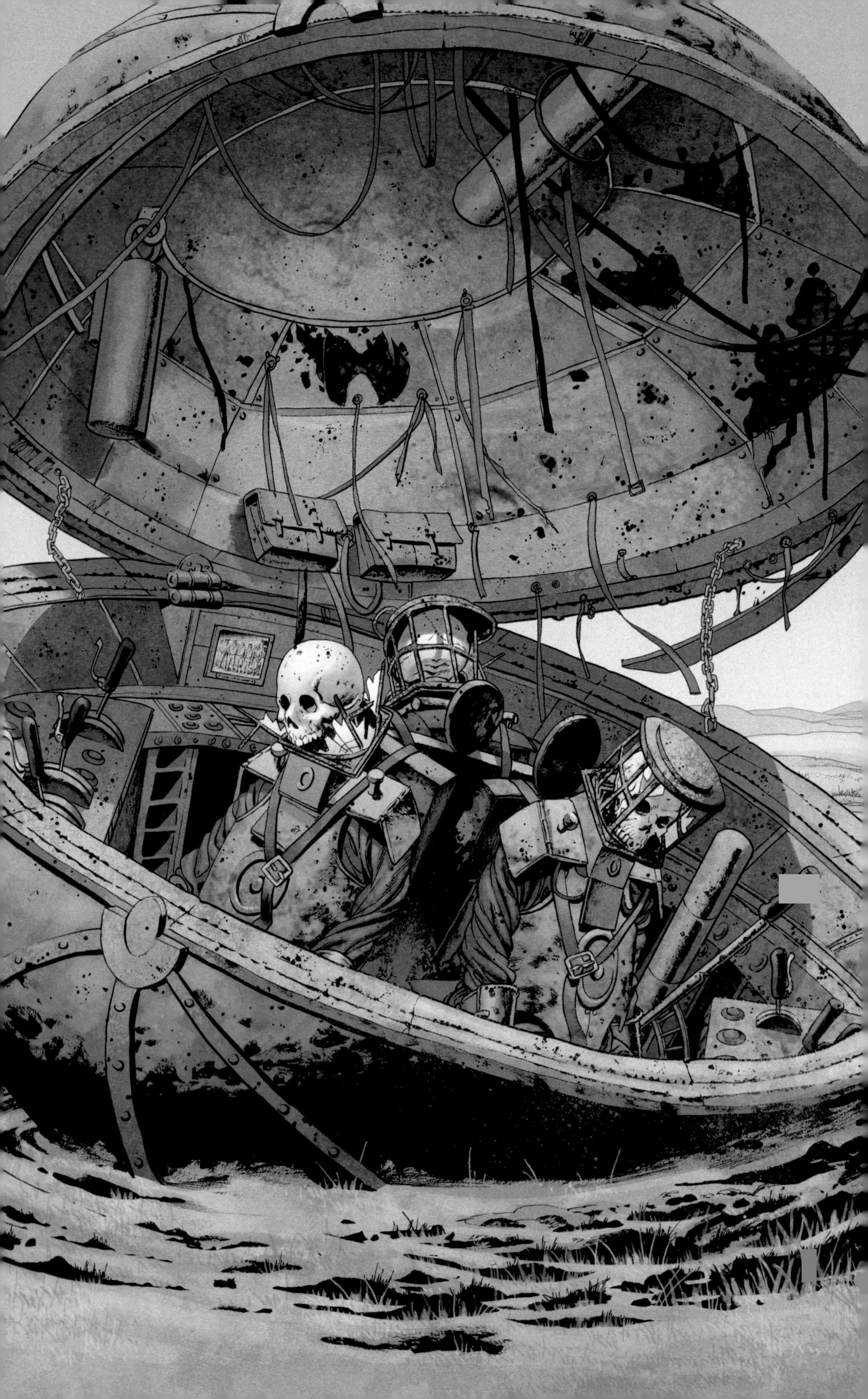

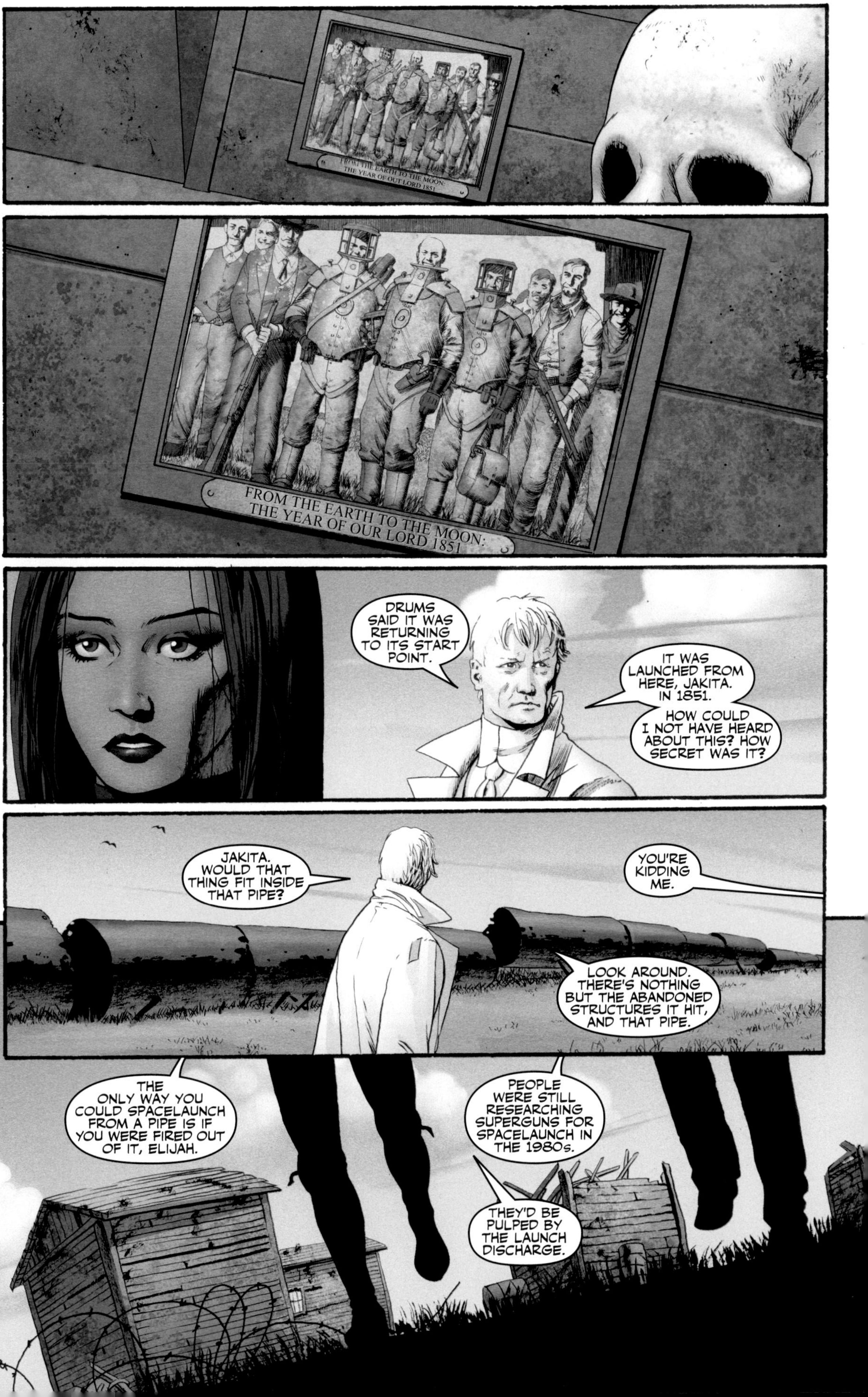
FROM THE EARTH TO THE MOON:
THE YEAR OF OUT LORD 1851
FROM THE EARTH TO THE MOON:
THE YEAR OF OUR LORD 1851
DRUMS SAID IT WAS RETURNING TO ITS START POINT.
IT WAS LAUNCHED FROM HERE, JAKITA. IN 1851.
HOW COULD I NOT HAVE HEARD ABOUT THIS? HOW SECRET WAS IT?
JAKITA. WOULD THAT THING FIT INSIDE THAT PIPE?
YOU'RE KIDDING ME.
LOOK AROUND. THERE'S NOTHING BUT THE ABANDONED STRUCTURES IT HIT, AND THAT PIPE.
THE ONLY WAY YOU COULD SPACELAUNCH FROM A PIPE IS IF YOU WERE FIRED OUT OF IT, ELIJAH.
PEOPLE WERE STILL RESEARCHING SUPERGUNS FOR SPACELAUNCH IN THE 1980s.
THEY'D BE PULPED BY THE LAUNCH DISCHARGE.

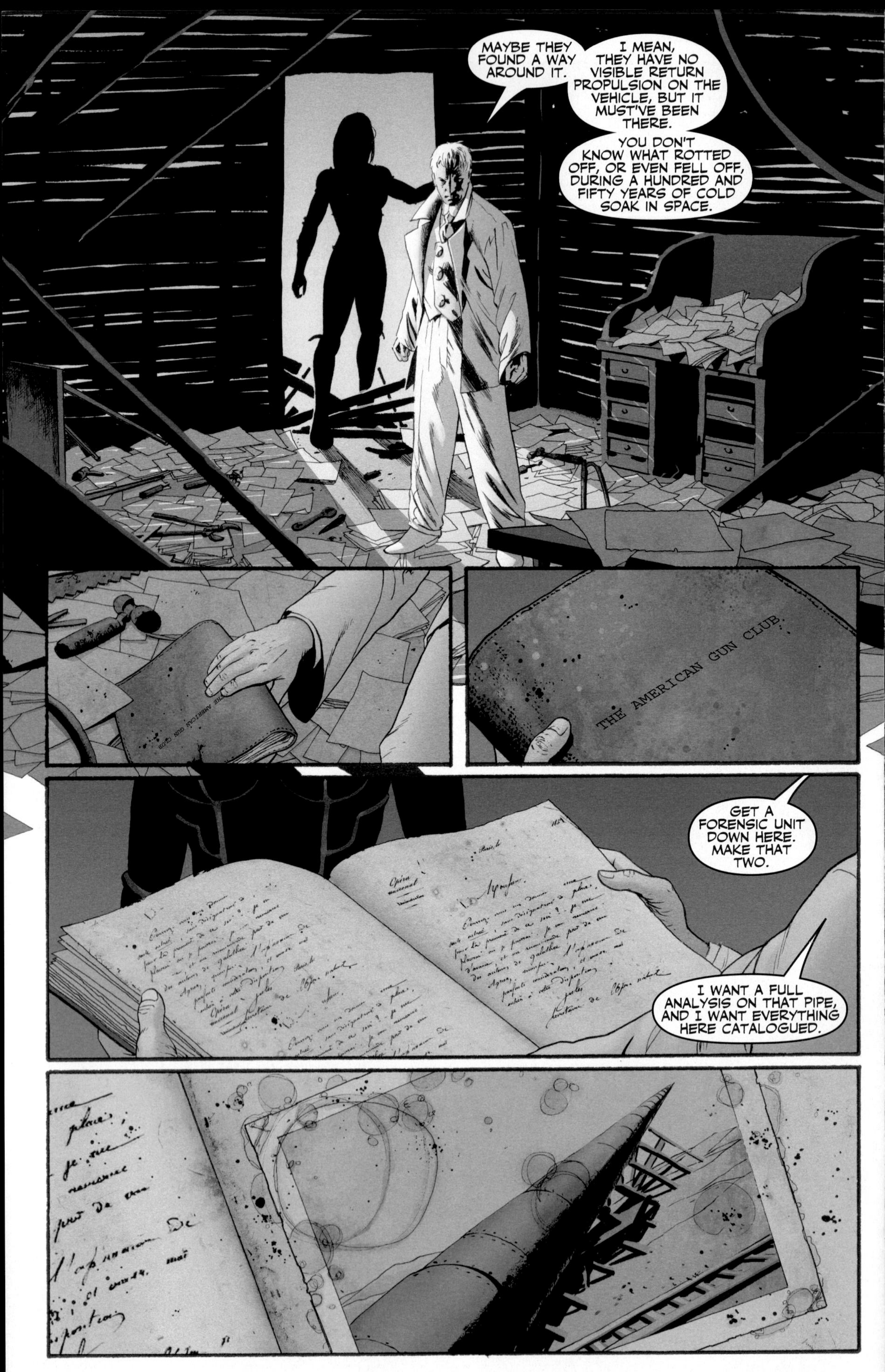
MAYBE THEY FOUND A WAY AROUND IT.
I MEAN, THEY HAVE NO VISIBLE RETURN PROPULSION ON THE VEHICLE, BUT IT MUST'VE BEEN THERE.
YOU DON'T KNOW WHAT ROTTED OFF, OR EVEN FELL OFF, DURING A HUNDRED AND FIFTY YEARS OF COLD SOAK IN SPACE.
THE AMERICAN GUN CLUB
GET A FORENSIC UNIT DOWN HERE. MAKE THAT TWO.
I WANT A FULL ANALYSIS ON THAT PIPE, AND I WANT EVERYTHING HERE CATALOGUED.

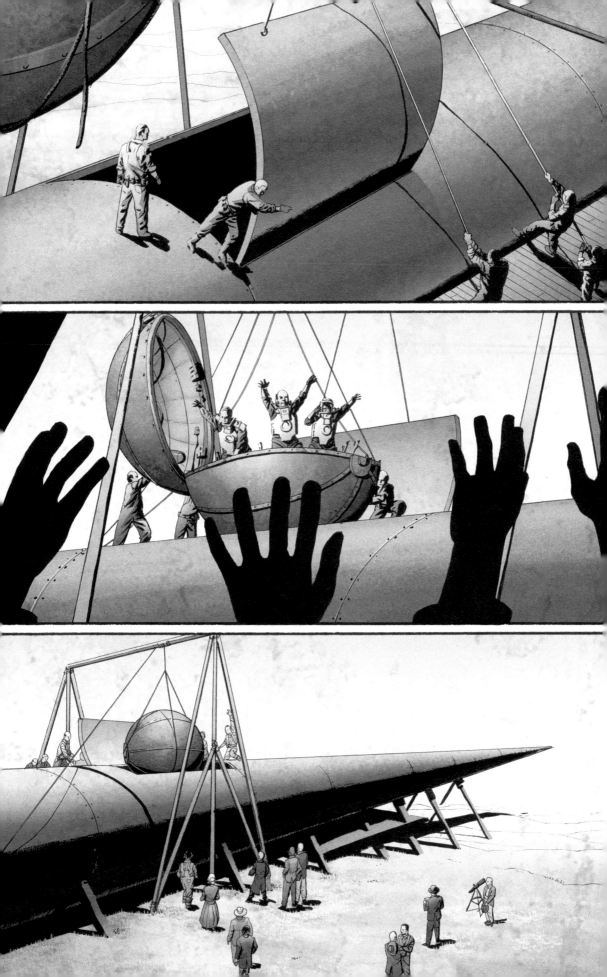

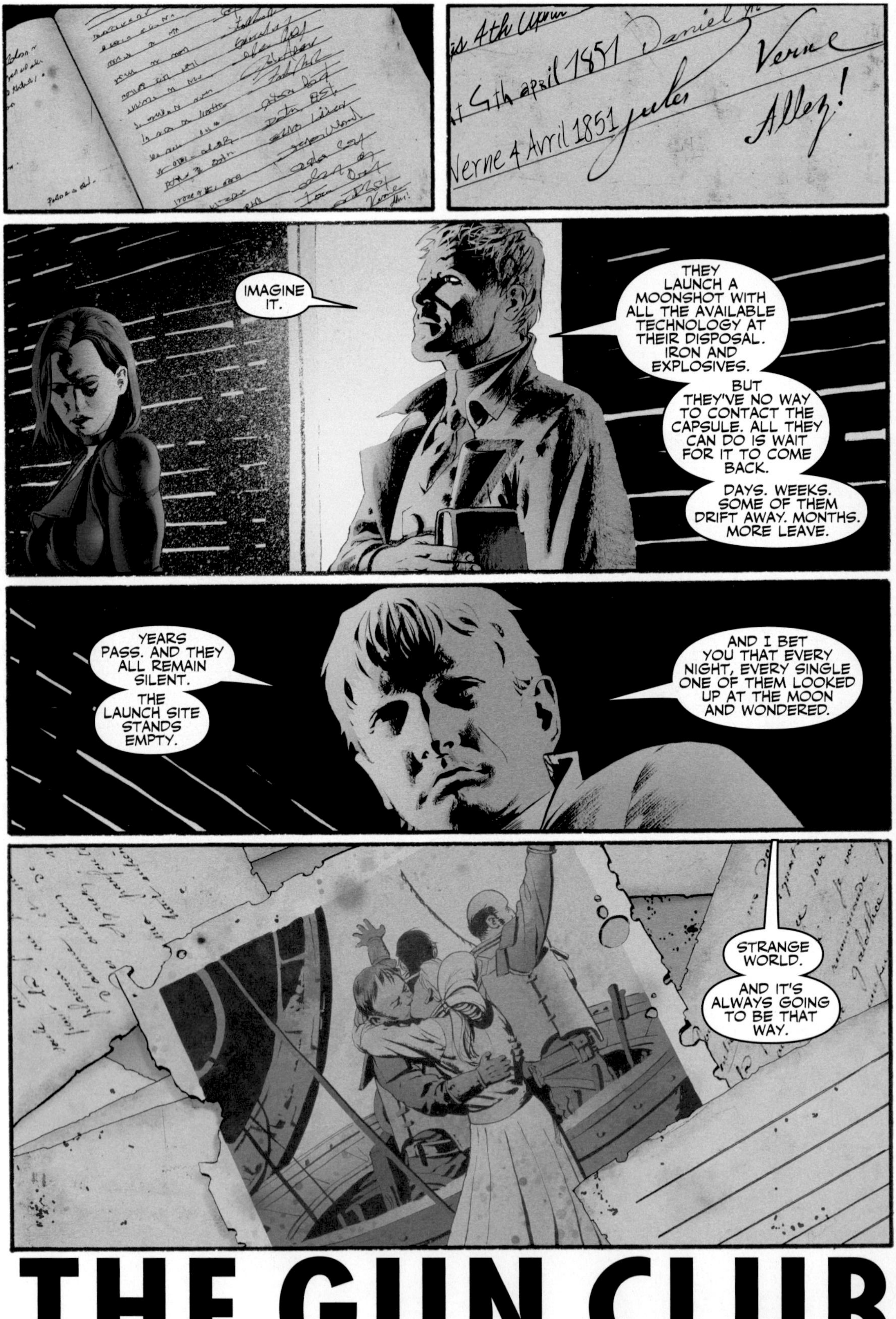
4th April 1851 Daniel
4th april 1851 Jules
Verne
Verne 4 Avril 1851
Allez!
IMAGINE IT.
THEY LAUNCH A MOONSHOT WITH ALL THE AVAILABLE TECHNOLOGY AT THEIR DISPOSAL. IRON AND EXPLOSIVES.
BUT THEY'VE NO WAY TO CONTACT THE CAPSULE. ALL THEY CAN DO IS WAIT FOR IT TO COME BACK.
DAYS. WEEKS. SOME OF THEM DRIFT AWAY. MONTHS. MORE LEAVE.
YEARS PASS. AND THEY ALL REMAIN SILENT.
THE LAUNCH SITE STANDS EMPTY.
AND I BET YOU THAT EVERY NIGHT, EVERY SINGLE ONE OF THEM LOOKED UP AT THE MOON AND WONDERED.
STRANGE WORLD.
AND IT'S ALWAYS GOING TO BE THAT WAY.

THE GUN CLUB

planetary
mystery
in space

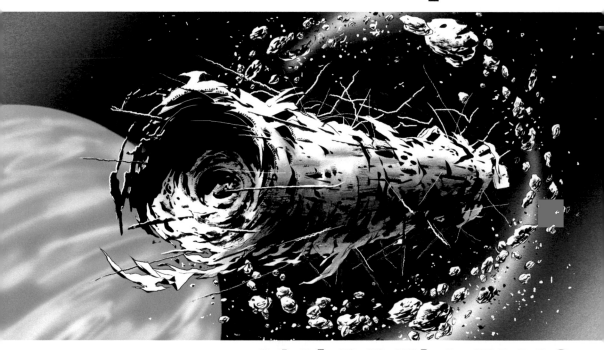

A COMIC BY WARREN ELLIS
JOHN CASSADAY

ADDITIONAL CONTRIBUTIONS BY
LAURA DEPUY MARTIN
and RICHARD STARKINGS

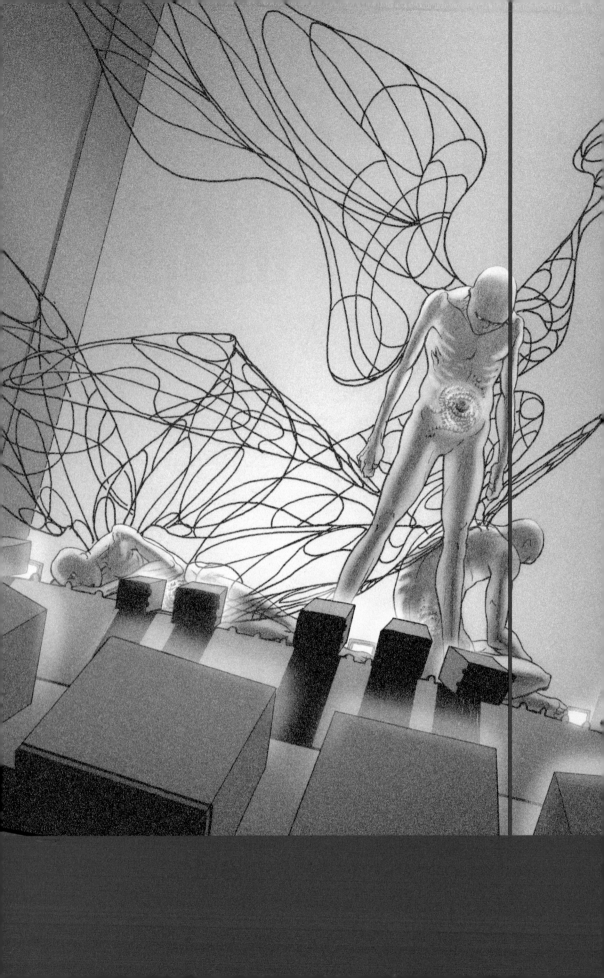

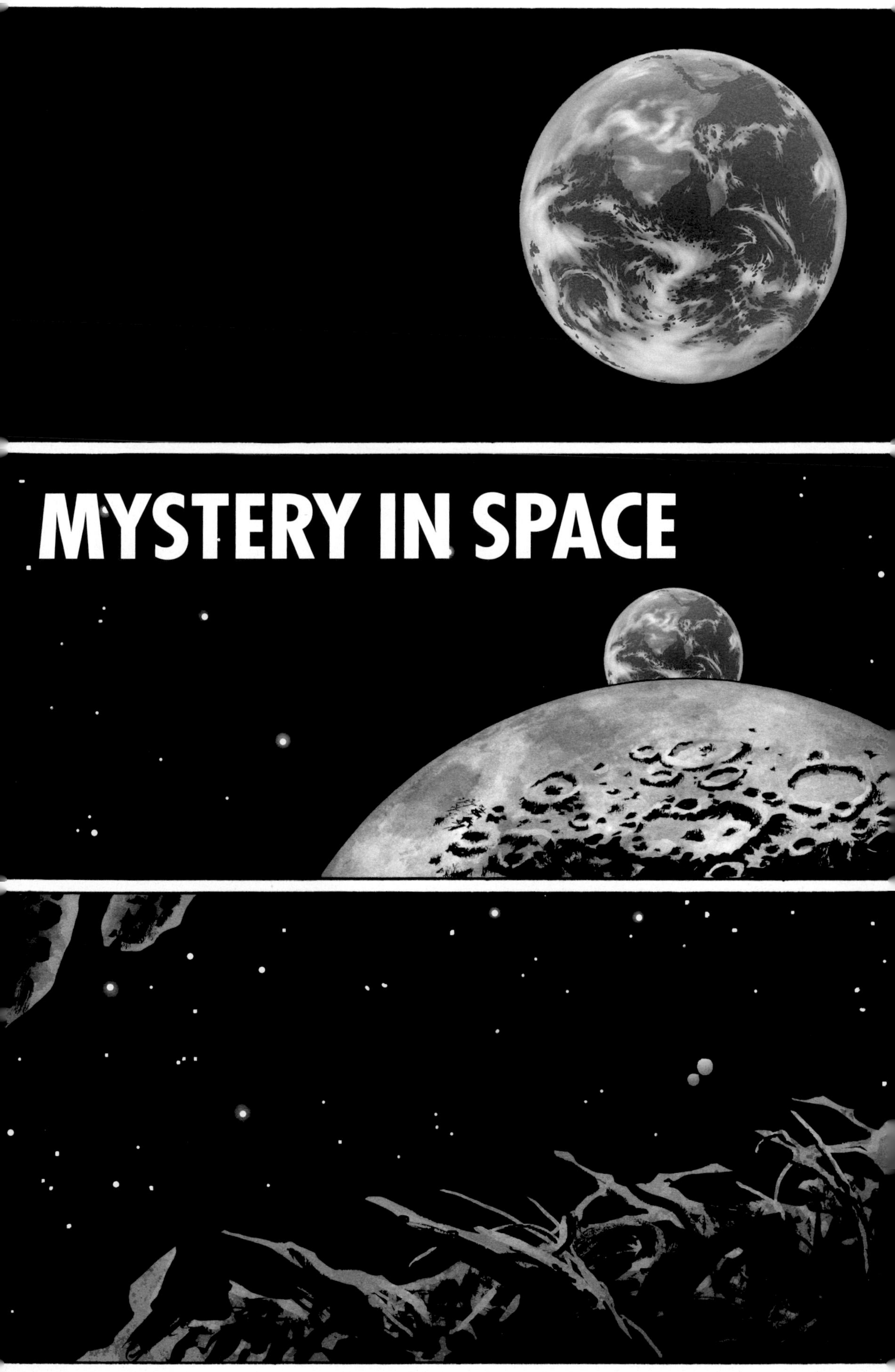
MYSTERY IN SPACE

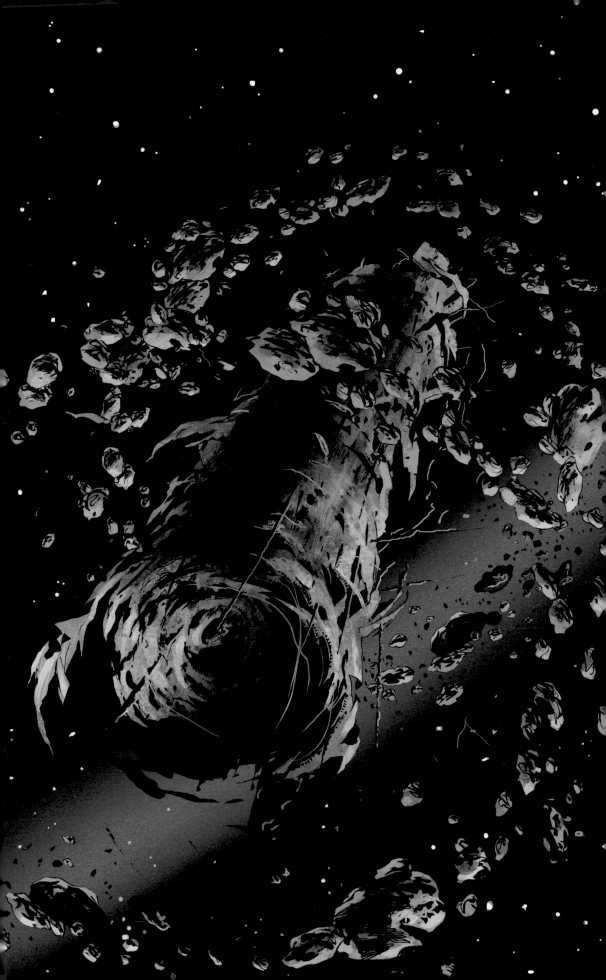

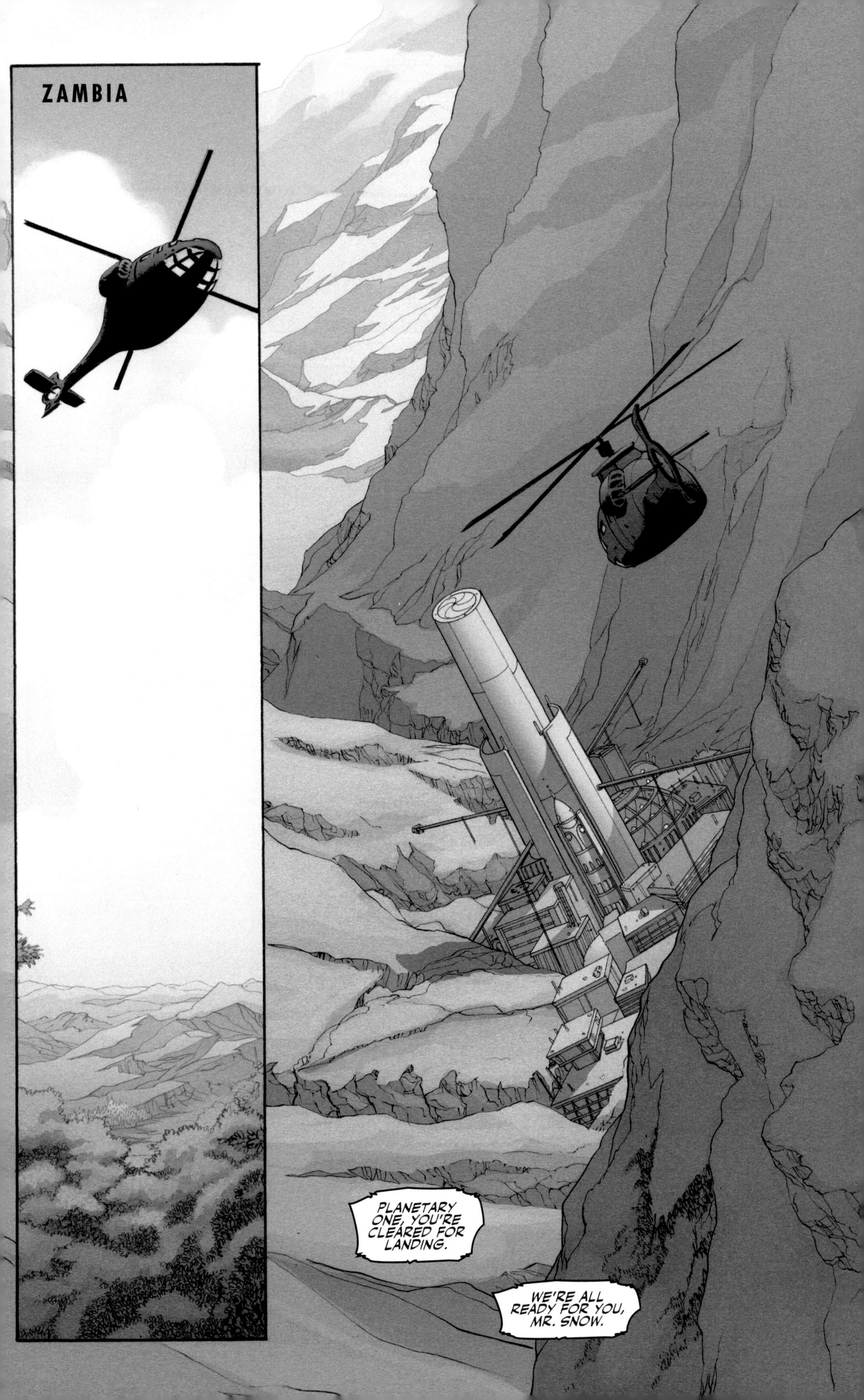
ZAMBIA
PLANETARY ONE, YOU'RE CLEARED FOR LANDING.
WE'RE ALL READY FOR YOU, MR. SNOW.

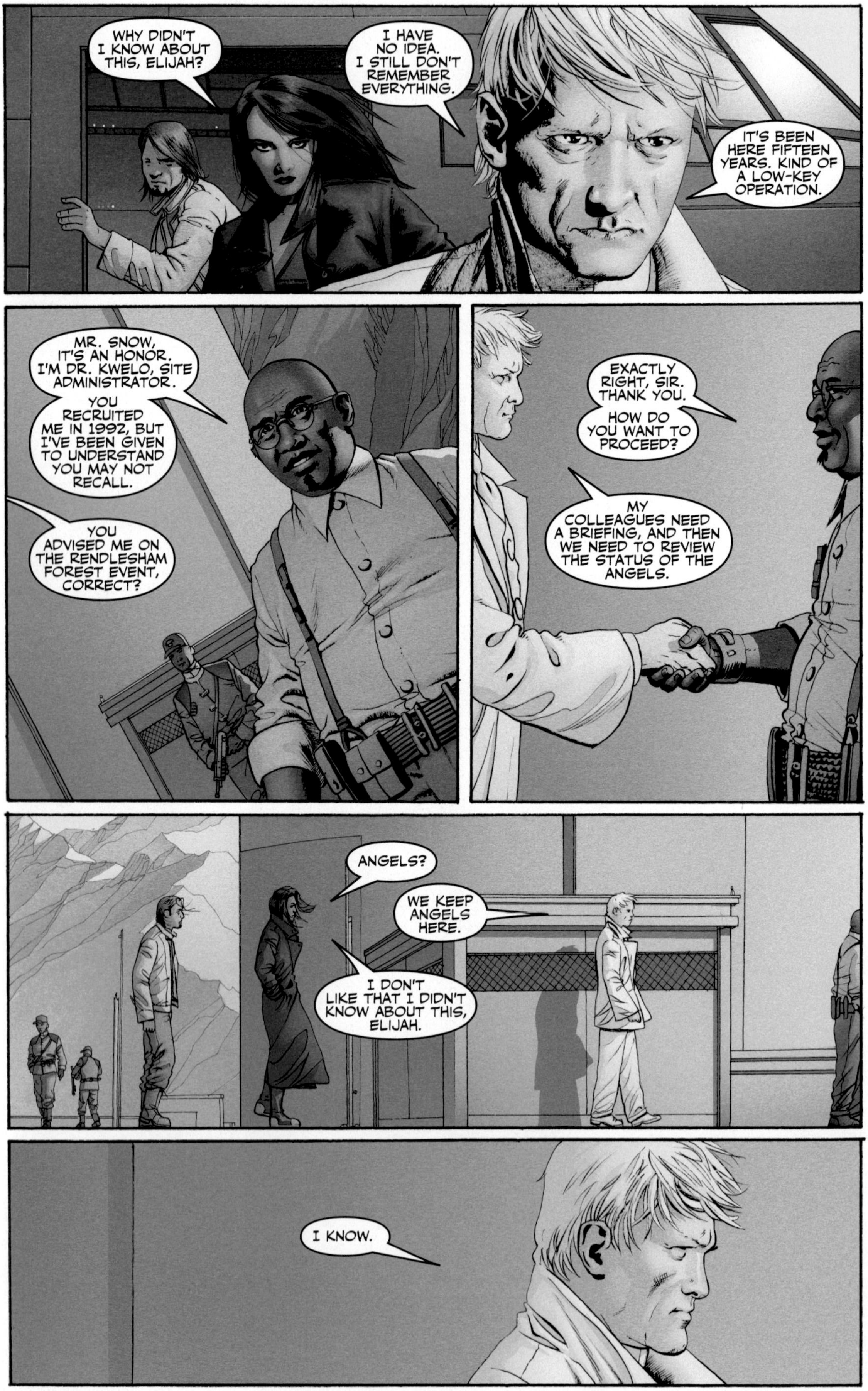
WHY DIDN'T I KNOW ABOUT THIS, ELIJAH?
I HAVE NO IDEA. I STILL DON'T REMEMBER EVERYTHING.
IT'S BEEN HERE FIFTEEN YEARS. KIND OF A LOW-KEY OPERATION.
MR. SNOW, IT'S AN HONOR. I'M DR. KWELO, SITE ADMINISTRATOR.
YOU RECRUITED ME IN 1992, BUT I'VE BEEN GIVEN TO UNDERSTAND YOU MAY NOT RECALL.
YOU ADVISED ME ON THE RENDLESHAM FOREST EVENT, CORRECT?
EXACTLY RIGHT, SIR. THANK YOU.
HOW DO YOU WANT TO PROCEED?
MY COLLEAGUES NEED A BRIEFING, AND THEN WE NEED TO REVIEW THE STATUS OF THE ANGELS.
ANGELS?
WE KEEP ANGELS HERE.
I DON'T LIKE THAT I DIDN'T KNOW ABOUT THIS, ELIJAH.
I KNOW.

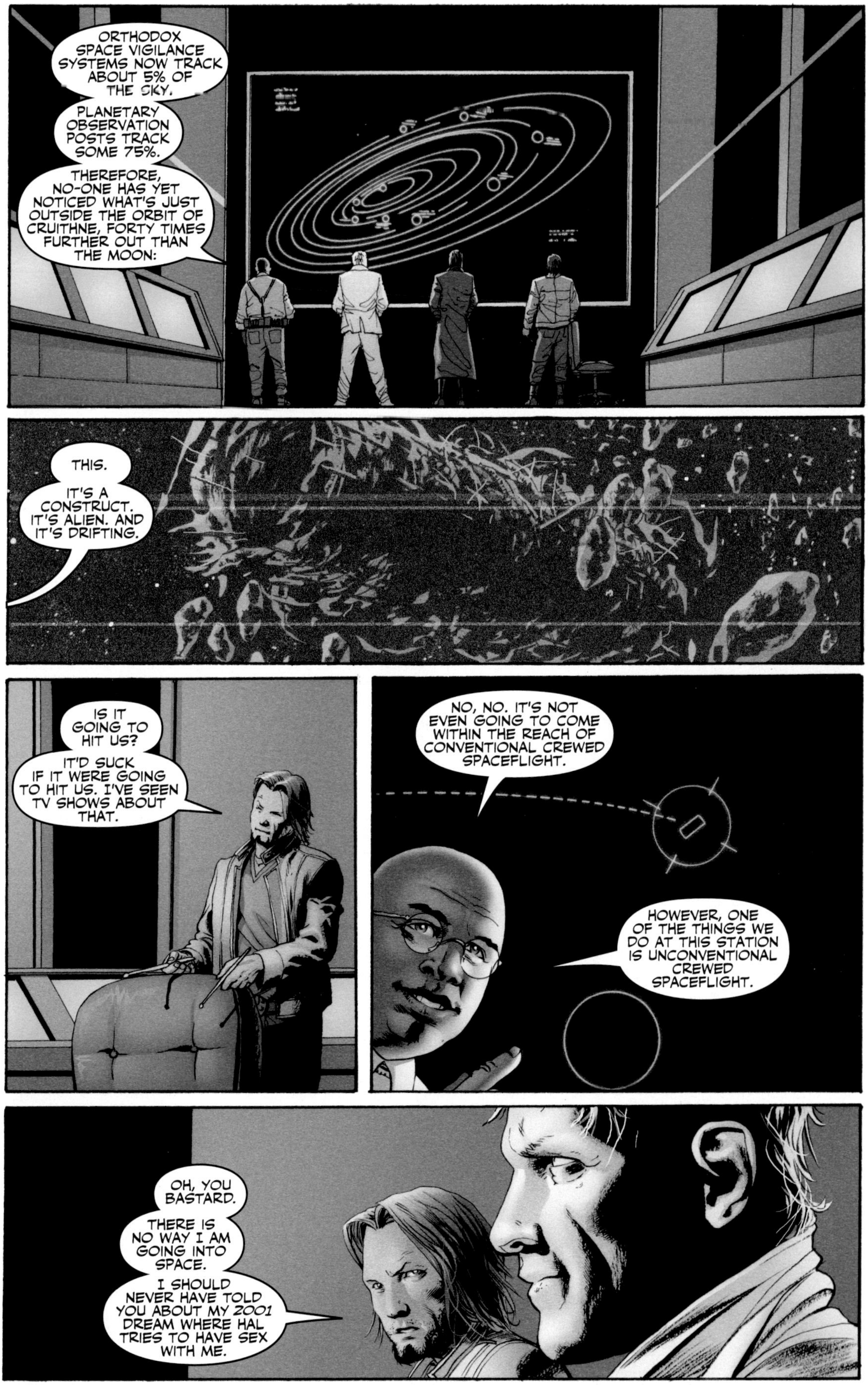
ORTHODOX SPACE VIGILANCE SYSTEMS NOW TRACK ABOUT 5% OF THE SKY.
PLANETARY OBSERVATION POSTS TRACK SOME 75%.
THEREFORE, NO-ONE HAS YET NOTICED WHAT'S JUST OUTSIDE THE ORBIT OF CRUITHNE, FORTY TIMES FURTHER OUT THAN THE MOON:
THIS.
IT'S A CONSTRUCT. IT'S ALIEN. AND IT'S DRIFTING.
IS IT GOING TO HIT US?
IT'D SUCK IF IT WERE GOING TO HIT US. I'VE SEEN TV SHOWS ABOUT THAT.
NO, NO. IT'S NOT EVEN GOING TO COME WITHIN THE REACH OF CONVENTIONAL CREWED SPACEFLIGHT.
HOWEVER, ONE OF THE THINGS WE DO AT THIS STATION IS UNCONVENTIONAL CREWED SPACEFLIGHT.
OH, YOU BASTARD.
THERE IS NO WAY I AM GOING INTO SPACE.
I SHOULD NEVER HAVE TOLD YOU ABOUT MY *2001* DREAM WHERE HAL TRIES TO HAVE SEX WITH ME.

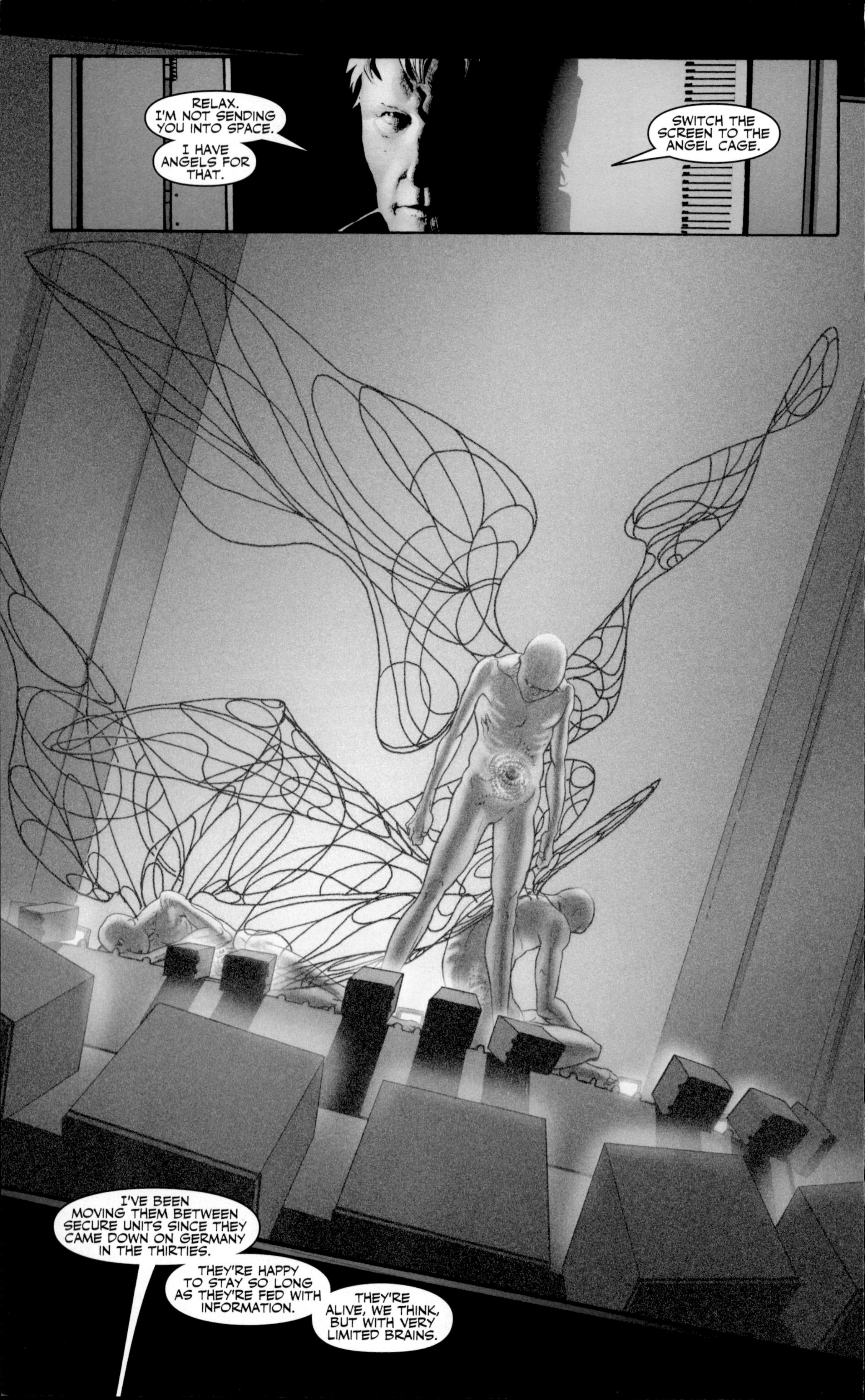
RELAX. I'M NOT SENDING YOU INTO SPACE.
I HAVE ANGELS FOR THAT.
SWITCH THE SCREEN TO THE ANGEL CAGE.
I'VE BEEN MOVING THEM BETWEEN SECURE UNITS SINCE THEY CAME DOWN ON GERMANY IN THE THIRTIES.
THEY'RE HAPPY TO STAY SO LONG AS THEY'RE FED WITH INFORMATION.
THEY'RE ALIVE, WE THINK, BUT WITH VERY LIMITED BRAINS.

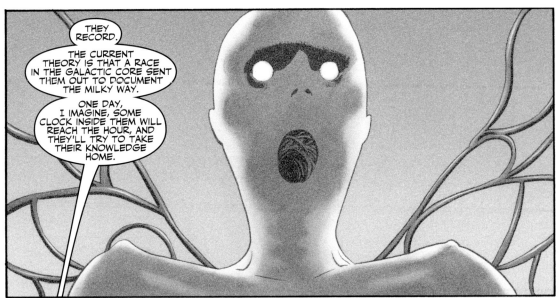

THEY RECORD.

THE CURRENT THEORY IS THAT A RACE IN THE GALACTIC CORE SENT THEM OUT TO DOCUMENT THE MILKY WAY.

ONE DAY, I IMAGINE, SOME CLOCK INSIDE THEM WILL REACH THE HOUR, AND THEY'LL TRY TO TAKE THEIR KNOWLEDGE HOME.

YOU'RE GOING TO SEND THEM UP?

THEY'RE PROGRAMMED TO PILOT SPACECRAFT. WE HAVE A VESSEL FROM 1951 THAT'LL DO THE JOB.

EXCUSE ME?

THERE WAS A FAILED ALIEN INVASION IN 1951. IT'S PROBABLY WHAT GALVANIZED THE COVERT SPACE PROGRAM THE FOUR WERE IN.

HOW MANY ALIEN SPACECRAFT DO WE HAVE, ELIJAH?

NINETEEN.

YOU'RE TELLING ME THAT WE'VE BEEN VISITED BY ALIENS NINETEEN TIMES, BUT SETI HAS NEVER HEARD A WHISPER OF AN ALIEN SIGNAL?

INTERESTING, ISN'T IT?

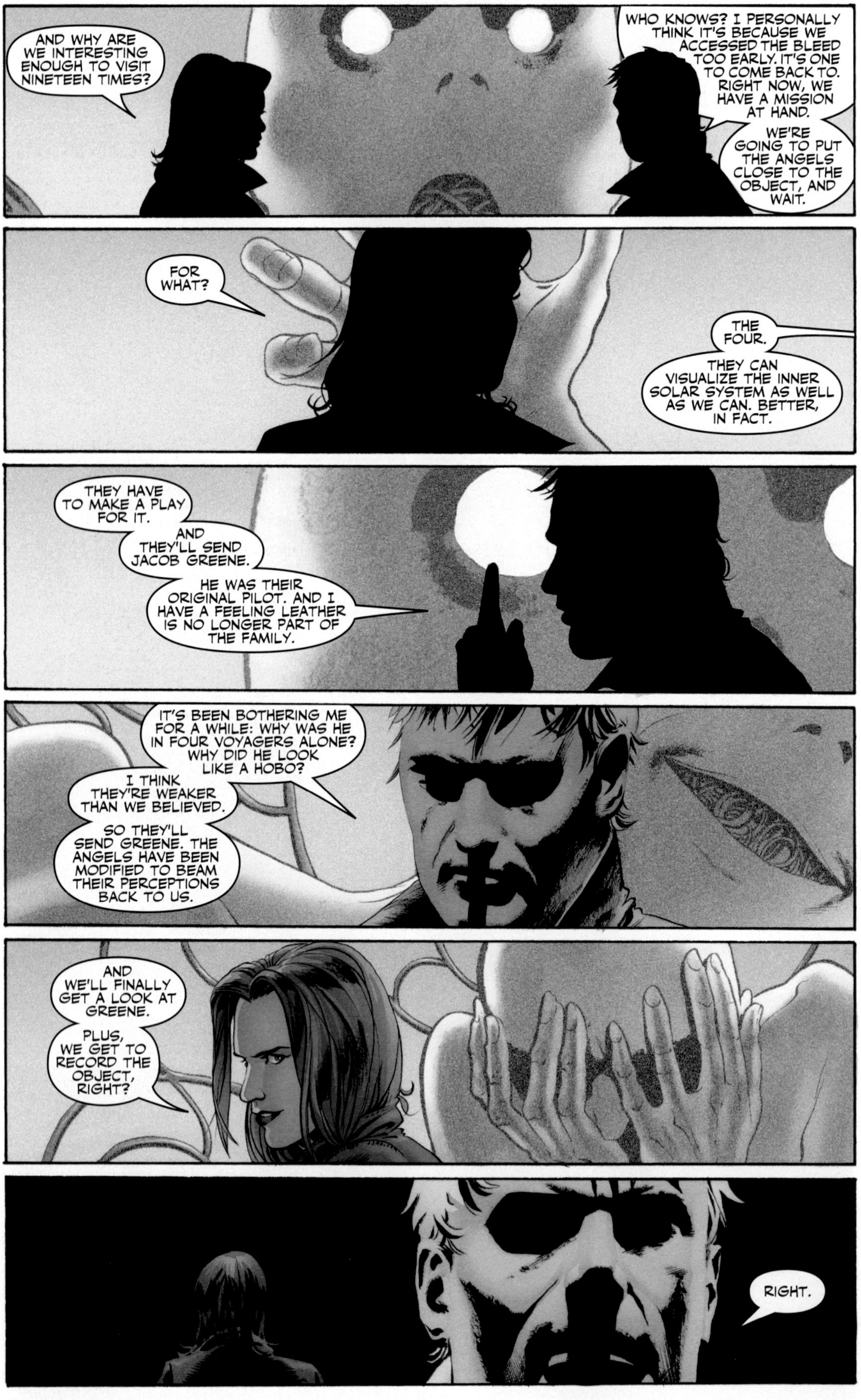
AND WHY ARE WE INTERESTING ENOUGH TO VISIT NINETEEN TIMES?
WHO KNOWS? I PERSONALLY THINK IT'S BECAUSE WE ACCESSED THE BLEED TOO EARLY. IT'S ONE TO COME BACK TO. RIGHT NOW, WE HAVE A MISSION AT HAND.
WE'RE GOING TO PUT THE ANGELS CLOSE TO THE OBJECT, AND WAIT.
FOR WHAT?
THE FOUR.
THEY CAN VISUALIZE THE INNER SOLAR SYSTEM AS WELL AS WE CAN. BETTER, IN FACT.
THEY HAVE TO MAKE A PLAY FOR IT.
AND THEY'LL SEND JACOB GREENE.
HE WAS THEIR ORIGINAL PILOT. AND I HAVE A FEELING LEATHER IS NO LONGER PART OF THE FAMILY.
IT'S BEEN BOTHERING ME FOR A WHILE: WHY WAS HE IN FOUR VOYAGERS ALONE? WHY DID HE LOOK LIKE A HOBO?
I THINK THEY'RE WEAKER THAN WE BELIEVED.
SO THEY'LL SEND GREENE. THE ANGELS HAVE BEEN MODIFIED TO BEAM THEIR PERCEPTIONS BACK TO US.
AND WE'LL FINALLY GET A LOOK AT GREENE.
PLUS, WE GET TO RECORD THE OBJECT, RIGHT?
RIGHT.

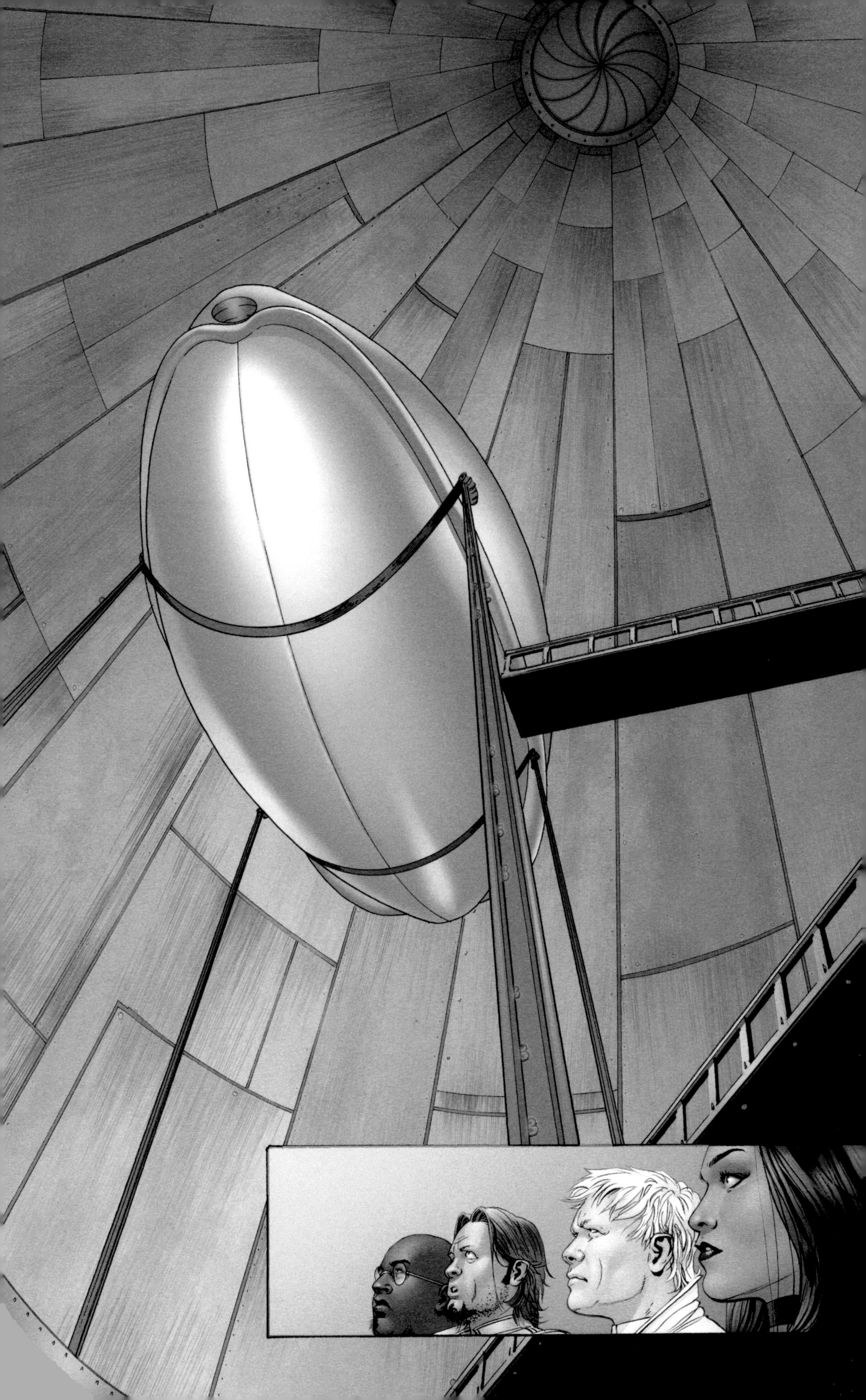

HOW DID YOU CONVINCE THEM TO GO?

ALL WE HAD TO DO WAS SHOW THEM OUR TELEMETRY ON THE OBJECT. THEY'D SEEN NOTHING LIKE IT.

THEY ASKED TO GO AND RECORD IT.

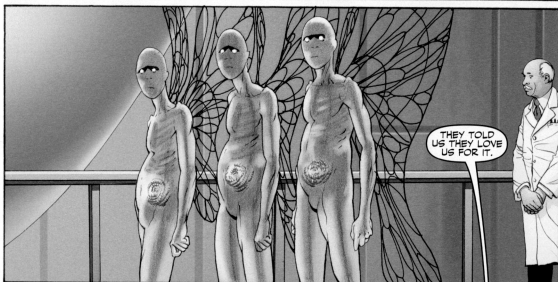

THEY TOLD US THEY LOVE US FOR IT.

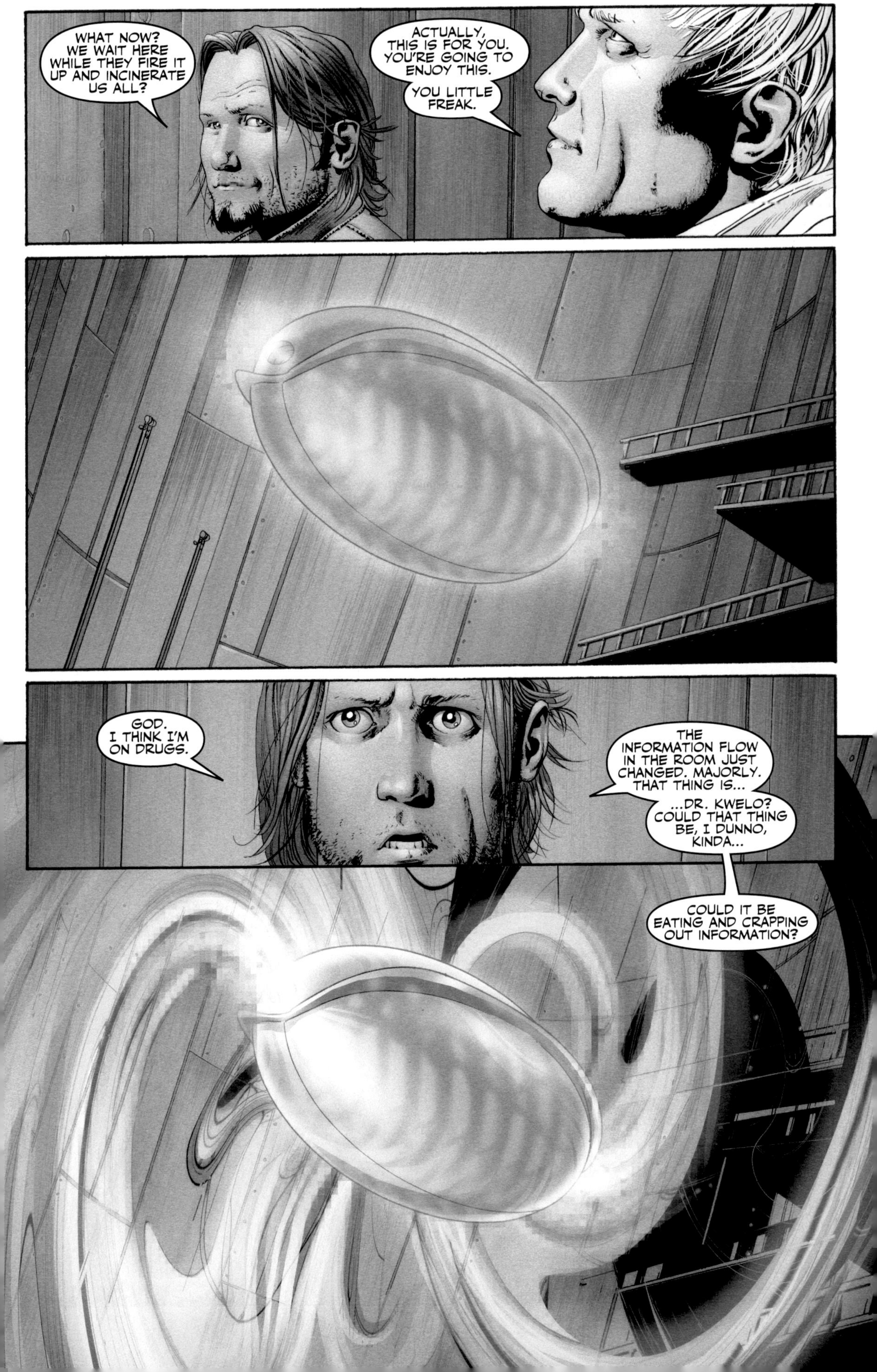
WHAT NOW? WE WAIT HERE WHILE THEY FIRE IT UP AND INCINERATE US ALL?
ACTUALLY, THIS IS FOR YOU. YOU'RE GOING TO ENJOY THIS.
YOU LITTLE FREAK.
GOD. I THINK I'M ON DRUGS.
THE INFORMATION FLOW IN THE ROOM JUST CHANGED. MAJORLY. THAT THING IS...
...DR. KWELO? COULD THAT THING BE, I DUNNO, KINDA...
COULD IT BE EATING AND CRAPPING OUT INFORMATION?

THAT'S VERY GOOD. OUR CURRENT BELIEF IS THAT THE CRAFT'S ENGINE IS AN INFORMATIONAL DRIVE.

THERE'S A THEORY THAT THE UNIVERSE'S UNDERPINNING IS INFORMATION, NOT MATTER AND ENERGY.

MATTER AND ENERGY MOVE IN VOLUME, BUT THE INFORMATIONAL CAPACITY OF THE UNIVERSE HAS BEEN FOUND TO RELY ONLY ON SURFACE AREA.

THAT MEANS THAT THE UNIVERSE IS TWO-DIMENSIONAL. MATTER, ENERGY, TIME, YOU, ME AND THE FLOOR ARE HOLOGRAMS.

EVERYTHING IN VOLUME IS AN EXPRESSION OF A TWO-DIMENSIONAL PLANE OF INFORMATION.

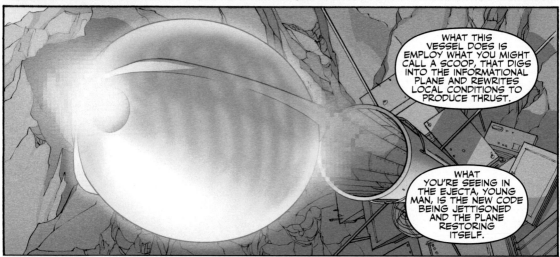

WHAT THIS VESSEL DOES IS EMPLOY WHAT YOU MIGHT CALL A SCOOP, THAT DIGS INTO THE INFORMATIONAL PLANE AND REWRITES LOCAL CONDITIONS TO PRODUCE THRUST.

WHAT YOU'RE SEEING IN THE EJECTA, YOUNG MAN, IS THE NEW CODE BEING JETTISONED AND THE PLANE RESTORING ITSELF.

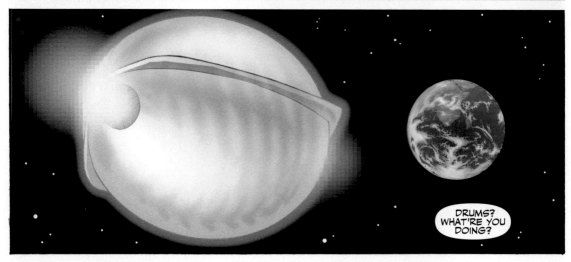

DRUMS? WHAT'RE YOU DOING?

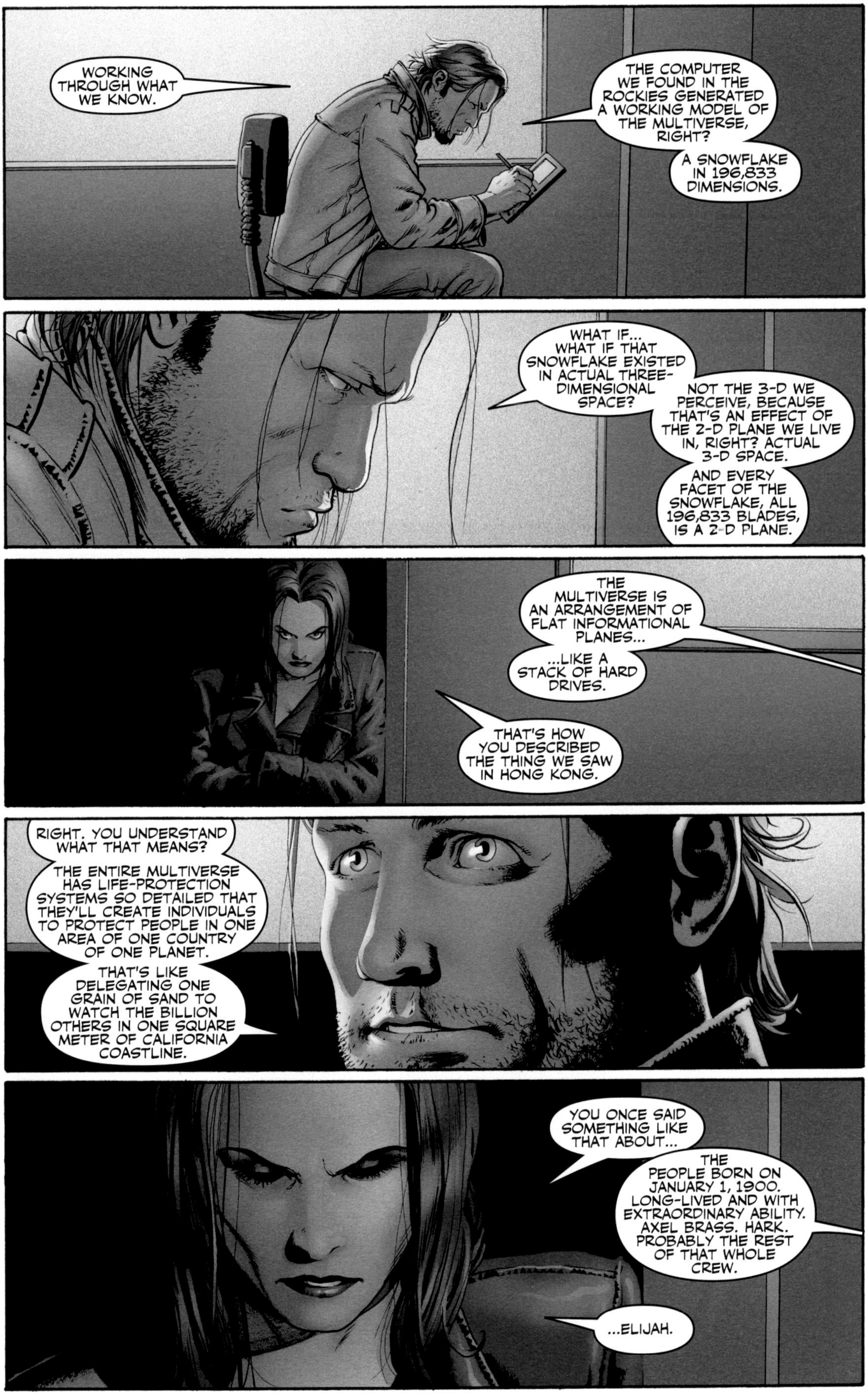
WORKING THROUGH WHAT WE KNOW.
THE COMPUTER WE FOUND IN THE ROCKIES GENERATED A WORKING MODEL OF THE MULTIVERSE, RIGHT?
A SNOWFLAKE IN 196,833 DIMENSIONS.
WHAT IF... WHAT IF THAT SNOWFLAKE EXISTED IN ACTUAL THREE-DIMENSIONAL SPACE?
NOT THE 3-D WE PERCEIVE, BECAUSE THAT'S AN EFFECT OF THE 2-D PLANE WE LIVE IN, RIGHT? ACTUAL 3-D SPACE.
AND EVERY FACET OF THE SNOWFLAKE, ALL 196,833 BLADES, IS A 2-D PLANE.
THE MULTIVERSE IS AN ARRANGEMENT OF FLAT INFORMATIONAL PLANES...
...LIKE A STACK OF HARD DRIVES.
THAT'S HOW YOU DESCRIBED THE THING WE SAW IN HONG KONG.
RIGHT. YOU UNDERSTAND WHAT THAT MEANS?
THE ENTIRE MULTIVERSE HAS LIFE-PROTECTION SYSTEMS SO DETAILED THAT THEY'LL CREATE INDIVIDUALS TO PROTECT PEOPLE IN ONE AREA OF ONE COUNTRY OF ONE PLANET.
THAT'S LIKE DELEGATING ONE GRAIN OF SAND TO WATCH THE BILLION OTHERS IN ONE SQUARE METER OF CALIFORNIA COASTLINE.
YOU ONCE SAID SOMETHING LIKE THAT ABOUT...
THE PEOPLE BORN ON JANUARY 1, 1900. LONG-LIVED AND WITH EXTRAORDINARY ABILITY. AXEL BRASS. HARK. PROBABLY THE REST OF THAT WHOLE CREW.
...ELIJAH.

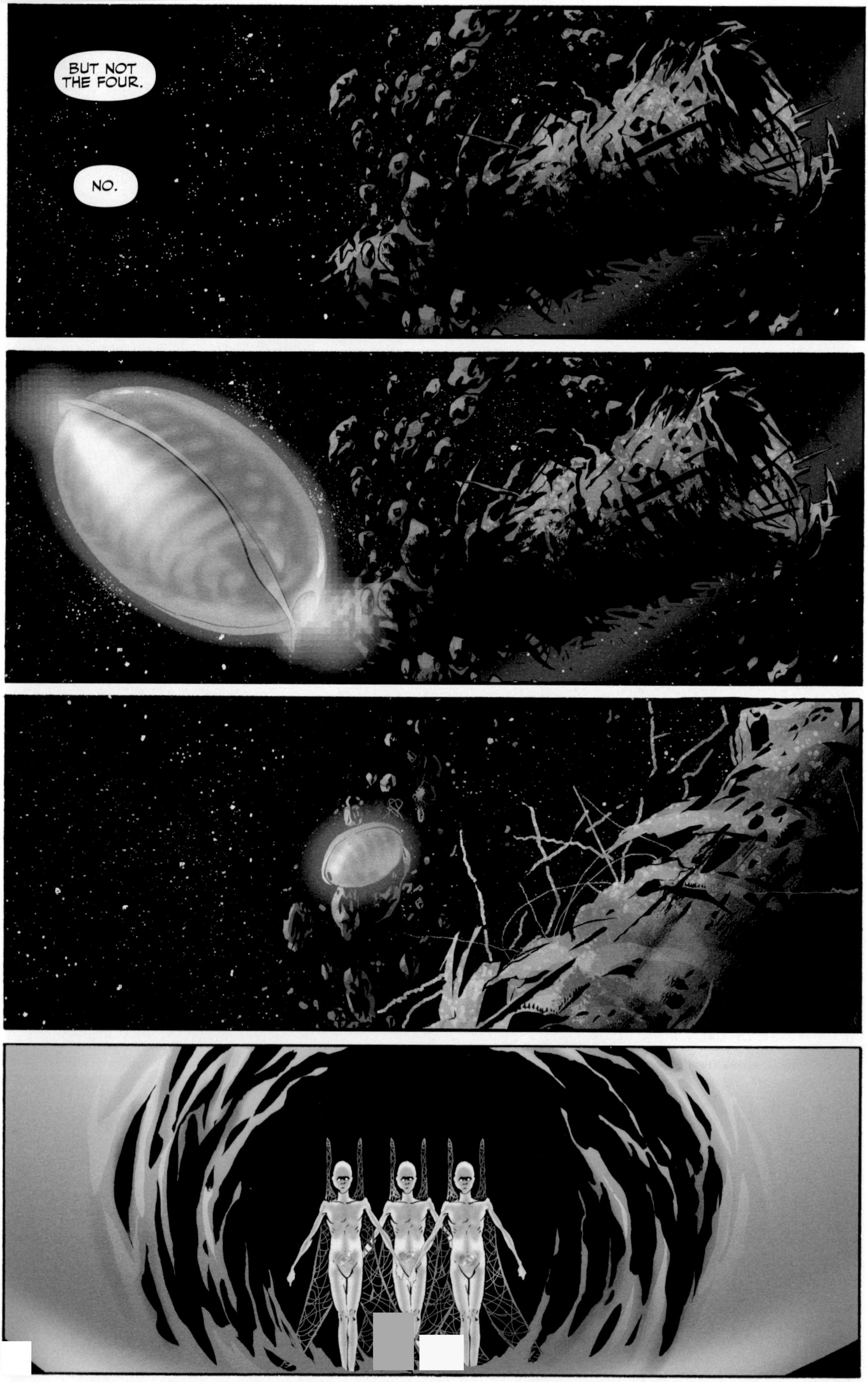
BUT NOT THE FOUR.
NO.

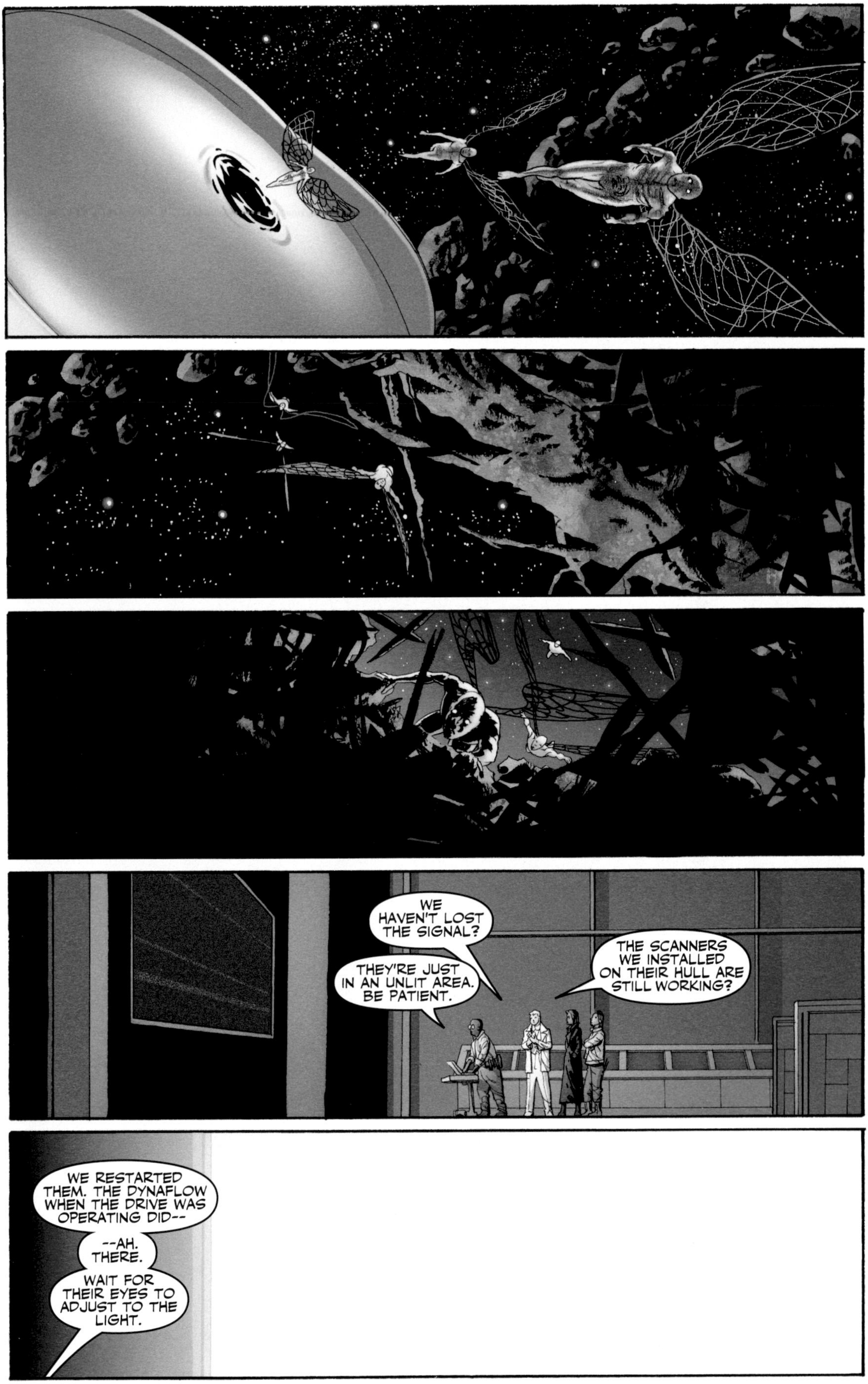
WE HAVEN'T LOST THE SIGNAL?
THEY'RE JUST IN AN UNLIT AREA. BE PATIENT.
THE SCANNERS WE INSTALLED ON THEIR HULL ARE STILL WORKING?
WE RESTARTED THEM. THE DYNAFLOW WHEN THE DRIVE WAS OPERATING DID--
--AH. THERE.
WAIT FOR THEIR EYES TO ADJUST TO THE LIGHT.

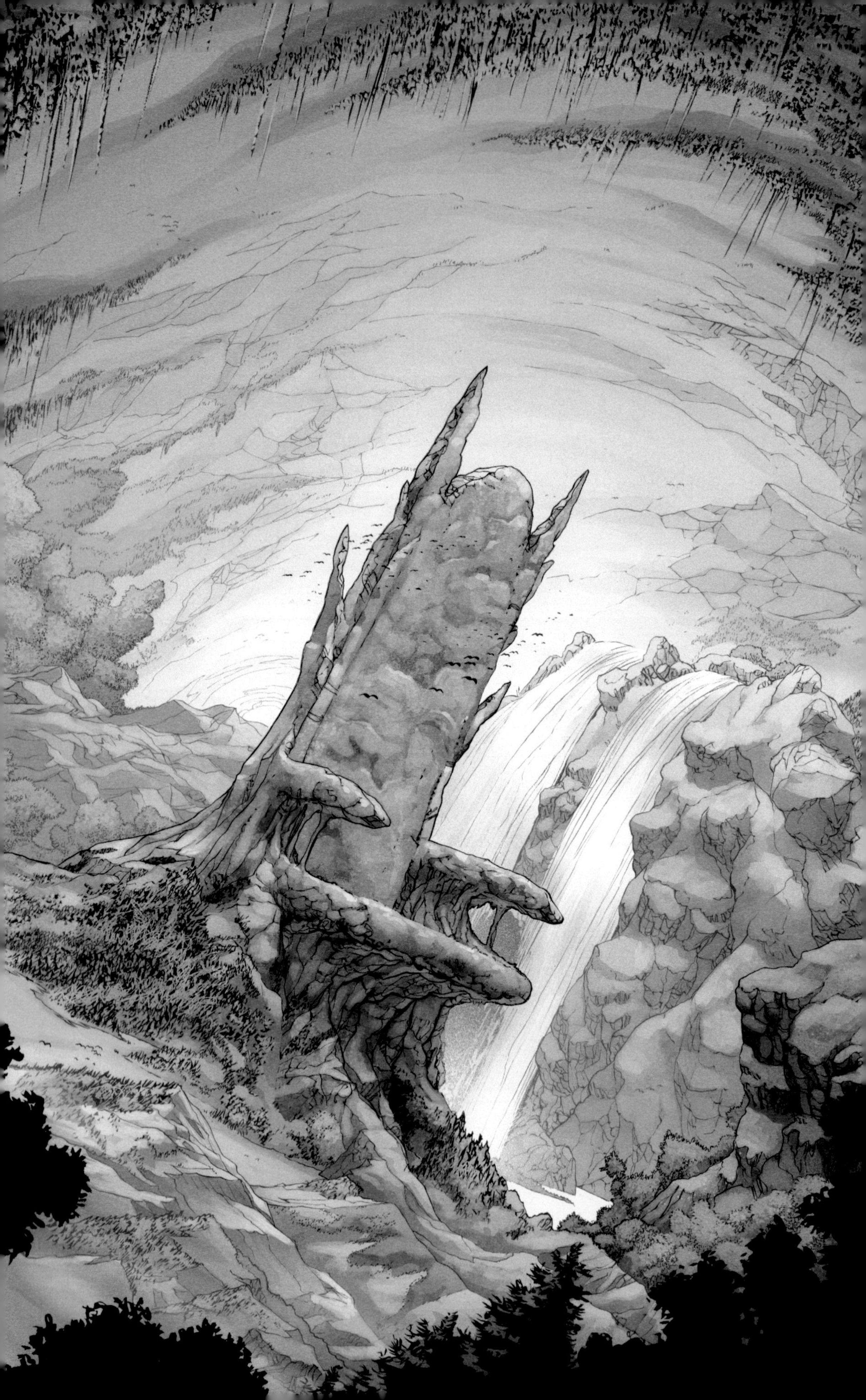

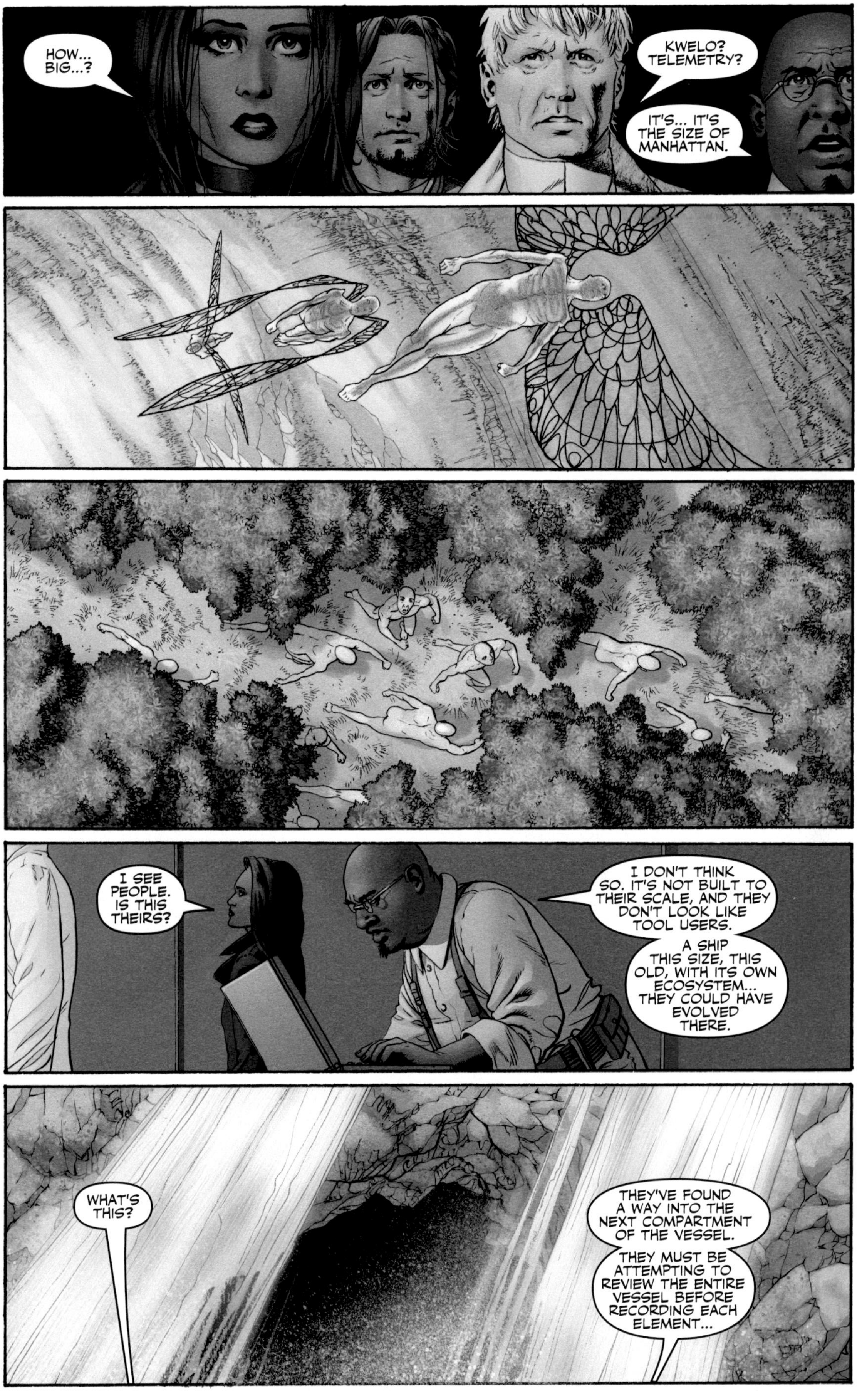
HOW... BIG...?
KWELO? TELEMETRY?
IT'S... IT'S THE SIZE OF MANHATTAN.
I SEE PEOPLE. IS THIS THEIRS?
I DON'T THINK SO. IT'S NOT BUILT TO THEIR SCALE, AND THEY DON'T LOOK LIKE TOOL USERS.
A SHIP THIS SIZE, THIS OLD, WITH ITS OWN ECOSYSTEM... THEY COULD HAVE EVOLVED THERE.
WHAT'S THIS?
THEY'VE FOUND A WAY INTO THE NEXT COMPARTMENT OF THE VESSEL.
THEY MUST BE ATTEMPTING TO REVIEW THE ENTIRE VESSEL BEFORE RECORDING EACH ELEMENT...

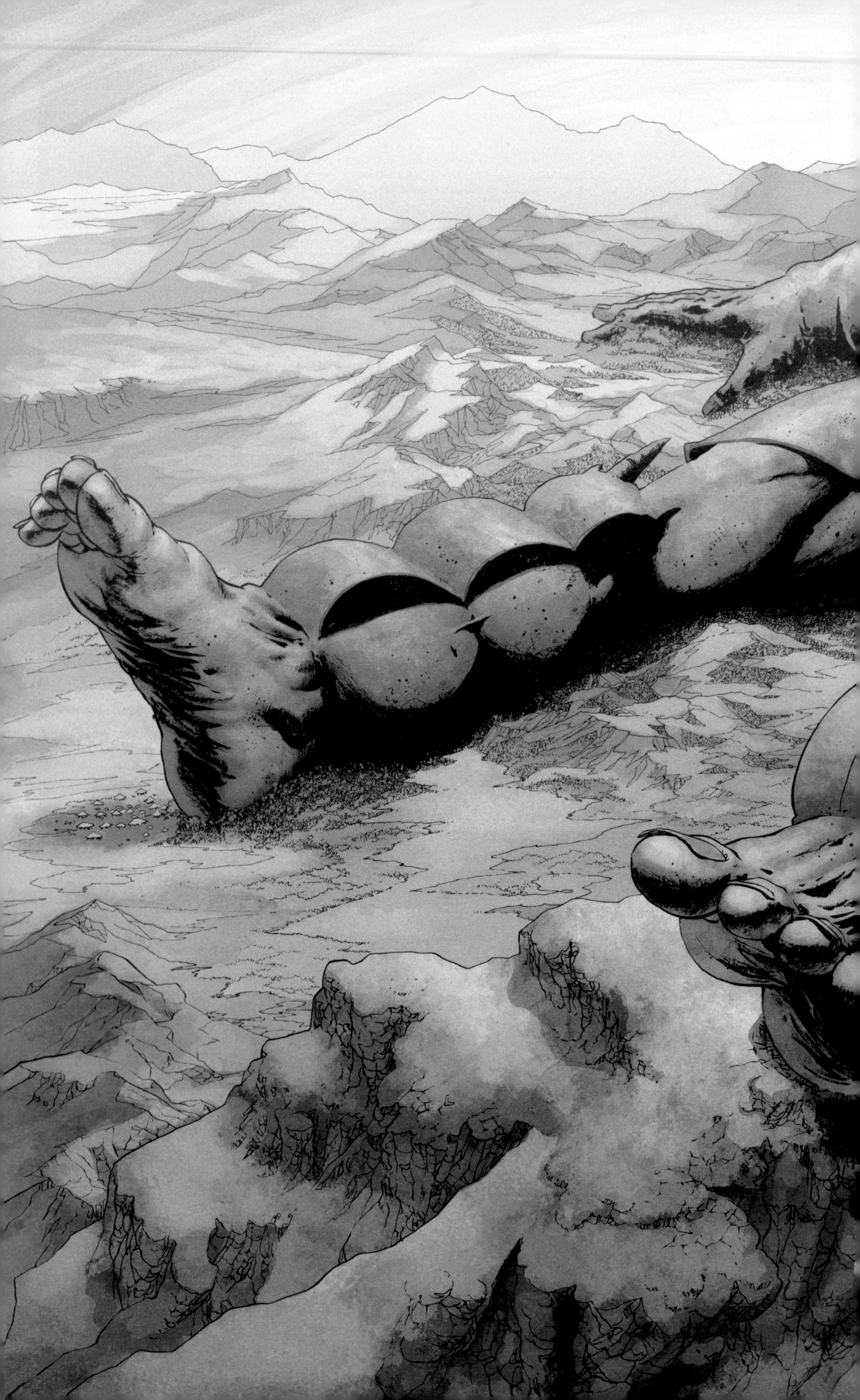

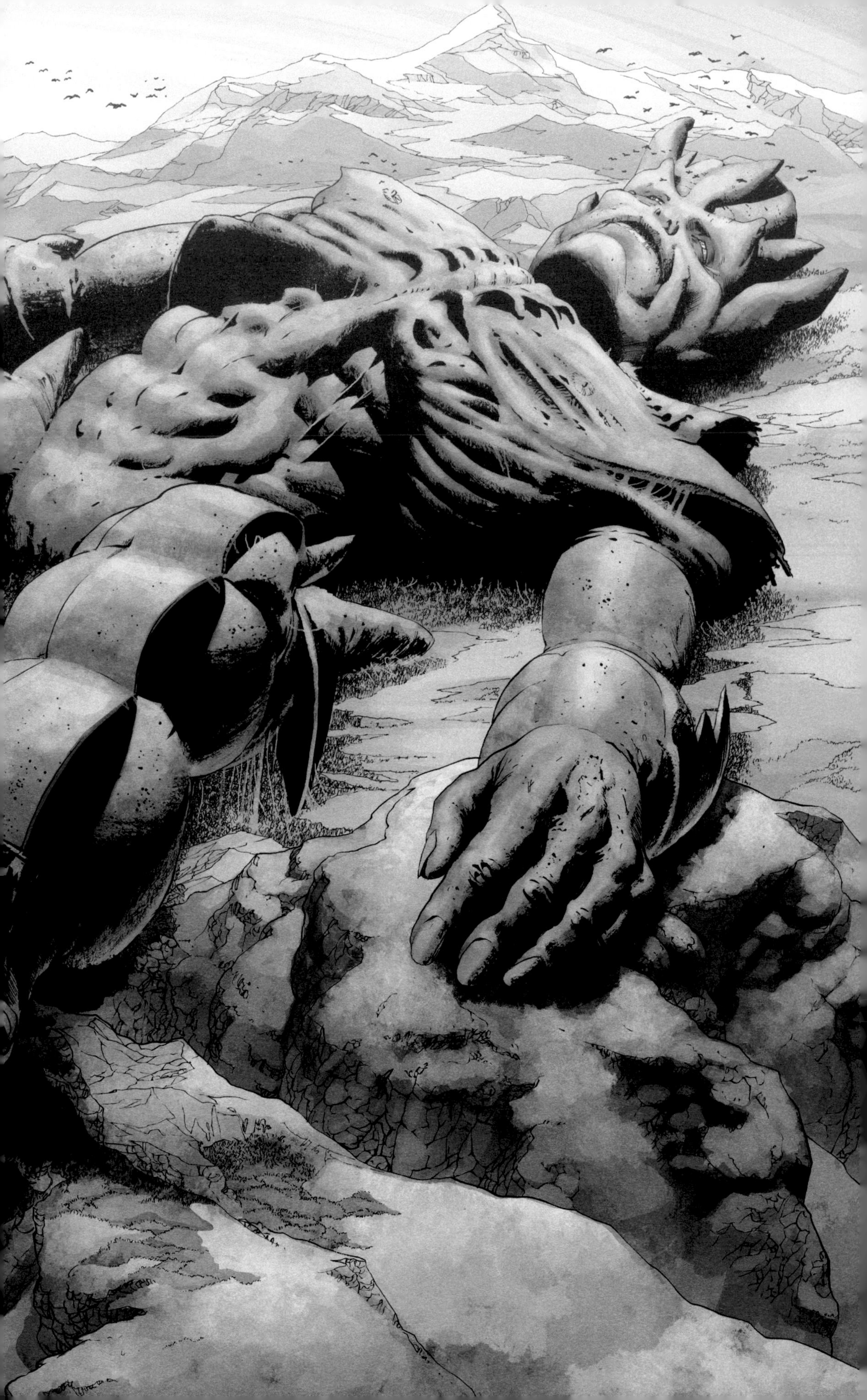

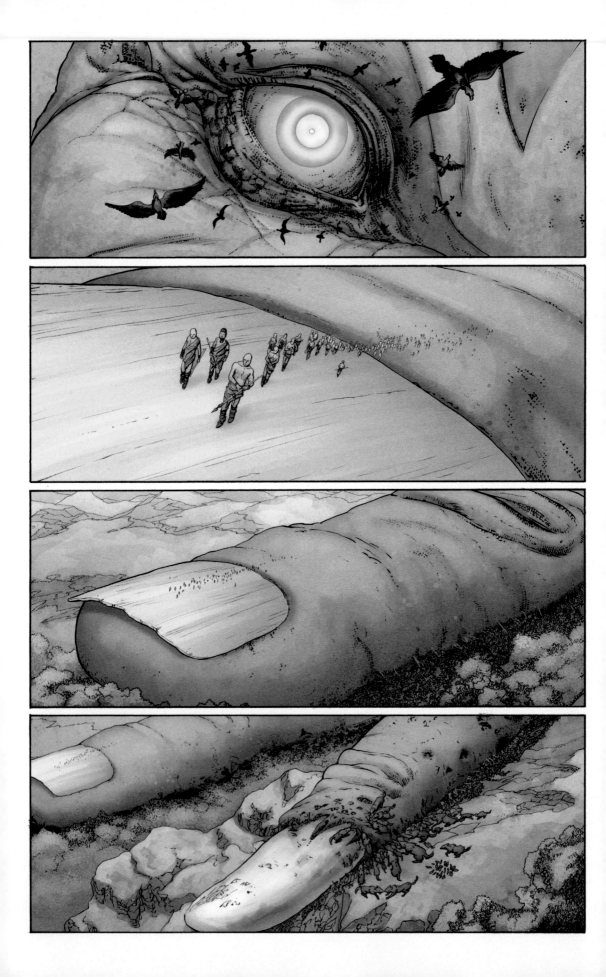

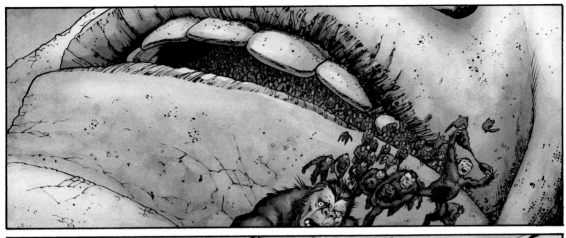

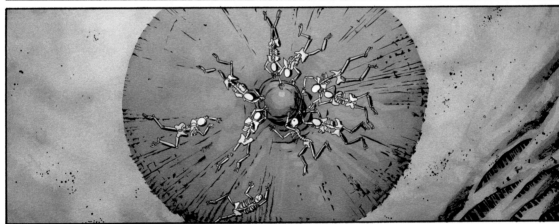

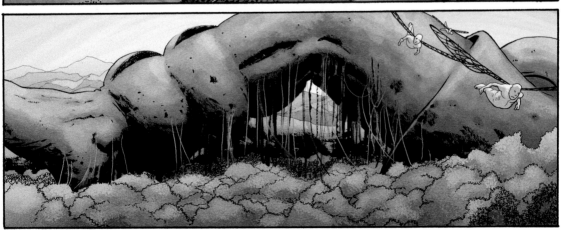

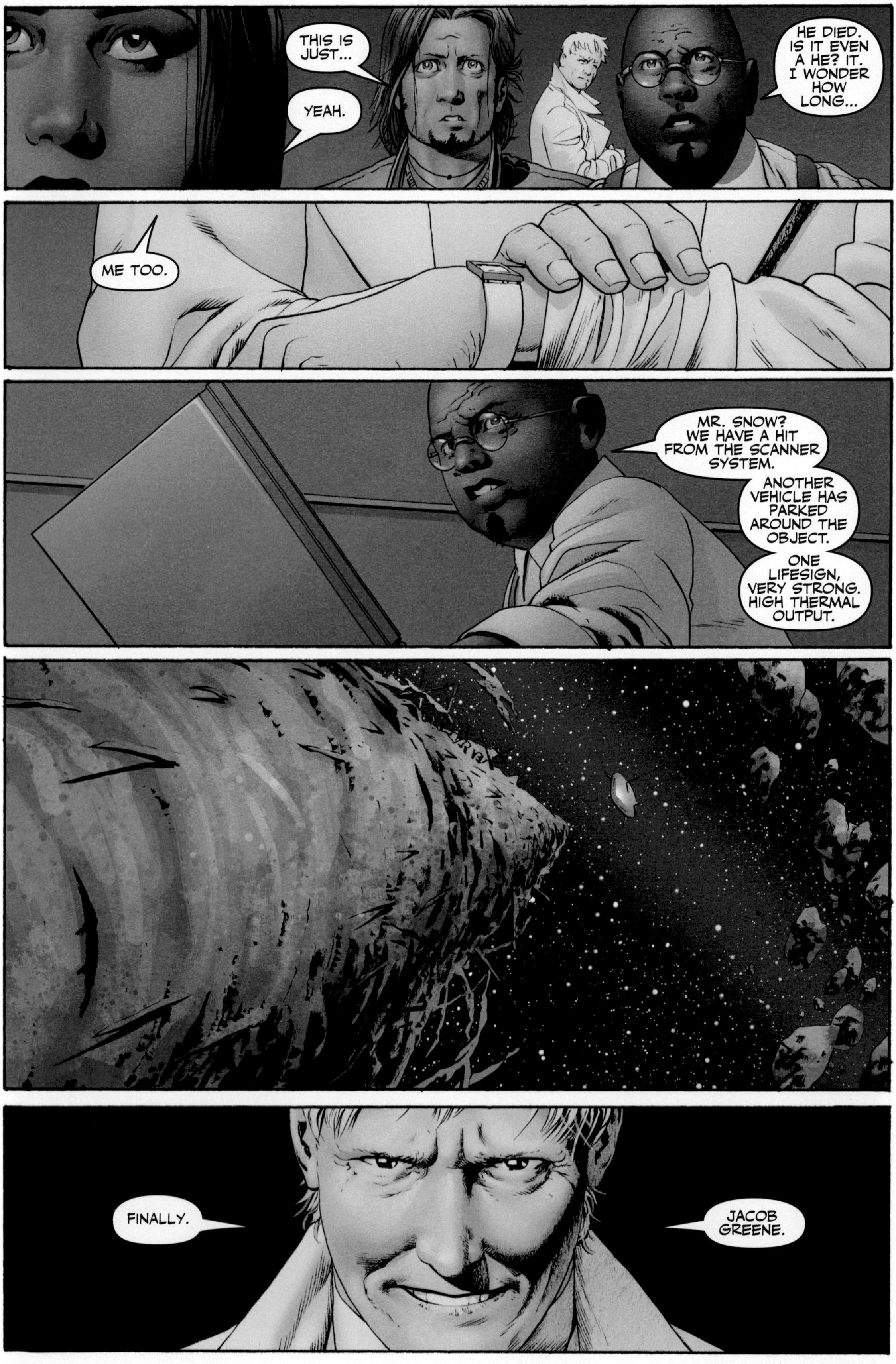
THIS IS JUST...
YEAH.
HE DIED. IS IT EVEN A HE? IT. I WONDER HOW LONG...
ME TOO.
MR. SNOW? WE HAVE A HIT FROM THE SCANNER SYSTEM.
ANOTHER VEHICLE HAS PARKED AROUND THE OBJECT.
ONE LIFESIGN, VERY STRONG. HIGH THERMAL OUTPUT.
FINALLY.
JACOB GREENE.

A WARREN ELLIS/JOHN CASSADAY PRODUCTION

PLANETARY

WILDSTORM UNIVERSE

ADDITIONAL CONTRIBUTIONS BY

LAURA MARTIN and RICHARD STARKINGS

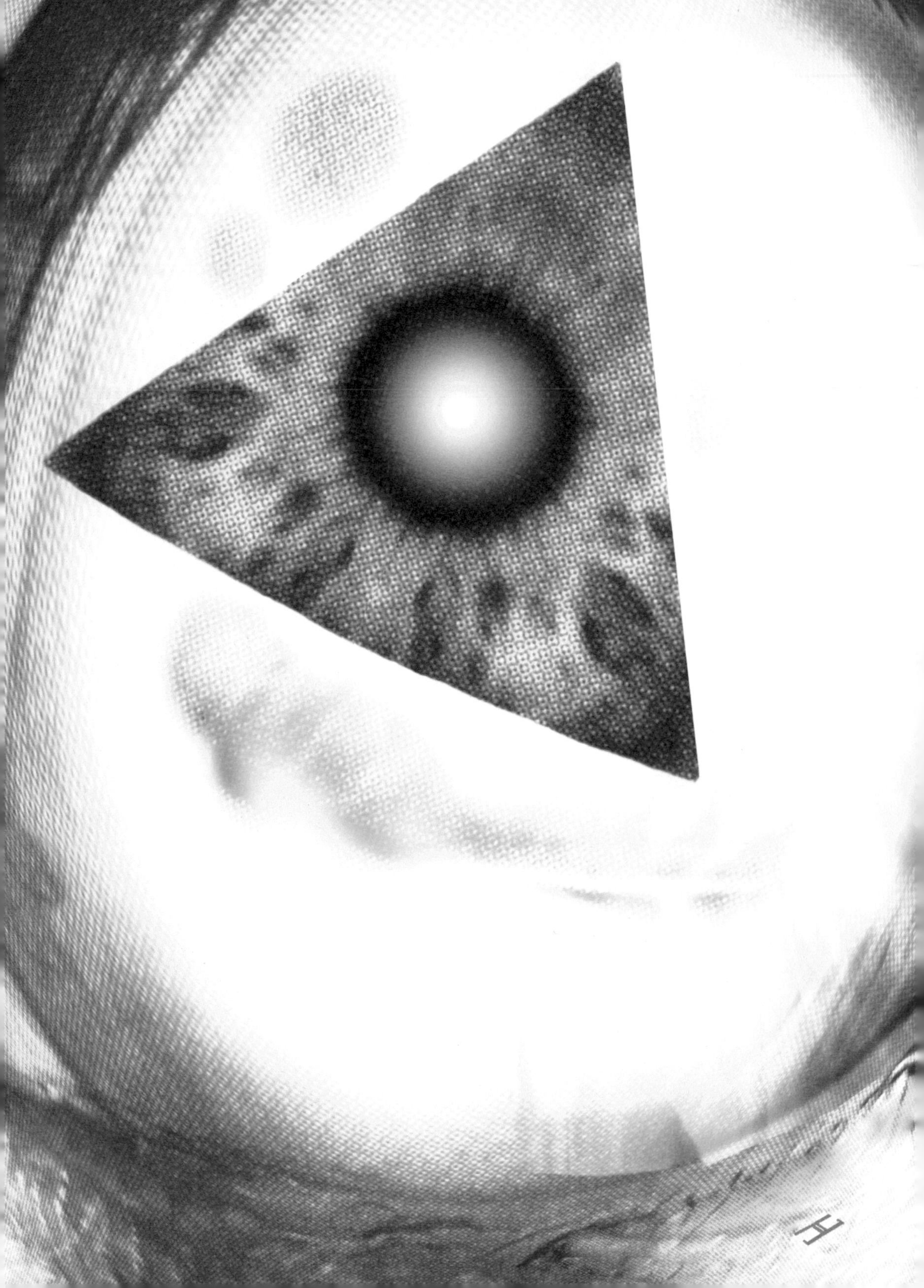

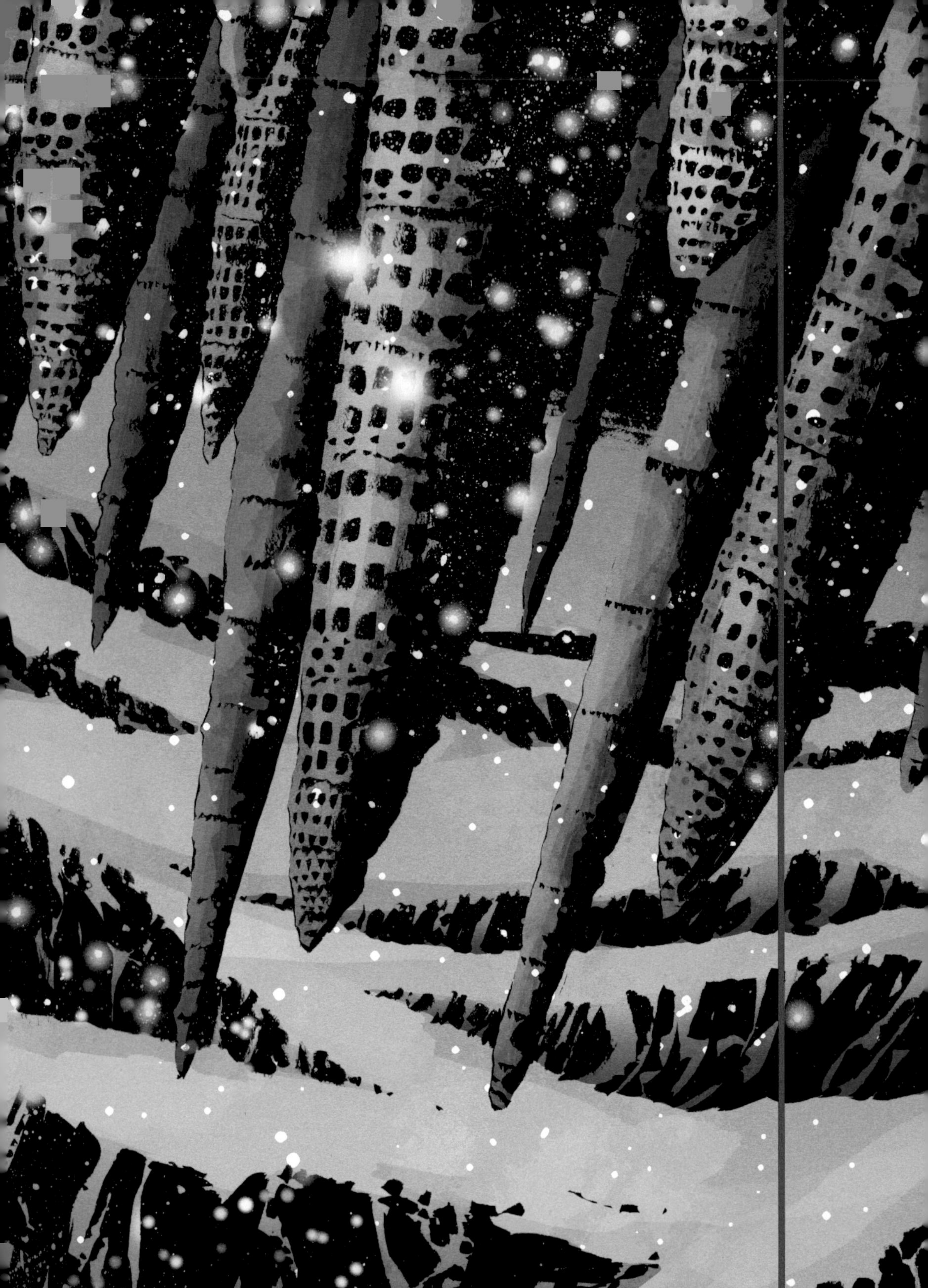

RENDEZVOUS

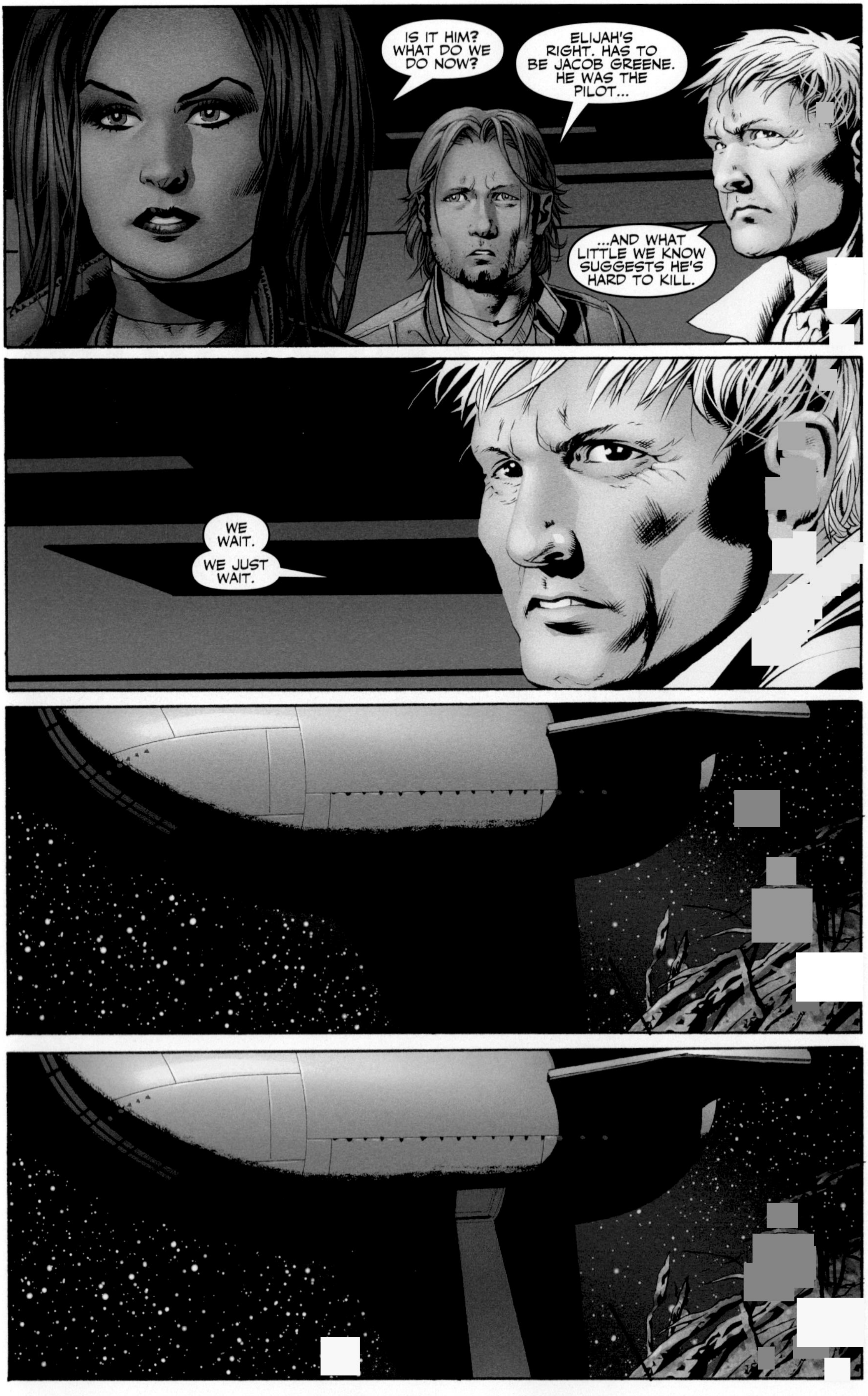
IS IT HIM? WHAT DO WE DO NOW?
ELIJAH'S RIGHT. HAS TO BE JACOB GREENE. HE WAS THE PILOT...
...AND WHAT LITTLE WE KNOW SUGGESTS HE'S HARD TO KILL.
WE WAIT.
WE JUST WAIT.

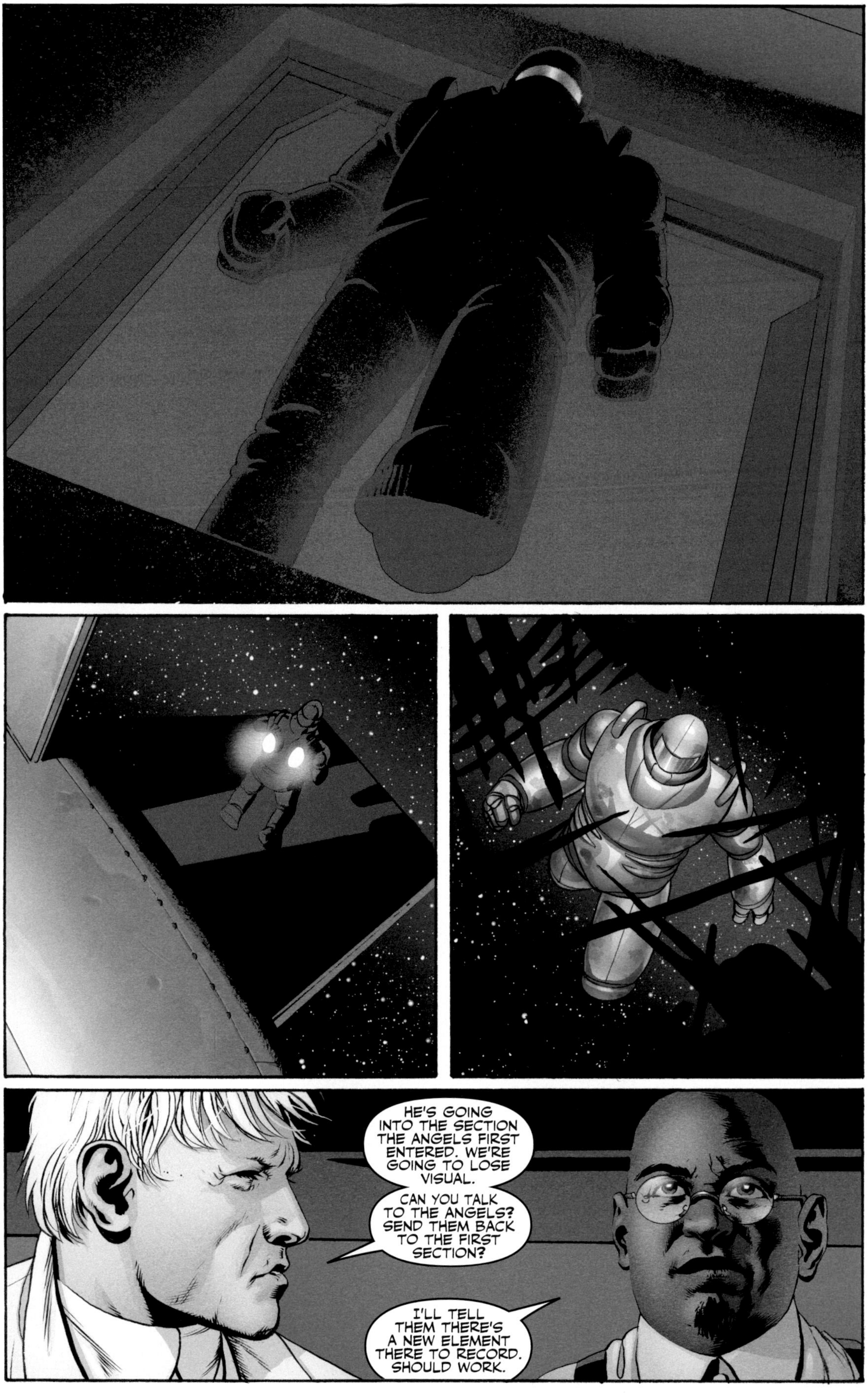
HE'S GOING INTO THE SECTION THE ANGELS FIRST ENTERED. WE'RE GOING TO LOSE VISUAL.
CAN YOU TALK TO THE ANGELS? SEND THEM BACK TO THE FIRST SECTION?
I'LL TELL THEM THERE'S A NEW ELEMENT THERE TO RECORD. SHOULD WORK.

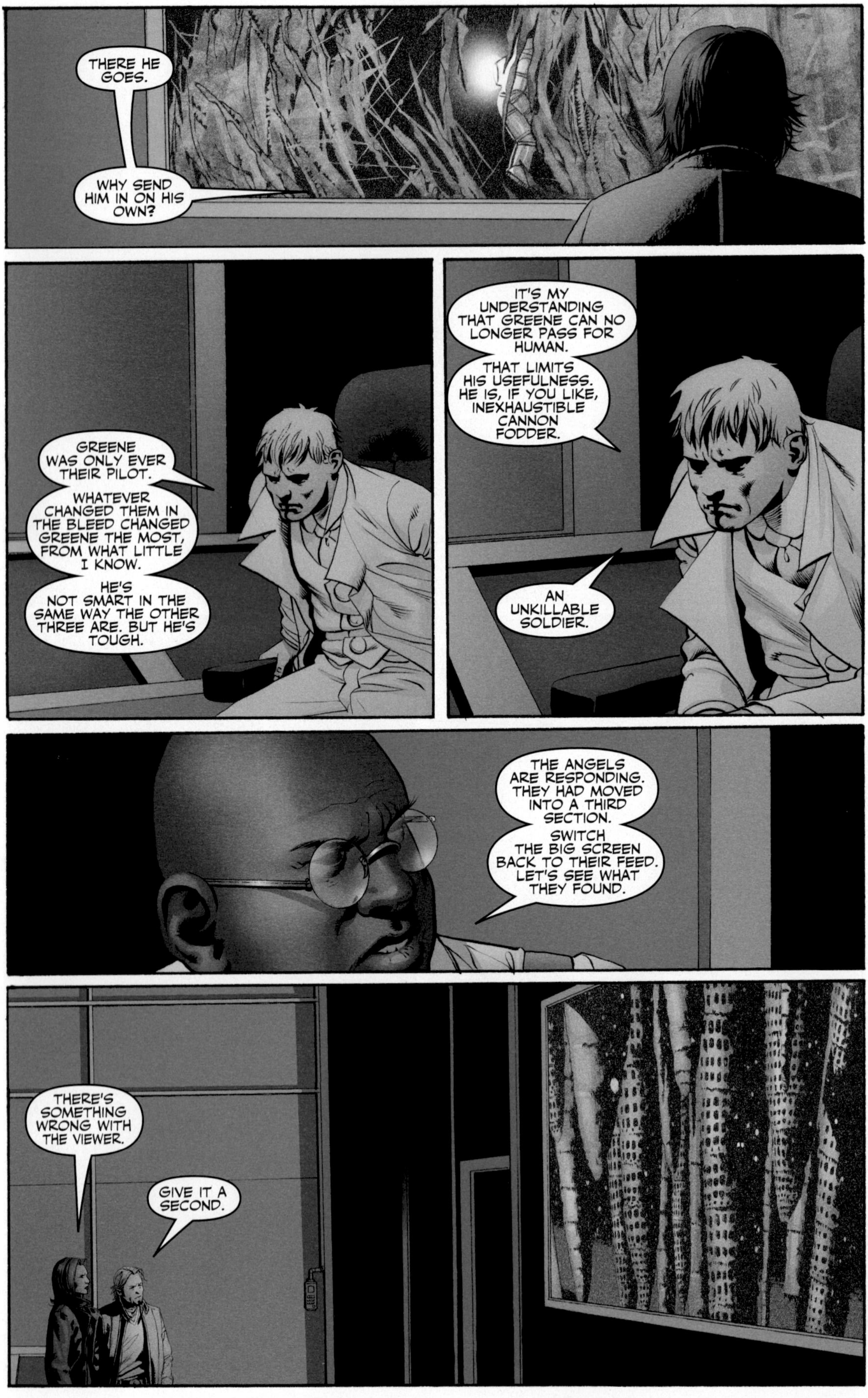
THERE HE GOES.
WHY SEND HIM IN ON HIS OWN?
GREENE WAS ONLY EVER THEIR PILOT.
WHATEVER CHANGED THEM IN THE BLEED CHANGED GREENE THE MOST, FROM WHAT LITTLE I KNOW.
HE'S NOT SMART IN THE SAME WAY THE OTHER THREE ARE. BUT HE'S TOUGH.
IT'S MY UNDERSTANDING THAT GREENE CAN NO LONGER PASS FOR HUMAN.
THAT LIMITS HIS USEFULNESS. HE IS, IF YOU LIKE, INEXHAUSTIBLE CANNON FODDER.
AN UNKILLABLE SOLDIER.
THE ANGELS ARE RESPONDING. THEY HAD MOVED INTO A THIRD SECTION.
SWITCH THE BIG SCREEN BACK TO THEIR FEED. LET'S SEE WHAT THEY FOUND.
THERE'S SOMETHING WRONG WITH THE VIEWER.
GIVE IT A SECOND.

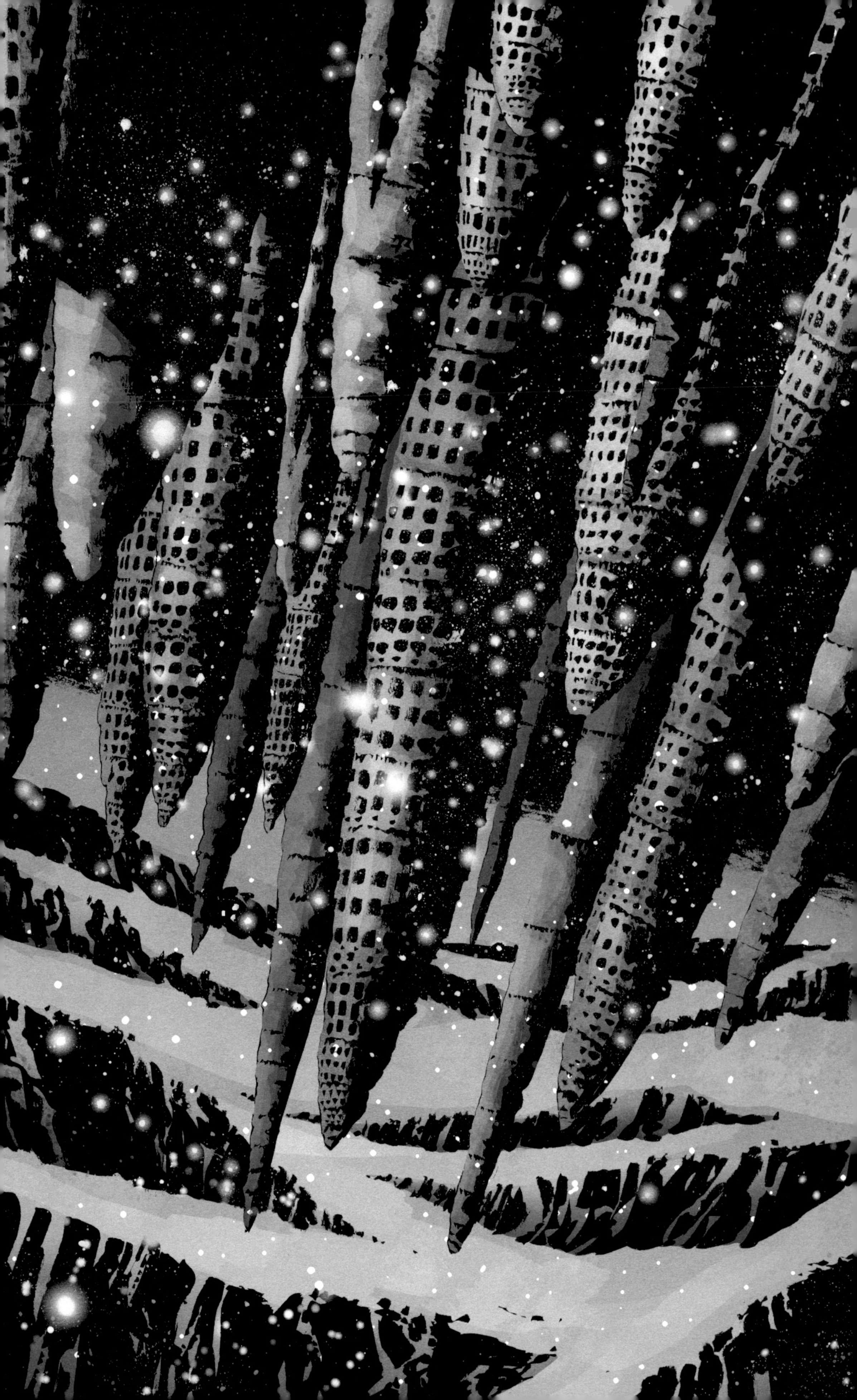

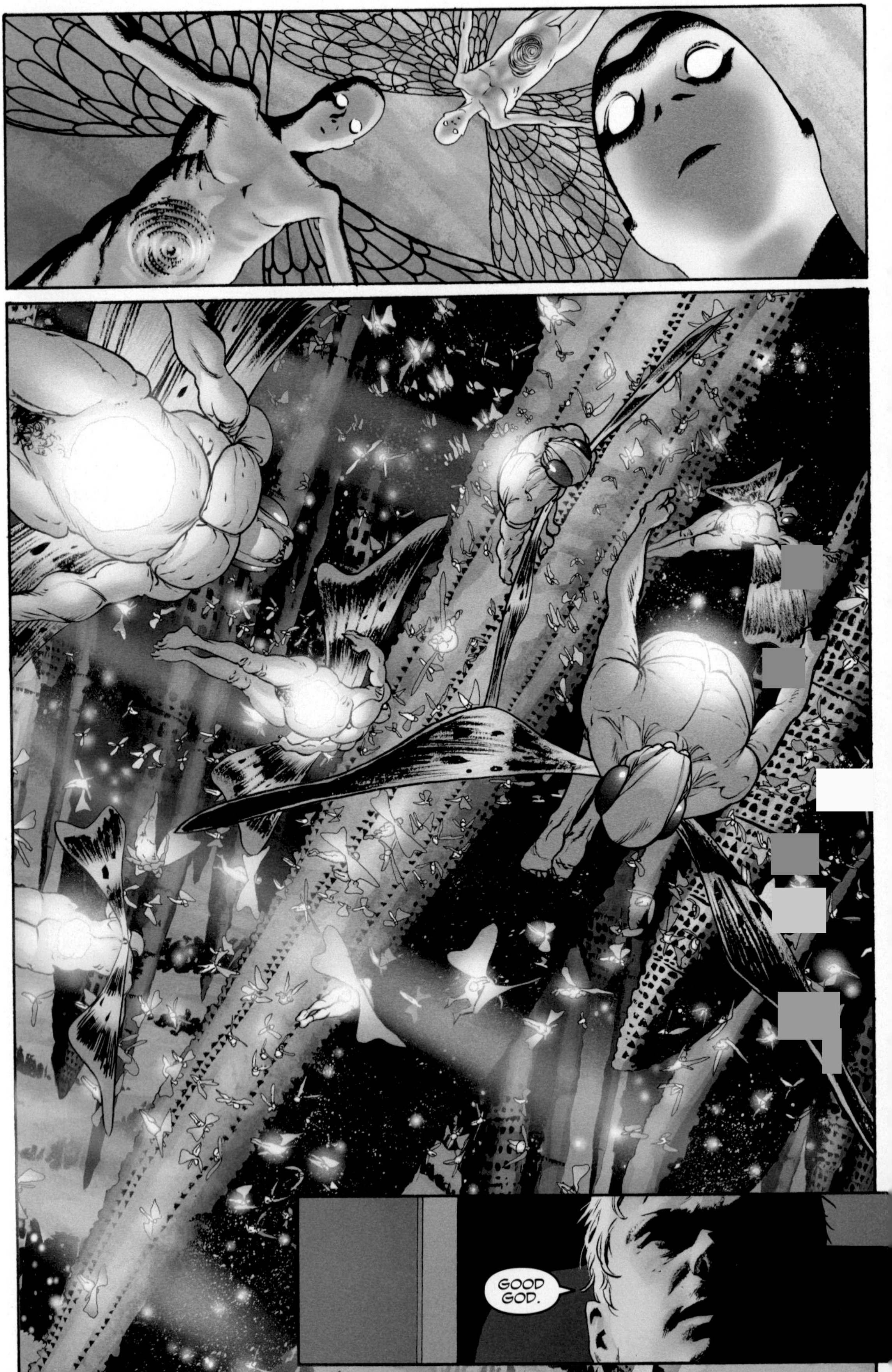
GOOD GOD.

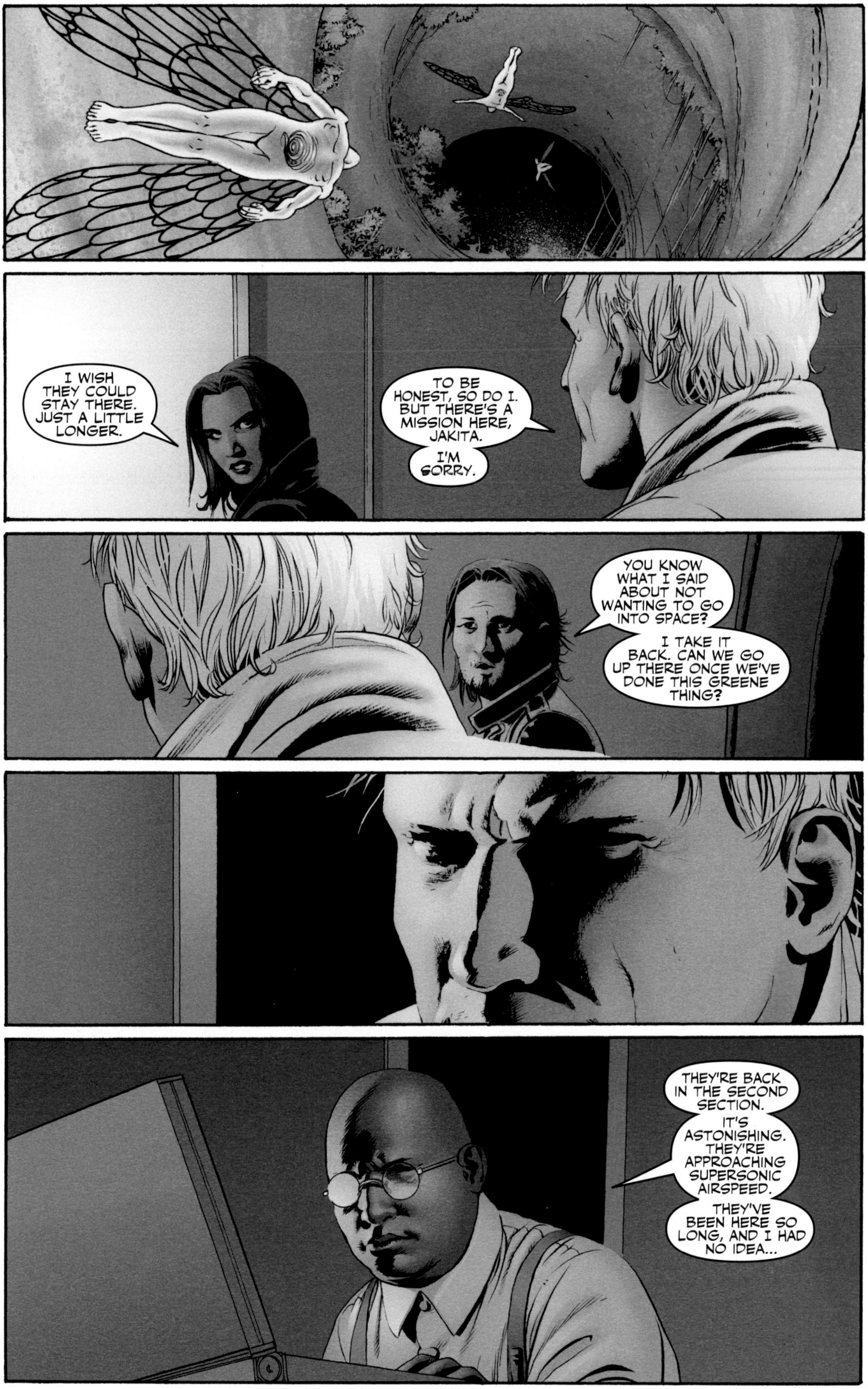
I WISH THEY COULD STAY THERE. JUST A LITTLE LONGER.
TO BE HONEST, SO DO I. BUT THERE'S A MISSION HERE, JAKITA.
I'M SORRY.
YOU KNOW WHAT I SAID ABOUT NOT WANTING TO GO INTO SPACE?
I TAKE IT BACK. CAN WE GO UP THERE ONCE WE'VE DONE THIS GREENE THING?
THEY'RE BACK IN THE SECOND SECTION.
IT'S ASTONISHING. THEY'RE APPROACHING SUPERSONIC AIRSPEED.
THEY'VE BEEN HERE SO LONG, AND I HAD NO IDEA...

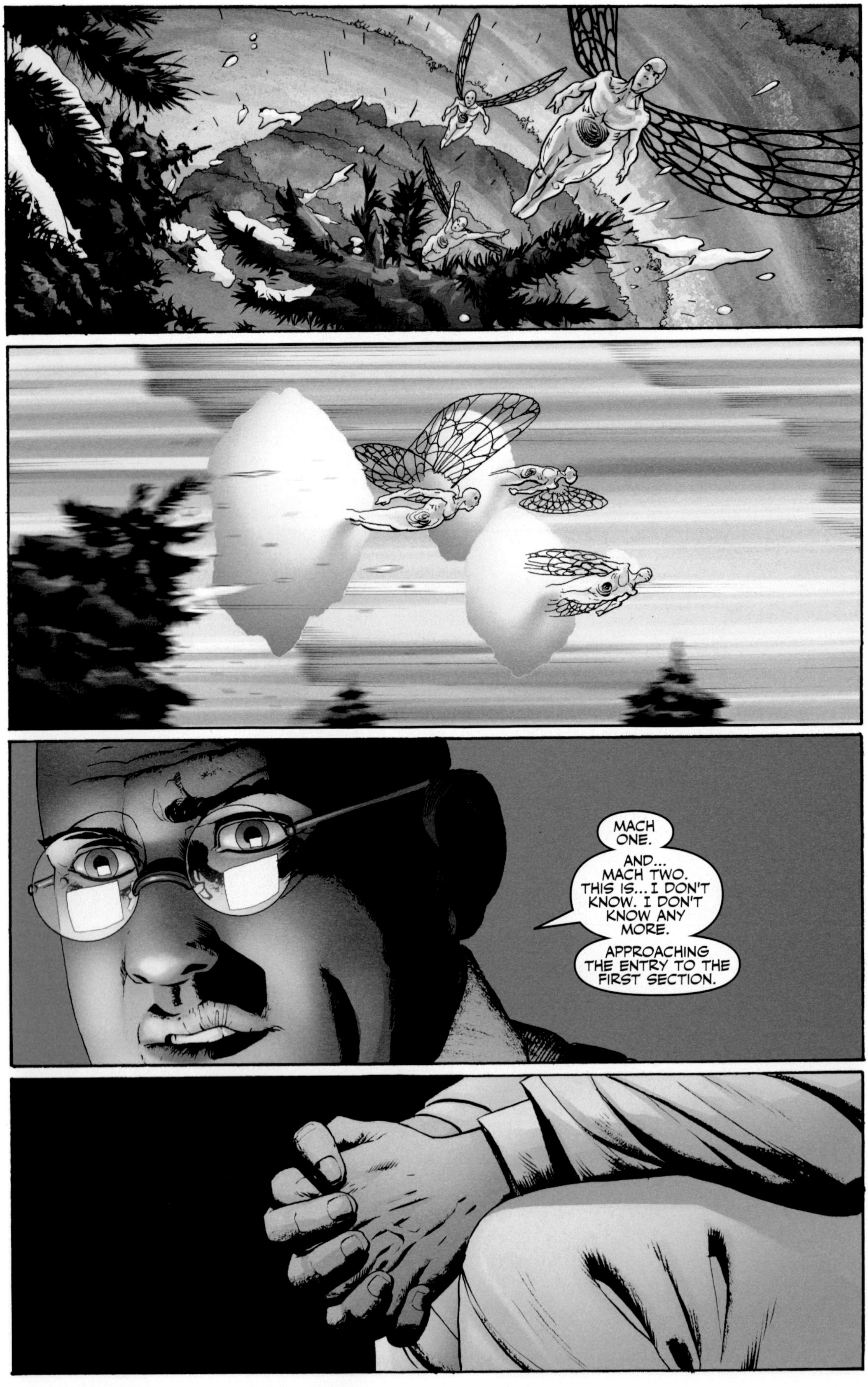
MACH ONE.
AND... MACH TWO. THIS IS... I DON'T KNOW. I DON'T KNOW ANY MORE.
APPROACHING THE ENTRY TO THE FIRST SECTION.

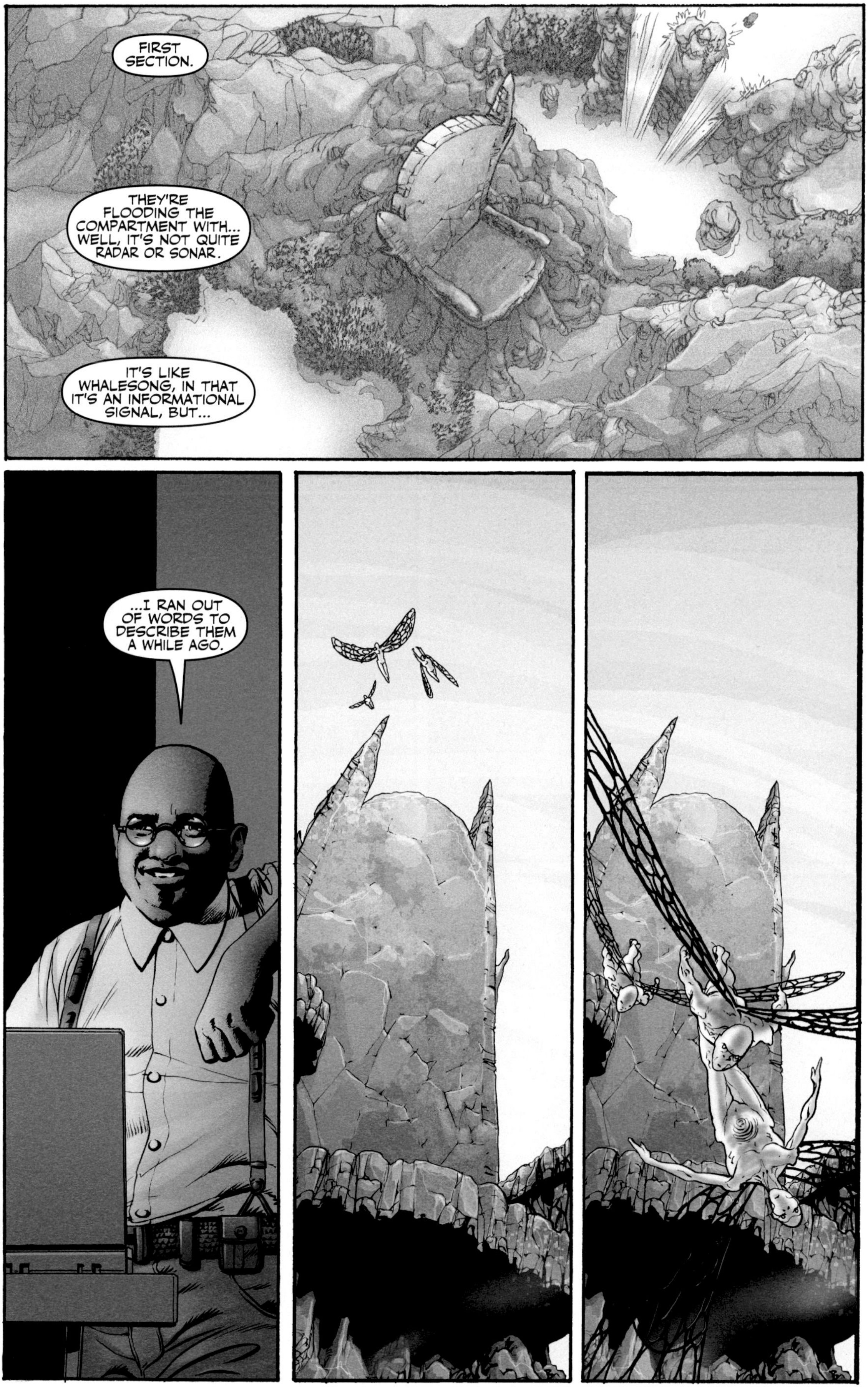
FIRST SECTION.
THEY'RE FLOODING THE COMPARTMENT WITH... WELL, IT'S NOT QUITE RADAR OR SONAR.
IT'S LIKE WHALESONG, IN THAT IT'S AN INFORMATIONAL SIGNAL, BUT...
...I RAN OUT OF WORDS TO DESCRIBE THEM A WHILE AGO.

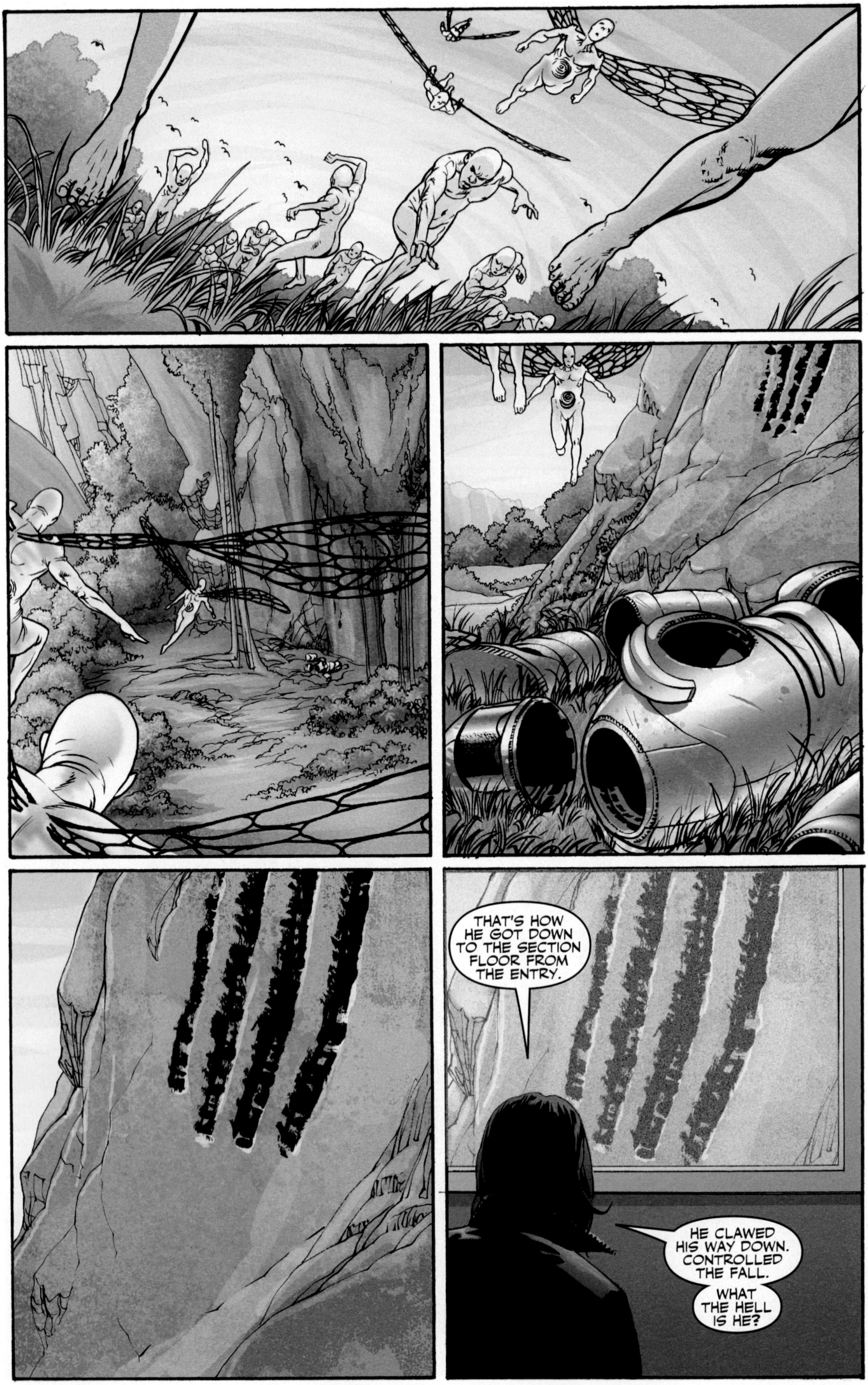
THAT'S HOW HE GOT DOWN TO THE SECTION FLOOR FROM THE ENTRY.
HE CLAWED HIS WAY DOWN. CONTROLLED THE FALL.
WHAT THE HELL IS HE?

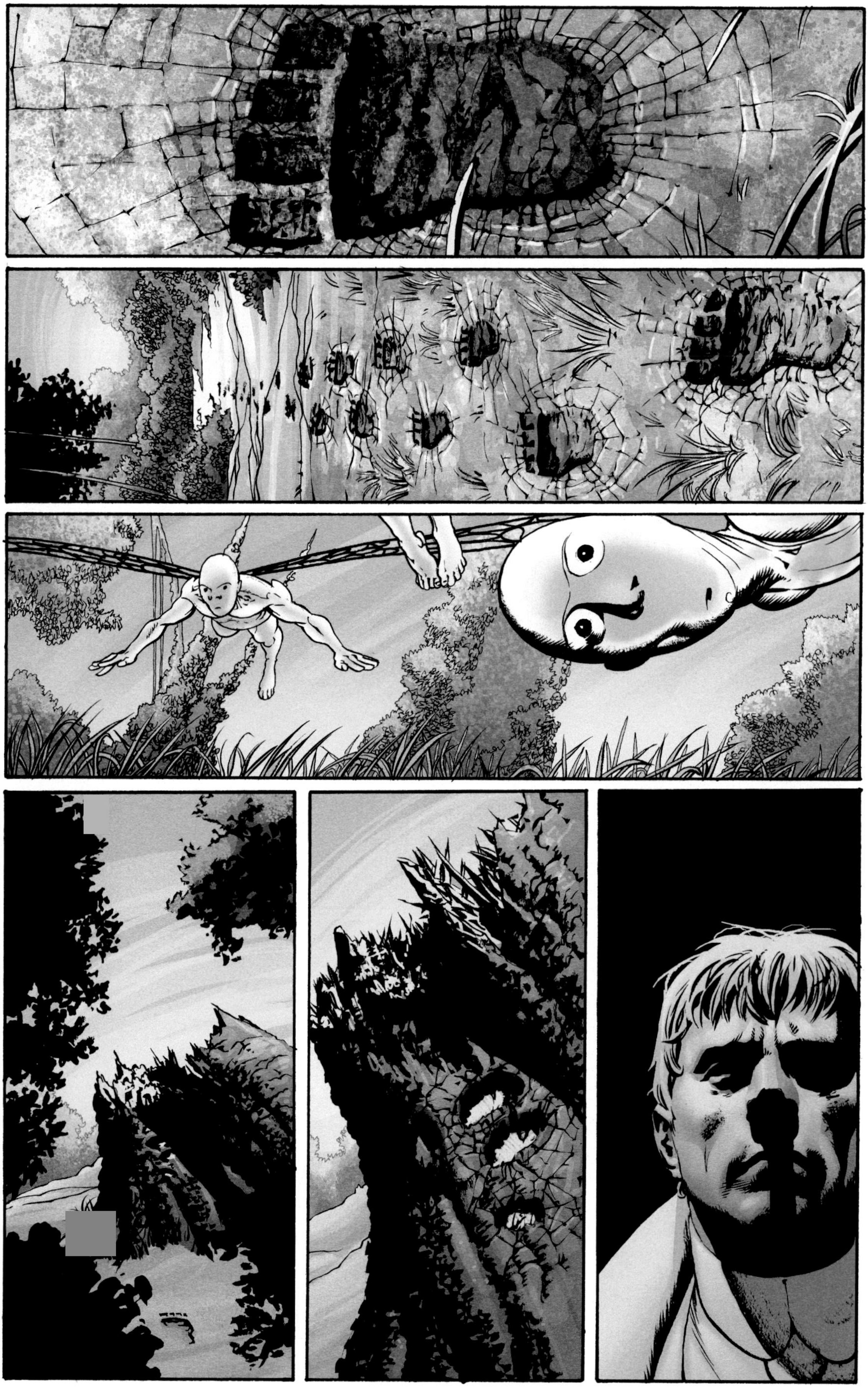

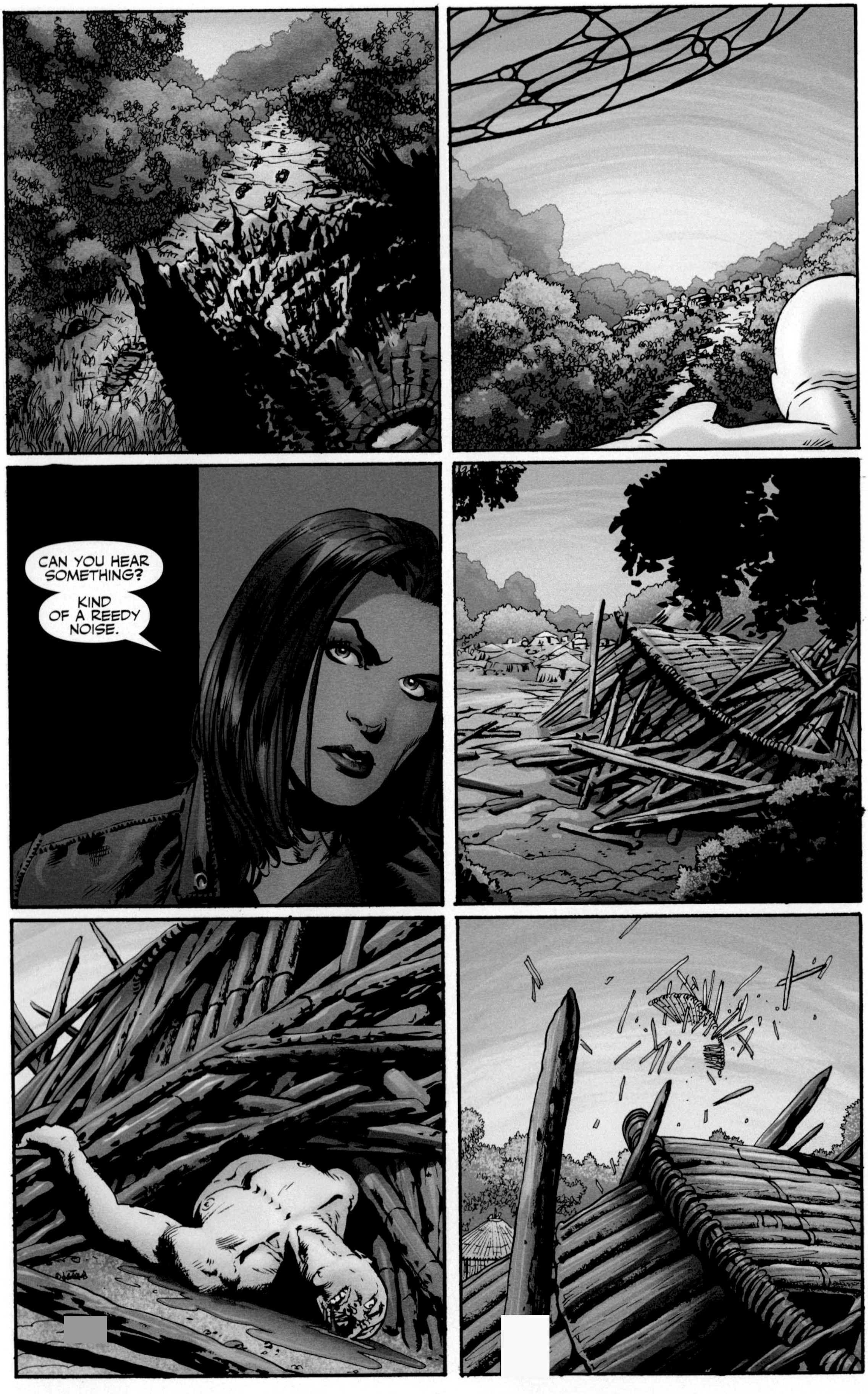
CAN YOU HEAR SOMETHING?
KIND OF A REEDY NOISE.

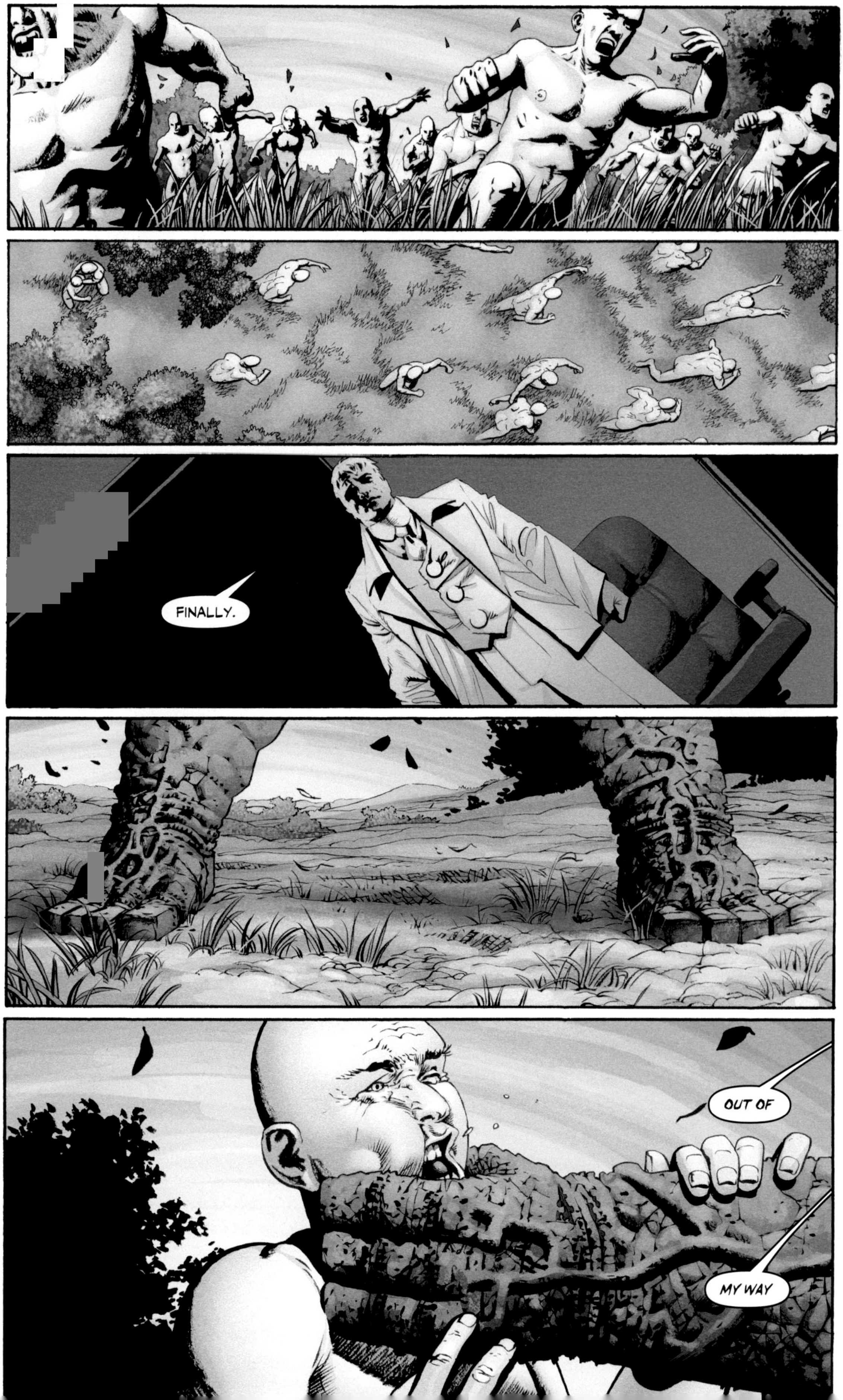
FINALLY.
OUT OF
MY WAY

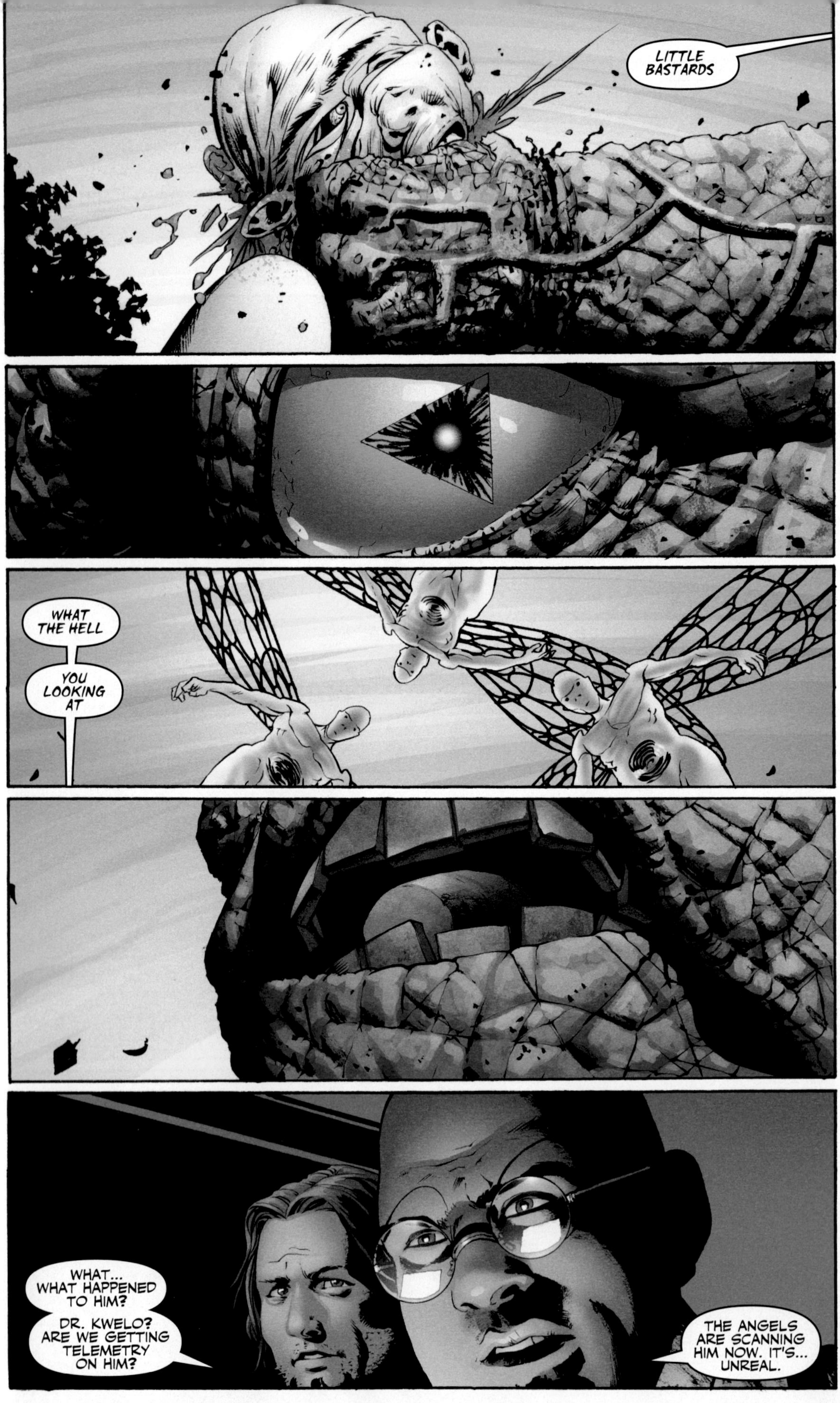
LITTLE BASTARDS
WHAT THE HELL
YOU LOOKING AT
WHAT... WHAT HAPPENED TO HIM?
DR. KWELO? ARE WE GETTING TELEMETRY ON HIM?
THE ANGELS ARE SCANNING HIM NOW. IT'S... UNREAL.

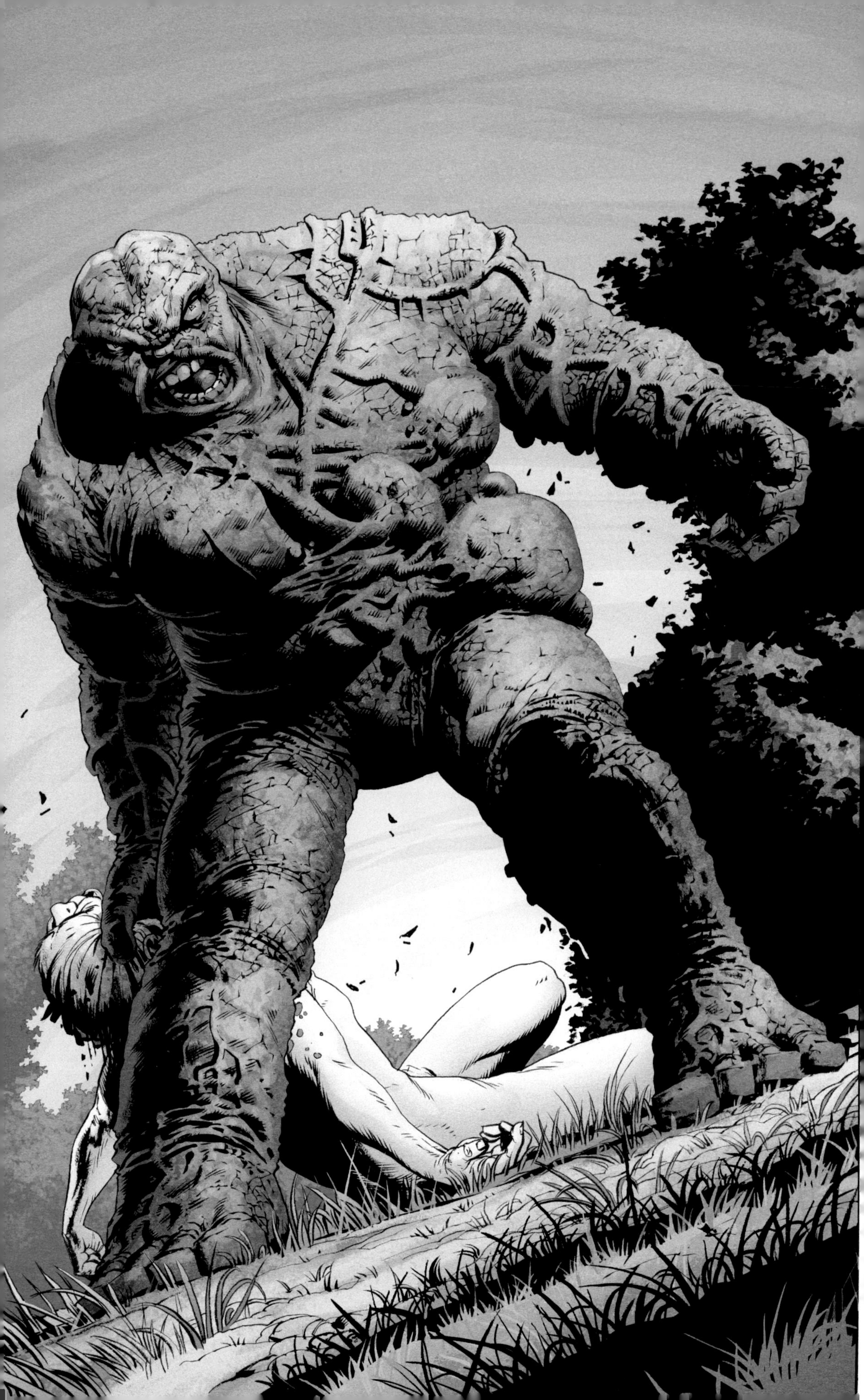

HOW'S THE TELEMETRY STREAM FROM THE ANGELS?

WE'RE HAVING TO REROUTE INTO TWO OF THE MAINFRAMES. JUST GIGABYTES OF STUFF...

THEY'RE RECORDING EVERY MILLIMETER OF HIM...

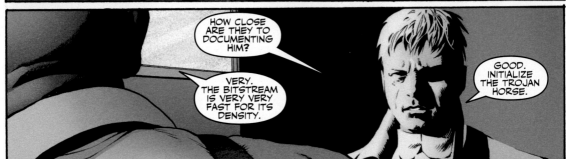

HOW CLOSE ARE THEY TO DOCUMENTING HIM?

VERY. THE BITSTREAM IS VERY VERY FAST FOR ITS DENSITY.

GOOD. INITIALIZE THE TROJAN HORSE.

THE WHAT?

MR. SNOW, PLEASE. I DON'T THINK THERE'S ANY--

I WASN'T INVITING A DEBATE. DO IT.

WHAT'RE YOU TALKING ABOUT, ELIJAH?

I KNEW THEY'D SEND GREENE UP.

AND I ALSO KNOW WE NEED GREENE OUT OF THE WAY. PERMANENTLY.

MR. SNOW HAD US FIT A DEVICE TO THE VESSEL'S POWERPLANT.

YOU'RE NOT SERIOUS.

YOU TRIED TO BRING ME BACK BY SHOWING ME A FILE DETAILING EVERY DISGUSTING THING THESE PEOPLE EVER DID.

WHAT DID YOU EXPECT TO HAPPEN?

DID YOU SOMEHOW BELIEVE I WOULD NOT USE EVERYTHING IN MY POWER TO WIPE THESE ANIMALS OUT?

CAMERA NINE HAS DETACHED FROM THE VESSEL AND THRUSTED TO A TWO HUNDRED MILE DISTANCE, MR. SNOW.

SWITCH OUR VIEW TO CAM NINE AND ACTUATE.

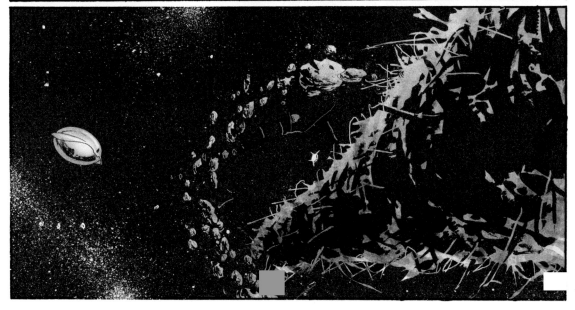

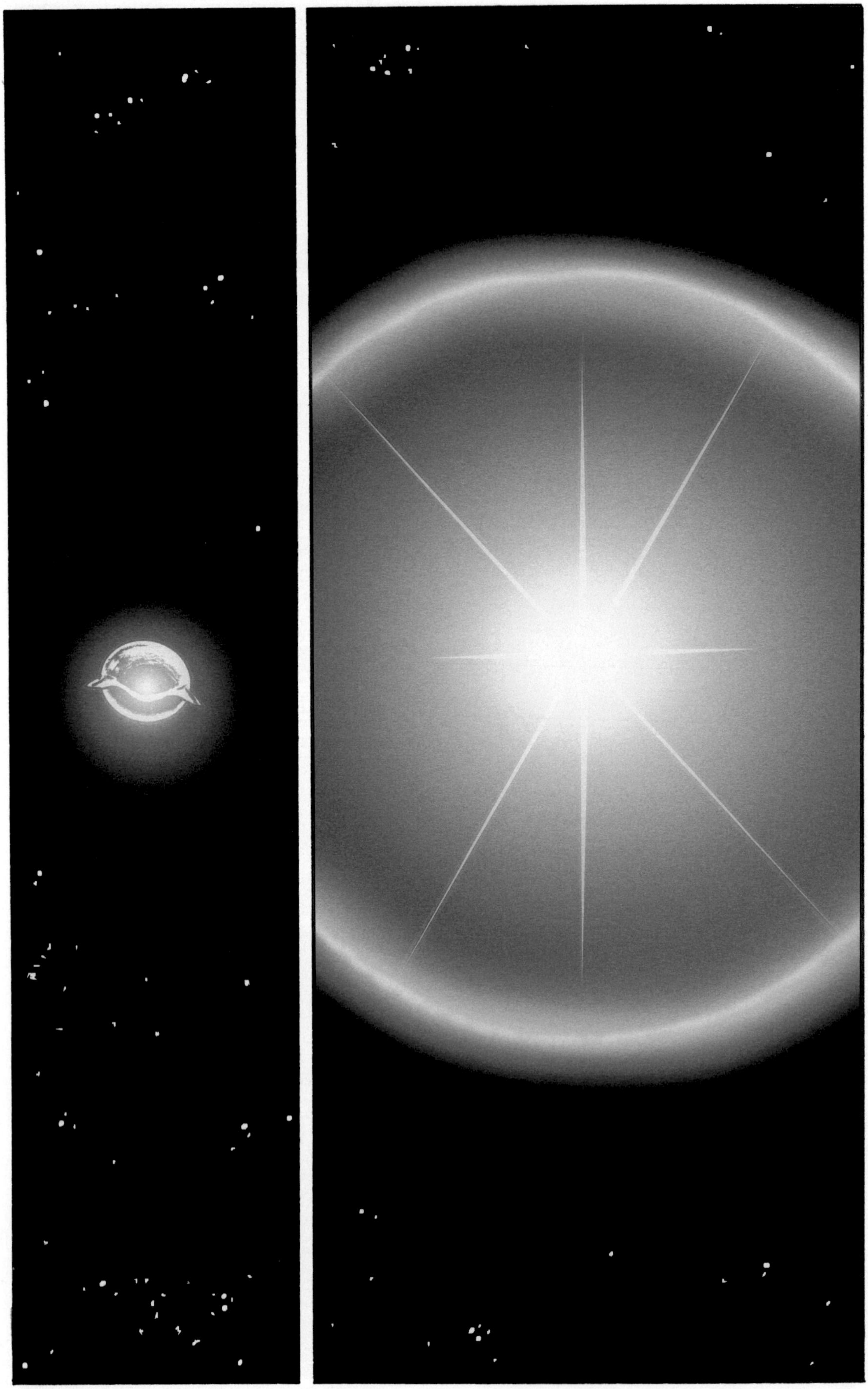

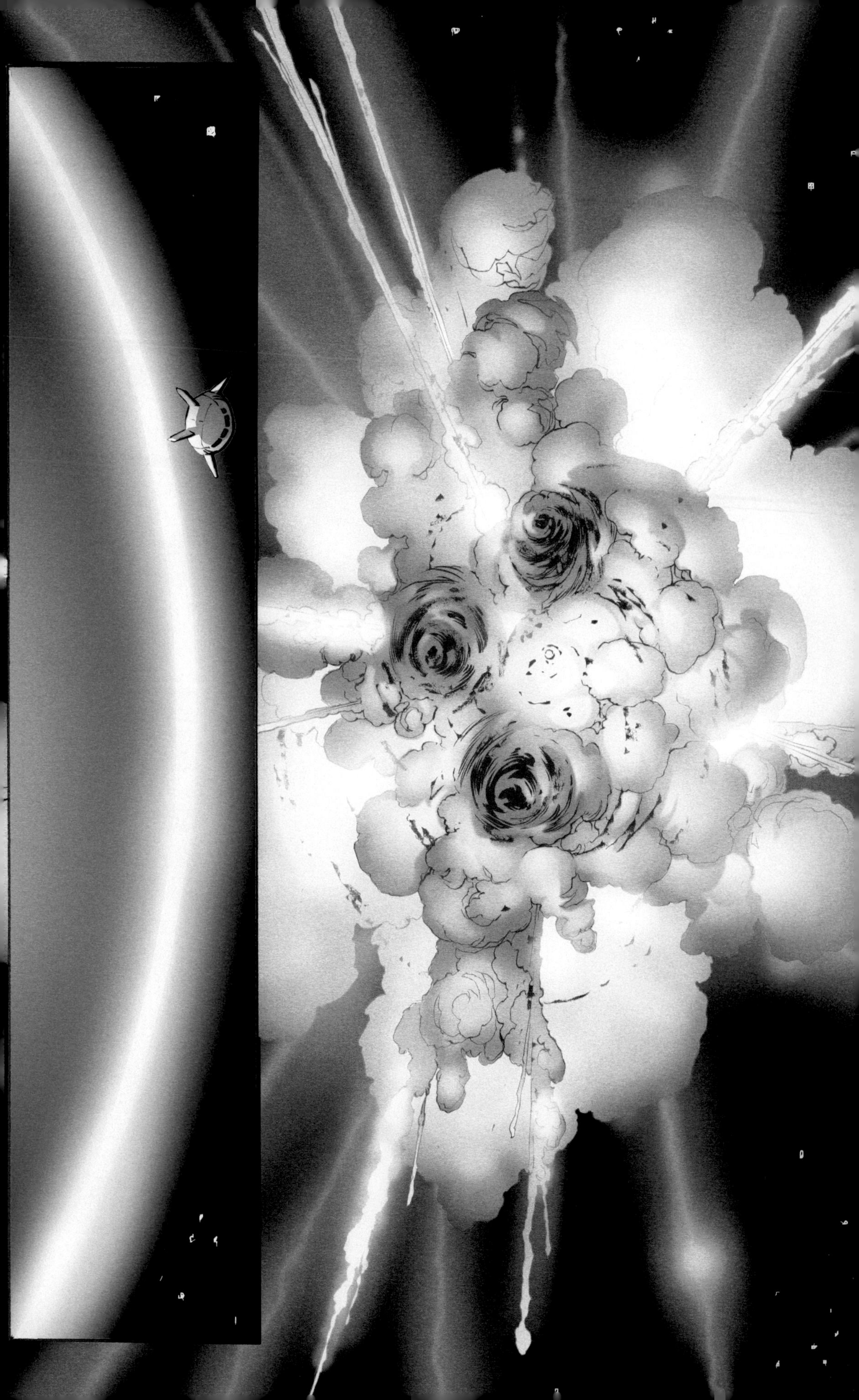

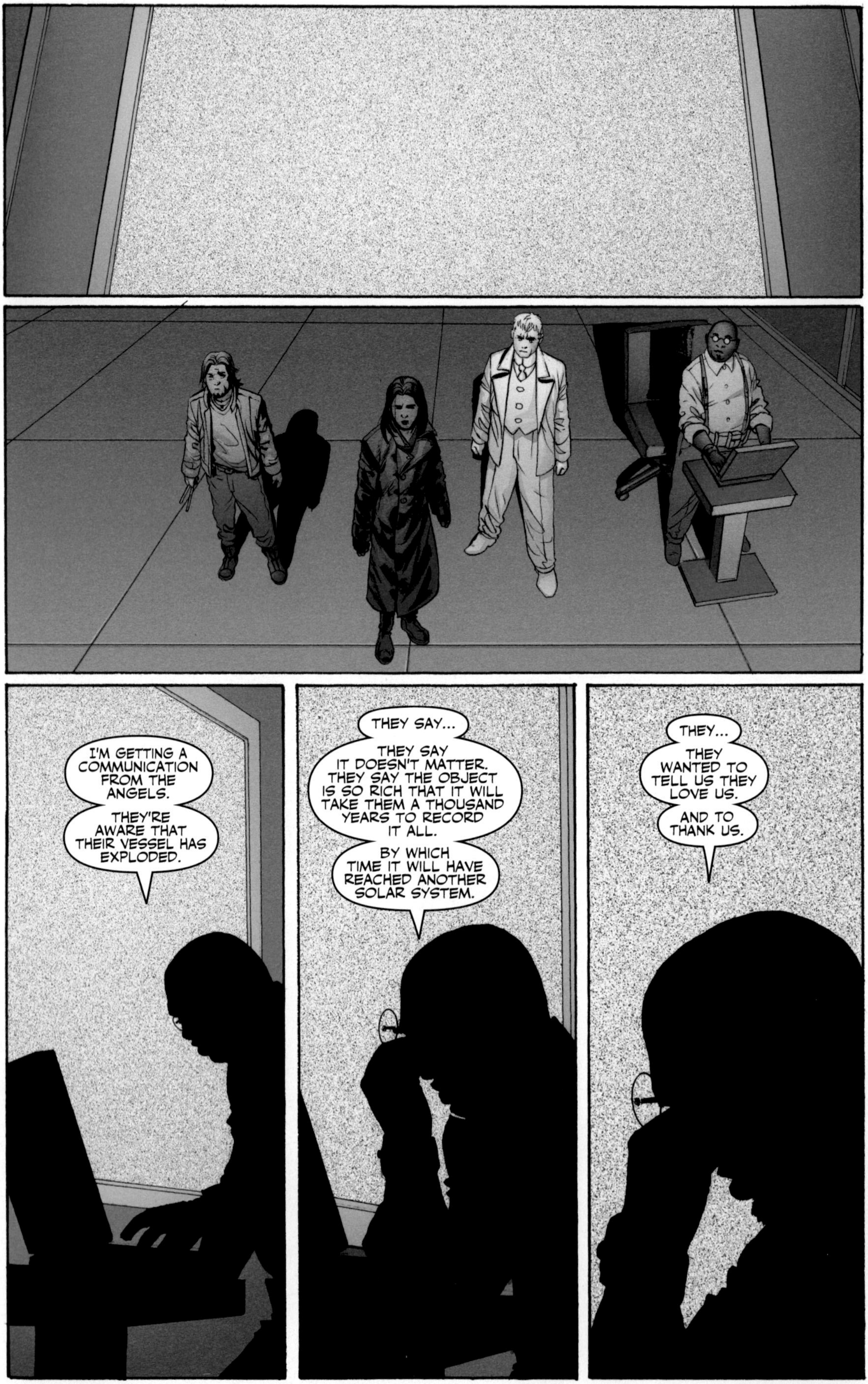
I'M GETTING A COMMUNICATION FROM THE ANGELS.
THEY'RE AWARE THAT THEIR VESSEL HAS EXPLODED.
THEY SAY...
THEY SAY IT DOESN'T MATTER. THEY SAY THE OBJECT IS SO RICH THAT IT WILL TAKE THEM A THOUSAND YEARS TO RECORD IT ALL.
BY WHICH TIME IT WILL HAVE REACHED ANOTHER SOLAR SYSTEM.
THEY...
THEY WANTED TO TELL US THEY LOVE US.
AND TO THANK US.

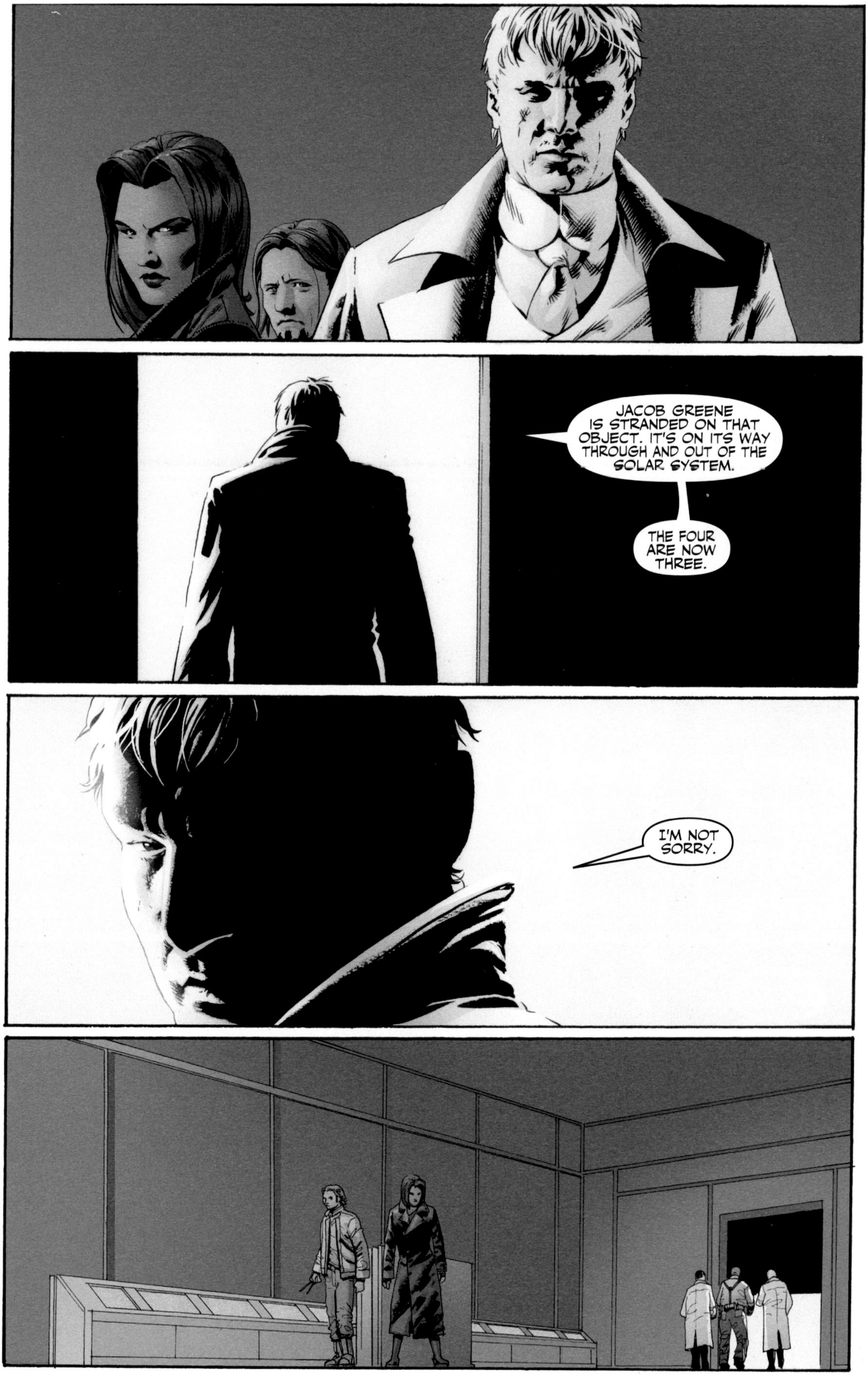
JACOB GREENE IS STRANDED ON THAT OBJECT. IT'S ON ITS WAY THROUGH AND OUT OF THE SOLAR SYSTEM.
THE FOUR ARE NOW THREE.
I'M NOT SORRY.

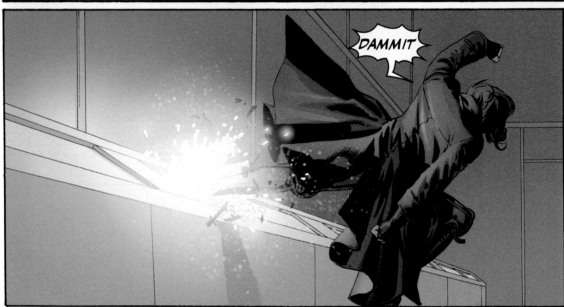

DAMMIT

I DON'T KNOW HIM ANYMORE.

WE BROUGHT HIM BACK.

BUT I SWEAR IT'S NOT HIM ANYMORE.

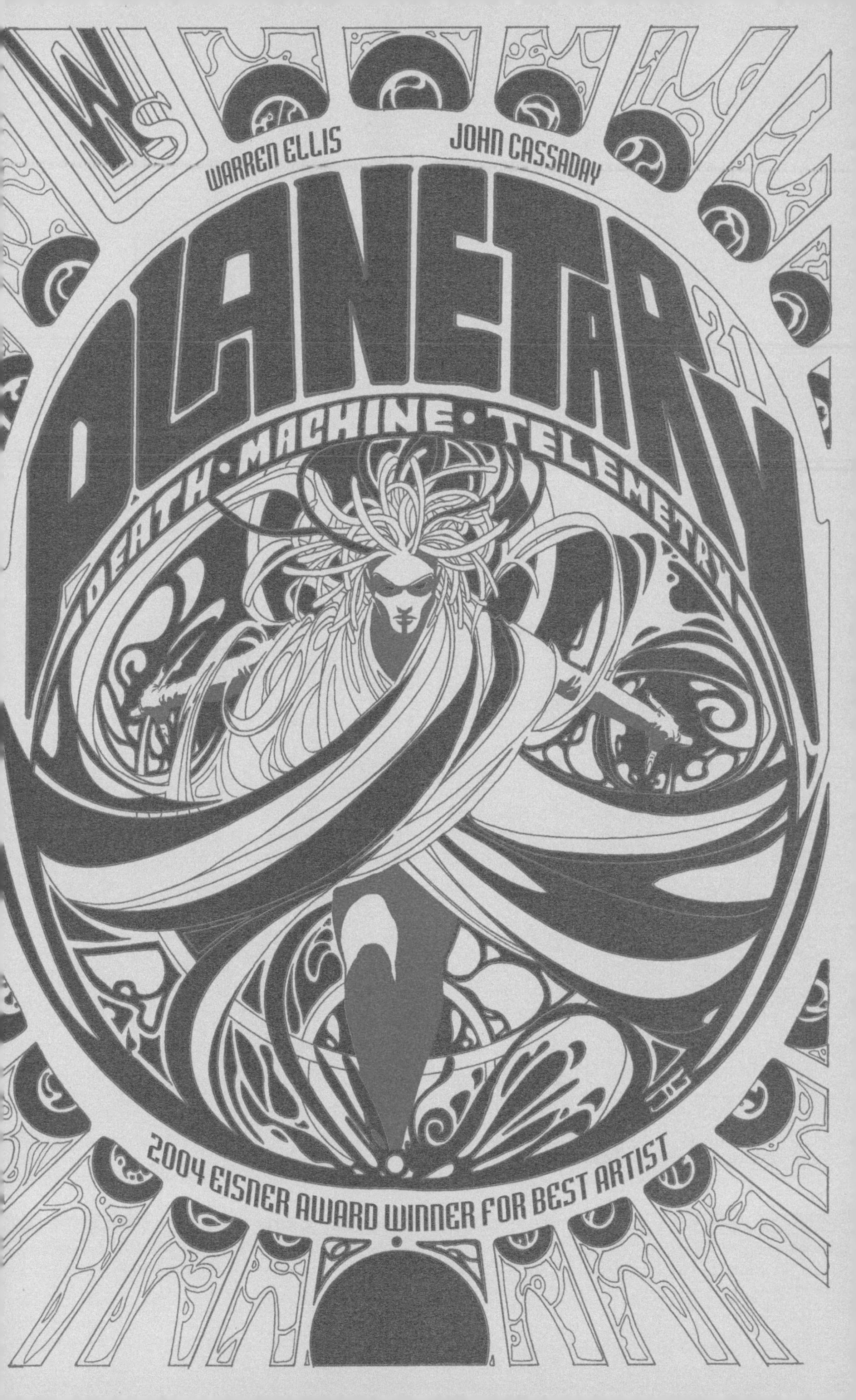
WS
WARREN ELLIS
JOHN CASSADAY
PLANETARY
21
DEATH • MACHINE • TELEMETRY
2004 EISNER AWARD WINNER FOR BEST ARTIST

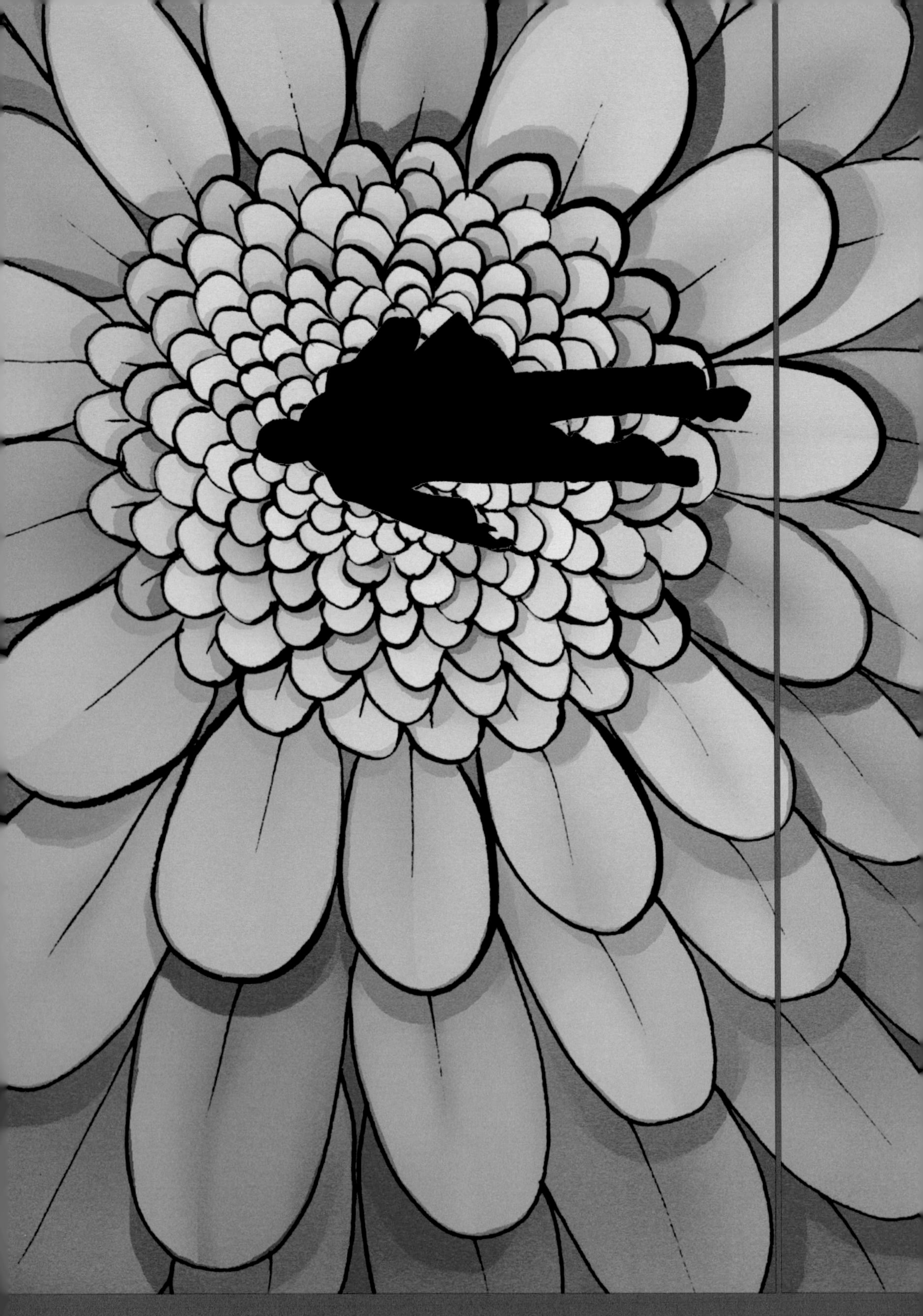

DEATH MACHINE TELEMETRY

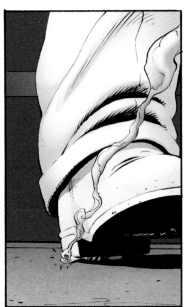

HELLO, MELANCTHA.

I'M HERE FOR MY CONSULTATION.

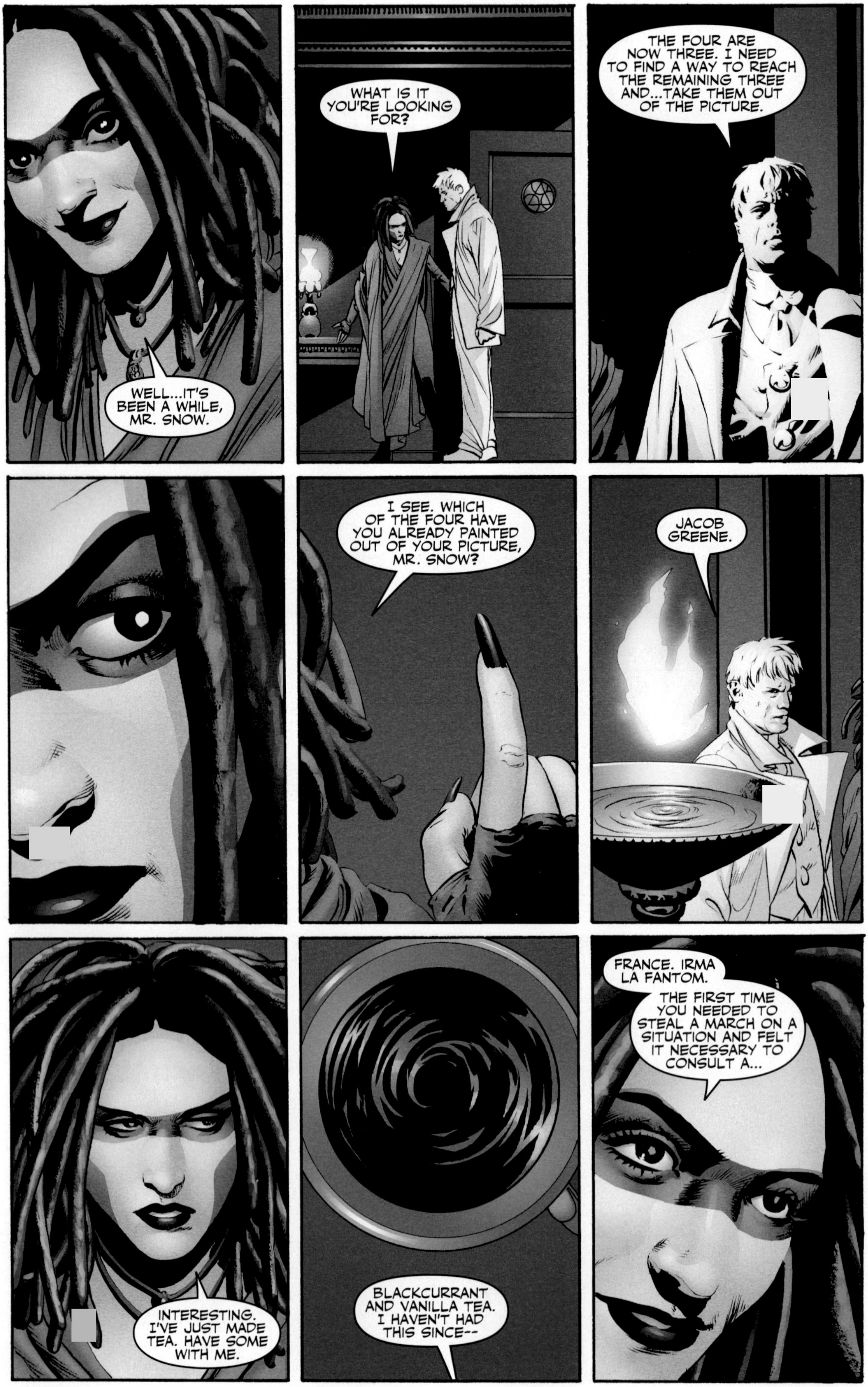
WELL...IT'S BEEN A WHILE, MR. SNOW.
WHAT IS IT YOU'RE LOOKING FOR?
THE FOUR ARE NOW THREE. I NEED TO FIND A WAY TO REACH THE REMAINING THREE AND...TAKE THEM OUT OF THE PICTURE.
I SEE. WHICH OF THE FOUR HAVE YOU ALREADY PAINTED OUT OF YOUR PICTURE, MR. SNOW?
JACOB GREENE.
INTERESTING. I'VE JUST MADE TEA. HAVE SOME WITH ME.
BLACKCURRANT AND VANILLA TEA. I HAVEN'T HAD THIS SINCE--
FRANCE. IRMA LA FANTOM.
THE FIRST TIME YOU NEEDED TO STEAL A MARCH ON A SITUATION AND FELT IT NECESSARY TO CONSULT A...

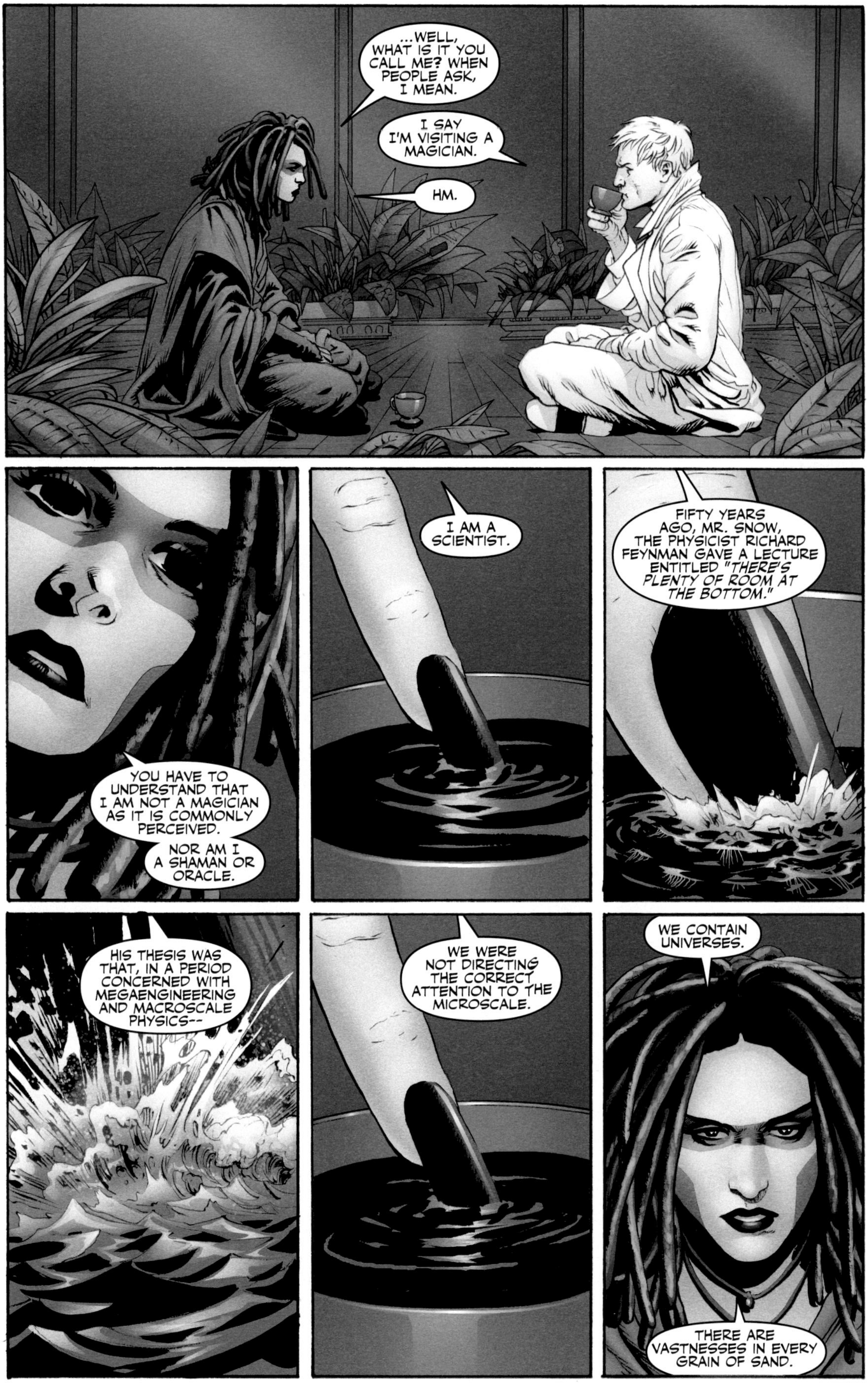
...WELL, WHAT IS IT YOU CALL ME? WHEN PEOPLE ASK, I MEAN.
I SAY I'M VISITING A MAGICIAN.
HM.
YOU HAVE TO UNDERSTAND THAT I AM NOT A MAGICIAN AS IT IS COMMONLY PERCEIVED.
NOR AM I A SHAMAN OR ORACLE.
I AM A SCIENTIST.
FIFTY YEARS AGO, MR. SNOW, THE PHYSICIST RICHARD FEYNMAN GAVE A LECTURE ENTITLED "THERE'S PLENTY OF ROOM AT THE BOTTOM."
HIS THESIS WAS THAT, IN A PERIOD CONCERNED WITH MEGAENGINEERING AND MACROSCALE PHYSICS--
WE WERE NOT DIRECTING THE CORRECT ATTENTION TO THE MICROSCALE.
WE CONTAIN UNIVERSES.
THERE ARE VASTNESSES IN EVERY GRAIN OF SAND.

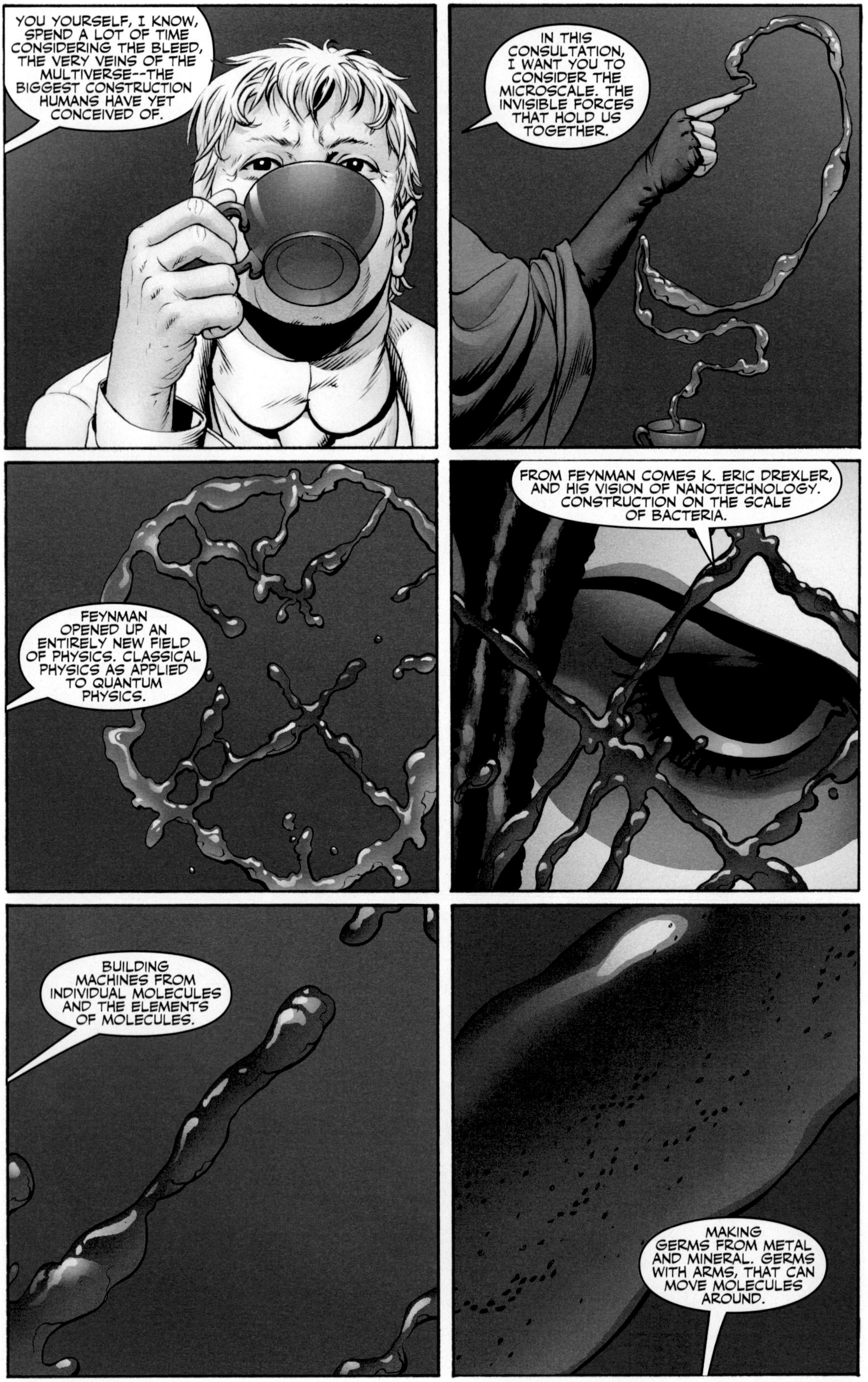
YOU YOURSELF, I KNOW, SPEND A LOT OF TIME CONSIDERING THE BLEED, THE VERY VEINS OF THE MULTIVERSE--THE BIGGEST CONSTRUCTION HUMANS HAVE YET CONCEIVED OF.
IN THIS CONSULTATION, I WANT YOU TO CONSIDER THE MICROSCALE. THE INVISIBLE FORCES THAT HOLD US TOGETHER.
FEYNMAN OPENED UP AN ENTIRELY NEW FIELD OF PHYSICS. CLASSICAL PHYSICS AS APPLIED TO QUANTUM PHYSICS.
FROM FEYNMAN COMES K. ERIC DREXLER, AND HIS VISION OF NANOTECHNOLOGY. CONSTRUCTION ON THE SCALE OF BACTERIA.
BUILDING MACHINES FROM INDIVIDUAL MOLECULES AND THE ELEMENTS OF MOLECULES.
MAKING GERMS FROM METAL AND MINERAL. GERMS WITH ARMS, THAT CAN MOVE MOLECULES AROUND.

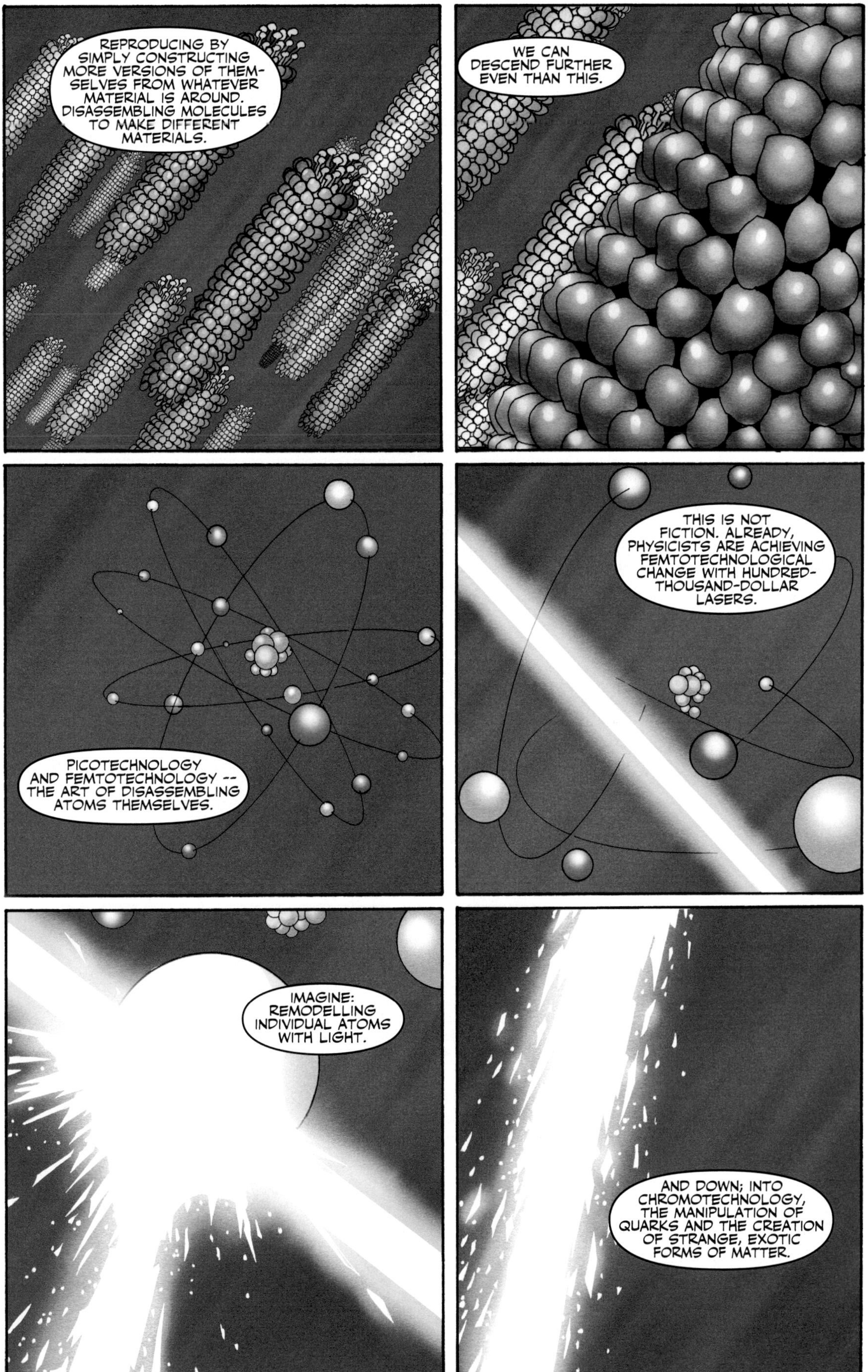
REPRODUCING BY SIMPLY CONSTRUCTING MORE VERSIONS OF THEMSELVES FROM WHATEVER MATERIAL IS AROUND. DISASSEMBLING MOLECULES TO MAKE DIFFERENT MATERIALS.
WE CAN DESCEND FURTHER EVEN THAN THIS.
PICOTECHNOLOGY AND FEMTOTECHNOLOGY -- THE ART OF DISASSEMBLING ATOMS THEMSELVES.
THIS IS NOT FICTION. ALREADY, PHYSICISTS ARE ACHIEVING FEMTOTECHNOLOGICAL CHANGE WITH HUNDRED-THOUSAND-DOLLAR LASERS.
IMAGINE: REMODELLING INDIVIDUAL ATOMS WITH LIGHT.
AND DOWN; INTO CHROMOTECHNOLOGY, THE MANIPULATION OF QUARKS AND THE CREATION OF STRANGE, EXOTIC FORMS OF MATTER.

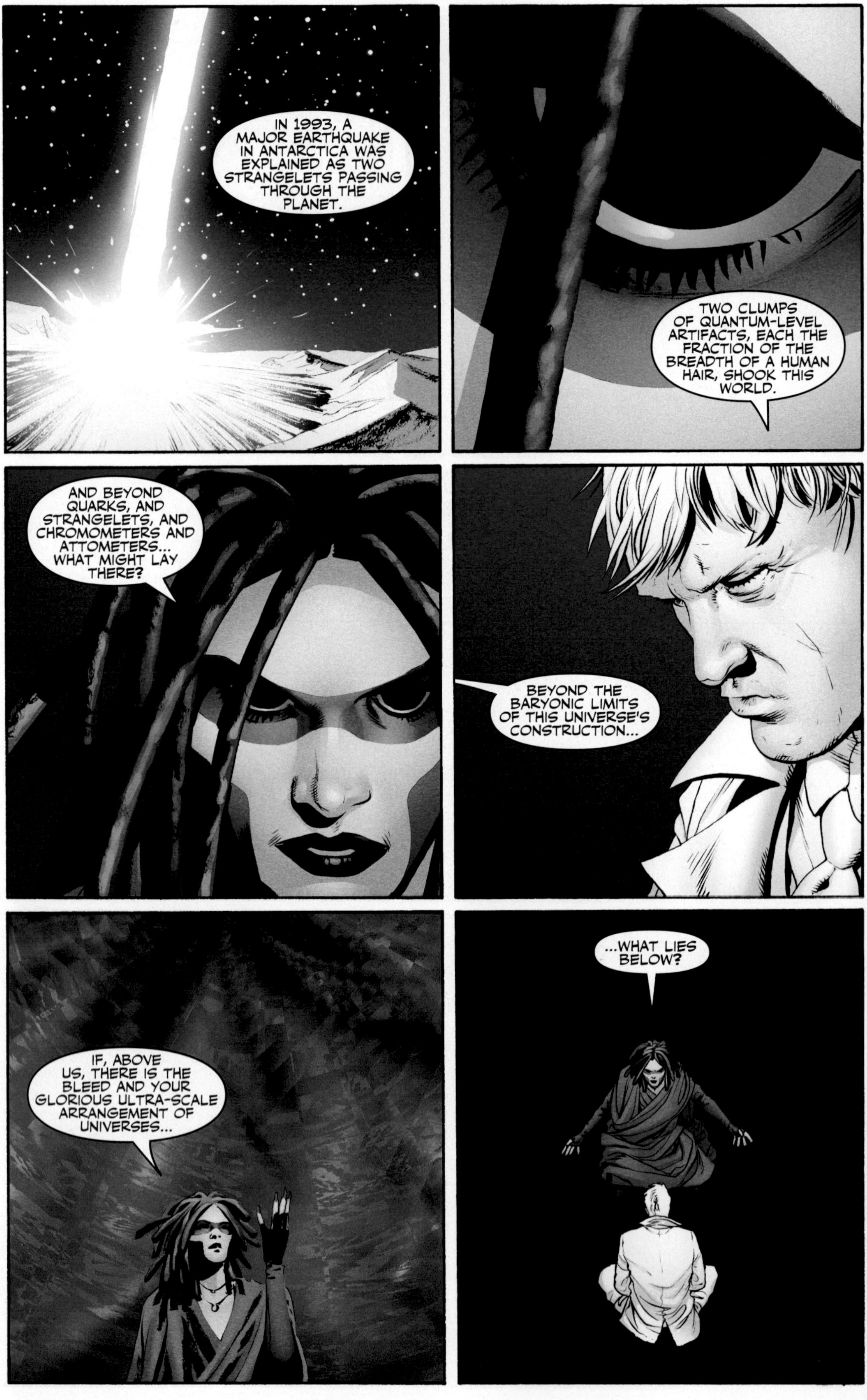
IN 1993, A MAJOR EARTHQUAKE IN ANTARCTICA WAS EXPLAINED AS TWO STRANGELETS PASSING THROUGH THE PLANET.
TWO CLUMPS OF QUANTUM-LEVEL ARTIFACTS, EACH THE FRACTION OF THE BREADTH OF A HUMAN HAIR, SHOOK THIS WORLD.
AND BEYOND QUARKS, AND STRANGELETS, AND CHROMOMETERS AND ATTOMETERS... WHAT MIGHT LAY THERE?
BEYOND THE BARYONIC LIMITS OF THIS UNIVERSE'S CONSTRUCTION...
IF, ABOVE US, THERE IS THE BLEED AND YOUR GLORIOUS ULTRA-SCALE ARRANGEMENT OF UNIVERSES...
...WHAT LIES BELOW?

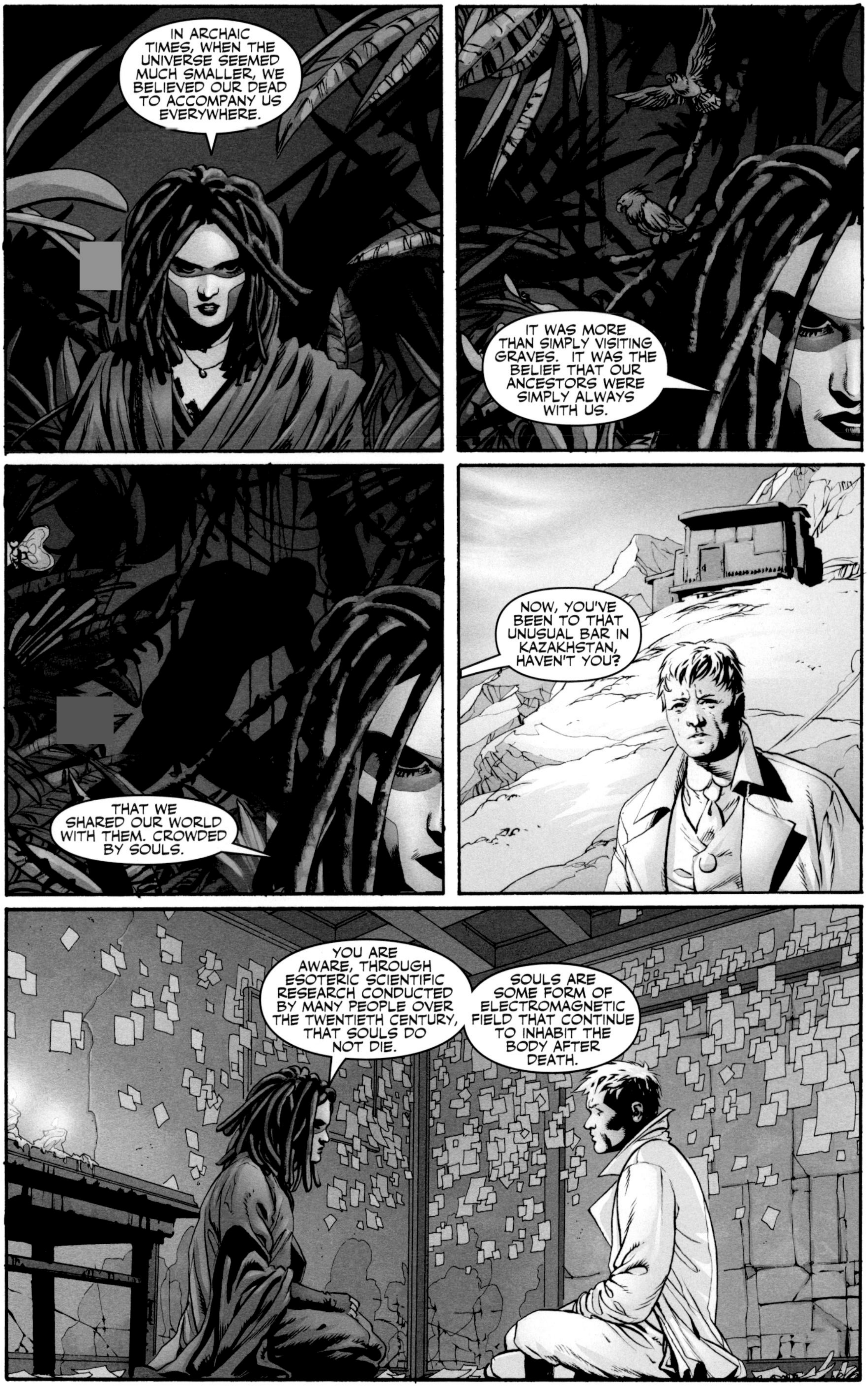
IN ARCHAIC TIMES, WHEN THE UNIVERSE SEEMED MUCH SMALLER, WE BELIEVED OUR DEAD TO ACCOMPANY US EVERYWHERE.
IT WAS MORE THAN SIMPLY VISITING GRAVES. IT WAS THE BELIEF THAT OUR ANCESTORS WERE SIMPLY ALWAYS WITH US.
THAT WE SHARED OUR WORLD WITH THEM. CROWDED BY SOULS.
NOW, YOU'VE BEEN TO THAT UNUSUAL BAR IN KAZAKHSTAN, HAVEN'T YOU?
YOU ARE AWARE, THROUGH ESOTERIC SCIENTIFIC RESEARCH CONDUCTED BY MANY PEOPLE OVER THE TWENTIETH CENTURY, THAT SOULS DO NOT DIE.
SOULS ARE SOME FORM OF ELECTROMAGNETIC FIELD THAT CONTINUE TO INHABIT THE BODY AFTER DEATH.

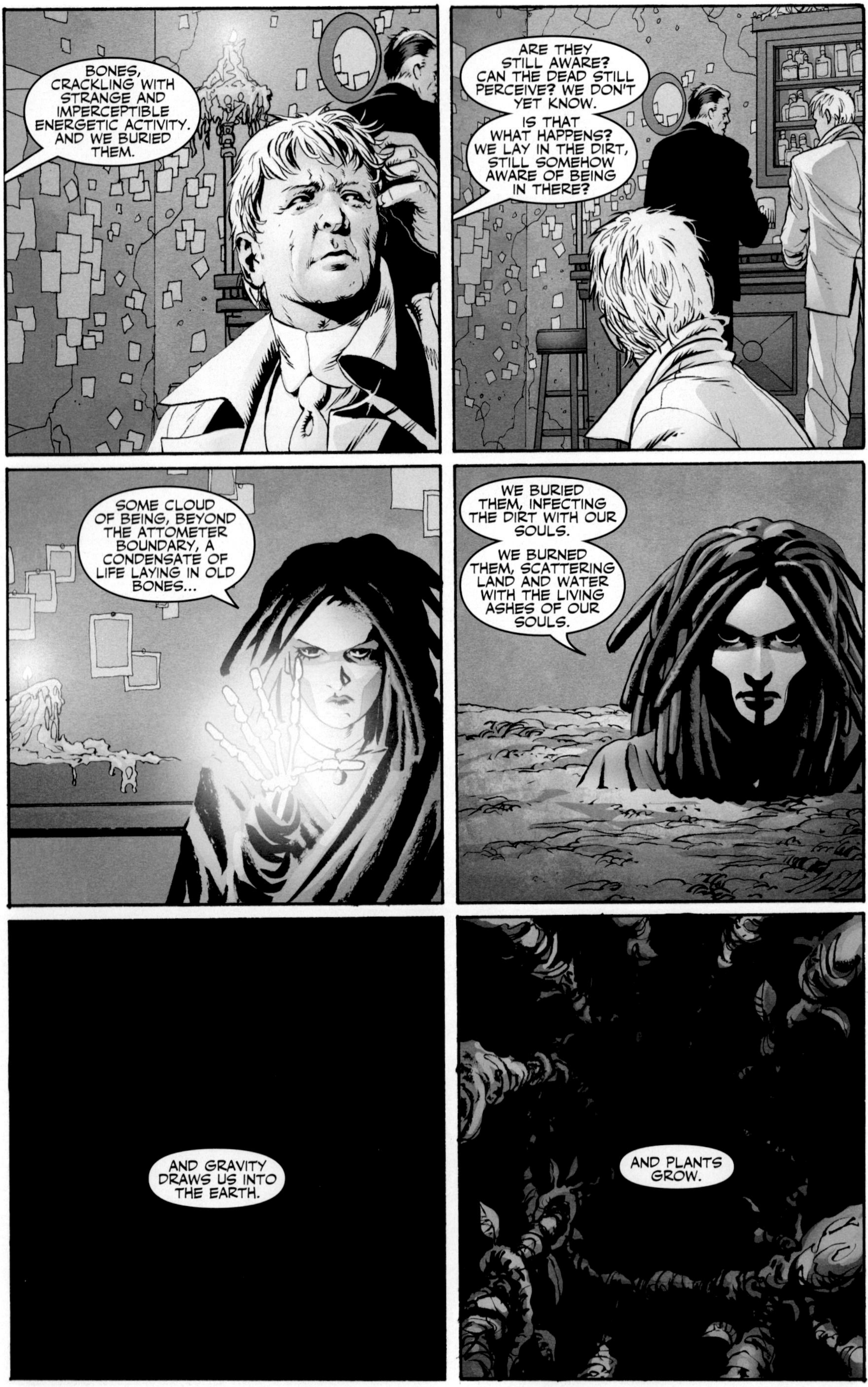
BONES, CRACKLING WITH STRANGE AND IMPERCEPTIBLE ENERGETIC ACTIVITY. AND WE BURIED THEM.
ARE THEY STILL AWARE? CAN THE DEAD STILL PERCEIVE? WE DON'T YET KNOW.
IS THAT WHAT HAPPENS? WE LAY IN THE DIRT, STILL SOMEHOW AWARE OF BEING IN THERE?
SOME CLOUD OF BEING, BEYOND THE ATTOMETER BOUNDARY, A CONDENSATE OF LIFE LAYING IN OLD BONES...
WE BURIED THEM, INFECTING THE DIRT WITH OUR SOULS.
WE BURNED THEM, SCATTERING LAND AND WATER WITH THE LIVING ASHES OF OUR SOULS.
AND GRAVITY DRAWS US INTO THE EARTH.
AND PLANTS GROW.

AYAHUASCA. PEYOTE. PSYLOCIBIN. STROPHARIA CUBENSIS.

THE DRUGS.

YES, HISTORICALLY, WE CONSIDER THEM SHAMANIC DRUGS, AND THEY WERE OVERLAID WITH RITUAL AND RELIGION AND THE OTHER CRAP OF ARCHAIC SOCIETIES.

BUT ALL SOCIETIES HAD THEIR SPEAKERS TO THE DEAD AND THEIR ORACLES WHO LOOKED INTO OTHER PLACES.

IN LEGEND, THE ORACLE AT DELPHI STOOD AT A POOL AND INHALED ITS VAPOR, THE PNEUMA, TO ORACULATE.

IT WAS RECENTLY FOUND THAT A VENT BENEATH THE POOL EXPRESSED ETHYLENE, A HYDROCARBON GAS THAT CREATES AN EUPHORIC DERANGEMENT, INTO THE WATER.

ETHYLENE, THE PNEUMA, IS A PLANT HORMONE.

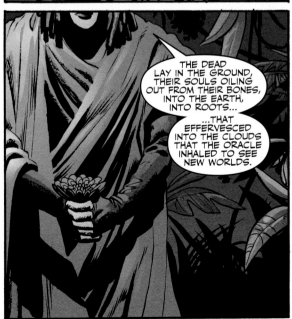

THE DEAD LAY IN THE GROUND, THEIR SOULS OILING OUT FROM THEIR BONES, INTO THE EARTH, INTO ROOTS...

...THAT EFFERVESCED INTO THE CLOUDS THAT THE ORACLE INHALED TO SEE NEW WORLDS.

INTO THE PLANTS THAT OUR SPEAKERS TO THE DEAD INGESTED TO DO THEIR BUSINESS.

THE DRUGS THAT WERE IN YOUR TEA, MR. SNOW.

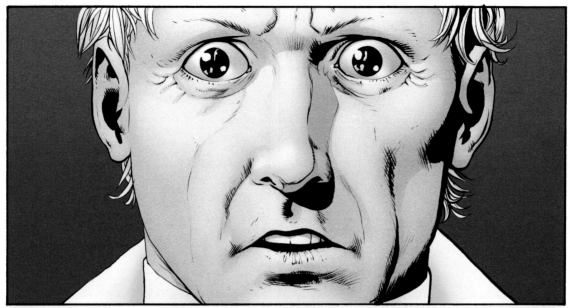

NO NEED TO PANIC. THE EFFECT WILL LAST ONLY FIVE MINUTES, AND YOU WILL HEAR MY VOICE THROUGHOUT.

I'M NOT SENDING YOU DOWN THERE ALONE.

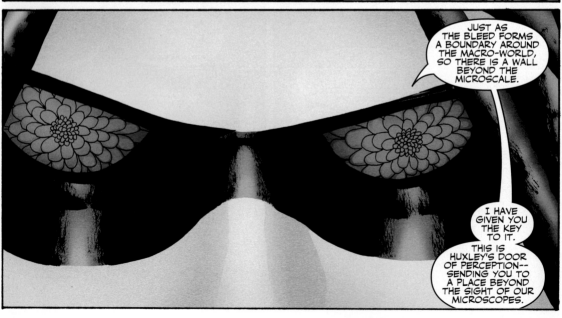

JUST AS THE BLEED FORMS A BOUNDARY AROUND THE MACRO-WORLD, SO THERE IS A WALL BEYOND THE MICROSCALE.

I HAVE GIVEN YOU THE KEY TO IT. THIS IS HUXLEY'S DOOR OF PERCEPTION-- SENDING YOU TO A PLACE BEYOND THE SIGHT OF OUR MICROSCOPES.

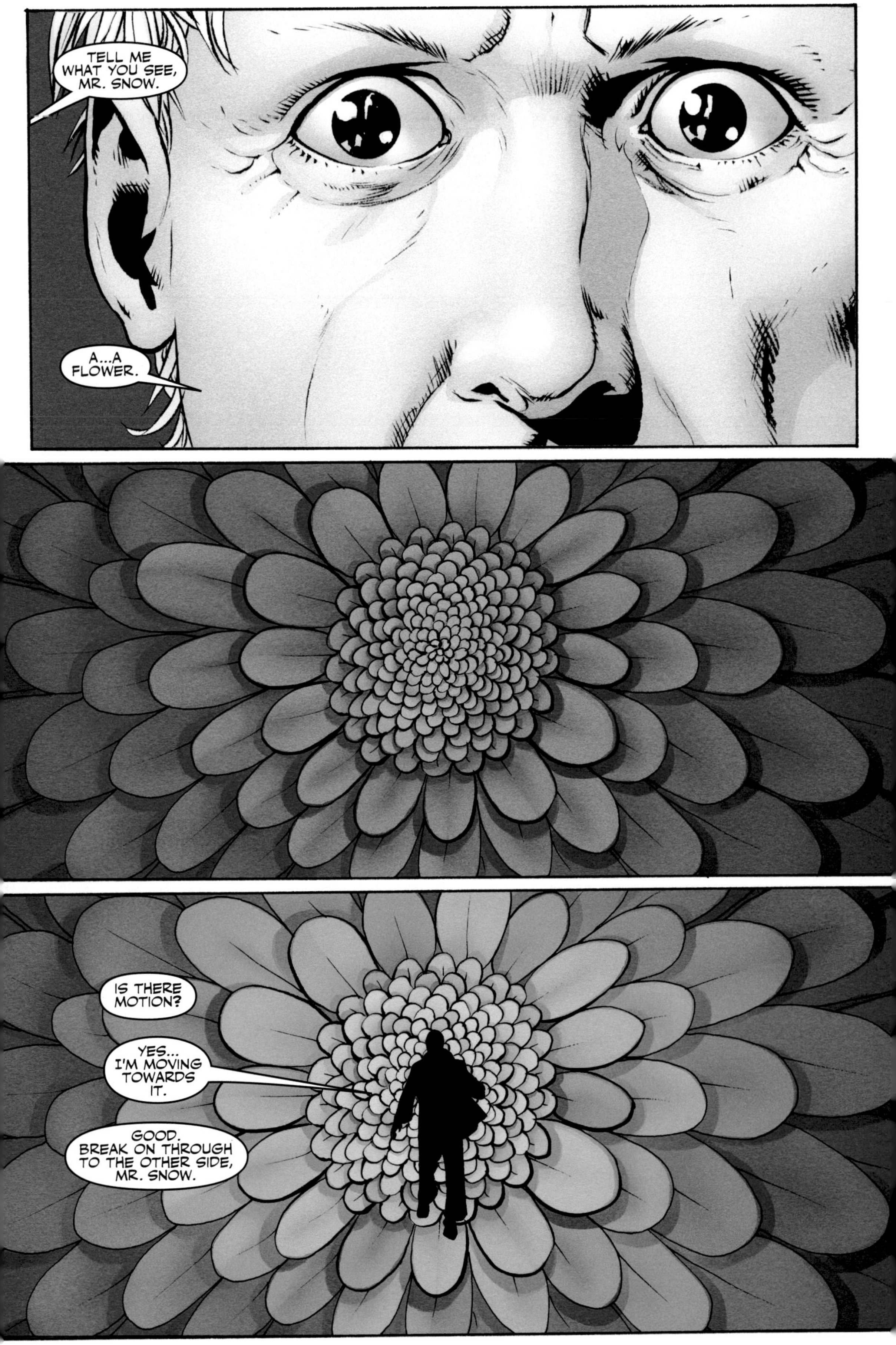
TELL ME WHAT YOU SEE, MR. SNOW.
A...A FLOWER.
IS THERE MOTION?
YES... I'M MOVING TOWARDS IT.
GOOD. BREAK ON THROUGH TO THE OTHER SIDE, MR. SNOW.

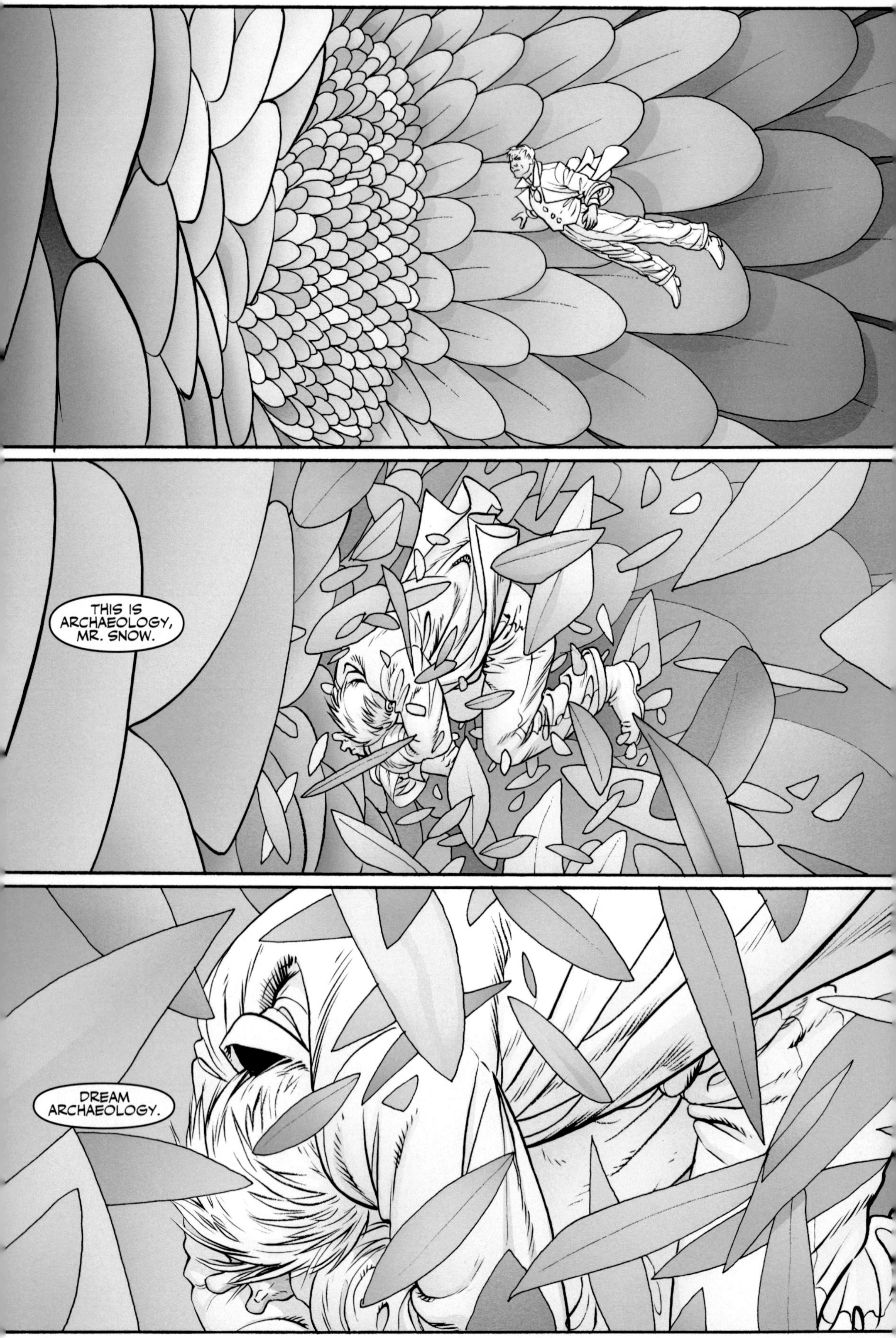
THIS IS ARCHAEOLOGY, MR. SNOW.
DREAM ARCHAEOLOGY.

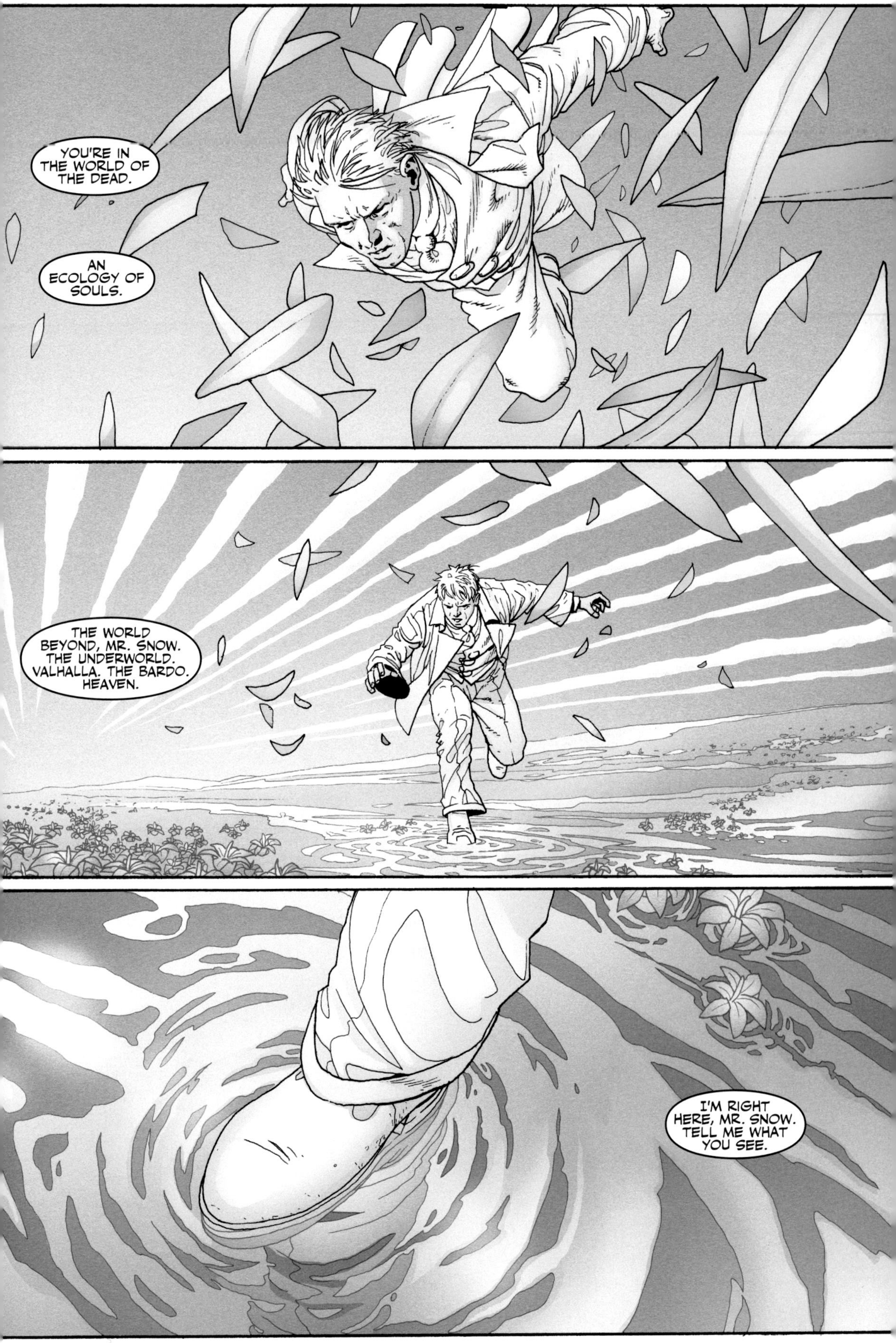
YOU'RE IN THE WORLD OF THE DEAD.
AN ECOLOGY OF SOULS.
THE WORLD BEYOND, MR. SNOW. THE UNDERWORLD. VALHALLA. THE BARDO. HEAVEN.
I'M RIGHT HERE, MR. SNOW. TELL ME WHAT YOU SEE.

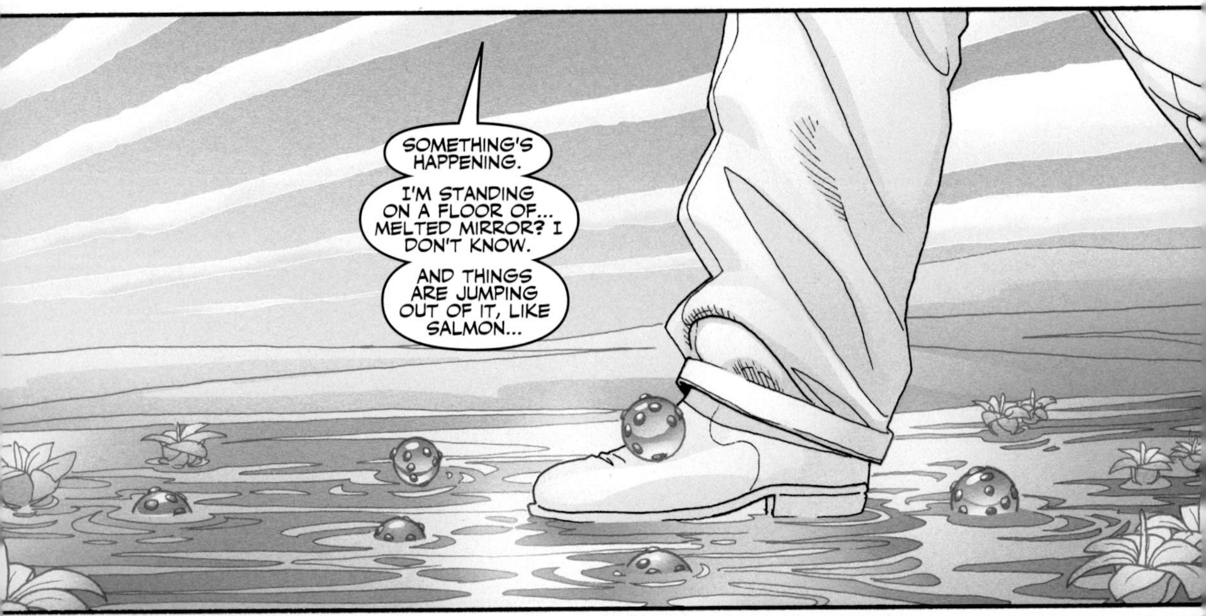
SOMETHING'S HAPPENING.
I'M STANDING ON A FLOOR OF... MELTED MIRROR? I DON'T KNOW.
AND THINGS ARE JUMPING OUT OF IT, LIKE SALMON...

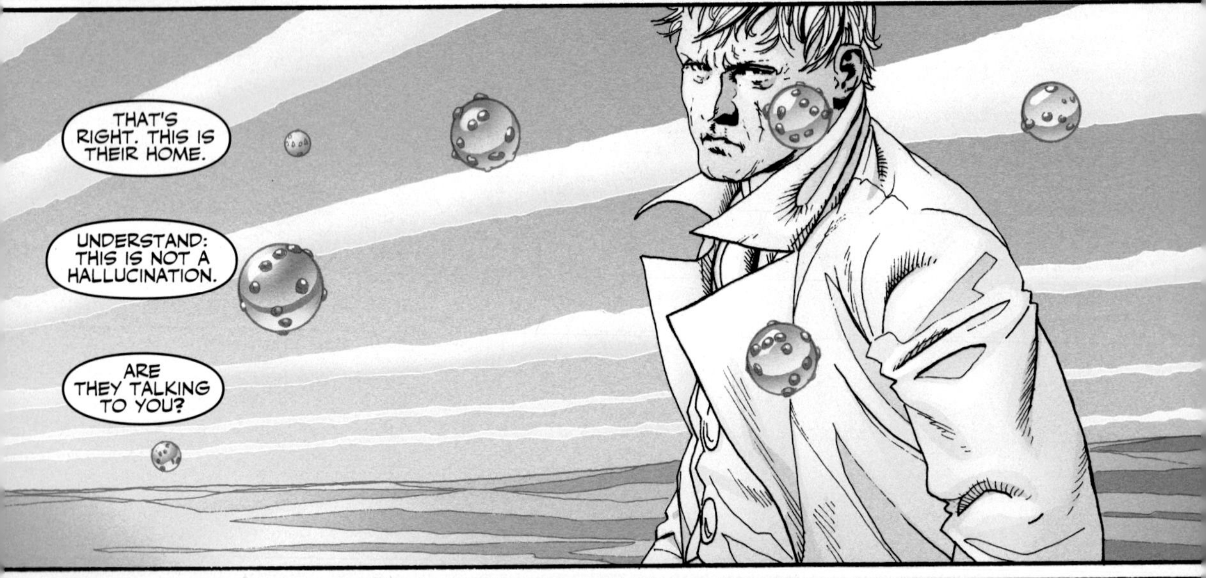
THAT'S RIGHT. THIS IS THEIR HOME.
UNDERSTAND: THIS IS NOT A HALLUCINATION.
ARE THEY TALKING TO YOU?

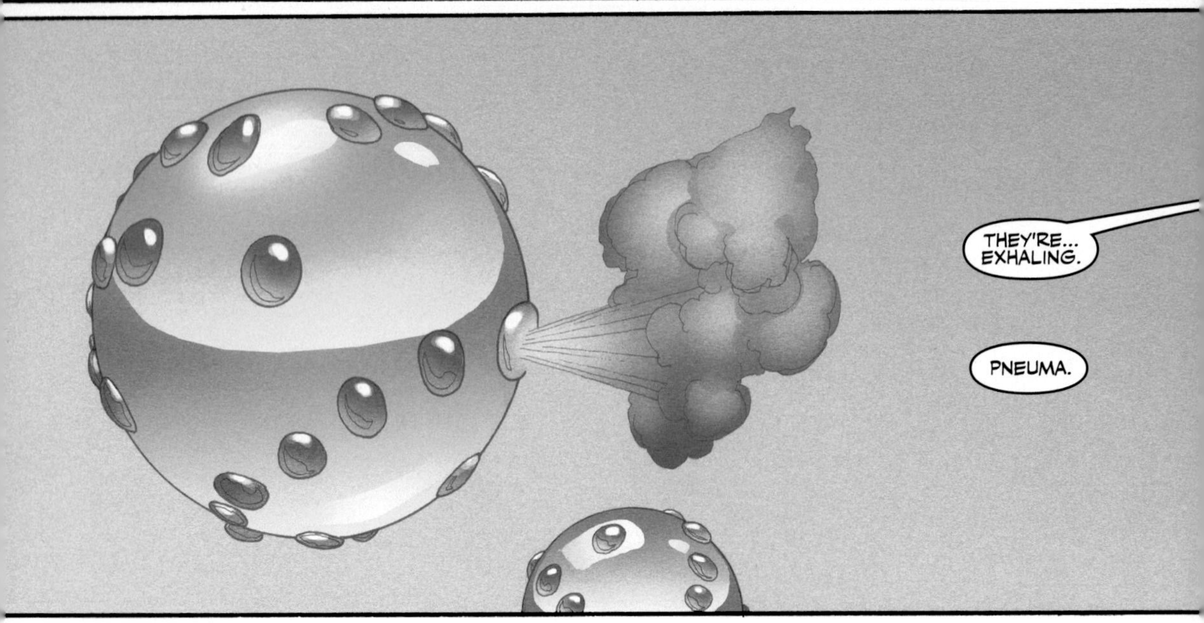
THEY'RE... EXHALING.
PNEUMA.

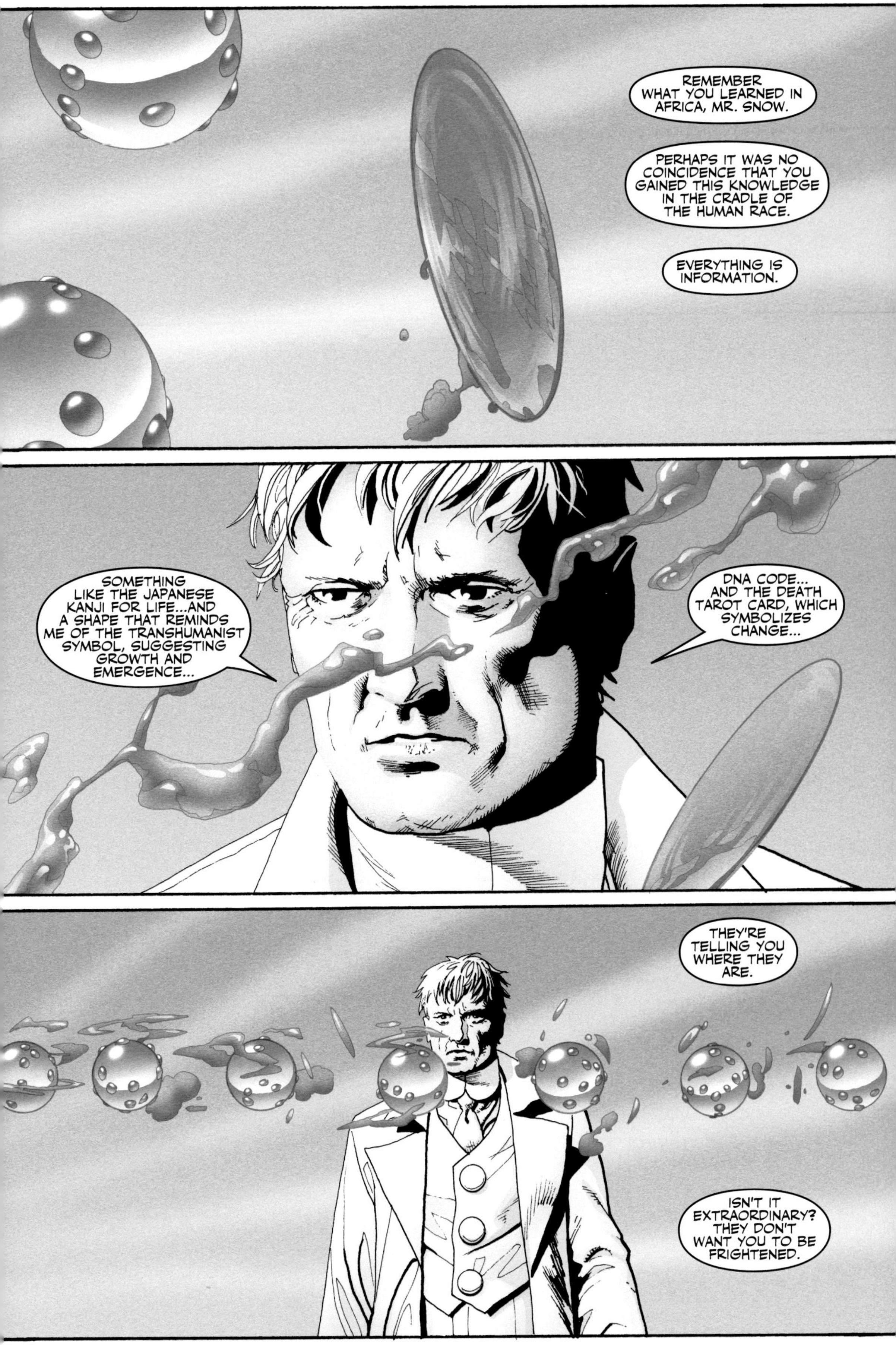
REMEMBER WHAT YOU LEARNED IN AFRICA, MR. SNOW.
PERHAPS IT WAS NO COINCIDENCE THAT YOU GAINED THIS KNOWLEDGE IN THE CRADLE OF THE HUMAN RACE.
EVERYTHING IS INFORMATION.
SOMETHING LIKE THE JAPANESE KANJI FOR LIFE...AND A SHAPE THAT REMINDS ME OF THE TRANSHUMANIST SYMBOL, SUGGESTING GROWTH AND EMERGENCE...
DNA CODE... AND THE DEATH TAROT CARD, WHICH SYMBOLIZES CHANGE...
THEY'RE TELLING YOU WHERE THEY ARE.
ISN'T IT EXTRAORDINARY? THEY DON'T WANT YOU TO BE FRIGHTENED.

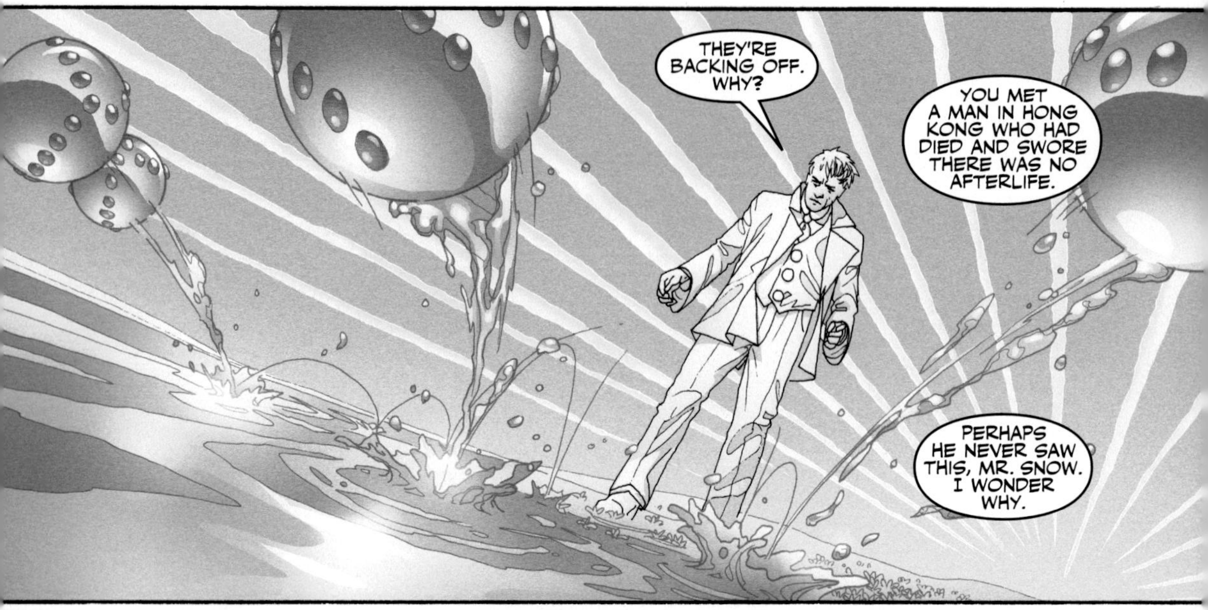
THEY'RE BACKING OFF. WHY?
YOU MET A MAN IN HONG KONG WHO HAD DIED AND SWORE THERE WAS NO AFTERLIFE.
PERHAPS HE NEVER SAW THIS, MR. SNOW. I WONDER WHY.

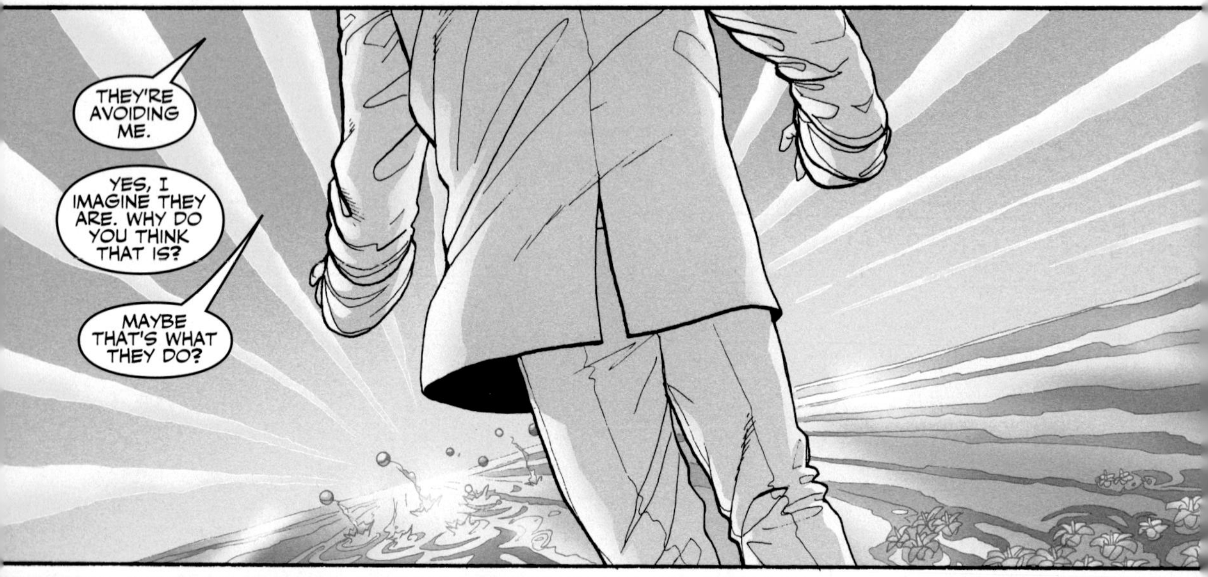
THEY'RE AVOIDING ME.
YES, I IMAGINE THEY ARE. WHY DO YOU THINK THAT IS?
MAYBE THAT'S WHAT THEY DO?

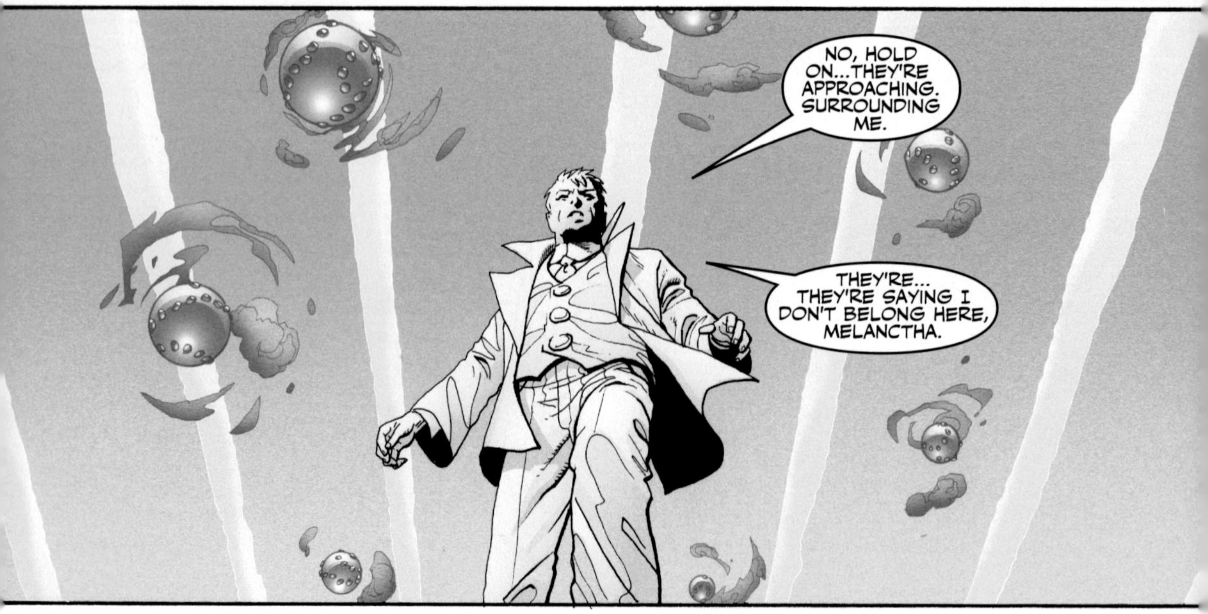
NO, HOLD ON...THEY'RE APPROACHING. SURROUNDING ME.
THEY'RE... THEY'RE SAYING I DON'T BELONG HERE, MELANCTHA.

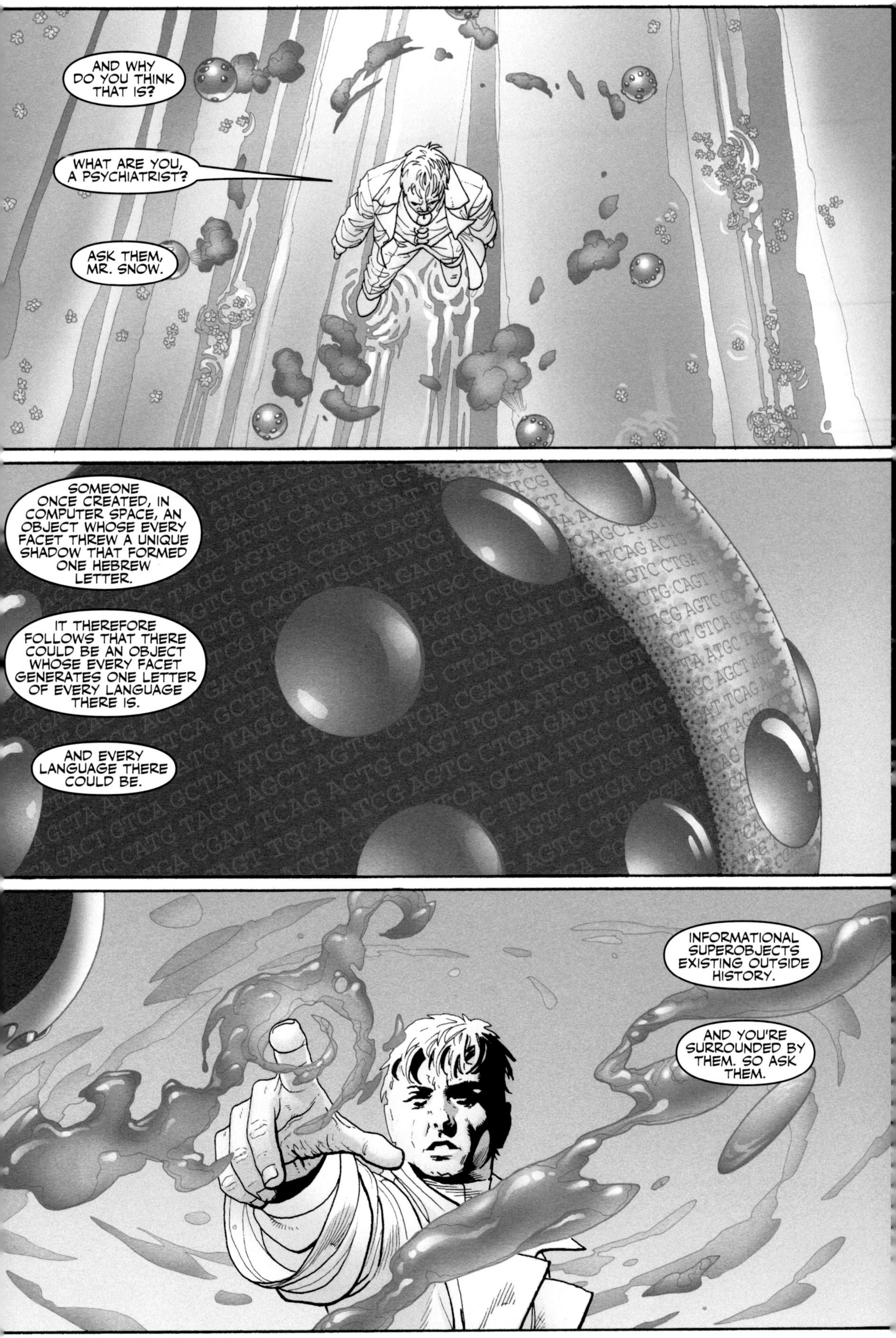
AND WHY DO YOU THINK THAT IS?
WHAT ARE YOU, A PSYCHIATRIST?
ASK THEM, MR. SNOW.
SOMEONE ONCE CREATED, IN COMPUTER SPACE, AN OBJECT WHOSE EVERY FACET THREW A UNIQUE SHADOW THAT FORMED ONE HEBREW LETTER.
IT THEREFORE FOLLOWS THAT THERE COULD BE AN OBJECT WHOSE EVERY FACET GENERATES ONE LETTER OF EVERY LANGUAGE THERE IS.
AND EVERY LANGUAGE THERE COULD BE.
INFORMATIONAL SUPEROBJECTS EXISTING OUTSIDE HISTORY.
AND YOU'RE SURROUNDED BY THEM. SO ASK THEM.

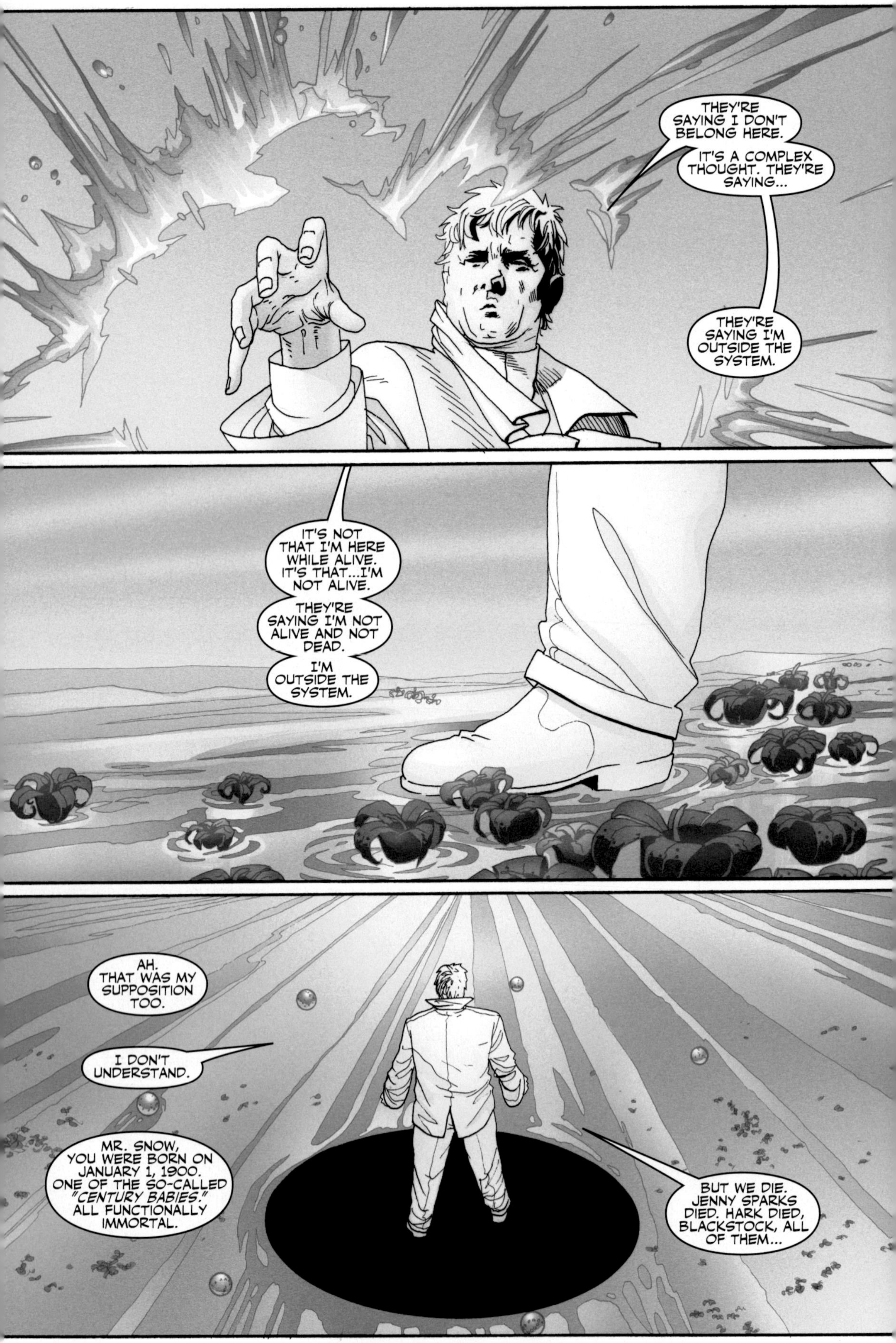
THEY'RE SAYING I DON'T BELONG HERE.
IT'S A COMPLEX THOUGHT. THEY'RE SAYING...
THEY'RE SAYING I'M OUTSIDE THE SYSTEM.
IT'S NOT THAT I'M HERE WHILE ALIVE. IT'S THAT...I'M NOT ALIVE.
THEY'RE SAYING I'M NOT ALIVE AND NOT DEAD.
I'M OUTSIDE THE SYSTEM.
AH. THAT WAS MY SUPPOSITION TOO.
I DON'T UNDERSTAND.
MR. SNOW, YOU WERE BORN ON JANUARY 1, 1900. ONE OF THE SO-CALLED "CENTURY BABIES." ALL FUNCTIONALLY IMMORTAL.
BUT WE DIE. JENNY SPARKS DIED. HARK DIED, BLACKSTOCK, ALL OF THEM...

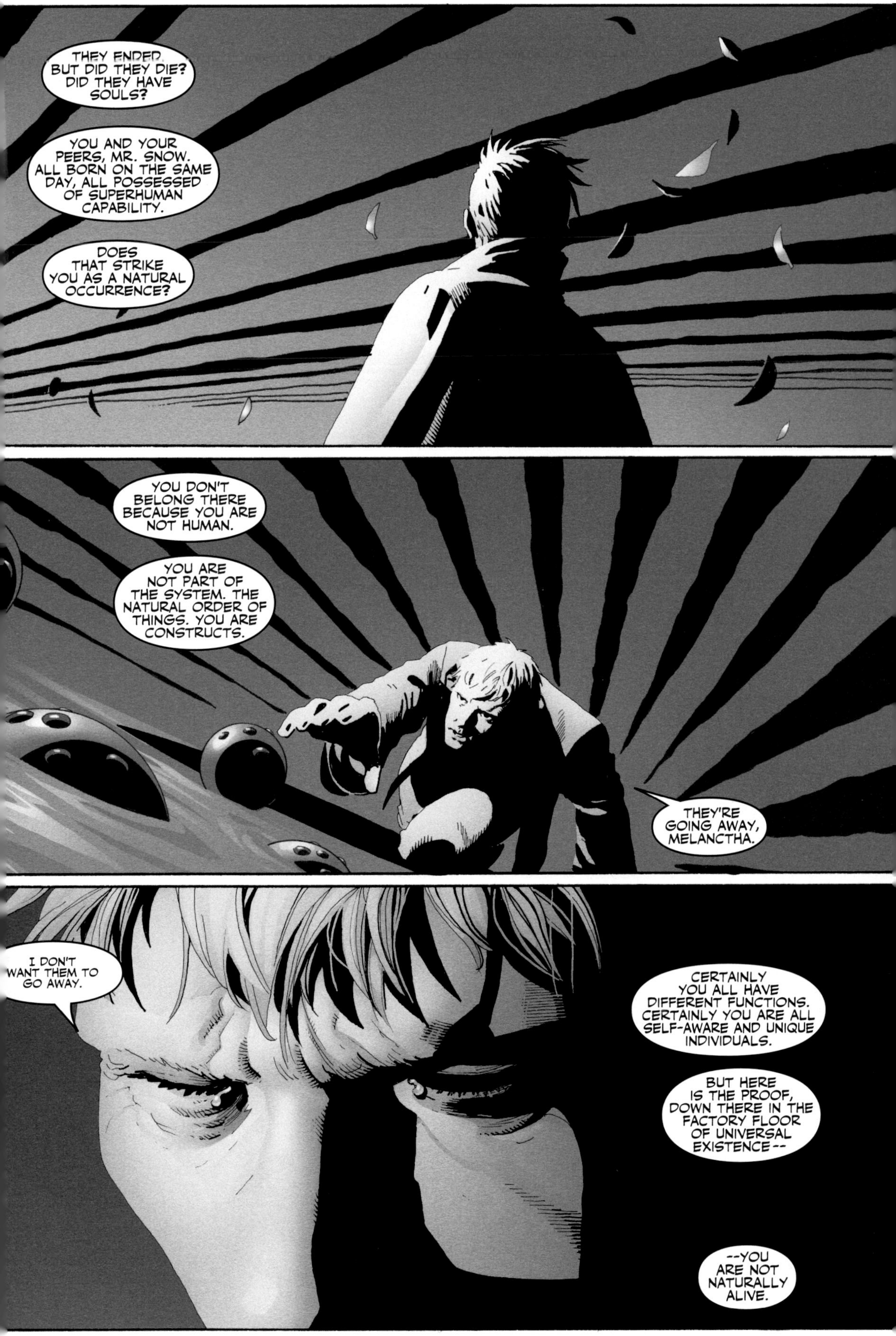
THEY ENDED. BUT DID THEY DIE? DID THEY HAVE SOULS?
YOU AND YOUR PEERS, MR. SNOW. ALL BORN ON THE SAME DAY, ALL POSSESSED OF SUPERHUMAN CAPABILITY.
DOES THAT STRIKE YOU AS A NATURAL OCCURRENCE?
YOU DON'T BELONG THERE BECAUSE YOU ARE NOT HUMAN.
YOU ARE NOT PART OF THE SYSTEM. THE NATURAL ORDER OF THINGS. YOU ARE CONSTRUCTS.
THEY'RE GOING AWAY, MELANCTHA.
I DON'T WANT THEM TO GO AWAY.
CERTAINLY YOU ALL HAVE DIFFERENT FUNCTIONS. CERTAINLY YOU ARE ALL SELF-AWARE AND UNIQUE INDIVIDUALS.
BUT HERE IS THE PROOF, DOWN THERE IN THE FACTORY FLOOR OF UNIVERSAL EXISTENCE--
--YOU ARE NOT NATURALLY ALIVE.

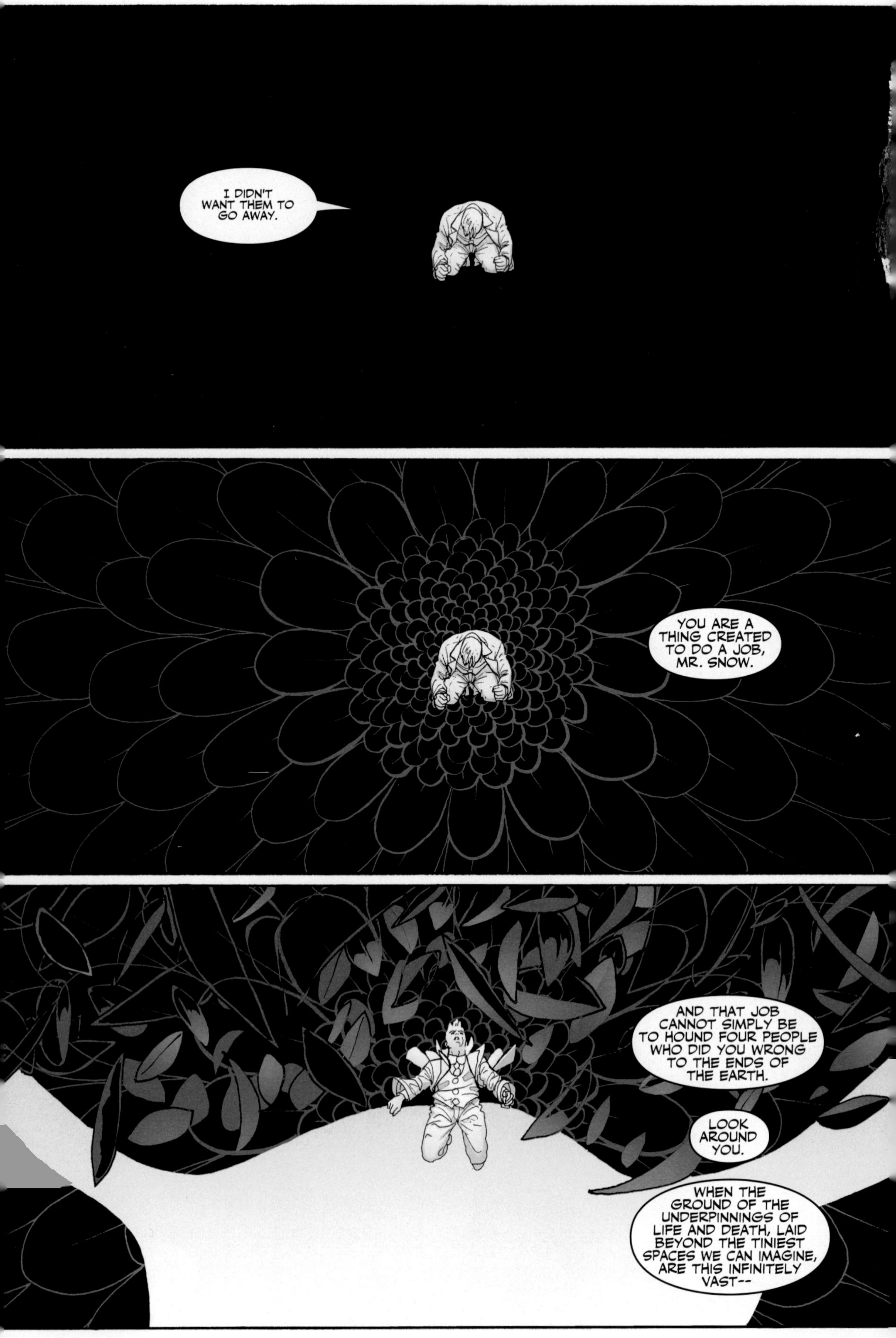
I DIDN'T WANT THEM TO GO AWAY.
YOU ARE A THING CREATED TO DO A JOB, MR. SNOW.
AND THAT JOB CANNOT SIMPLY BE TO HOUND FOUR PEOPLE WHO DID YOU WRONG TO THE ENDS OF THE EARTH.
LOOK AROUND YOU.
WHEN THE GROUND OF THE UNDERPINNINGS OF LIFE AND DEATH, LAID BEYOND THE TINIEST SPACES WE CAN IMAGINE, ARE THIS INFINITELY VAST--

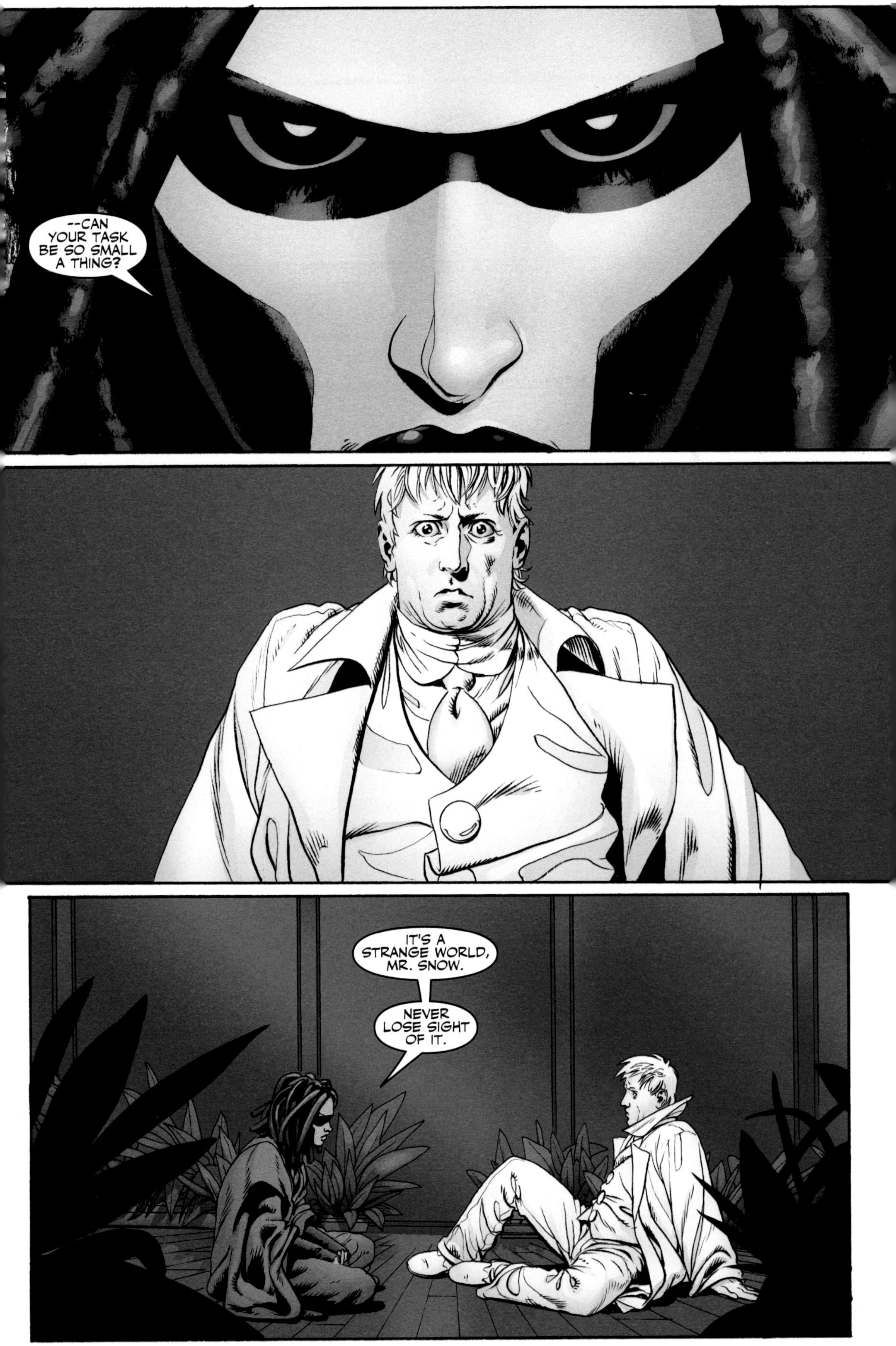
--CAN YOUR TASK BE SO SMALL A THING?
IT'S A STRANGE WORLD, MR. SNOW.
NEVER LOSE SIGHT OF IT.

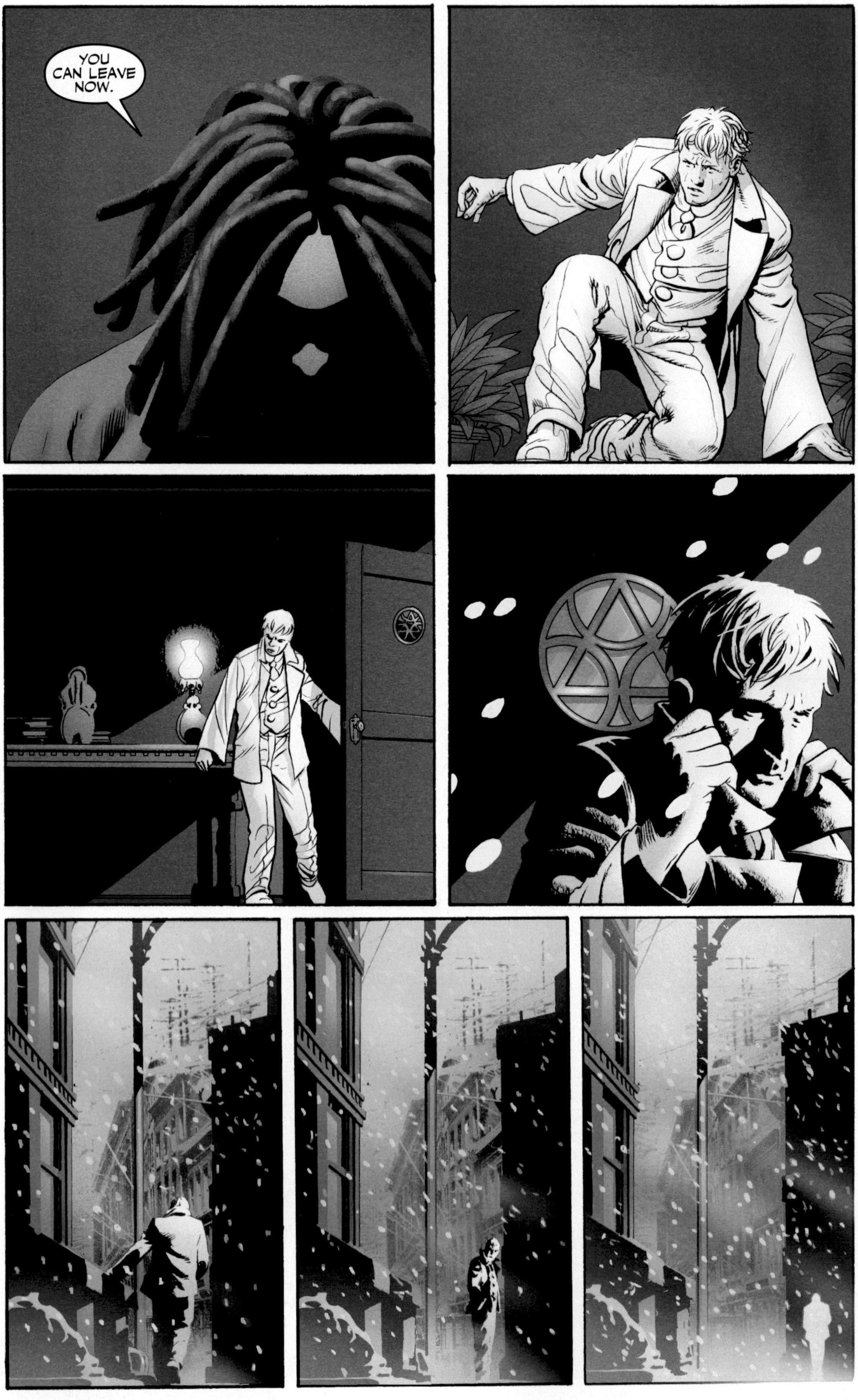
YOU CAN LEAVE NOW.

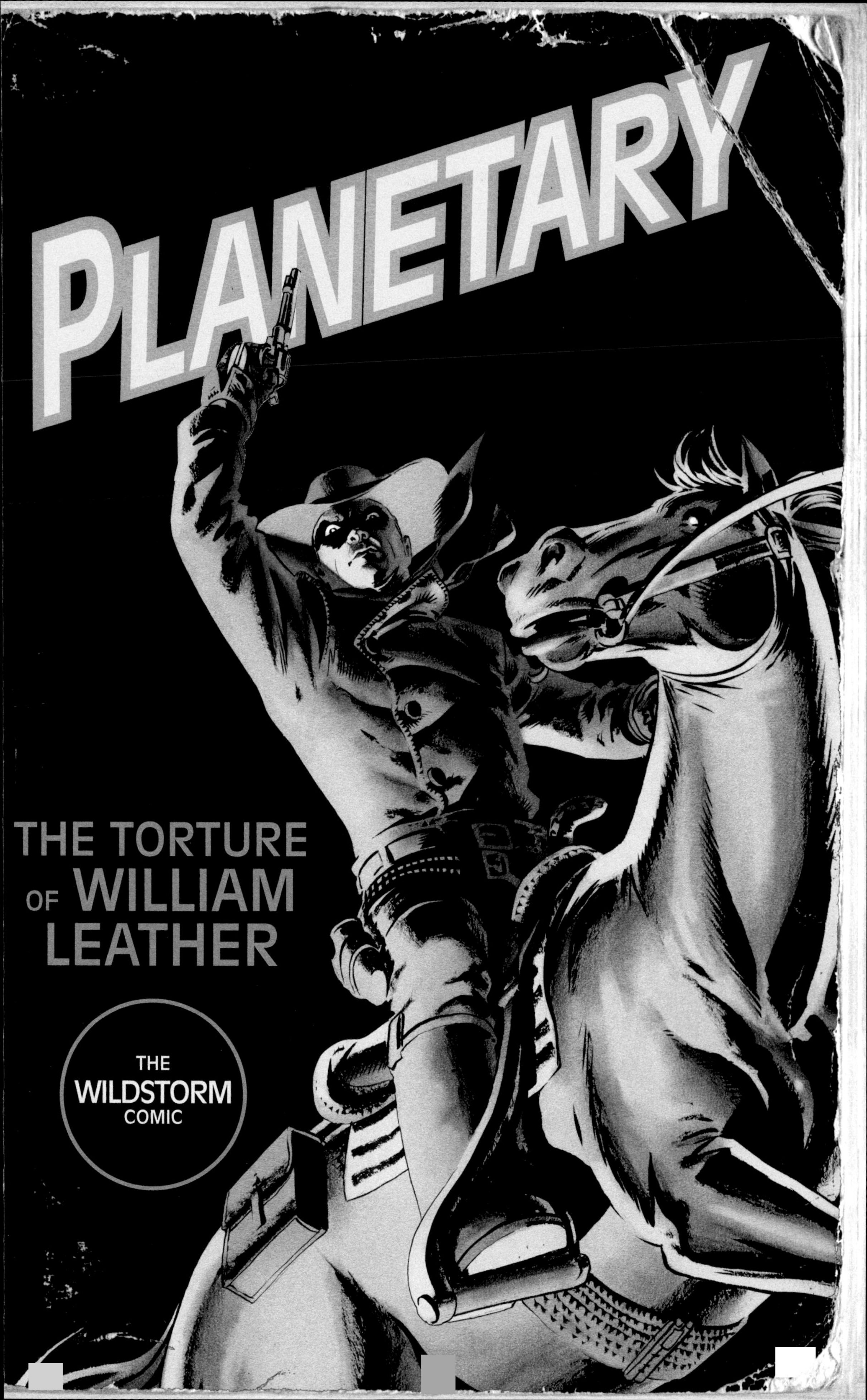

PLANETARY
THE TORTURE OF WILLIAM LEATHER
THE WILDSTORM COMIC

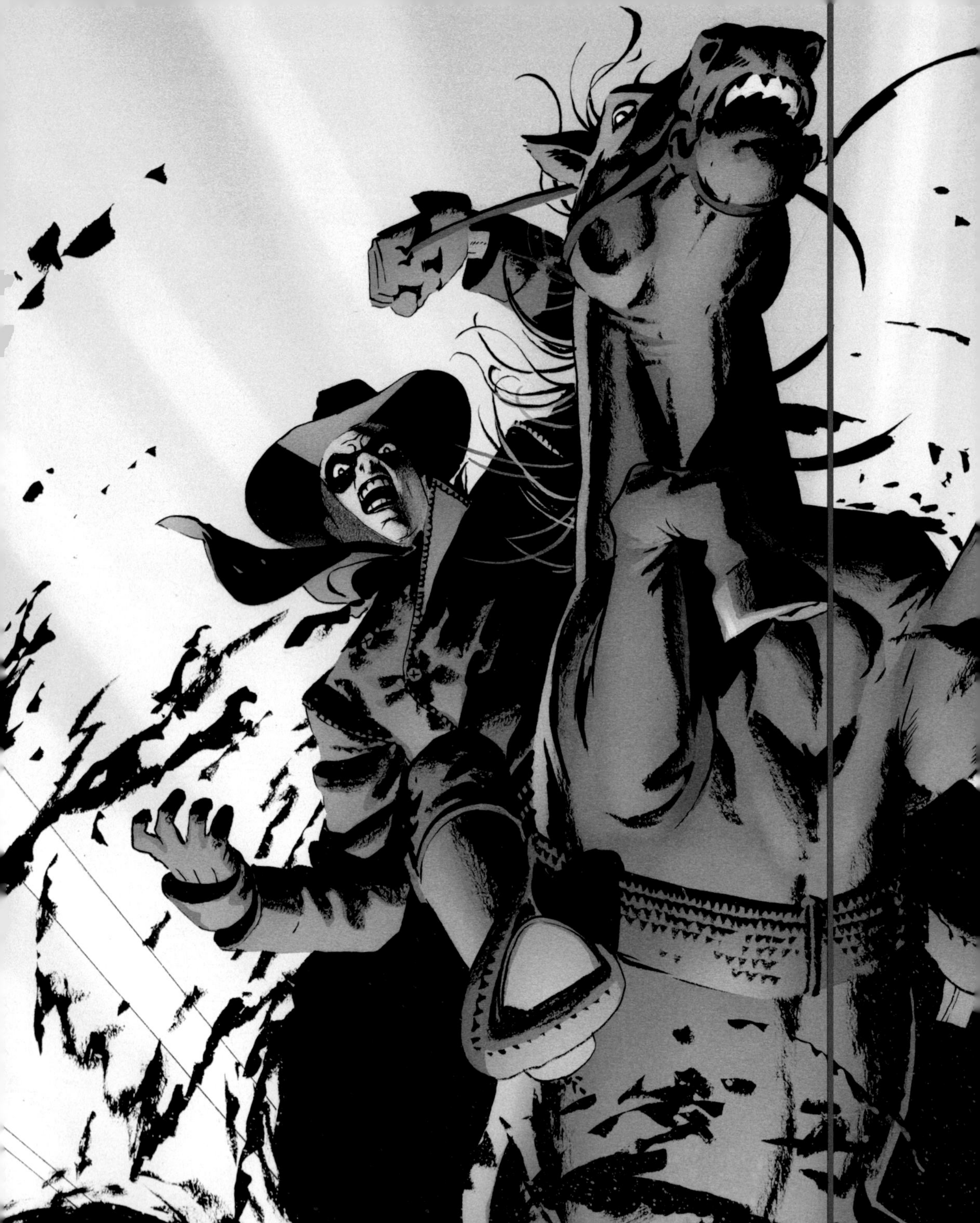

THE TORTURE OF WILLIAM LEATHER

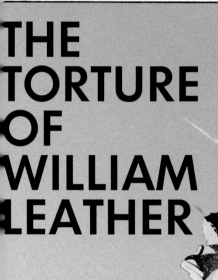

I'M WILLIAM LEATHER.

JOHN LEATHER WAS MY GRANDFATHER.

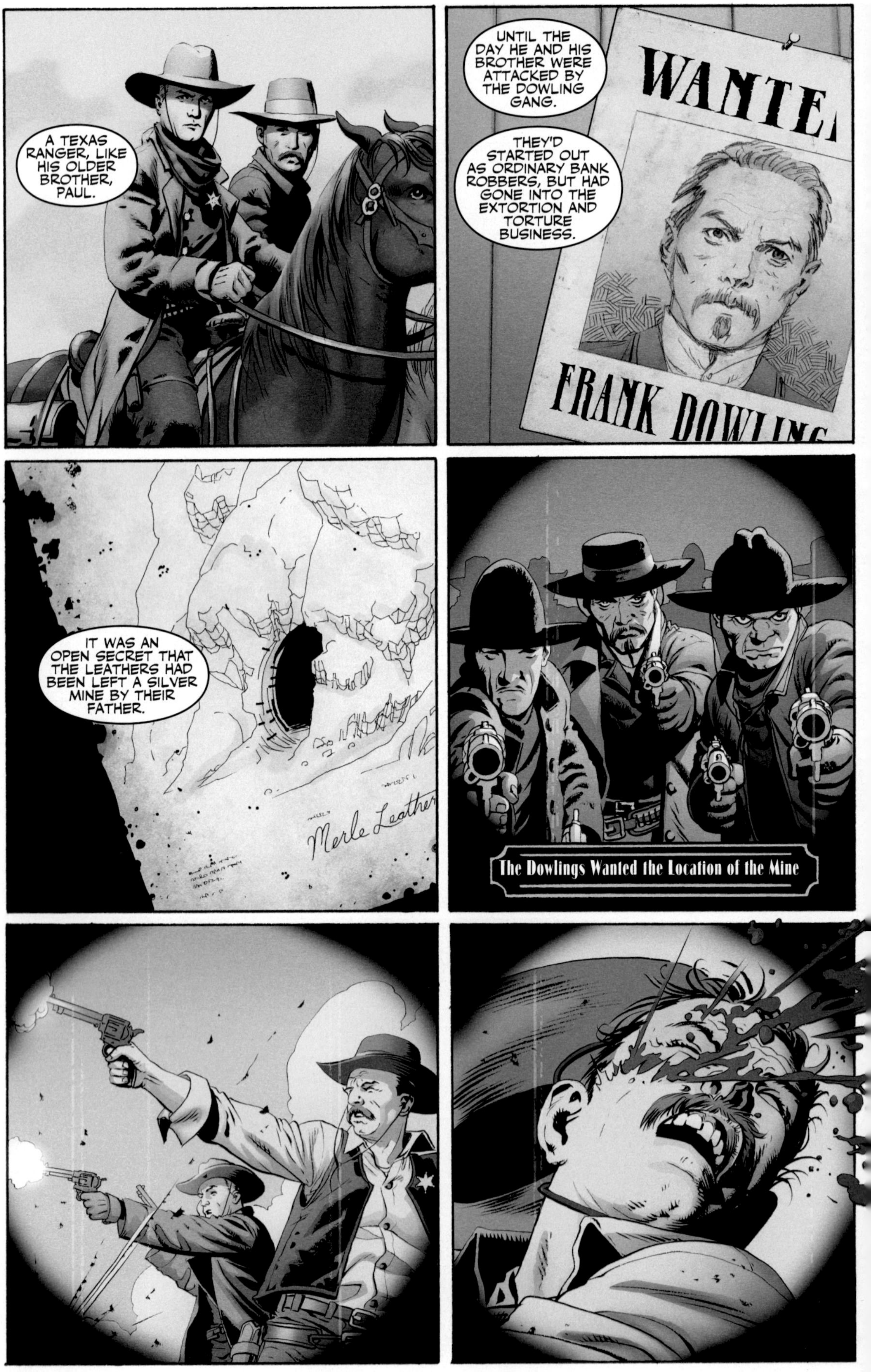
A TEXAS RANGER, LIKE HIS OLDER BROTHER, PAUL.
UNTIL THE DAY HE AND HIS BROTHER WERE ATTACKED BY THE DOWLING GANG.
WANTE
FRANK DOWLIN
THEY'D STARTED OUT AS ORDINARY BANK ROBBERS, BUT HAD GONE INTO THE EXTORTION AND TORTURE BUSINESS.
IT WAS AN OPEN SECRET THAT THE LEATHERS HAD BEEN LEFT A SILVER MINE BY THEIR FATHER.
Merle Leather
The Dowlings Wanted the Location of the Mine

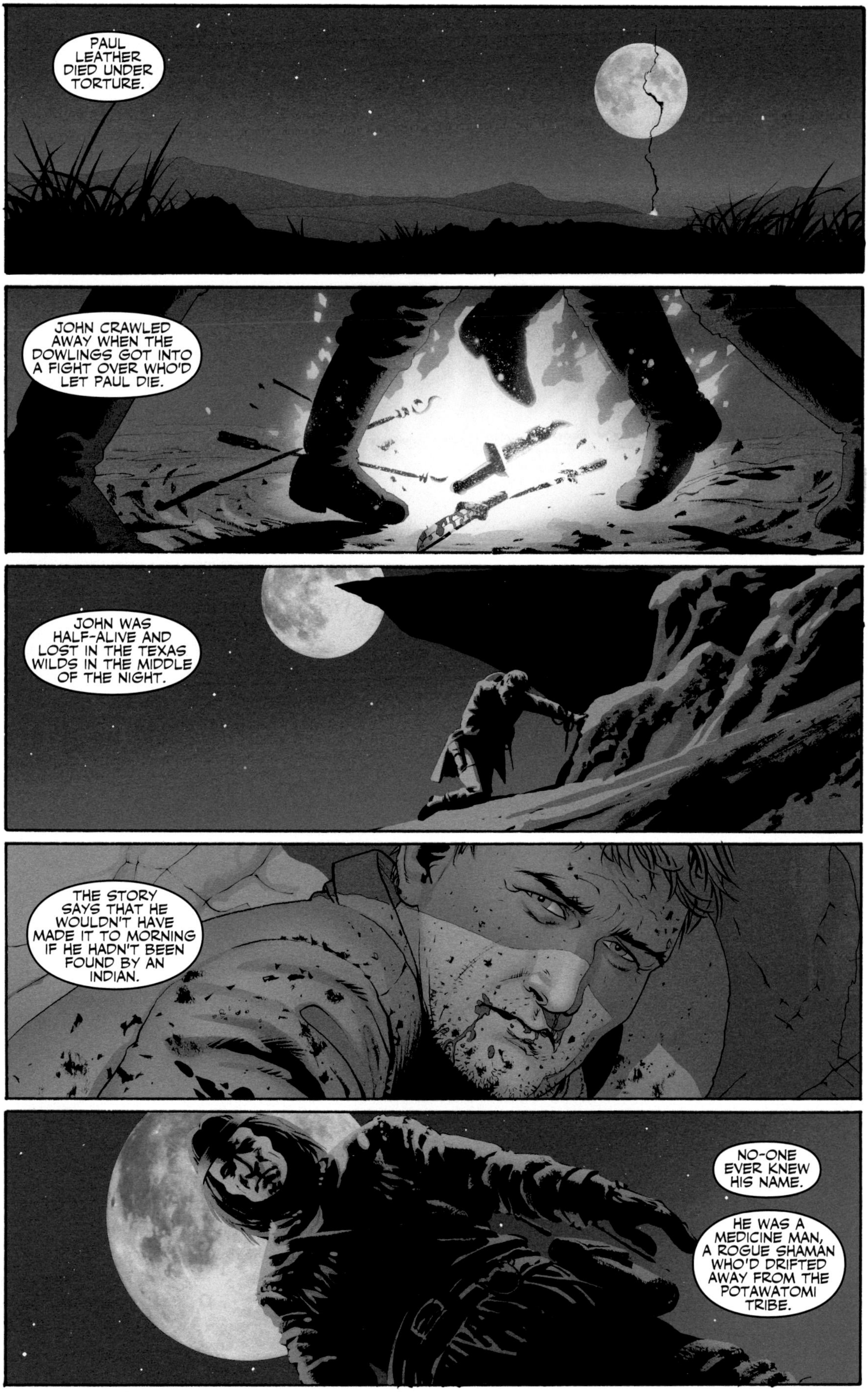
PAUL LEATHER DIED UNDER TORTURE.
JOHN CRAWLED AWAY WHEN THE DOWLINGS GOT INTO A FIGHT OVER WHO'D LET PAUL DIE.
JOHN WAS HALF-ALIVE AND LOST IN THE TEXAS WILDS IN THE MIDDLE OF THE NIGHT.
THE STORY SAYS THAT HE WOULDN'T HAVE MADE IT TO MORNING IF HE HADN'T BEEN FOUND BY AN INDIAN.
NO-ONE EVER KNEW HIS NAME.
HE WAS A MEDICINE MAN, A ROGUE SHAMAN WHO'D DRIFTED AWAY FROM THE POTAWATOMI TRIBE.

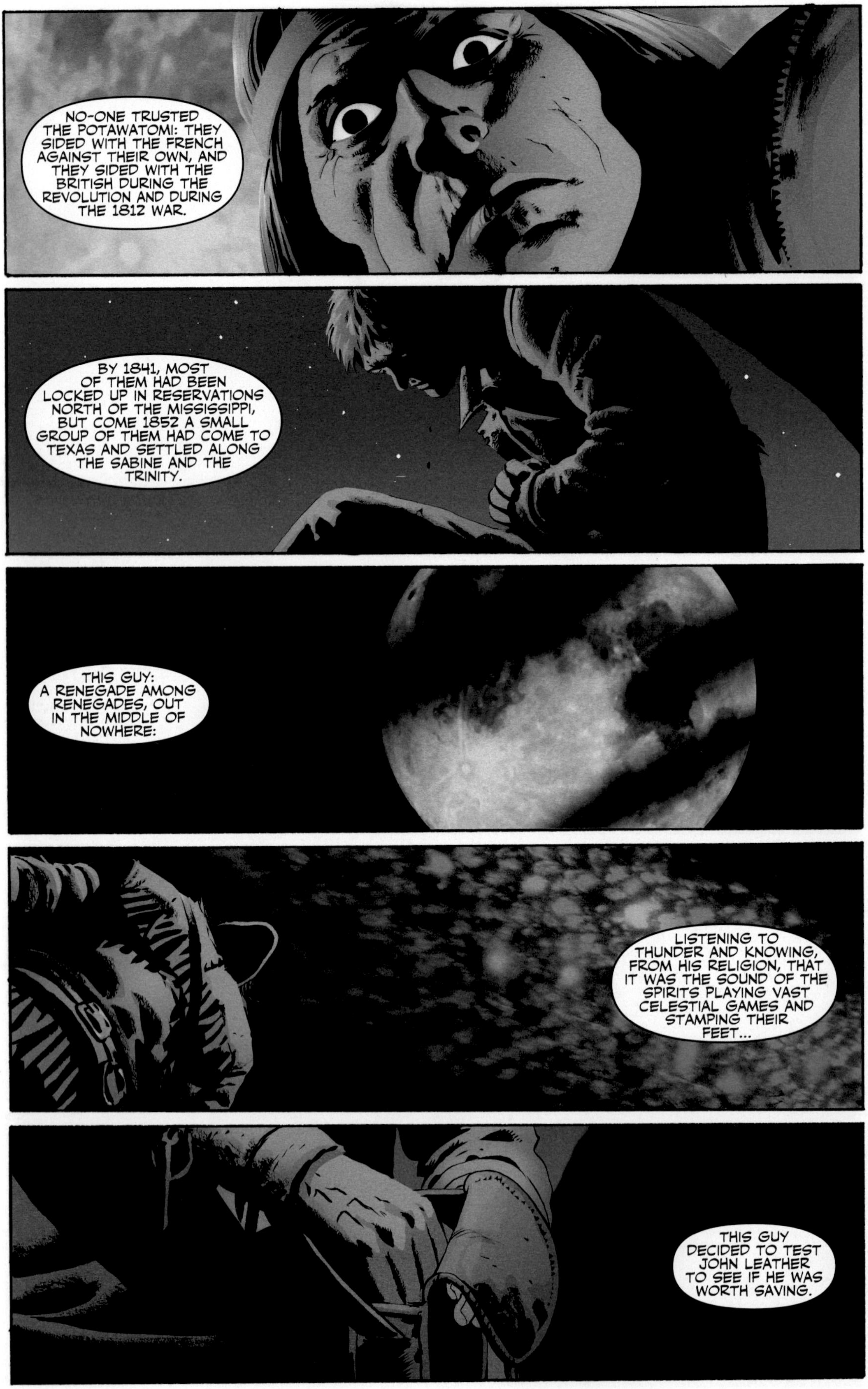
NO-ONE TRUSTED THE POTAWATOMI: THEY SIDED WITH THE FRENCH AGAINST THEIR OWN, AND THEY SIDED WITH THE BRITISH DURING THE REVOLUTION AND DURING THE 1812 WAR.
BY 1841, MOST OF THEM HAD BEEN LOCKED UP IN RESERVATIONS NORTH OF THE MISSISSIPPI, BUT COME 1852 A SMALL GROUP OF THEM HAD COME TO TEXAS AND SETTLED ALONG THE SABINE AND THE TRINITY.
THIS GUY: A RENEGADE AMONG RENEGADES, OUT IN THE MIDDLE OF NOWHERE:
LISTENING TO THUNDER AND KNOWING, FROM HIS RELIGION, THAT IT WAS THE SOUND OF THE SPIRITS PLAYING VAST CELESTIAL GAMES AND STAMPING THEIR FEET...
THIS GUY DECIDED TO TEST JOHN LEATHER TO SEE IF HE WAS WORTH SAVING.

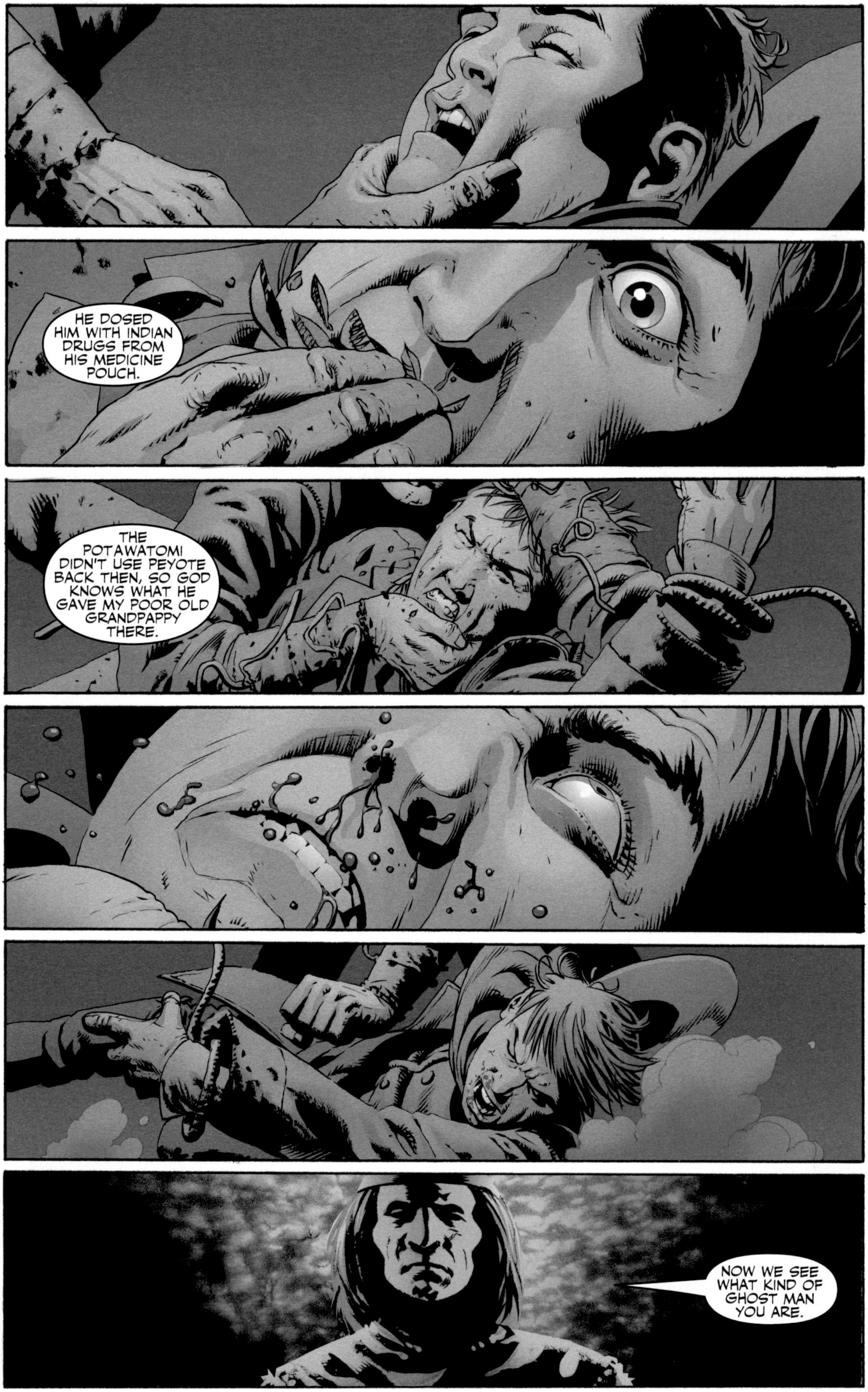
HE DOSED HIM WITH INDIAN DRUGS FROM HIS MEDICINE POUCH.
THE POTAWATOMI DIDN'T USE PEYOTE BACK THEN, SO GOD KNOWS WHAT HE GAVE MY POOR OLD GRANDPAPPY THERE.
NOW WE SEE WHAT KIND OF GHOST MAN YOU ARE.

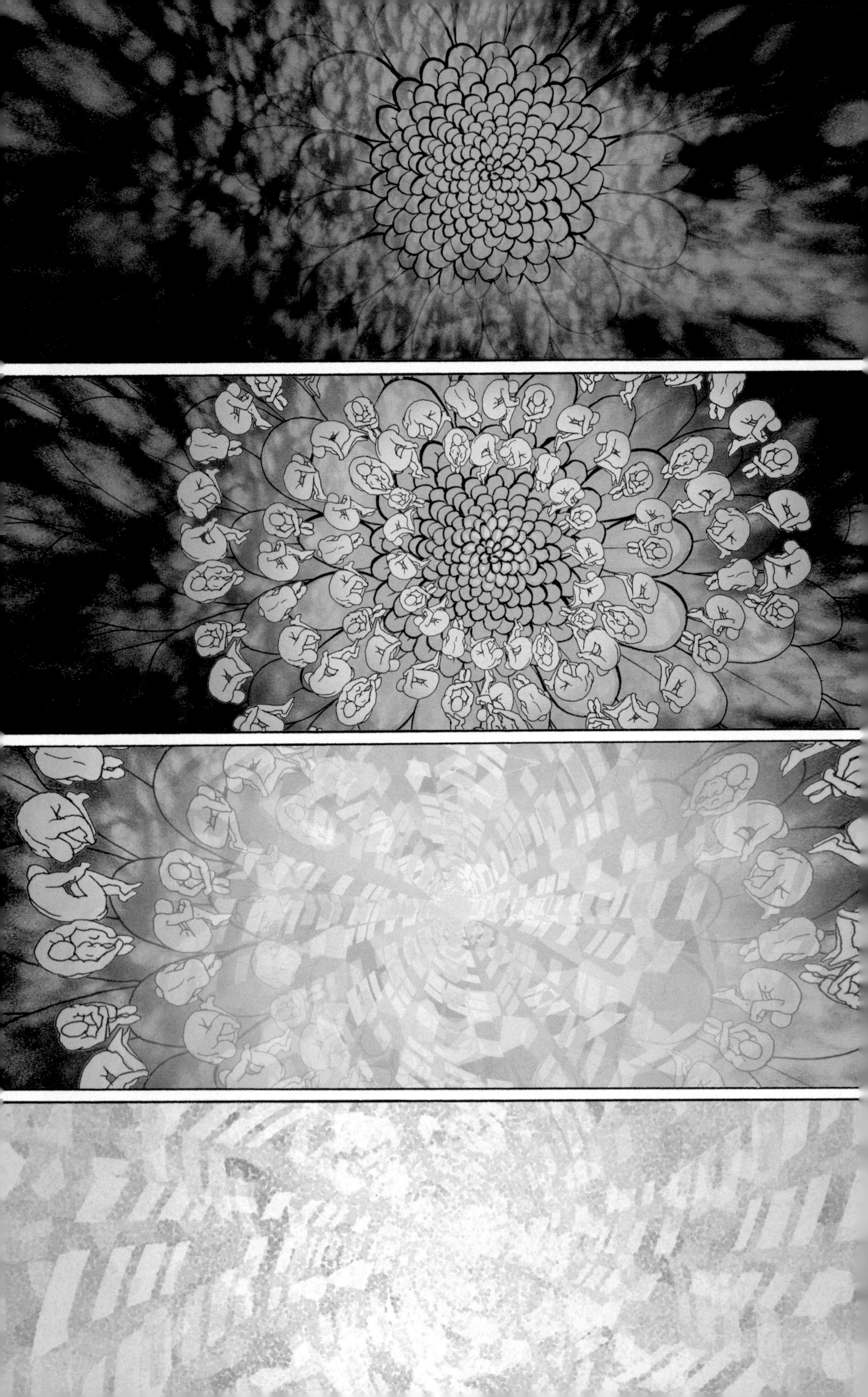

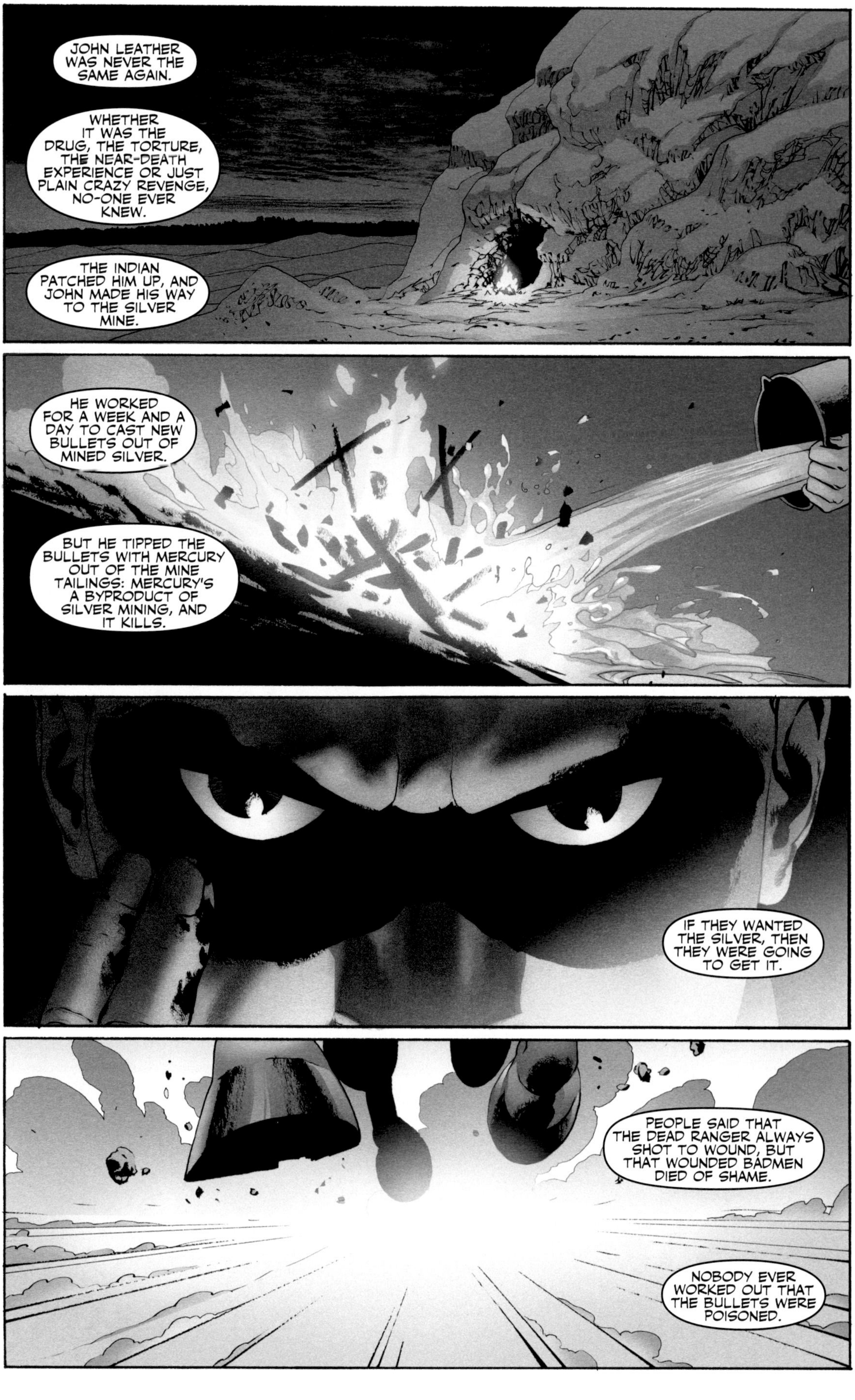
JOHN LEATHER WAS NEVER THE SAME AGAIN.
WHETHER IT WAS THE DRUG, THE TORTURE, THE NEAR-DEATH EXPERIENCE OR JUST PLAIN CRAZY REVENGE, NO-ONE EVER KNEW.
THE INDIAN PATCHED HIM UP, AND JOHN MADE HIS WAY TO THE SILVER MINE.
HE WORKED FOR A WEEK AND A DAY TO CAST NEW BULLETS OUT OF MINED SILVER.
BUT HE TIPPED THE BULLETS WITH MERCURY OUT OF THE MINE TAILINGS: MERCURY'S A BYPRODUCT OF SILVER MINING, AND IT KILLS.
IF THEY WANTED THE SILVER, THEN THEY WERE GOING TO GET IT.
PEOPLE SAID THAT THE DEAD RANGER ALWAYS SHOT TO WOUND, BUT THAT WOUNDED BADMEN DIED OF SHAME.
NOBODY EVER WORKED OUT THAT THE BULLETS WERE POISONED.

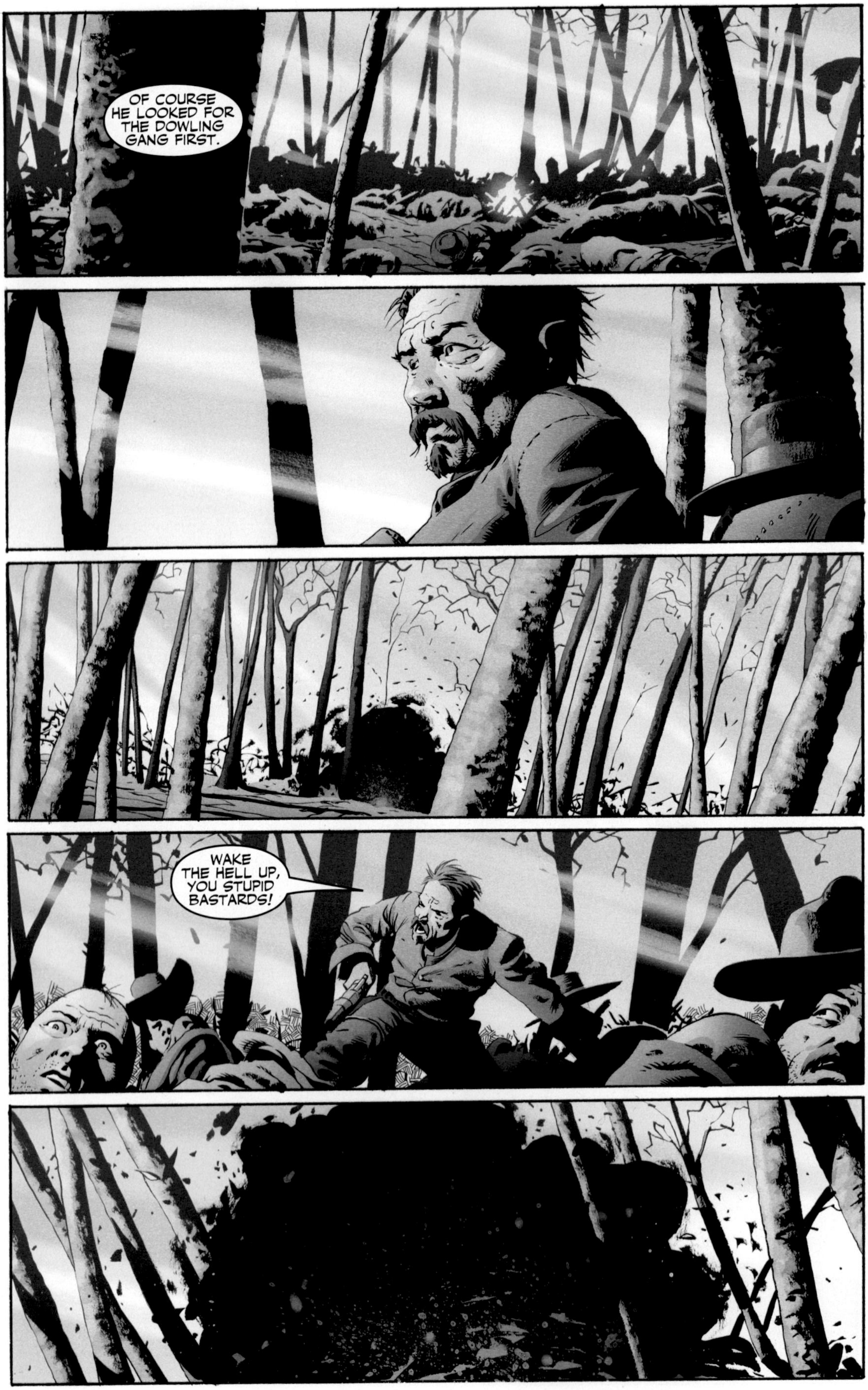
OF COURSE HE LOOKED FOR THE DOWLING GANG FIRST.
WAKE THE HELL UP, YOU STUPID BASTARDS!

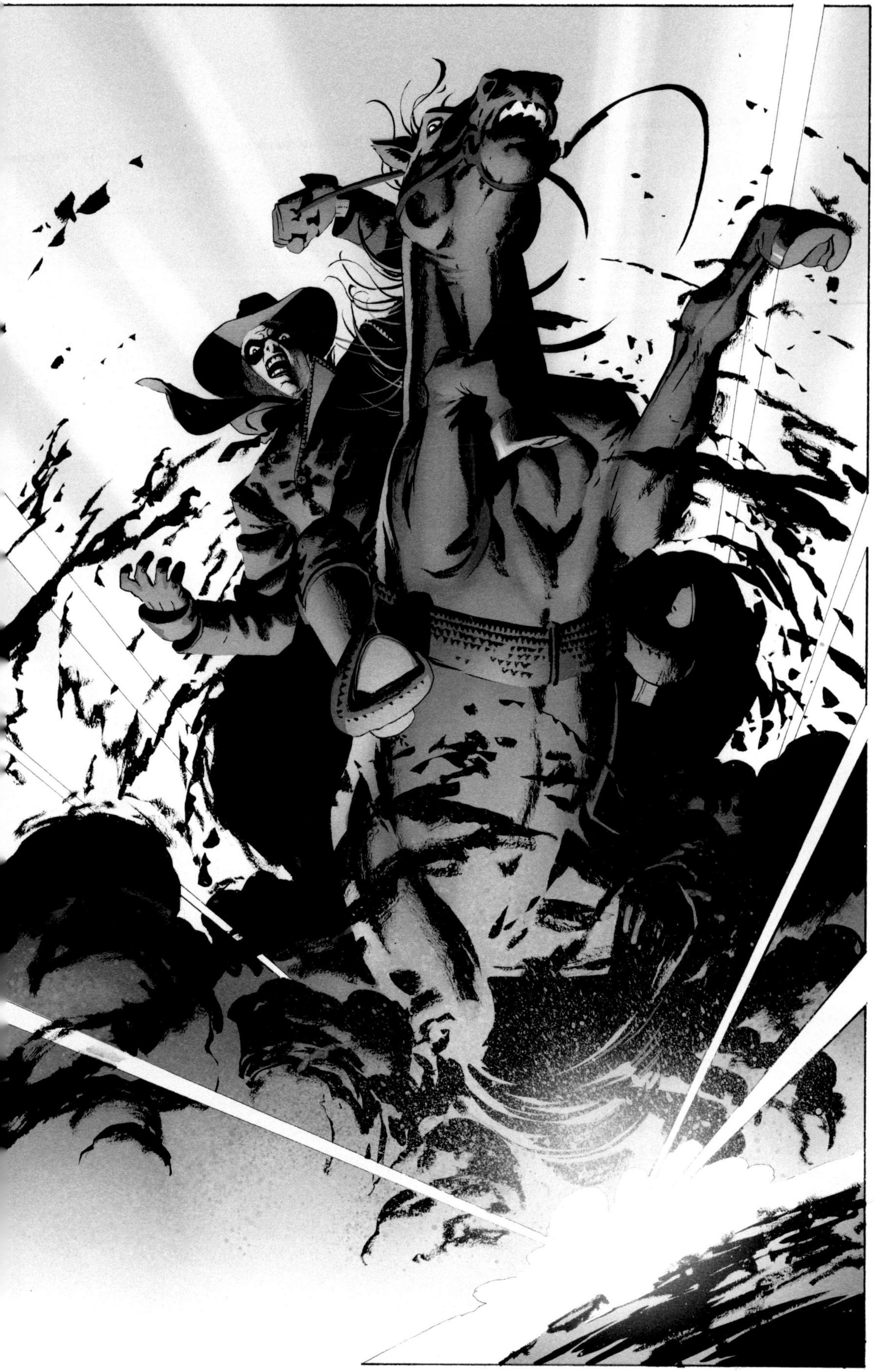

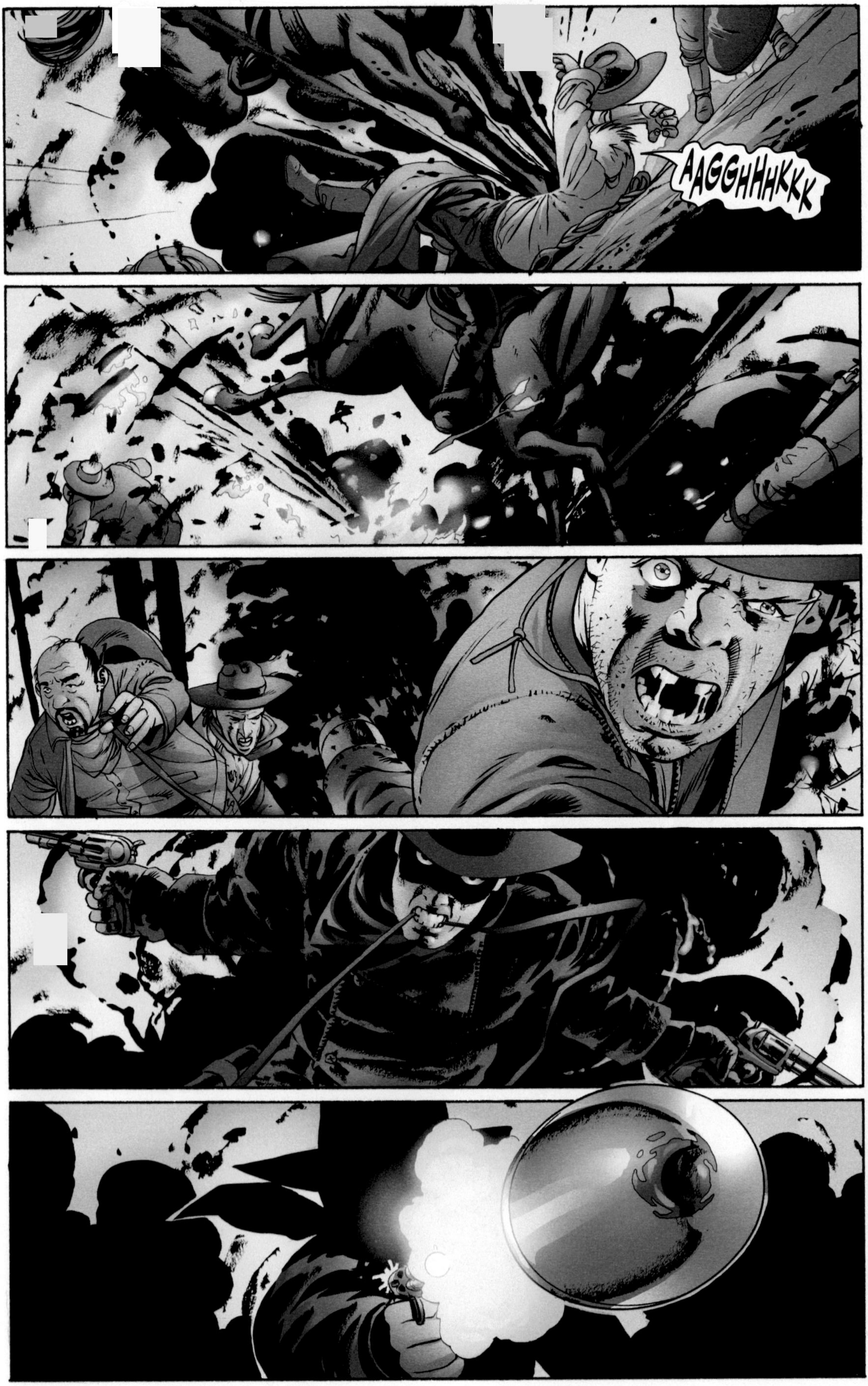
AAGGHHHKKK

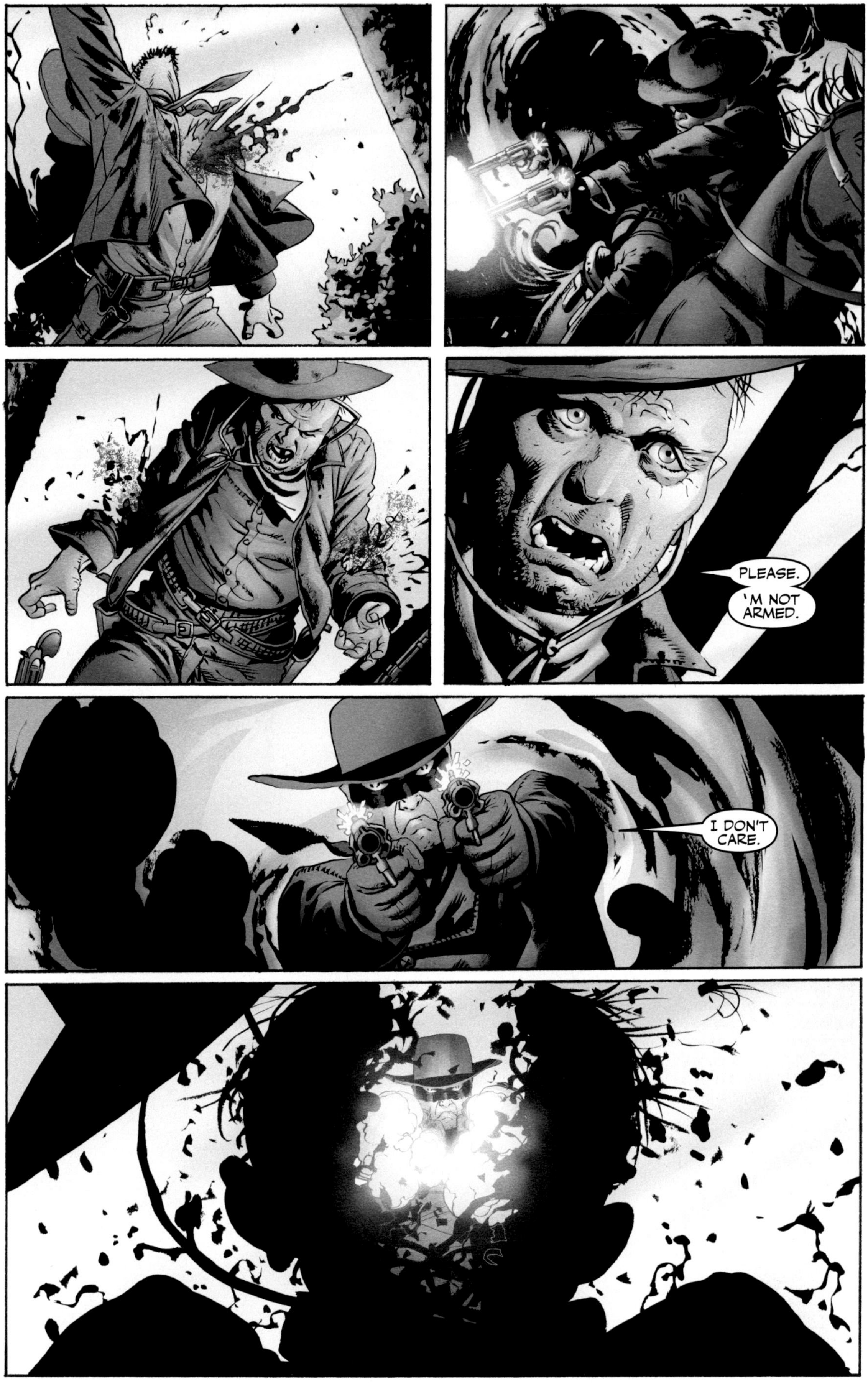
PLEASE.
'M NOT ARMED.
I DON'T CARE.

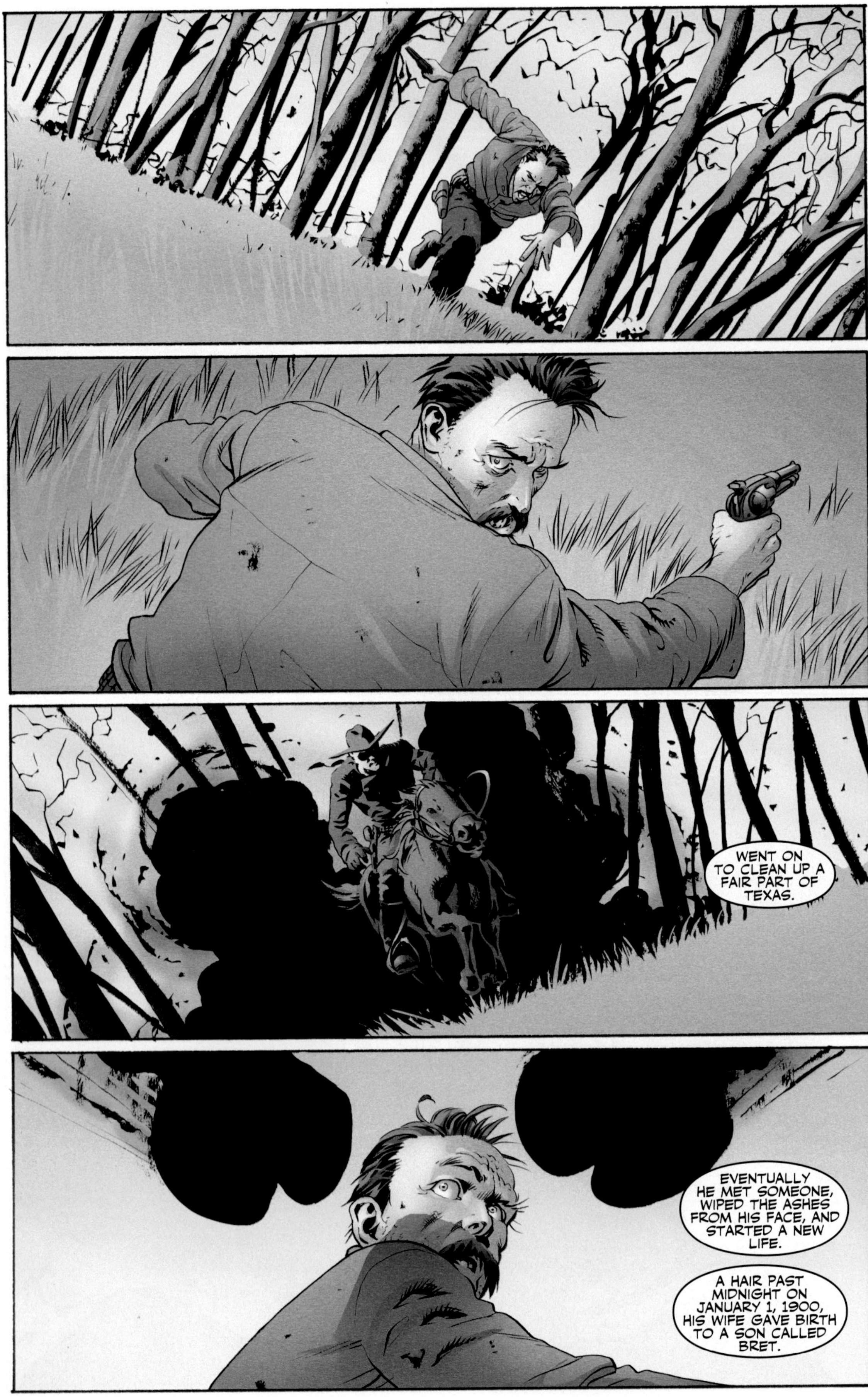
WENT ON TO CLEAN UP A FAIR PART OF TEXAS.
EVENTUALLY HE MET SOMEONE, WIPED THE ASHES FROM HIS FACE, AND STARTED A NEW LIFE.
A HAIR PAST MIDNIGHT ON JANUARY 1, 1900, HIS WIFE GAVE BIRTH TO A SON CALLED BRET.

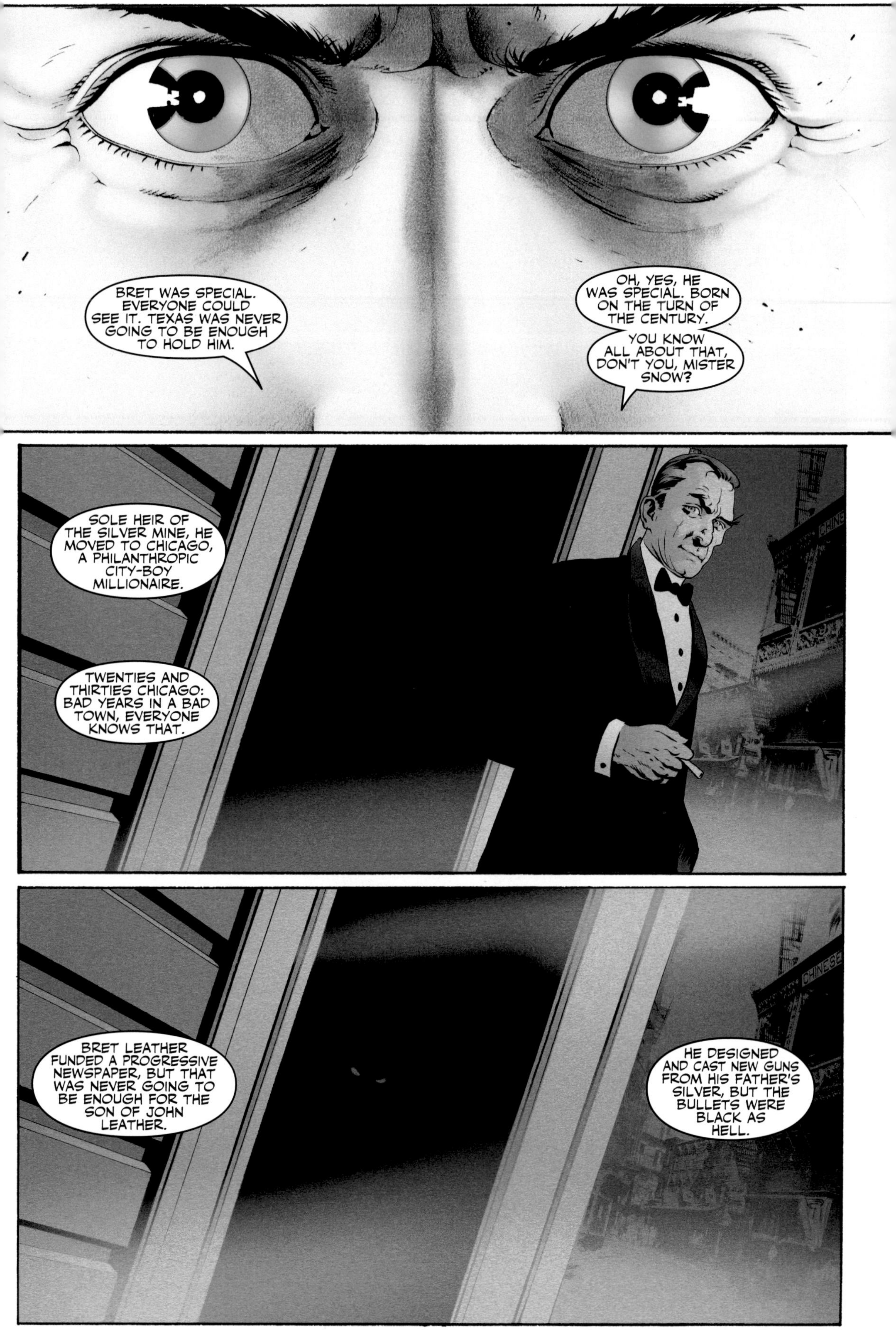
BRET WAS SPECIAL. EVERYONE COULD SEE IT. TEXAS WAS NEVER GOING TO BE ENOUGH TO HOLD HIM.
OH, YES, HE WAS SPECIAL. BORN ON THE TURN OF THE CENTURY.
YOU KNOW ALL ABOUT THAT, DON'T YOU, MISTER SNOW?
SOLE HEIR OF THE SILVER MINE, HE MOVED TO CHICAGO, A PHILANTHROPIC CITY-BOY MILLIONAIRE.
TWENTIES AND THIRTIES CHICAGO: BAD YEARS IN A BAD TOWN, EVERYONE KNOWS THAT.
BRET LEATHER FUNDED A PROGRESSIVE NEWSPAPER, BUT THAT WAS NEVER GOING TO BE ENOUGH FOR THE SON OF JOHN LEATHER.
HE DESIGNED AND CAST NEW GUNS FROM HIS FATHER'S SILVER, BUT THE BULLETS WERE BLACK AS HELL.

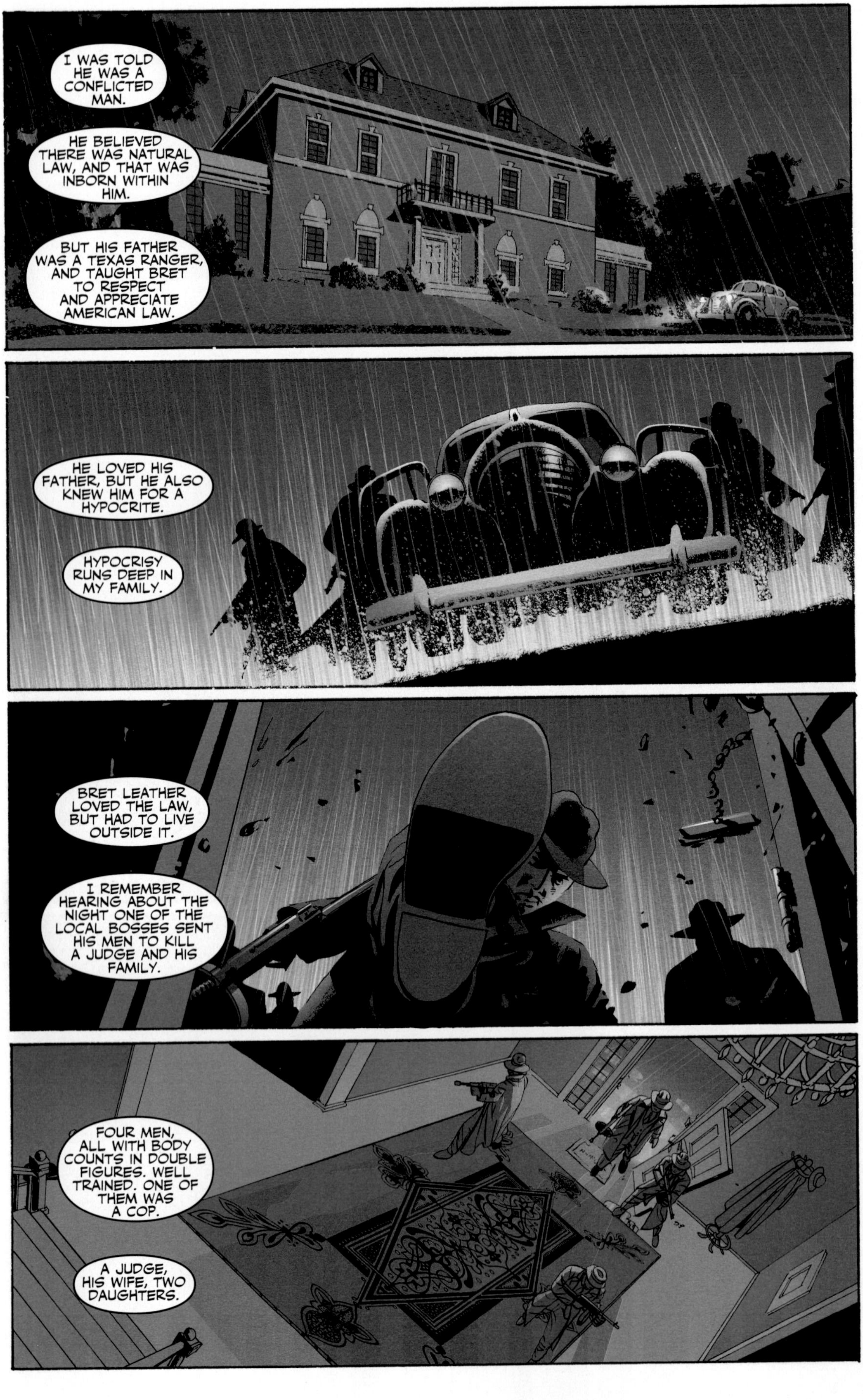
I WAS TOLD HE WAS A CONFLICTED MAN.
HE BELIEVED THERE WAS NATURAL LAW, AND THAT WAS INBORN WITHIN HIM.
BUT HIS FATHER WAS A TEXAS RANGER, AND TAUGHT BRET TO RESPECT AND APPRECIATE AMERICAN LAW.
HE LOVED HIS FATHER, BUT HE ALSO KNEW HIM FOR A HYPOCRITE.
HYPOCRISY RUNS DEEP IN MY FAMILY.
BRET LEATHER LOVED THE LAW, BUT HAD TO LIVE OUTSIDE IT.
I REMEMBER HEARING ABOUT THE NIGHT ONE OF THE LOCAL BOSSES SENT HIS MEN TO KILL A JUDGE AND HIS FAMILY.
FOUR MEN, ALL WITH BODY COUNTS IN DOUBLE FIGURES. WELL TRAINED. ONE OF THEM WAS A COP.
A JUDGE, HIS WIFE, TWO DAUGHTERS.

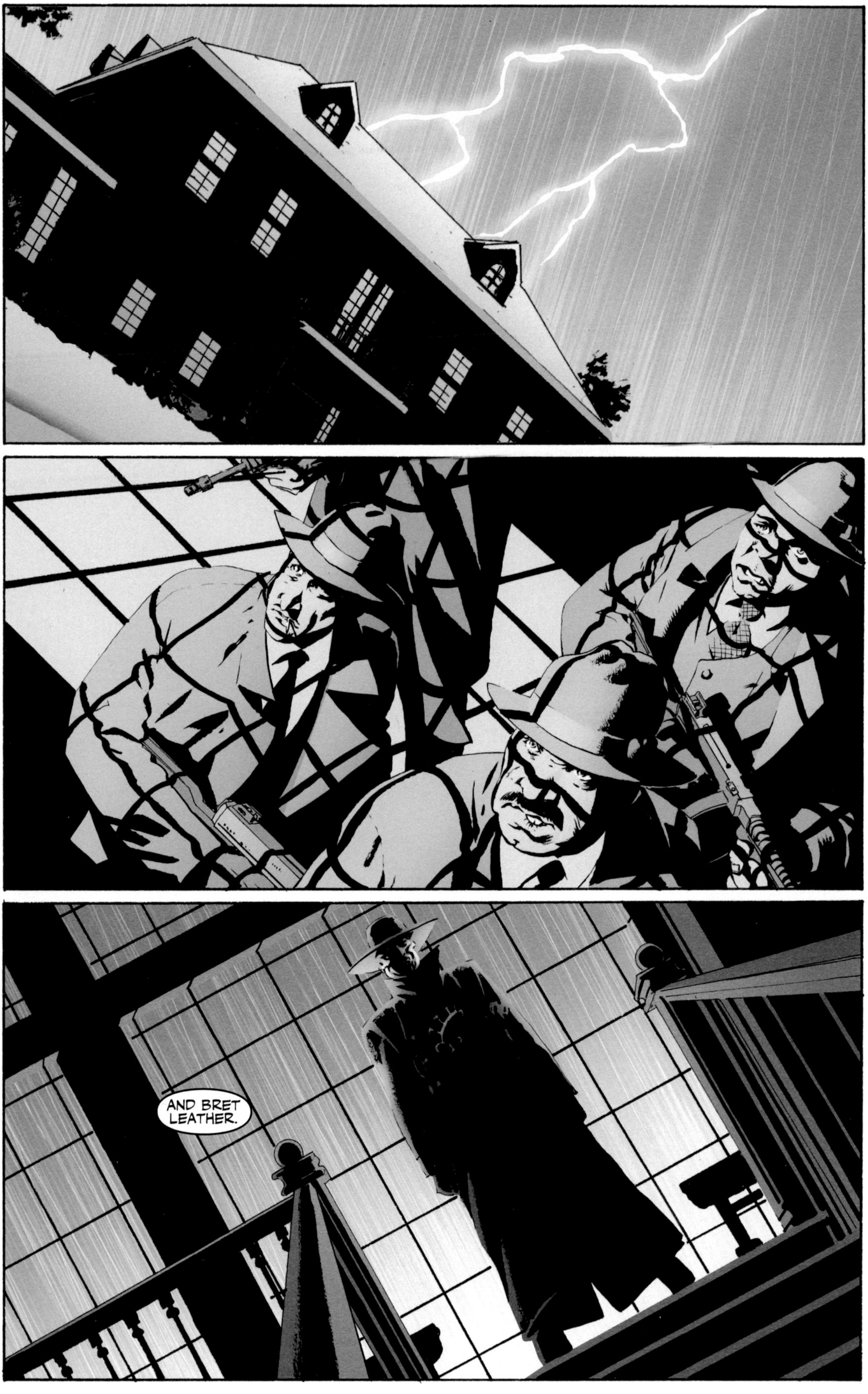
AND BRET LEATHER.

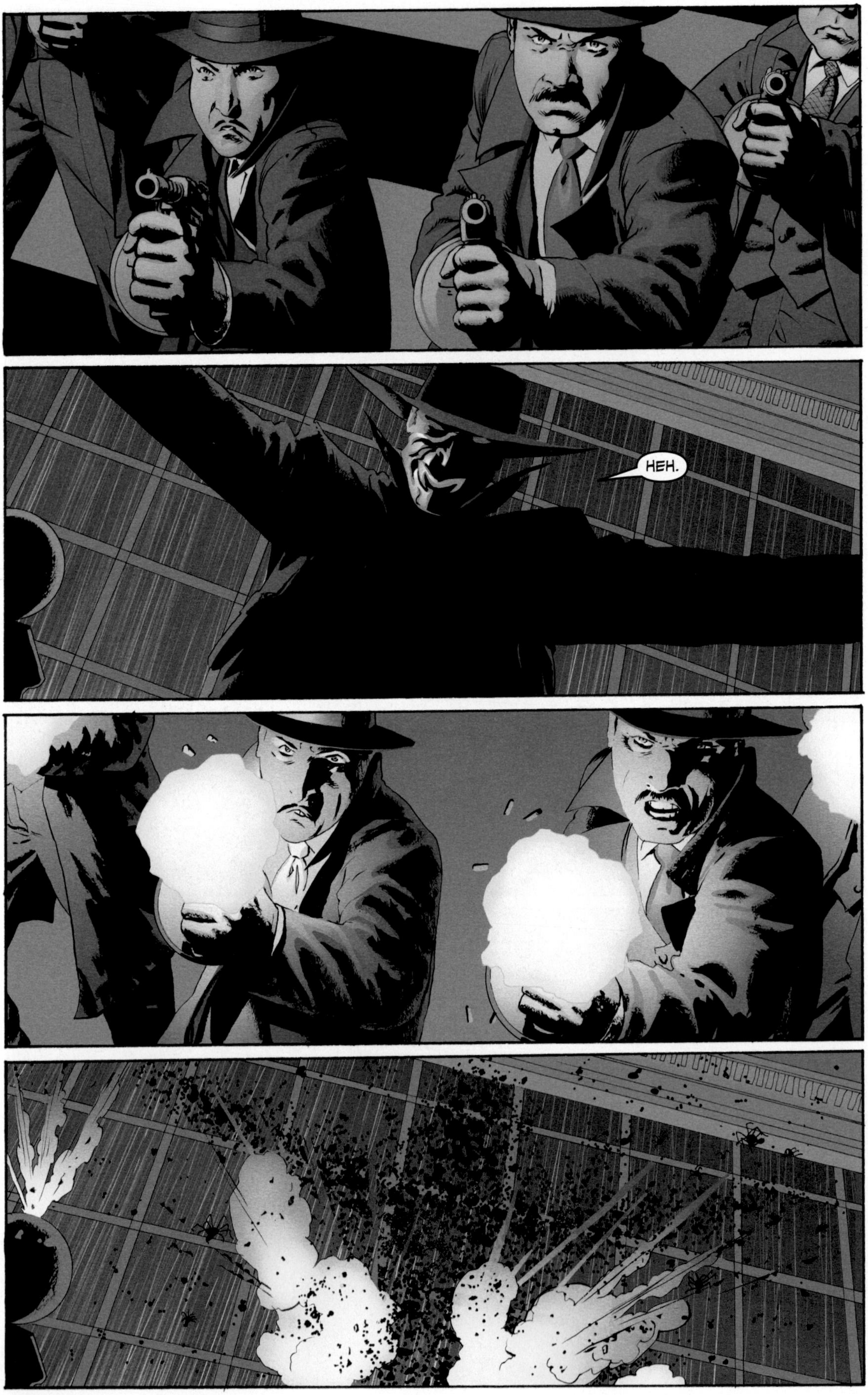
HEH.

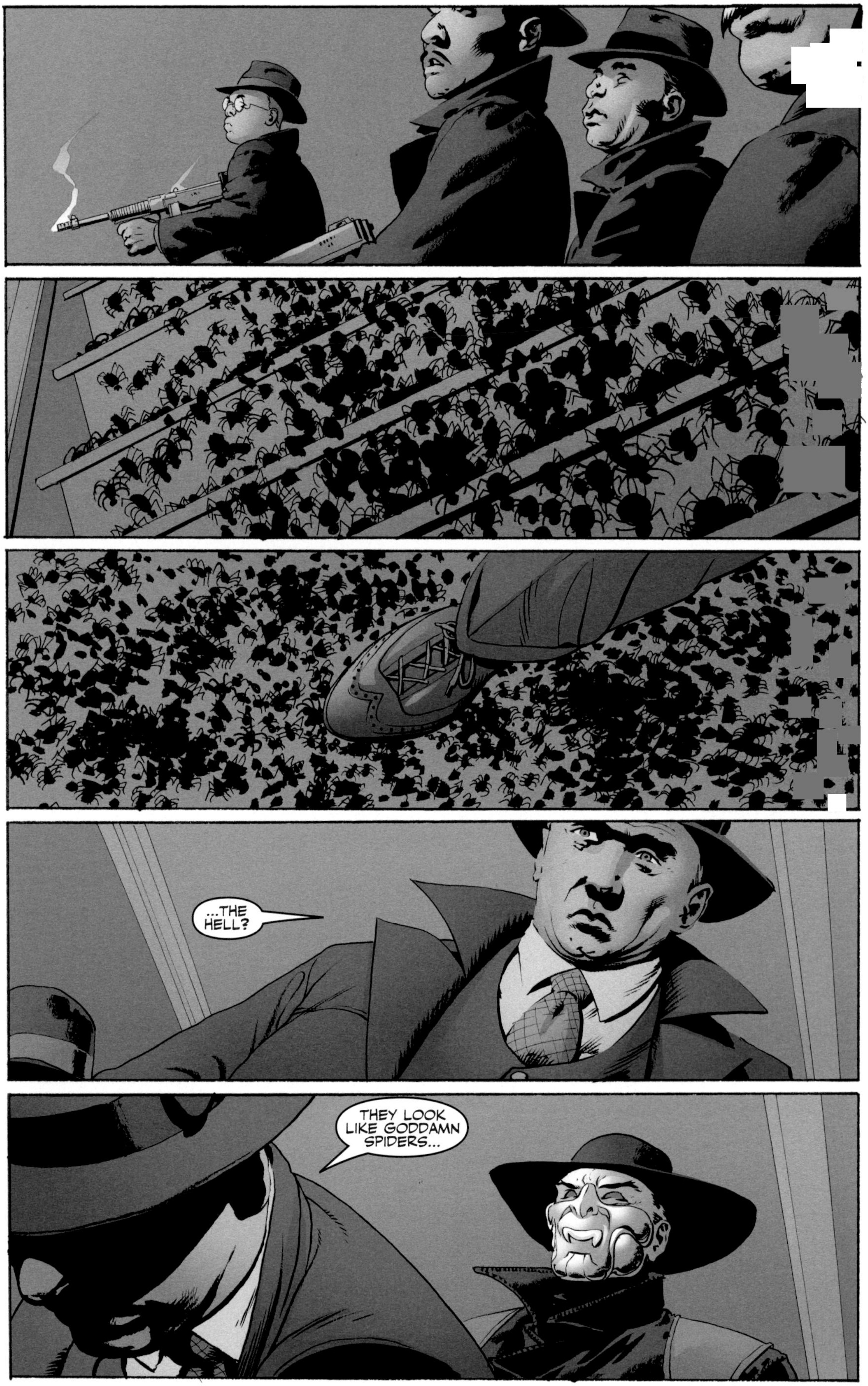
...THE HELL?
THEY LOOK LIKE GODDAMN SPIDERS...

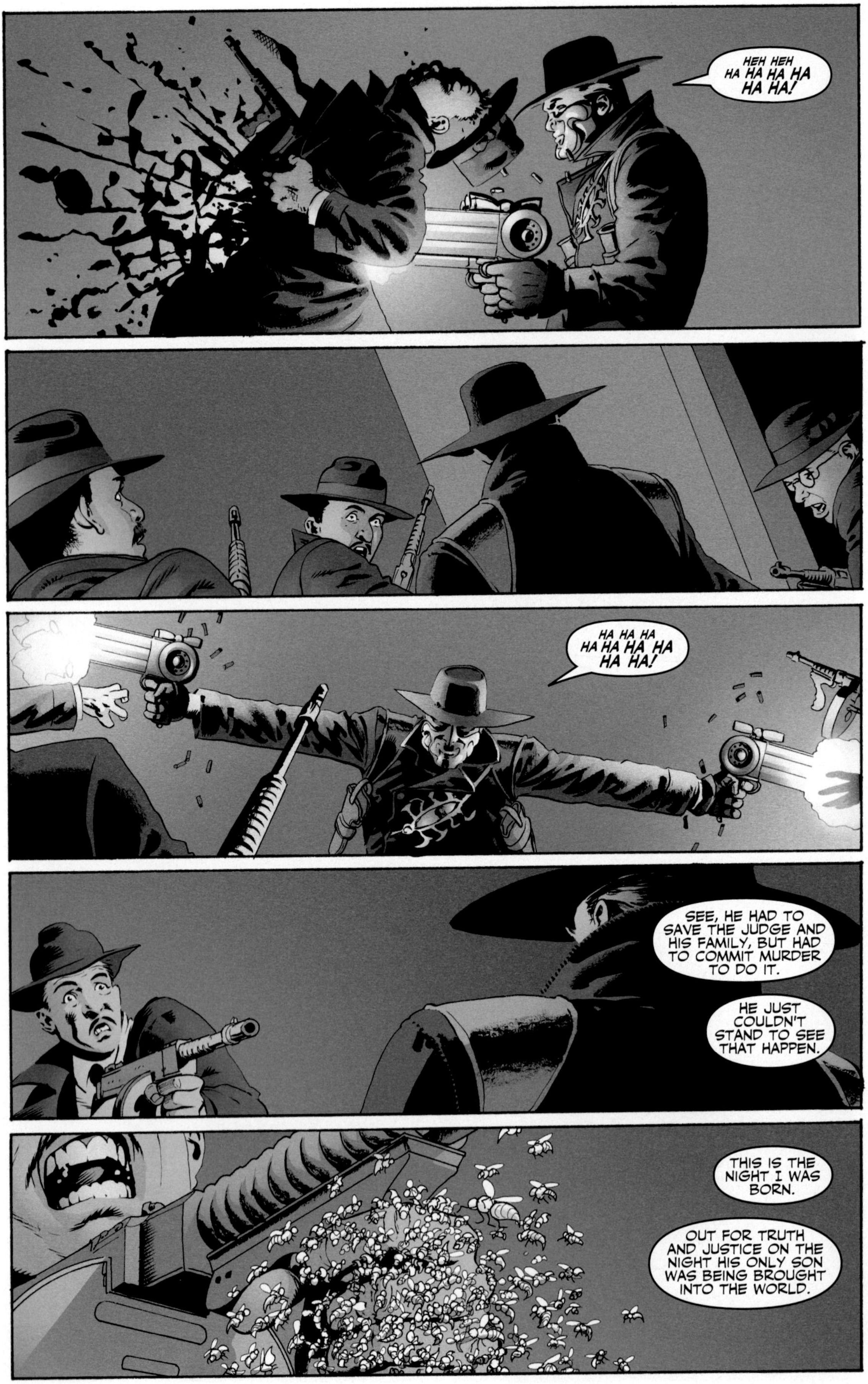
HEH HEH HA HA HA HA HA HA!
HA HA HA HA HA HA HA HA HA HA!
SEE, HE HAD TO SAVE THE JUDGE AND HIS FAMILY, BUT HAD TO COMMIT MURDER TO DO IT.
HE JUST COULDN'T STAND TO SEE THAT HAPPEN.
THIS IS THE NIGHT I WAS BORN.
OUT FOR TRUTH AND JUSTICE ON THE NIGHT HIS ONLY SON WAS BEING BROUGHT INTO THE WORLD.

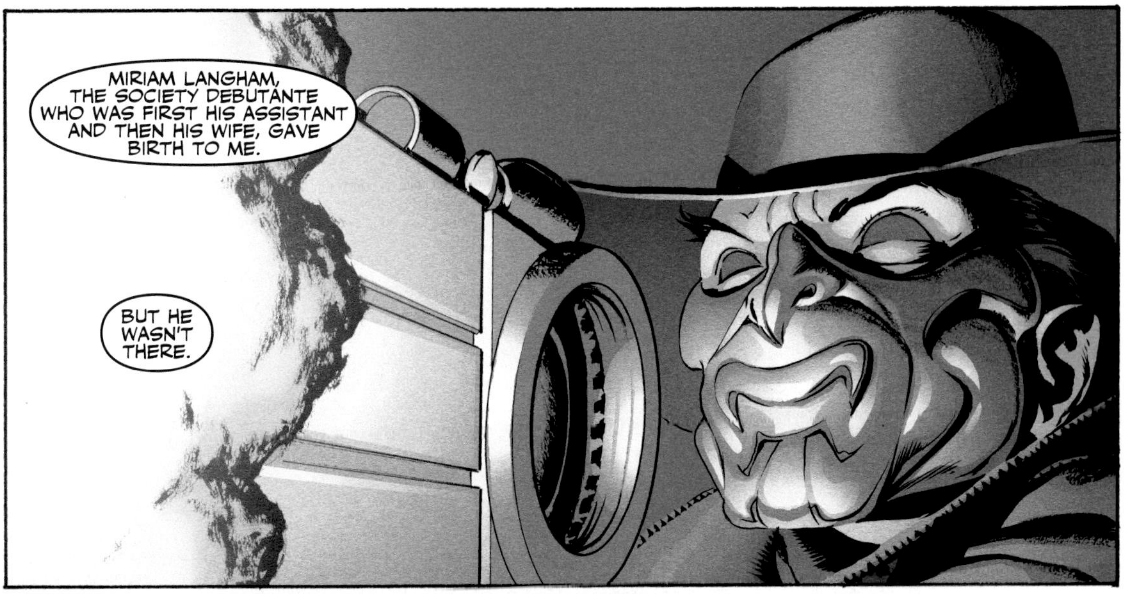
MIRIAM LANGHAM, THE SOCIETY DEBUTANTE WHO WAS FIRST HIS ASSISTANT AND THEN HIS WIFE, GAVE BIRTH TO ME.
BUT HE WASN'T THERE.

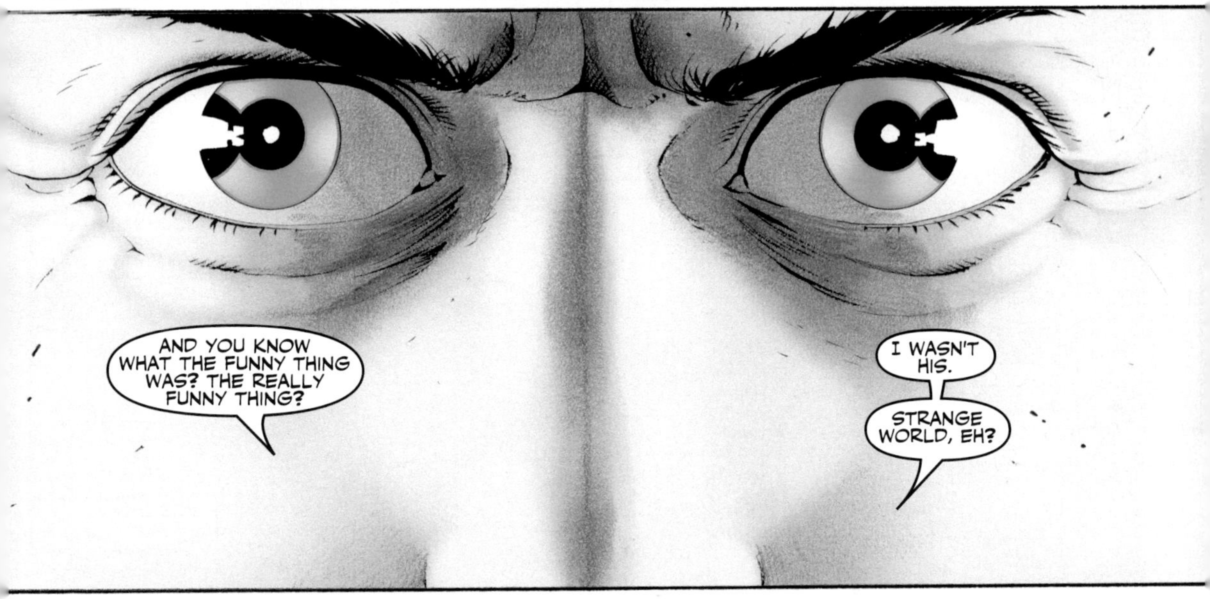
AND YOU KNOW WHAT THE FUNNY THING WAS? THE REALLY FUNNY THING?
I WASN'T HIS.
STRANGE WORLD, EH?

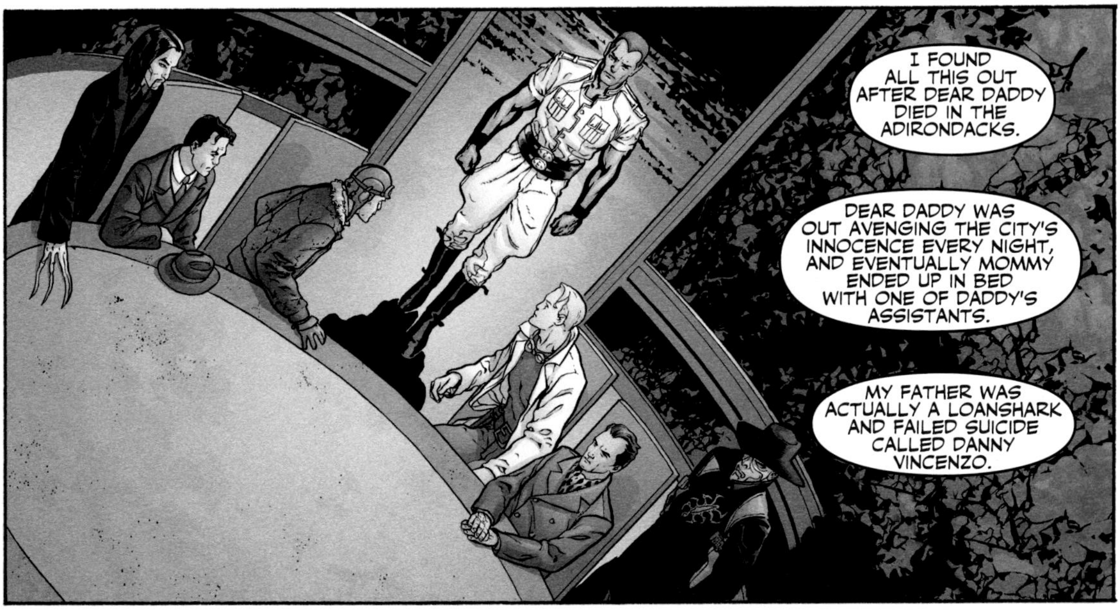
I FOUND ALL THIS OUT AFTER DEAR DADDY DIED IN THE ADIRONDACKS.
DEAR DADDY WAS OUT AVENGING THE CITY'S INNOCENCE EVERY NIGHT, AND EVENTUALLY MOMMY ENDED UP IN BED WITH ONE OF DADDY'S ASSISTANTS.
MY FATHER WAS ACTUALLY A LOANSHARK AND FAILED SUICIDE CALLED DANNY VINCENZO.

FUNNY; HE COULD TELL WHENEVER ANYONE WAS LYING TO HIM--ANYONE EXCEPT HER.

IT WASN'T UNTIL AFTER THE WAR THAT I REALIZED WHAT I'D BEEN CHEATED OUT OF.

WHEN I MET RANDALL DOWLING.

STRANGE WORLD: HE REALLY WAS RELATED TO THE DOWLING MY GRANDPAPPY STAMPED TO DEATH IN THE TEXAS WOODS.

DOWLING EXPLAINED THE WAY OF THE WORLD TO ME.

IF I'D BEEN BRET LEATHER'S SON, I WOULD BE SUPERHUMAN.

I WOULD BE ABLE TO DO EVERYTHING HE'D BEEN CAPABLE OF.

AND I WOULD VERY PROBABLY BE FUNCTIONALLY IMMORTAL.

YOU KNOW WHAT HE SAID TO ME?

"WE'LL PUNISH THEM ALL. THE LIARS AND THE CHEATS AND THE PEOPLE WHO'D STEAL YOUR BIRTHRIGHT.

"WE WILL PUNISH THEM ALL BY BECOMING GREAT."

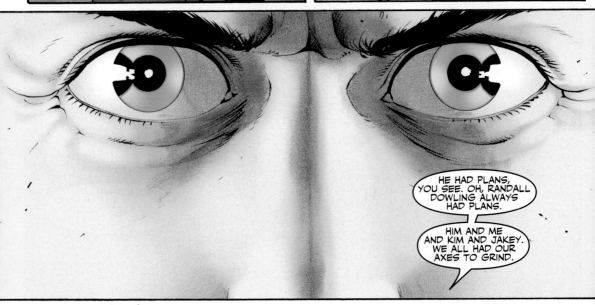

HE HAD PLANS, YOU SEE. OH, RANDALL DOWLING ALWAYS HAD PLANS.

HIM AND ME AND KIM AND JAKEY. WE ALL HAD OUR AXES TO GRIND.

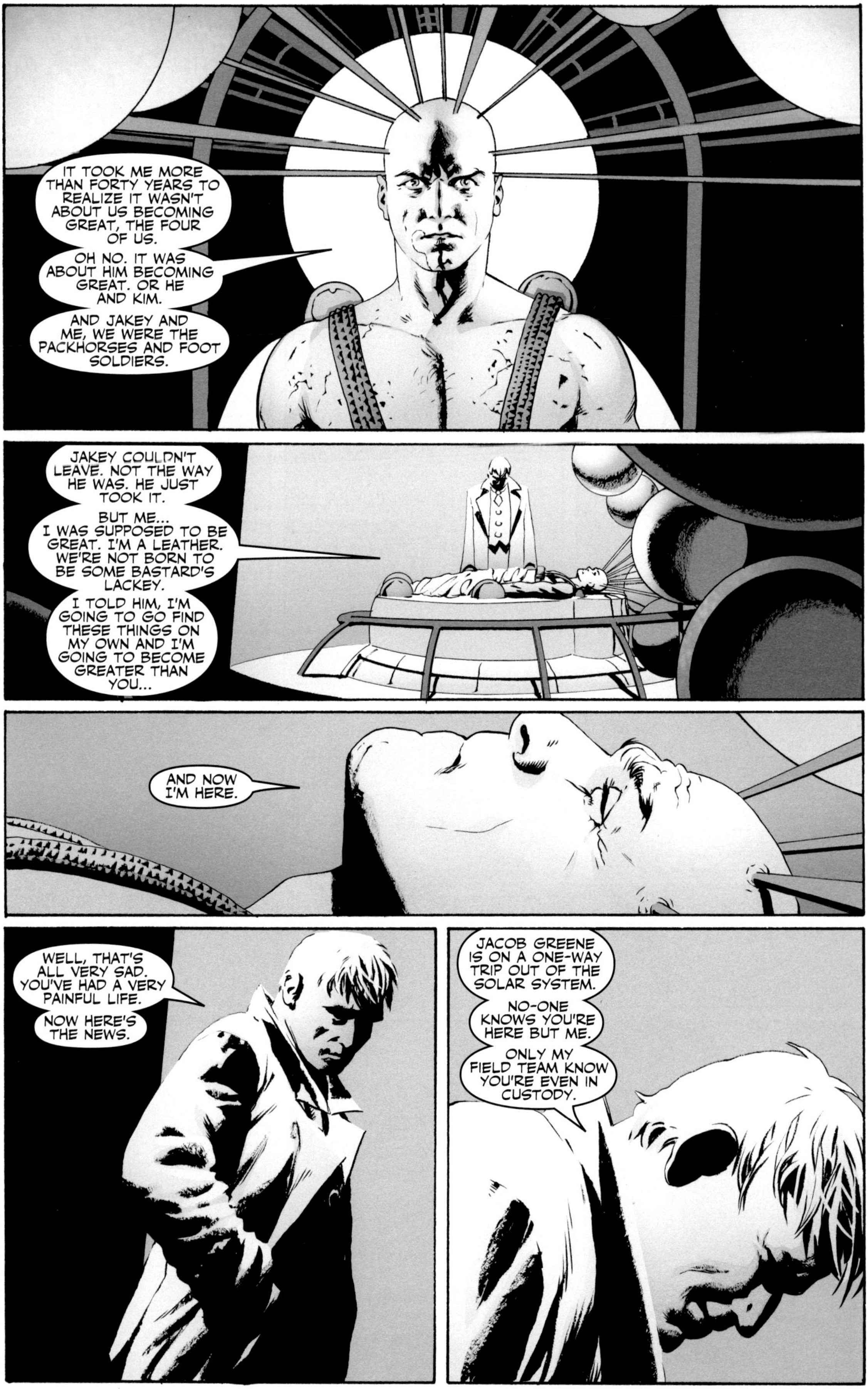
IT TOOK ME MORE THAN FORTY YEARS TO REALIZE IT WASN'T ABOUT US BECOMING GREAT, THE FOUR OF US.
OH NO. IT WAS ABOUT HIM BECOMING GREAT. OR HE AND KIM.
AND JAKEY AND ME, WE WERE THE PACKHORSES AND FOOT SOLDIERS.
JAKEY COULDN'T LEAVE. NOT THE WAY HE WAS. HE JUST TOOK IT.
BUT ME... I WAS SUPPOSED TO BE GREAT. I'M A LEATHER. WE'RE NOT BORN TO BE SOME BASTARD'S LACKEY.
I TOLD HIM, I'M GOING TO GO FIND THESE THINGS ON MY OWN AND I'M GOING TO BECOME GREATER THAN YOU...
AND NOW I'M HERE.
WELL, THAT'S ALL VERY SAD. YOU'VE HAD A VERY PAINFUL LIFE.
NOW HERE'S THE NEWS.
JACOB GREENE IS ON A ONE-WAY TRIP OUT OF THE SOLAR SYSTEM.
NO-ONE KNOWS YOU'RE HERE BUT ME.
ONLY MY FIELD TEAM KNOW YOU'RE EVEN IN CUSTODY.

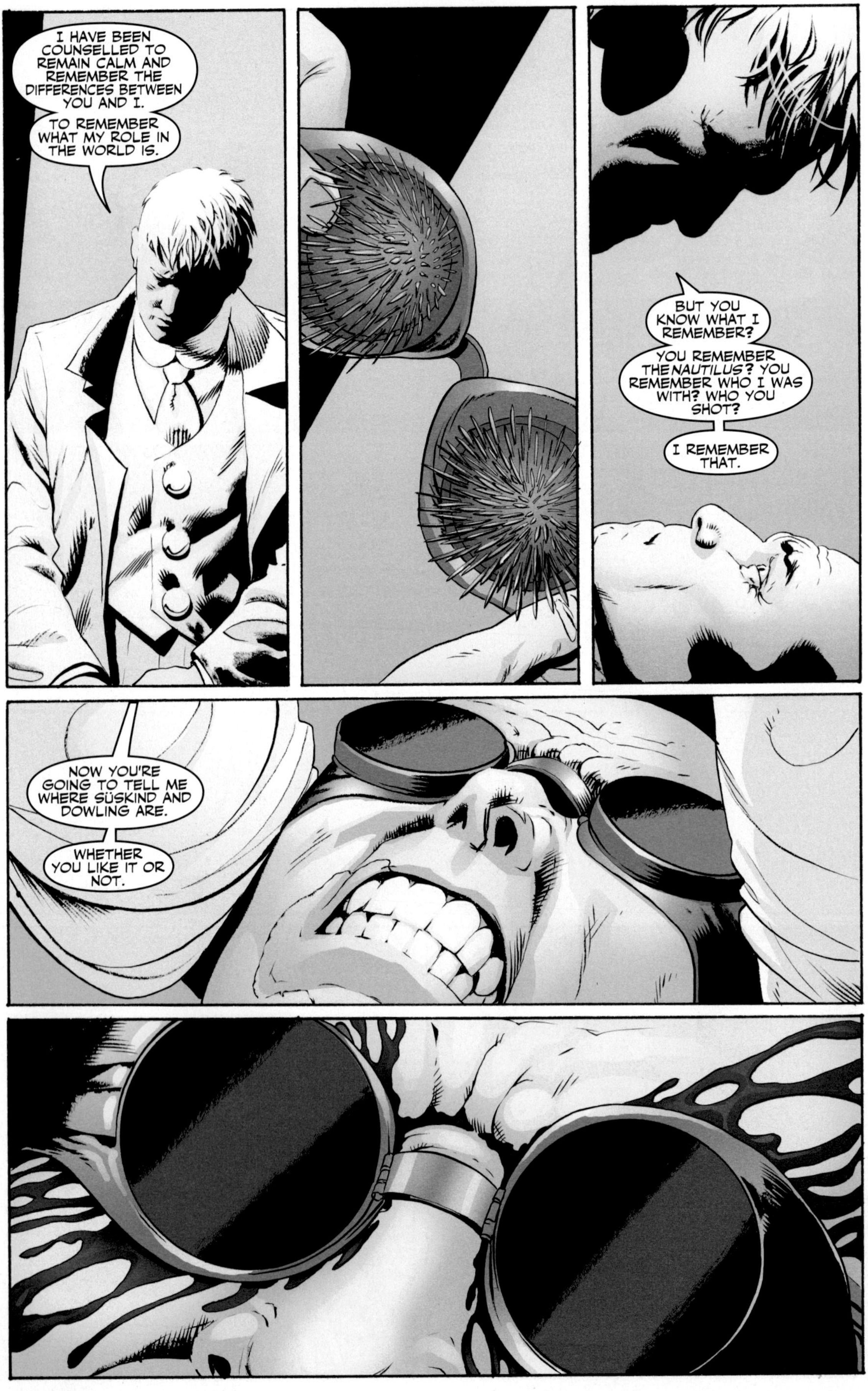
I HAVE BEEN COUNSELLED TO REMAIN CALM AND REMEMBER THE DIFFERENCES BETWEEN YOU AND I.
TO REMEMBER WHAT MY ROLE IN THE WORLD IS.
BUT YOU KNOW WHAT I REMEMBER?
YOU REMEMBER THE *NAUTILUS*? YOU REMEMBER WHO I WAS WITH? WHO YOU SHOT?
I REMEMBER THAT.
NOW YOU'RE GOING TO TELL ME WHERE SÜSKIND AND DOWLING ARE.
WHETHER YOU LIKE IT OR NOT.

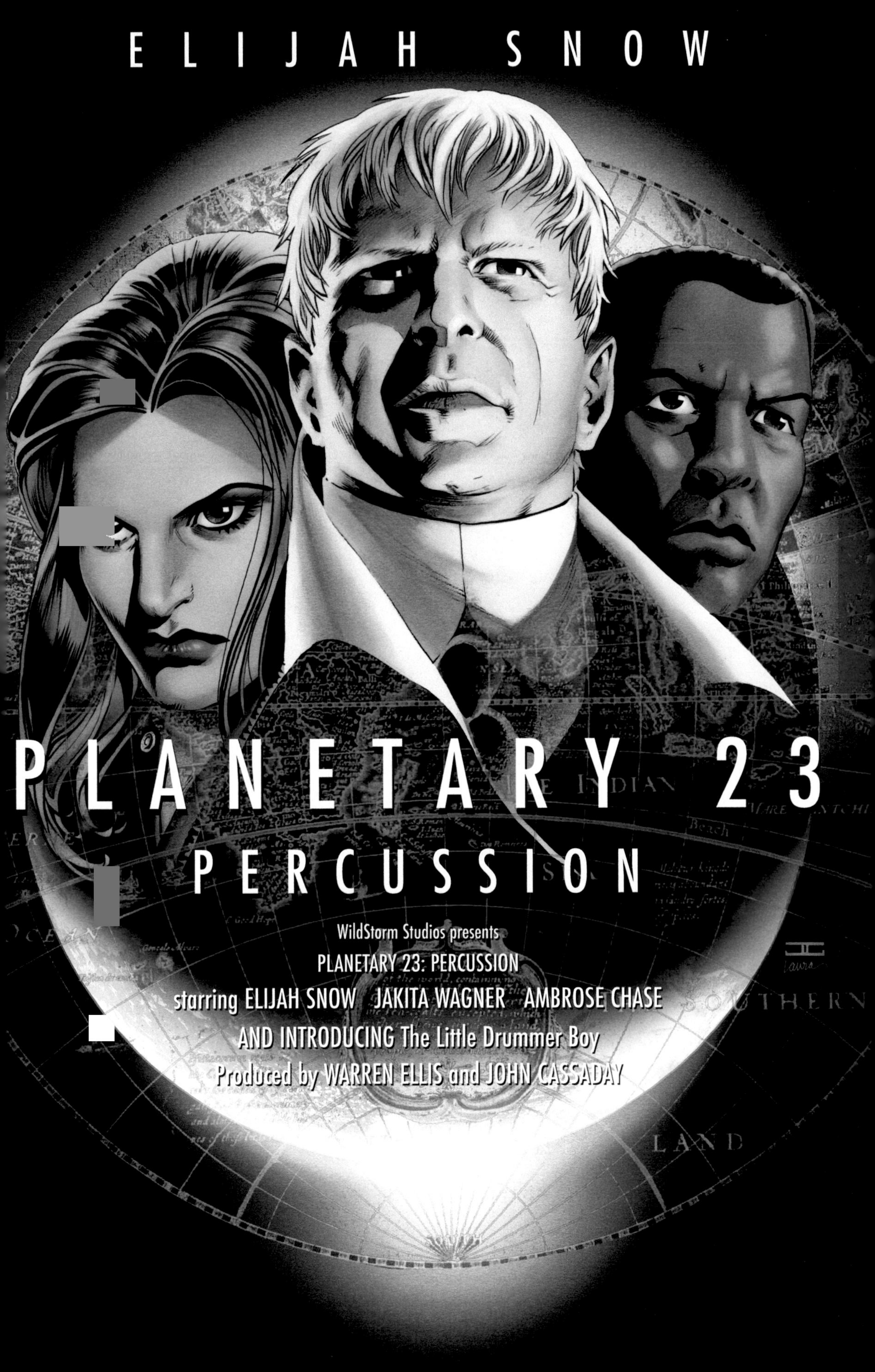
ELIJAH SNOW
PLANETARY 23
PERCUSSION
WildStorm Studios presents
PLANETARY 23: PERCUSSION
starring ELIJAH SNOW JAKITA WAGNER AMBROSE CHASE
AND INTRODUCING The Little Drummer Boy
Produced by WARREN ELLIS and JOHN CASSADAY

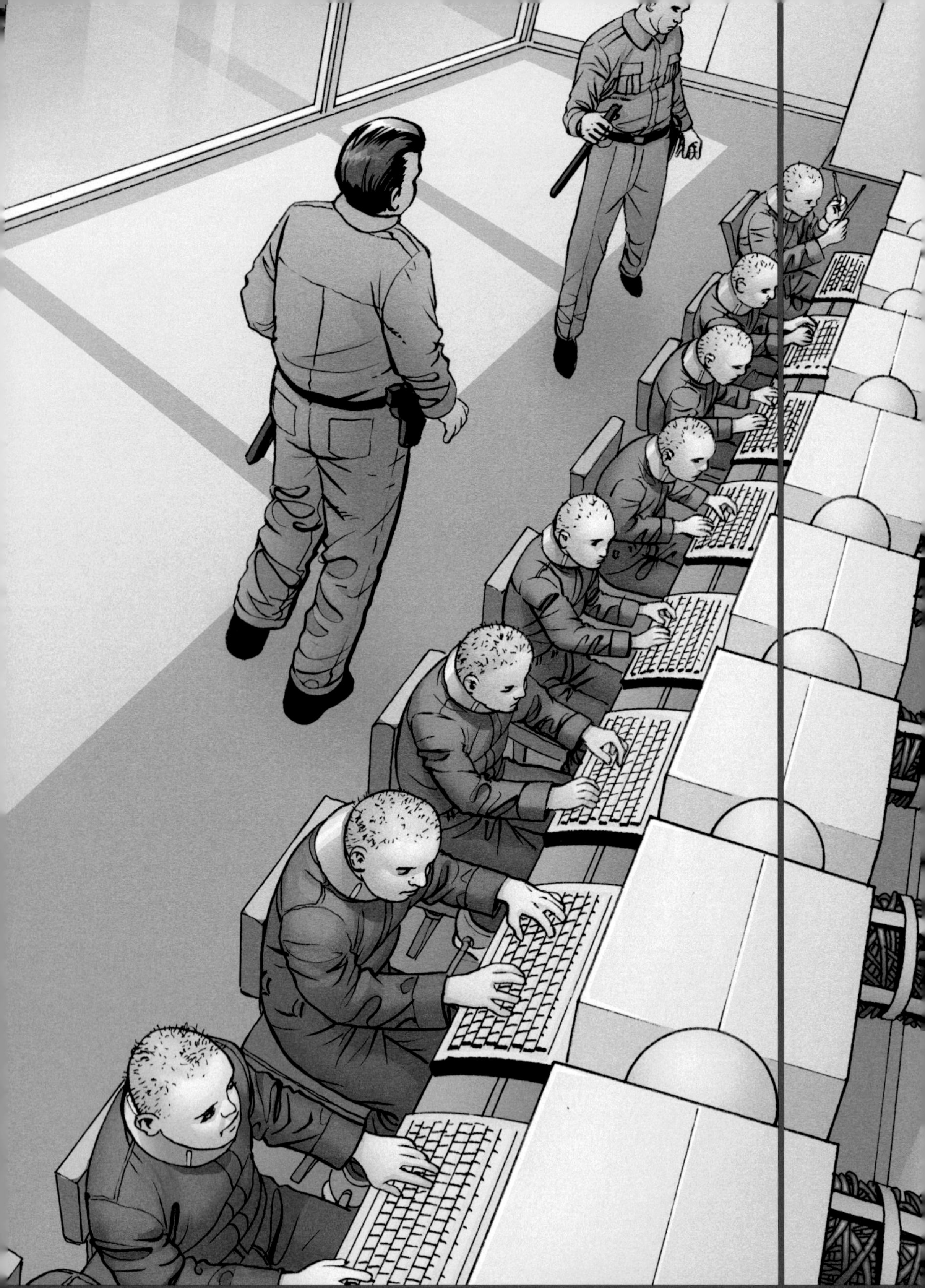

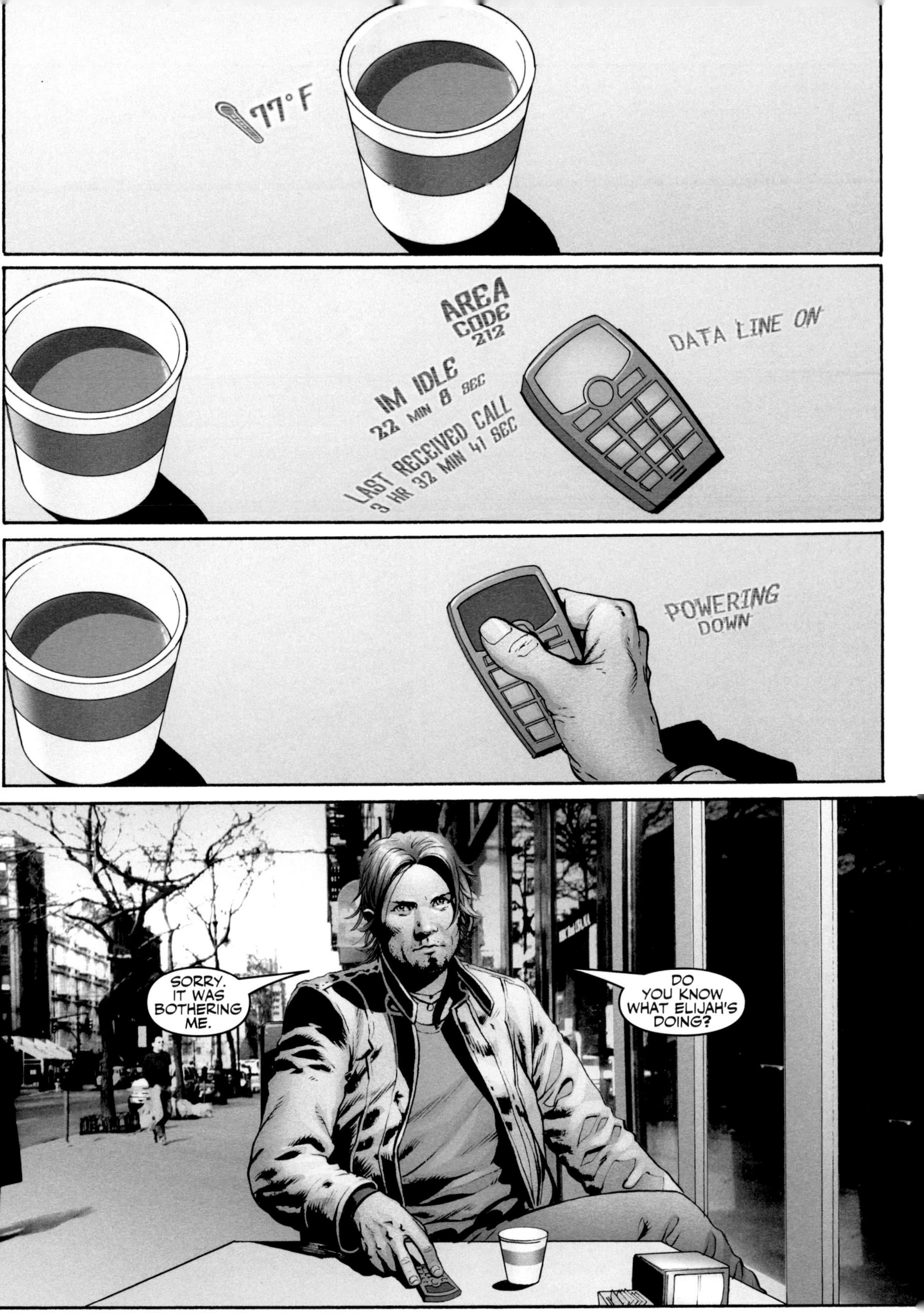
77°F
AREA CODE 212
IM IDLE
22 MIN 8 SEC
LAST RECEIVED CALL
3 HR 32 MIN 41 SEC
DATA LINE ON
POWERING DOWN
SORRY. IT WAS BOTHERING ME.
DO YOU KNOW WHAT ELIJAH'S DOING?

PERCUSSION

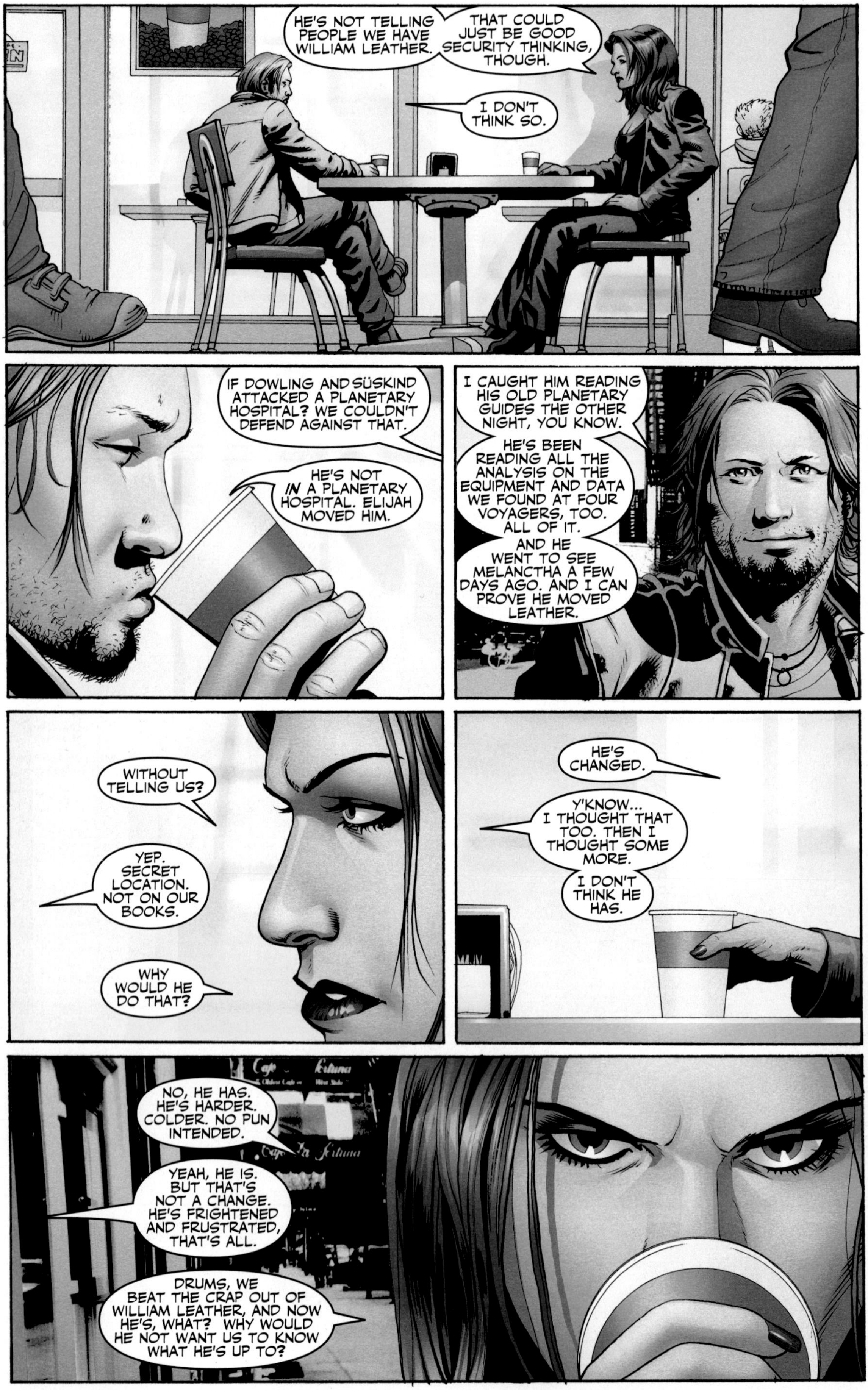
HE'S NOT TELLING PEOPLE WE HAVE WILLIAM LEATHER.
THAT COULD JUST BE GOOD SECURITY THINKING, THOUGH.
I DON'T THINK SO.
IF DOWLING AND SÜSKIND ATTACKED A PLANETARY HOSPITAL? WE COULDN'T DEFEND AGAINST THAT.
HE'S NOT IN A PLANETARY HOSPITAL. ELIJAH MOVED HIM.
I CAUGHT HIM READING HIS OLD PLANETARY GUIDES THE OTHER NIGHT, YOU KNOW.
HE'S BEEN READING ALL THE ANALYSIS ON THE EQUIPMENT AND DATA WE FOUND AT FOUR VOYAGERS, TOO. ALL OF IT.
AND HE WENT TO SEE MELANCTHA A FEW DAYS AGO. AND I CAN PROVE HE MOVED LEATHER.
WITHOUT TELLING US?
YEP. SECRET LOCATION. NOT ON OUR BOOKS.
WHY WOULD HE DO THAT?
HE'S CHANGED.
Y'KNOW... I THOUGHT THAT TOO. THEN I THOUGHT SOME MORE.
I DON'T THINK HE HAS.
NO, HE HAS. HE'S HARDER. COLDER. NO PUN INTENDED.
YEAH, HE IS. BUT THAT'S NOT A CHANGE. HE'S FRIGHTENED AND FRUSTRATED, THAT'S ALL.
DRUMS, WE BEAT THE CRAP OUT OF WILLIAM LEATHER, AND NOW HE'S, WHAT? WHY WOULD HE NOT WANT US TO KNOW WHAT HE'S UP TO?

HE'S TORTURING HIM.

OH MY GOD. DRUMS, HOW CAN YOU SAY HE'S NOT CHANGED?

LOOK AT WHAT HE DID WITH JACOB GREENE!

I KNOW. HE SAVED HIM.

...WHAT?

IF HE SENT GREENE AWAY, HE DIDN'T HAVE TO KILL HIM. THE GUY WILL PROBABLY HAVE A NATURAL LIFESPAN, WHATEVER THAT MIGHT TURN OUT TO BE.

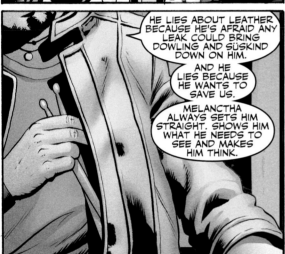

HE LIES ABOUT LEATHER BECAUSE HE'S AFRAID ANY LEAK COULD BRING DOWLING AND SÜSKIND DOWN ON HIM.

AND HE LIES BECAUSE HE WANTS TO SAVE US.

MELANCTHA ALWAYS SETS HIM STRAIGHT. SHOWS HIM WHAT HE NEEDS TO SEE AND MAKES HIM THINK.

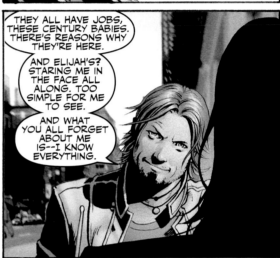

THEY ALL HAVE JOBS, THESE CENTURY BABIES. THERE'S REASONS WHY THEY'RE HERE.

AND ELIJAH'S? STARING ME IN THE FACE ALL ALONG. TOO SIMPLE FOR ME TO SEE.

AND WHAT YOU ALL FORGET ABOUT ME IS--I KNOW EVERYTHING.

OF COURSE YOU'RE DEFENDING HIM...

WELL, IT'S NOT LIKE I DON'T HAVE A GOOD REASON TO DEFEND ANYONE WHO WANTS TO GO AFTER THE FOUR, RIGHT?

OH, PUT THOSE FRIGGING THINGS DOWN FOR A MINUTE, WOULD YOU?

YOU'VE GOT STUFF TO DO, YOU LITTLE BASTARD.

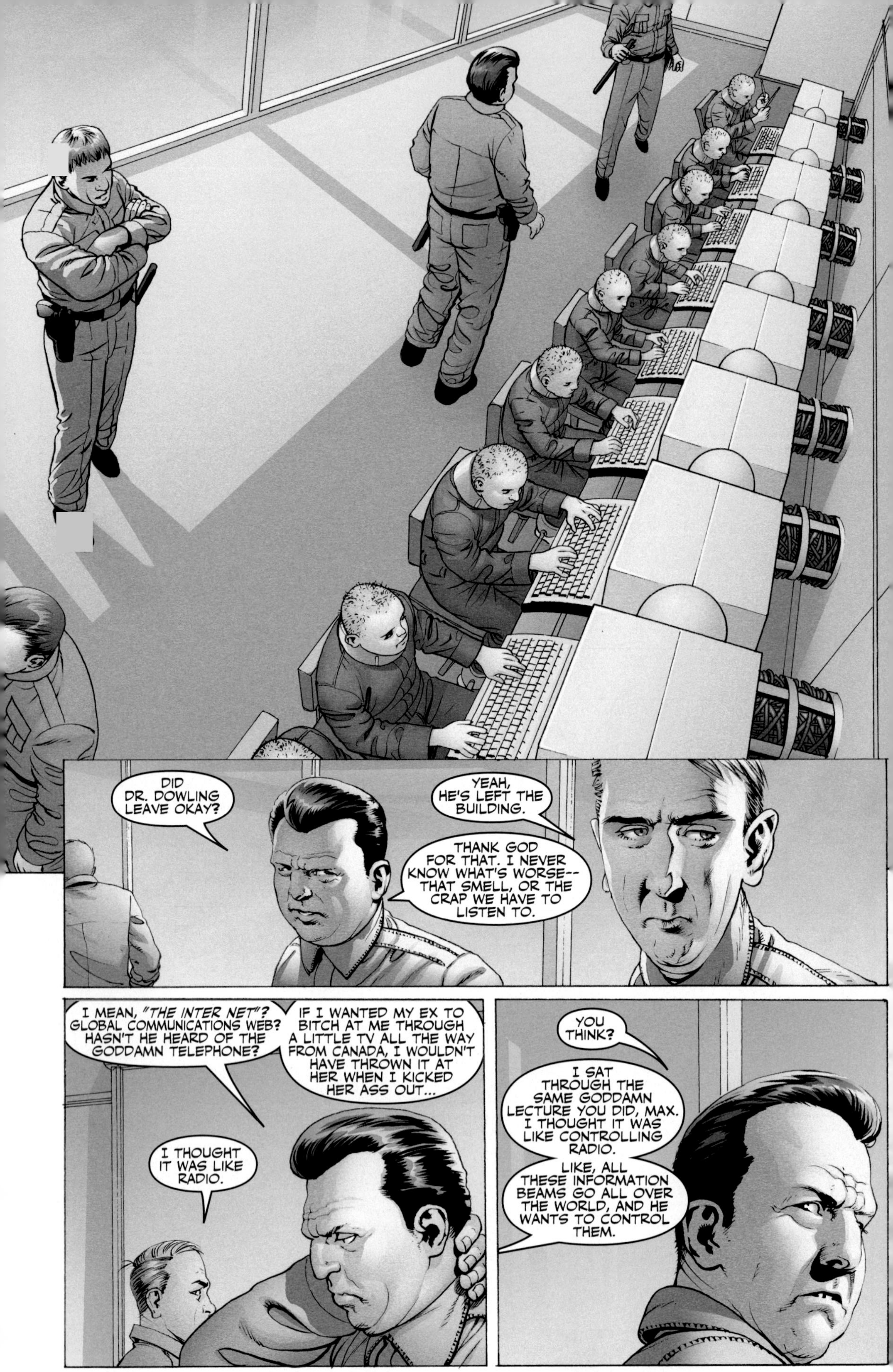
DID DR. DOWLING LEAVE OKAY?
YEAH, HE'S LEFT THE BUILDING.
THANK GOD FOR THAT. I NEVER KNOW WHAT'S WORSE-- THAT SMELL, OR THE CRAP WE HAVE TO LISTEN TO.
I MEAN, "THE INTER NET"? GLOBAL COMMUNICATIONS WEB? HASN'T HE HEARD OF THE GODDAMN TELEPHONE?
IF I WANTED MY EX TO BITCH AT ME THROUGH A LITTLE TV ALL THE WAY FROM CANADA, I WOULDN'T HAVE THROWN IT AT HER WHEN I KICKED HER ASS OUT...
I THOUGHT IT WAS LIKE RADIO.
YOU THINK?
I SAT THROUGH THE SAME GODDAMN LECTURE YOU DID, MAX. I THOUGHT IT WAS LIKE CONTROLLING RADIO.
LIKE, ALL THESE INFORMATION BEAMS GO ALL OVER THE WORLD, AND HE WANTS TO CONTROL THEM.

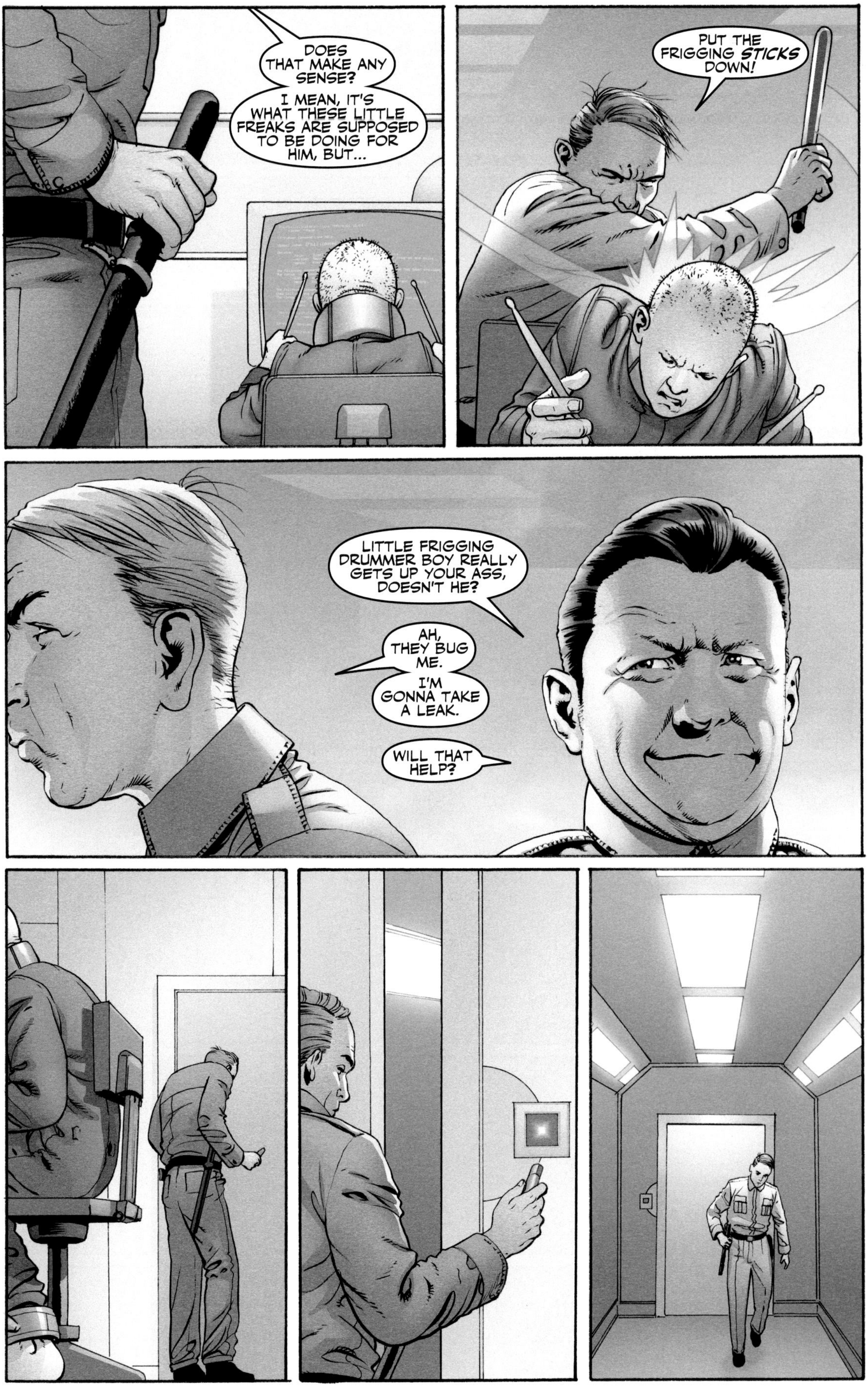
DOES THAT MAKE ANY SENSE?
I MEAN, IT'S WHAT THESE LITTLE FREAKS ARE SUPPOSED TO BE DOING FOR HIM, BUT...
PUT THE FRIGGING STICKS DOWN!
LITTLE FRIGGING DRUMMER BOY REALLY GETS UP YOUR ASS, DOESN'T HE?
AH, THEY BUG ME.
I'M GONNA TAKE A LEAK.
WILL THAT HELP?

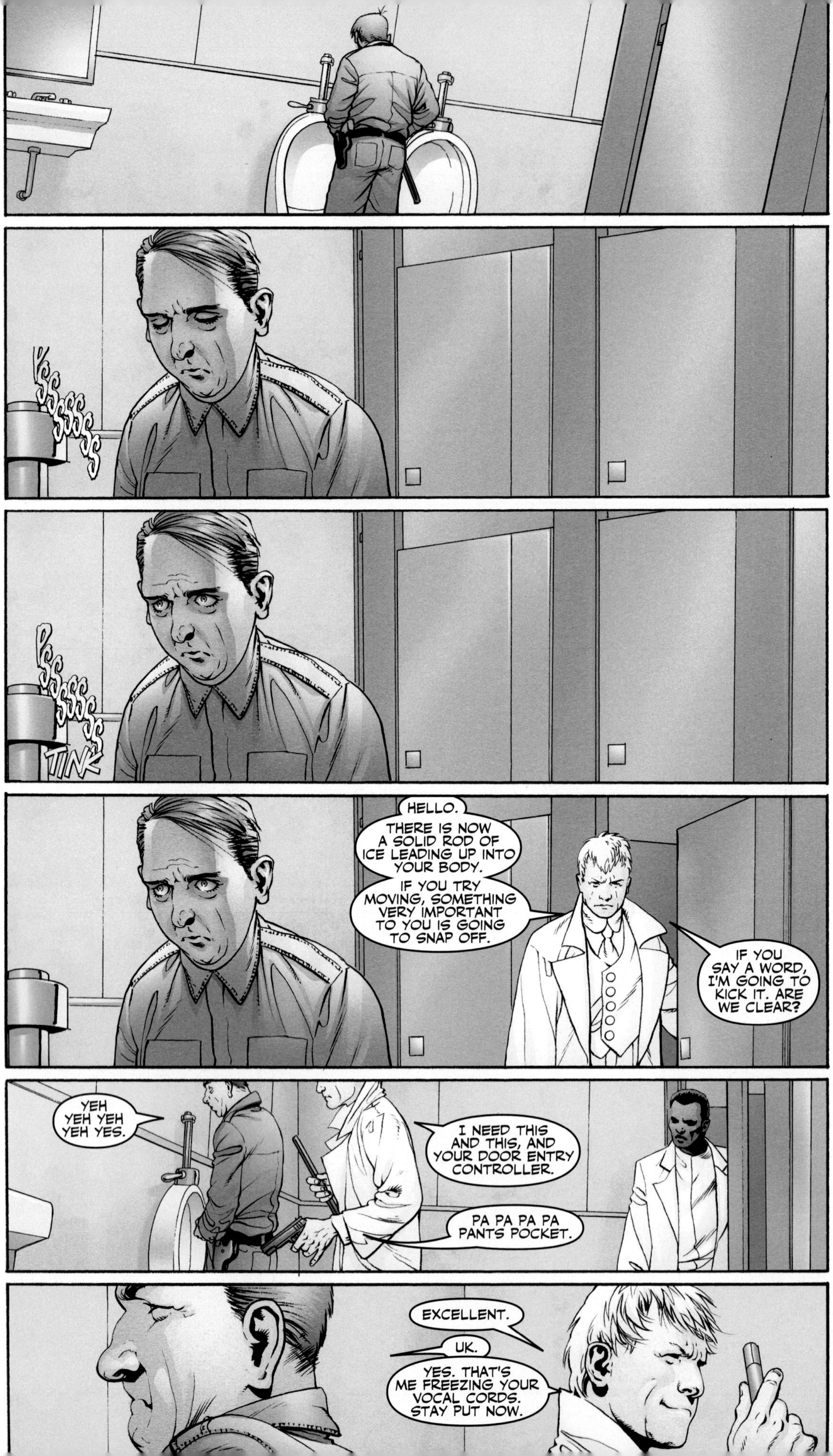
PSSSSSSSS
PSSSSSSSS
TINK
HELLO.
THERE IS NOW A SOLID ROD OF ICE LEADING UP INTO YOUR BODY.
IF YOU TRY MOVING, SOMETHING VERY IMPORTANT TO YOU IS GOING TO SNAP OFF.
IF YOU SAY A WORD, I'M GOING TO KICK IT. ARE WE CLEAR?
YEH YEH YEH YEH YES.
I NEED THIS AND THIS, AND YOUR DOOR ENTRY CONTROLLER.
PA PA PA PA PANTS POCKET.
EXCELLENT.
UK.
YES. THAT'S ME FREEZING YOUR VOCAL CORDS. STAY PUT NOW.

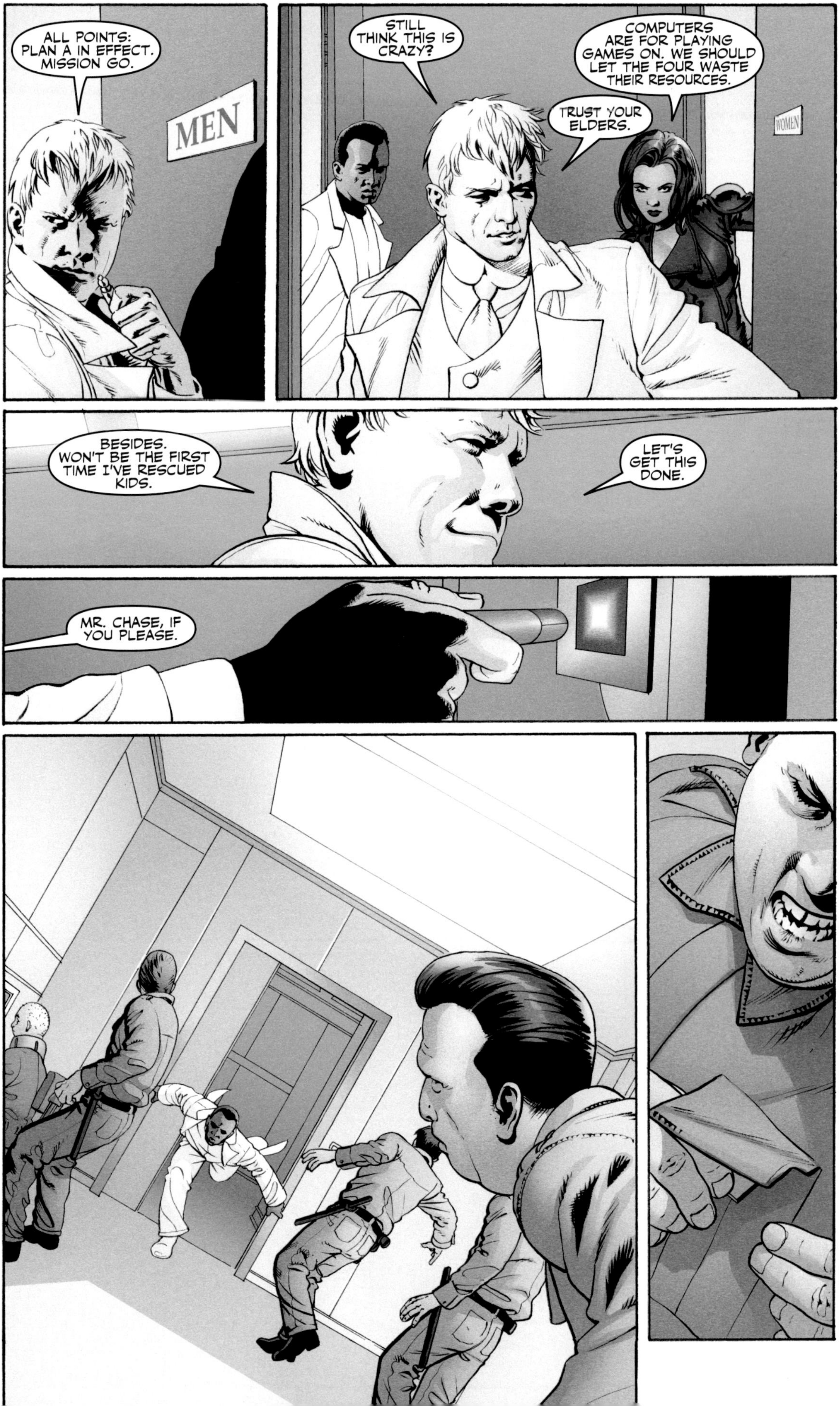
ALL POINTS: PLAN A IN EFFECT. MISSION GO.
MEN
STILL THINK THIS IS CRAZY?
COMPUTERS ARE FOR PLAYING GAMES ON. WE SHOULD LET THE FOUR WASTE THEIR RESOURCES.
TRUST YOUR ELDERS.
WOMEN
BESIDES. WON'T BE THE FIRST TIME I'VE RESCUED KIDS.
LET'S GET THIS DONE.
MR. CHASE, IF YOU PLEASE.

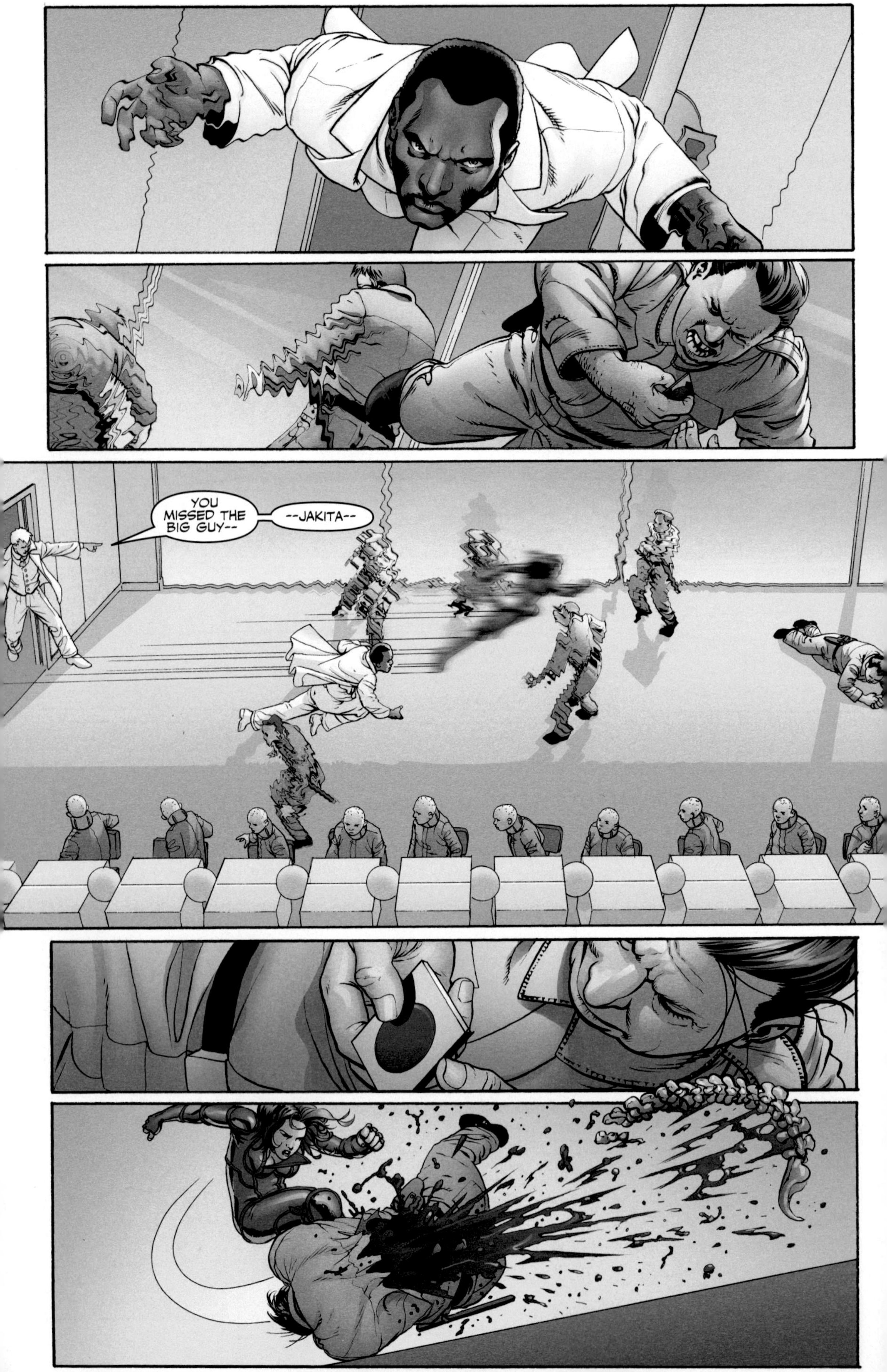
YOU MISSED THE BIG GUY--
--JAKITA--

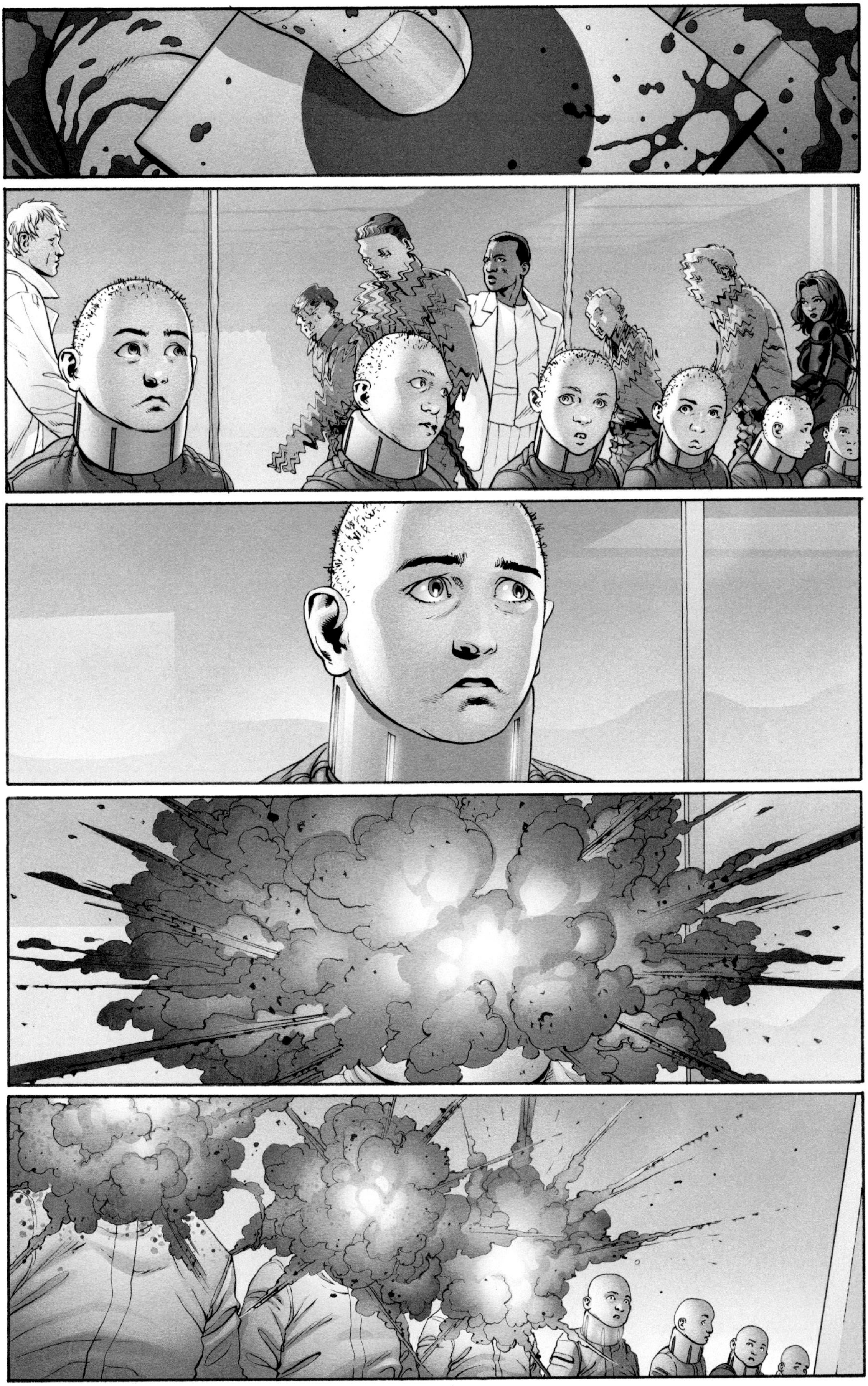

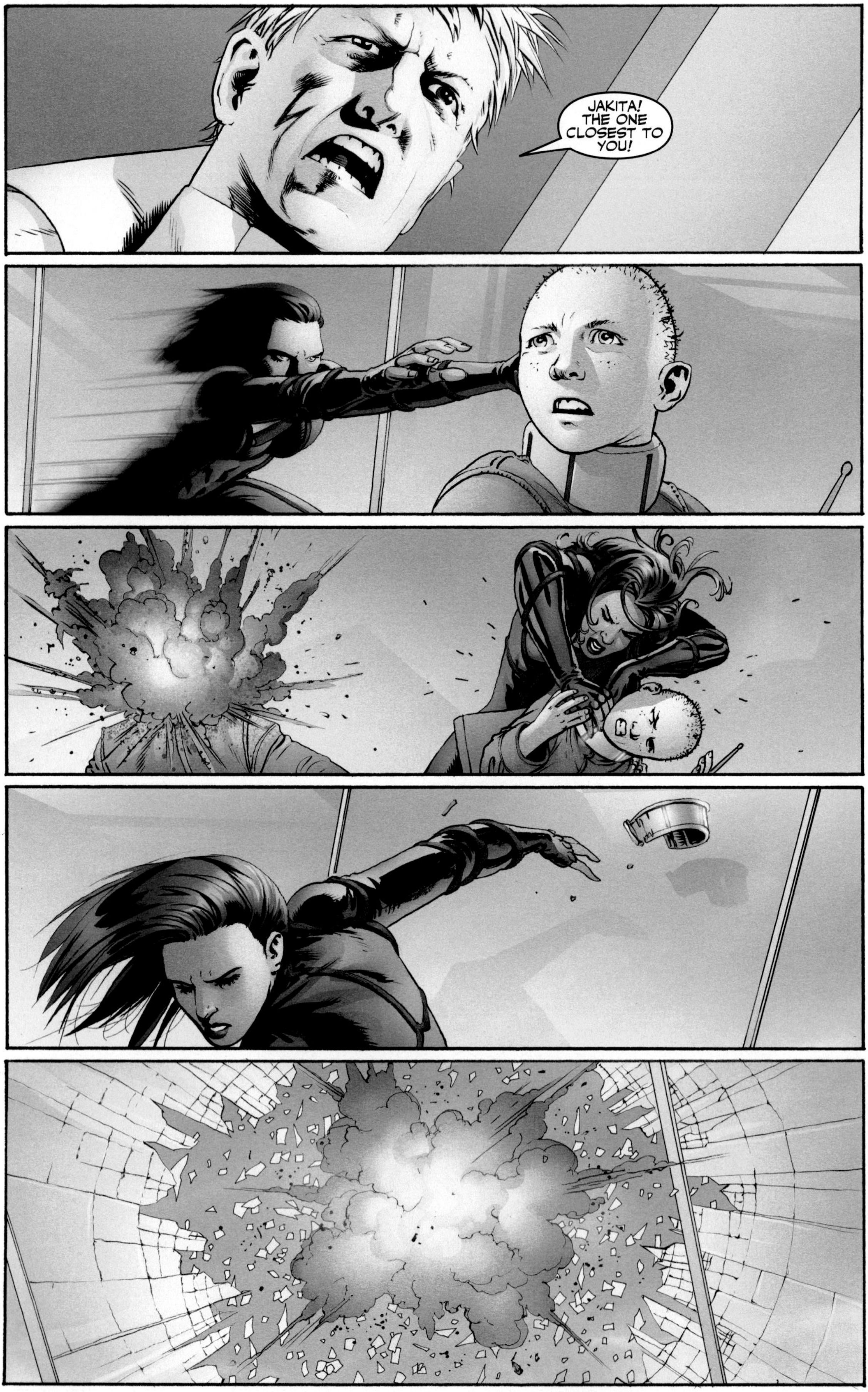
JAKITA! THE ONE CLOSEST TO YOU!

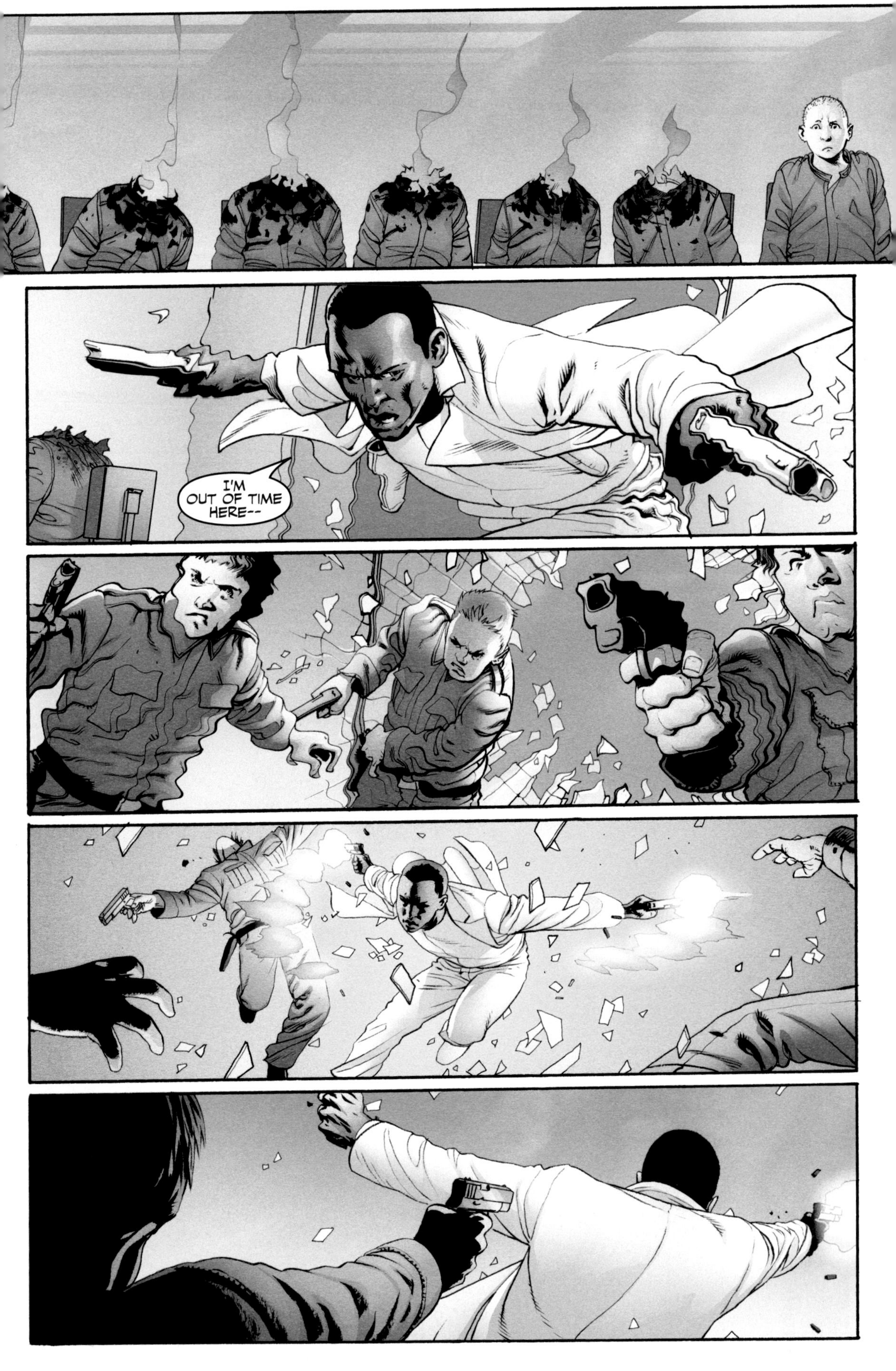
I'M OUT OF TIME HERE--

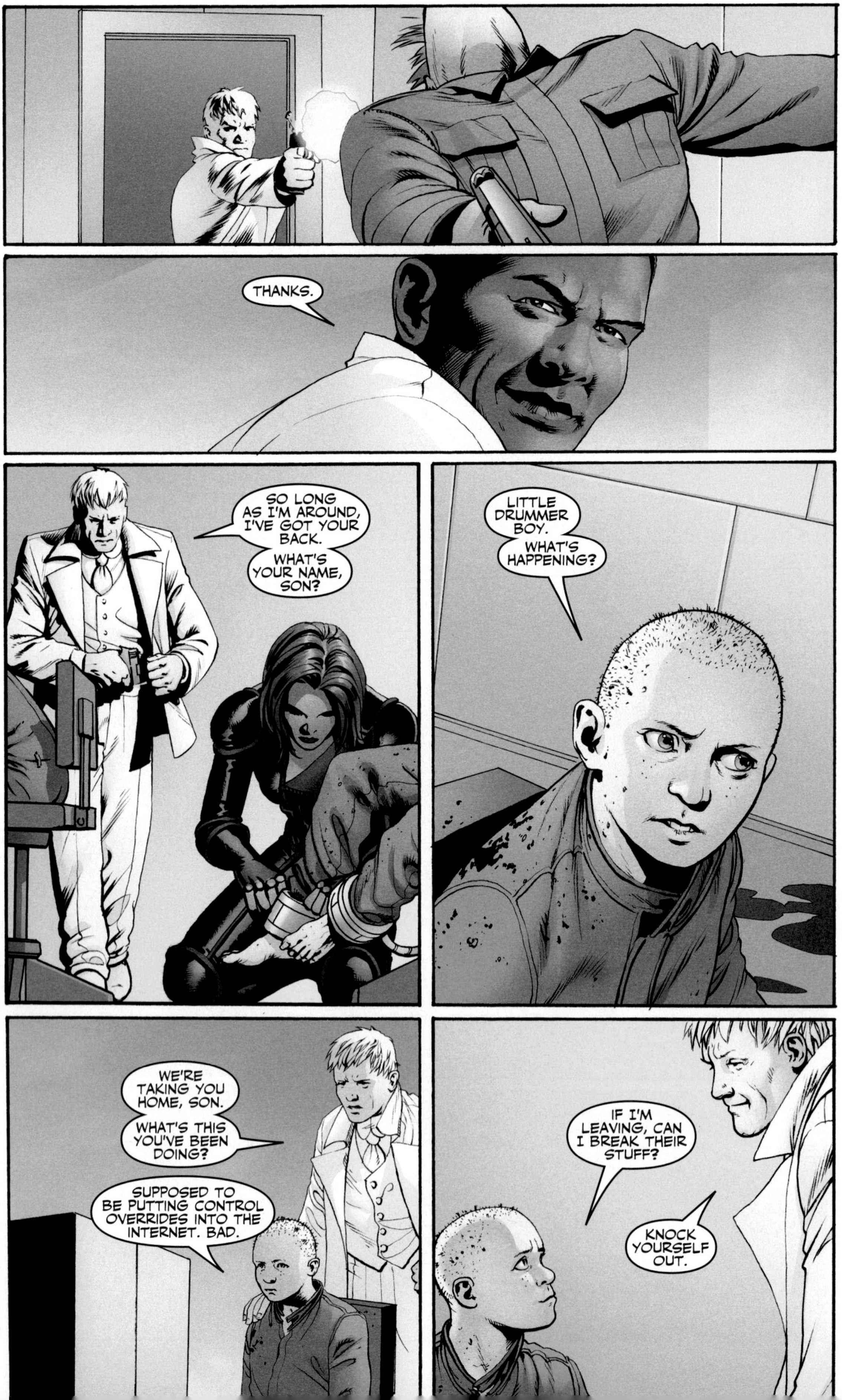
THANKS.
SO LONG AS I'M AROUND, I'VE GOT YOUR BACK.
WHAT'S YOUR NAME, SON?
LITTLE DRUMMER BOY.
WHAT'S HAPPENING?
WE'RE TAKING YOU HOME, SON.
WHAT'S THIS YOU'VE BEEN DOING?
SUPPOSED TO BE PUTTING CONTROL OVERRIDES INTO THE INTERNET. BAD.
IF I'M LEAVING, CAN I BREAK THEIR STUFF?
KNOCK YOURSELF OUT.

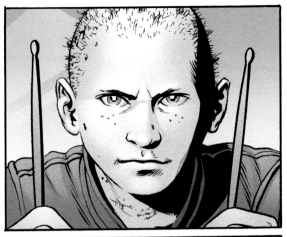

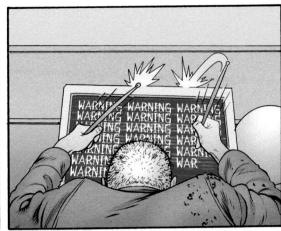

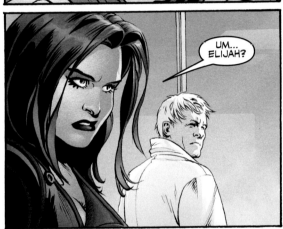

WARNING WARNING WARNING
UM... ELIJAH?
HA HA SCREW YOU STINKY DOCTOR DOWLING AND YOUR CRAPPY FOOD AND ROUGH TOILET PAPER.
CRASH

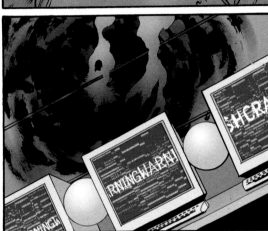

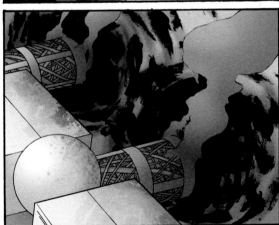

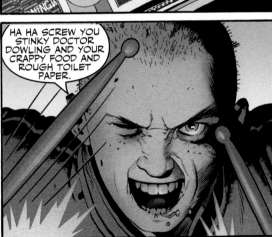

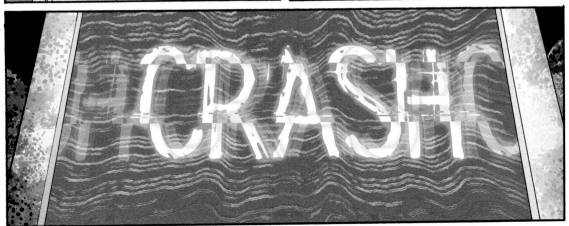

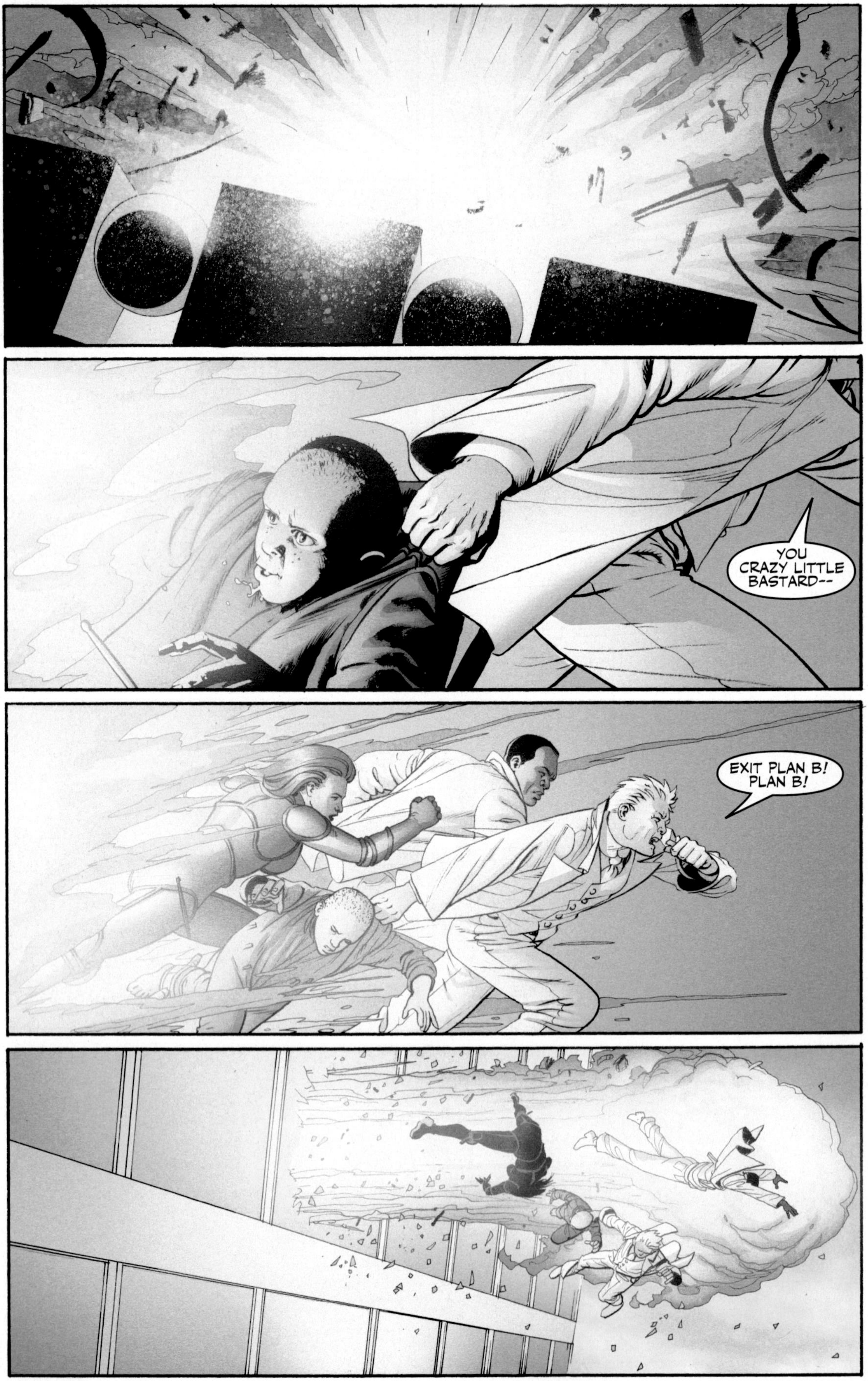
YOU CRAZY LITTLE BASTARD--
EXIT PLAN B! PLAN B!

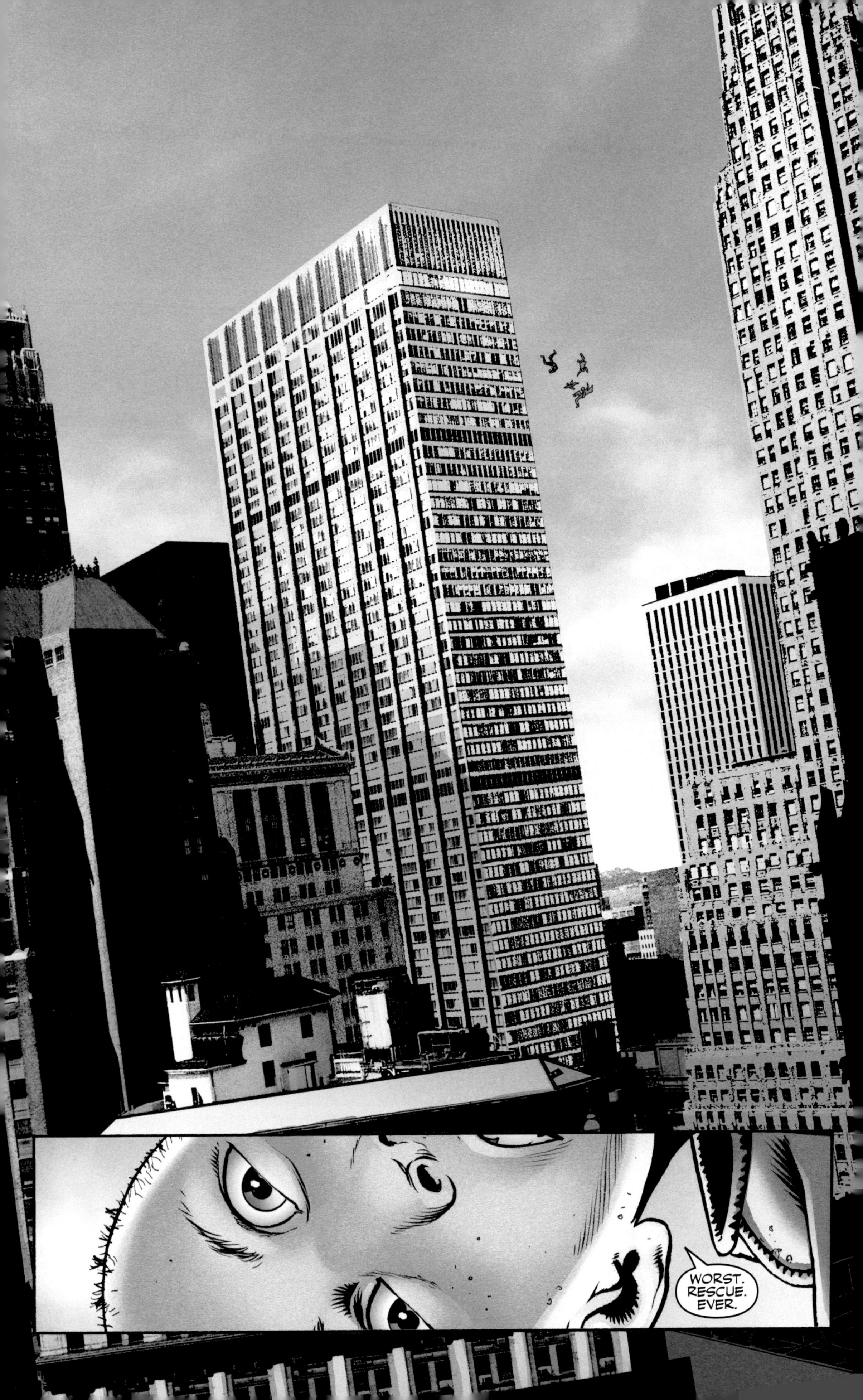
WORST. RESCUE. EVER.

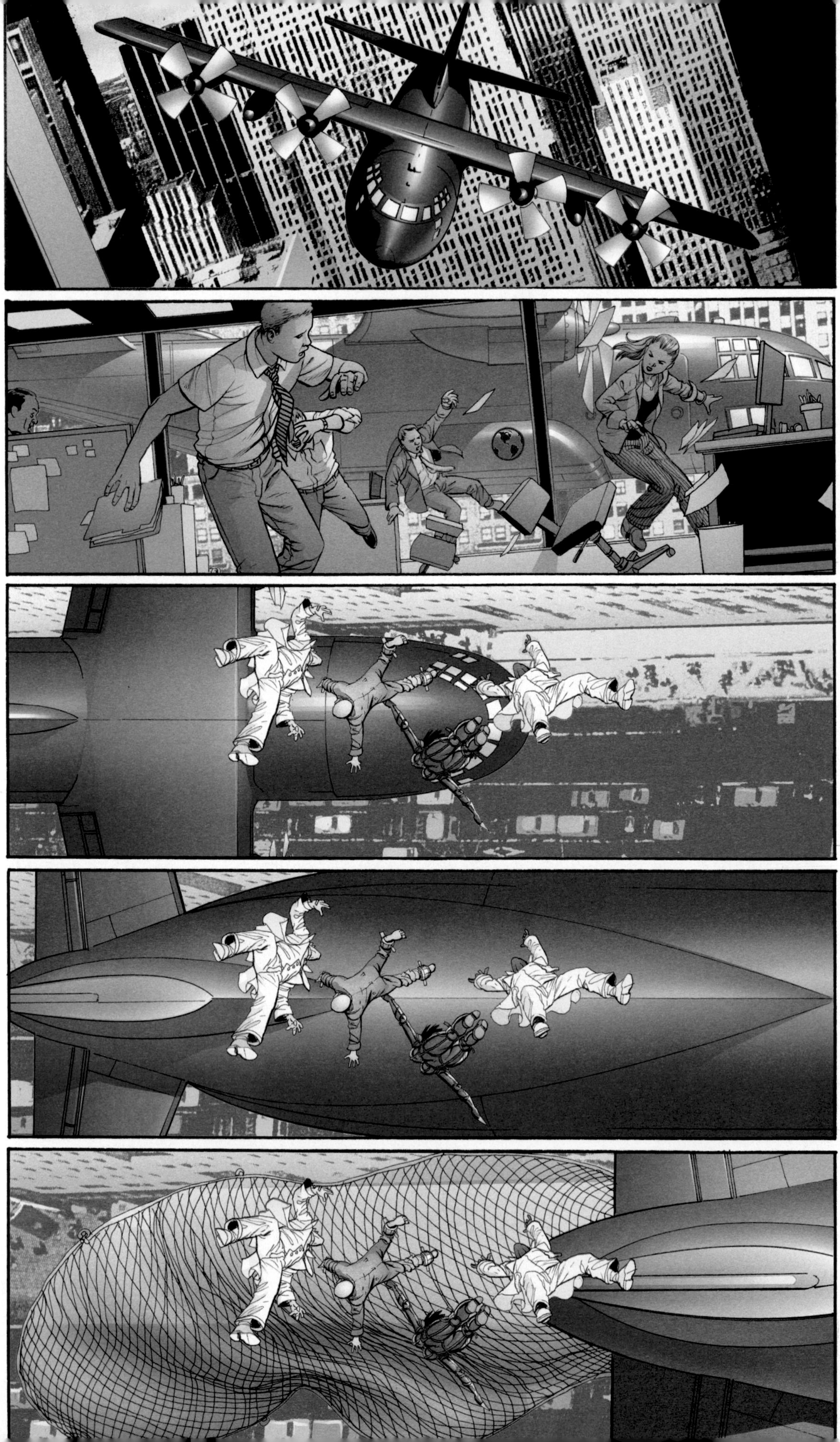

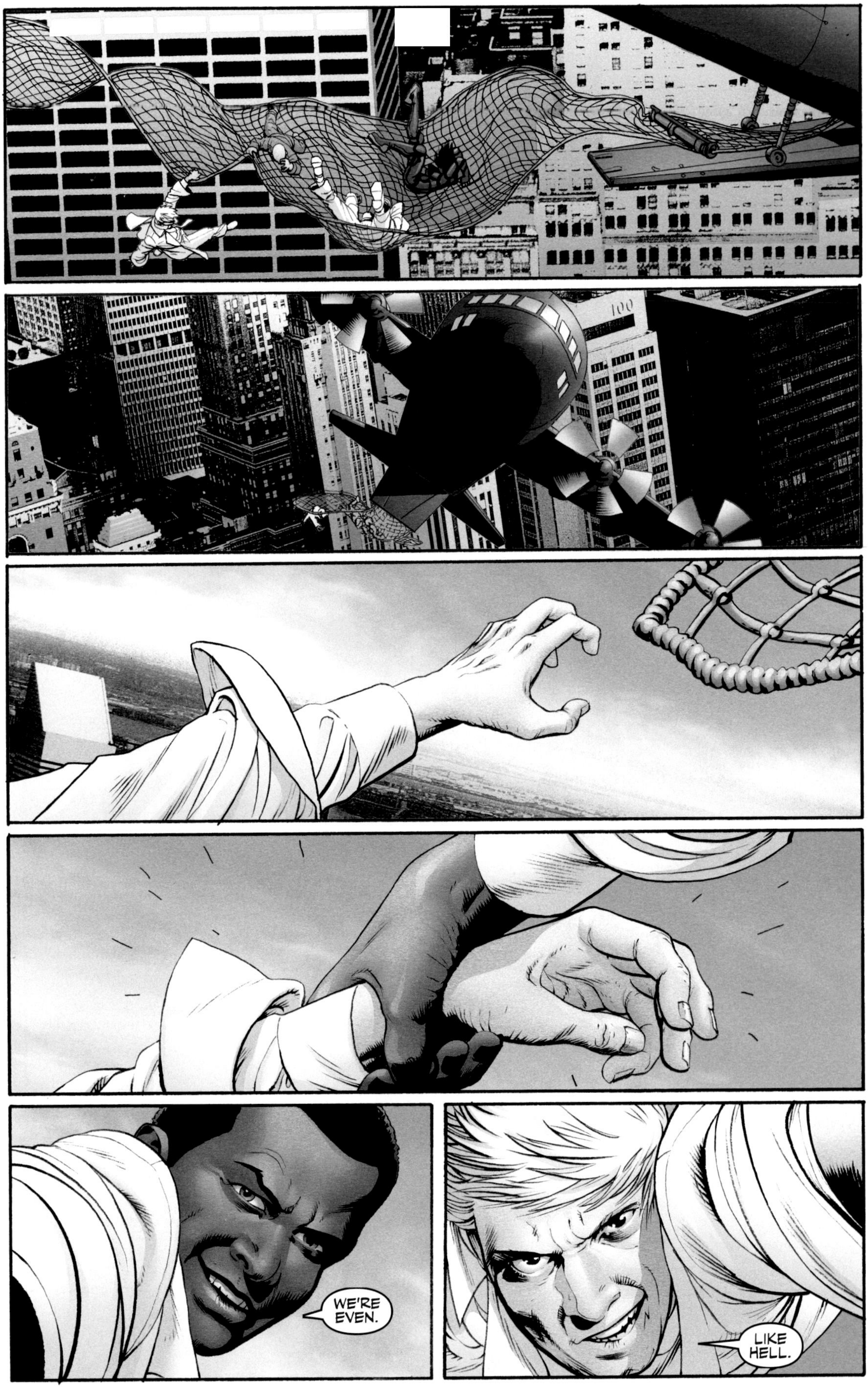
WE'RE EVEN.
LIKE HELL.

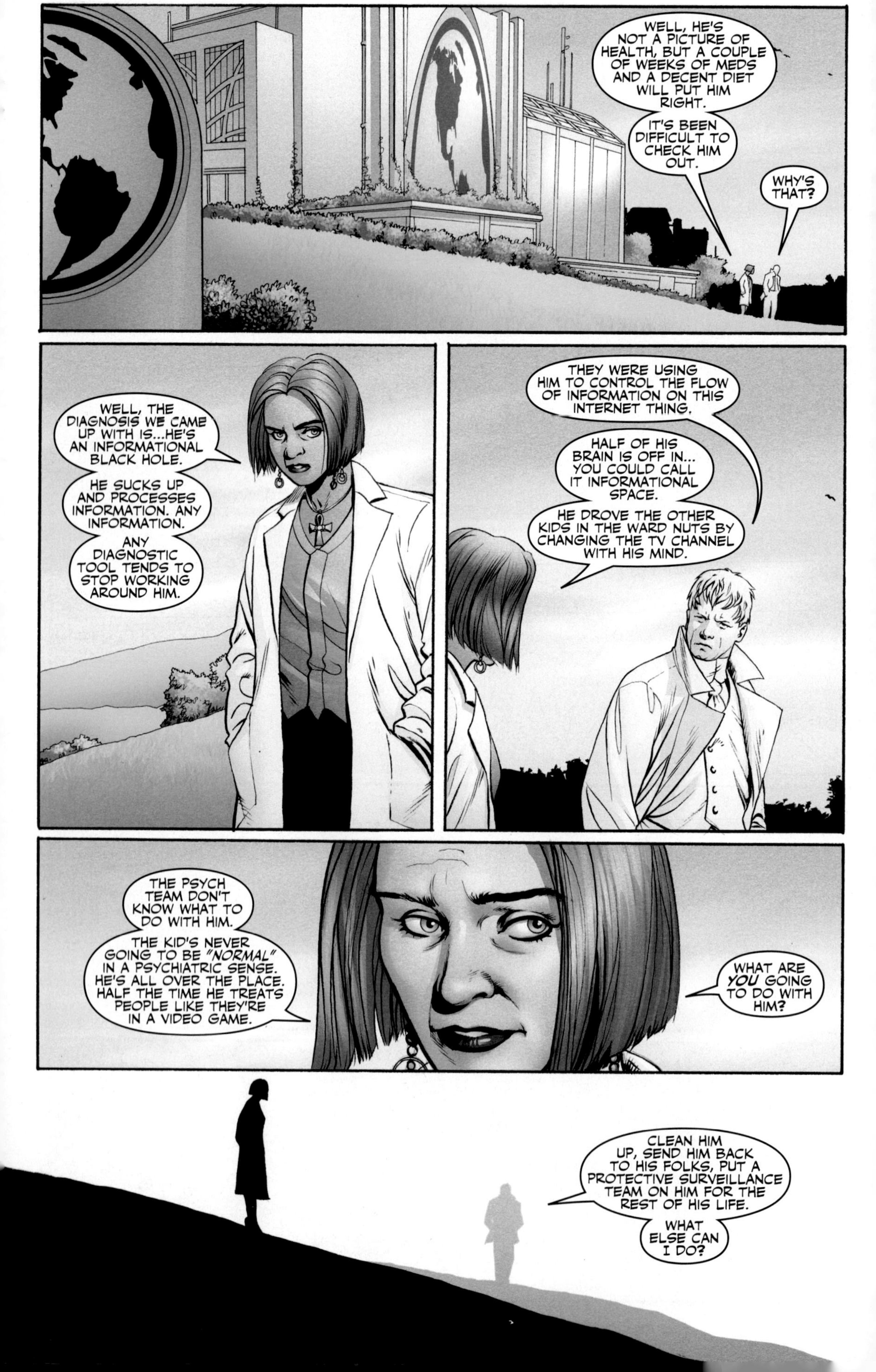
WELL, HE'S NOT A PICTURE OF HEALTH, BUT A COUPLE OF WEEKS OF MEDS AND A DECENT DIET WILL PUT HIM RIGHT.
IT'S BEEN DIFFICULT TO CHECK HIM OUT.
WHY'S THAT?
WELL, THE DIAGNOSIS WE CAME UP WITH IS...HE'S AN INFORMATIONAL BLACK HOLE.
HE SUCKS UP AND PROCESSES INFORMATION. ANY INFORMATION.
ANY DIAGNOSTIC TOOL TENDS TO STOP WORKING AROUND HIM.
THEY WERE USING HIM TO CONTROL THE FLOW OF INFORMATION ON THIS INTERNET THING.
HALF OF HIS BRAIN IS OFF IN... YOU COULD CALL IT INFORMATIONAL SPACE.
HE DROVE THE OTHER KIDS IN THE WARD NUTS BY CHANGING THE TV CHANNEL WITH HIS MIND.
THE PSYCH TEAM DON'T KNOW WHAT TO DO WITH HIM.
THE KID'S NEVER GOING TO BE "NORMAL" IN A PSYCHIATRIC SENSE. HE'S ALL OVER THE PLACE. HALF THE TIME HE TREATS PEOPLE LIKE THEY'RE IN A VIDEO GAME.
WHAT ARE YOU GOING TO DO WITH HIM?
CLEAN HIM UP, SEND HIM BACK TO HIS FOLKS, PUT A PROTECTIVE SURVEILLANCE TEAM ON HIM FOR THE REST OF HIS LIFE.
WHAT ELSE CAN I DO?

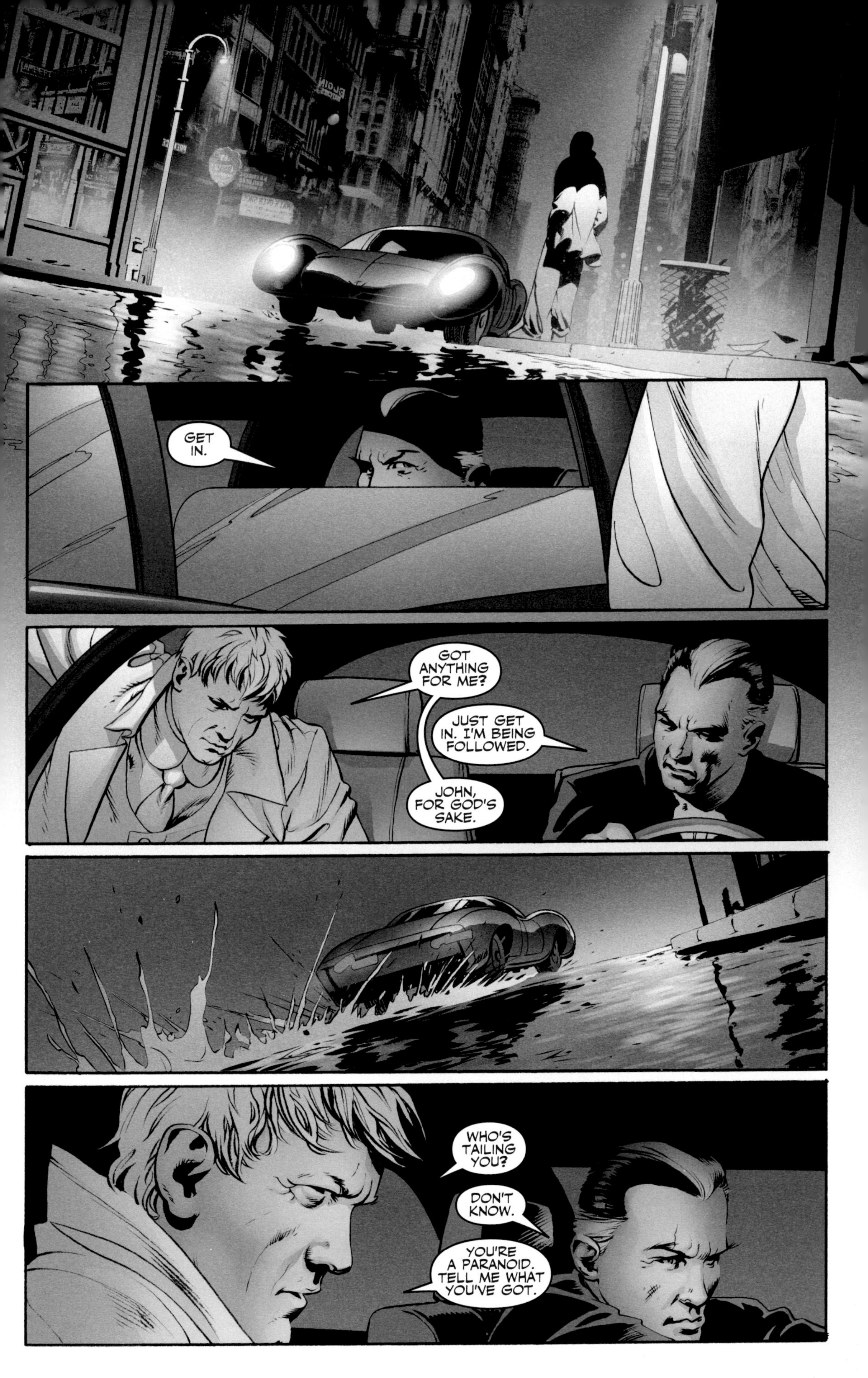
GET IN.
GOT ANYTHING FOR ME?
JUST GET IN. I'M BEING FOLLOWED.
JOHN, FOR GOD'S SAKE.
WHO'S TAILING YOU?
DON'T KNOW.
YOU'RE A PARANOID. TELL ME WHAT YOU'VE GOT.

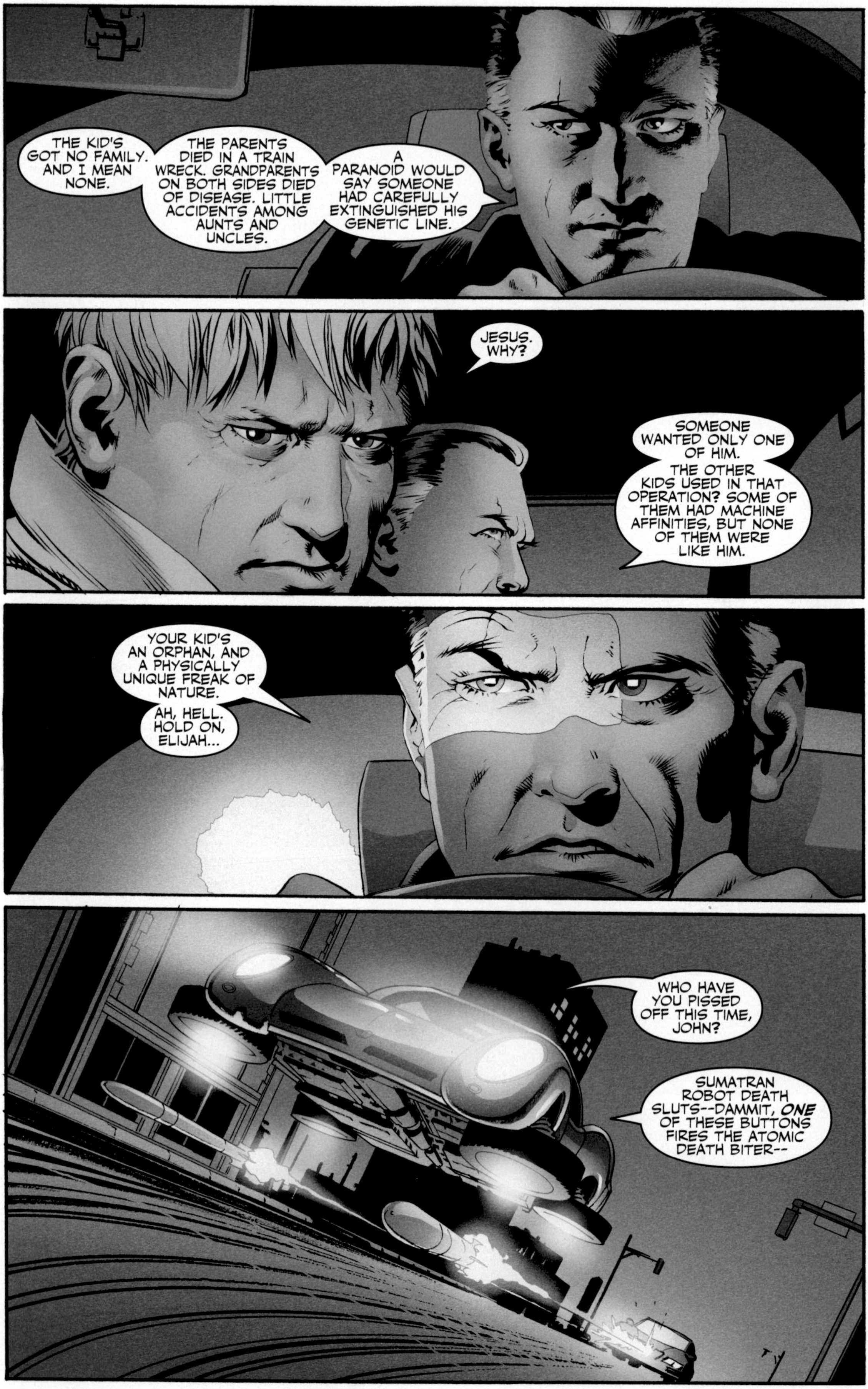
THE KID'S GOT NO FAMILY. AND I MEAN NONE.
THE PARENTS DIED IN A TRAIN WRECK. GRANDPARENTS ON BOTH SIDES DIED OF DISEASE. LITTLE ACCIDENTS AMONG AUNTS AND UNCLES.
A PARANOID WOULD SAY SOMEONE HAD CAREFULLY EXTINGUISHED HIS GENETIC LINE.
JESUS. WHY?
SOMEONE WANTED ONLY ONE OF HIM.
THE OTHER KIDS USED IN THAT OPERATION? SOME OF THEM HAD MACHINE AFFINITIES, BUT NONE OF THEM WERE LIKE HIM.
YOUR KID'S AN ORPHAN, AND A PHYSICALLY UNIQUE FREAK OF NATURE.
AH, HELL. HOLD ON, ELIJAH...
WHO HAVE YOU PISSED OFF THIS TIME, JOHN?
SUMATRAN ROBOT DEATH SLUTS--DAMMIT, ONE OF THESE BUTTONS FIRES THE ATOMIC DEATH BITER--

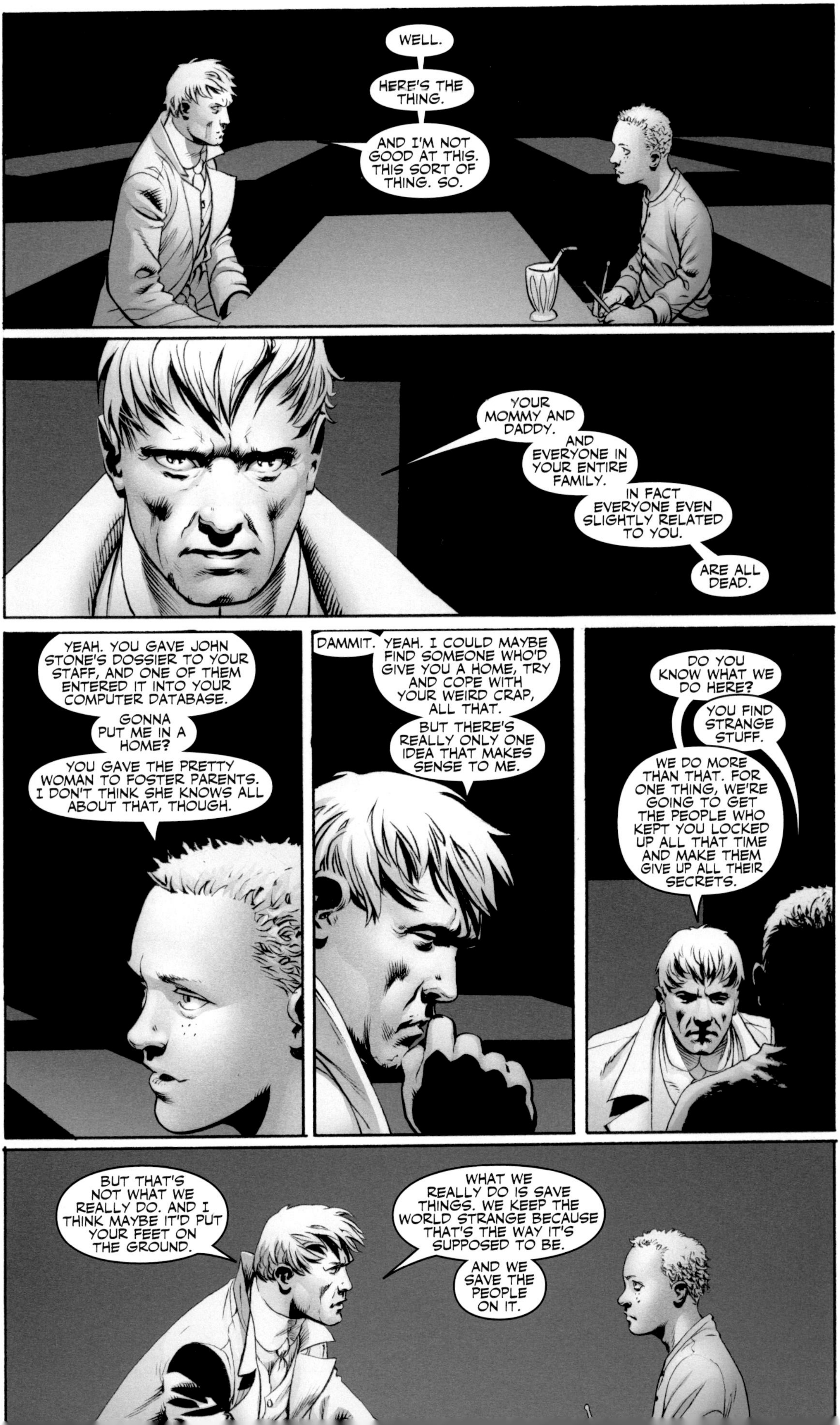
WELL.
HERE'S THE THING.
AND I'M NOT GOOD AT THIS. THIS SORT OF THING. SO.
YOUR MOMMY AND DADDY.
AND EVERYONE IN YOUR ENTIRE FAMILY.
IN FACT EVERYONE EVEN SLIGHTLY RELATED TO YOU.
ARE ALL DEAD.
YEAH. YOU GAVE JOHN STONE'S DOSSIER TO YOUR STAFF, AND ONE OF THEM ENTERED IT INTO YOUR COMPUTER DATABASE.
GONNA PUT ME IN A HOME?
YOU GAVE THE PRETTY WOMAN TO FOSTER PARENTS. I DON'T THINK SHE KNOWS ALL ABOUT THAT, THOUGH.
DAMMIT.
YEAH. I COULD MAYBE FIND SOMEONE WHO'D GIVE YOU A HOME, TRY AND COPE WITH YOUR WEIRD CRAP, ALL THAT.
BUT THERE'S REALLY ONLY ONE IDEA THAT MAKES SENSE TO ME.
DO YOU KNOW WHAT WE DO HERE?
YOU FIND STRANGE STUFF.
WE DO MORE THAN THAT. FOR ONE THING, WE'RE GOING TO GET THE PEOPLE WHO KEPT YOU LOCKED UP ALL THAT TIME AND MAKE THEM GIVE UP ALL THEIR SECRETS.
BUT THAT'S NOT WHAT WE REALLY DO. AND I THINK MAYBE IT'D PUT YOUR FEET ON THE GROUND.
WHAT WE REALLY DO IS SAVE THINGS. WE KEEP THE WORLD STRANGE BECAUSE THAT'S THE WAY IT'S SUPPOSED TO BE.
AND WE SAVE THE PEOPLE ON IT.

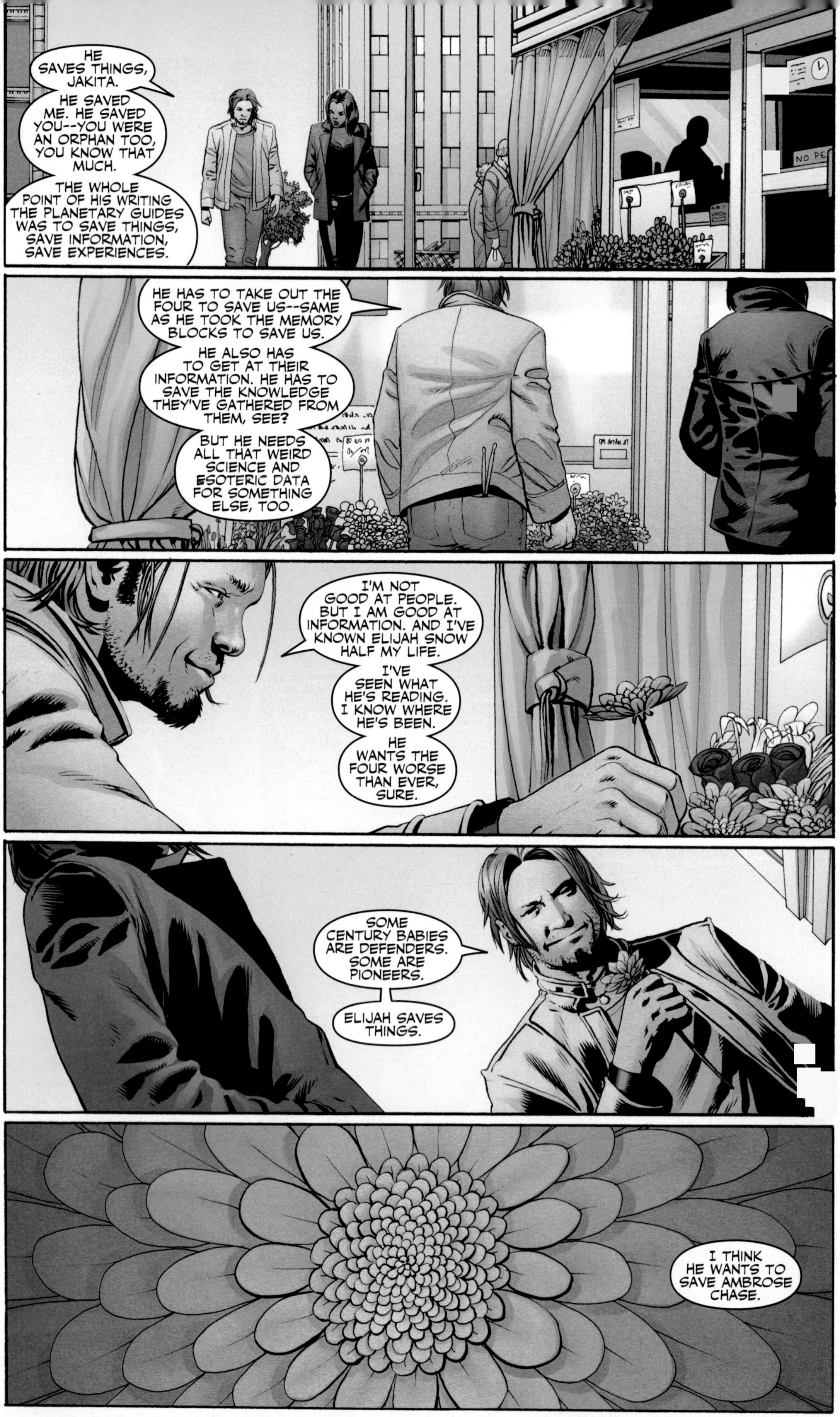
HE SAVES THINGS, JAKITA.
HE SAVED ME. HE SAVED YOU--YOU WERE AN ORPHAN TOO, YOU KNOW THAT MUCH.
THE WHOLE POINT OF HIS WRITING THE PLANETARY GUIDES WAS TO SAVE THINGS, SAVE INFORMATION, SAVE EXPERIENCES.
HE HAS TO TAKE OUT THE FOUR TO SAVE US--SAME AS HE TOOK THE MEMORY BLOCKS TO SAVE US.
HE ALSO HAS TO GET AT THEIR INFORMATION. HE HAS TO SAVE THE KNOWLEDGE THEY'VE GATHERED FROM THEM, SEE?
BUT HE NEEDS ALL THAT WEIRD SCIENCE AND ESOTERIC DATA FOR SOMETHING ELSE, TOO.
I'M NOT GOOD AT PEOPLE. BUT I AM GOOD AT INFORMATION. AND I'VE KNOWN ELIJAH SNOW HALF MY LIFE.
I'VE SEEN WHAT HE'S READING. I KNOW WHERE HE'S BEEN.
HE WANTS THE FOUR WORSE THAN EVER, SURE.
SOME CENTURY BABIES ARE DEFENDERS. SOME ARE PIONEERS.
ELIJAH SAVES THINGS.
I THINK HE WANTS TO SAVE AMBROSE CHASE.

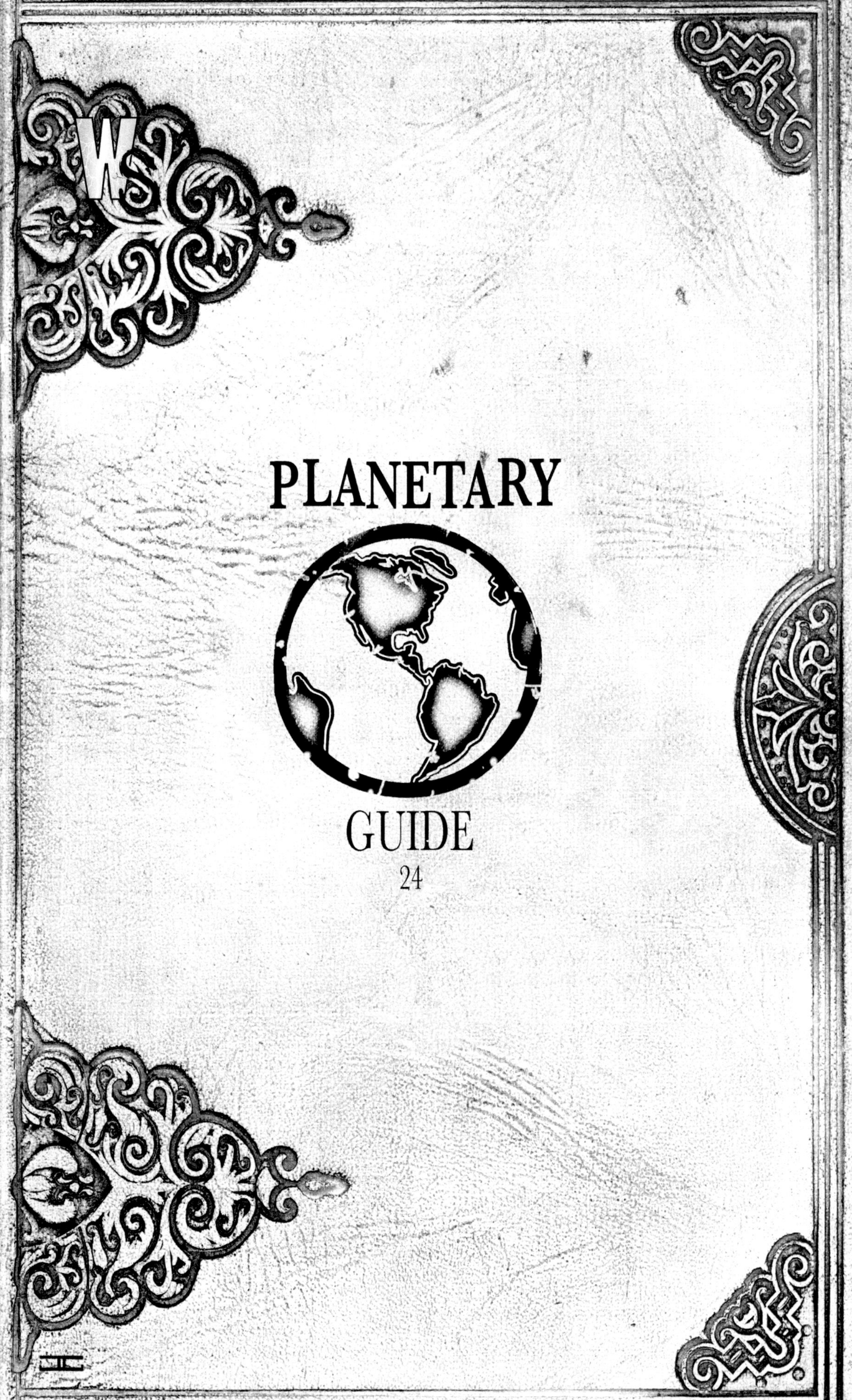
PLANETARY
GUIDE
24

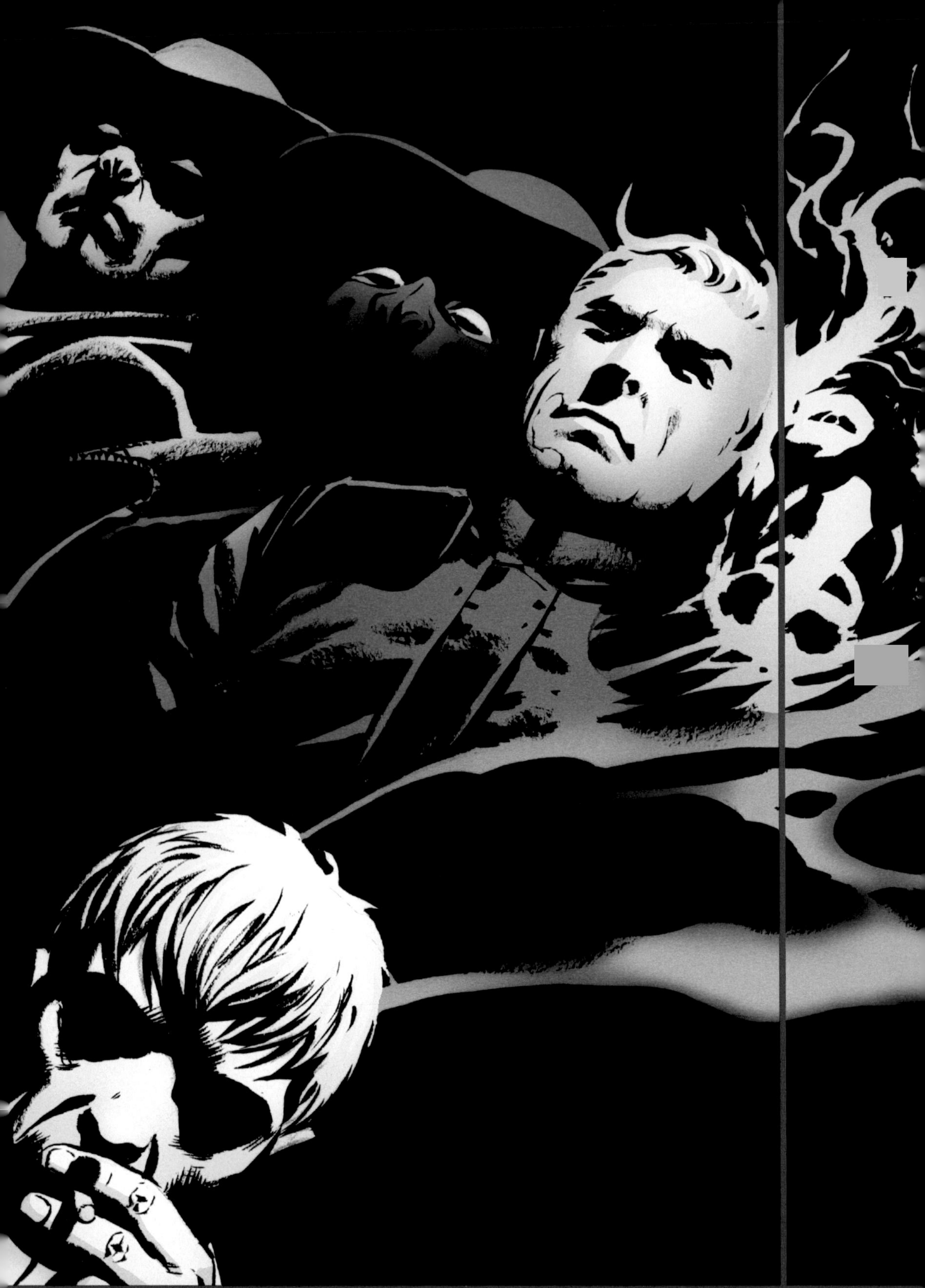

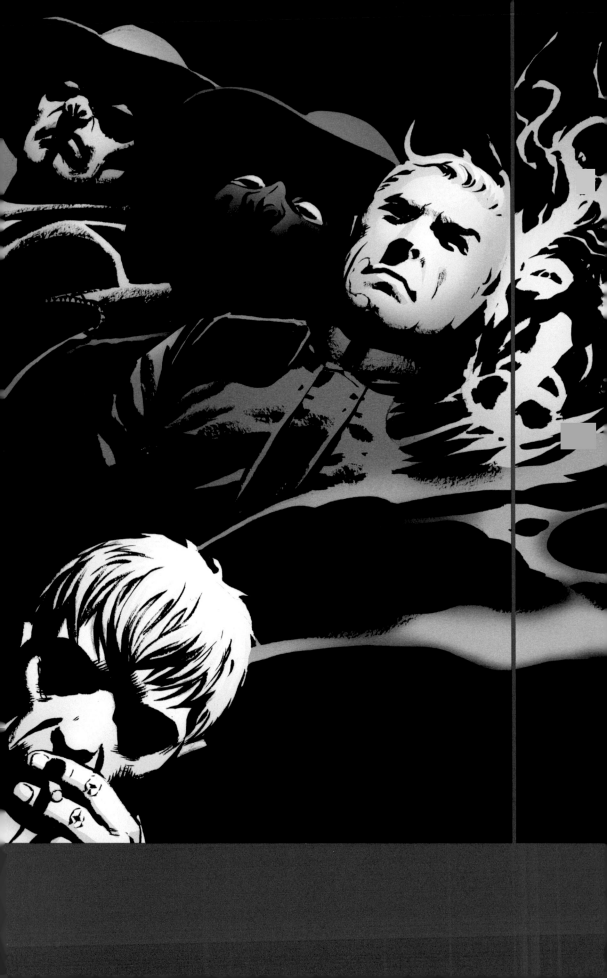

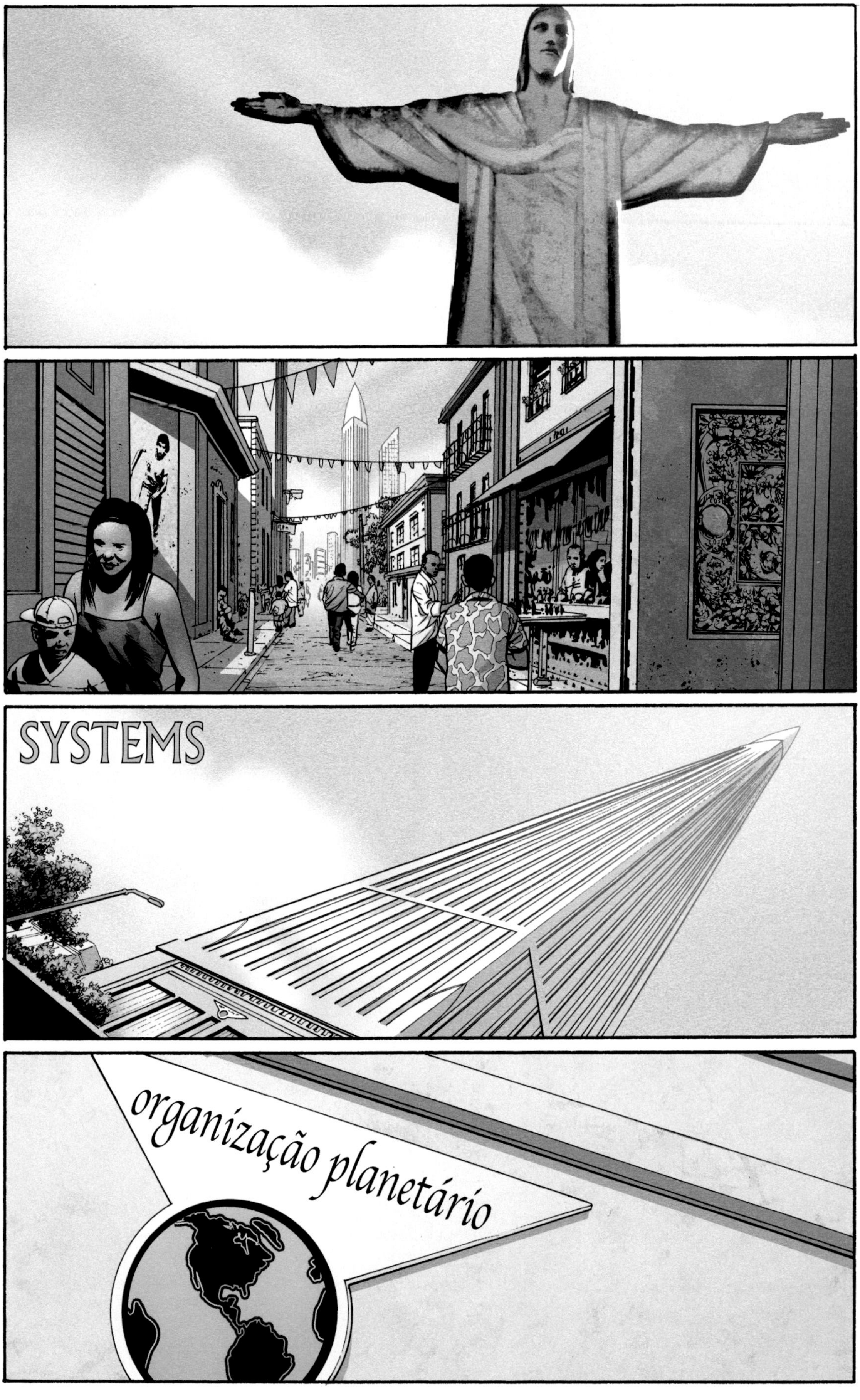
SYSTEMS
organização planetário

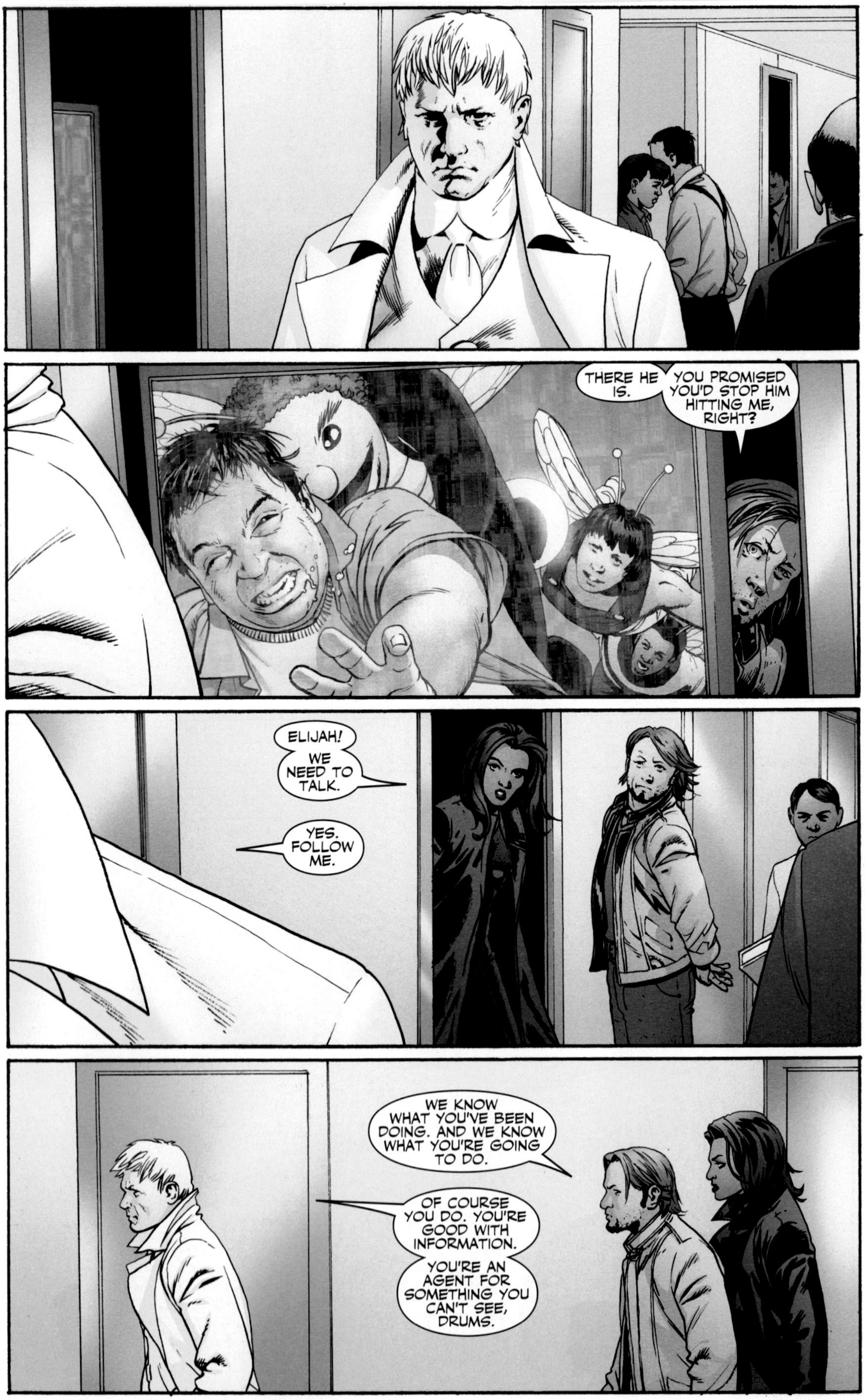
THERE HE IS.
YOU PROMISED YOU'D STOP HIM HITTING ME, RIGHT?
ELIJAH! WE NEED TO TALK.
YES. FOLLOW ME.
WE KNOW WHAT YOU'VE BEEN DOING. AND WE KNOW WHAT YOU'RE GOING TO DO.
OF COURSE YOU DO. YOU'RE GOOD WITH INFORMATION.
YOU'RE AN AGENT FOR SOMETHING YOU CAN'T SEE, DRUMS.

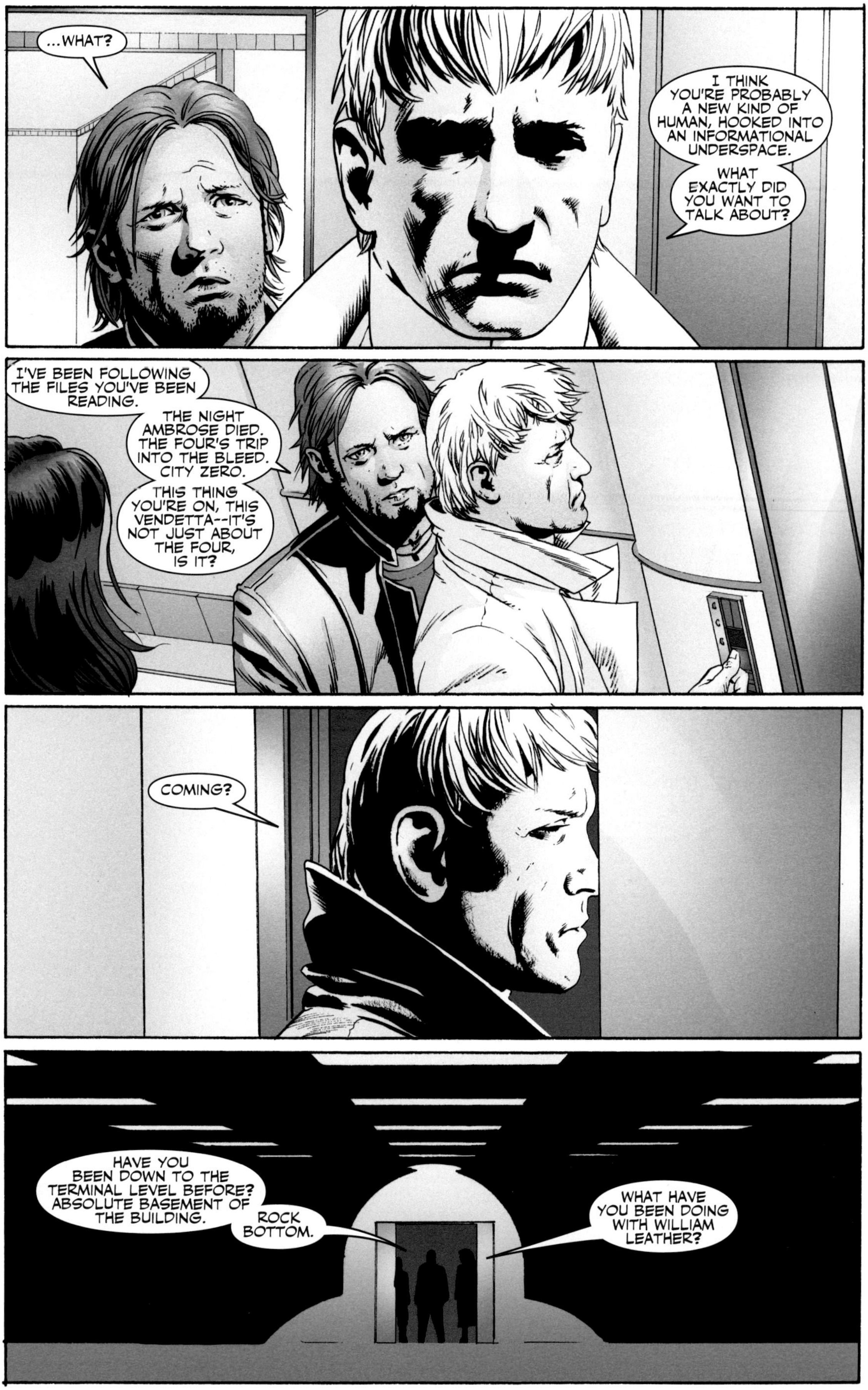
...WHAT?
I THINK YOU'RE PROBABLY A NEW KIND OF HUMAN, HOOKED INTO AN INFORMATIONAL UNDERSPACE.
WHAT EXACTLY DID YOU WANT TO TALK ABOUT?
I'VE BEEN FOLLOWING THE FILES YOU'VE BEEN READING.
THE NIGHT AMBROSE DIED. THE FOUR'S TRIP INTO THE BLEED. CITY ZERO.
THIS THING YOU'RE ON, THIS VENDETTA--IT'S NOT JUST ABOUT THE FOUR, IS IT?
COMING?
HAVE YOU BEEN DOWN TO THE TERMINAL LEVEL BEFORE? ABSOLUTE BASEMENT OF THE BUILDING.
ROCK BOTTOM.
WHAT HAVE YOU BEEN DOING WITH WILLIAM LEATHER?

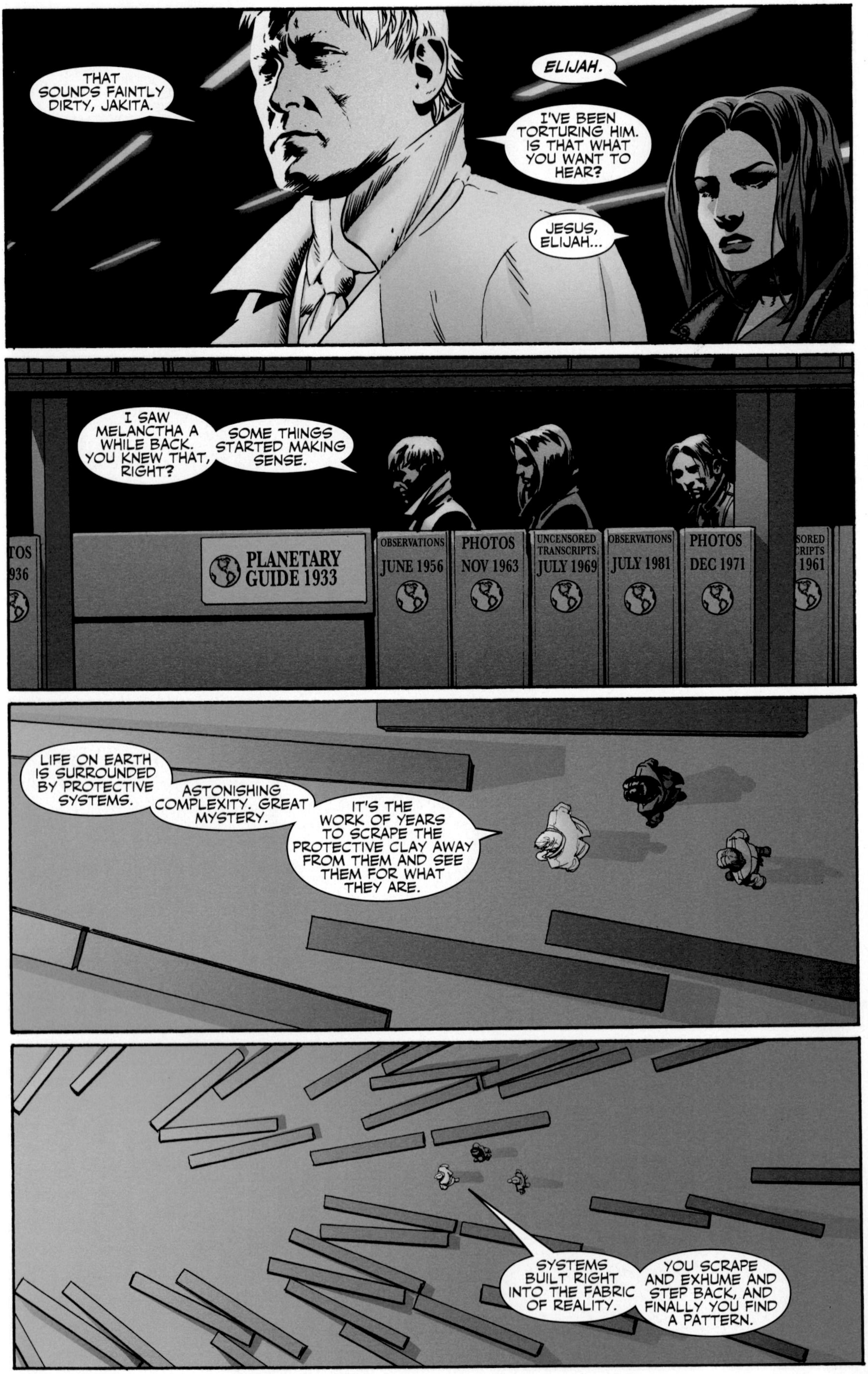
THAT SOUNDS FAINTLY DIRTY, JAKITA.
ELIJAH.
I'VE BEEN TORTURING HIM. IS THAT WHAT YOU WANT TO HEAR?
JESUS, ELIJAH...
I SAW MELANCTHA A WHILE BACK. YOU KNEW THAT, RIGHT?
SOME THINGS STARTED MAKING SENSE.
TOS
936
PLANETARY GUIDE 1933
OBSERVATIONS JUNE 1956
PHOTOS NOV 1963
UNCENSORED TRANSCRIPTS JULY 1969
OBSERVATIONS JULY 1981
PHOTOS DEC 1971
SORED CRIPTS 1961
LIFE ON EARTH IS SURROUNDED BY PROTECTIVE SYSTEMS.
ASTONISHING COMPLEXITY. GREAT MYSTERY.
IT'S THE WORK OF YEARS TO SCRAPE THE PROTECTIVE CLAY AWAY FROM THEM AND SEE THEM FOR WHAT THEY ARE.
SYSTEMS BUILT RIGHT INTO THE FABRIC OF REALITY.
YOU SCRAPE AND EXHUME AND STEP BACK, AND FINALLY YOU FIND A PATTERN.

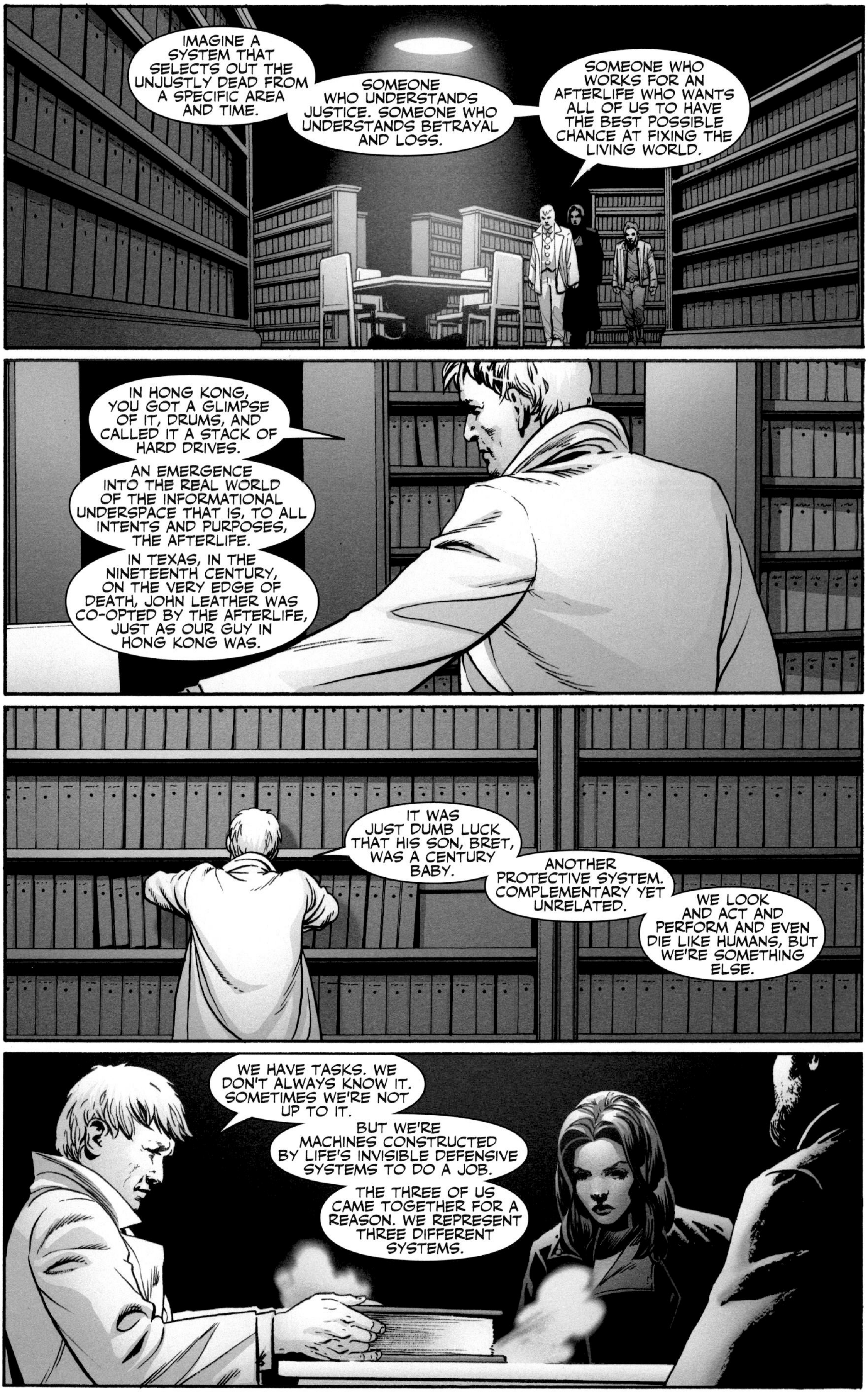
IMAGINE A SYSTEM THAT SELECTS OUT THE UNJUSTLY DEAD FROM A SPECIFIC AREA AND TIME.
SOMEONE WHO UNDERSTANDS JUSTICE. SOMEONE WHO UNDERSTANDS BETRAYAL AND LOSS.
SOMEONE WHO WORKS FOR AN AFTERLIFE WHO WANTS ALL OF US TO HAVE THE BEST POSSIBLE CHANCE AT FIXING THE LIVING WORLD.
IN HONG KONG, YOU GOT A GLIMPSE OF IT, DRUMS, AND CALLED IT A STACK OF HARD DRIVES.
AN EMERGENCE INTO THE REAL WORLD OF THE INFORMATIONAL UNDERSPACE THAT IS, TO ALL INTENTS AND PURPOSES, THE AFTERLIFE.
IN TEXAS, IN THE NINETEENTH CENTURY, ON THE VERY EDGE OF DEATH, JOHN LEATHER WAS CO-OPTED BY THE AFTERLIFE, JUST AS OUR GUY IN HONG KONG WAS.
IT WAS JUST DUMB LUCK THAT HIS SON, BRET, WAS A CENTURY BABY.
ANOTHER PROTECTIVE SYSTEM. COMPLEMENTARY YET UNRELATED.
WE LOOK AND ACT AND PERFORM AND EVEN DIE LIKE HUMANS, BUT WE'RE SOMETHING ELSE.
WE HAVE TASKS. WE DON'T ALWAYS KNOW IT. SOMETIMES WE'RE NOT UP TO IT.
BUT WE'RE MACHINES CONSTRUCTED BY LIFE'S INVISIBLE DEFENSIVE SYSTEMS TO DO A JOB.
THE THREE OF US CAME TOGETHER FOR A REASON. WE REPRESENT THREE DIFFERENT SYSTEMS.

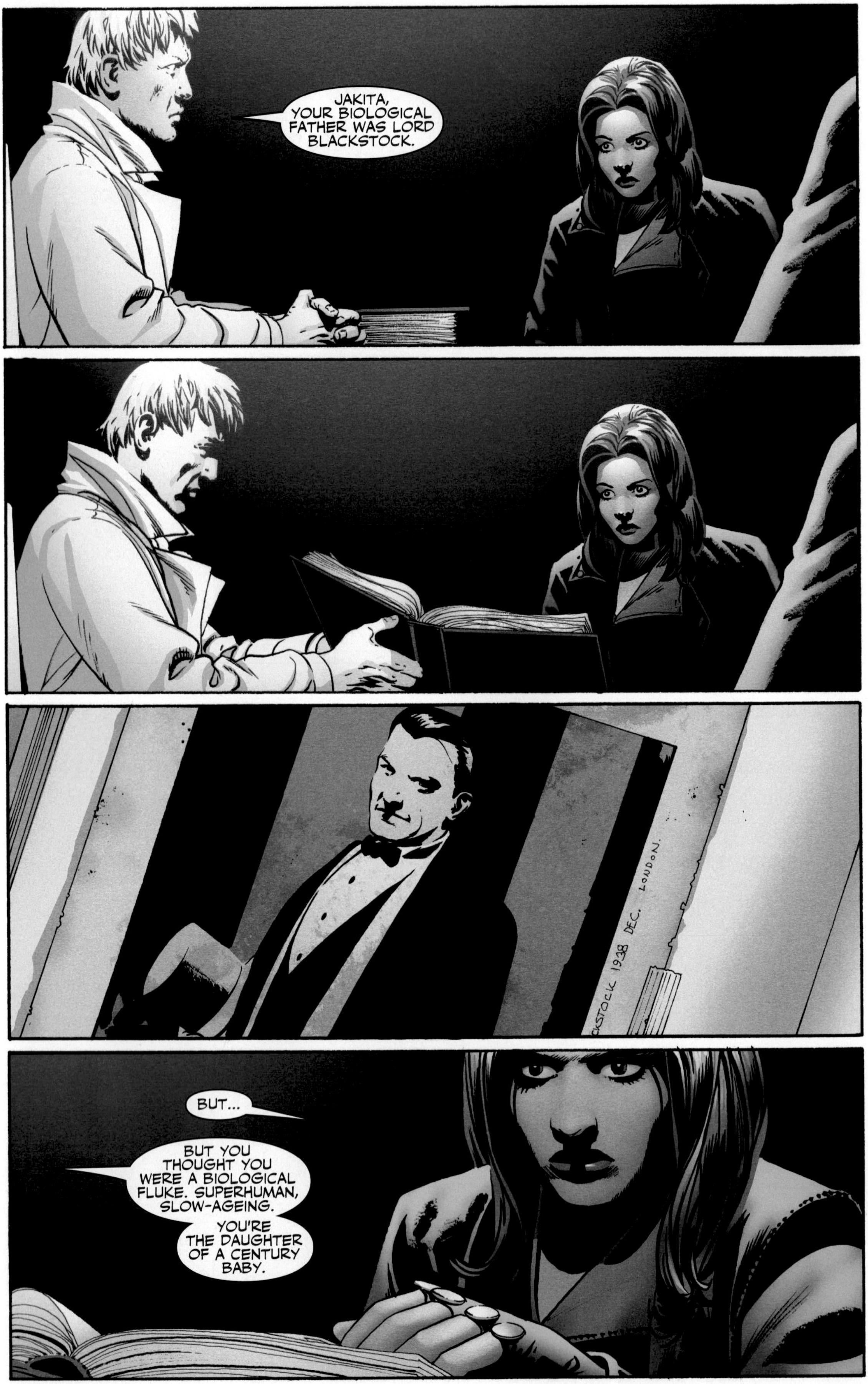
JAKITA, YOUR BIOLOGICAL FATHER WAS LORD BLACKSTOCK.
CKSTOCK 1938 DEC. LONDON.
BUT...
BUT YOU THOUGHT YOU WERE A BIOLOGICAL FLUKE. SUPERHUMAN, SLOW-AGEING.
YOU'RE THE DAUGHTER OF A CENTURY BABY.

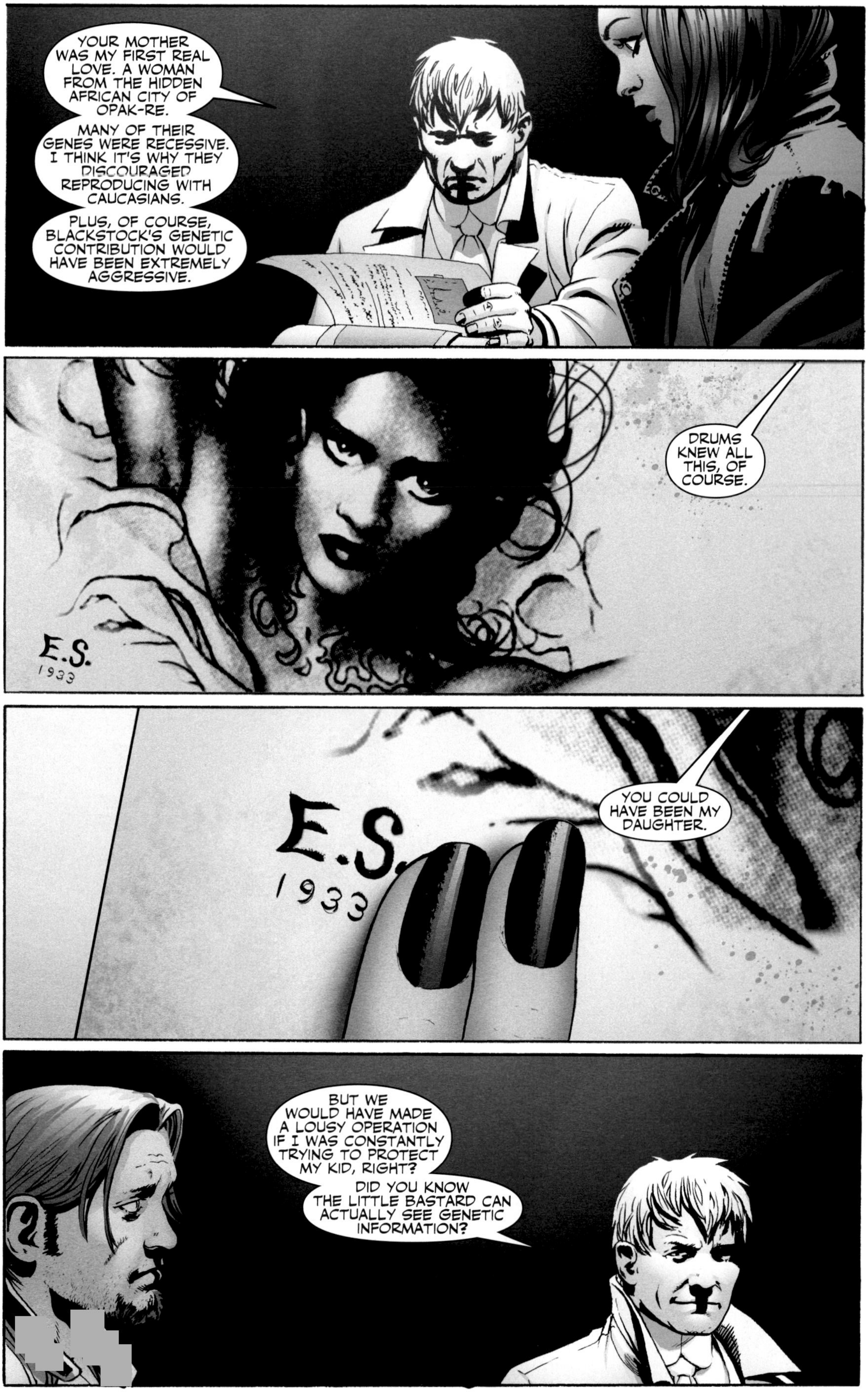

YOUR MOTHER WAS MY FIRST REAL LOVE. A WOMAN FROM THE HIDDEN AFRICAN CITY OF OPAK-RE.
MANY OF THEIR GENES WERE RECESSIVE. I THINK IT'S WHY THEY DISCOURAGED REPRODUCING WITH CAUCASIANS.
PLUS, OF COURSE, BLACKSTOCK'S GENETIC CONTRIBUTION WOULD HAVE BEEN EXTREMELY AGGRESSIVE.
DRUMS KNEW ALL THIS, OF COURSE.
E.S.
1933
E.S.
1933
YOU COULD HAVE BEEN MY DAUGHTER.
BUT WE WOULD HAVE MADE A LOUSY OPERATION IF I WAS CONSTANTLY TRYING TO PROTECT MY KID, RIGHT?
DID YOU KNOW THE LITTLE BASTARD CAN ACTUALLY SEE GENETIC INFORMATION?

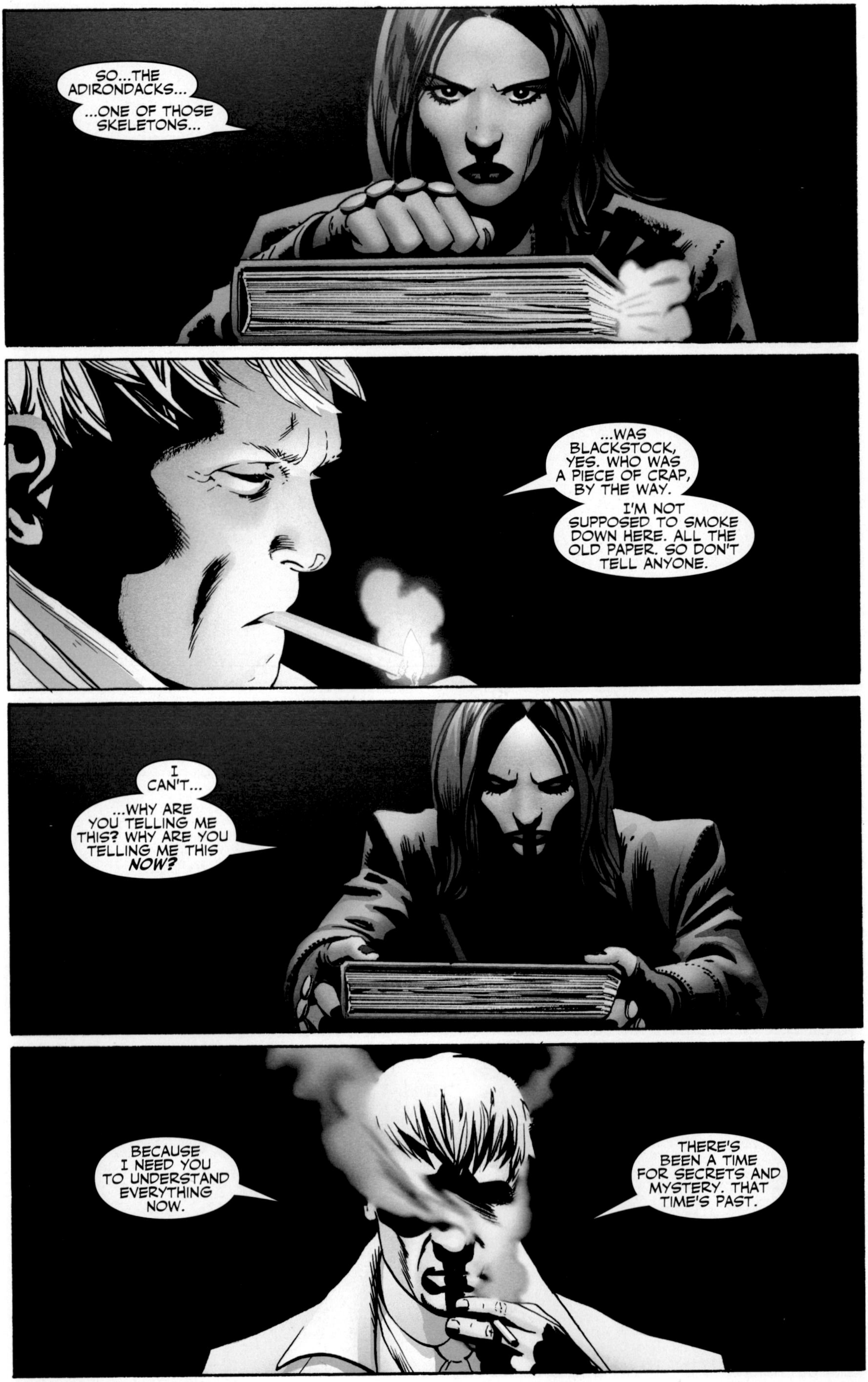
SO...THE ADIRONDACKS...
...ONE OF THOSE SKELETONS...
...WAS BLACKSTOCK, YES. WHO WAS A PIECE OF CRAP, BY THE WAY.
I'M NOT SUPPOSED TO SMOKE DOWN HERE. ALL THE OLD PAPER. SO DON'T TELL ANYONE.
I CAN'T...
...WHY ARE YOU TELLING ME THIS? WHY ARE YOU TELLING ME THIS *NOW?*
BECAUSE I NEED YOU TO UNDERSTAND EVERYTHING NOW.
THERE'S BEEN A TIME FOR SECRETS AND MYSTERY. THAT TIME'S PAST.

...SO BRET LEATHER IS RELATED TO WILLIAM LEATHER?

BRET LEATHER'S WIFE WAS UNFAITHFUL. WILLIAM LEATHER DIDN'T INHERIT A THING FROM BRET.

THAT'S HOW DOWLING GOT HIS HOOKS INTO WILLIAM. REAL LIFE CHEATED HIM OUT OF INHERITING POWER.

DOWLING'S LIFE HAS BEEN ALL ABOUT FINDING WAYS TO APPROXIMATE THE ABILITIES WE ALL HAVE--

--AND THEN LOCKING THEM AWAY OR KILLING THEM.

WHICH BRINGS ME TO THE QUESTION OF WHY HE LEFT US ALL ALIVE.

WE FIND THINGS. WE PROTECT THEM.

"IT'S A STRANGE WORLD. LETS KEEP IT THAT WAY."

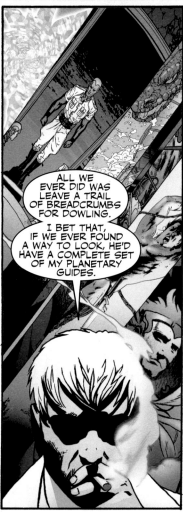

ALL WE EVER DID WAS LEAVE A TRAIL OF BREADCRUMBS FOR DOWLING.

I BET THAT, IF WE EVER FOUND A WAY TO LOOK, HE'D HAVE A COMPLETE SET OF MY PLANETARY GUIDES.

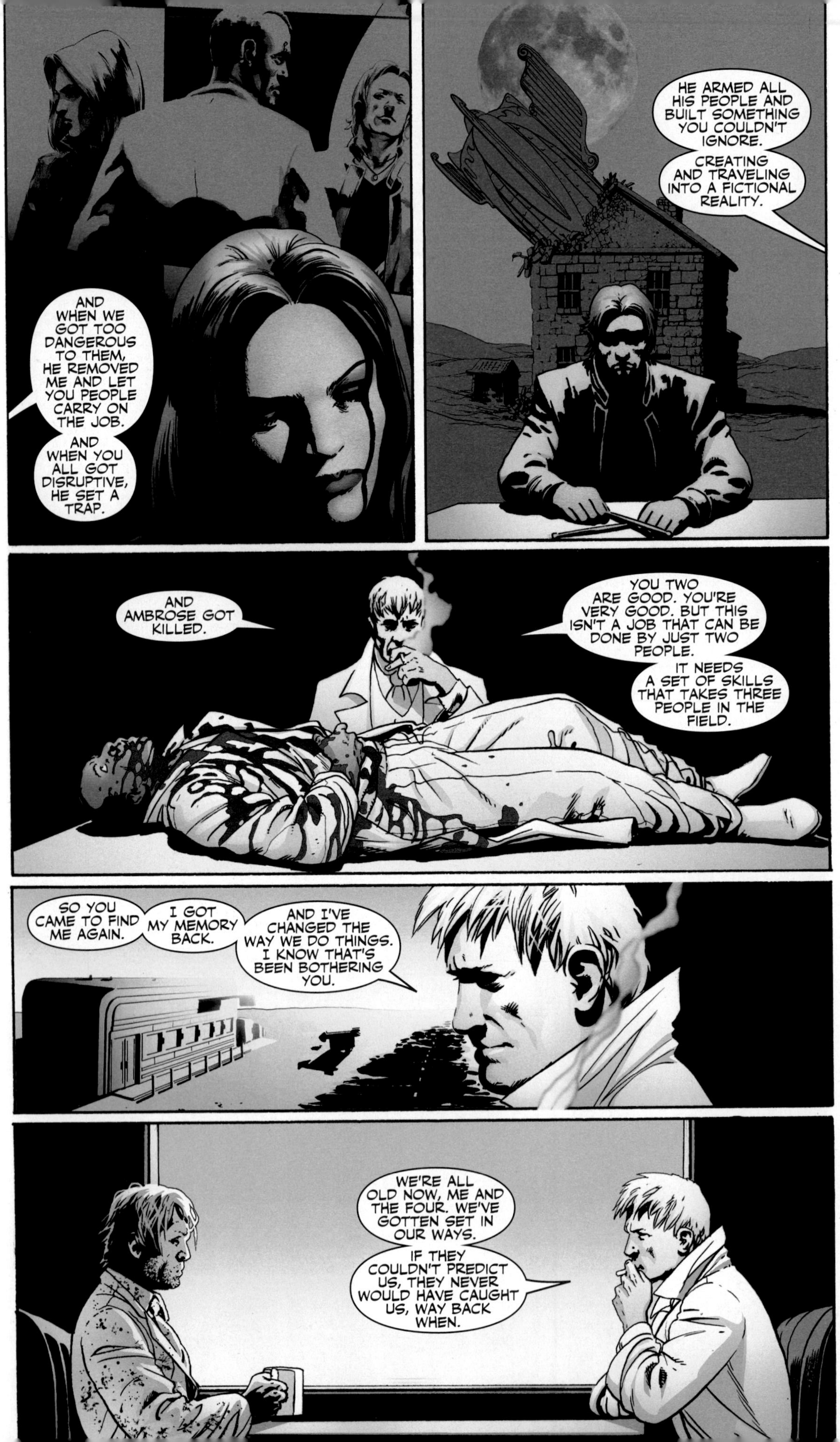
AND WHEN WE GOT TOO DANGEROUS TO THEM, HE REMOVED ME AND LET YOU PEOPLE CARRY ON THE JOB.
AND WHEN YOU ALL GOT DISRUPTIVE, HE SET A TRAP.
HE ARMED ALL HIS PEOPLE AND BUILT SOMETHING YOU COULDN'T IGNORE.
CREATING AND TRAVELING INTO A FICTIONAL REALITY.
AND AMBROSE GOT KILLED.
YOU TWO ARE GOOD. YOU'RE VERY GOOD. BUT THIS ISN'T A JOB THAT CAN BE DONE BY JUST TWO PEOPLE.
IT NEEDS A SET OF SKILLS THAT TAKES THREE PEOPLE IN THE FIELD.
SO YOU CAME TO FIND ME AGAIN.
I GOT MY MEMORY BACK.
AND I'VE CHANGED THE WAY WE DO THINGS. I KNOW THAT'S BEEN BOTHERING YOU.
WE'RE ALL OLD NOW, ME AND THE FOUR. WE'VE GOTTEN SET IN OUR WAYS.
IF THEY COULDN'T PREDICT US, THEY NEVER WOULD HAVE CAUGHT US, WAY BACK WHEN.

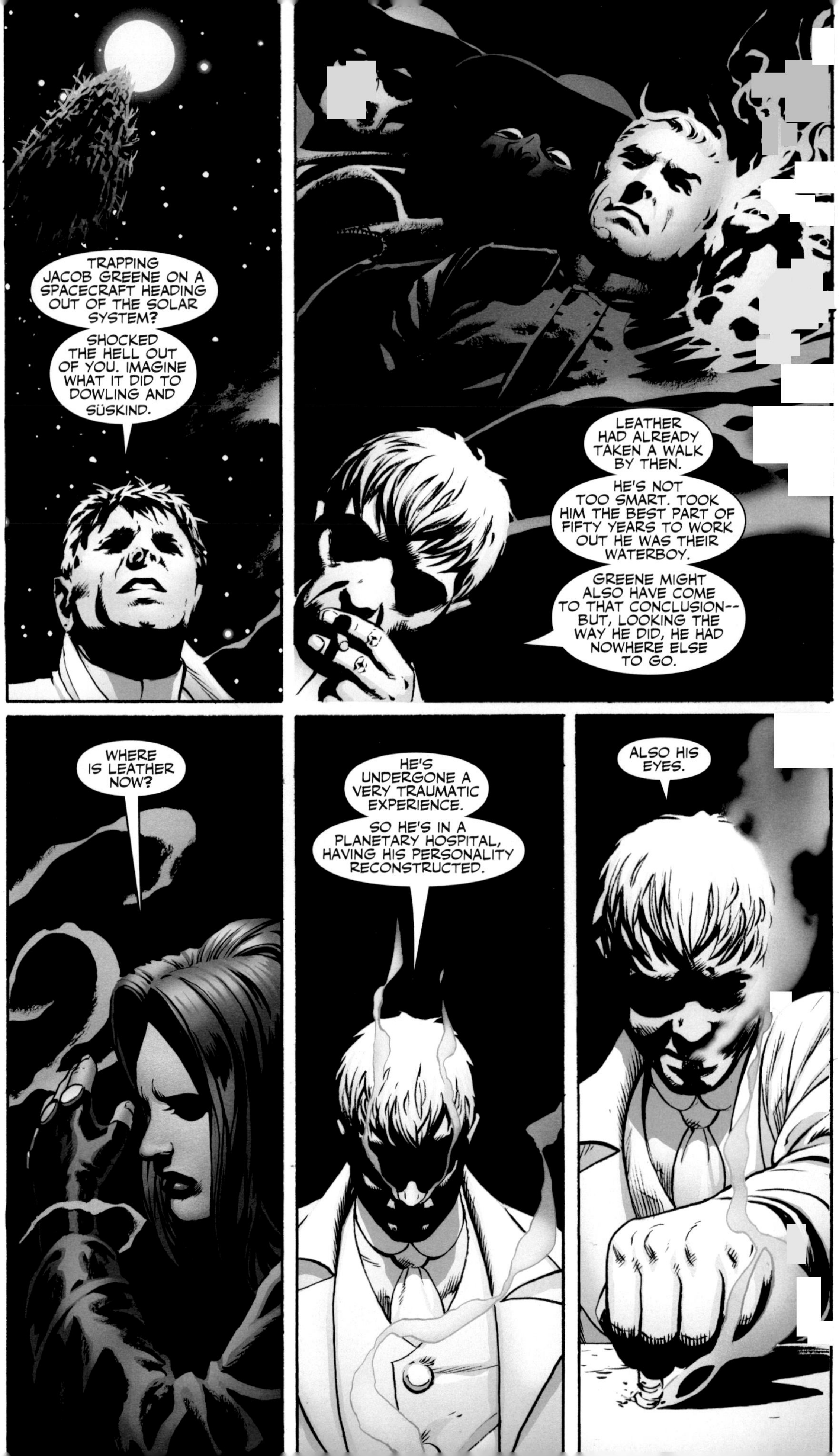
TRAPPING JACOB GREENE ON A SPACECRAFT HEADING OUT OF THE SOLAR SYSTEM?
SHOCKED THE HELL OUT OF YOU. IMAGINE WHAT IT DID TO DOWLING AND SÜSKIND.
LEATHER HAD ALREADY TAKEN A WALK BY THEN.
HE'S NOT TOO SMART. TOOK HIM THE BEST PART OF FIFTY YEARS TO WORK OUT HE WAS THEIR WATERBOY.
GREENE MIGHT ALSO HAVE COME TO THAT CONCLUSION-- BUT, LOOKING THE WAY HE DID, HE HAD NOWHERE ELSE TO GO.
WHERE IS LEATHER NOW?
HE'S UNDERGONE A VERY TRAUMATIC EXPERIENCE.
SO HE'S IN A PLANETARY HOSPITAL, HAVING HIS PERSONALITY RECONSTRUCTED.
ALSO HIS EYES.

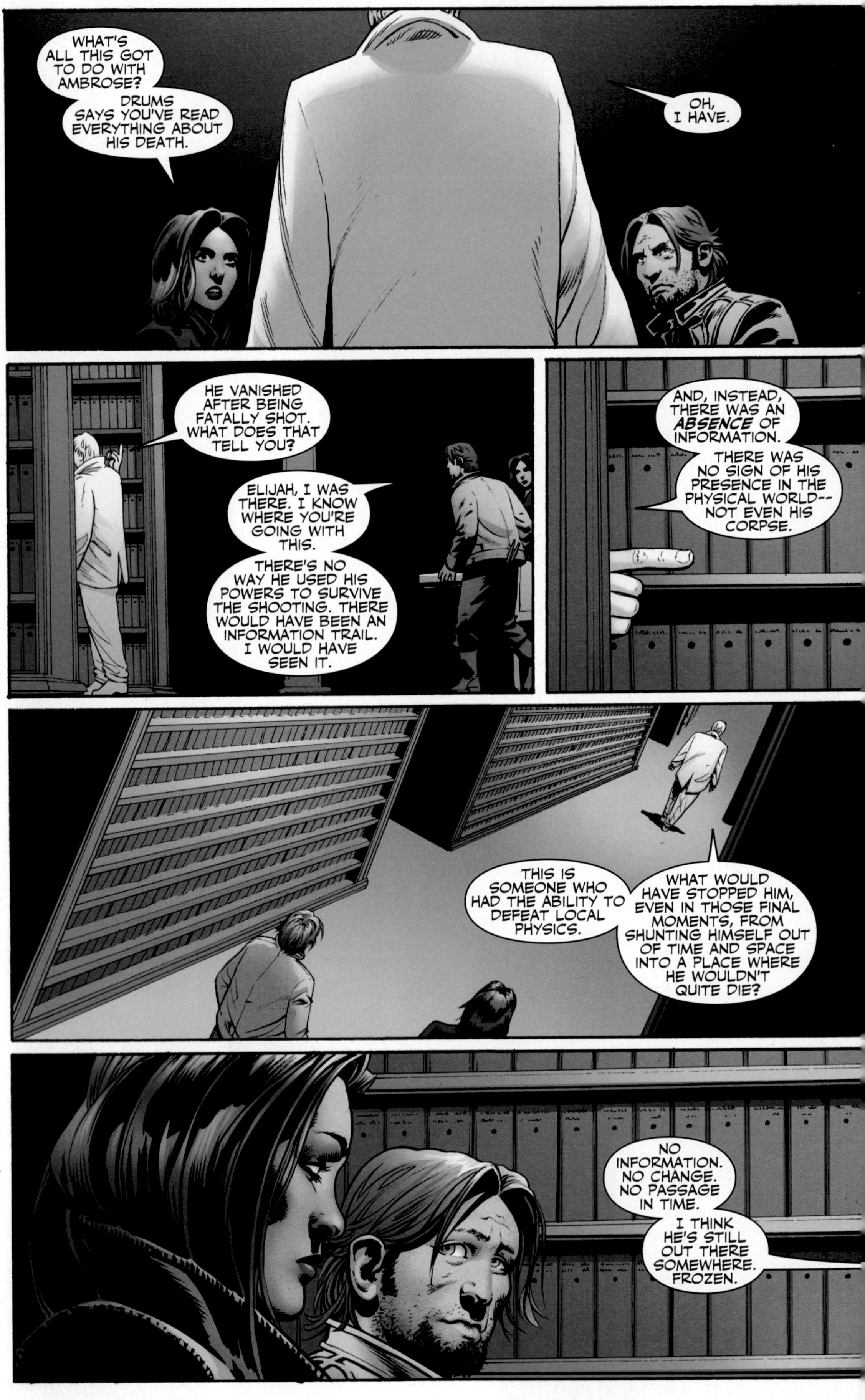
WHAT'S ALL THIS GOT TO DO WITH AMBROSE?
DRUMS SAYS YOU'VE READ EVERYTHING ABOUT HIS DEATH.
OH, I HAVE.
HE VANISHED AFTER BEING FATALLY SHOT. WHAT DOES THAT TELL YOU?
ELIJAH, I WAS THERE. I KNOW WHERE YOU'RE GOING WITH THIS.
THERE'S NO WAY HE USED HIS POWERS TO SURVIVE THE SHOOTING. THERE WOULD HAVE BEEN AN INFORMATION TRAIL. I WOULD HAVE SEEN IT.
AND, INSTEAD, THERE WAS AN *ABSENCE* OF INFORMATION.
THERE WAS NO SIGN OF HIS PRESENCE IN THE PHYSICAL WORLD-- NOT EVEN HIS CORPSE.
THIS IS SOMEONE WHO HAD THE ABILITY TO DEFEAT LOCAL PHYSICS.
WHAT WOULD HAVE STOPPED HIM, EVEN IN THOSE FINAL MOMENTS, FROM SHUNTING HIMSELF OUT OF TIME AND SPACE INTO A PLACE WHERE HE WOULDN'T QUITE DIE?
NO INFORMATION. NO CHANGE. NO PASSAGE IN TIME.
I THINK HE'S STILL OUT THERE SOMEWHERE. FROZEN.

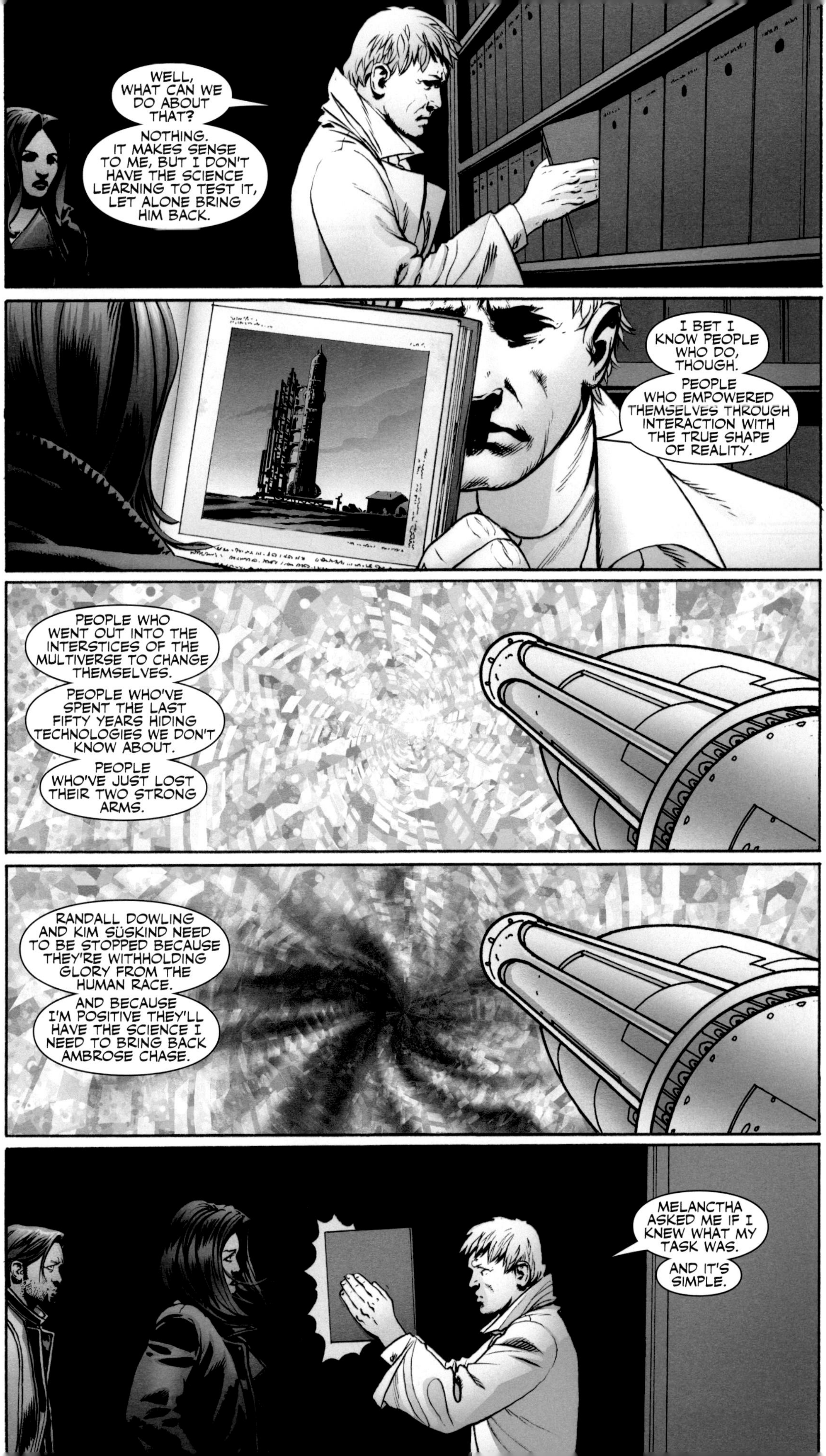
WELL, WHAT CAN WE DO ABOUT THAT?
NOTHING. IT MAKES SENSE TO ME, BUT I DON'T HAVE THE SCIENCE LEARNING TO TEST IT, LET ALONE BRING HIM BACK.
I BET I KNOW PEOPLE WHO DO, THOUGH.
PEOPLE WHO EMPOWERED THEMSELVES THROUGH INTERACTION WITH THE TRUE SHAPE OF REALITY.
PEOPLE WHO WENT OUT INTO THE INTERSTICES OF THE MULTIVERSE TO CHANGE THEMSELVES.
PEOPLE WHO'VE SPENT THE LAST FIFTY YEARS HIDING TECHNOLOGIES WE DON'T KNOW ABOUT.
PEOPLE WHO'VE JUST LOST THEIR TWO STRONG ARMS.
RANDALL DOWLING AND KIM SÜSKIND NEED TO BE STOPPED BECAUSE THEY'RE WITHHOLDING GLORY FROM THE HUMAN RACE.
AND BECAUSE I'M POSITIVE THEY'LL HAVE THE SCIENCE I NEED TO BRING BACK AMBROSE CHASE.
MELANCTHA ASKED ME IF I KNEW WHAT MY TASK WAS.
AND IT'S SIMPLE.

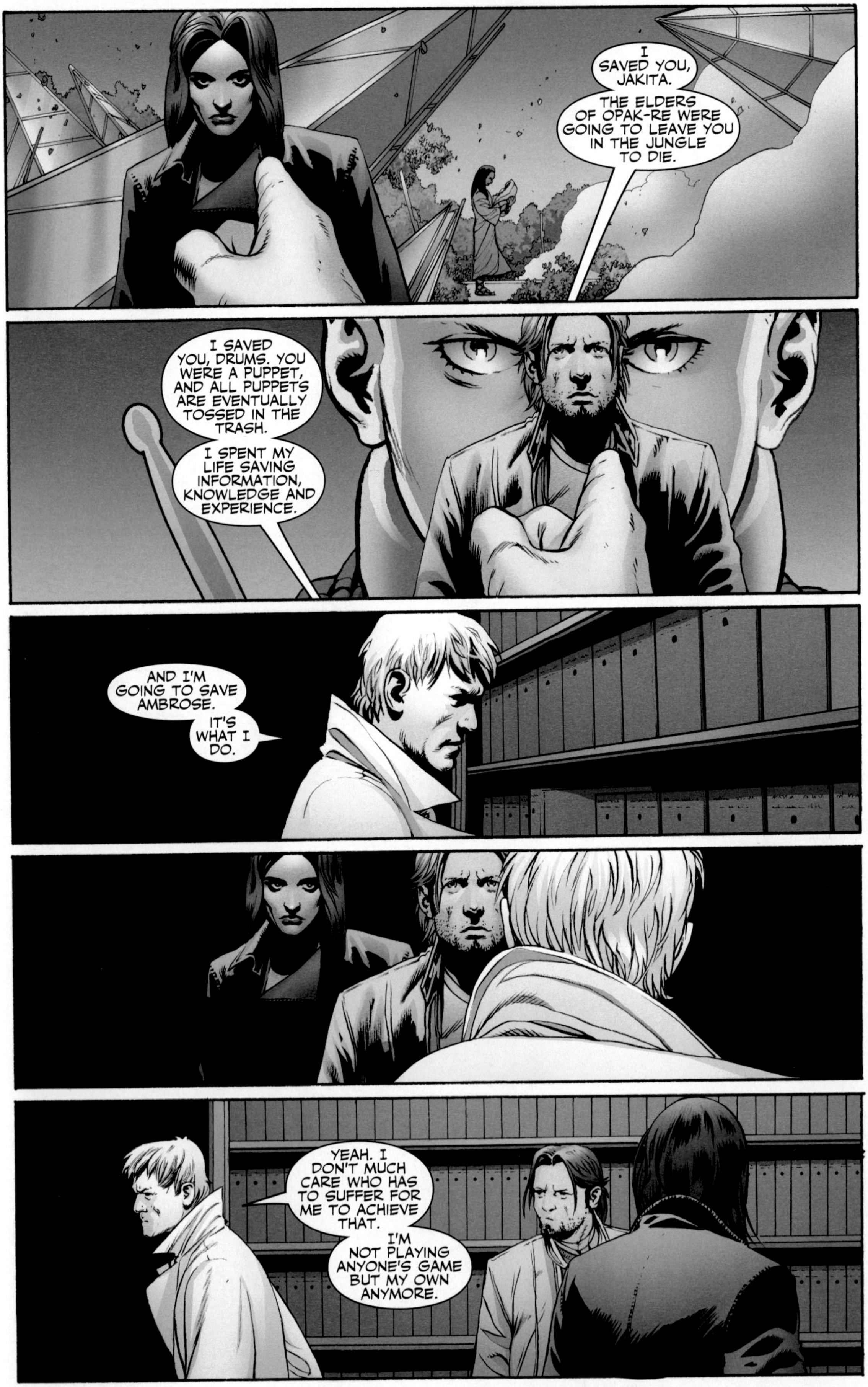
I SAVED YOU, JAKITA.
THE ELDERS OF OPAK-RE WERE GOING TO LEAVE YOU IN THE JUNGLE TO DIE.
I SAVED YOU, DRUMS. YOU WERE A PUPPET, AND ALL PUPPETS ARE EVENTUALLY TOSSED IN THE TRASH.
I SPENT MY LIFE SAVING INFORMATION, KNOWLEDGE AND EXPERIENCE.
AND I'M GOING TO SAVE AMBROSE.
IT'S WHAT I DO.
YEAH. I DON'T MUCH CARE WHO HAS TO SUFFER FOR ME TO ACHIEVE THAT.
I'M NOT PLAYING ANYONE'S GAME BUT MY OWN ANYMORE.

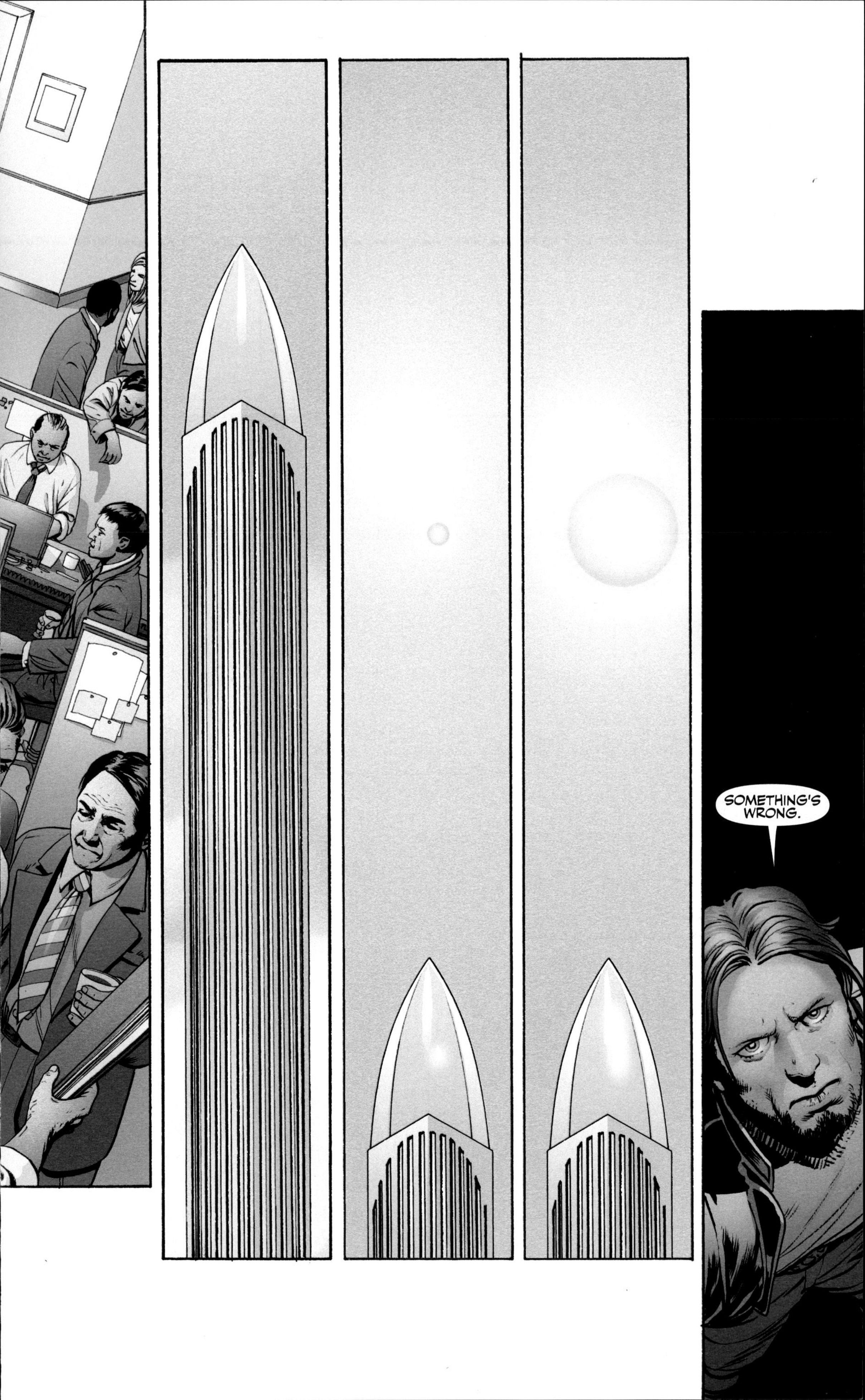
SOMETHING'S WRONG.

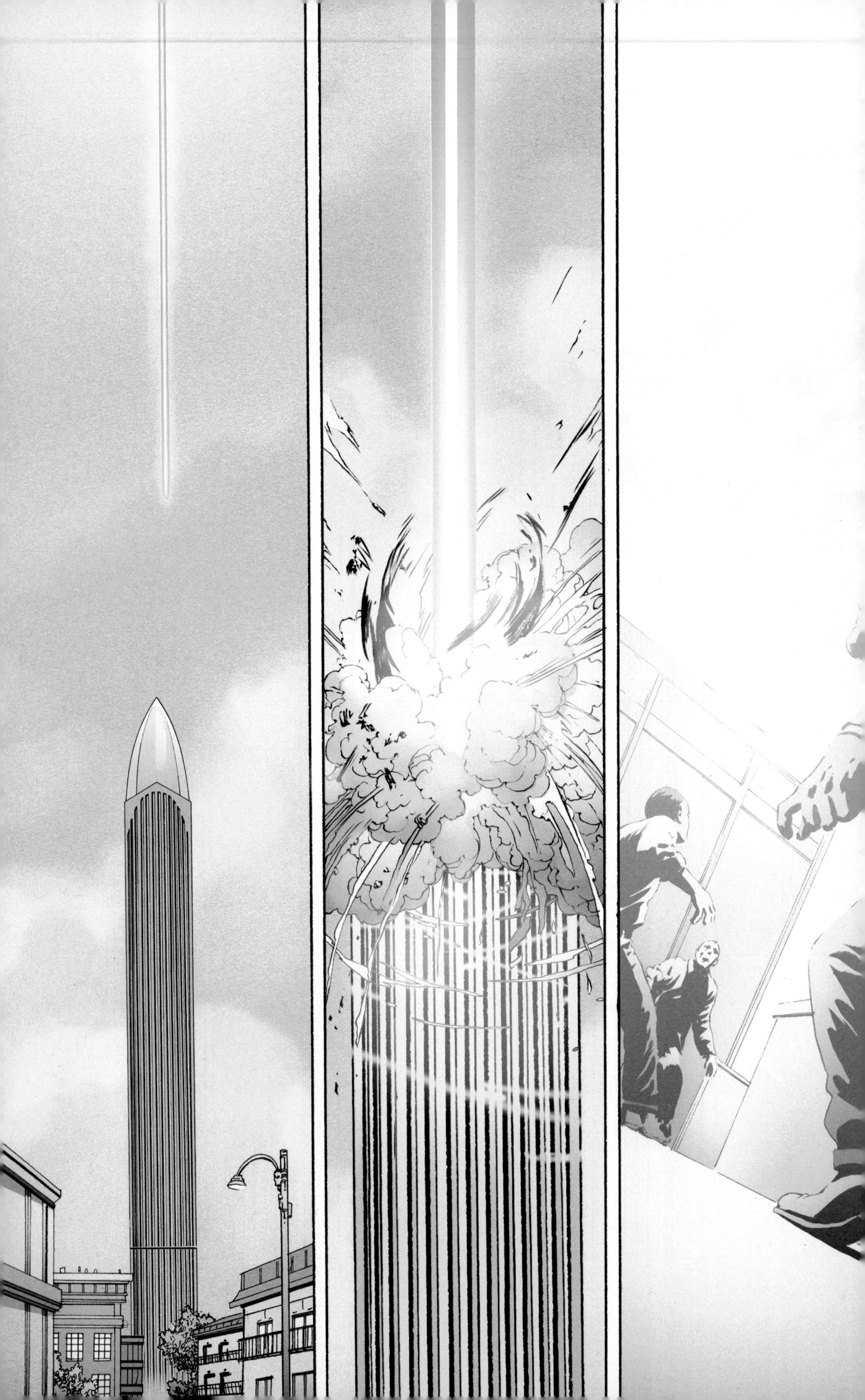

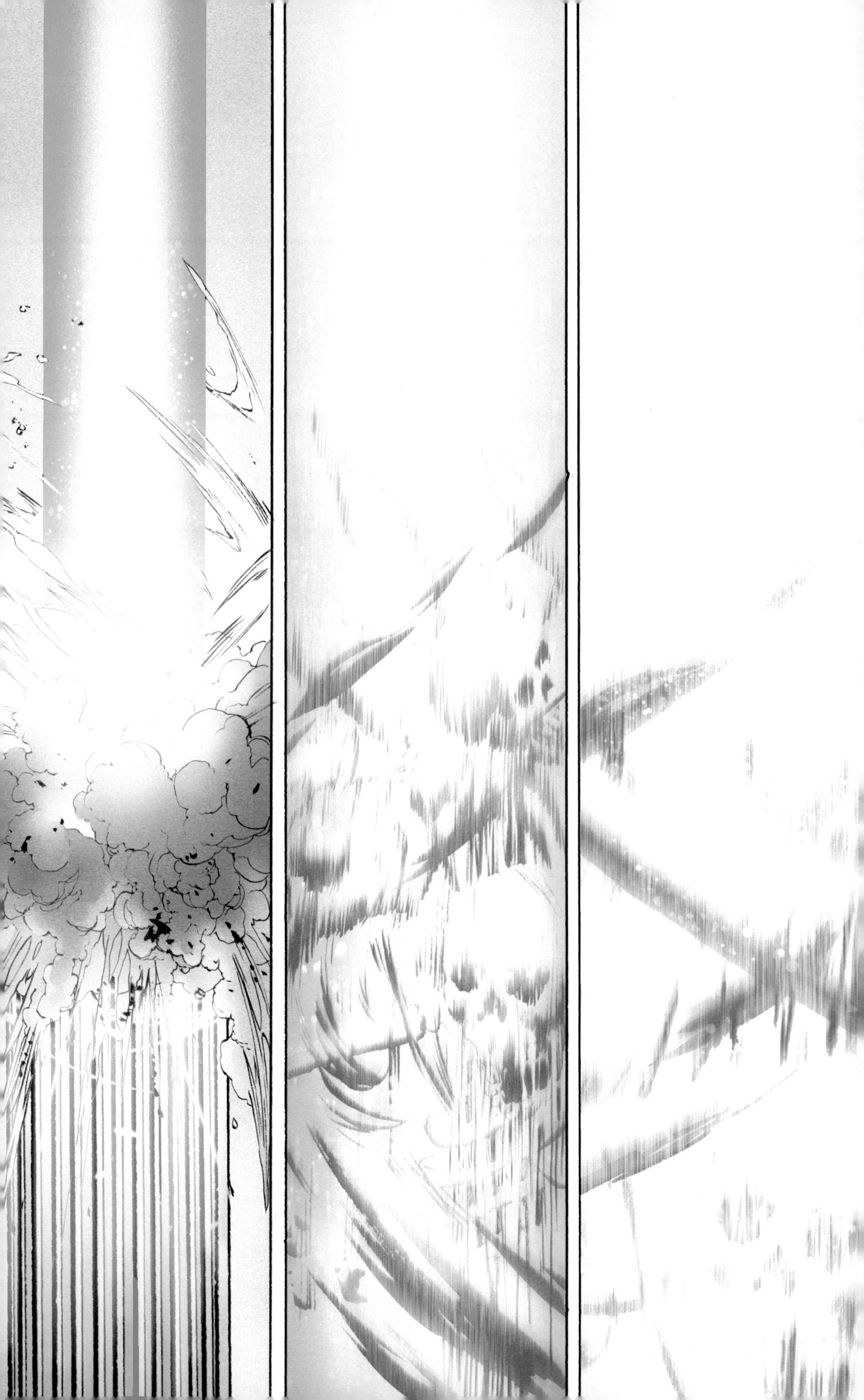

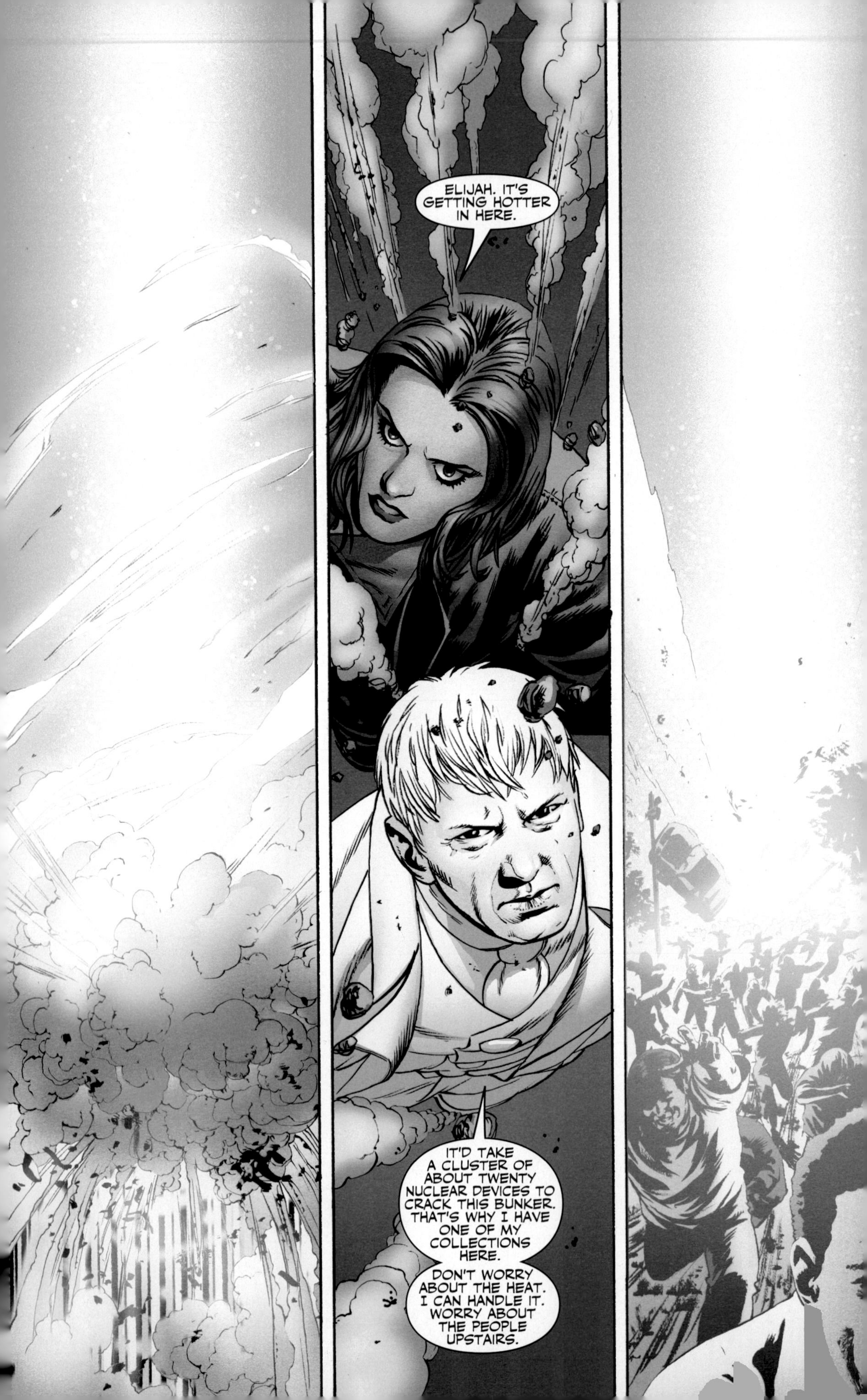
ELIJAH. IT'S GETTING HOTTER IN HERE.
IT'D TAKE A CLUSTER OF ABOUT TWENTY NUCLEAR DEVICES TO CRACK THIS BUNKER. THAT'S WHY I HAVE ONE OF MY COLLECTIONS HERE.
DON'T WORRY ABOUT THE HEAT. I CAN HANDLE IT. WORRY ABOUT THE PEOPLE UPSTAIRS.

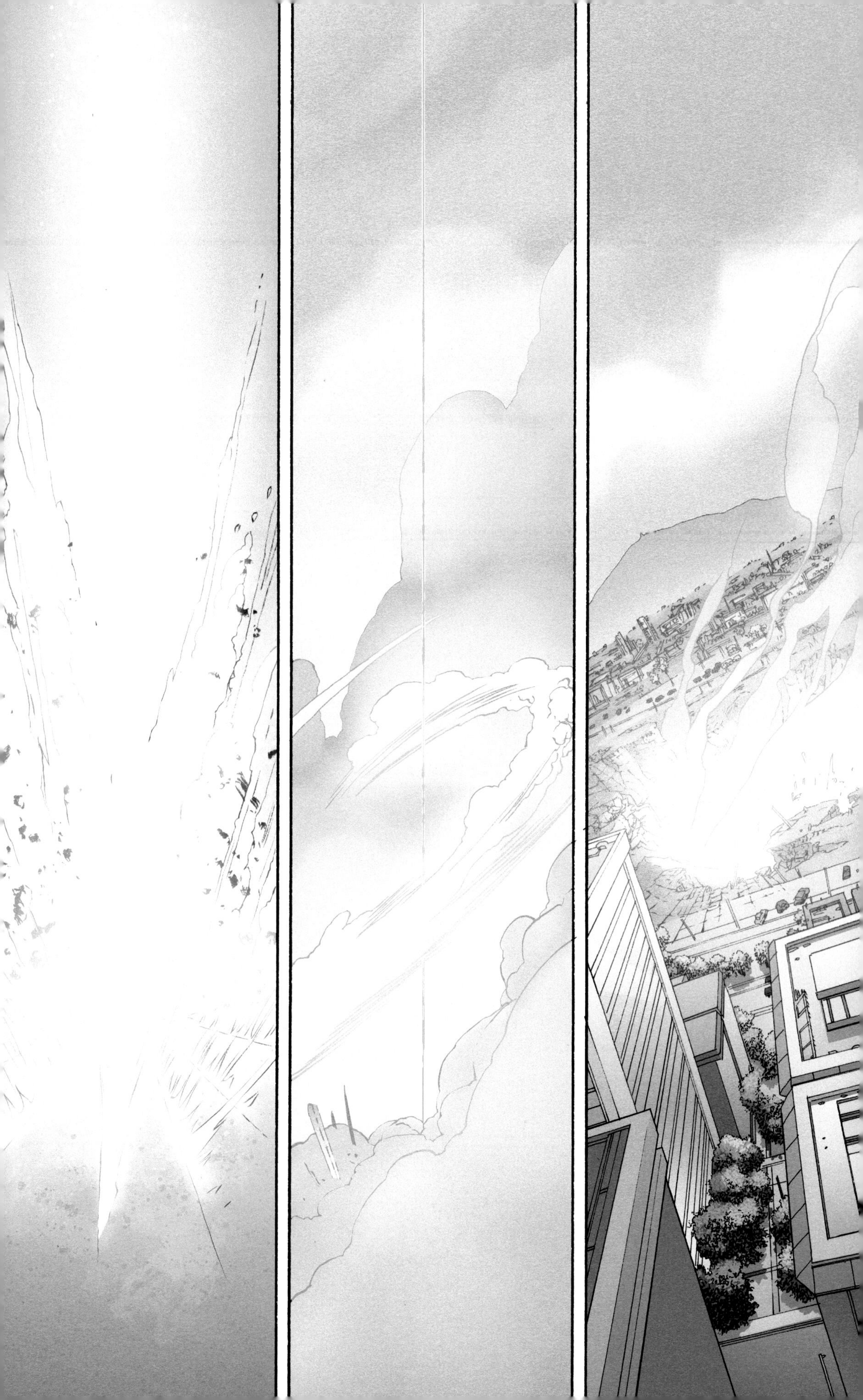

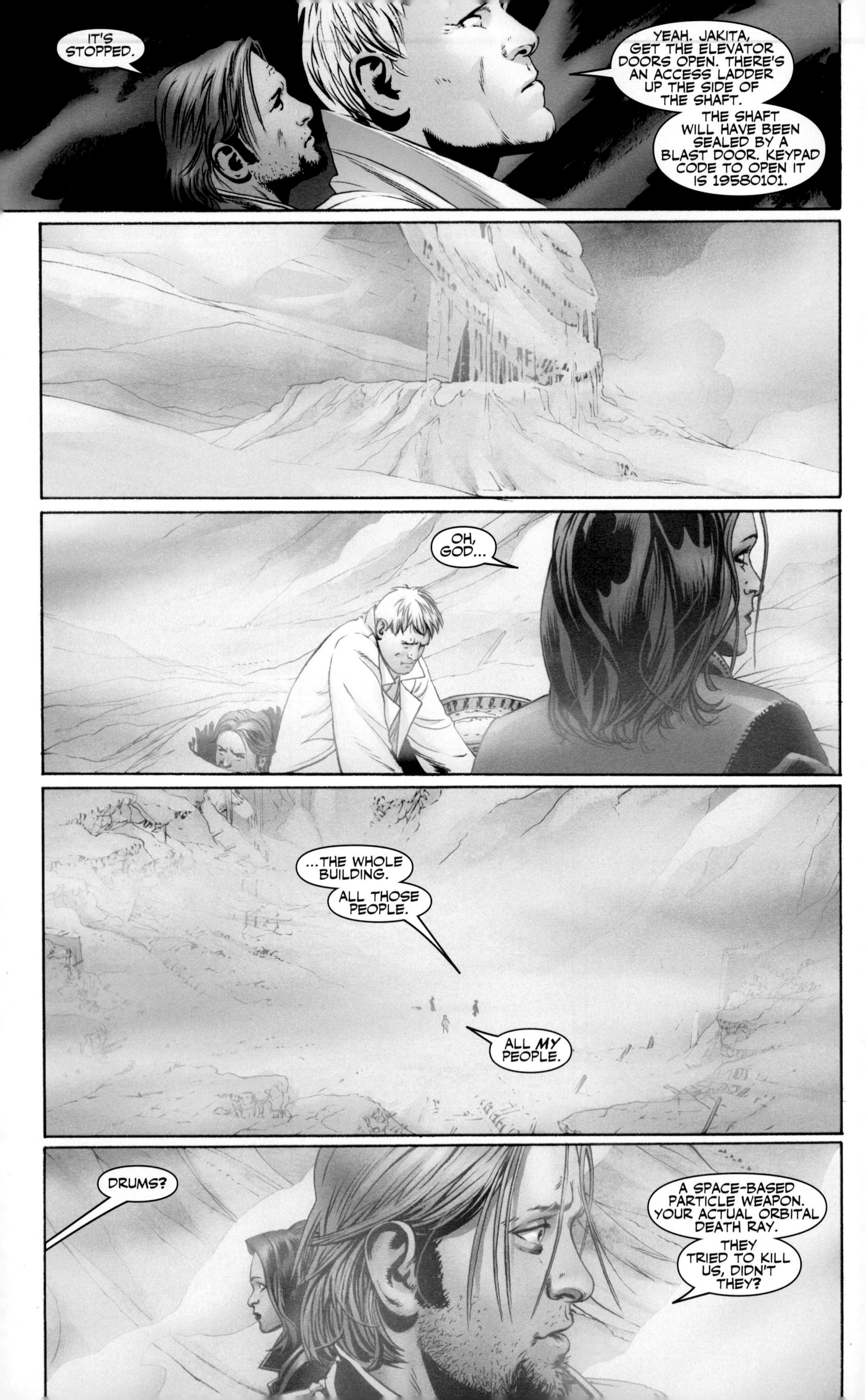
IT'S STOPPED.
YEAH. JAKITA, GET THE ELEVATOR DOORS OPEN. THERE'S AN ACCESS LADDER UP THE SIDE OF THE SHAFT.
THE SHAFT WILL HAVE BEEN SEALED BY A BLAST DOOR. KEYPAD CODE TO OPEN IT IS 19580101.
OH, GOD...
...THE WHOLE BUILDING.
ALL THOSE PEOPLE.
ALL *MY* PEOPLE.
DRUMS?
A SPACE-BASED PARTICLE WEAPON. YOUR ACTUAL ORBITAL DEATH RAY.
THEY TRIED TO KILL US, DIDN'T THEY?

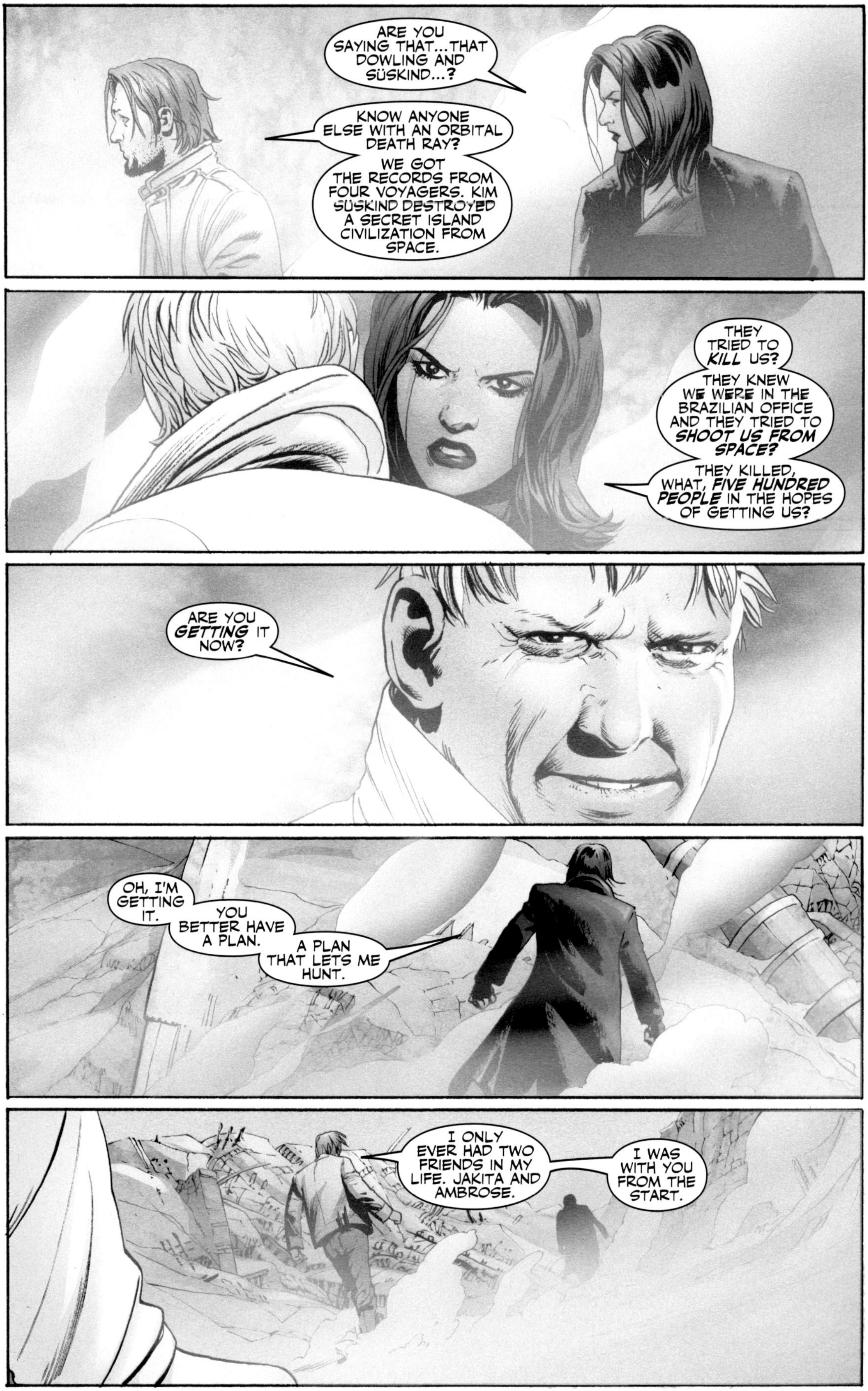
ARE YOU SAYING THAT...THAT DOWLING AND SÜSKIND...?
KNOW ANYONE ELSE WITH AN ORBITAL DEATH RAY?
WE GOT THE RECORDS FROM FOUR VOYAGERS. KIM SÜSKIND DESTROYED A SECRET ISLAND CIVILIZATION FROM SPACE.
THEY TRIED TO KILL US?
THEY KNEW WE WERE IN THE BRAZILIAN OFFICE AND THEY TRIED TO SHOOT US FROM SPACE?
THEY KILLED, WHAT, FIVE HUNDRED PEOPLE IN THE HOPES OF GETTING US?
ARE YOU GETTING IT NOW?
OH, I'M GETTING IT.
YOU BETTER HAVE A PLAN.
A PLAN THAT LETS ME HUNT.
I ONLY EVER HAD TWO FRIENDS IN MY LIFE. JAKITA AND AMBROSE.
I WAS WITH YOU FROM THE START.

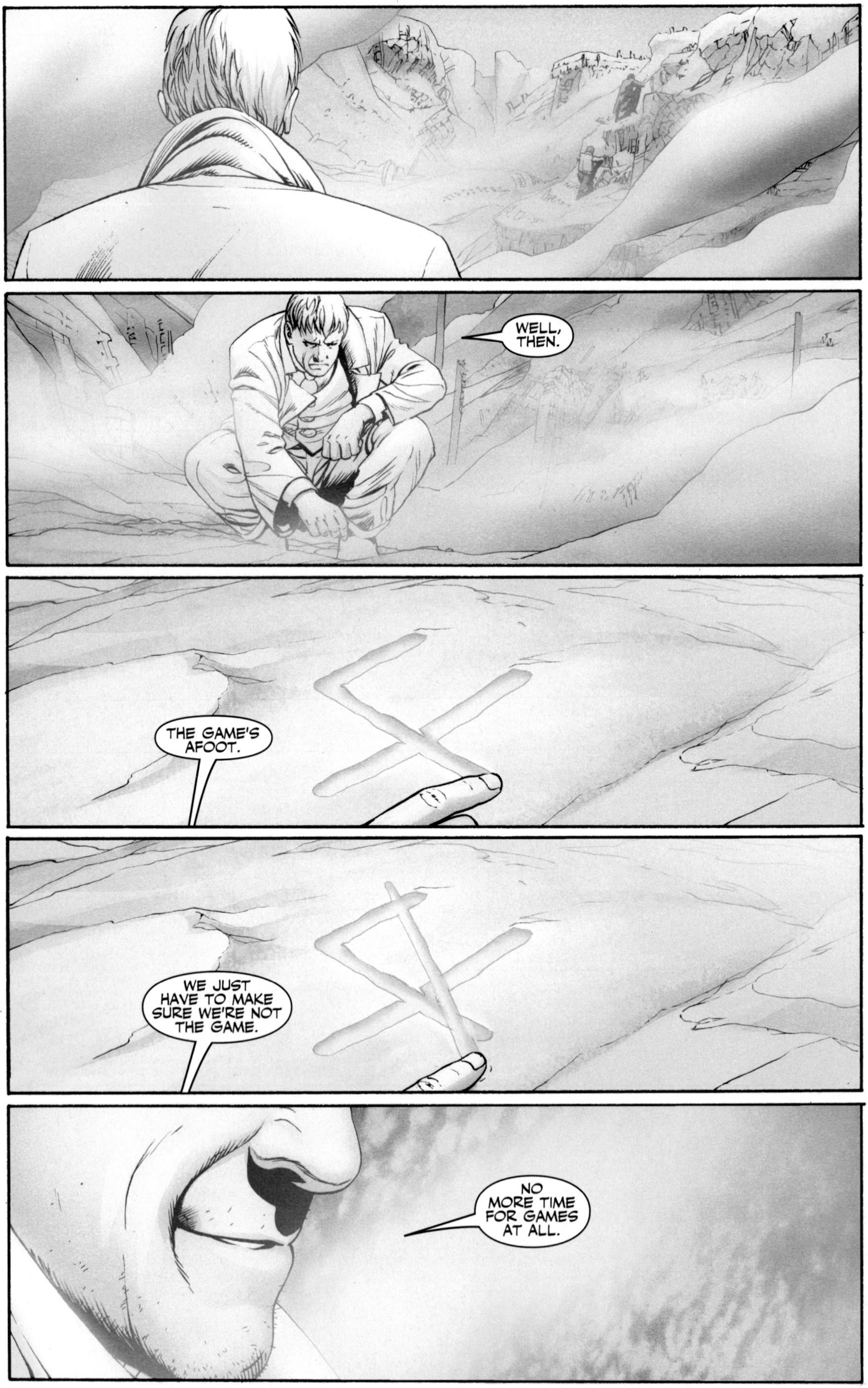
WELL, THEN.
THE GAME'S AFOOT.
WE JUST HAVE TO MAKE SURE WE'RE NOT THE GAME.
NO MORE TIME FOR GAMES AT ALL.

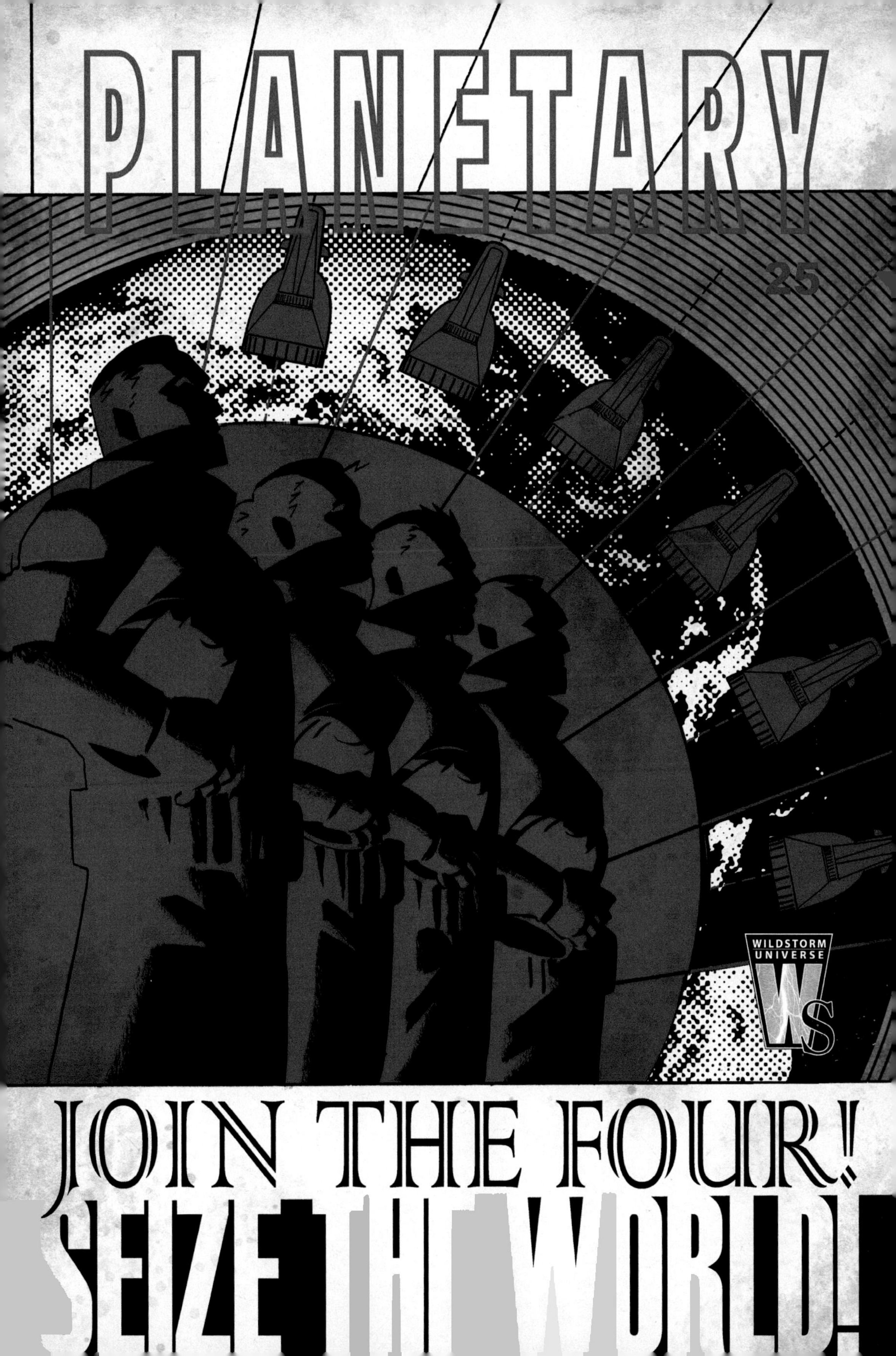
PLANETARY
25
WILDSTORM UNIVERSE
JOIN THE FOUR!
SEIZE THE WORLD!

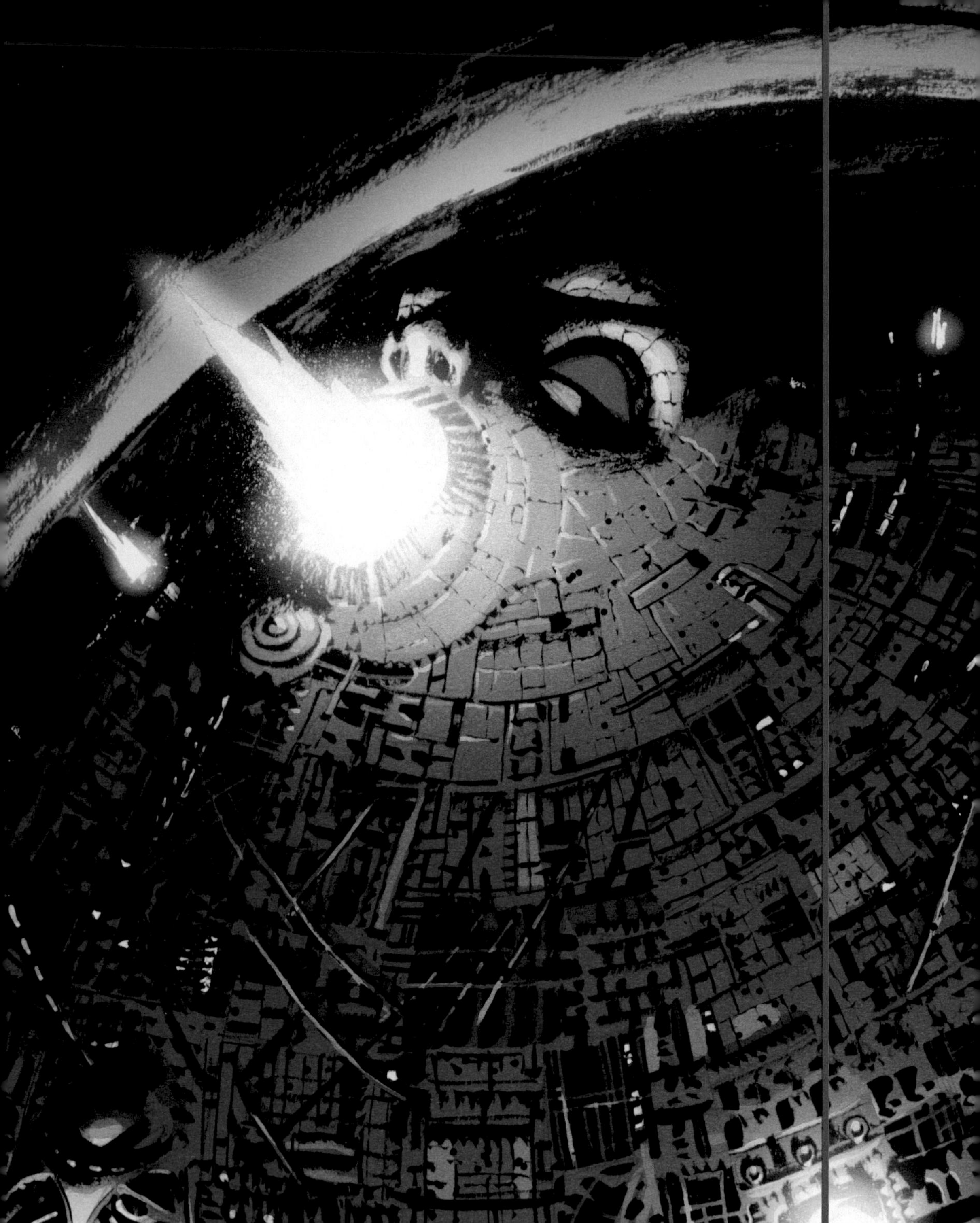

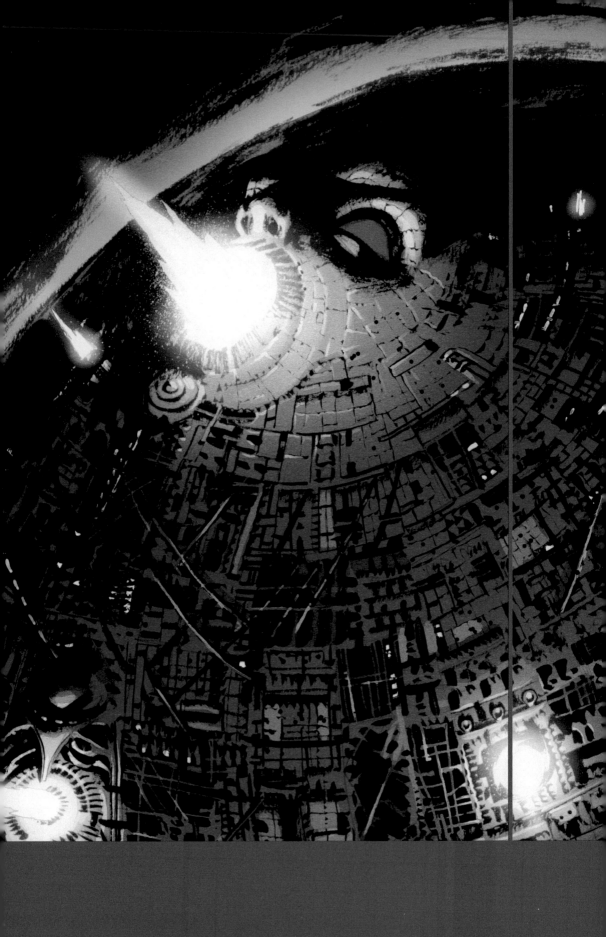

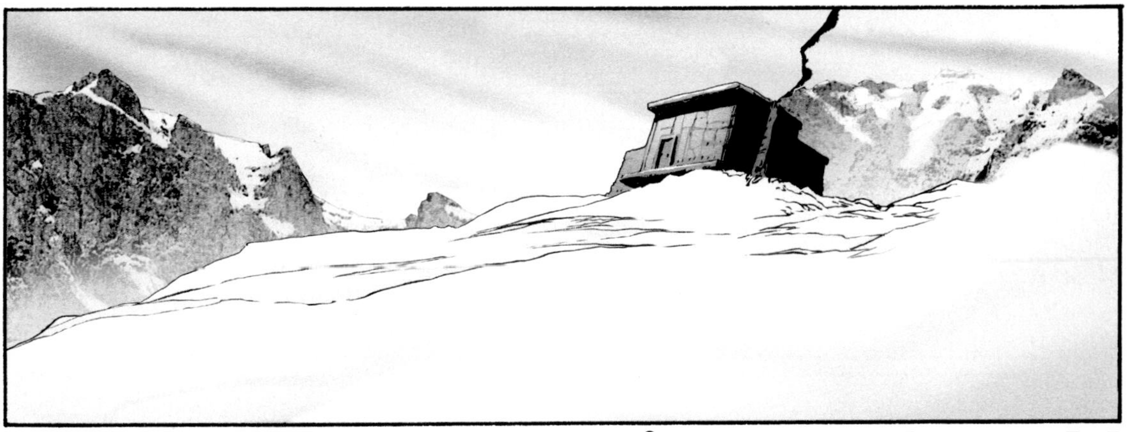

in from the cold

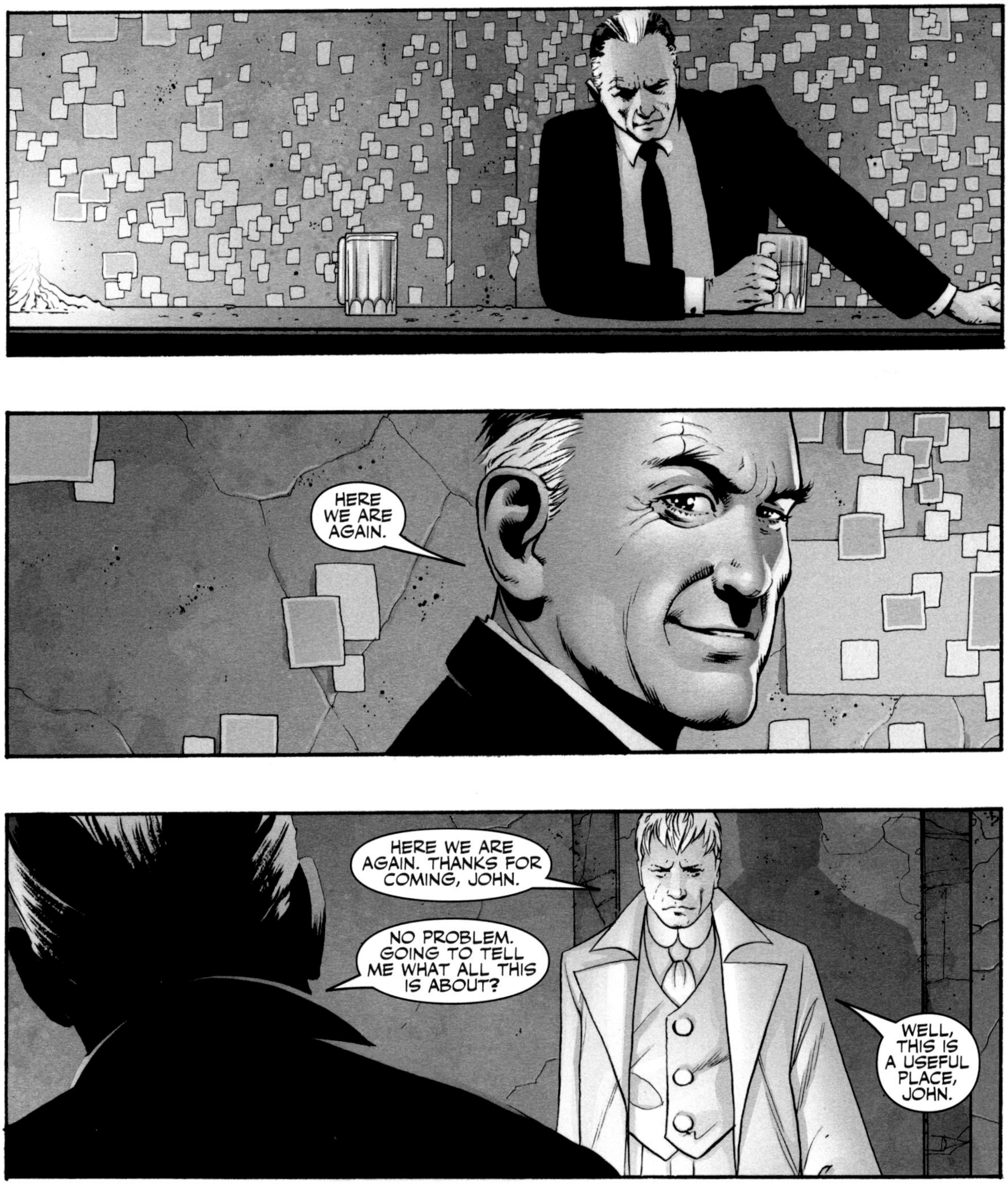
HERE WE ARE AGAIN.
HERE WE ARE AGAIN. THANKS FOR COMING, JOHN.
NO PROBLEM. GOING TO TELL ME WHAT ALL THIS IS ABOUT?
WELL, THIS IS A USEFUL PLACE, JOHN.

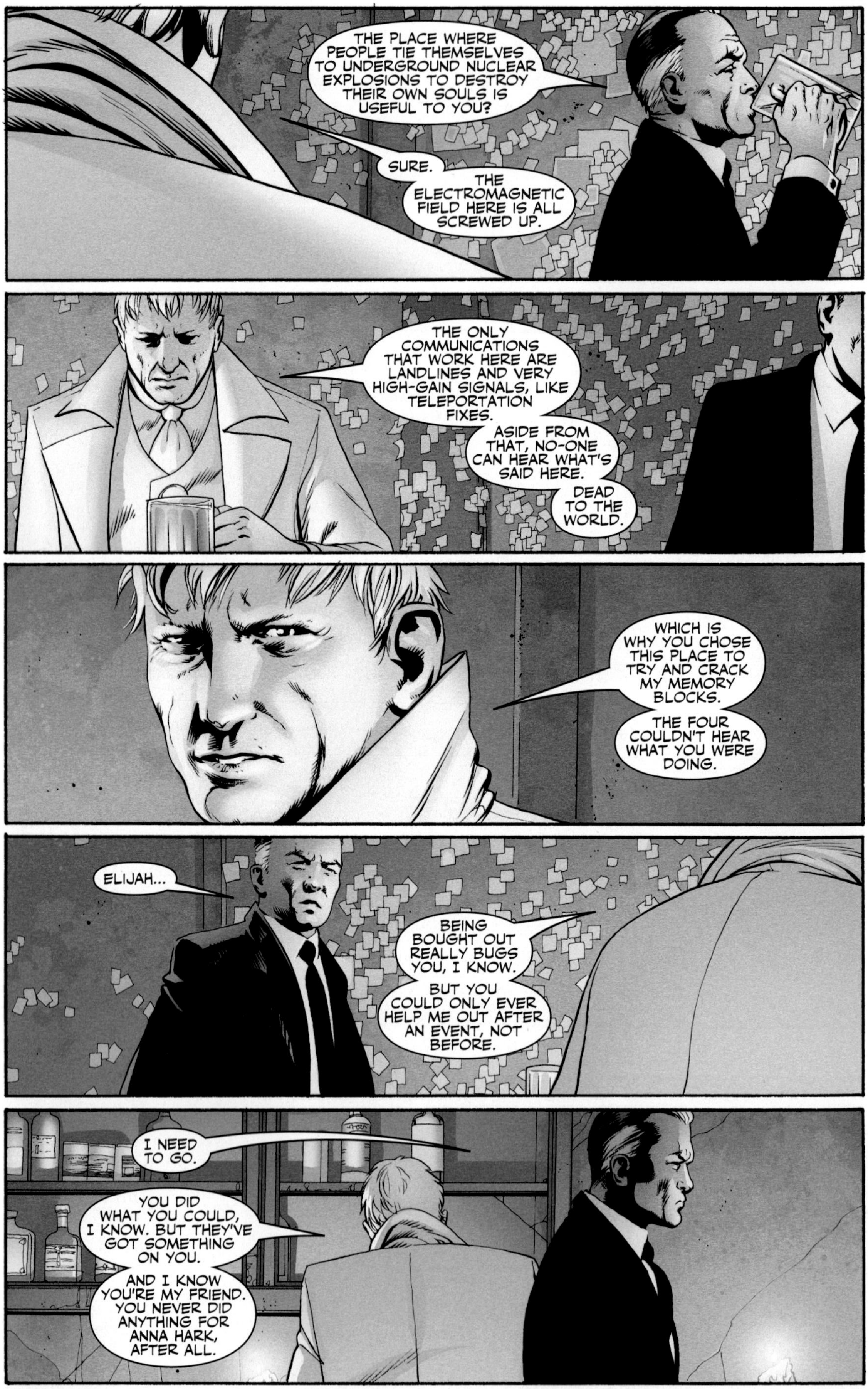
THE PLACE WHERE PEOPLE TIE THEMSELVES TO UNDERGROUND NUCLEAR EXPLOSIONS TO DESTROY THEIR OWN SOULS IS USEFUL TO YOU?
SURE.
THE ELECTROMAGNETIC FIELD HERE IS ALL SCREWED UP.
THE ONLY COMMUNICATIONS THAT WORK HERE ARE LANDLINES AND VERY HIGH-GAIN SIGNALS, LIKE TELEPORTATION FIXES.
ASIDE FROM THAT, NO-ONE CAN HEAR WHAT'S SAID HERE.
DEAD TO THE WORLD.
WHICH IS WHY YOU CHOSE THIS PLACE TO TRY AND CRACK MY MEMORY BLOCKS.
THE FOUR COULDN'T HEAR WHAT YOU WERE DOING.
ELIJAH...
BEING BOUGHT OUT REALLY BUGS YOU, I KNOW.
BUT YOU COULD ONLY EVER HELP ME OUT AFTER AN EVENT, NOT BEFORE.
I NEED TO GO.
YOU DID WHAT YOU COULD, I KNOW. BUT THEY'VE GOT SOMETHING ON YOU.
AND I KNOW YOU'RE MY FRIEND. YOU NEVER DID ANYTHING FOR ANNA HARK, AFTER ALL.

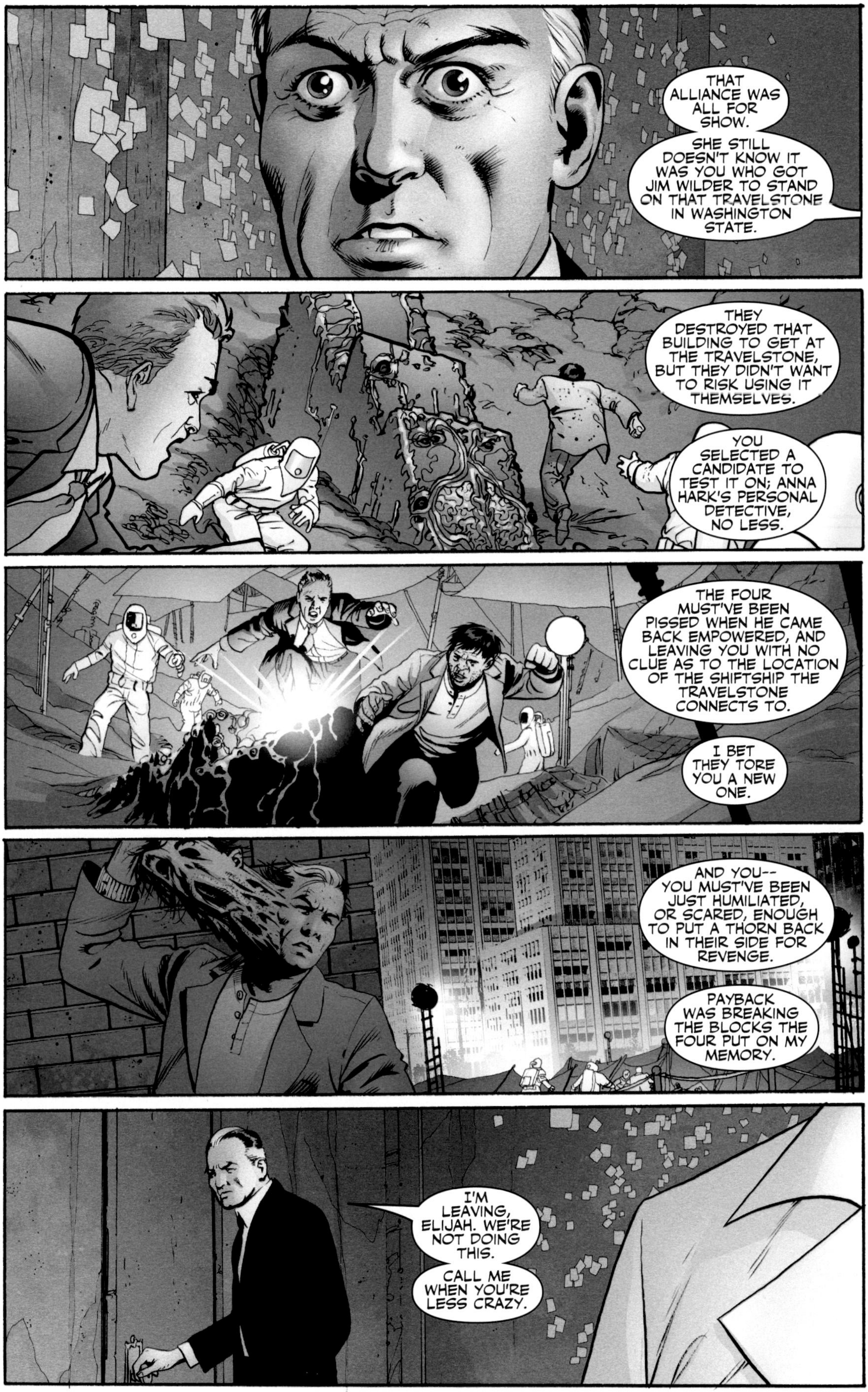
THAT ALLIANCE WAS ALL FOR SHOW.
SHE STILL DOESN'T KNOW IT WAS YOU WHO GOT JIM WILDER TO STAND ON THAT TRAVELSTONE IN WASHINGTON STATE.
THEY DESTROYED THAT BUILDING TO GET AT THE TRAVELSTONE, BUT THEY DIDN'T WANT TO RISK USING IT THEMSELVES.
YOU SELECTED A CANDIDATE TO TEST IT ON; ANNA HARK'S PERSONAL DETECTIVE, NO LESS.
THE FOUR MUST'VE BEEN PISSED WHEN HE CAME BACK EMPOWERED, AND LEAVING YOU WITH NO CLUE AS TO THE LOCATION OF THE SHIFTSHIP THE TRAVELSTONE CONNECTS TO.
I BET THEY TORE YOU A NEW ONE.
AND YOU-- YOU MUST'VE BEEN JUST HUMILIATED, OR SCARED, ENOUGH TO PUT A THORN BACK IN THEIR SIDE FOR REVENGE.
PAYBACK WAS BREAKING THE BLOCKS THE FOUR PUT ON MY MEMORY.
I'M LEAVING, ELIJAH. WE'RE NOT DOING THIS.
CALL ME WHEN YOU'RE LESS CRAZY.

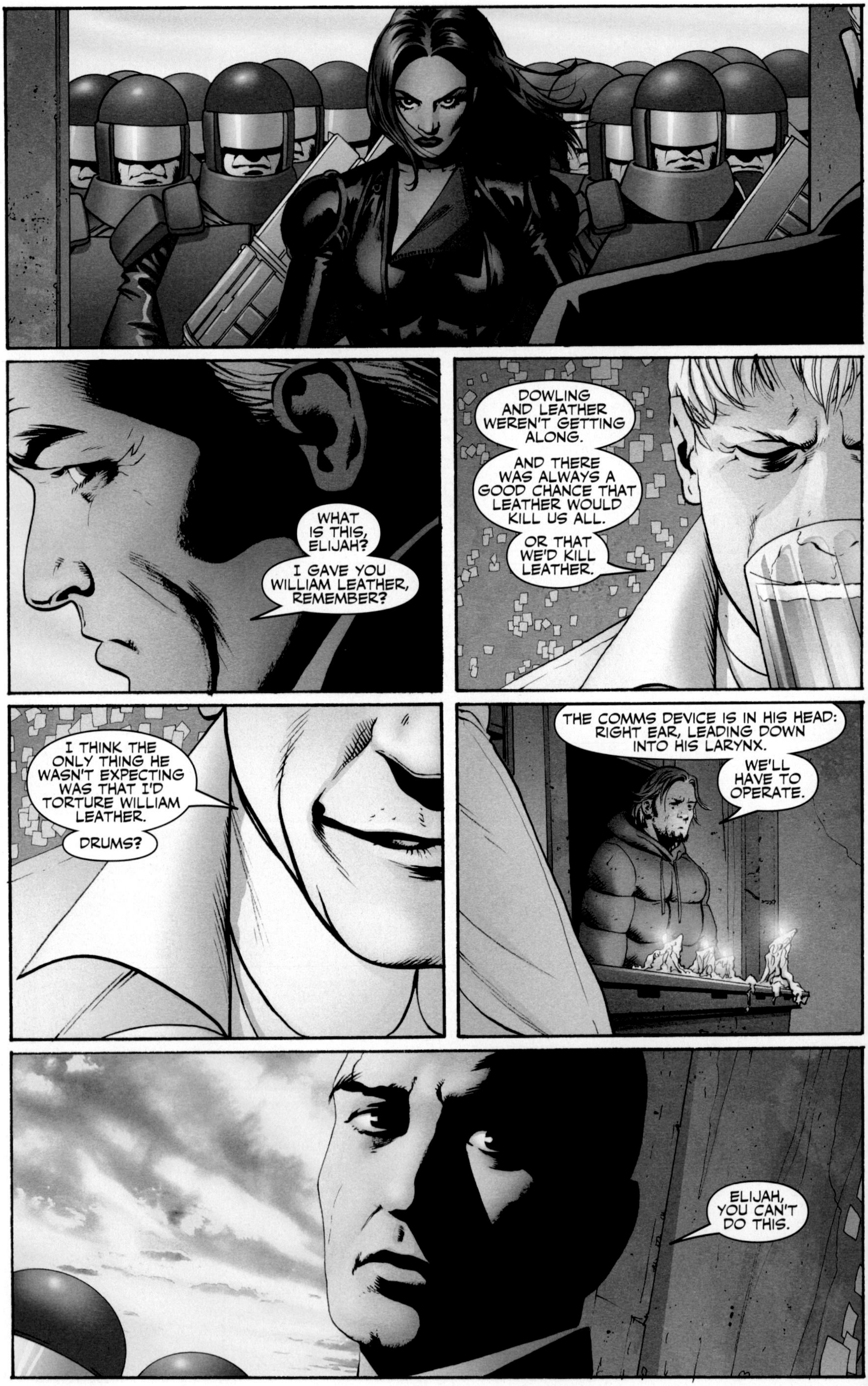
WHAT IS THIS, ELIJAH?
I GAVE YOU WILLIAM LEATHER, REMEMBER?
DOWLING AND LEATHER WEREN'T GETTING ALONG.
AND THERE WAS ALWAYS A GOOD CHANCE THAT LEATHER WOULD KILL US ALL.
OR THAT WE'D KILL LEATHER.
I THINK THE ONLY THING HE WASN'T EXPECTING WAS THAT I'D TORTURE WILLIAM LEATHER.
DRUMS?
THE COMMS DEVICE IS IN HIS HEAD: RIGHT EAR, LEADING DOWN INTO HIS LARYNX.
WE'LL HAVE TO OPERATE.
ELIJAH, YOU CAN'T DO THIS.

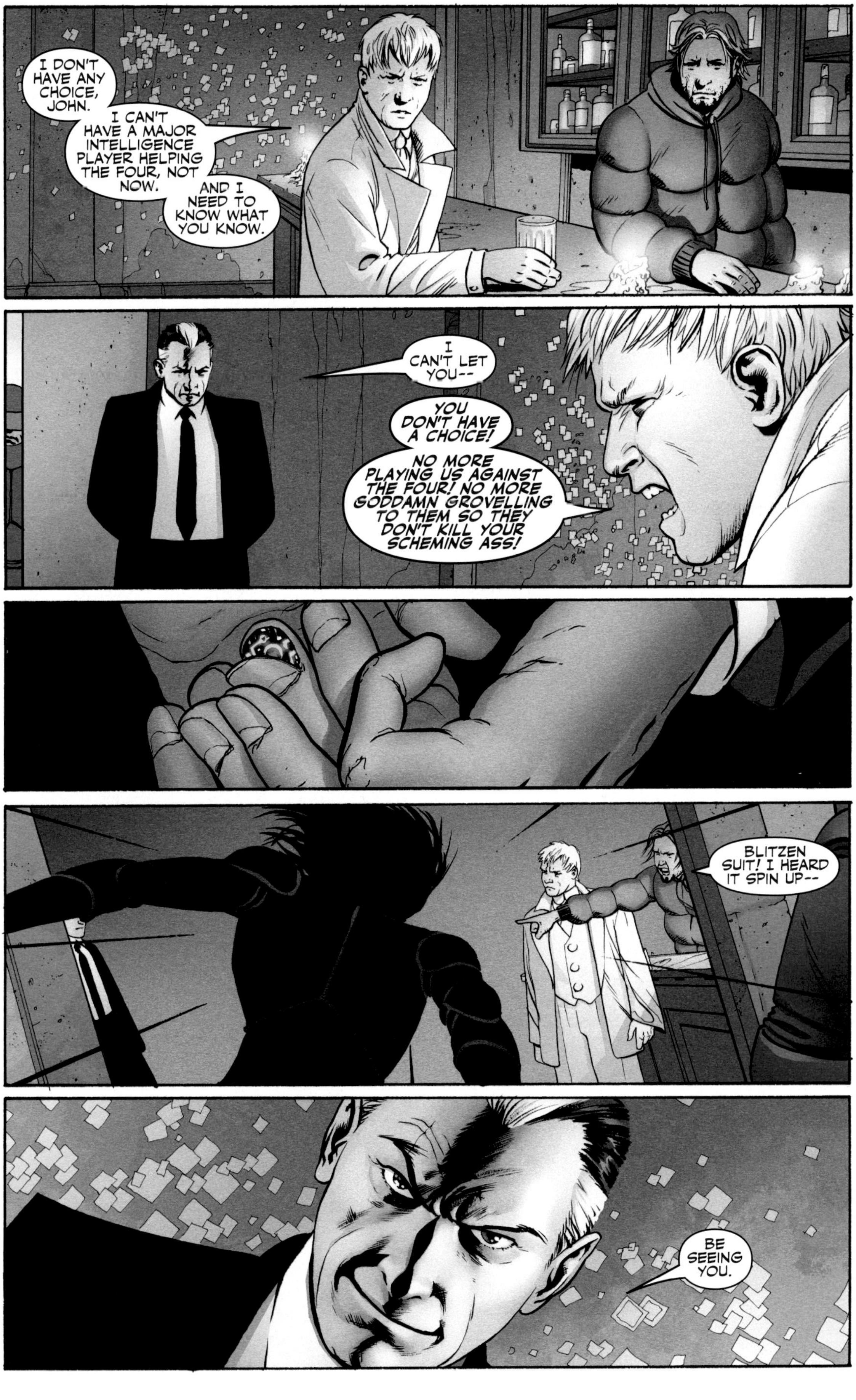
I DON'T HAVE ANY CHOICE, JOHN.
I CAN'T HAVE A MAJOR INTELLIGENCE PLAYER HELPING THE FOUR, NOT NOW.
AND I NEED TO KNOW WHAT YOU KNOW.
I CAN'T LET YOU--
YOU DON'T HAVE A CHOICE!
NO MORE PLAYING US AGAINST THE FOUR! NO MORE GODDAMN GROVELLING TO THEM SO THEY DON'T KILL YOUR SCHEMING ASS!
BLITZEN SUIT! I HEARD IT SPIN UP--
BE SEEING YOU.

MINES?

ENJOY.

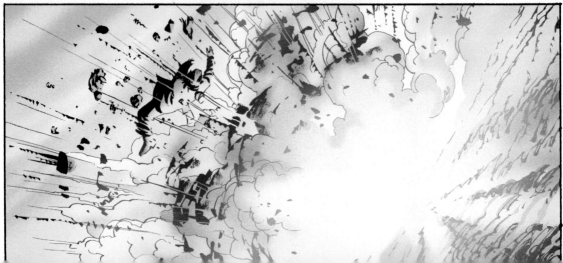

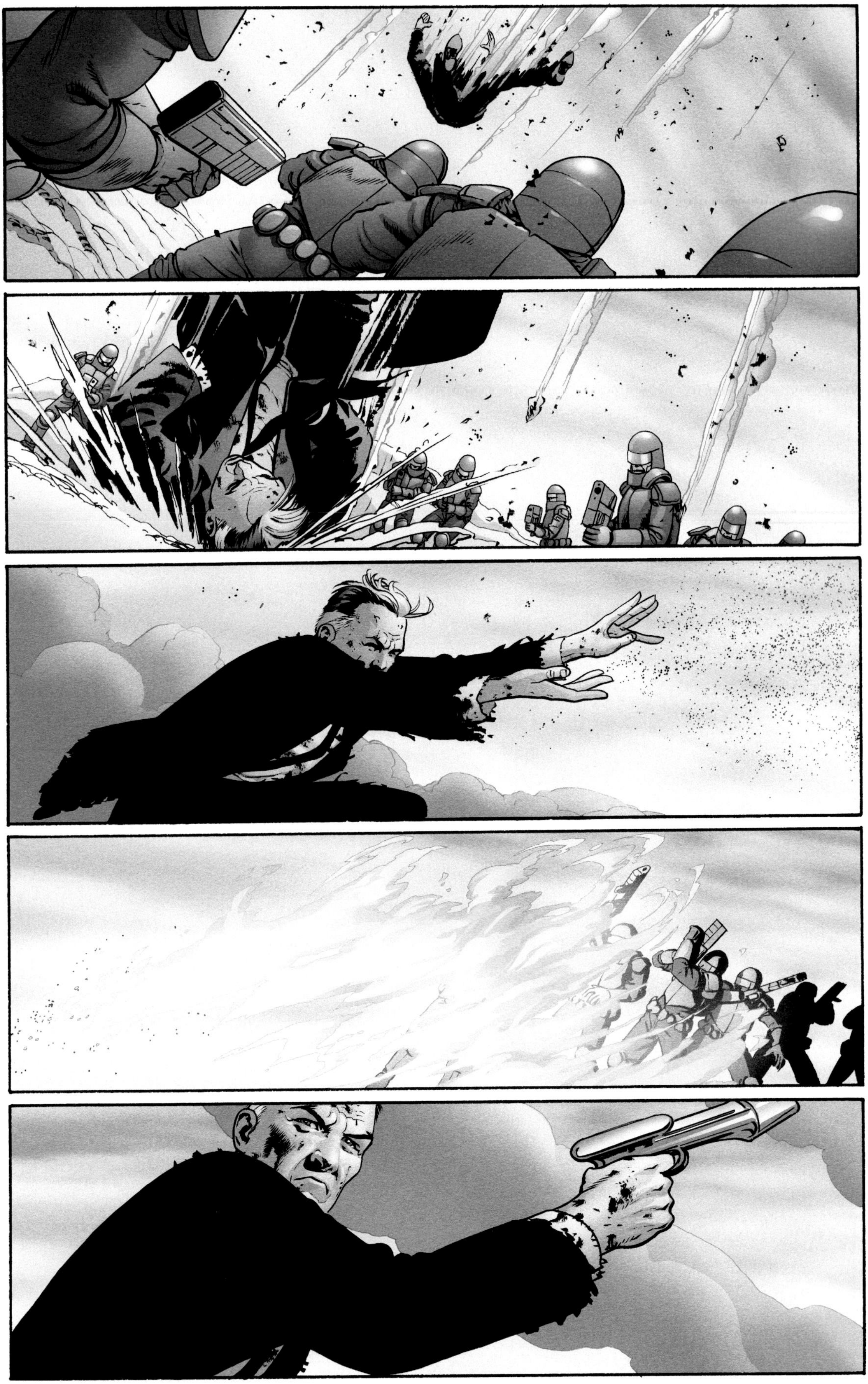

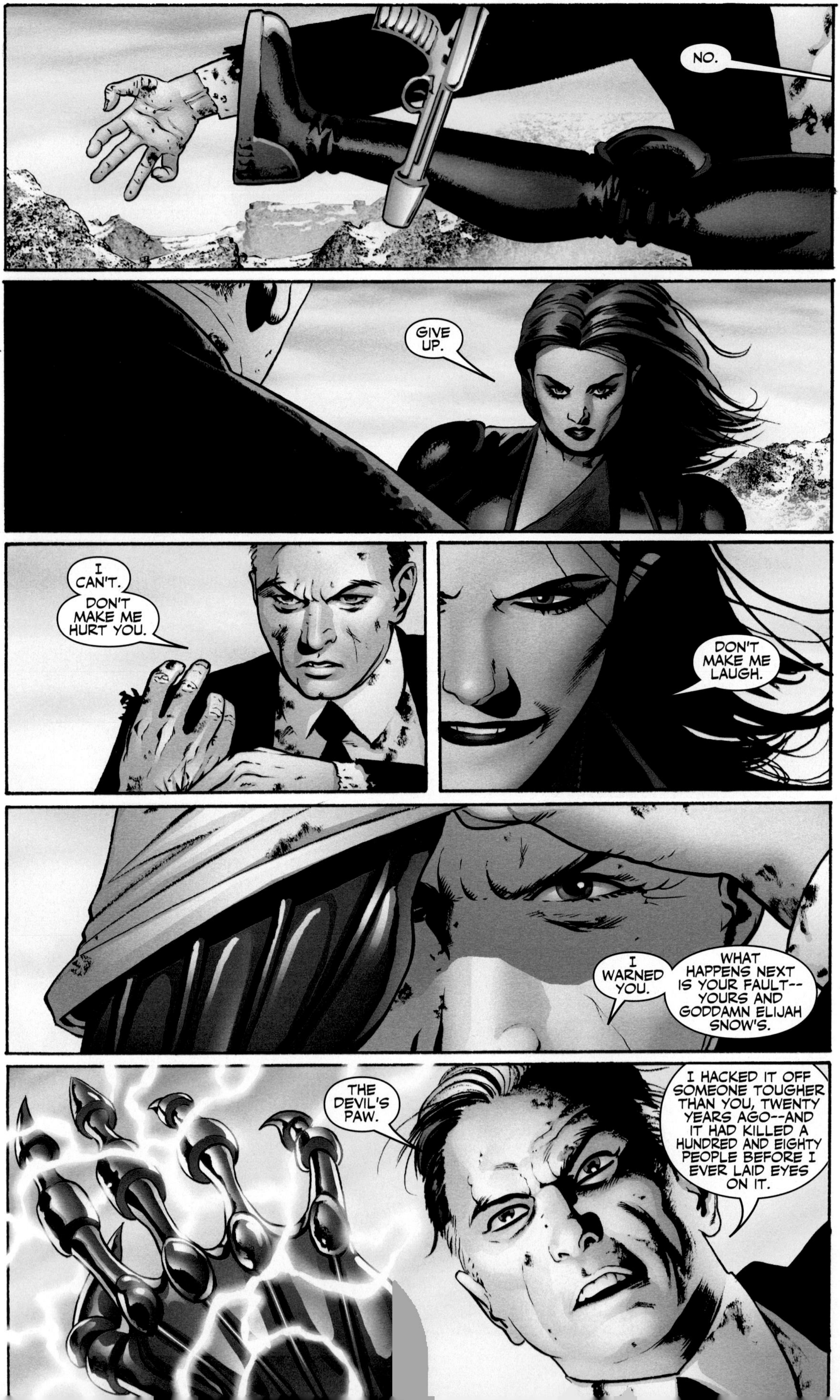
NO.
GIVE UP.
I CAN'T. DON'T MAKE ME HURT YOU.
DON'T MAKE ME LAUGH.
I WARNED YOU.
WHAT HAPPENS NEXT IS YOUR FAULT-- YOURS AND GODDAMN ELIJAH SNOW'S.
THE DEVIL'S PAW.
I HACKED IT OFF SOMEONE TOUGHER THAN YOU, TWENTY YEARS AGO--AND IT HAD KILLED A HUNDRED AND EIGHTY PEOPLE BEFORE I EVER LAID EYES ON IT.

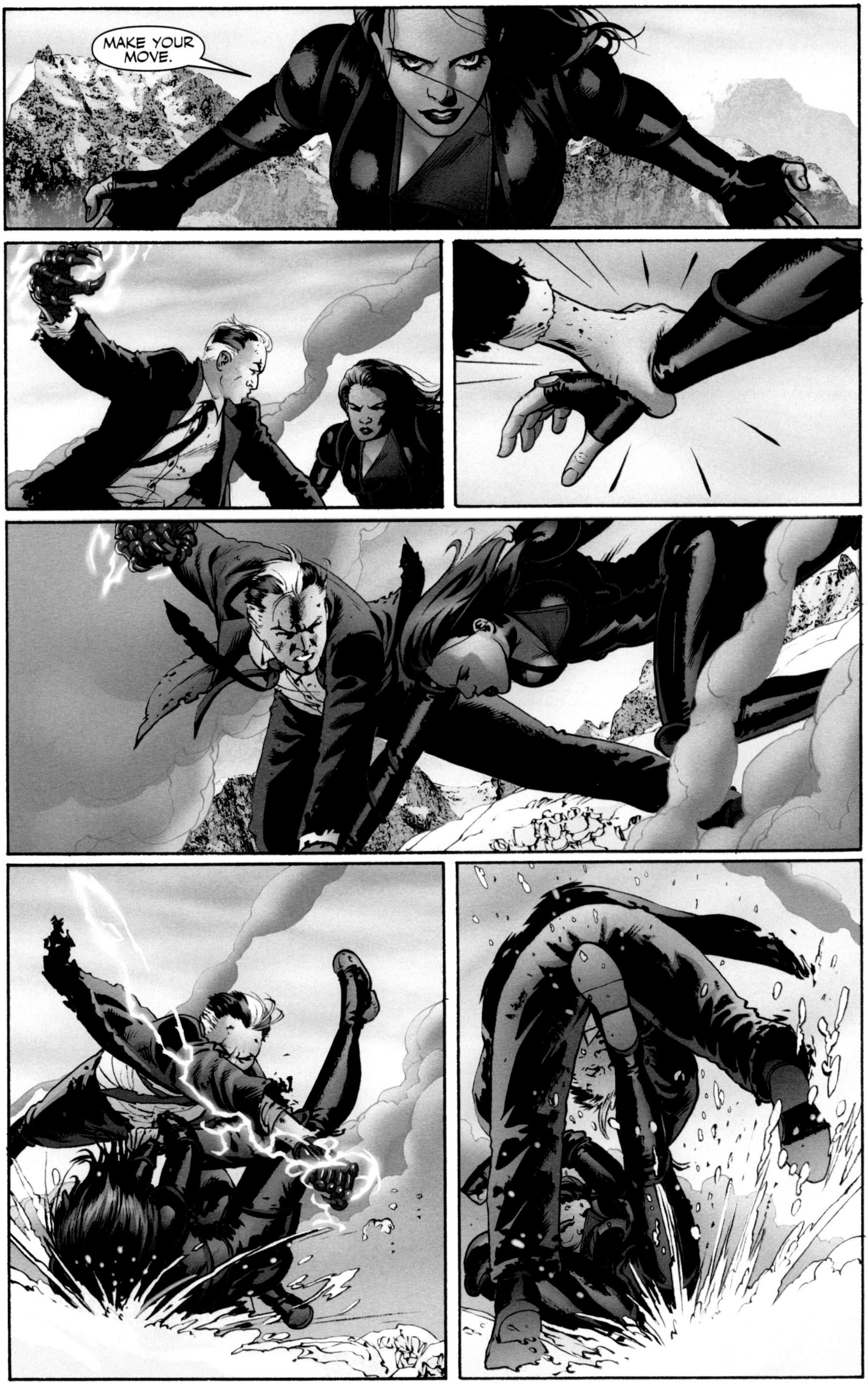
MAKE YOUR MOVE.

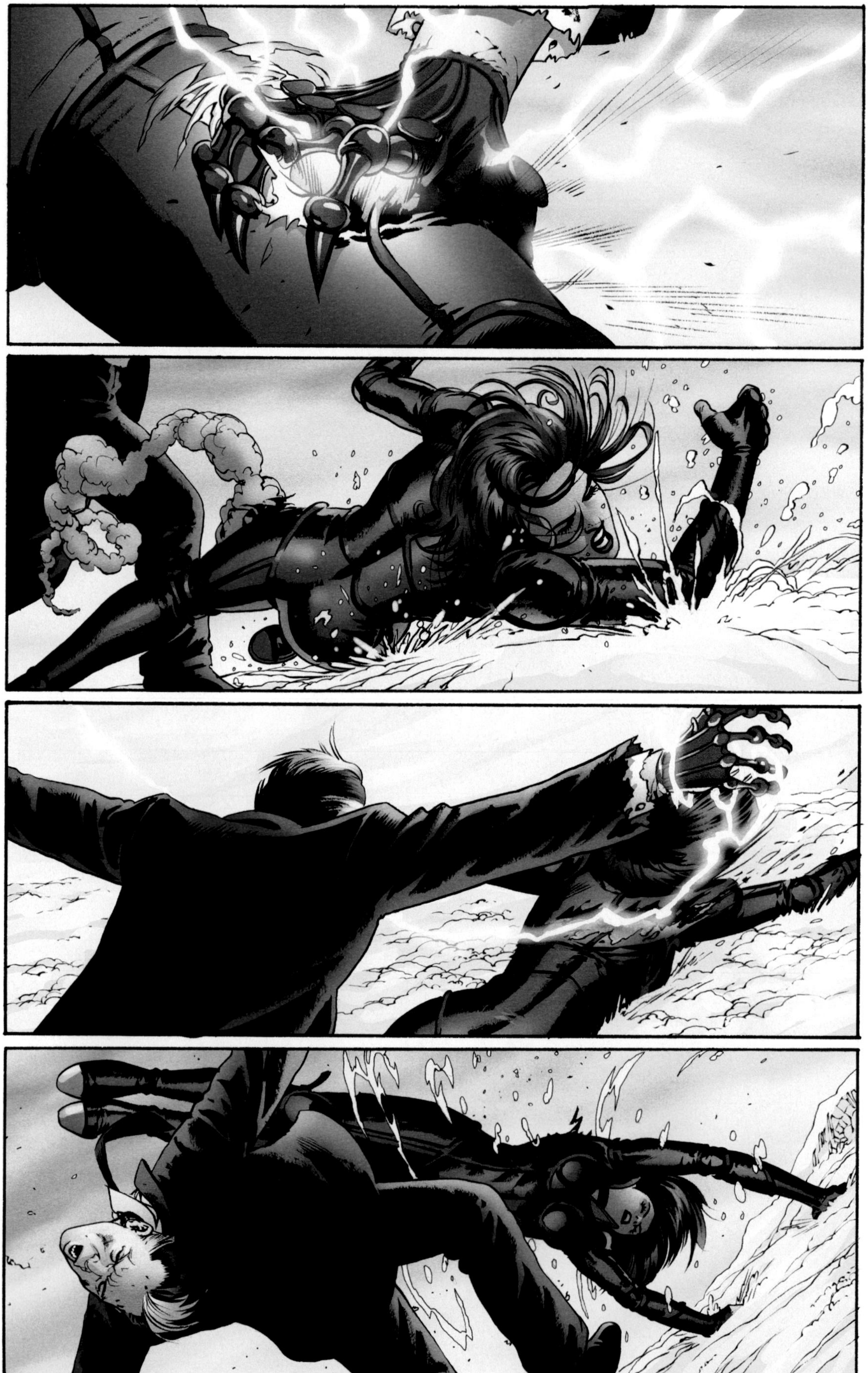

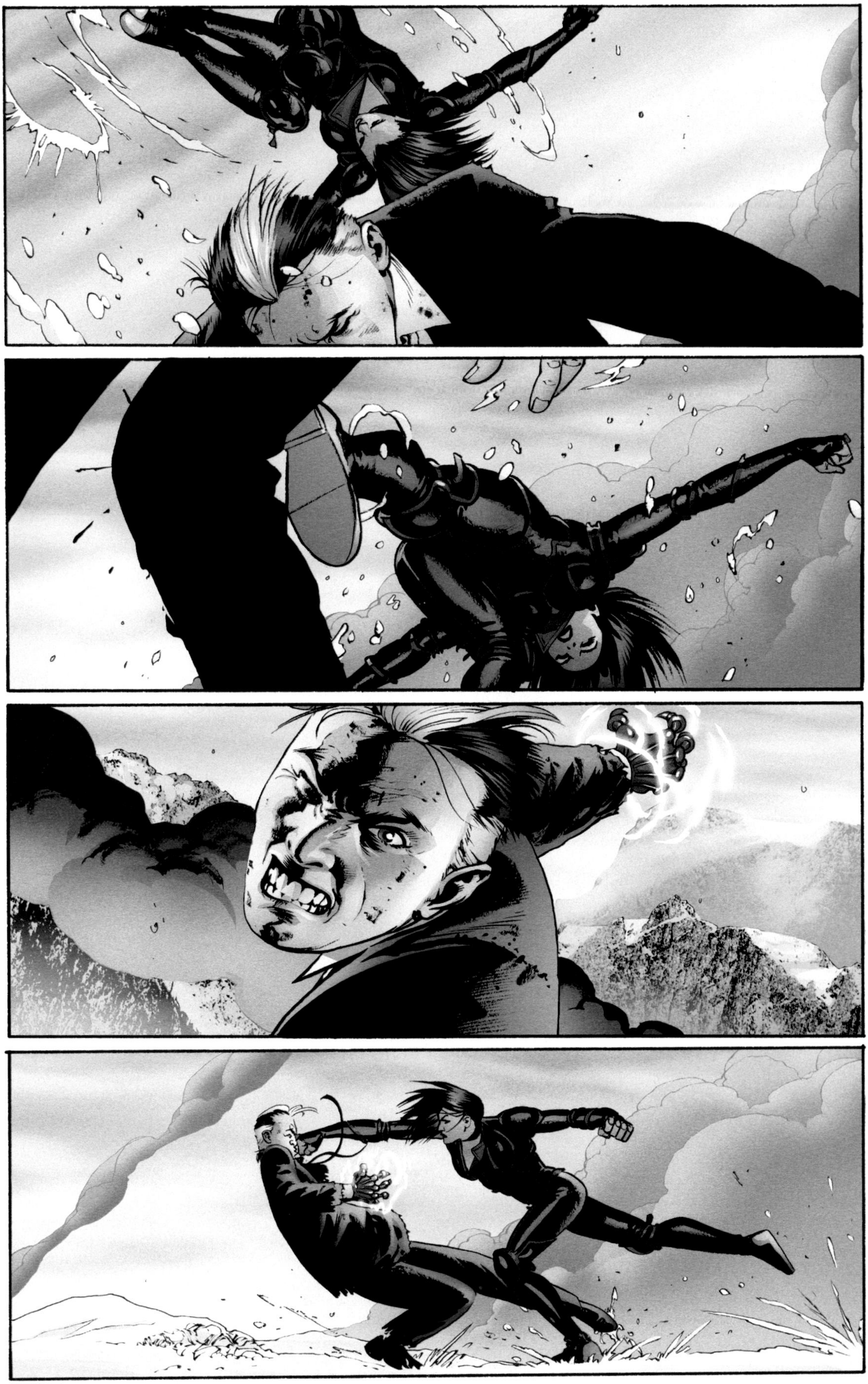

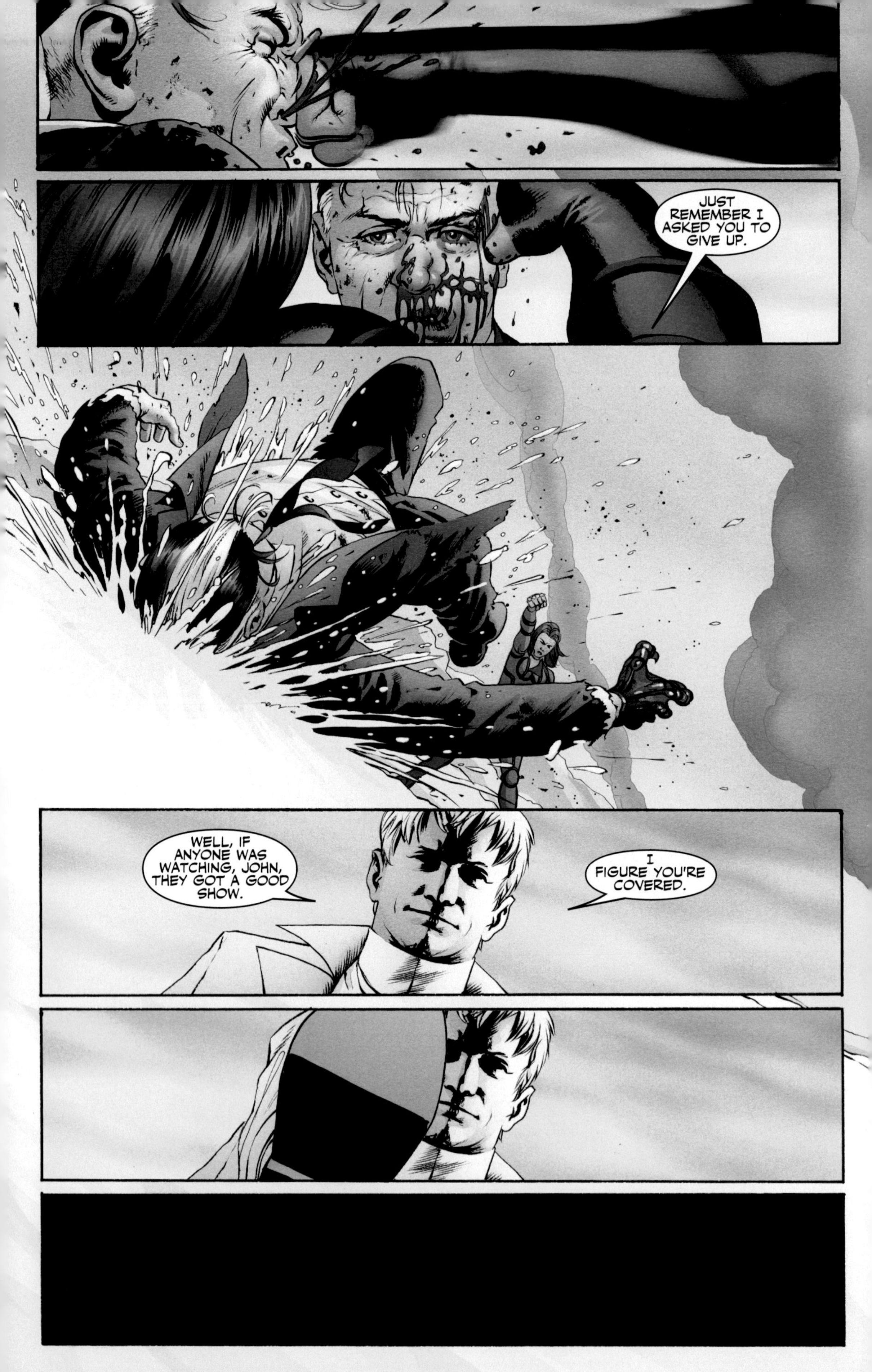
JUST REMEMBER I ASKED YOU TO GIVE UP.
WELL, IF ANYONE WAS WATCHING, JOHN, THEY GOT A GOOD SHOW.
I FIGURE YOU'RE COVERED.

WELL, I'M SO GLAD YOU SAVED ME FROM THE FOUR.

I MEAN, THEY MIGHT HAVE *HURT* ME.

YOU *BASTARDS.*

AH, QUIT WHINING. IF YOU'D TOLD US THERE WAS A BOMB IN YOUR CHEST, WE WOULD HAVE BEEN PREPARED IN ADVANCE.

THE DRUMMER DIDN'T HEAR IT UNTIL WE WERE LOADING YOU ON THE CHOPPER.

I HAD TO FREEZE IT AND KEEP IT THAT WAY UNTIL WE GOT HERE.

WHATEVER. I'M DEAD ANYWAY, NOW.

WHAT DO YOU WANT TO KNOW, ELIJAH?

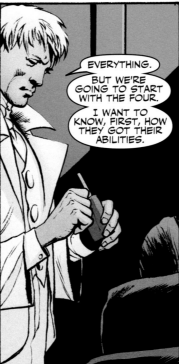

EVERYTHING.

BUT WE'RE GOING TO START WITH THE FOUR.

I WANT TO KNOW, FIRST, HOW THEY GOT THEIR ABILITIES.

ALL WE KNOW IS THAT THEIR 1961 MOONSHOT TOOK THEM INTO THE BLEED SOMEHOW.

THEY SENT A PROBE FIRST.

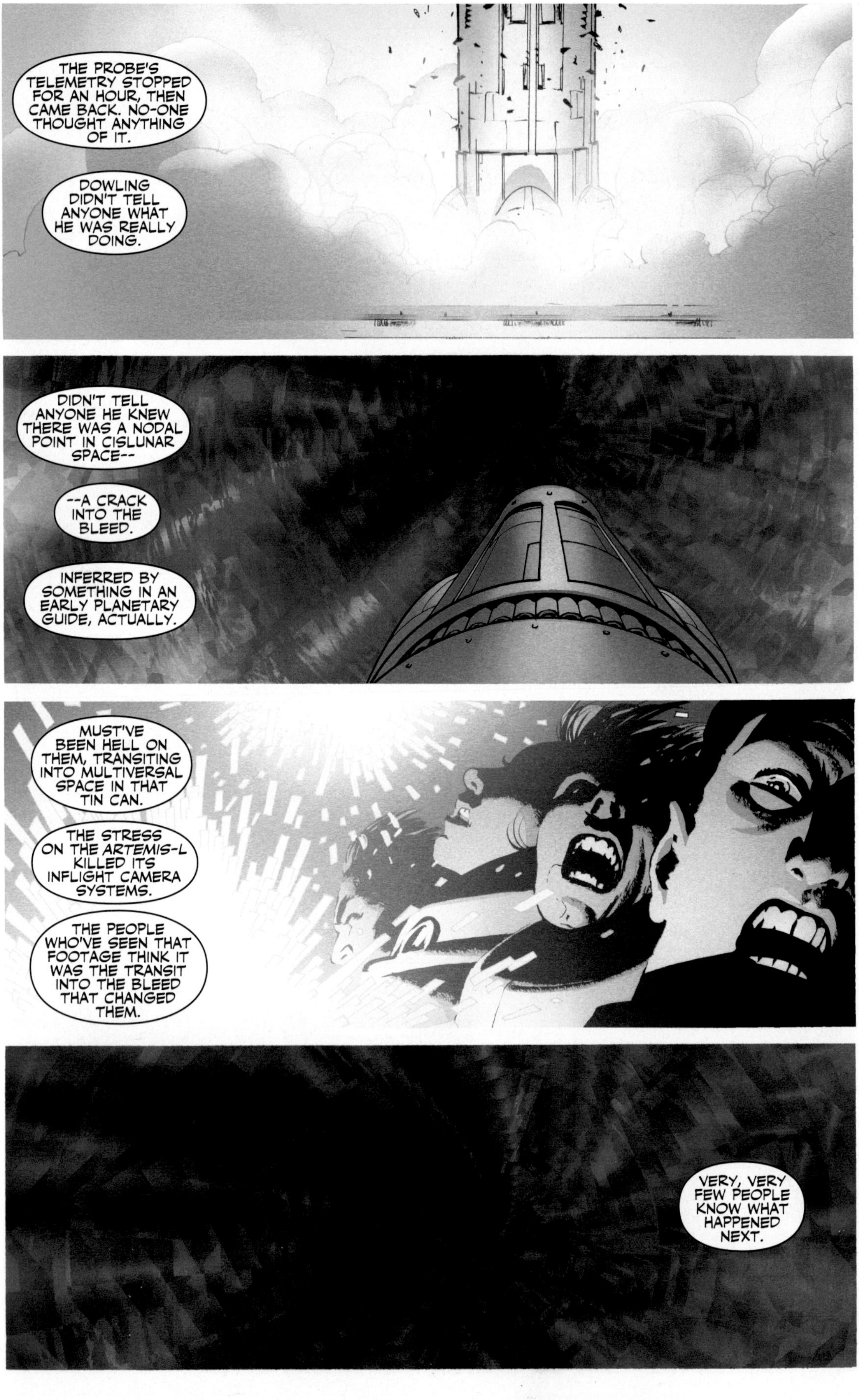
THE PROBE'S TELEMETRY STOPPED FOR AN HOUR, THEN CAME BACK. NO-ONE THOUGHT ANYTHING OF IT.
DOWLING DIDN'T TELL ANYONE WHAT HE WAS REALLY DOING.
DIDN'T TELL ANYONE HE KNEW THERE WAS A NODAL POINT IN CISLUNAR SPACE--
--A CRACK INTO THE BLEED.
INFERRED BY SOMETHING IN AN EARLY PLANETARY GUIDE, ACTUALLY.
MUST'VE BEEN HELL ON THEM, TRANSITING INTO MULTIVERSAL SPACE IN THAT TIN CAN.
THE STRESS ON THE *ARTEMIS-L* KILLED ITS INFLIGHT CAMERA SYSTEMS.
THE PEOPLE WHO'VE SEEN THAT FOOTAGE THINK IT WAS THE TRANSIT INTO THE BLEED THAT CHANGED THEM.
VERY, VERY FEW PEOPLE KNOW WHAT HAPPENED NEXT.

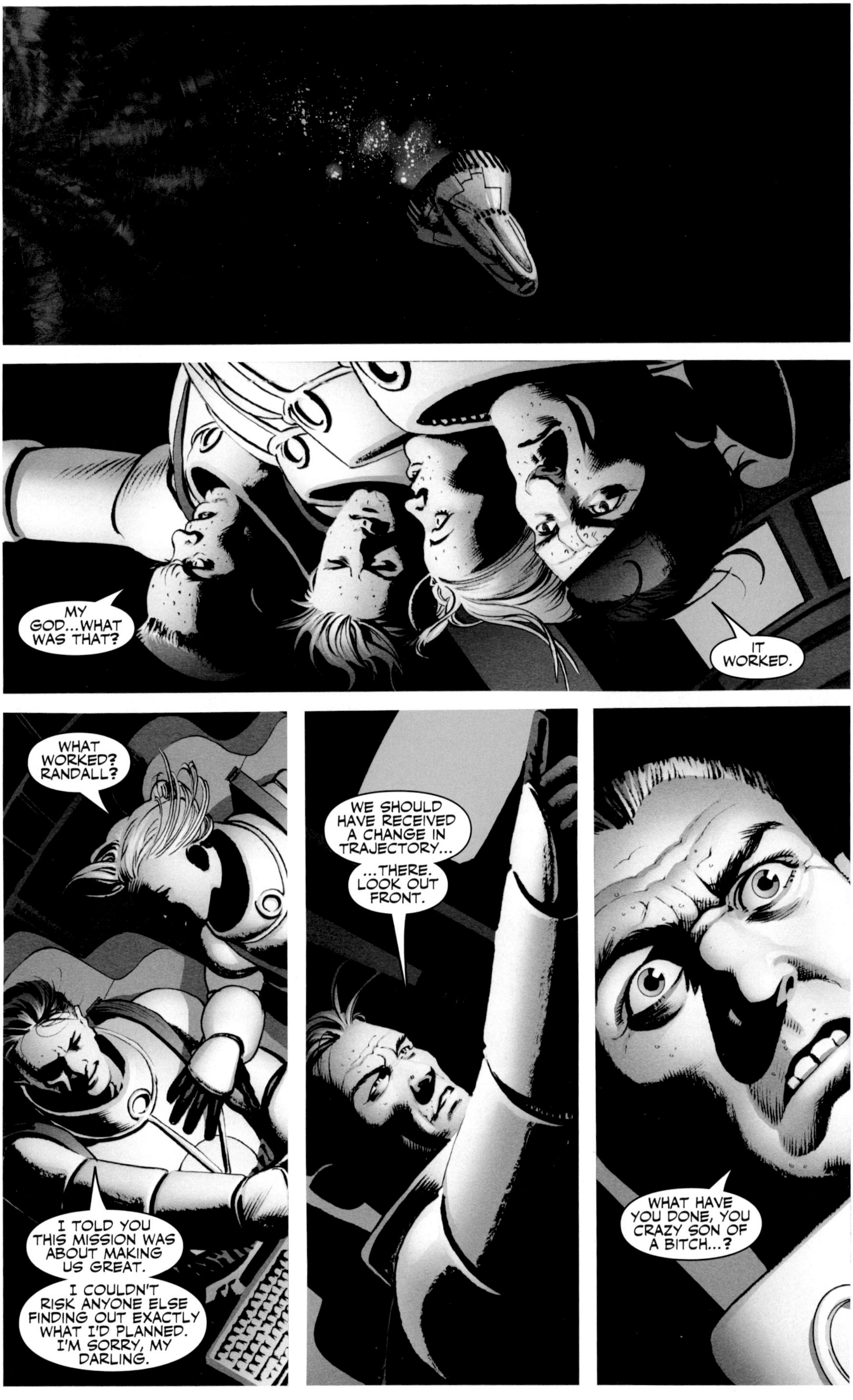
MY GOD...WHAT WAS THAT?
IT WORKED.
WHAT WORKED? RANDALL?
I TOLD YOU THIS MISSION WAS ABOUT MAKING US GREAT.
I COULDN'T RISK ANYONE ELSE FINDING OUT EXACTLY WHAT I'D PLANNED. I'M SORRY, MY DARLING.
WE SHOULD HAVE RECEIVED A CHANGE IN TRAJECTORY...
...THERE. LOOK OUT FRONT.
WHAT HAVE YOU DONE, YOU CRAZY SON OF A BITCH...?

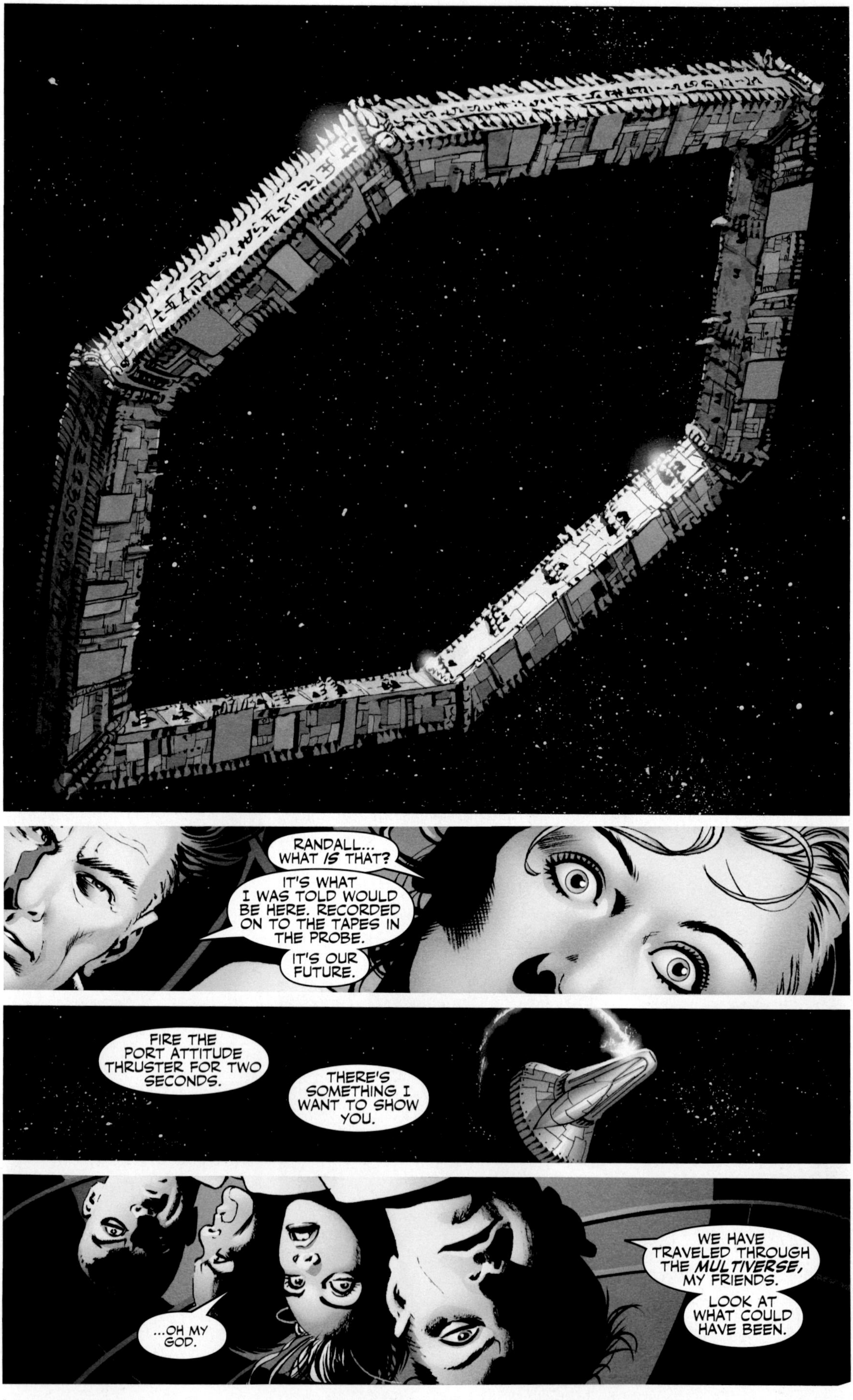

RANDALL... WHAT *IS* THAT?
IT'S WHAT I WAS TOLD WOULD BE HERE. RECORDED ON TO THE TAPES IN THE PROBE.
IT'S OUR FUTURE.
FIRE THE PORT ATTITUDE THRUSTER FOR TWO SECONDS.
THERE'S SOMETHING I WANT TO SHOW YOU.
WE HAVE TRAVELED THROUGH THE *MULTIVERSE,* MY FRIENDS.
LOOK AT WHAT COULD HAVE BEEN.
...OH MY GOD.

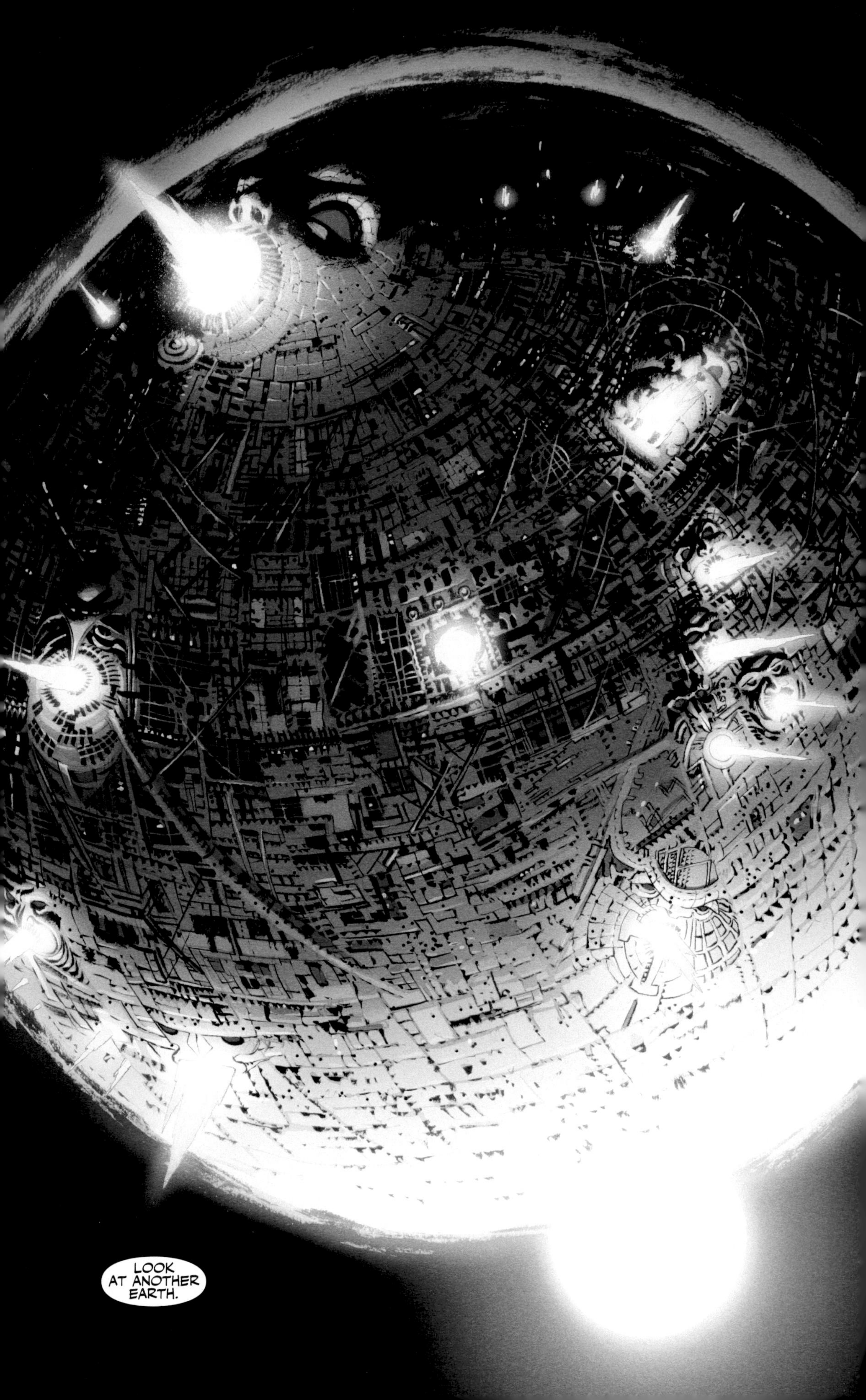
LOOK AT ANOTHER EARTH.

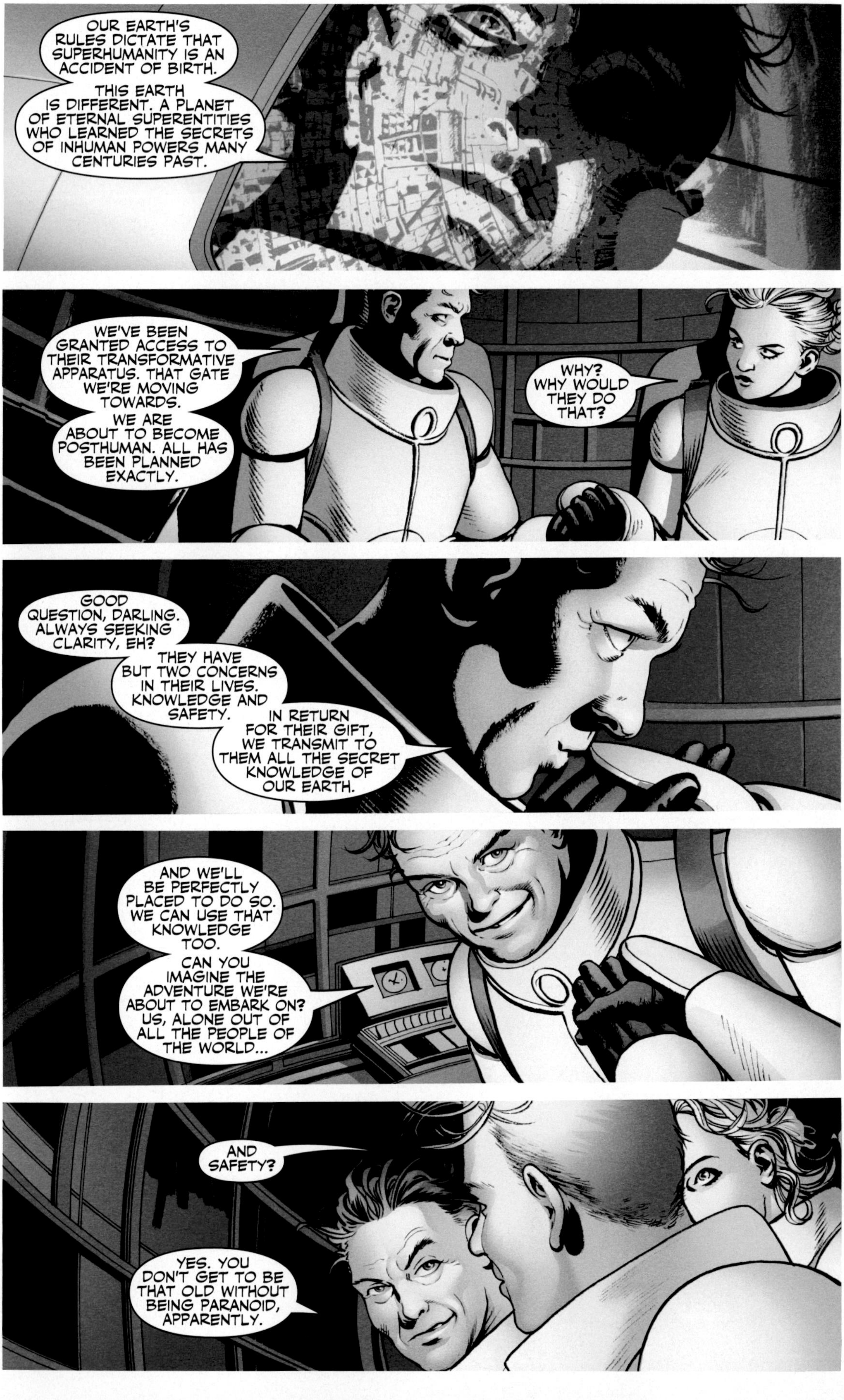
OUR EARTH'S RULES DICTATE THAT SUPERHUMANITY IS AN ACCIDENT OF BIRTH.
THIS EARTH IS DIFFERENT. A PLANET OF ETERNAL SUPERENTITIES WHO LEARNED THE SECRETS OF INHUMAN POWERS MANY CENTURIES PAST.
WE'VE BEEN GRANTED ACCESS TO THEIR TRANSFORMATIVE APPARATUS. THAT GATE WE'RE MOVING TOWARDS.
WE ARE ABOUT TO BECOME POSTHUMAN. ALL HAS BEEN PLANNED EXACTLY.
WHY? WHY WOULD THEY DO THAT?
GOOD QUESTION, DARLING. ALWAYS SEEKING CLARITY, EH?
THEY HAVE BUT TWO CONCERNS IN THEIR LIVES. KNOWLEDGE AND SAFETY.
IN RETURN FOR THEIR GIFT, WE TRANSMIT TO THEM ALL THE SECRET KNOWLEDGE OF OUR EARTH.
AND WE'LL BE PERFECTLY PLACED TO DO SO. WE CAN USE THAT KNOWLEDGE TOO.
CAN YOU IMAGINE THE ADVENTURE WE'RE ABOUT TO EMBARK ON? US, ALONE OUT OF ALL THE PEOPLE OF THE WORLD...
AND SAFETY?
YES. YOU DON'T GET TO BE THAT OLD WITHOUT BEING PARANOID, APPARENTLY.

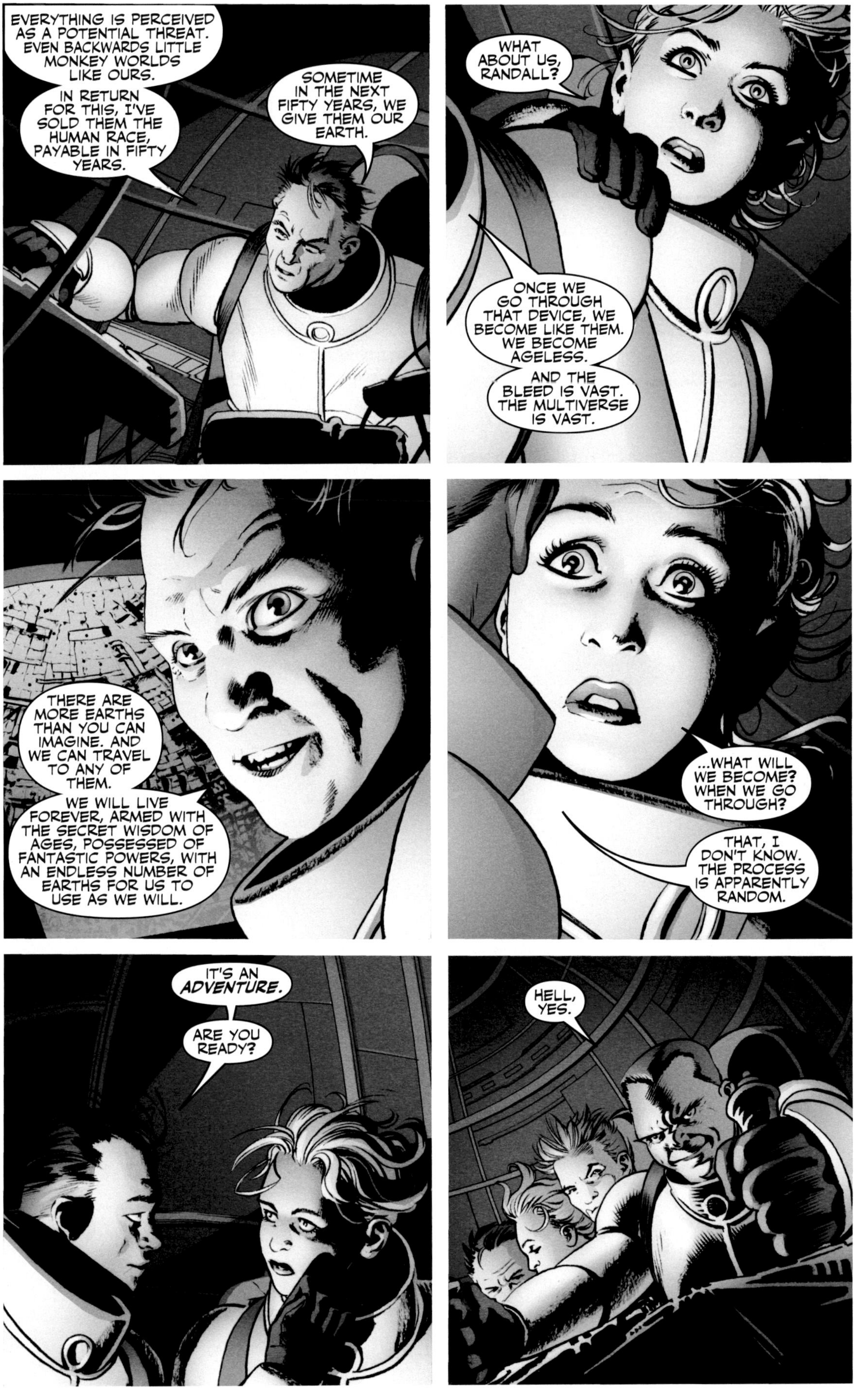
EVERYTHING IS PERCEIVED AS A POTENTIAL THREAT. EVEN BACKWARDS LITTLE MONKEY WORLDS LIKE OURS.
IN RETURN FOR THIS, I'VE SOLD THEM THE HUMAN RACE, PAYABLE IN FIFTY YEARS.
SOMETIME IN THE NEXT FIFTY YEARS, WE GIVE THEM OUR EARTH.
WHAT ABOUT US, RANDALL?
ONCE WE GO THROUGH THAT DEVICE, WE BECOME LIKE THEM. WE BECOME AGELESS.
AND THE BLEED IS VAST. THE MULTIVERSE IS VAST.
THERE ARE MORE EARTHS THAN YOU CAN IMAGINE. AND WE CAN TRAVEL TO ANY OF THEM.
WE WILL LIVE FOREVER, ARMED WITH THE SECRET WISDOM OF AGES, POSSESSED OF FANTASTIC POWERS, WITH AN ENDLESS NUMBER OF EARTHS FOR US TO USE AS WE WILL.
...WHAT WILL WE BECOME? WHEN WE GO THROUGH?
THAT, I DON'T KNOW. THE PROCESS IS APPARENTLY RANDOM.
IT'S AN *ADVENTURE.*
ARE YOU READY?
HELL, YES.

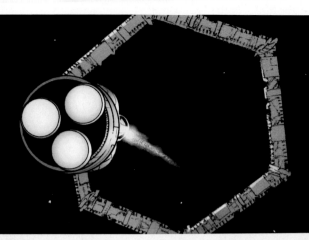

"SOMETIME IN THE NEXT FIFTY YEARS," THEY SAID TO DOWLING.

THAT WAS IN 1961.

WE'RE INTO THE 21ST CENTURY NOW.

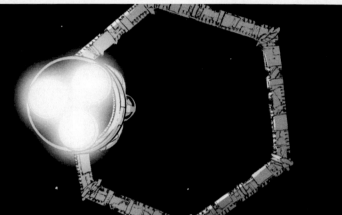

THE BEST CASE SCENARIO IS THAT A PARALLEL WORLD FULL OF PARANOID, AGELESS POSTHUMANS IS GOING TO COME FOR US IN 2011.

PRESUMABLY EXPECTING US TO HAVE BEEN SUBJUGATED BY THE FOUR PREVIOUS TO THEIR ARRIVAL.

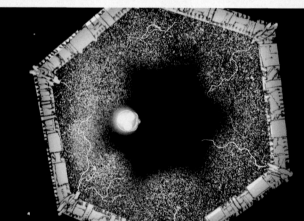

AND WHO'S TO SAY? MAYBE WE HAVE. THE WONDERS THEY'VE WITHHELD FROM US...PERHAPS WE'VE BEEN MADE A THIRD-WORLD VERSION OF THE EARTH.

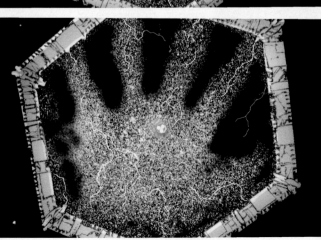

BUT YOU COMING BACK, AND YOU GETTING SERIOUS...THAT SCARED THEM.

TIME COULD BE RUNNING OUT FOR THEM AS WELL AS FOR US.

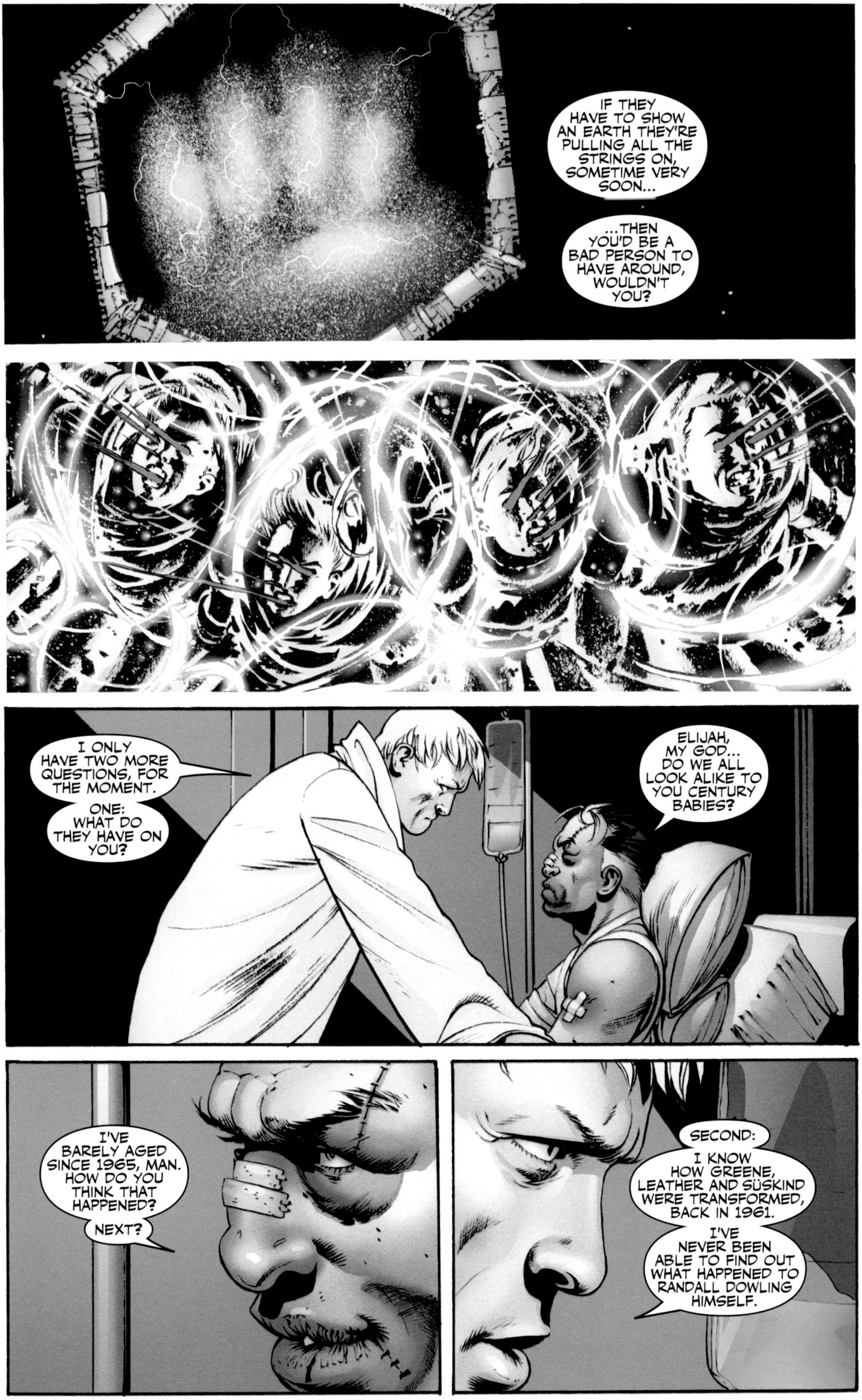
IF THEY HAVE TO SHOW AN EARTH THEY'RE PULLING ALL THE STRINGS ON, SOMETIME VERY SOON...
...THEN YOU'D BE A BAD PERSON TO HAVE AROUND, WOULDN'T YOU?
I ONLY HAVE TWO MORE QUESTIONS, FOR THE MOMENT.
ONE: WHAT DO THEY HAVE ON YOU?
ELIJAH, MY GOD... DO WE ALL LOOK ALIKE TO YOU CENTURY BABIES?
I'VE BARELY AGED SINCE 1965, MAN. HOW DO YOU THINK THAT HAPPENED?
NEXT?
SECOND:
I KNOW HOW GREENE, LEATHER AND SÜSKIND WERE TRANSFORMED, BACK IN 1961.
I'VE NEVER BEEN ABLE TO FIND OUT WHAT HAPPENED TO RANDALL DOWLING HIMSELF.

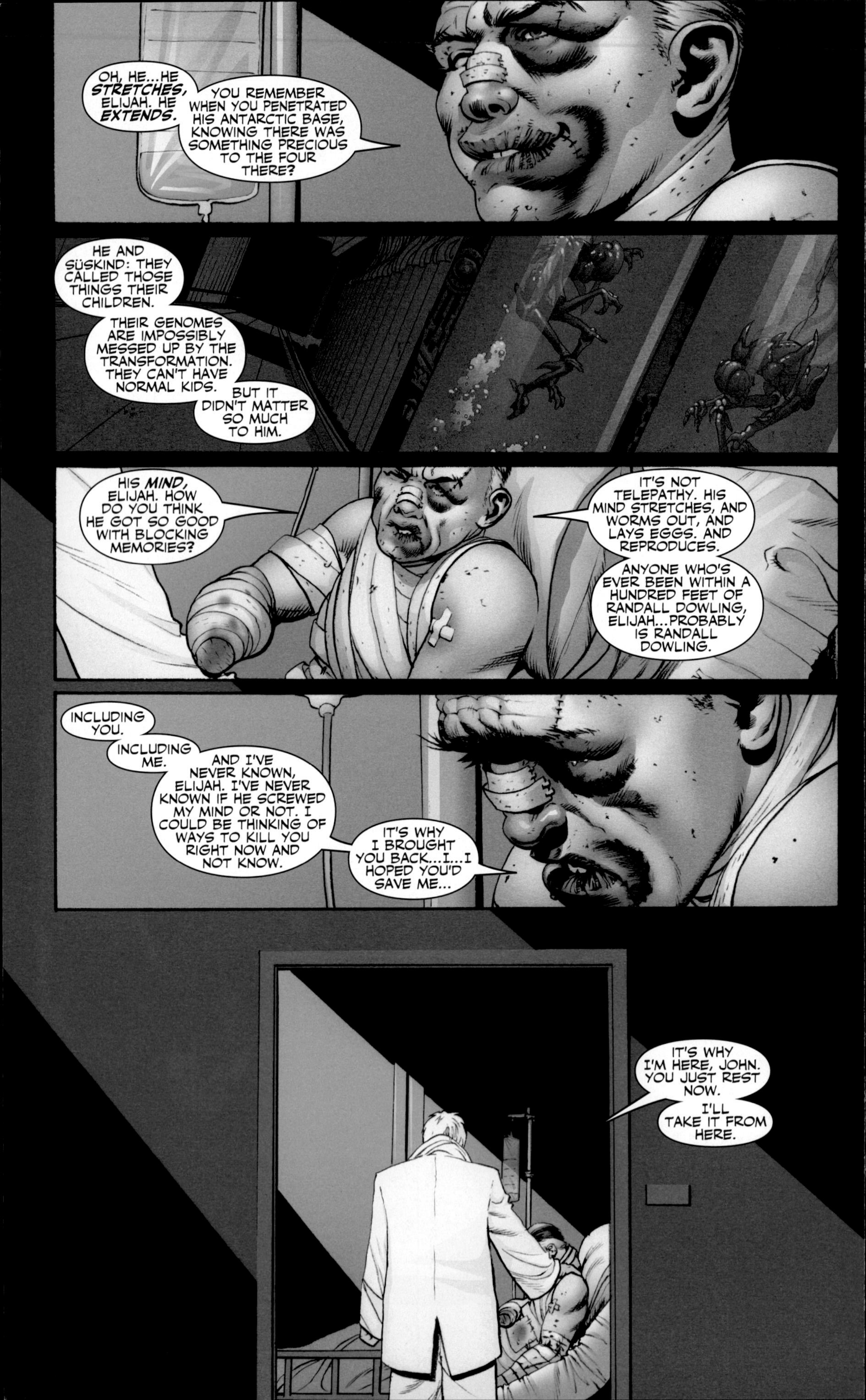
OH, HE...HE STRETCHES, ELIJAH. HE EXTENDS.
YOU REMEMBER WHEN YOU PENETRATED HIS ANTARCTIC BASE, KNOWING THERE WAS SOMETHING PRECIOUS TO THE FOUR THERE?
HE AND SÜSKIND: THEY CALLED THOSE THINGS THEIR CHILDREN.
THEIR GENOMES ARE IMPOSSIBLY MESSED UP BY THE TRANSFORMATION. THEY CAN'T HAVE NORMAL KIDS.
BUT IT DIDN'T MATTER SO MUCH TO HIM.
HIS MIND, ELIJAH. HOW DO YOU THINK HE GOT SO GOOD WITH BLOCKING MEMORIES?
IT'S NOT TELEPATHY. HIS MIND STRETCHES, AND WORMS OUT, AND LAYS EGGS. AND REPRODUCES.
ANYONE WHO'S EVER BEEN WITHIN A HUNDRED FEET OF RANDALL DOWLING, ELIJAH...PROBABLY IS RANDALL DOWLING.
INCLUDING YOU.
INCLUDING ME.
AND I'VE NEVER KNOWN, ELIJAH. I'VE NEVER KNOWN IF HE SCREWED MY MIND OR NOT. I COULD BE THINKING OF WAYS TO KILL YOU RIGHT NOW AND NOT KNOW.
IT'S WHY I BROUGHT YOU BACK...I...I HOPED YOU'D SAVE ME...
IT'S WHY I'M HERE, JOHN. YOU JUST REST NOW.
I'LL TAKE IT FROM HERE.

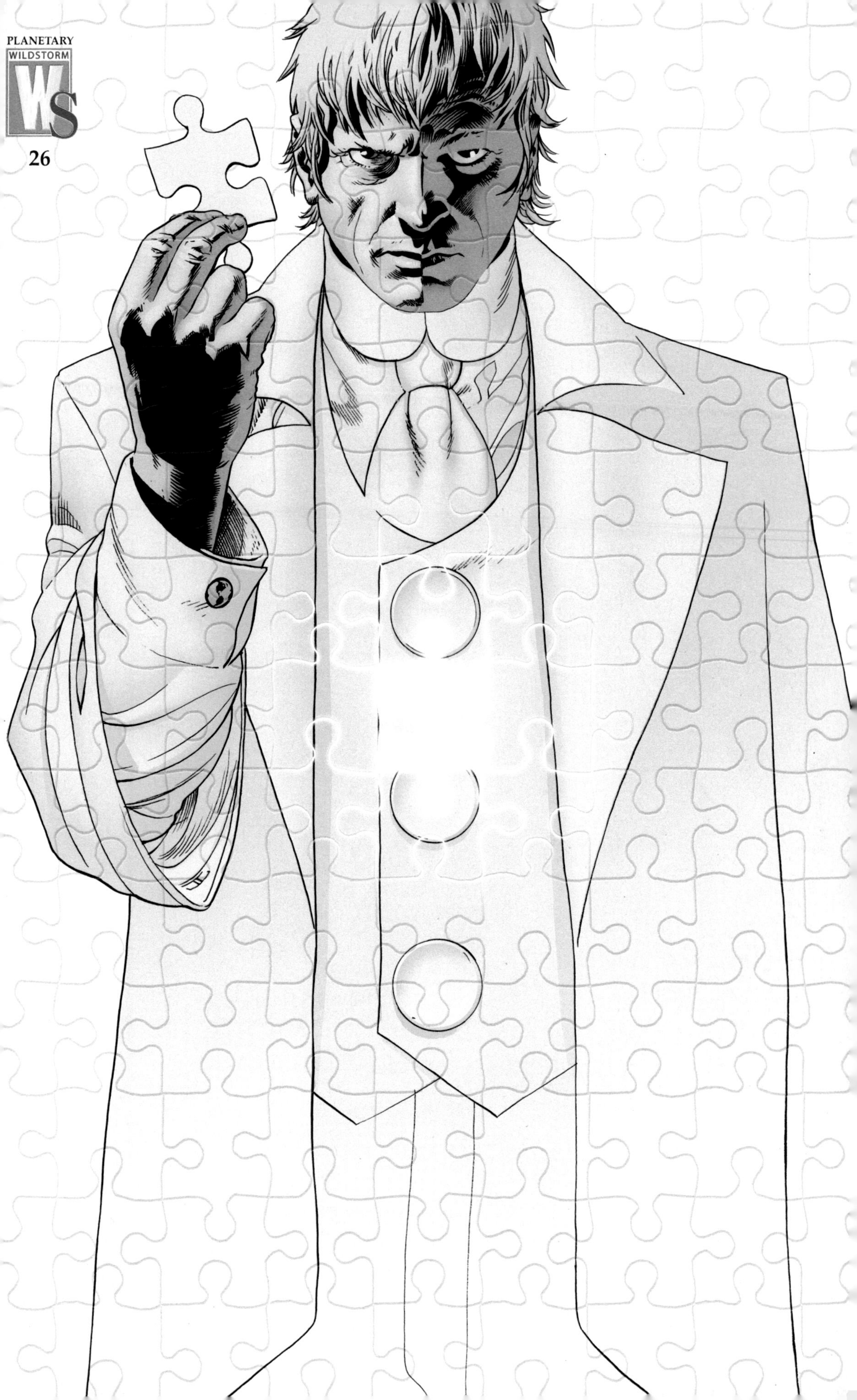
PLANETARY
WILDSTORM
26

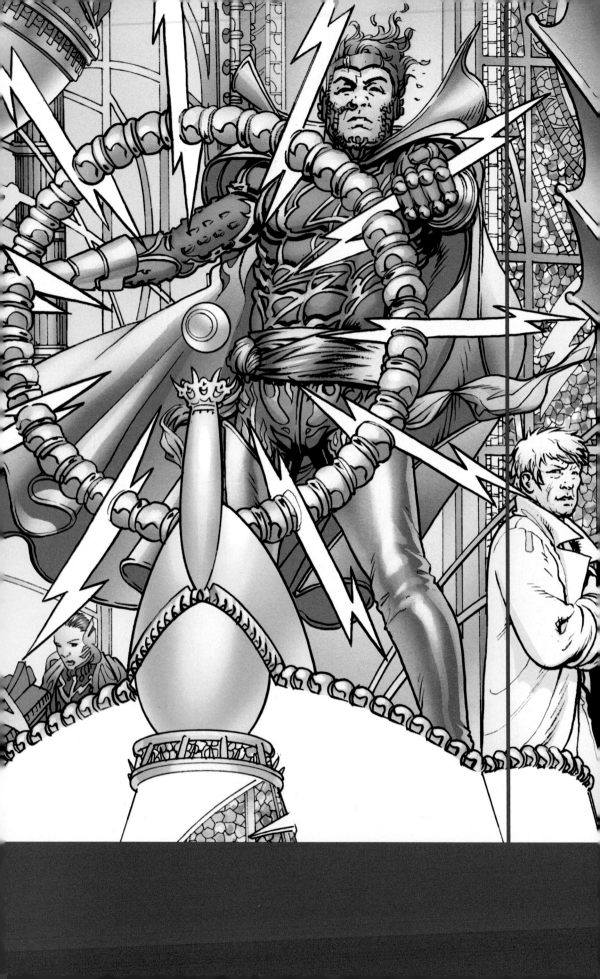

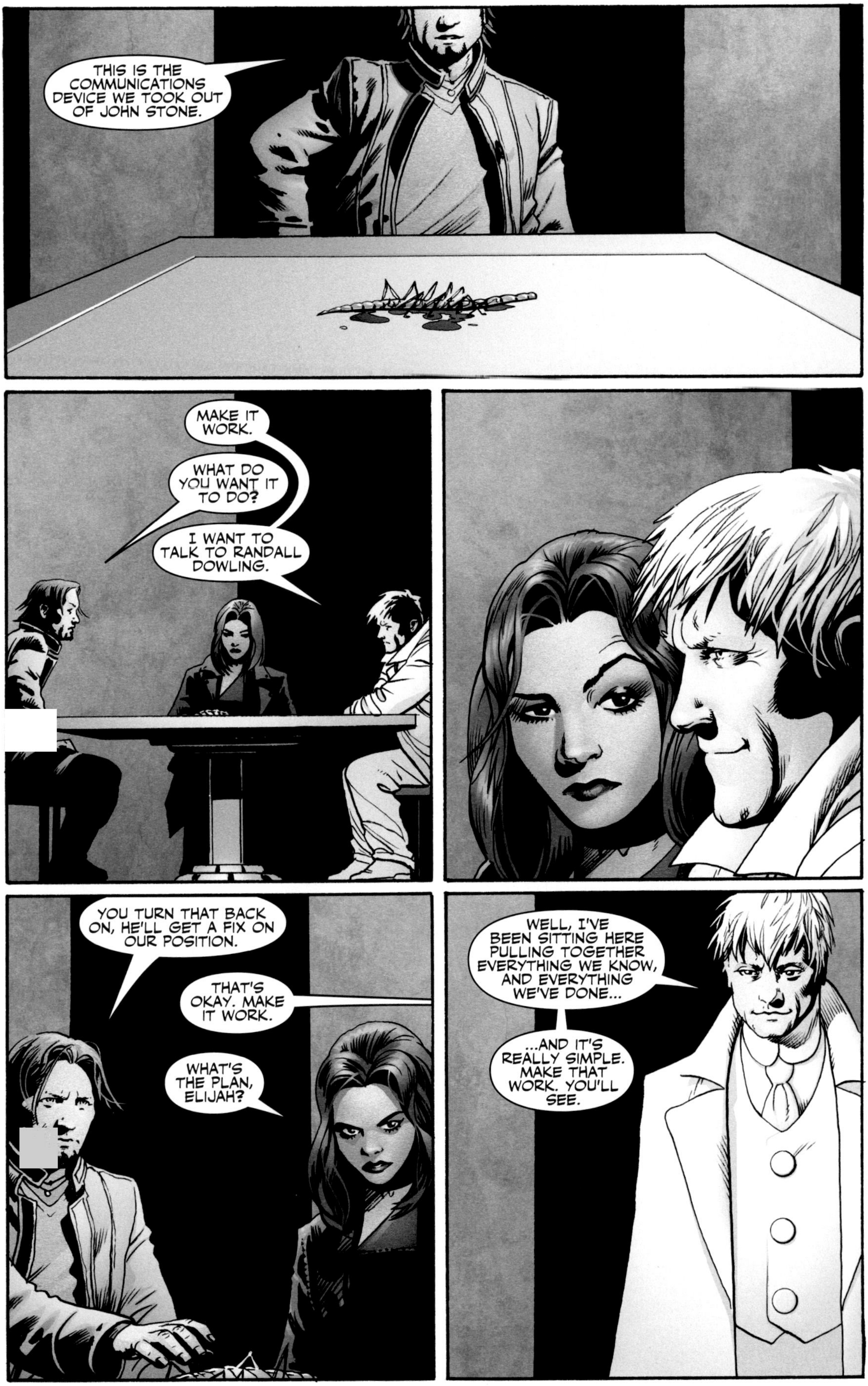
THIS IS THE COMMUNICATIONS DEVICE WE TOOK OUT OF JOHN STONE.
MAKE IT WORK.
WHAT DO YOU WANT IT TO DO?
I WANT TO TALK TO RANDALL DOWLING.
YOU TURN THAT BACK ON, HE'LL GET A FIX ON OUR POSITION.
THAT'S OKAY. MAKE IT WORK.
WHAT'S THE PLAN, ELIJAH?
WELL, I'VE BEEN SITTING HERE PULLING TOGETHER EVERYTHING WE KNOW, AND EVERYTHING WE'VE DONE...
...AND IT'S REALLY SIMPLE. MAKE THAT WORK. YOU'LL SEE.

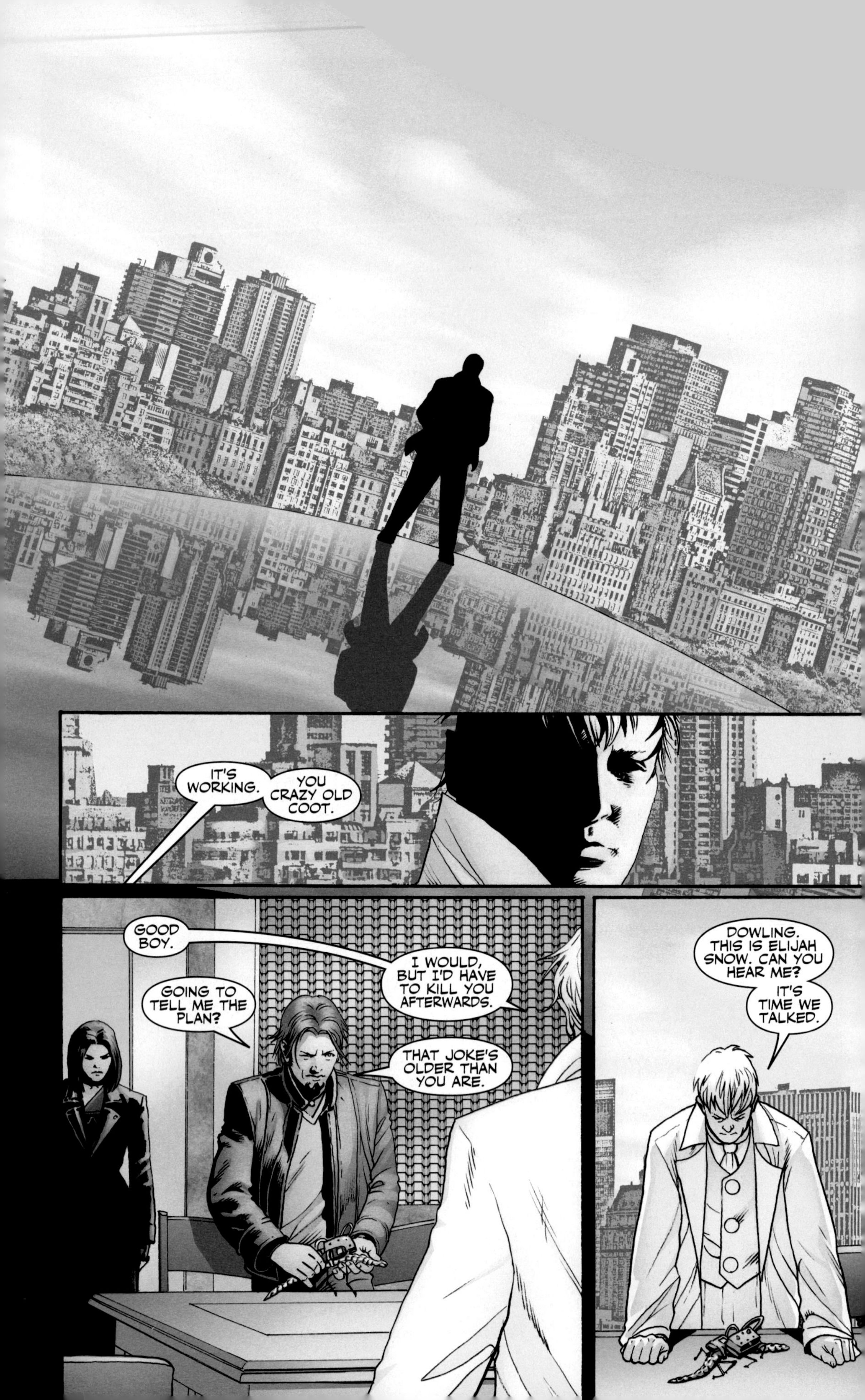
IT'S WORKING.
YOU CRAZY OLD COOT.
GOOD BOY.
GOING TO TELL ME THE PLAN?
I WOULD, BUT I'D HAVE TO KILL YOU AFTERWARDS.
THAT JOKE'S OLDER THAN YOU ARE.
DOWLING. THIS IS ELIJAH SNOW. CAN YOU HEAR ME?
IT'S TIME WE TALKED.

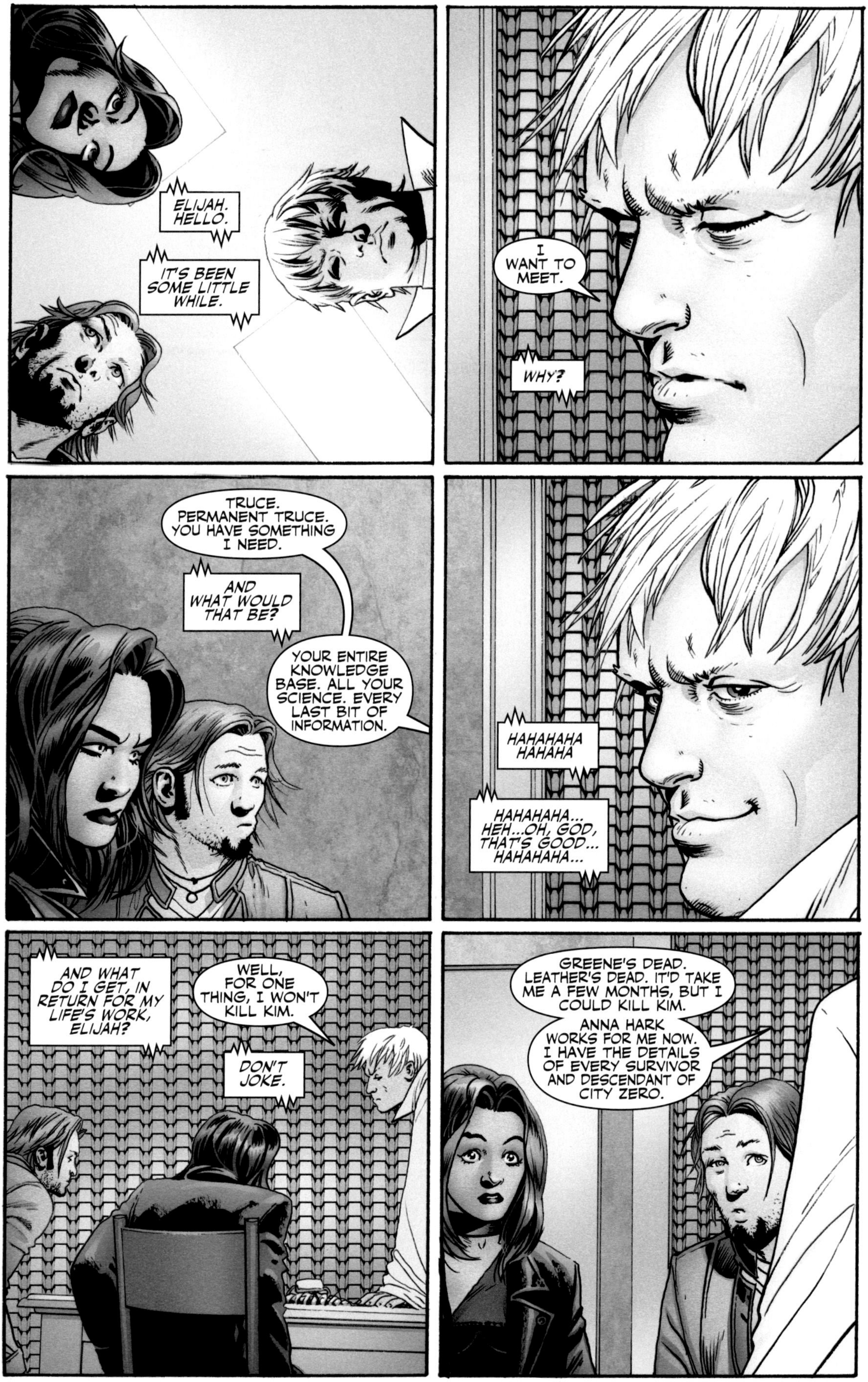
ELIJAH. HELLO.
IT'S BEEN SOME LITTLE WHILE.
I WANT TO MEET.
WHY?
TRUCE. PERMANENT TRUCE. YOU HAVE SOMETHING I NEED.
AND WHAT WOULD THAT BE?
YOUR ENTIRE KNOWLEDGE BASE. ALL YOUR SCIENCE. EVERY LAST BIT OF INFORMATION.
HAHAHAHA HAHAHA
HAHAHAHA... HEH...OH, GOD, THAT'S GOOD... HAHAHAHA...
AND WHAT DO I GET, IN RETURN FOR MY LIFE'S WORK, ELIJAH?
WELL, FOR ONE THING, I WON'T KILL KIM.
DON'T JOKE.
GREENE'S DEAD. LEATHER'S DEAD. IT'D TAKE ME A FEW MONTHS, BUT I COULD KILL KIM.
ANNA HARK WORKS FOR ME NOW. I HAVE THE DETAILS OF EVERY SURVIVOR AND DESCENDANT OF CITY ZERO.

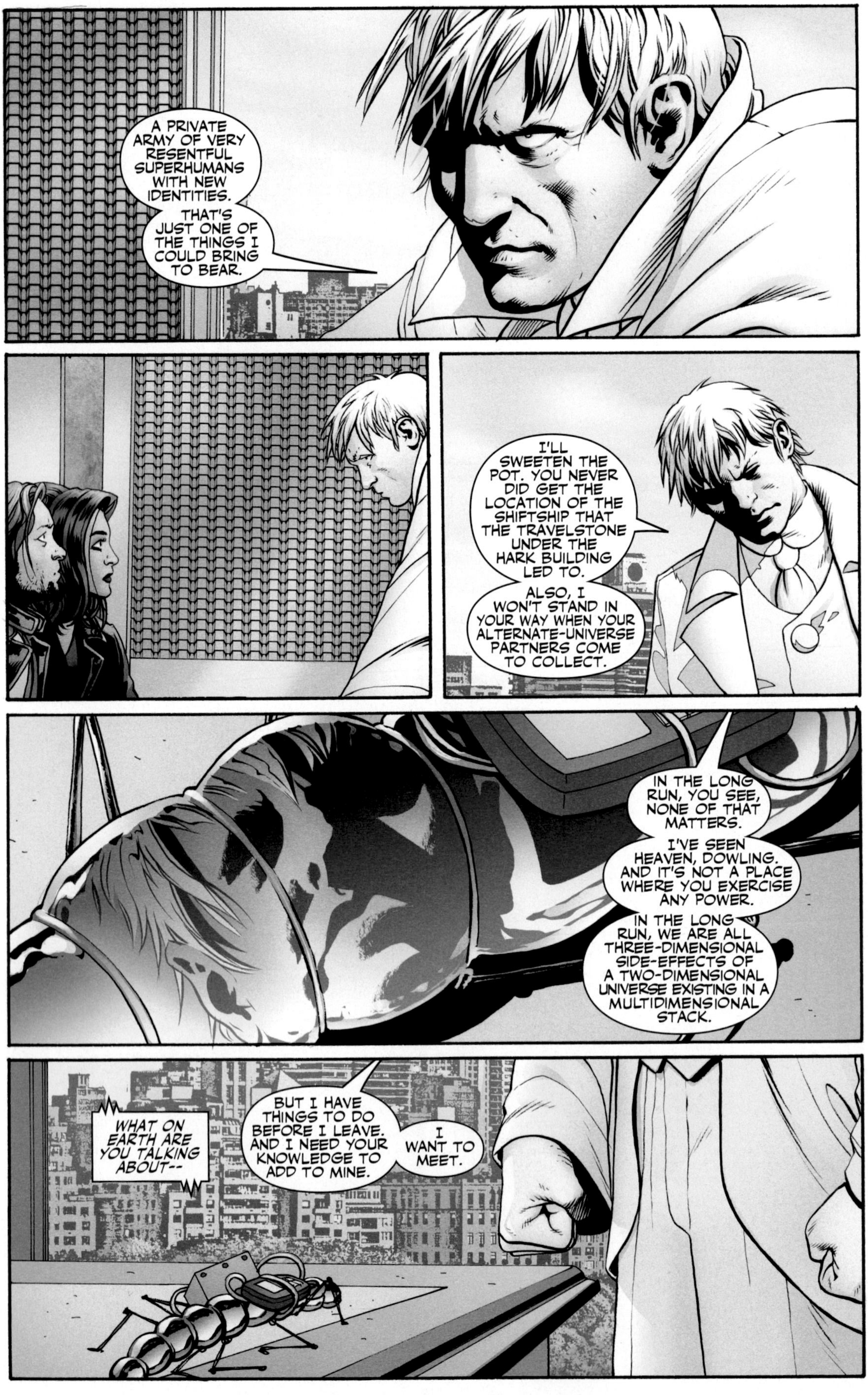
A PRIVATE ARMY OF VERY RESENTFUL SUPERHUMANS WITH NEW IDENTITIES.
THAT'S JUST ONE OF THE THINGS I COULD BRING TO BEAR.
I'LL SWEETEN THE POT. YOU NEVER DID GET THE LOCATION OF THE SHIFTSHIP THAT THE TRAVELSTONE UNDER THE HARK BUILDING LED TO.
ALSO, I WON'T STAND IN YOUR WAY WHEN YOUR ALTERNATE-UNIVERSE PARTNERS COME TO COLLECT.
IN THE LONG RUN, YOU SEE, NONE OF THAT MATTERS.
I'VE SEEN HEAVEN, DOWLING. AND IT'S NOT A PLACE WHERE YOU EXERCISE ANY POWER.
IN THE LONG RUN, WE ARE ALL THREE-DIMENSIONAL SIDE-EFFECTS OF A TWO-DIMENSIONAL UNIVERSE EXISTING IN A MULTIDIMENSIONAL STACK.
WHAT ON EARTH ARE YOU TALKING ABOUT--
BUT I HAVE THINGS TO DO BEFORE I LEAVE. AND I NEED YOUR KNOWLEDGE TO ADD TO MINE.
I WANT TO MEET.

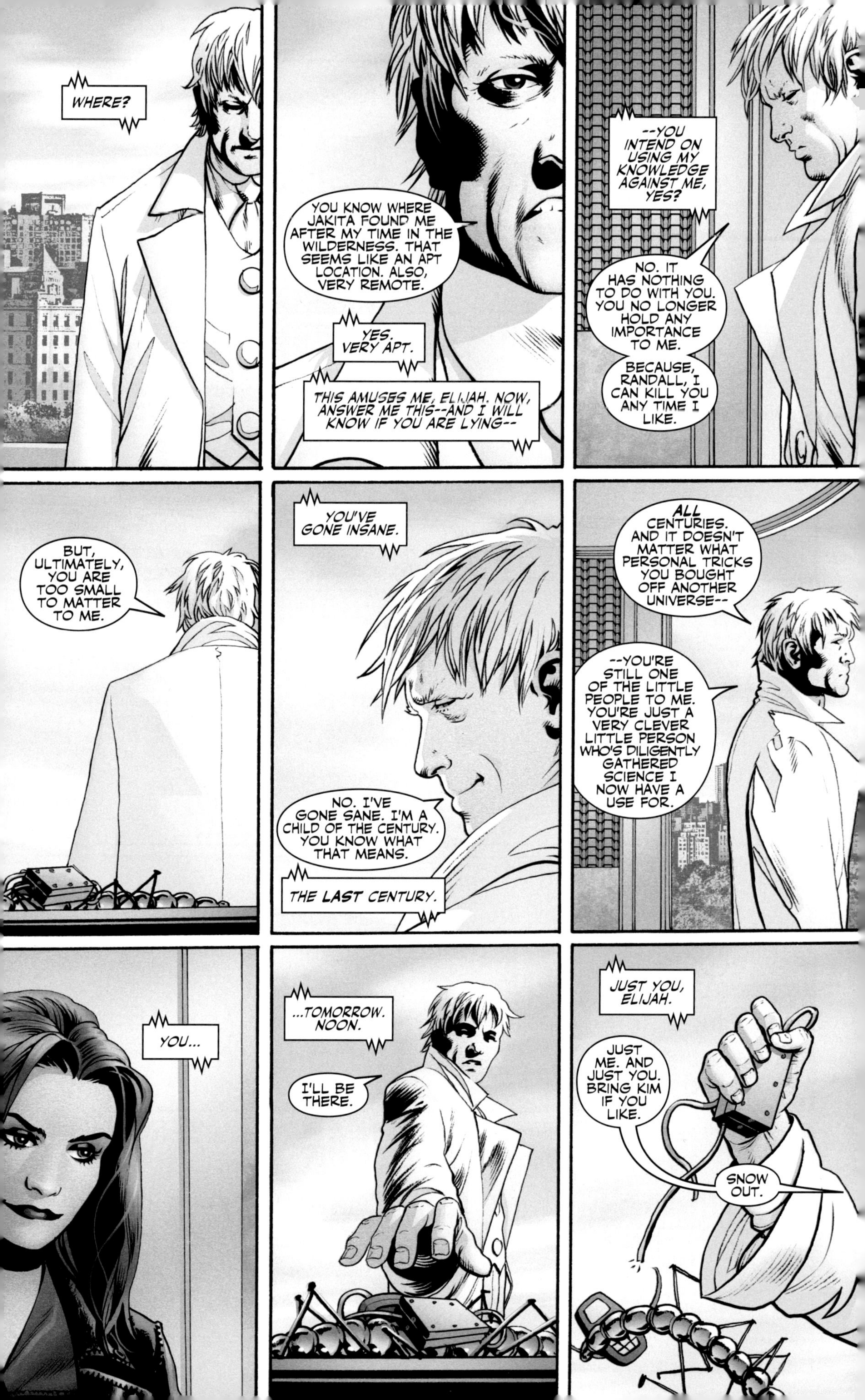
WHERE?
YOU KNOW WHERE JAKITA FOUND ME AFTER MY TIME IN THE WILDERNESS. THAT SEEMS LIKE AN APT LOCATION. ALSO, VERY REMOTE.
YES. VERY APT.
THIS AMUSES ME, ELIJAH. NOW, ANSWER ME THIS--AND I WILL KNOW IF YOU ARE LYING--
--YOU INTEND ON USING MY KNOWLEDGE AGAINST ME, YES?
NO. IT HAS NOTHING TO DO WITH YOU. YOU NO LONGER HOLD ANY IMPORTANCE TO ME.
BECAUSE, RANDALL, I CAN KILL YOU ANY TIME I LIKE.
BUT, ULTIMATELY, YOU ARE TOO SMALL TO MATTER TO ME.
YOU'VE GONE INSANE.
NO. I'VE GONE SANE. I'M A CHILD OF THE CENTURY. YOU KNOW WHAT THAT MEANS.
THE LAST CENTURY.
ALL CENTURIES. AND IT DOESN'T MATTER WHAT PERSONAL TRICKS YOU BOUGHT OFF ANOTHER UNIVERSE--
--YOU'RE STILL ONE OF THE LITTLE PEOPLE TO ME. YOU'RE JUST A VERY CLEVER LITTLE PERSON WHO'S DILIGENTLY GATHERED SCIENCE I NOW HAVE A USE FOR.
YOU...
...TOMORROW. NOON.
I'LL BE THERE.
JUST YOU, ELIJAH.
JUST ME. AND JUST YOU. BRING KIM IF YOU LIKE.
SNOW OUT.

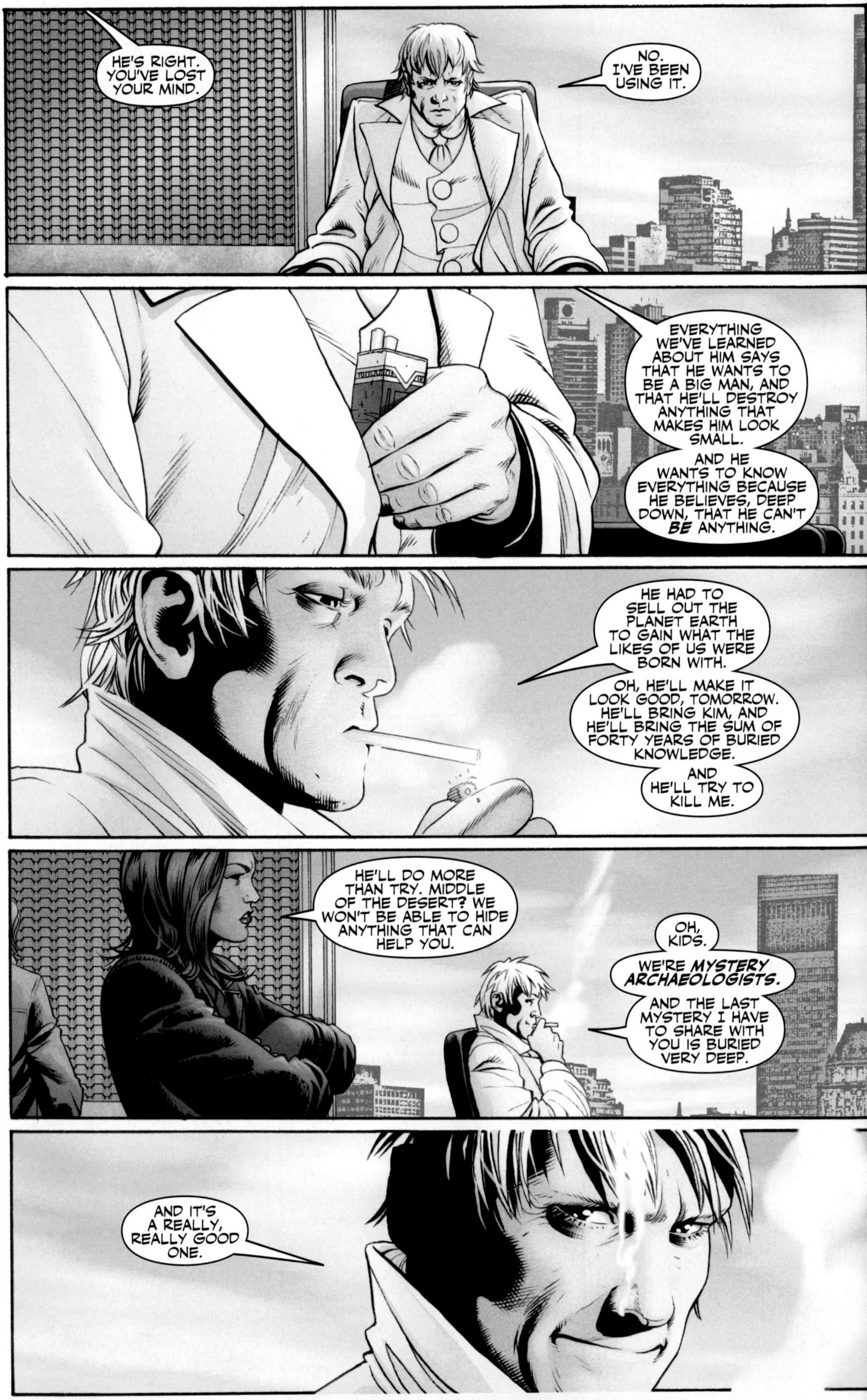
HE'S RIGHT. YOU'VE LOST YOUR MIND.
NO. I'VE BEEN USING IT.
EVERYTHING WE'VE LEARNED ABOUT HIM SAYS THAT HE WANTS TO BE A BIG MAN, AND THAT HE'LL DESTROY ANYTHING THAT MAKES HIM LOOK SMALL.
AND HE WANTS TO KNOW EVERYTHING BECAUSE HE BELIEVES, DEEP DOWN, THAT HE CAN'T *BE* ANYTHING.
HE HAD TO SELL OUT THE PLANET EARTH TO GAIN WHAT THE LIKES OF US WERE BORN WITH.
OH, HE'LL MAKE IT LOOK GOOD, TOMORROW. HE'LL BRING KIM, AND HE'LL BRING THE SUM OF FORTY YEARS OF BURIED KNOWLEDGE.
AND HE'LL TRY TO KILL ME.
HE'LL DO MORE THAN TRY. MIDDLE OF THE DESERT? WE WON'T BE ABLE TO HIDE ANYTHING THAT CAN HELP YOU.
OH, KIDS.
WE'RE *MYSTERY ARCHAEOLOGISTS.*
AND THE LAST MYSTERY I HAVE TO SHARE WITH YOU IS BURIED VERY DEEP.
AND IT'S A REALLY, REALLY GOOD ONE.

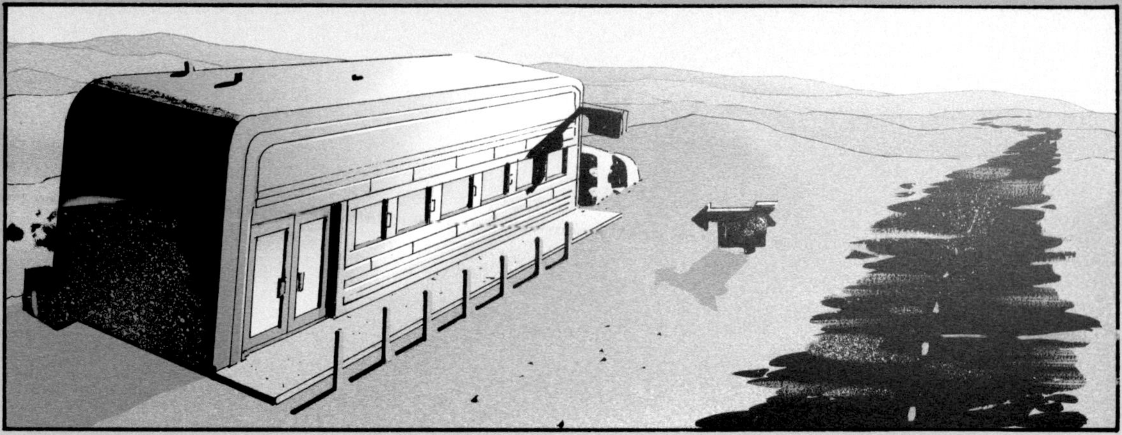

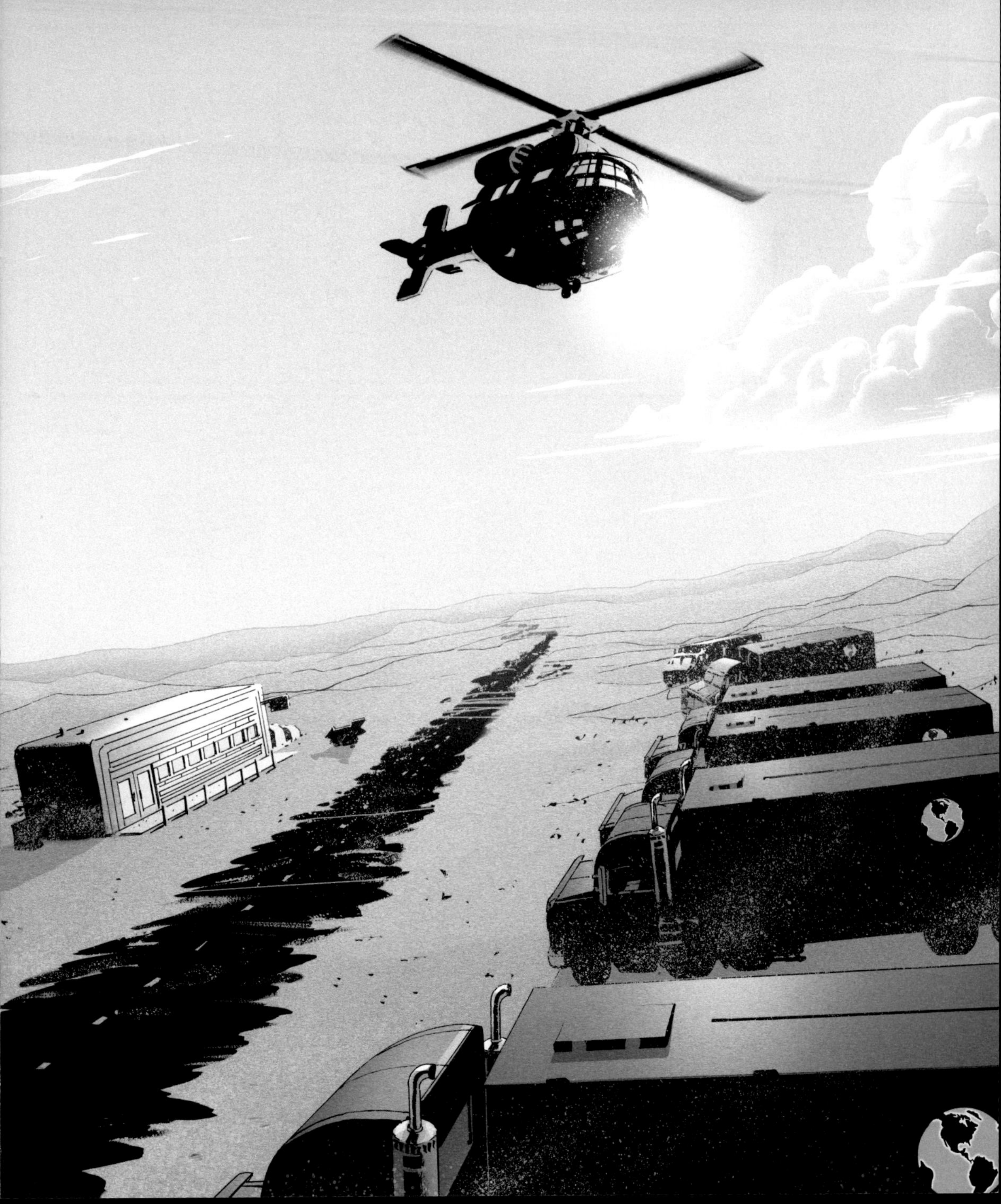

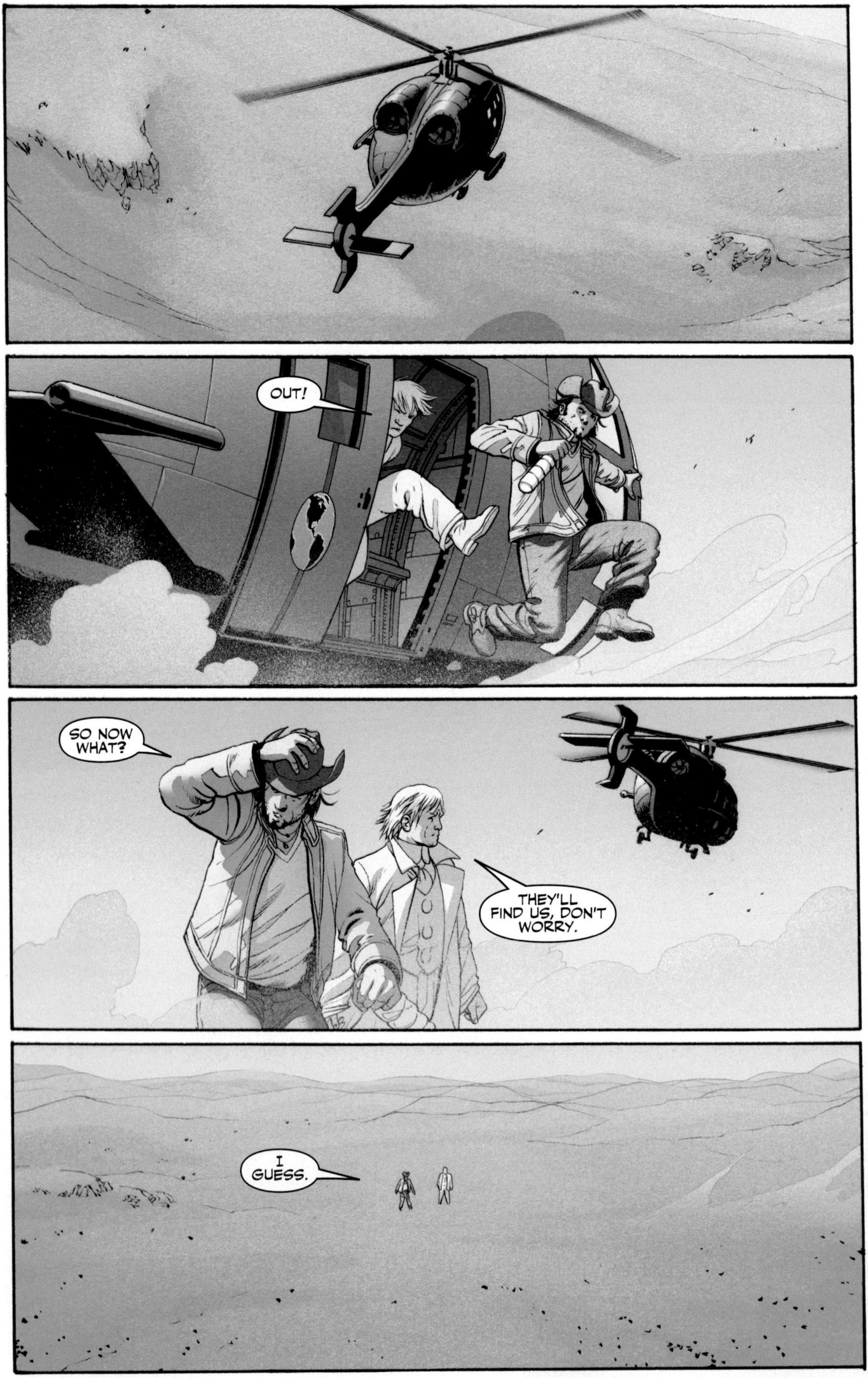
OUT!
SO NOW WHAT?
THEY'LL FIND US, DON'T WORRY.
I GUESS.

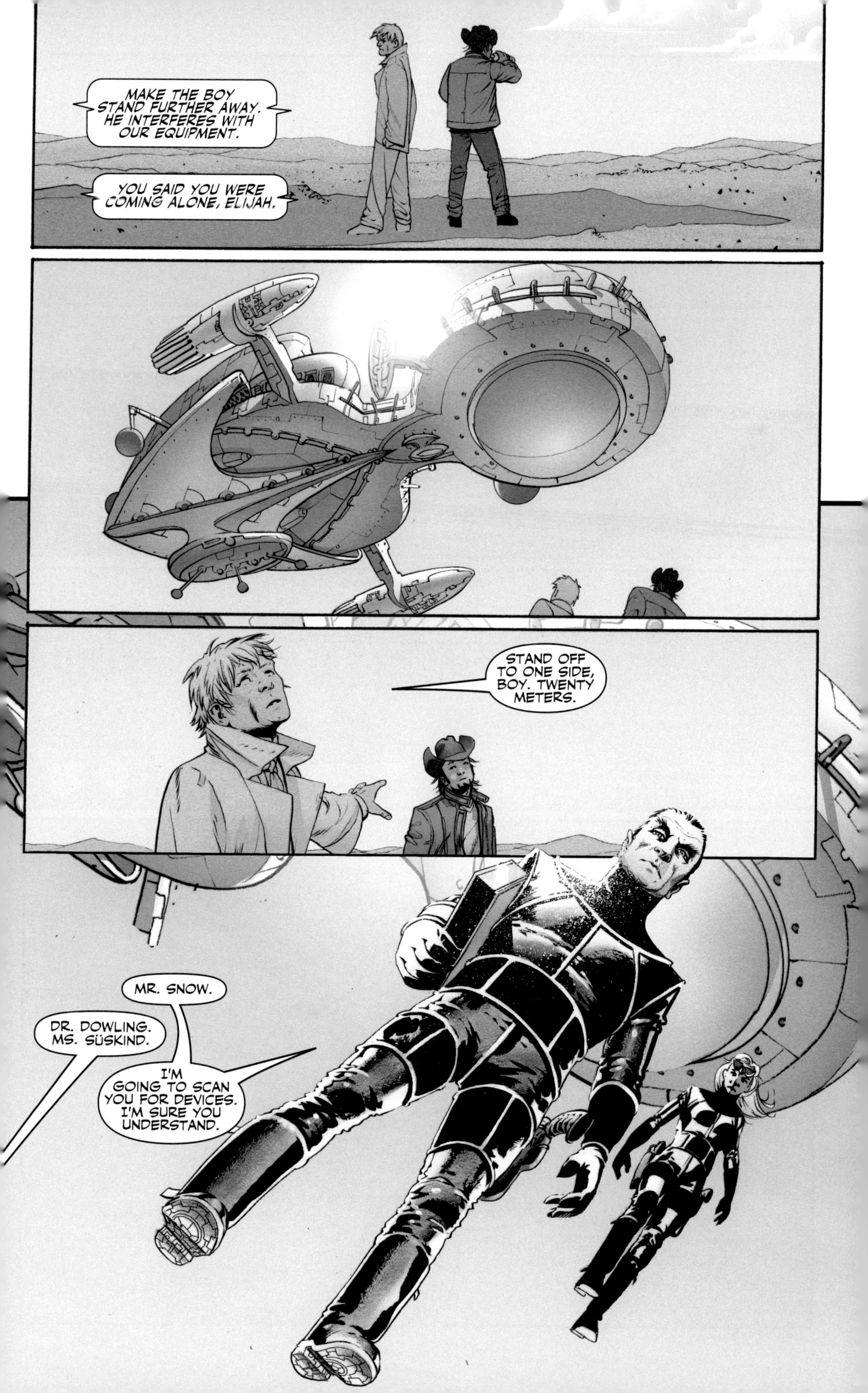
MAKE THE BOY STAND FURTHER AWAY. HE INTERFERES WITH OUR EQUIPMENT.
YOU SAID YOU WERE COMING ALONE, ELIJAH.
STAND OFF TO ONE SIDE, BOY. TWENTY METERS.
MR. SNOW.
DR. DOWLING. MS. SÜSKIND.
I'M GOING TO SCAN YOU FOR DEVICES. I'M SURE YOU UNDERSTAND.

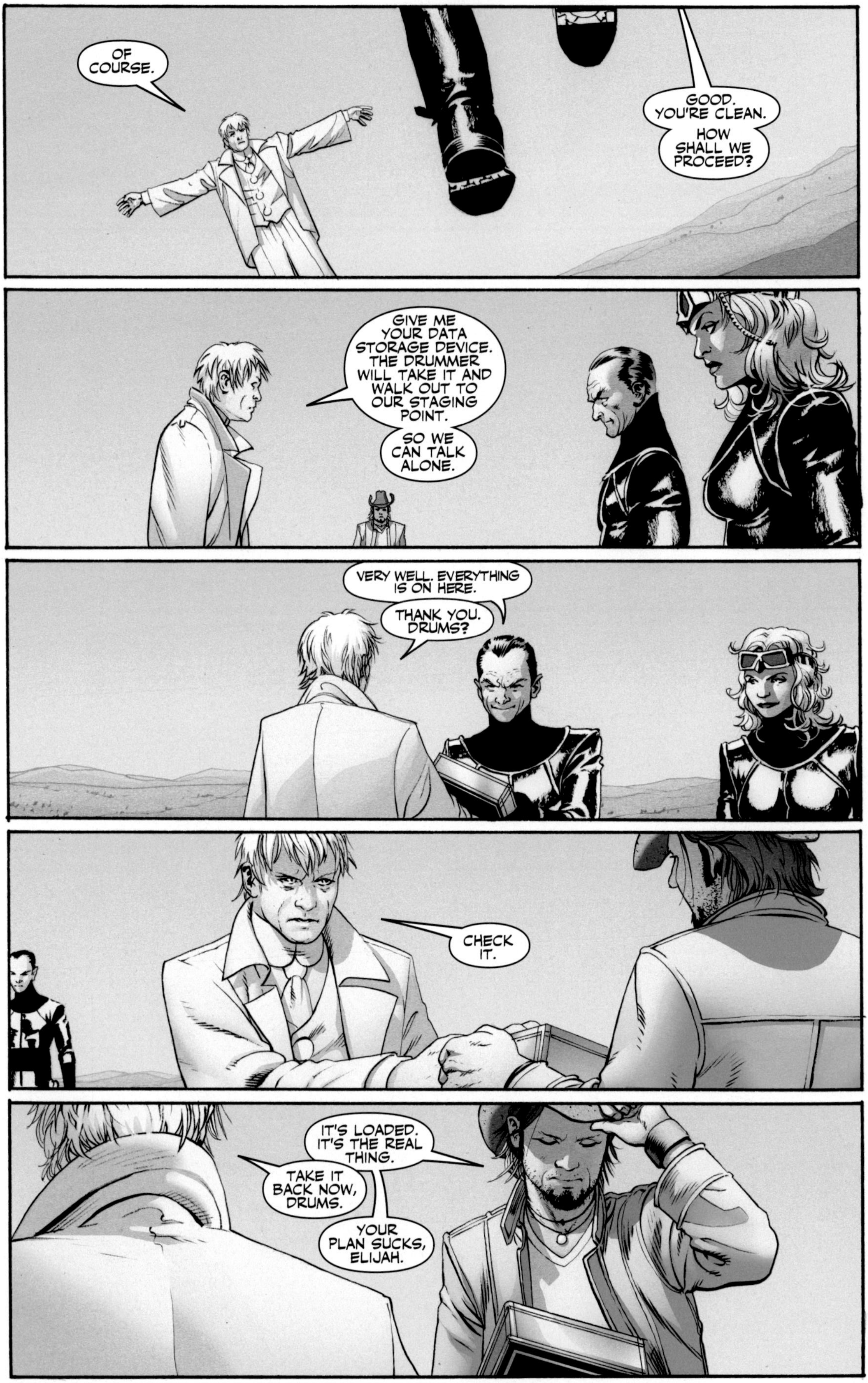
OF COURSE.
GOOD. YOU'RE CLEAN.
HOW SHALL WE PROCEED?
GIVE ME YOUR DATA STORAGE DEVICE. THE DRUMMER WILL TAKE IT AND WALK OUT TO OUR STAGING POINT.
SO WE CAN TALK ALONE.
VERY WELL. EVERYTHING IS ON HERE.
THANK YOU. DRUMS?
CHECK IT.
IT'S LOADED. IT'S THE REAL THING.
TAKE IT BACK NOW, DRUMS.
YOUR PLAN SUCKS, ELIJAH.

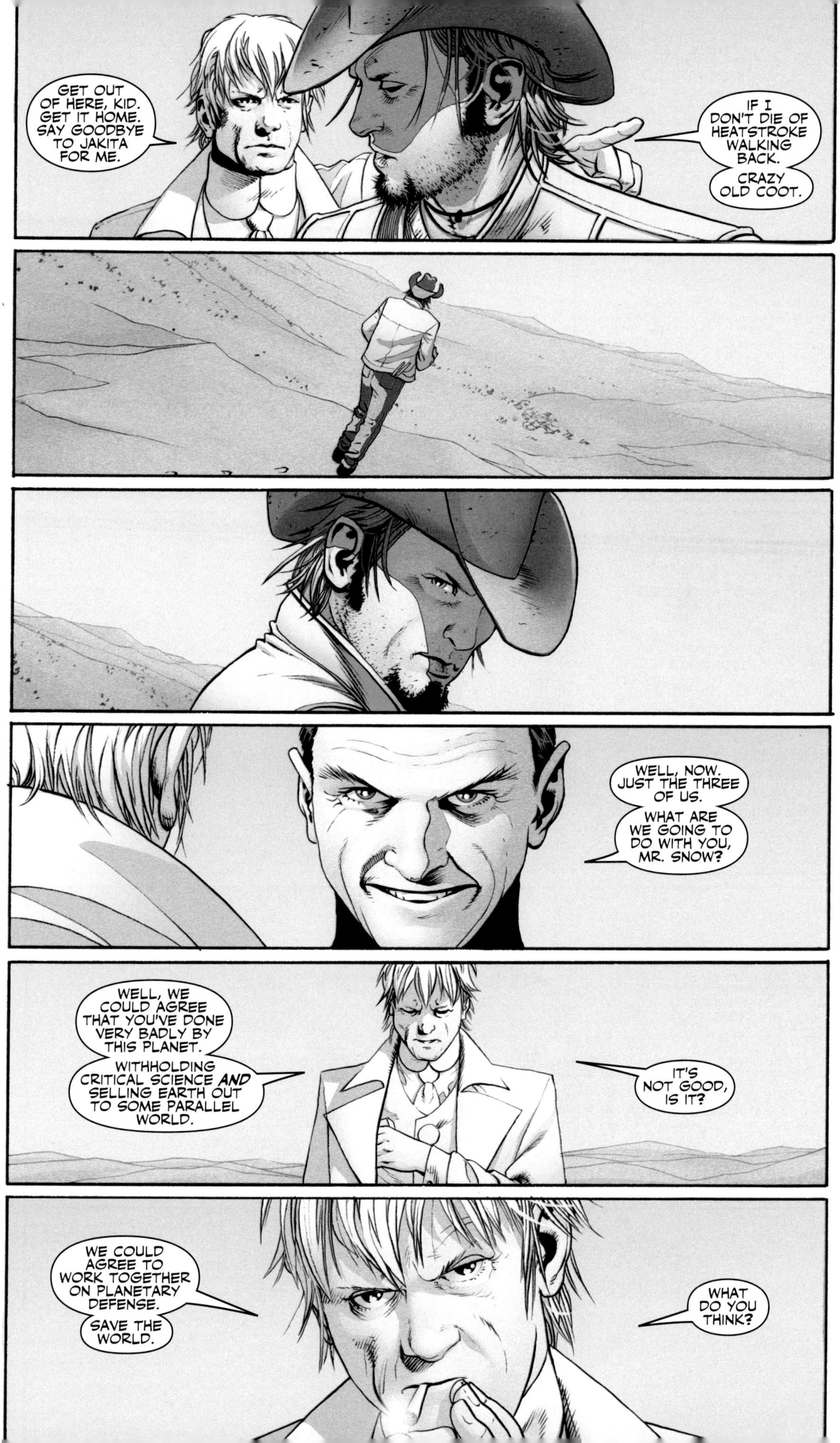
GET OUT OF HERE, KID. GET IT HOME. SAY GOODBYE TO JAKITA FOR ME.
IF I DON'T DIE OF HEATSTROKE WALKING BACK.
CRAZY OLD COOT.
WELL, NOW. JUST THE THREE OF US.
WHAT ARE WE GOING TO DO WITH YOU, MR. SNOW?
WELL, WE COULD AGREE THAT YOU'VE DONE VERY BADLY BY THIS PLANET.
WITHHOLDING CRITICAL SCIENCE *AND* SELLING EARTH OUT TO SOME PARALLEL WORLD.
IT'S NOT GOOD, IS IT?
WE COULD AGREE TO WORK TOGETHER ON PLANETARY DEFENSE.
SAVE THE WORLD.
WHAT DO YOU THINK?

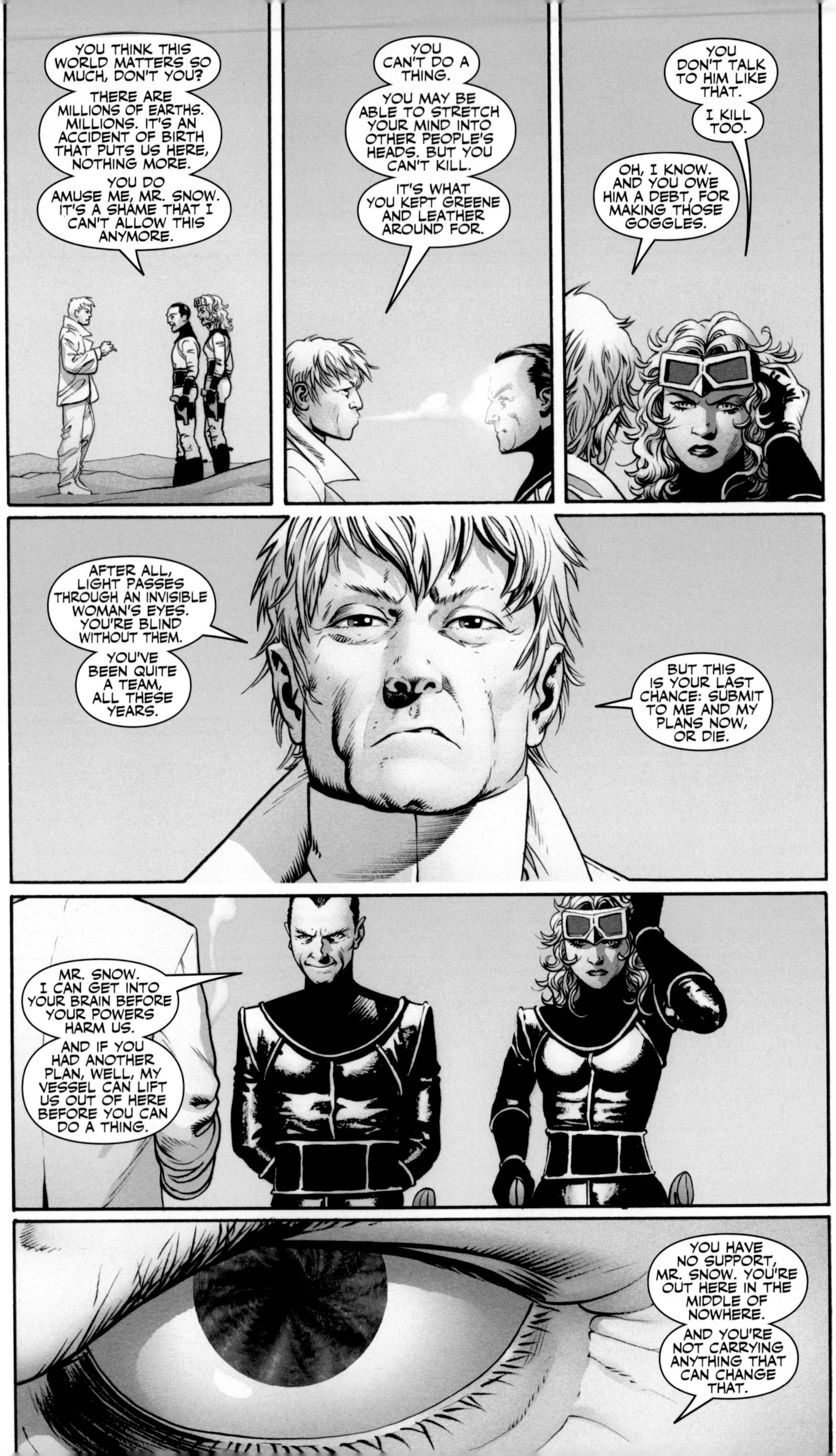
YOU THINK THIS WORLD MATTERS SO MUCH, DON'T YOU?
THERE ARE MILLIONS OF EARTHS. MILLIONS. IT'S AN ACCIDENT OF BIRTH THAT PUTS US HERE, NOTHING MORE.
YOU DO AMUSE ME, MR. SNOW. IT'S A SHAME THAT I CAN'T ALLOW THIS ANYMORE.
YOU CAN'T DO A THING.
YOU MAY BE ABLE TO STRETCH YOUR MIND INTO OTHER PEOPLE'S HEADS. BUT YOU CAN'T KILL.
IT'S WHAT YOU KEPT GREENE AND LEATHER AROUND FOR.
YOU DON'T TALK TO HIM LIKE THAT.
I KILL TOO.
OH, I KNOW. AND YOU OWE HIM A DEBT, FOR MAKING THOSE GOGGLES.
AFTER ALL, LIGHT PASSES THROUGH AN INVISIBLE WOMAN'S EYES. YOU'RE BLIND WITHOUT THEM.
YOU'VE BEEN QUITE A TEAM, ALL THESE YEARS.
BUT THIS IS YOUR LAST CHANCE: SUBMIT TO ME AND MY PLANS NOW, OR DIE.
MR. SNOW. I CAN GET INTO YOUR BRAIN BEFORE YOUR POWERS HARM US.
AND IF YOU HAD ANOTHER PLAN, WELL, MY VESSEL CAN LIFT US OUT OF HERE BEFORE YOU CAN DO A THING.
YOU HAVE NO SUPPORT, MR. SNOW. YOU'RE OUT HERE IN THE MIDDLE OF NOWHERE.
AND YOU'RE NOT CARRYING ANYTHING THAT CAN CHANGE THAT.

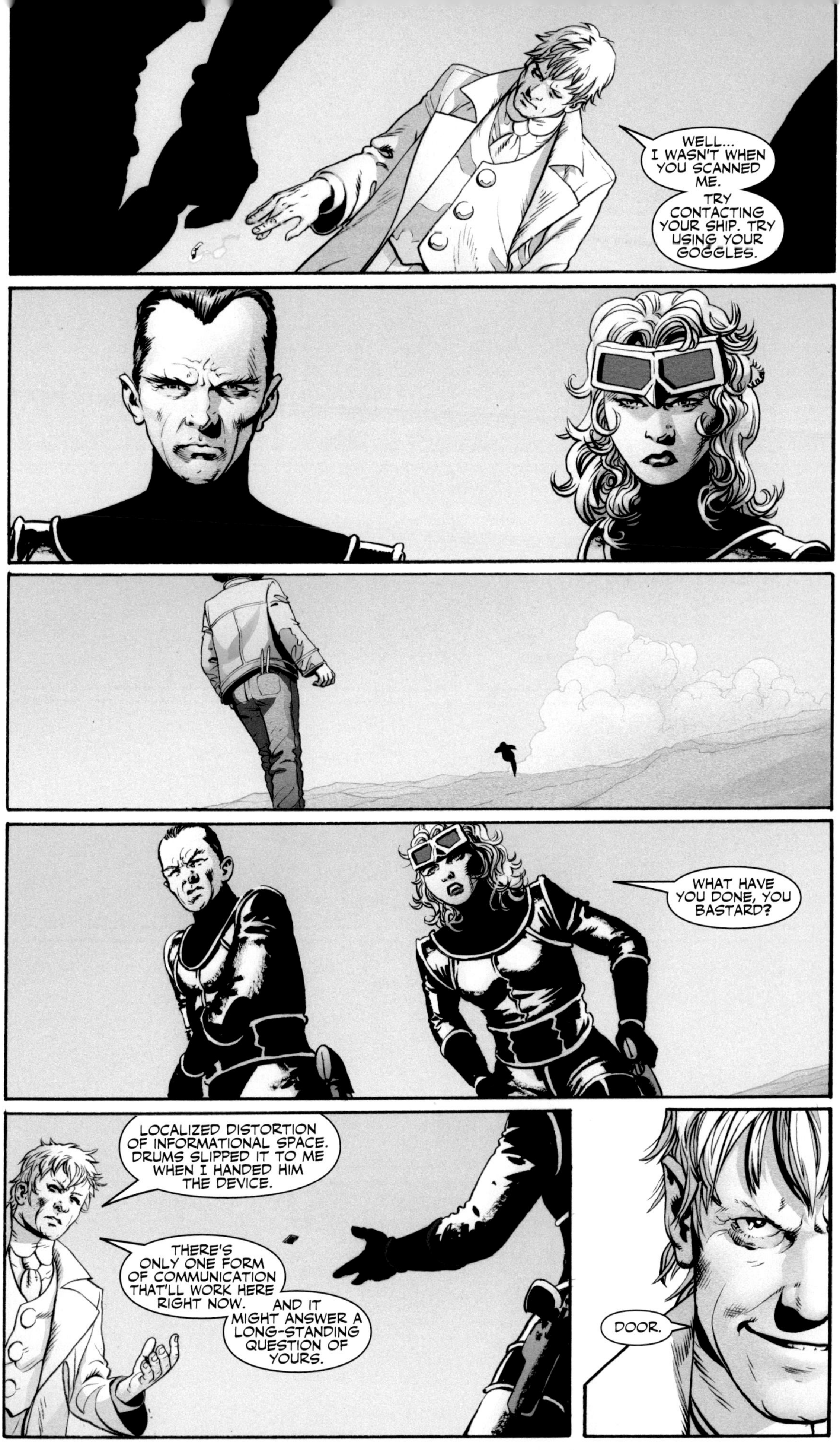
WELL... I WASN'T WHEN YOU SCANNED ME.
TRY CONTACTING YOUR SHIP. TRY USING YOUR GOGGLES.
WHAT HAVE YOU DONE, YOU BASTARD?
LOCALIZED DISTORTION OF INFORMATIONAL SPACE. DRUMS SLIPPED IT TO ME WHEN I HANDED HIM THE DEVICE.
THERE'S ONLY ONE FORM OF COMMUNICATION THAT'LL WORK HERE RIGHT NOW.
AND IT MIGHT ANSWER A LONG-STANDING QUESTION OF YOURS.
DOOR.

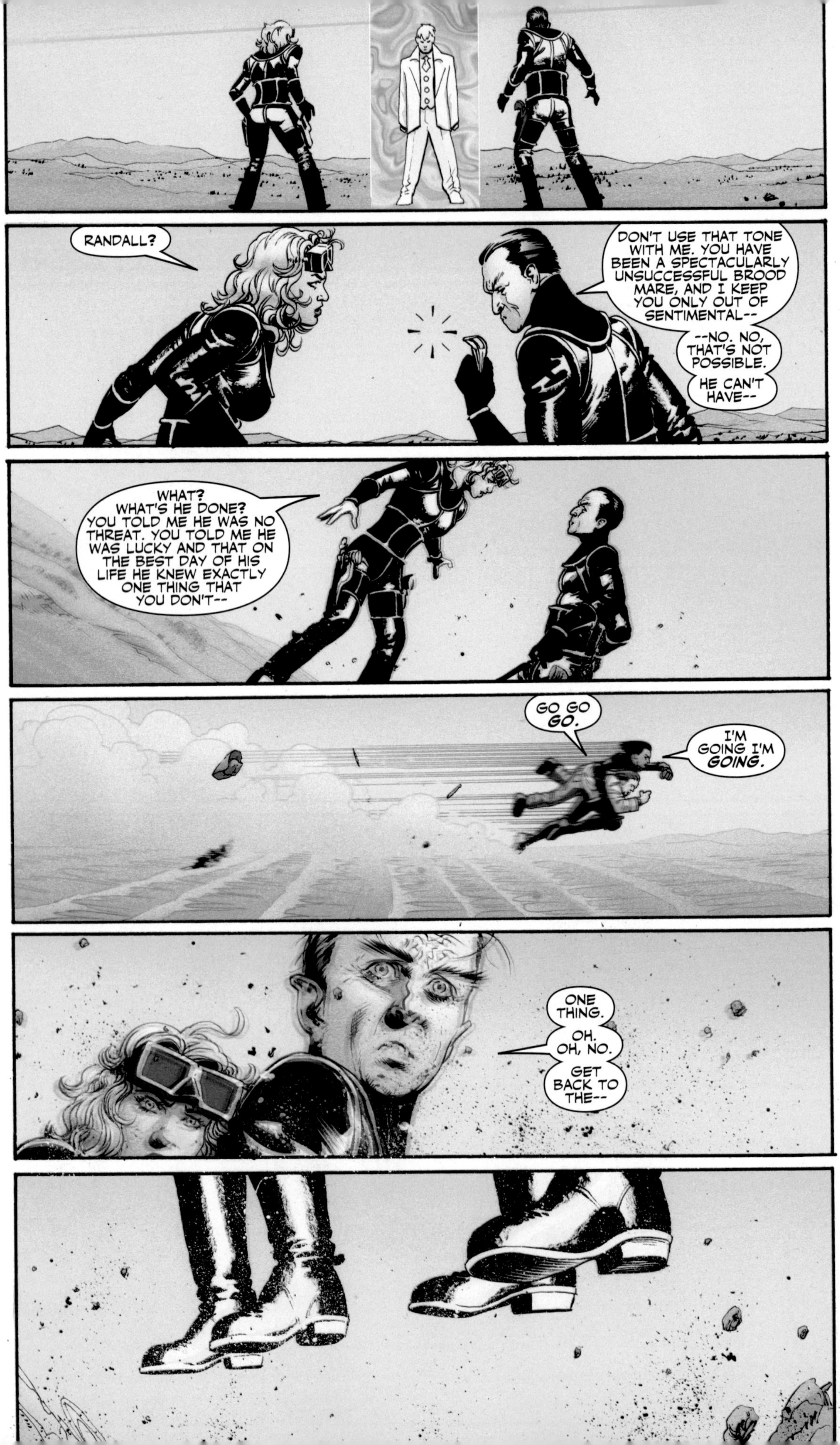
RANDALL?
DON'T USE THAT TONE WITH ME. YOU HAVE BEEN A SPECTACULARLY UNSUCCESSFUL BROOD MARE, AND I KEEP YOU ONLY OUT OF SENTIMENTAL--
--NO. NO, THAT'S NOT POSSIBLE.
HE CAN'T HAVE--
WHAT? WHAT'S HE DONE? YOU TOLD ME HE WAS NO THREAT. YOU TOLD ME HE WAS LUCKY AND THAT ON THE BEST DAY OF HIS LIFE HE KNEW EXACTLY ONE THING THAT YOU DON'T--
GO GO *GO.*
I'M GOING I'M *GOING.*
ONE THING.
OH. OH, NO.
GET BACK TO THE--

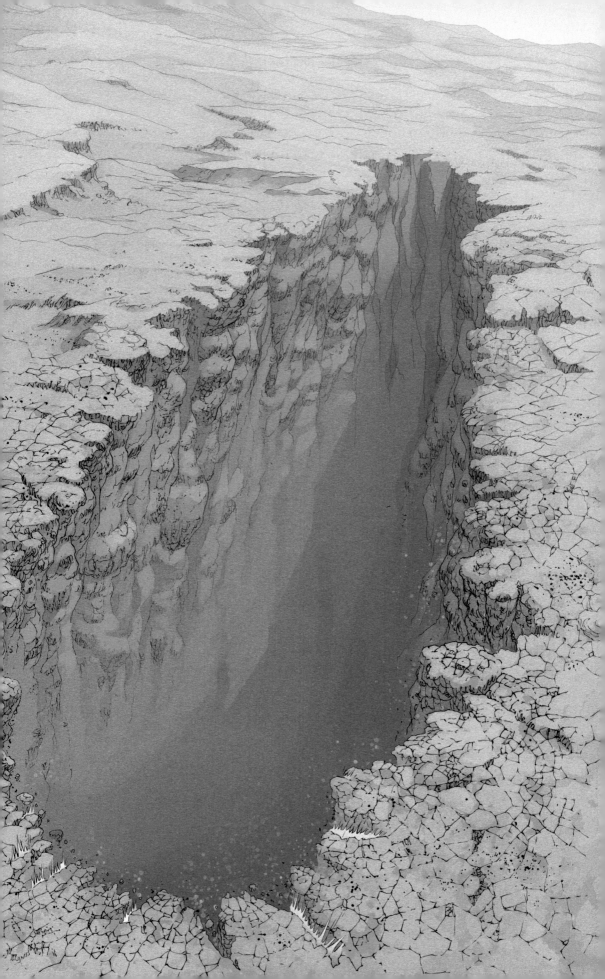

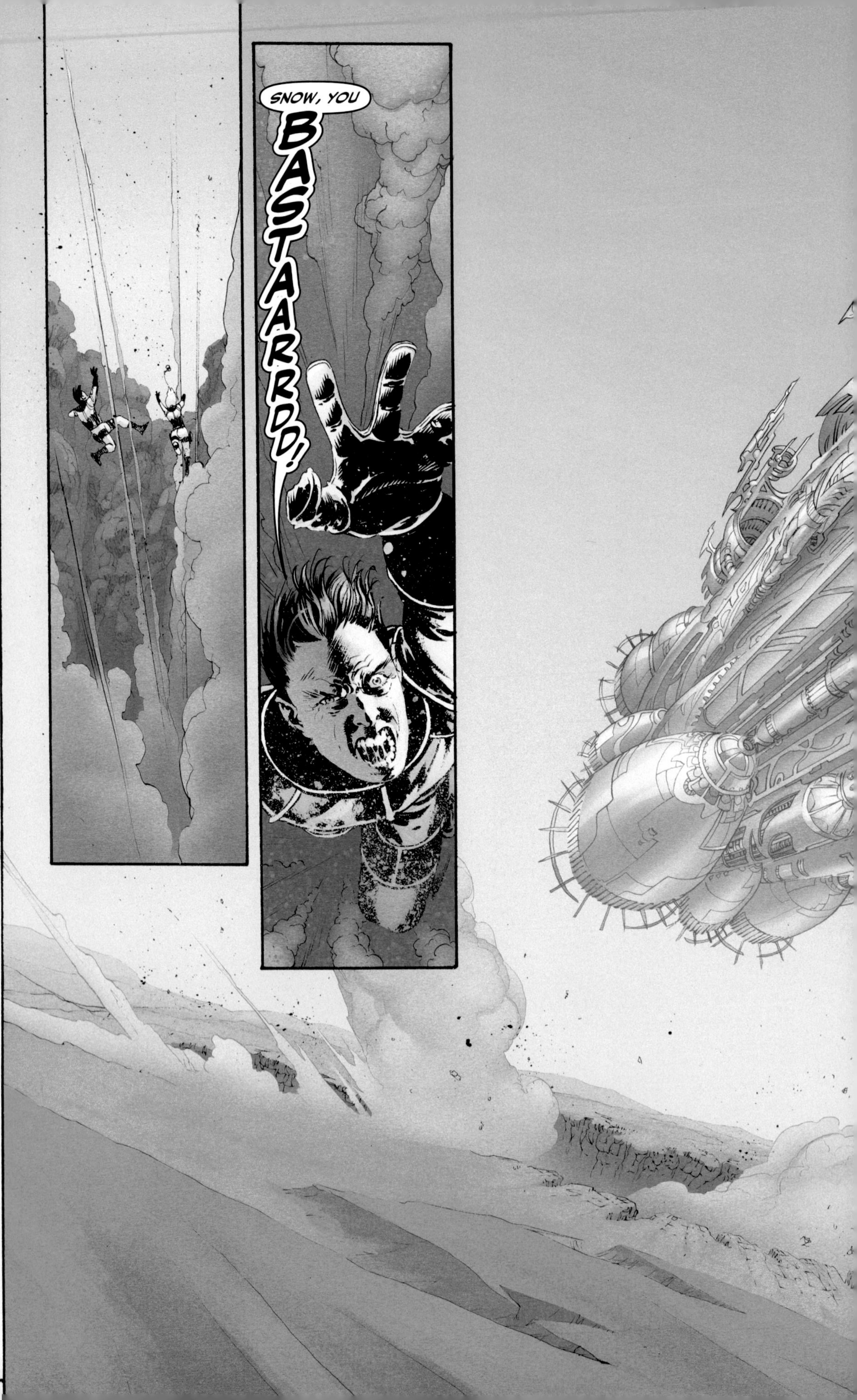
SNOW, YOU
BASTAARRDD!

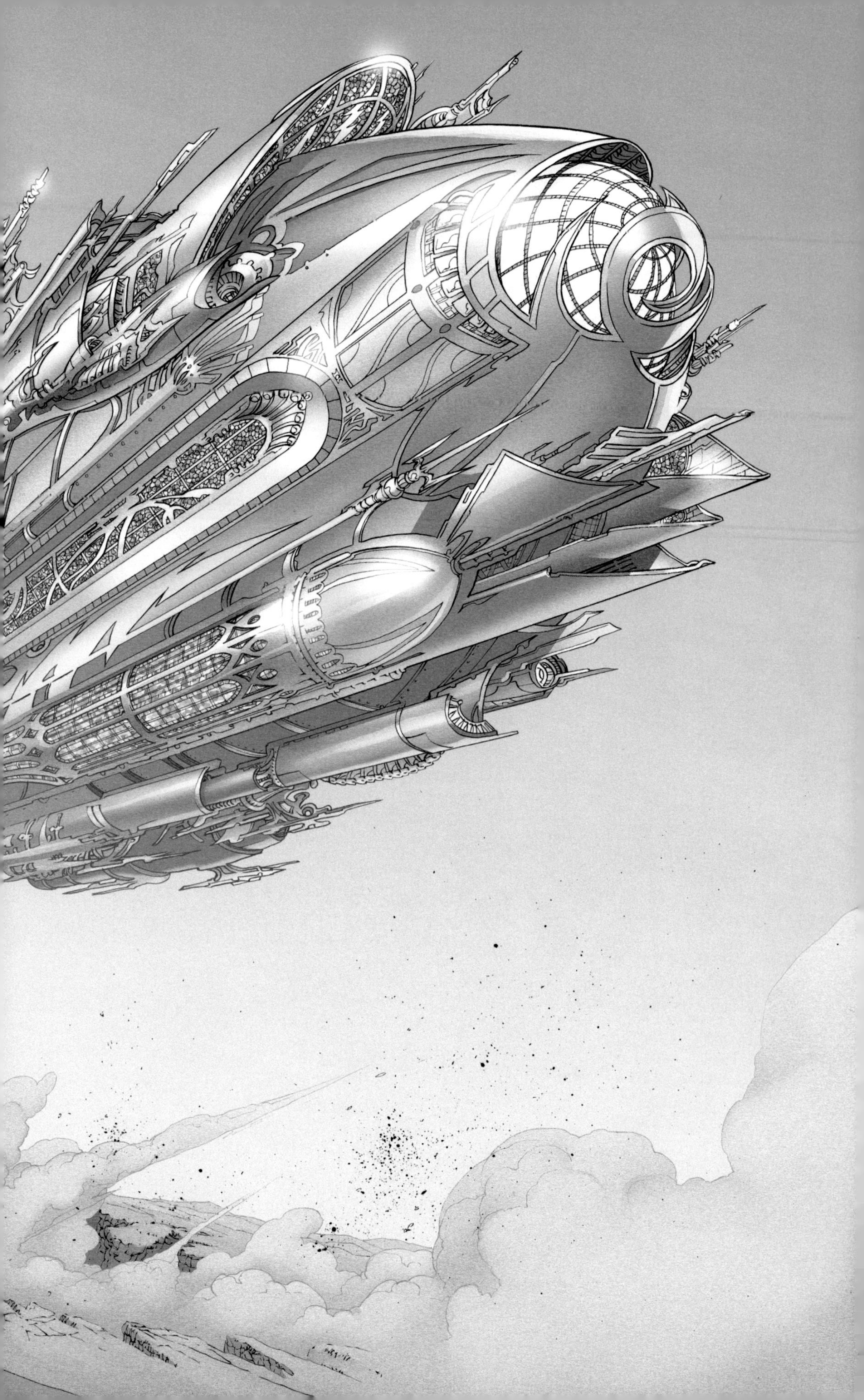

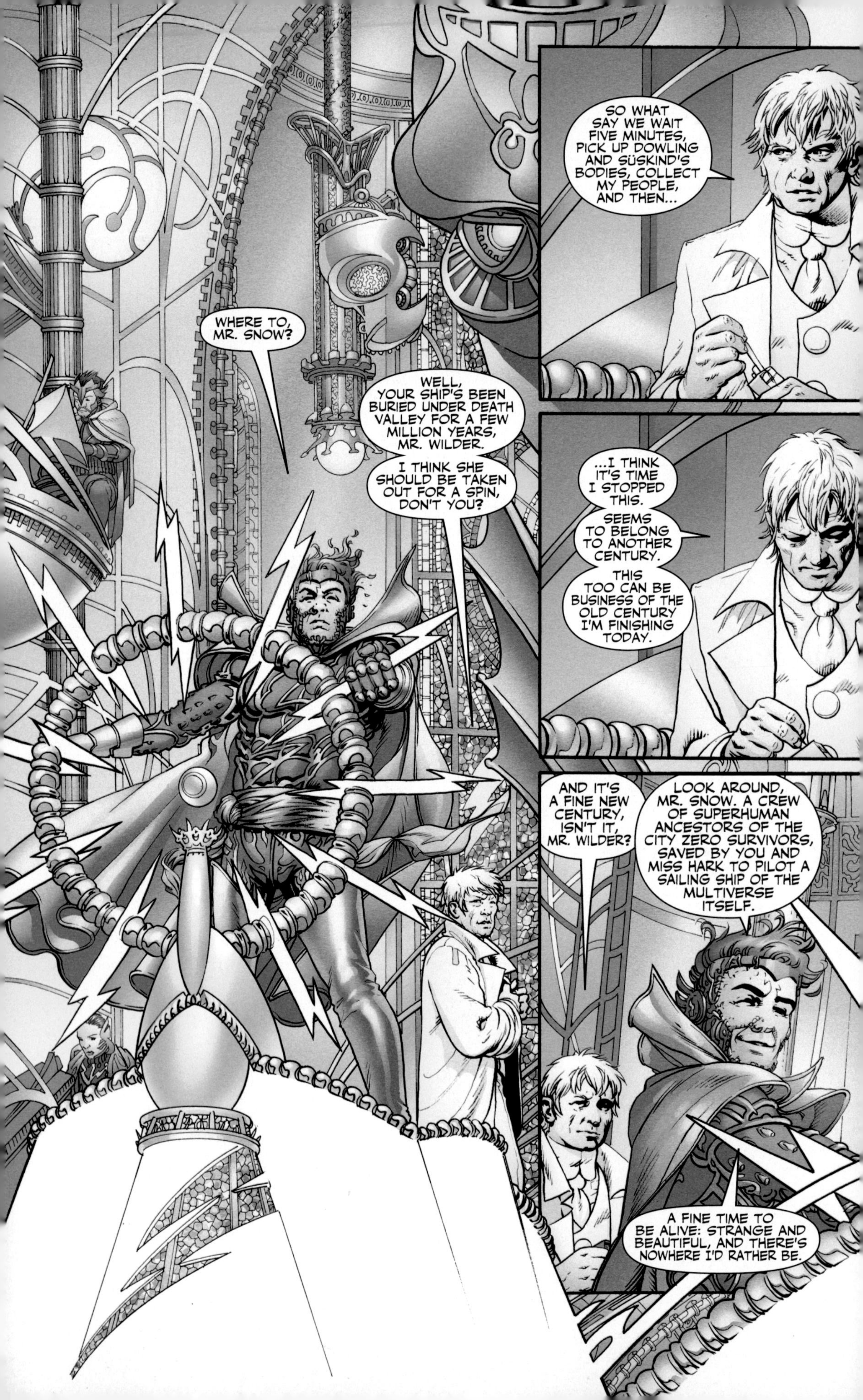
WHERE TO, MR. SNOW?
WELL, YOUR SHIP'S BEEN BURIED UNDER DEATH VALLEY FOR A FEW MILLION YEARS, MR. WILDER.
I THINK SHE SHOULD BE TAKEN OUT FOR A SPIN, DON'T YOU?
SO WHAT SAY WE WAIT FIVE MINUTES, PICK UP DOWLING AND SÜSKIND'S BODIES, COLLECT MY PEOPLE, AND THEN...
...I THINK IT'S TIME I STOPPED THIS.
SEEMS TO BELONG TO ANOTHER CENTURY.
THIS TOO CAN BE BUSINESS OF THE OLD CENTURY I'M FINISHING TODAY.
AND IT'S A FINE NEW CENTURY, ISN'T IT, MR. WILDER?
LOOK AROUND, MR. SNOW. A CREW OF SUPERHUMAN ANCESTORS OF THE CITY ZERO SURVIVORS, SAVED BY YOU AND MISS HARK TO PILOT A SAILING SHIP OF THE MULTIVERSE ITSELF.
A FINE TIME TO BE ALIVE: STRANGE AND BEAUTIFUL, AND THERE'S NOWHERE I'D RATHER BE.

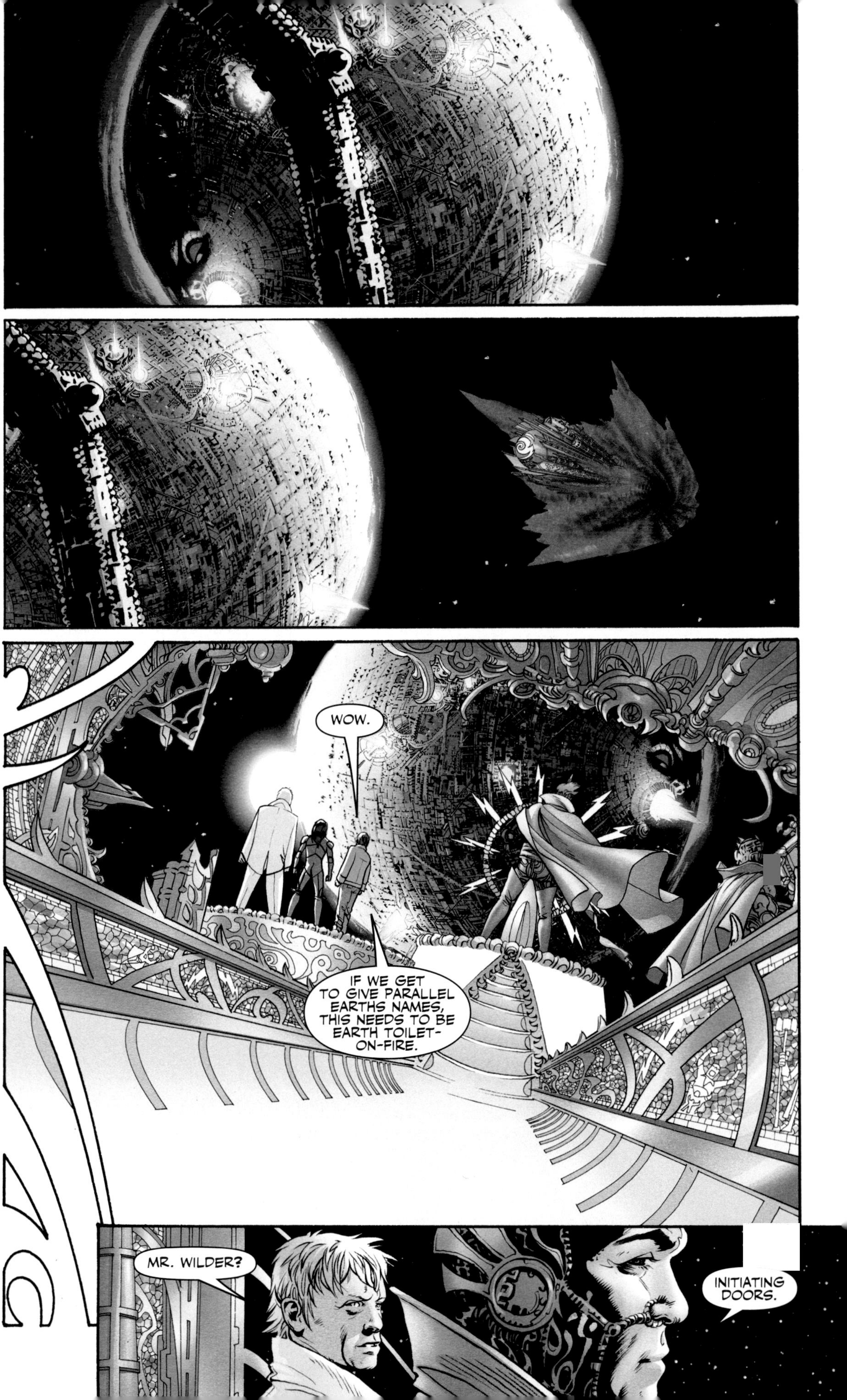
WOW.
IF WE GET TO GIVE PARALLEL EARTHS NAMES, THIS NEEDS TO BE EARTH TOILET-ON-FIRE.
MR. WILDER?
INITIATING DOORS.

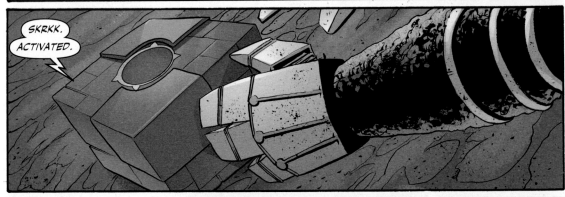

SKRKK. ACTIVATED.

HELLO. MY NAME IS ELIJAH SNOW. I AM PART OF THE DEFENSE SYSTEM OF THE EARTH RANDALL DOWLING SOLD TO YOU.

THAT'S HIS BODY. I DROPPED IT FROM A GREAT HEIGHT, WHICH MAY BE WHY YOU DON'T IMMEDIATELY RECOGNIZE HIM.

THE SALE IS OFF. YOUR MONEY'S NO GOOD.

ANY INCURSION INTO MY UNIVERSE WILL SEE THE BLEED RIPPED OPEN AROUND YOUR PLANET AND YOU FED TO THE THINGS THAT WAIT THERE.

THINGS MY PEOPLE LEARNED HOW TO KILL MORE THAN FIFTY YEARS AGO, BY THE WAY.

THAT'S IF I DON'T JUST DELETE YOUR UNIVERSE FROM THE INFORMATIONAL SUPERSTRUCTURE OF REALITY.

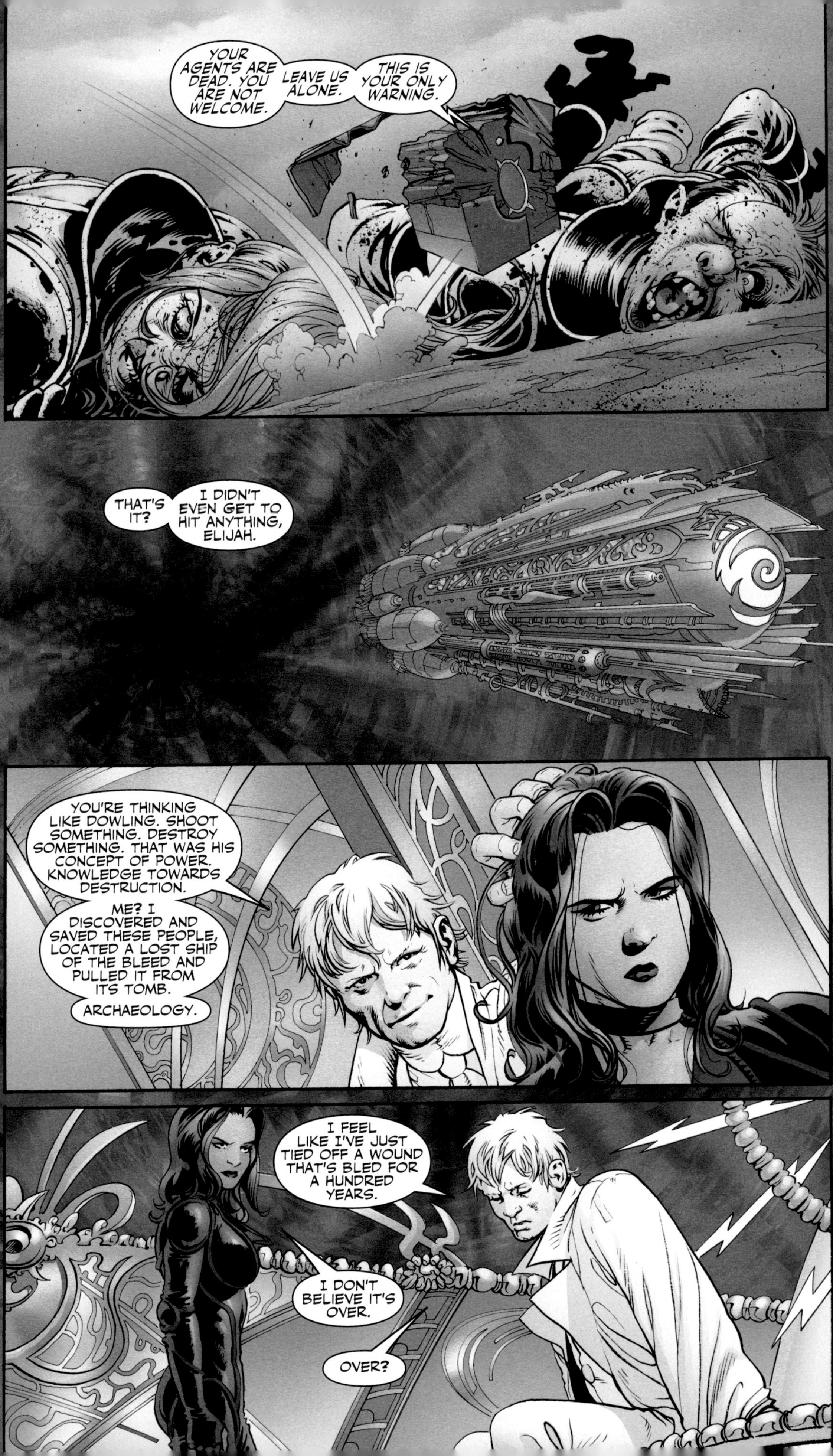

YOUR AGENTS ARE DEAD. YOU ARE NOT WELCOME.
LEAVE US ALONE.
THIS IS YOUR ONLY WARNING.
THAT'S IT?
I DIDN'T EVEN GET TO HIT ANYTHING, ELIJAH.
YOU'RE THINKING LIKE DOWLING. SHOOT SOMETHING. DESTROY SOMETHING. THAT WAS HIS CONCEPT OF POWER. KNOWLEDGE TOWARDS DESTRUCTION.
ME? I DISCOVERED AND SAVED THESE PEOPLE, LOCATED A LOST SHIP OF THE BLEED AND PULLED IT FROM ITS TOMB.
ARCHAEOLOGY.
I FEEL LIKE I'VE JUST TIED OFF A WOUND THAT'S BLED FOR A HUNDRED YEARS.
I DON'T BELIEVE IT'S OVER.
OVER?

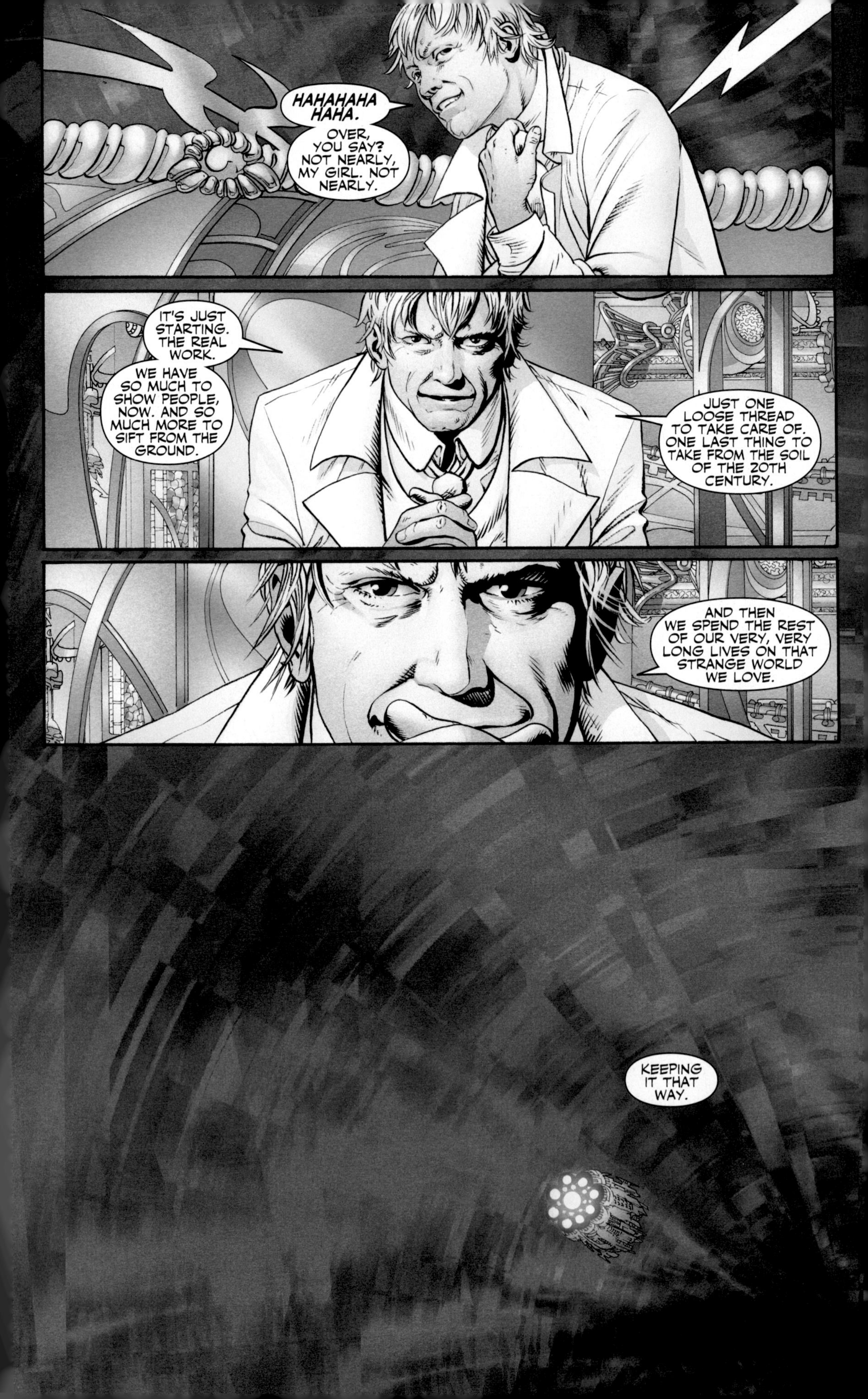
HAHAHAHA HAHA.
OVER, YOU SAY? NOT NEARLY, MY GIRL. NOT NEARLY.
IT'S JUST STARTING. THE REAL WORK.
WE HAVE SO MUCH TO SHOW PEOPLE, NOW. AND SO MUCH MORE TO SIFT FROM THE GROUND.
JUST ONE LOOSE THREAD TO TAKE CARE OF. ONE LAST THING TO TAKE FROM THE SOIL OF THE 20TH CENTURY.
AND THEN WE SPEND THE REST OF OUR VERY, VERY LONG LIVES ON THAT STRANGE WORLD WE LOVE.
KEEPING IT THAT WAY.

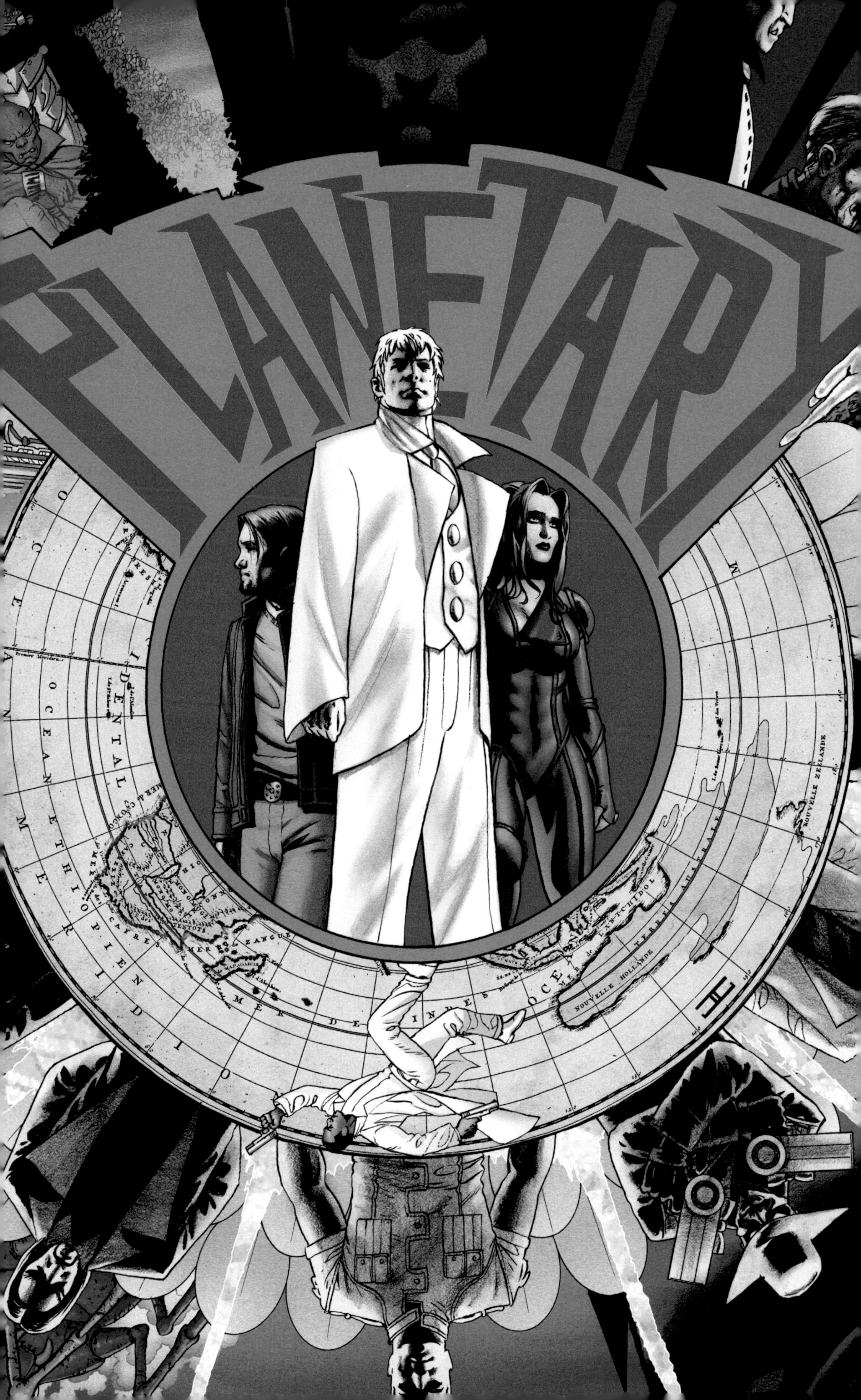
PLANETARY
NOUVELLE ZELANDE
NOUVELLE HOLLANDE

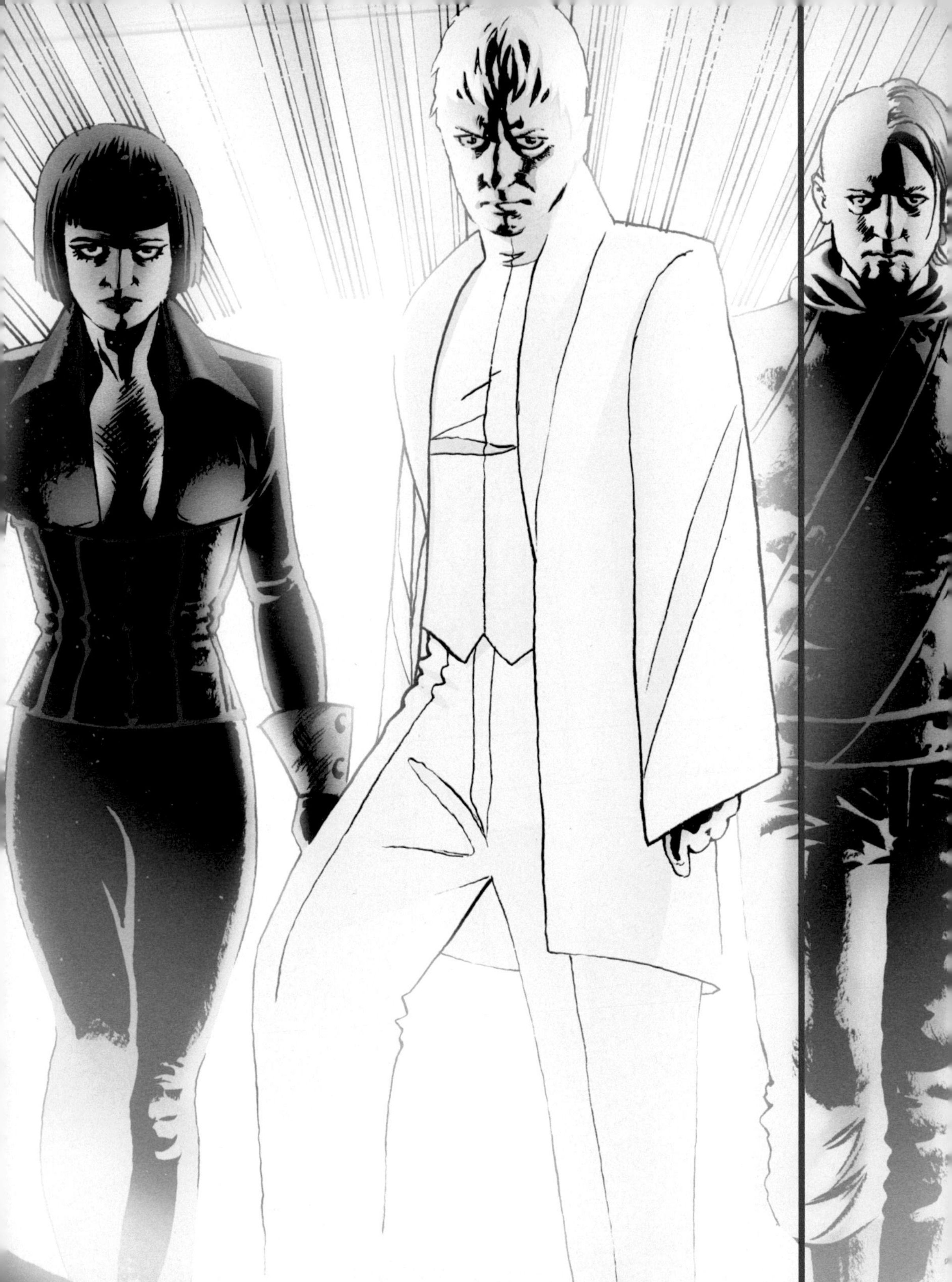

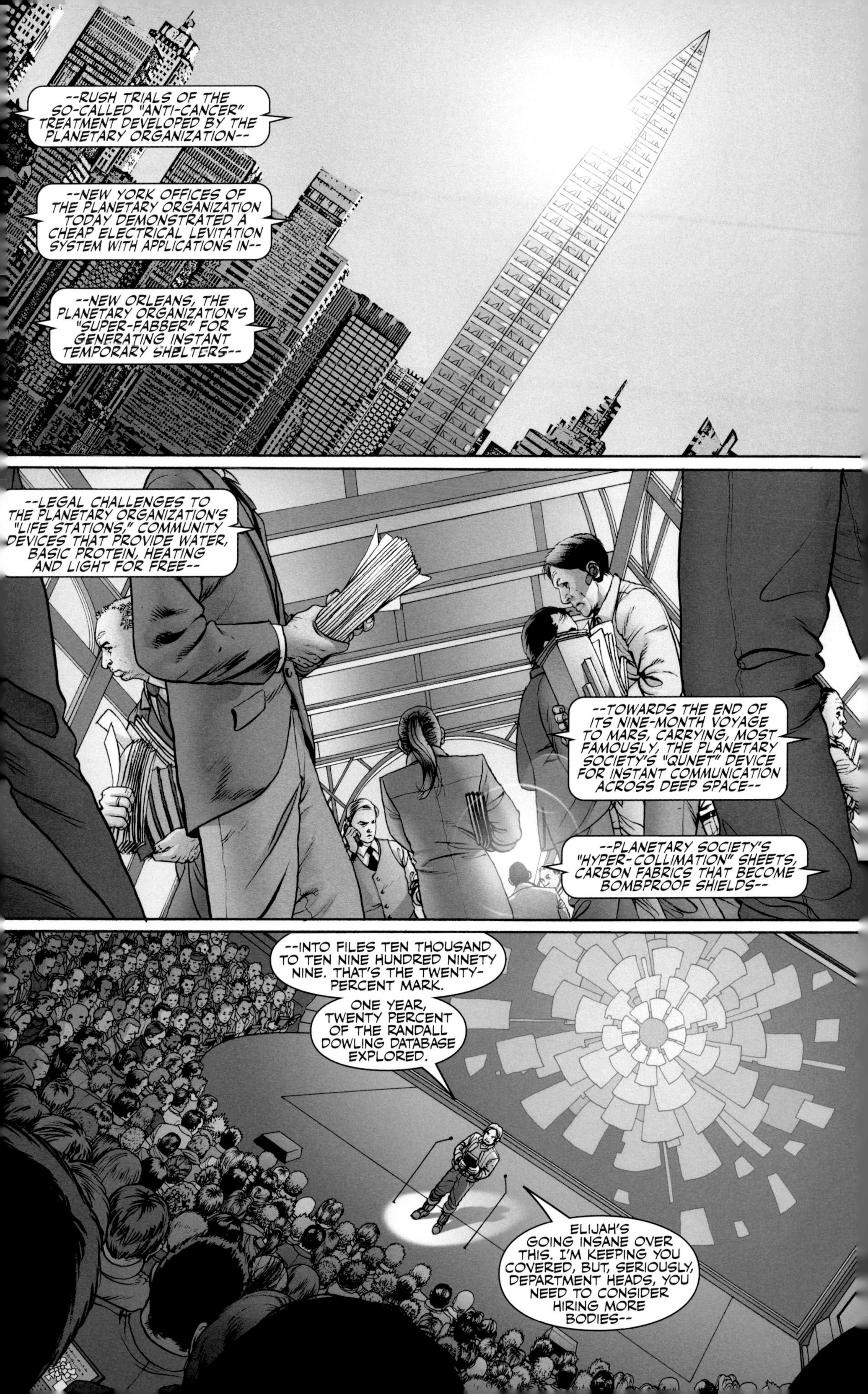
--RUSH TRIALS OF THE SO-CALLED "ANTI-CANCER" TREATMENT DEVELOPED BY THE PLANETARY ORGANIZATION--
--NEW YORK OFFICES OF THE PLANETARY ORGANIZATION TODAY DEMONSTRATED A CHEAP ELECTRICAL LEVITATION SYSTEM WITH APPLICATIONS IN--
--NEW ORLEANS, THE PLANETARY ORGANIZATION'S "SUPER-FABBER" FOR GENERATING INSTANT TEMPORARY SHELTERS--
--LEGAL CHALLENGES TO THE PLANETARY ORGANIZATION'S "LIFE STATIONS," COMMUNITY DEVICES THAT PROVIDE WATER, BASIC PROTEIN, HEATING AND LIGHT FOR FREE--
--TOWARDS THE END OF ITS NINE-MONTH VOYAGE TO MARS, CARRYING, MOST FAMOUSLY, THE PLANETARY SOCIETY'S "QUNET" DEVICE FOR INSTANT COMMUNICATION ACROSS DEEP SPACE--
--PLANETARY SOCIETY'S "HYPER-COLLIMATION" SHEETS, CARBON FABRICS THAT BECOME BOMBPROOF SHIELDS--
--INTO FILES TEN THOUSAND TO TEN NINE HUNDRED NINETY NINE. THAT'S THE TWENTY-PERCENT MARK.
ONE YEAR, TWENTY PERCENT OF THE RANDALL DOWLING DATABASE EXPLORED.
ELIJAH'S GOING INSANE OVER THIS. I'M KEEPING YOU COVERED, BUT, SERIOUSLY, DEPARTMENT HEADS, YOU NEED TO CONSIDER HIRING MORE BODIES--

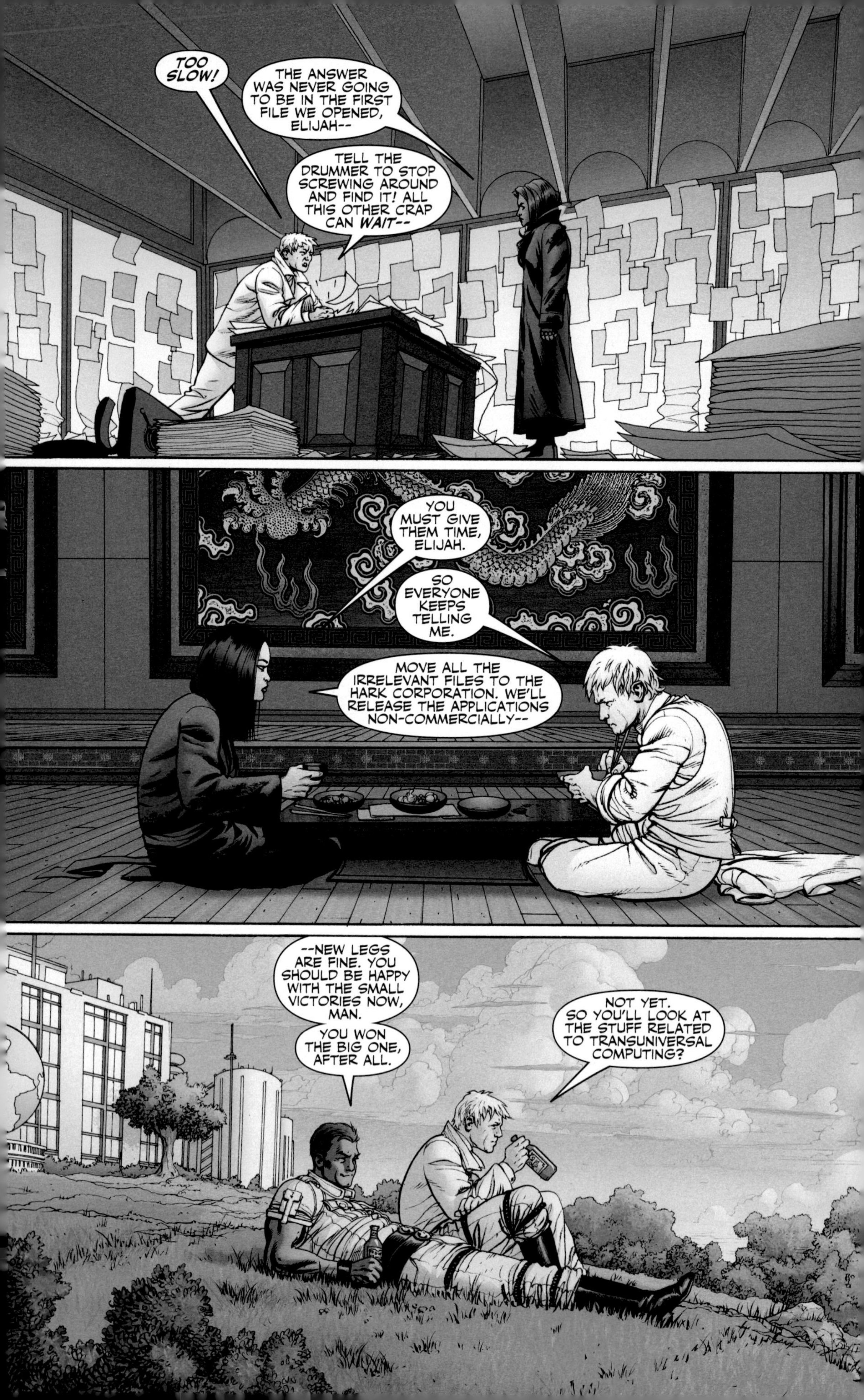
TOO SLOW!
THE ANSWER WAS NEVER GOING TO BE IN THE FIRST FILE WE OPENED, ELIJAH--
TELL THE DRUMMER TO STOP SCREWING AROUND AND FIND IT! ALL THIS OTHER CRAP CAN WAIT--
YOU MUST GIVE THEM TIME, ELIJAH.
SO EVERYONE KEEPS TELLING ME.
MOVE ALL THE IRRELEVANT FILES TO THE HARK CORPORATION. WE'LL RELEASE THE APPLICATIONS NON-COMMERCIALLY--
--NEW LEGS ARE FINE. YOU SHOULD BE HAPPY WITH THE SMALL VICTORIES NOW, MAN.
YOU WON THE BIG ONE, AFTER ALL.
NOT YET. SO YOU'LL LOOK AT THE STUFF RELATED TO TRANSUNIVERSAL COMPUTING?

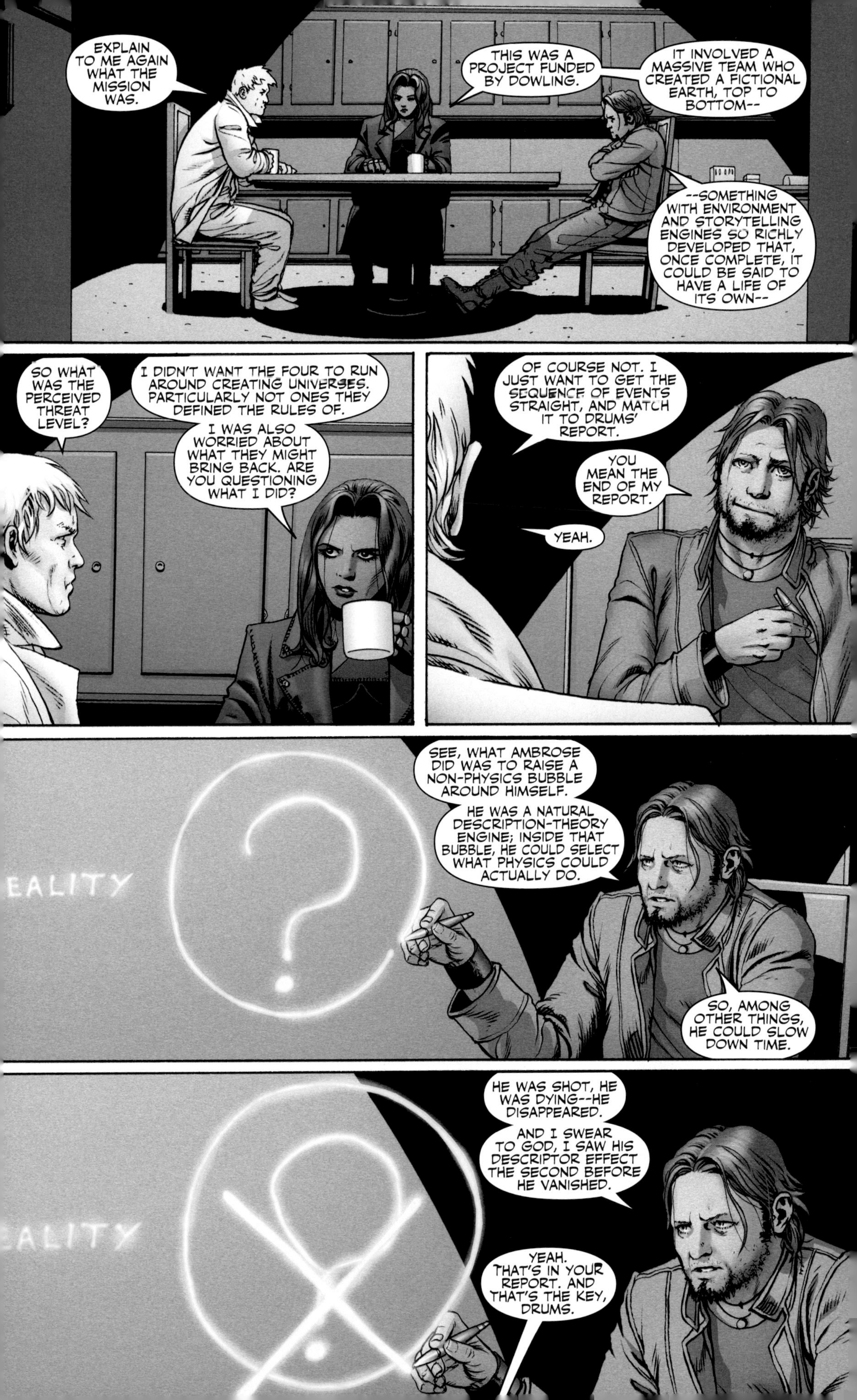
EXPLAIN TO ME AGAIN WHAT THE MISSION WAS.
THIS WAS A PROJECT FUNDED BY DOWLING.
IT INVOLVED A MASSIVE TEAM WHO CREATED A FICTIONAL EARTH, TOP TO BOTTOM--
--SOMETHING WITH ENVIRONMENT AND STORYTELLING ENGINES SO RICHLY DEVELOPED THAT, ONCE COMPLETE, IT COULD BE SAID TO HAVE A LIFE OF ITS OWN--
SO WHAT WAS THE PERCEIVED THREAT LEVEL?
I DIDN'T WANT THE FOUR TO RUN AROUND CREATING UNIVERSES. PARTICULARLY NOT ONES THEY DEFINED THE RULES OF.
I WAS ALSO WORRIED ABOUT WHAT THEY MIGHT BRING BACK. ARE YOU QUESTIONING WHAT I DID?
OF COURSE NOT. I JUST WANT TO GET THE SEQUENCE OF EVENTS STRAIGHT, AND MATCH IT TO DRUMS' REPORT.
YOU MEAN THE END OF MY REPORT.
YEAH.
REALITY
SEE, WHAT AMBROSE DID WAS TO RAISE A NON-PHYSICS BUBBLE AROUND HIMSELF.
HE WAS A NATURAL DESCRIPTION-THEORY ENGINE; INSIDE THAT BUBBLE, HE COULD SELECT WHAT PHYSICS COULD ACTUALLY DO.
SO, AMONG OTHER THINGS, HE COULD SLOW DOWN TIME.
REALITY
HE WAS SHOT, HE WAS DYING--HE DISAPPEARED.
AND I SWEAR TO GOD, I SAW HIS DESCRIPTOR EFFECT THE SECOND BEFORE HE VANISHED.
YEAH. THAT'S IN YOUR REPORT. AND THAT'S THE KEY, DRUMS.

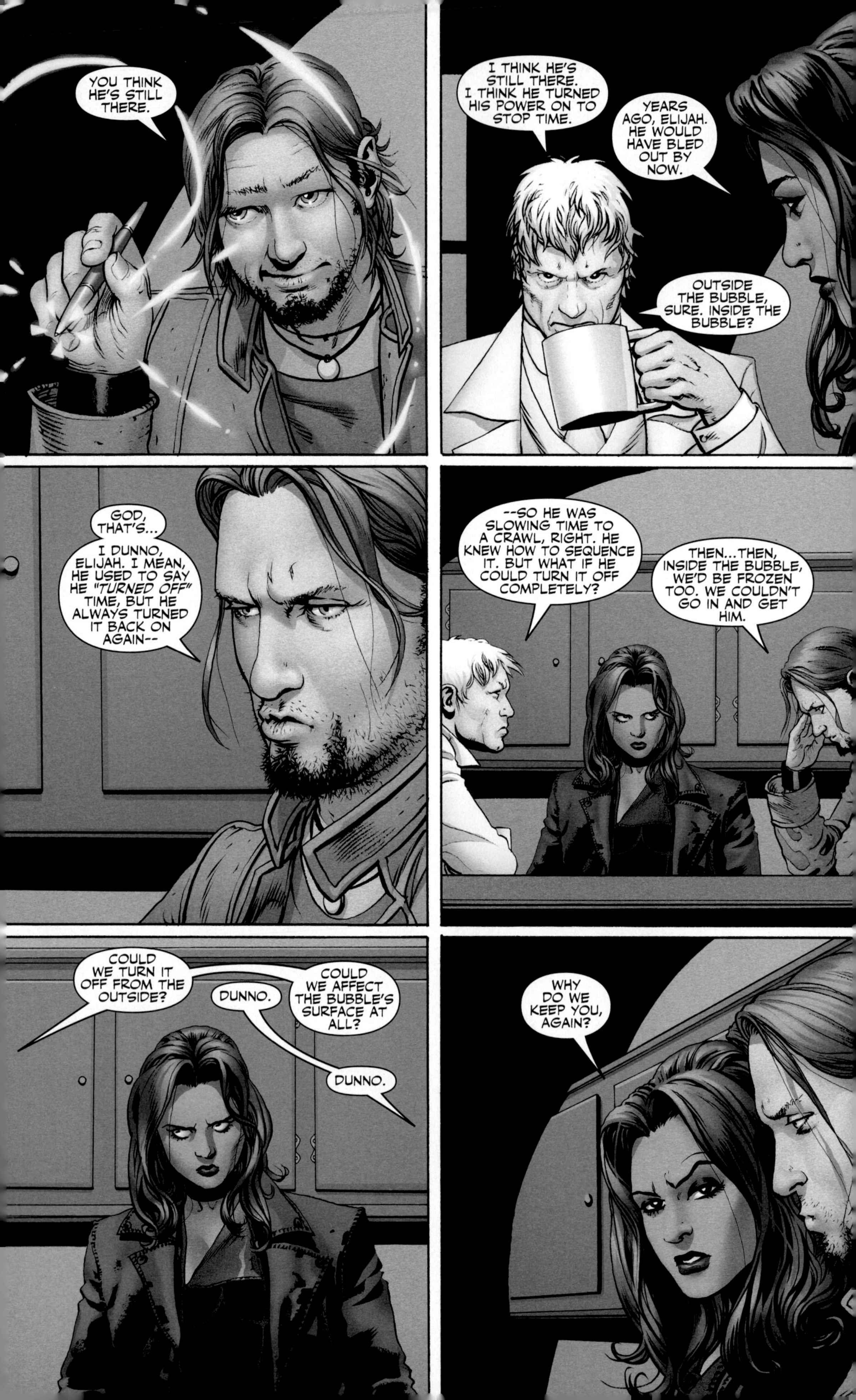
YOU THINK HE'S STILL THERE.
I THINK HE'S STILL THERE. I THINK HE TURNED HIS POWER ON TO STOP TIME.
YEARS AGO, ELIJAH. HE WOULD HAVE BLED OUT BY NOW.
OUTSIDE THE BUBBLE, SURE. INSIDE THE BUBBLE?
GOD, THAT'S...
I DUNNO, ELIJAH. I MEAN, HE USED TO SAY HE *"TURNED OFF"* TIME, BUT HE ALWAYS TURNED IT BACK ON AGAIN--
--SO HE WAS SLOWING TIME TO A CRAWL, RIGHT. HE KNEW HOW TO SEQUENCE IT. BUT WHAT IF HE COULD TURN IT OFF COMPLETELY?
THEN...THEN, INSIDE THE BUBBLE, WE'D BE FROZEN TOO. WE COULDN'T GO IN AND GET HIM.
COULD WE TURN IT OFF FROM THE OUTSIDE?
DUNNO.
COULD WE AFFECT THE BUBBLE'S SURFACE AT ALL?
DUNNO.
WHY DO WE KEEP YOU, AGAIN?

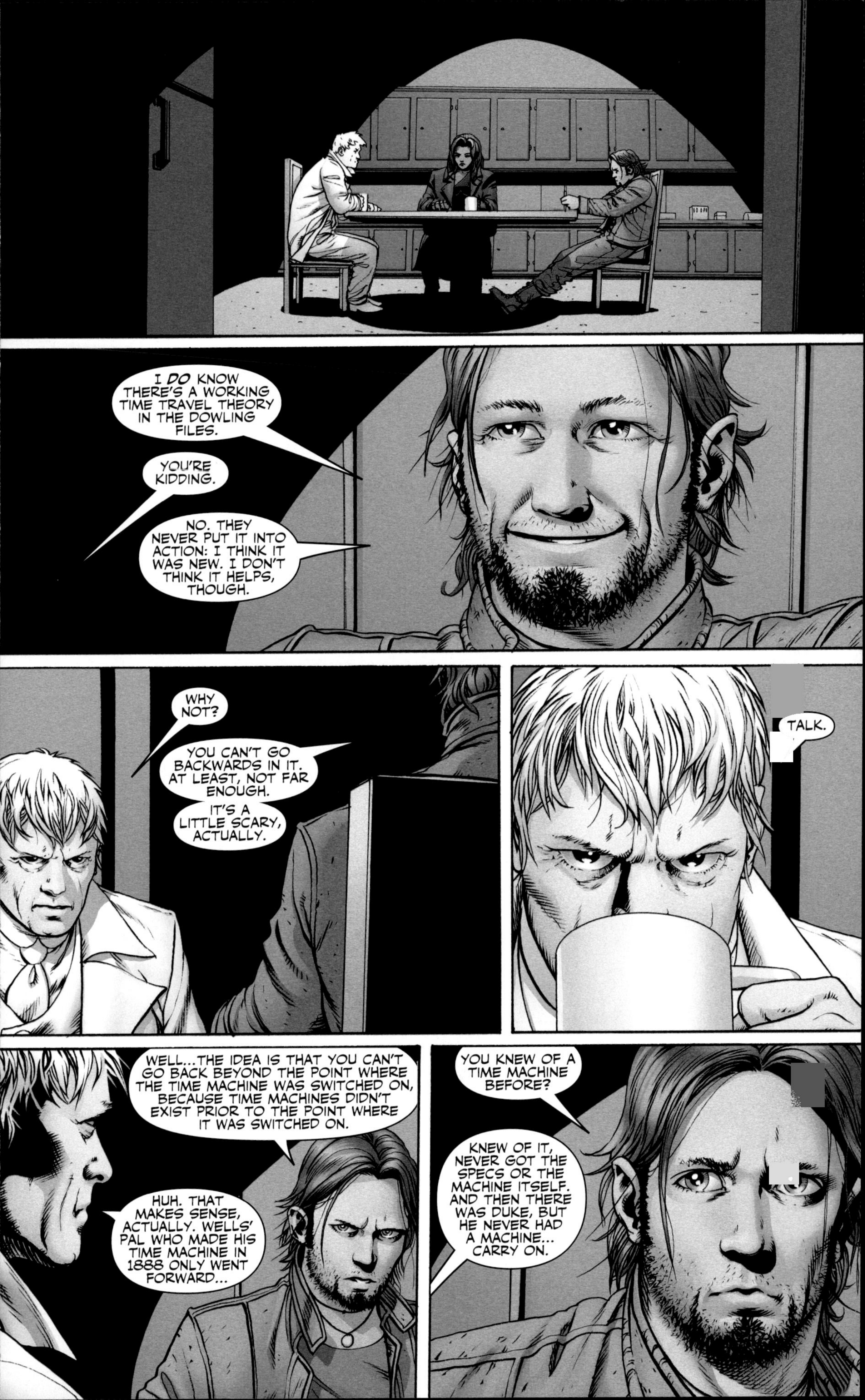
I DO KNOW THERE'S A WORKING TIME TRAVEL THEORY IN THE DOWLING FILES.
YOU'RE KIDDING.
NO. THEY NEVER PUT IT INTO ACTION: I THINK IT WAS NEW. I DON'T THINK IT HELPS, THOUGH.
WHY NOT?
YOU CAN'T GO BACKWARDS IN IT. AT LEAST, NOT FAR ENOUGH.
IT'S A LITTLE SCARY, ACTUALLY.
TALK.
WELL...THE IDEA IS THAT YOU CAN'T GO BACK BEYOND THE POINT WHERE THE TIME MACHINE WAS SWITCHED ON, BECAUSE TIME MACHINES DIDN'T EXIST PRIOR TO THE POINT WHERE IT WAS SWITCHED ON.
HUH. THAT MAKES SENSE, ACTUALLY. WELLS' PAL WHO MADE HIS TIME MACHINE IN 1888 ONLY WENT FORWARD...
YOU KNEW OF A TIME MACHINE BEFORE?
KNEW OF IT, NEVER GOT THE SPECS OR THE MACHINE ITSELF. AND THEN THERE WAS DUKE, BUT HE NEVER HAD A MACHINE... CARRY ON.

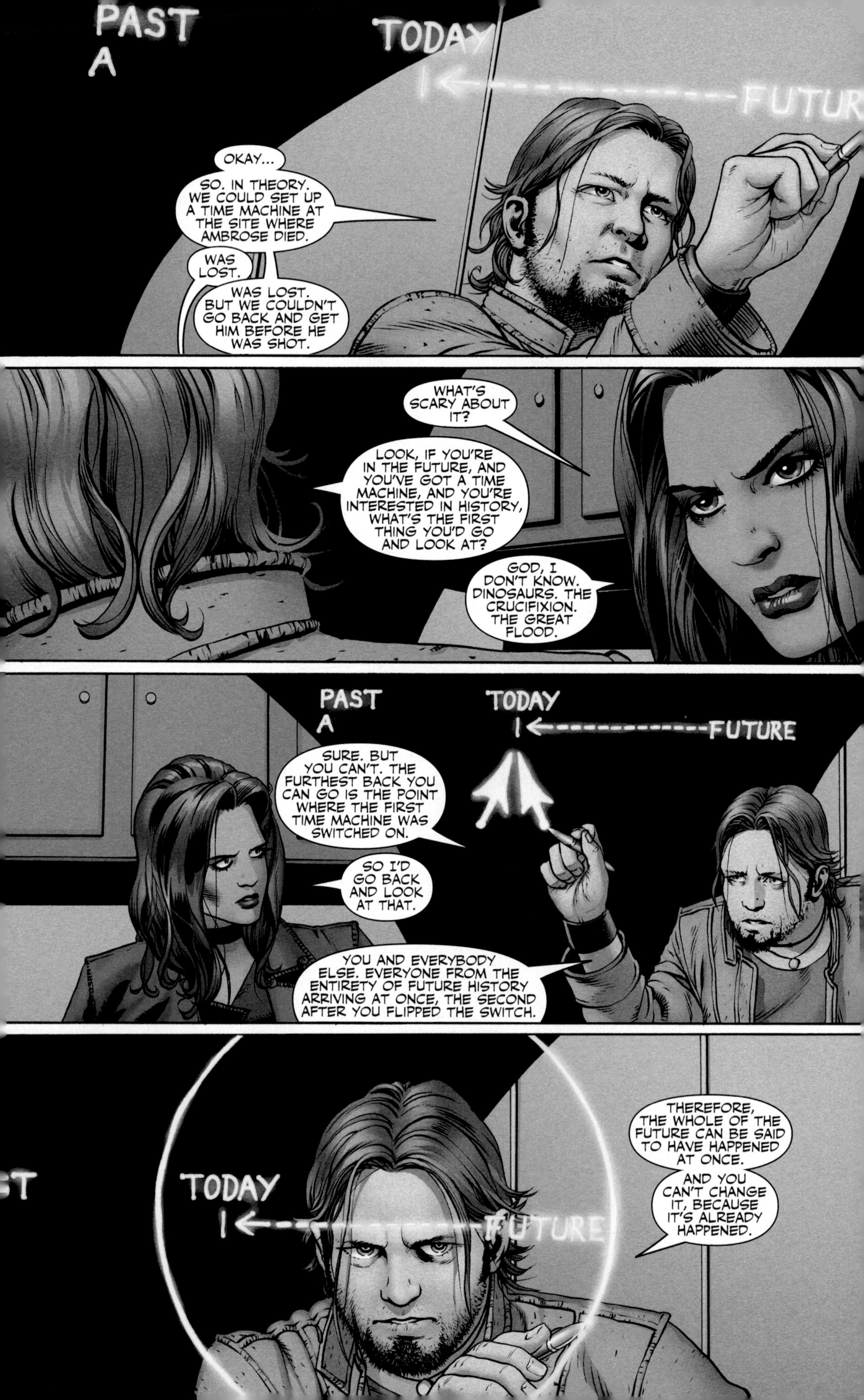
PAST
A
TODAY
FUTURE
OKAY...
SO. IN THEORY. WE COULD SET UP A TIME MACHINE AT THE SITE WHERE AMBROSE DIED.
WAS LOST.
WAS LOST. BUT WE COULDN'T GO BACK AND GET HIM BEFORE HE WAS SHOT.
WHAT'S SCARY ABOUT IT?
LOOK, IF YOU'RE IN THE FUTURE, AND YOU'VE GOT A TIME MACHINE, AND YOU'RE INTERESTED IN HISTORY, WHAT'S THE FIRST THING YOU'D GO AND LOOK AT?
GOD, I DON'T KNOW. DINOSAURS. THE CRUCIFIXION. THE GREAT FLOOD.
PAST
A
TODAY
FUTURE
SURE. BUT YOU CAN'T. THE FURTHEST BACK YOU CAN GO IS THE POINT WHERE THE FIRST TIME MACHINE WAS SWITCHED ON.
SO I'D GO BACK AND LOOK AT THAT.
YOU AND EVERYBODY ELSE. EVERYONE FROM THE ENTIRETY OF FUTURE HISTORY ARRIVING AT ONCE, THE SECOND AFTER YOU FLIPPED THE SWITCH.
TODAY
FUTURE
THEREFORE, THE WHOLE OF THE FUTURE CAN BE SAID TO HAVE HAPPENED AT ONCE.
AND YOU CAN'T CHANGE IT, BECAUSE IT'S ALREADY HAPPENED.

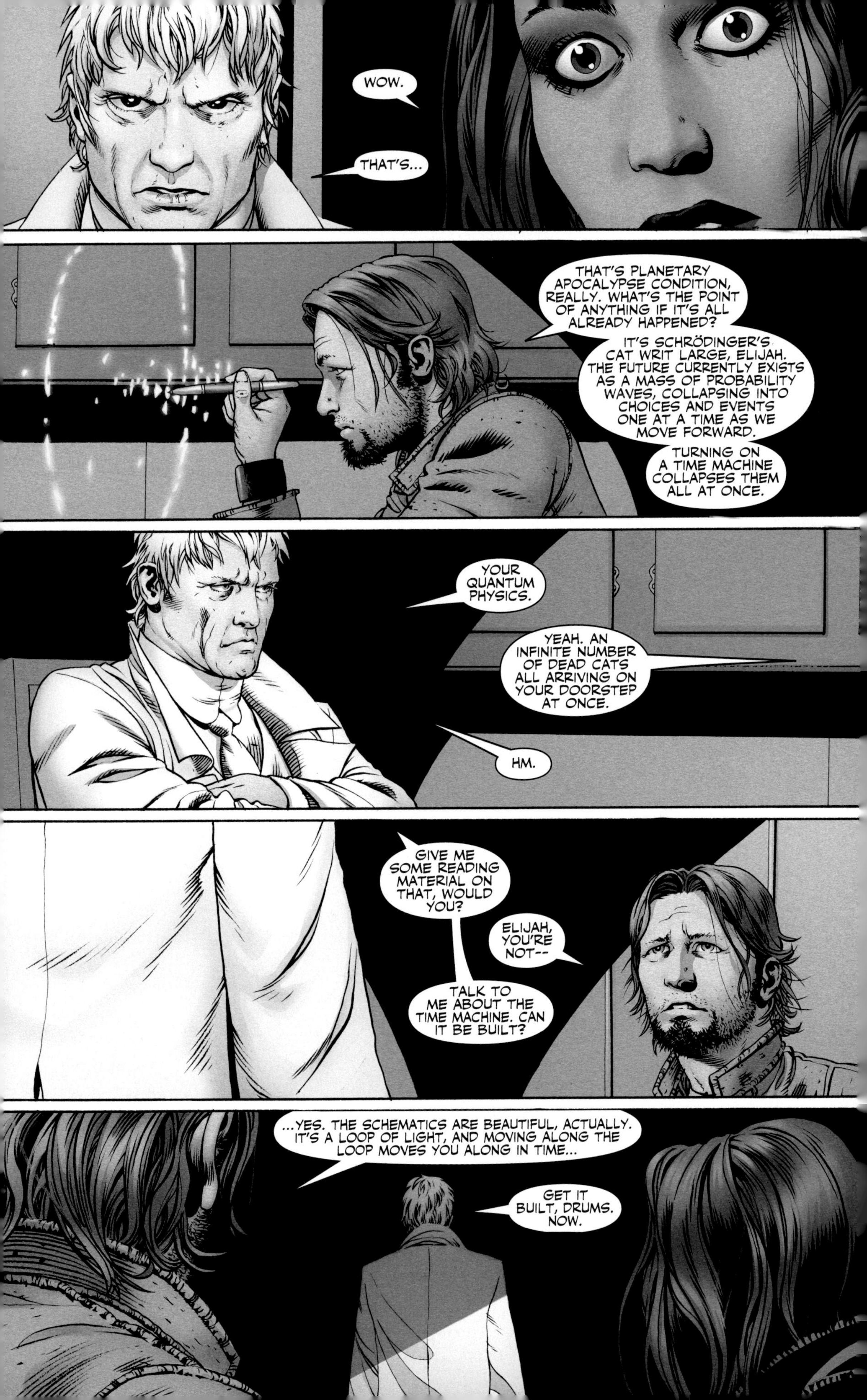
WOW.
THAT'S...
THAT'S PLANETARY APOCALYPSE CONDITION, REALLY. WHAT'S THE POINT OF ANYTHING IF IT'S ALL ALREADY HAPPENED?
IT'S SCHRÖDINGER'S CAT WRIT LARGE, ELIJAH. THE FUTURE CURRENTLY EXISTS AS A MASS OF PROBABILITY WAVES, COLLAPSING INTO CHOICES AND EVENTS ONE AT A TIME AS WE MOVE FORWARD.
TURNING ON A TIME MACHINE COLLAPSES THEM ALL AT ONCE.
YOUR QUANTUM PHYSICS.
YEAH. AN INFINITE NUMBER OF DEAD CATS ALL ARRIVING ON YOUR DOORSTEP AT ONCE.
HM.
GIVE ME SOME READING MATERIAL ON THAT, WOULD YOU?
ELIJAH, YOU'RE NOT--
TALK TO ME ABOUT THE TIME MACHINE. CAN IT BE BUILT?
...YES. THE SCHEMATICS ARE BEAUTIFUL, ACTUALLY. IT'S A LOOP OF LIGHT, AND MOVING ALONG THE LOOP MOVES YOU ALONG IN TIME...
GET IT BUILT, DRUMS. NOW.

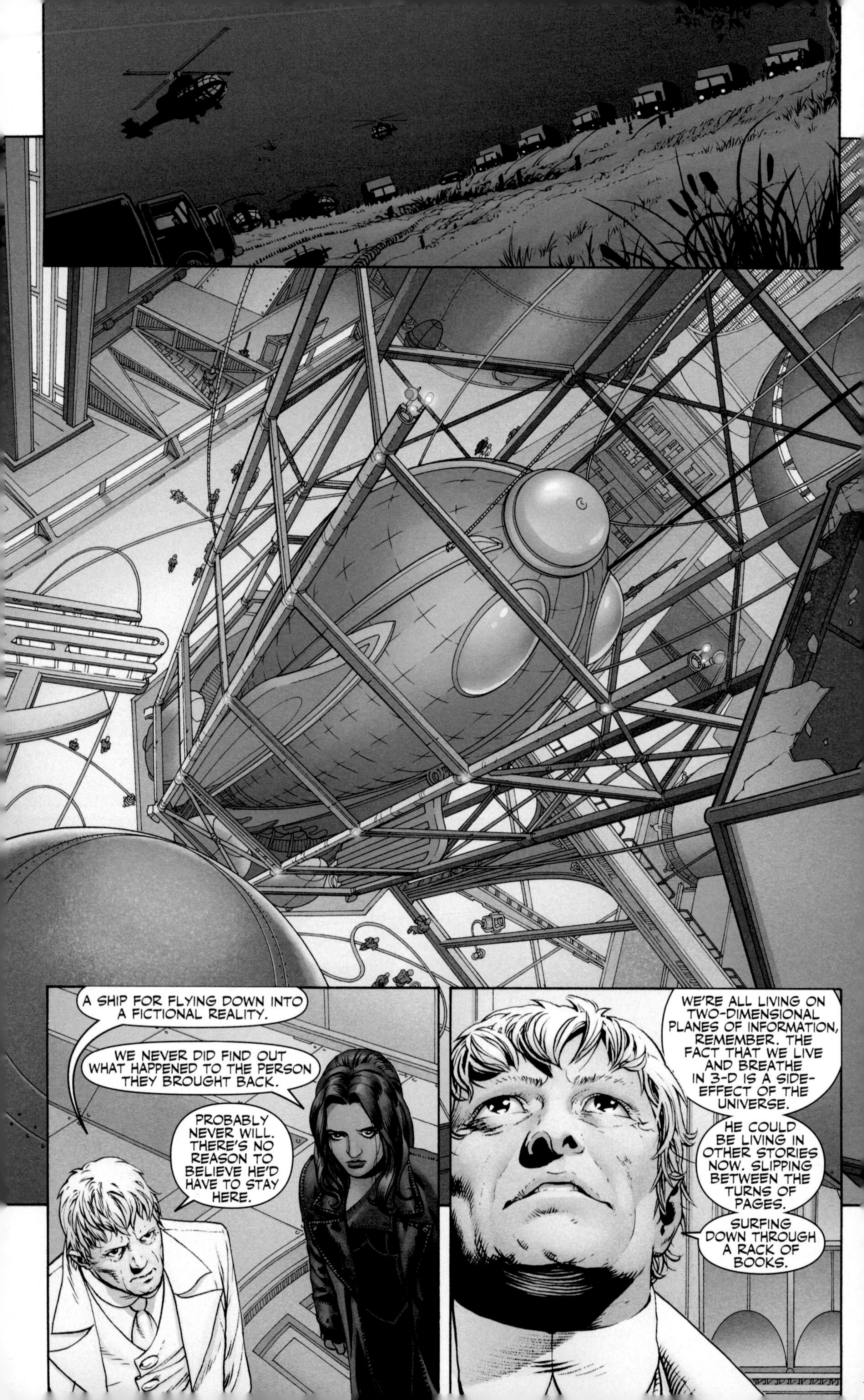
A SHIP FOR FLYING DOWN INTO A FICTIONAL REALITY.
WE NEVER DID FIND OUT WHAT HAPPENED TO THE PERSON THEY BROUGHT BACK.
PROBABLY NEVER WILL. THERE'S NO REASON TO BELIEVE HE'D HAVE TO STAY HERE.
WE'RE ALL LIVING ON TWO-DIMENSIONAL PLANES OF INFORMATION, REMEMBER. THE FACT THAT WE LIVE AND BREATHE IN 3-D IS A SIDE-EFFECT OF THE UNIVERSE.
HE COULD BE LIVING IN OTHER STORIES NOW. SLIPPING BETWEEN THE TURNS OF PAGES.
SURFING DOWN THROUGH A RACK OF BOOKS.

WHAT'S THIS?

THE HUNTING PARTY.

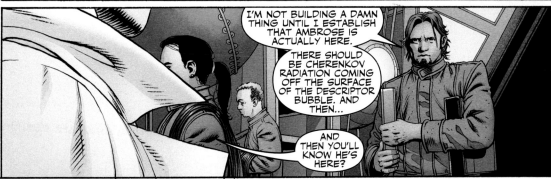

I'M NOT BUILDING A DAMN THING UNTIL I ESTABLISH THAT AMBROSE IS ACTUALLY HERE.

THERE SHOULD BE CHERENKOV RADIATION COMING OFF THE SURFACE OF THE DESCRIPTOR BUBBLE. AND THEN...

AND THEN YOU'LL KNOW HE'S HERE?

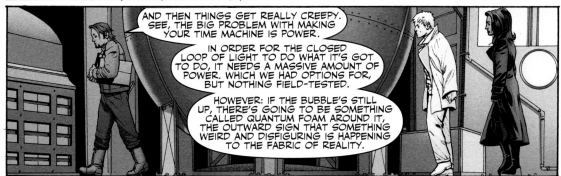

AND THEN THINGS GET REALLY CREEPY. SEE, THE BIG PROBLEM WITH MAKING YOUR TIME MACHINE IS POWER.

IN ORDER FOR THE CLOSED LOOP OF LIGHT TO DO WHAT IT'S GOT TO DO, IT NEEDS A MASSIVE AMOUNT OF POWER. WHICH WE HAD OPTIONS FOR, BUT NOTHING FIELD-TESTED.

HOWEVER: IF THE BUBBLE'S STILL UP, THERE'S GOING TO BE SOMETHING CALLED QUANTUM FOAM AROUND IT, THE OUTWARD SIGN THAT SOMETHING WEIRD AND DISFIGURING IS HAPPENING TO THE FABRIC OF REALITY.

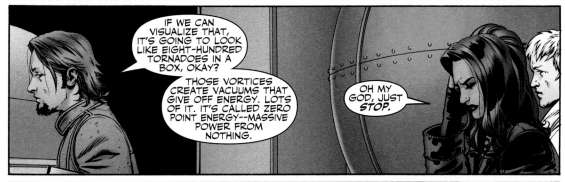

IF WE CAN VISUALIZE THAT, IT'S GOING TO LOOK LIKE EIGHT-HUNDRED TORNADOES IN A BOX, OKAY?

THOSE VORTICES CREATE VACUUMS THAT GIVE OFF ENERGY. LOTS OF IT. IT'S CALLED ZERO POINT ENERGY--MASSIVE POWER FROM NOTHING.

OH MY GOD, JUST *STOP*.

WHICH WOULD MEAN THAT AMBROSE WAS GENERATING THE POWER TO SAVE HIMSELF ALL ALONG.

WHICH IS CREEPY.

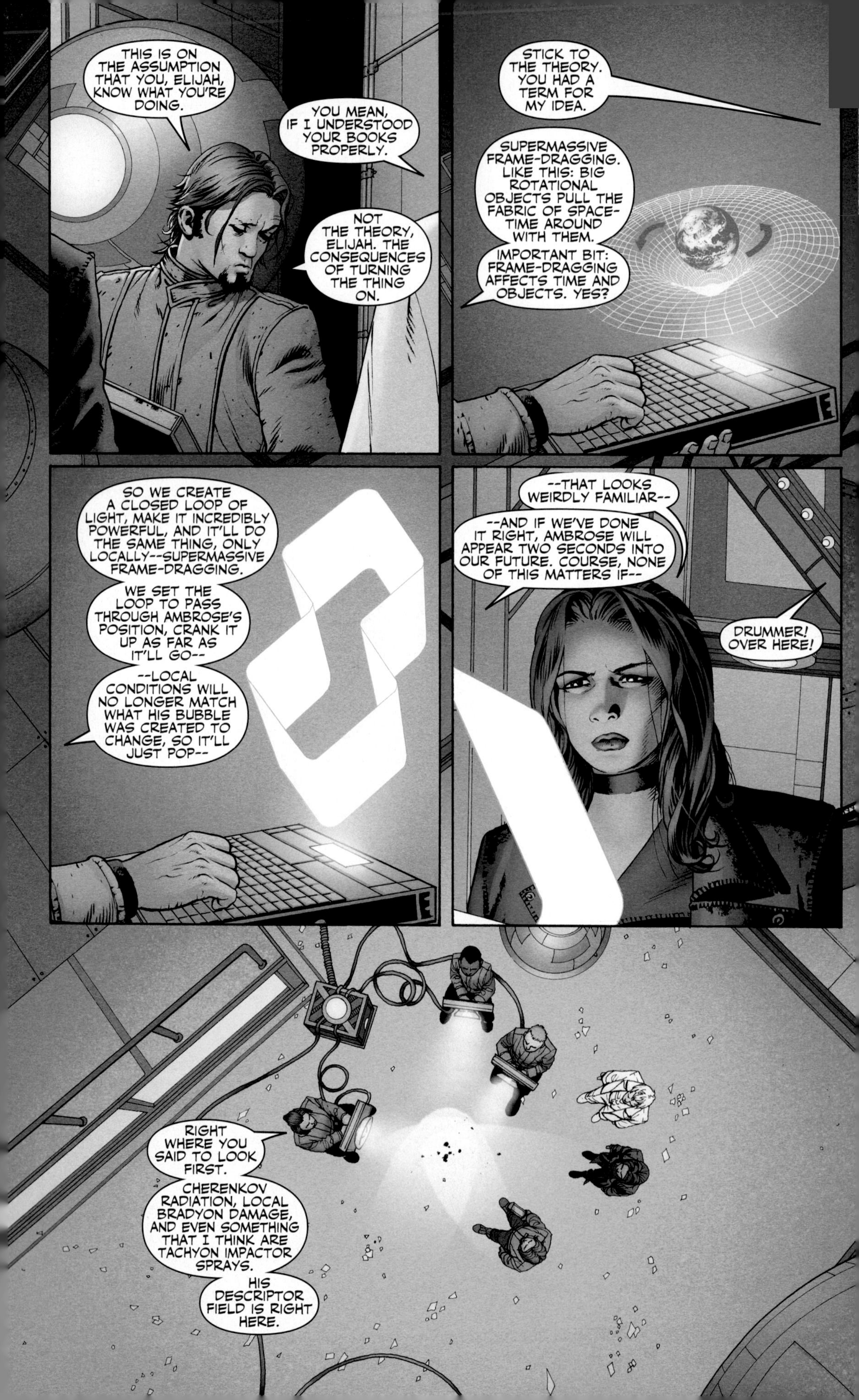
THIS IS ON THE ASSUMPTION THAT YOU, ELIJAH, KNOW WHAT YOU'RE DOING.
YOU MEAN, IF I UNDERSTOOD YOUR BOOKS PROPERLY.
NOT THE THEORY, ELIJAH. THE CONSEQUENCES OF TURNING THE THING ON.
STICK TO THE THEORY. YOU HAD A TERM FOR MY IDEA.
SUPERMASSIVE FRAME-DRAGGING. LIKE THIS: BIG ROTATIONAL OBJECTS PULL THE FABRIC OF SPACE-TIME AROUND WITH THEM.
IMPORTANT BIT: FRAME-DRAGGING AFFECTS TIME AND OBJECTS. YES?
SO WE CREATE A CLOSED LOOP OF LIGHT, MAKE IT INCREDIBLY POWERFUL, AND IT'LL DO THE SAME THING, ONLY LOCALLY--SUPERMASSIVE FRAME-DRAGGING.
WE SET THE LOOP TO PASS THROUGH AMBROSE'S POSITION, CRANK IT UP AS FAR AS IT'LL GO--
--LOCAL CONDITIONS WILL NO LONGER MATCH WHAT HIS BUBBLE WAS CREATED TO CHANGE, SO IT'LL JUST POP--
--THAT LOOKS WEIRDLY FAMILIAR--
--AND IF WE'VE DONE IT RIGHT, AMBROSE WILL APPEAR TWO SECONDS INTO OUR FUTURE. COURSE, NONE OF THIS MATTERS IF--
DRUMMER! OVER HERE!
RIGHT WHERE YOU SAID TO LOOK FIRST.
CHERENKOV RADIATION, LOCAL BRADYON DAMAGE, AND EVEN SOMETHING THAT I THINK ARE TACHYON IMPACTOR SPRAYS.
HIS DESCRIPTOR FIELD IS RIGHT HERE.

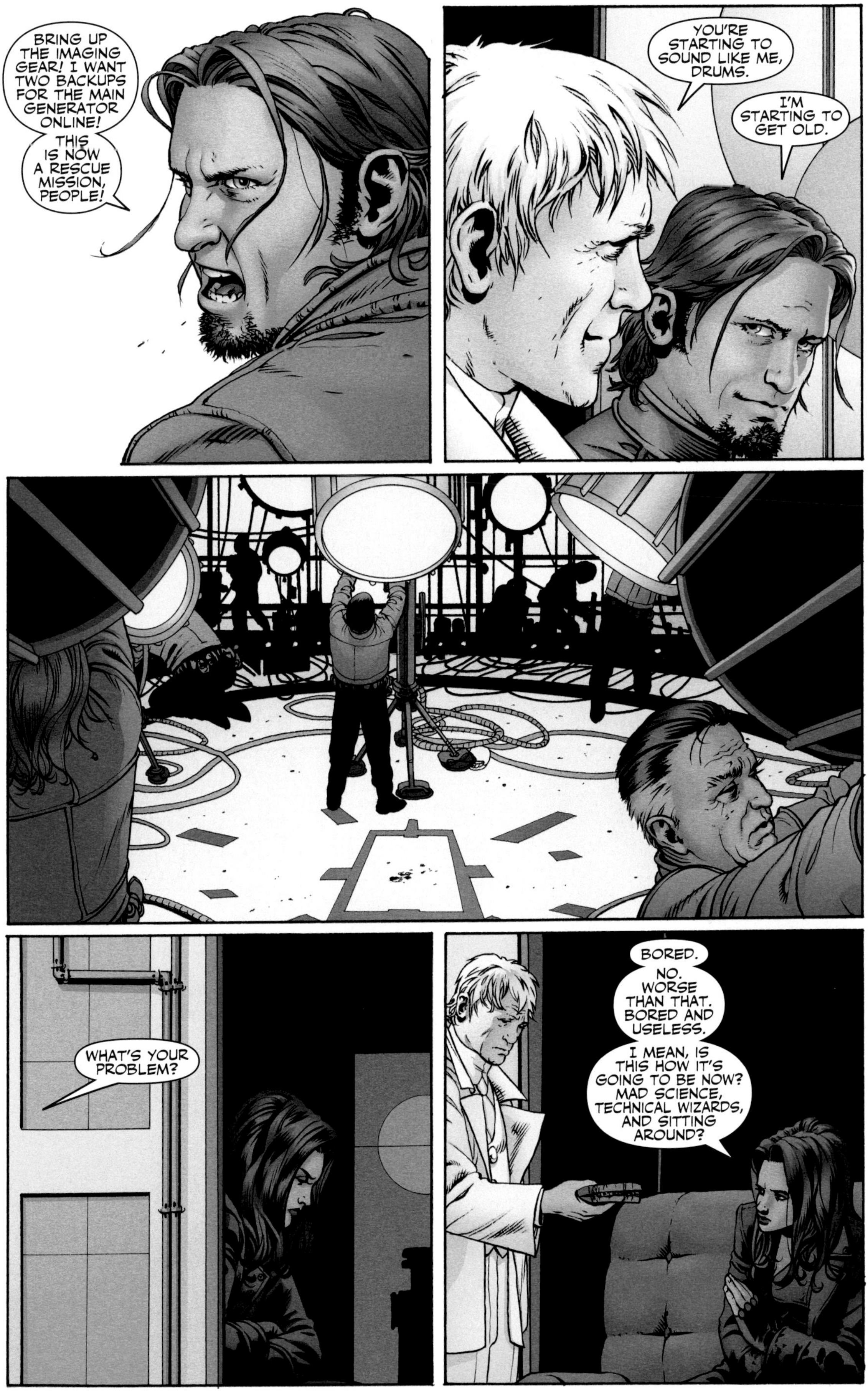
BRING UP THE IMAGING GEAR! I WANT TWO BACKUPS FOR THE MAIN GENERATOR ONLINE!
THIS IS NOW A RESCUE MISSION, PEOPLE!
YOU'RE STARTING TO SOUND LIKE ME, DRUMS.
I'M STARTING TO GET OLD.
WHAT'S YOUR PROBLEM?
BORED.
NO. WORSE THAN THAT. BORED AND USELESS.
I MEAN, IS THIS HOW IT'S GOING TO BE NOW? MAD SCIENCE, TECHNICAL WIZARDS, AND SITTING AROUND?

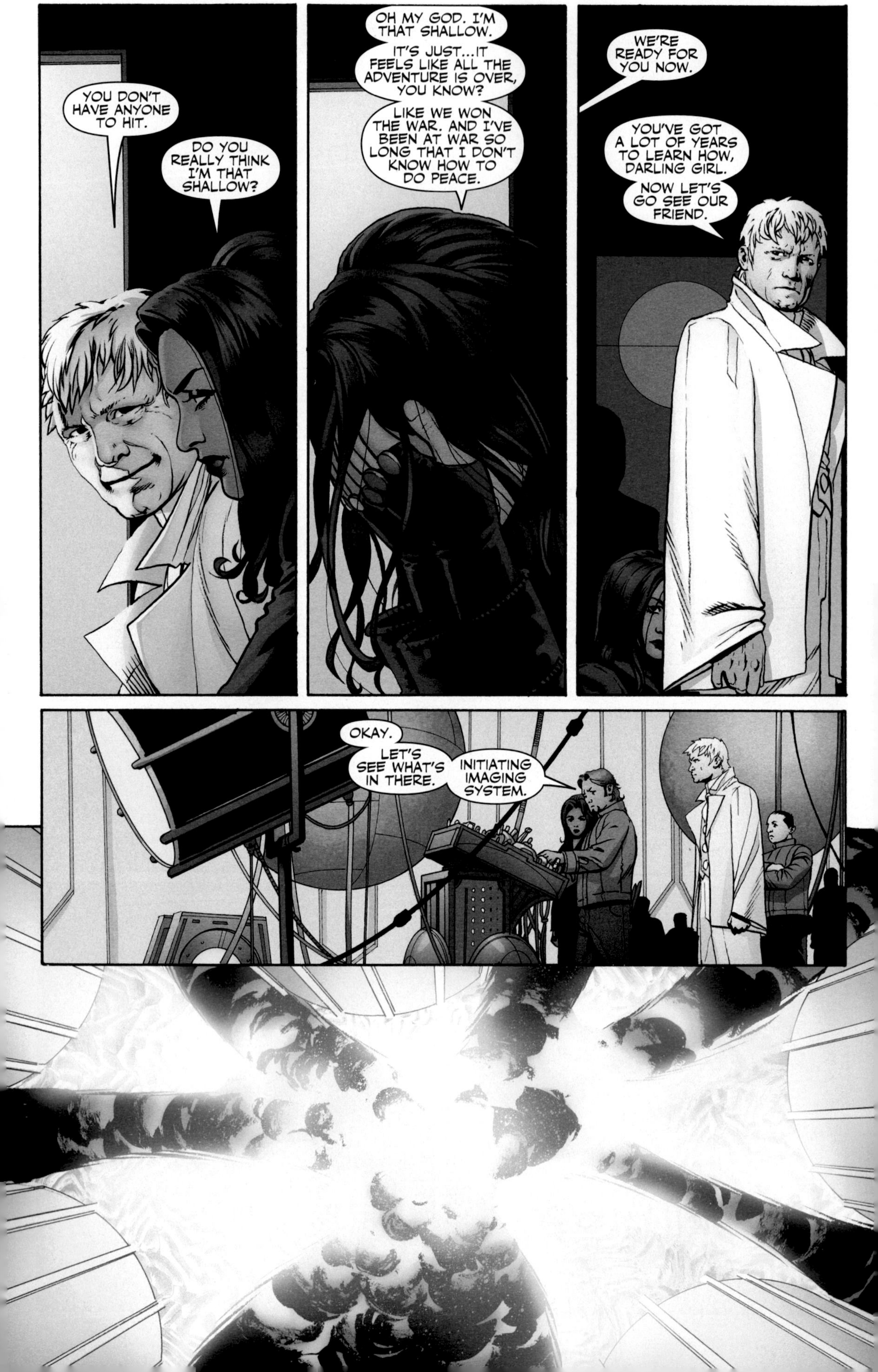
YOU DON'T HAVE ANYONE TO HIT.
DO YOU REALLY THINK I'M THAT SHALLOW?
OH MY GOD. I'M THAT SHALLOW.
IT'S JUST...IT FEELS LIKE ALL THE ADVENTURE IS OVER, YOU KNOW?
LIKE WE WON THE WAR. AND I'VE BEEN AT WAR SO LONG THAT I DON'T KNOW HOW TO DO PEACE.
WE'RE READY FOR YOU NOW.
YOU'VE GOT A LOT OF YEARS TO LEARN HOW, DARLING GIRL.
NOW LET'S GO SEE OUR FRIEND.
OKAY.
LET'S SEE WHAT'S IN THERE.
INITIATING IMAGING SYSTEM.

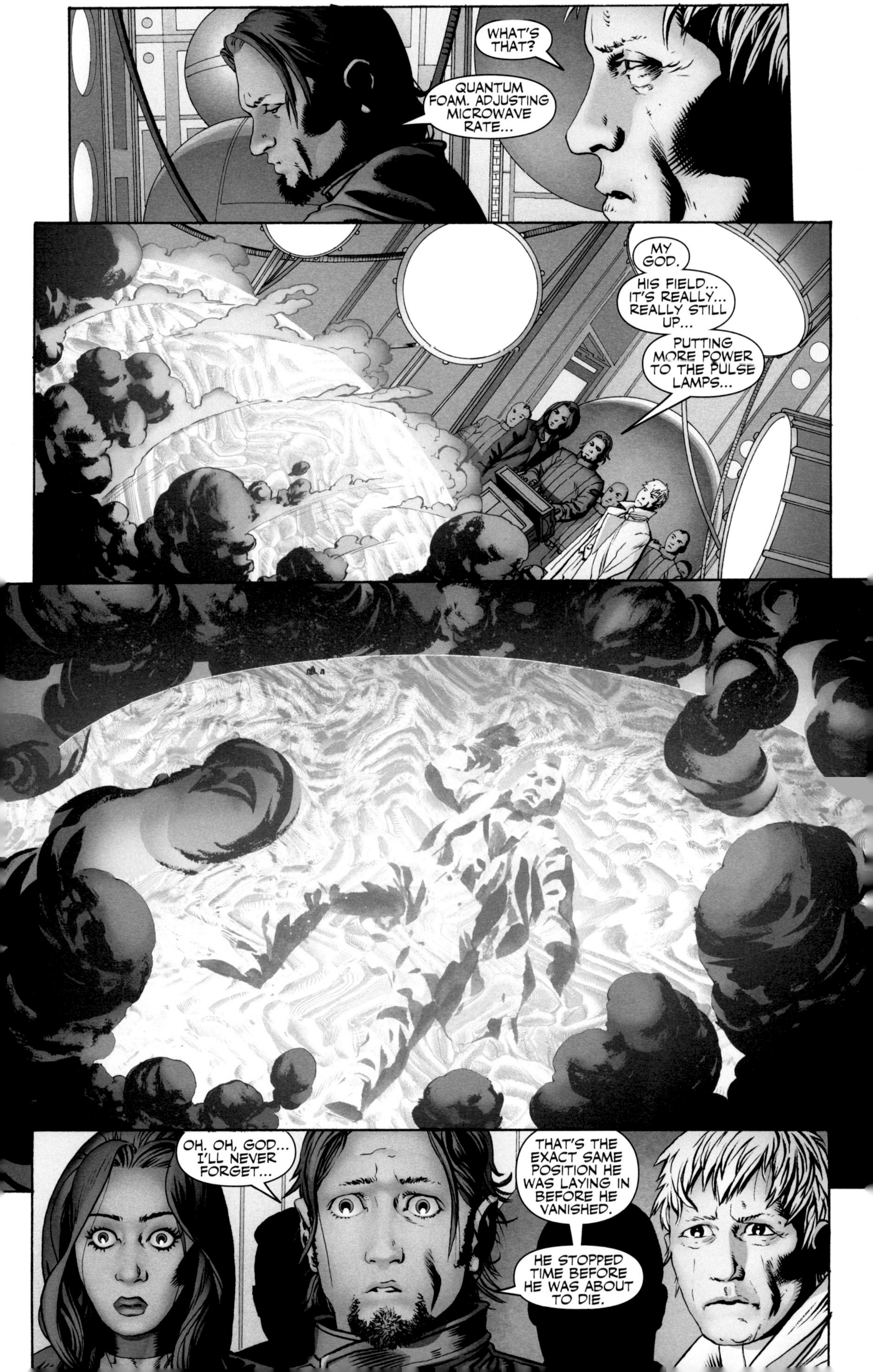
WHAT'S THAT?
QUANTUM FOAM. ADJUSTING MICROWAVE RATE...
MY GOD.
HIS FIELD... IT'S REALLY... REALLY STILL UP...
PUTTING MORE POWER TO THE PULSE LAMPS...
OH. OH, GOD... I'LL NEVER FORGET...
THAT'S THE EXACT SAME POSITION HE WAS LAYING IN BEFORE HE VANISHED.
HE STOPPED TIME BEFORE HE WAS ABOUT TO DIE.

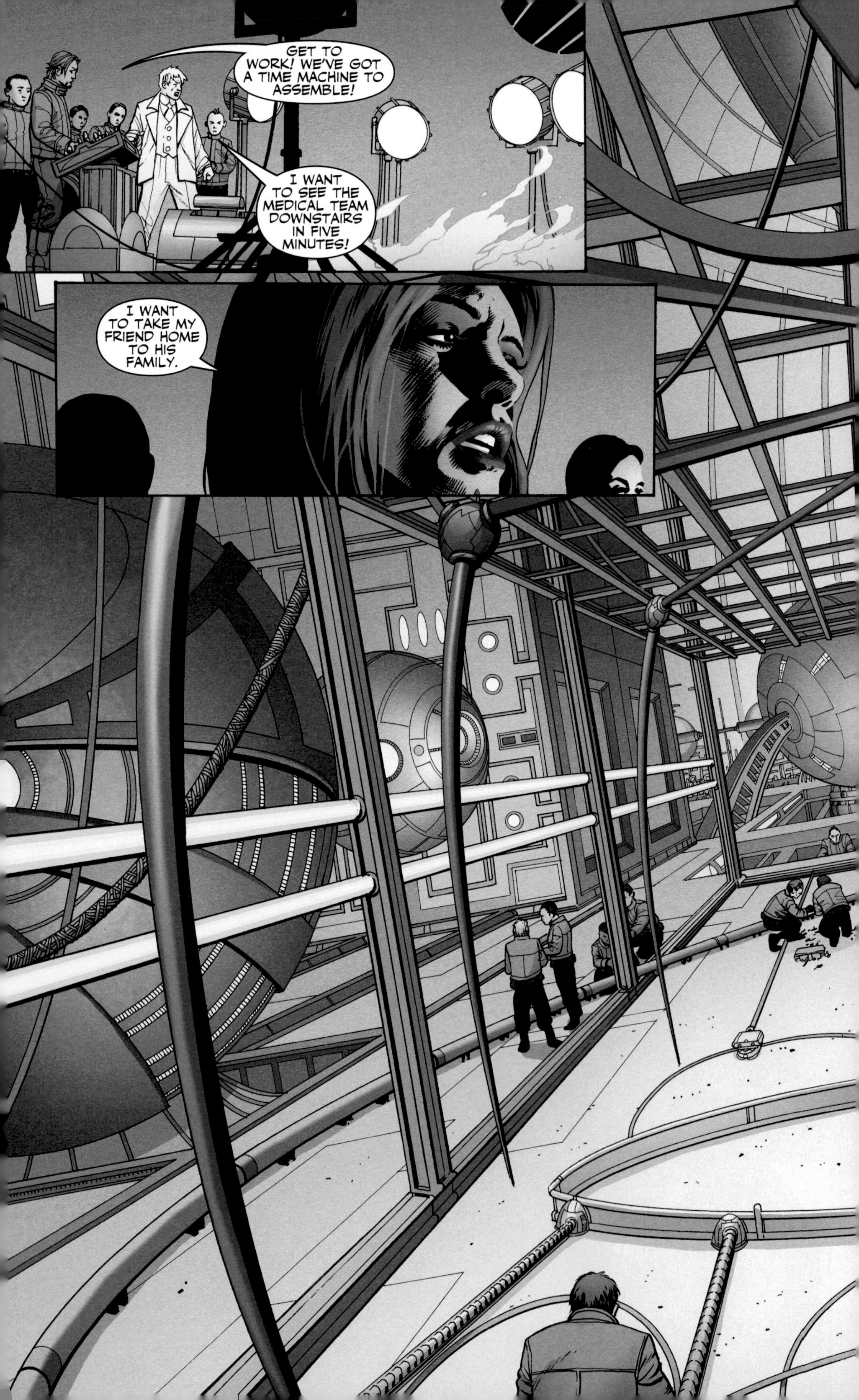
GET TO WORK! WE'VE GOT A TIME MACHINE TO ASSEMBLE!
I WANT TO SEE THE MEDICAL TEAM DOWNSTAIRS IN FIVE MINUTES!
I WANT TO TAKE MY FRIEND HOME TO HIS FAMILY.

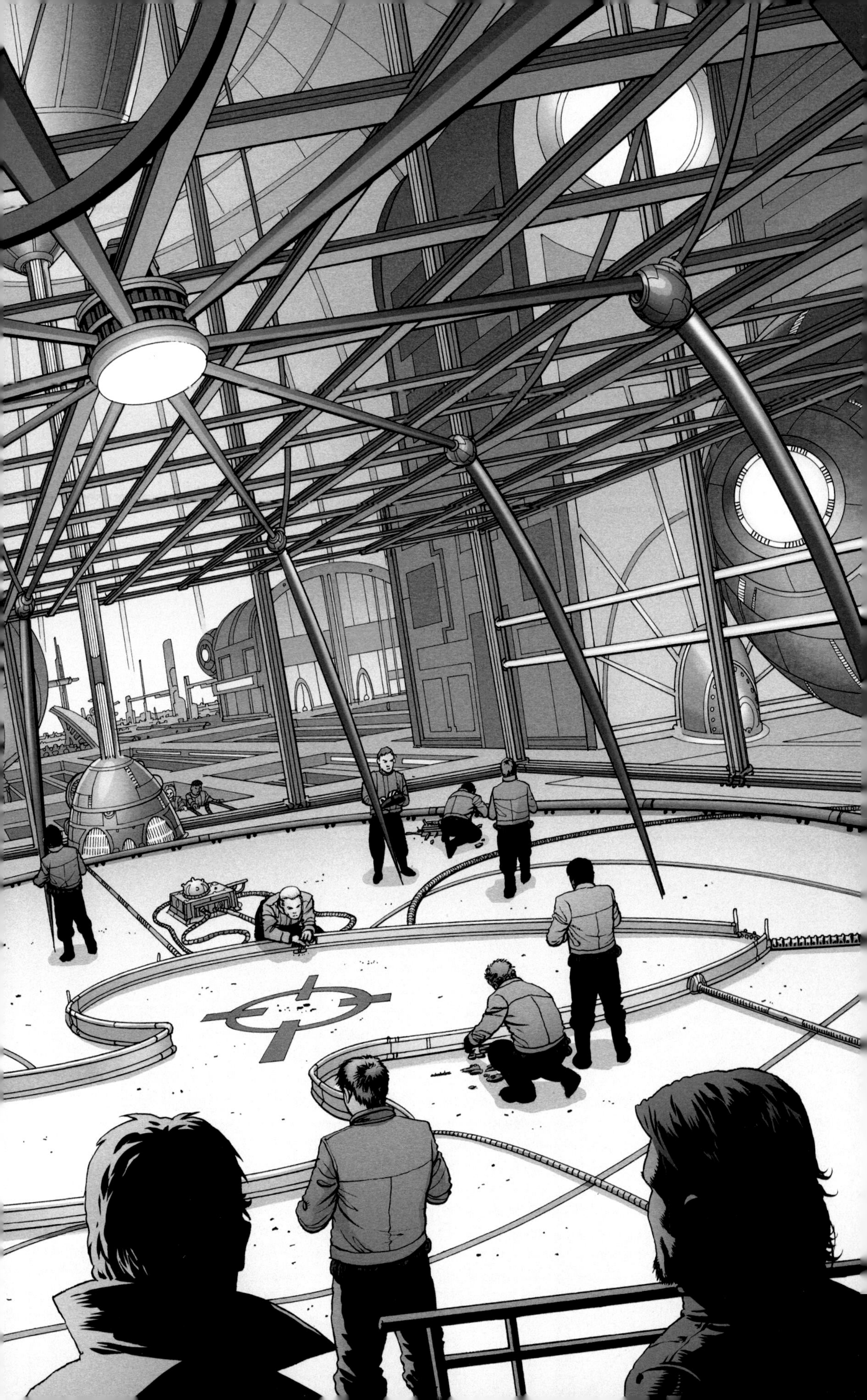

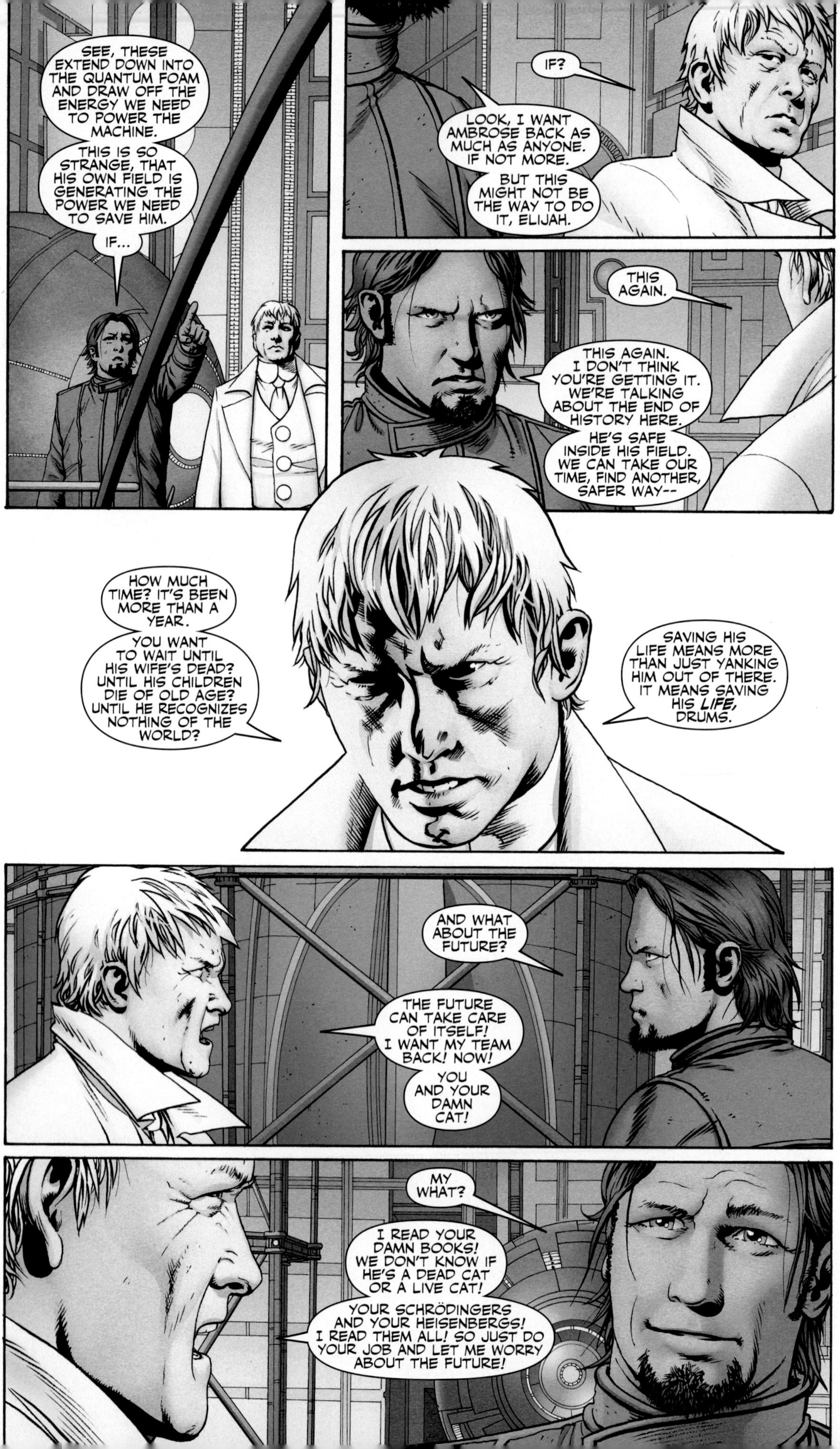

SEE, THESE EXTEND DOWN INTO THE QUANTUM FOAM AND DRAW OFF THE ENERGY WE NEED TO POWER THE MACHINE.
THIS IS SO STRANGE, THAT HIS OWN FIELD IS GENERATING THE POWER WE NEED TO SAVE HIM.
IF...
IF?
LOOK, I WANT AMBROSE BACK AS MUCH AS ANYONE. IF NOT MORE.
BUT THIS MIGHT NOT BE THE WAY TO DO IT, ELIJAH.
THIS AGAIN.
THIS AGAIN. I DON'T THINK YOU'RE GETTING IT. WE'RE TALKING ABOUT THE END OF HISTORY HERE.
HE'S SAFE INSIDE HIS FIELD. WE CAN TAKE OUR TIME, FIND ANOTHER, SAFER WAY--
HOW MUCH TIME? IT'S BEEN MORE THAN A YEAR.
YOU WANT TO WAIT UNTIL HIS WIFE'S DEAD? UNTIL HIS CHILDREN DIE OF OLD AGE? UNTIL HE RECOGNIZES NOTHING OF THE WORLD?
SAVING HIS LIFE MEANS MORE THAN JUST YANKING HIM OUT OF THERE. IT MEANS SAVING HIS LIFE, DRUMS.
AND WHAT ABOUT THE FUTURE?
THE FUTURE CAN TAKE CARE OF ITSELF! I WANT MY TEAM BACK! NOW!
YOU AND YOUR DAMN CAT!
MY WHAT?
I READ YOUR DAMN BOOKS! WE DON'T KNOW IF HE'S A DEAD CAT OR A LIVE CAT!
YOUR SCHRÖDINGERS AND YOUR HEISENBERGS! I READ THEM ALL! SO JUST DO YOUR JOB AND LET ME WORRY ABOUT THE FUTURE!

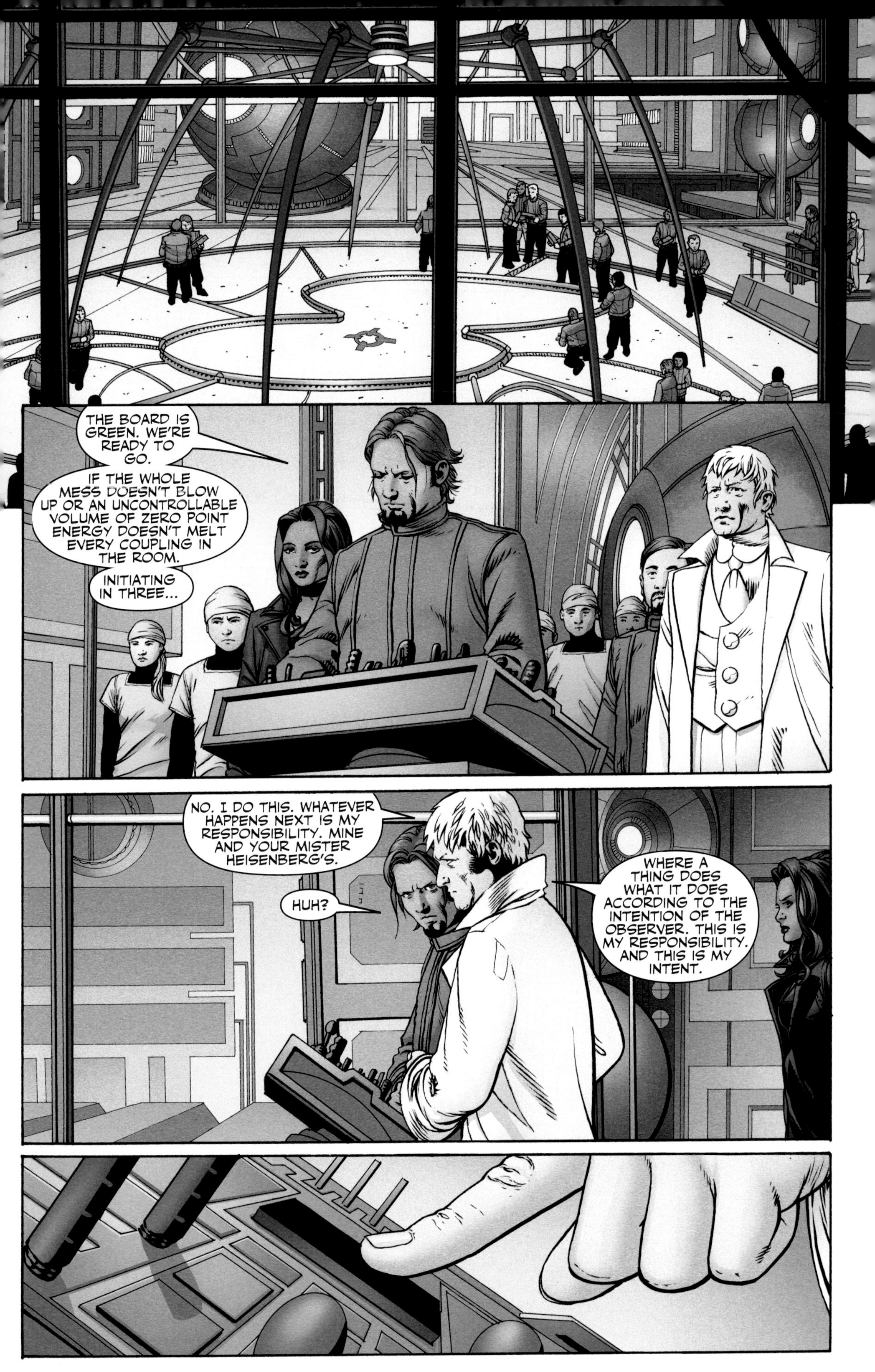
THE BOARD IS GREEN. WE'RE READY TO GO.
IF THE WHOLE MESS DOESN'T BLOW UP OR AN UNCONTROLLABLE VOLUME OF ZERO POINT ENERGY DOESN'T MELT EVERY COUPLING IN THE ROOM.
INITIATING IN THREE...
NO. I DO THIS. WHATEVER HAPPENS NEXT IS MY RESPONSIBILITY. MINE AND YOUR MISTER HEISENBERG'S.
HUH?
WHERE A THING DOES WHAT IT DOES ACCORDING TO THE INTENTION OF THE OBSERVER. THIS IS MY RESPONSIBILITY. AND THIS IS MY INTENT.

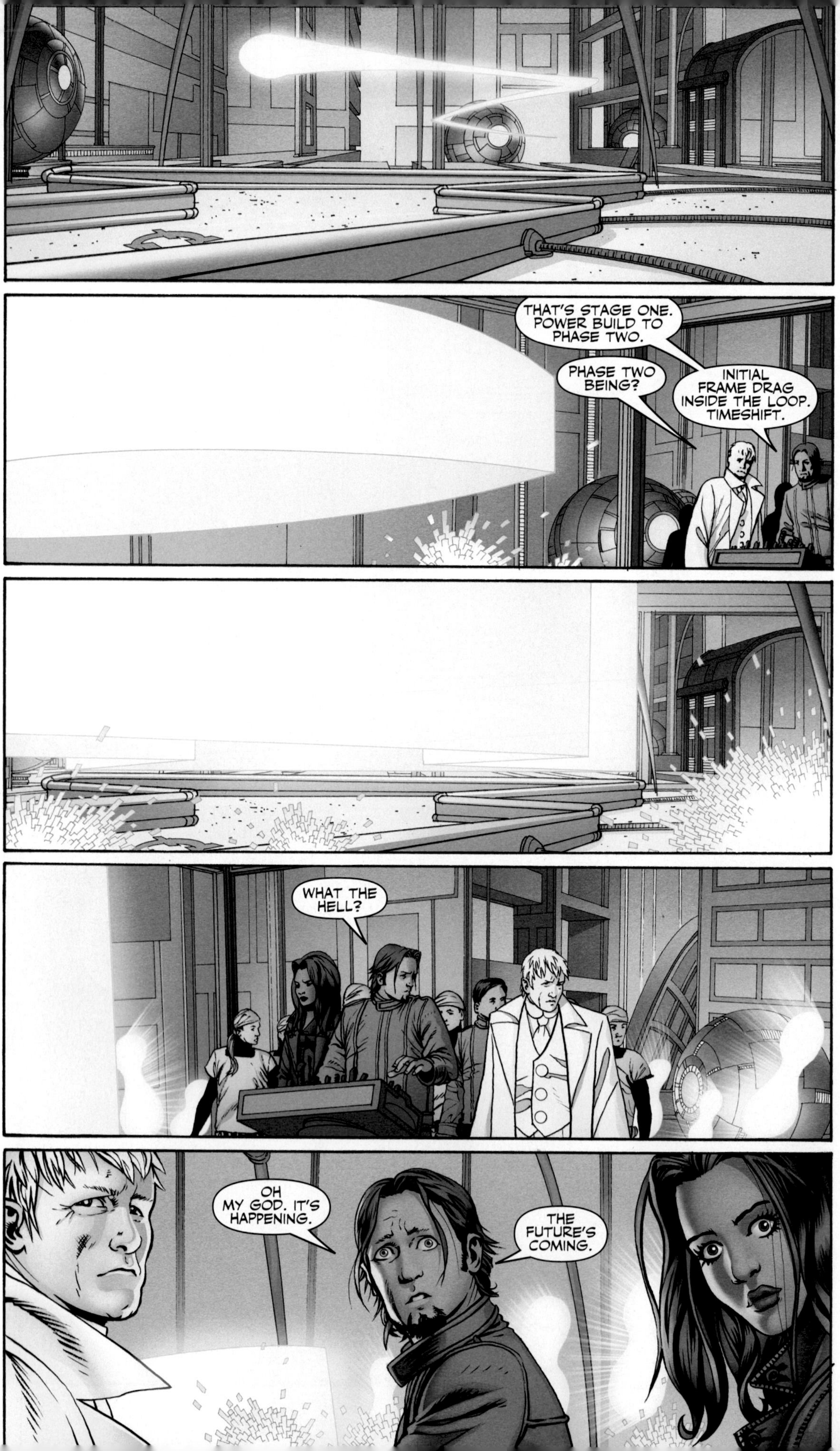
THAT'S STAGE ONE. POWER BUILD TO PHASE TWO.
PHASE TWO BEING?
INITIAL FRAME DRAG INSIDE THE LOOP. TIMESHIFT.
WHAT THE HELL?
OH MY GOD. IT'S HAPPENING.
THE FUTURE'S COMING.

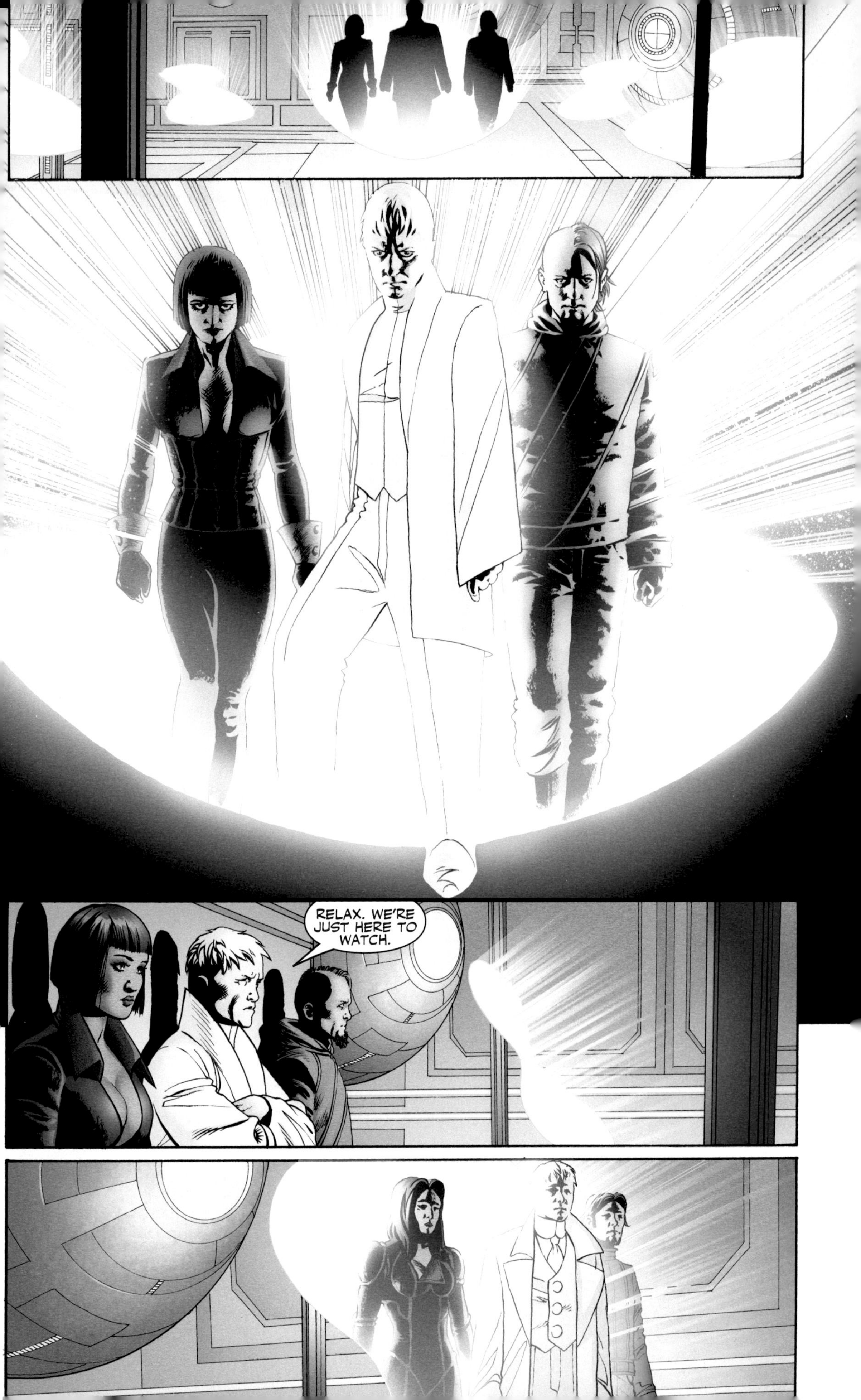
RELAX. WE'RE JUST HERE TO WATCH.

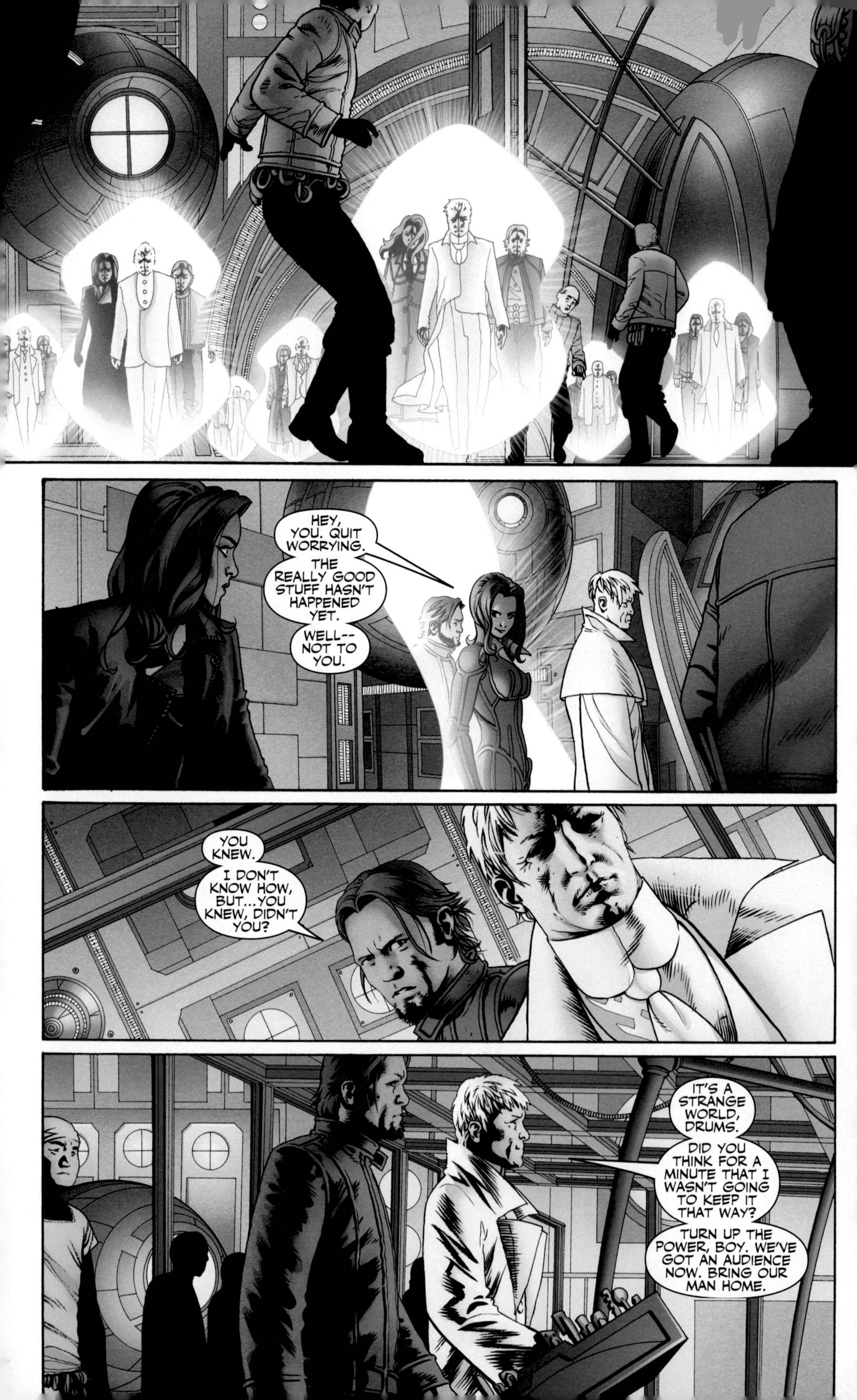
HEY, YOU. QUIT WORRYING.
THE REALLY GOOD STUFF HASN'T HAPPENED YET.
WELL-- NOT TO YOU.
YOU KNEW.
I DON'T KNOW HOW, BUT...YOU KNEW, DIDN'T YOU?
IT'S A STRANGE WORLD, DRUMS.
DID YOU THINK FOR A MINUTE THAT I WASN'T GOING TO KEEP IT THAT WAY?
TURN UP THE POWER, BOY. WE'VE GOT AN AUDIENCE NOW. BRING OUR MAN HOME.

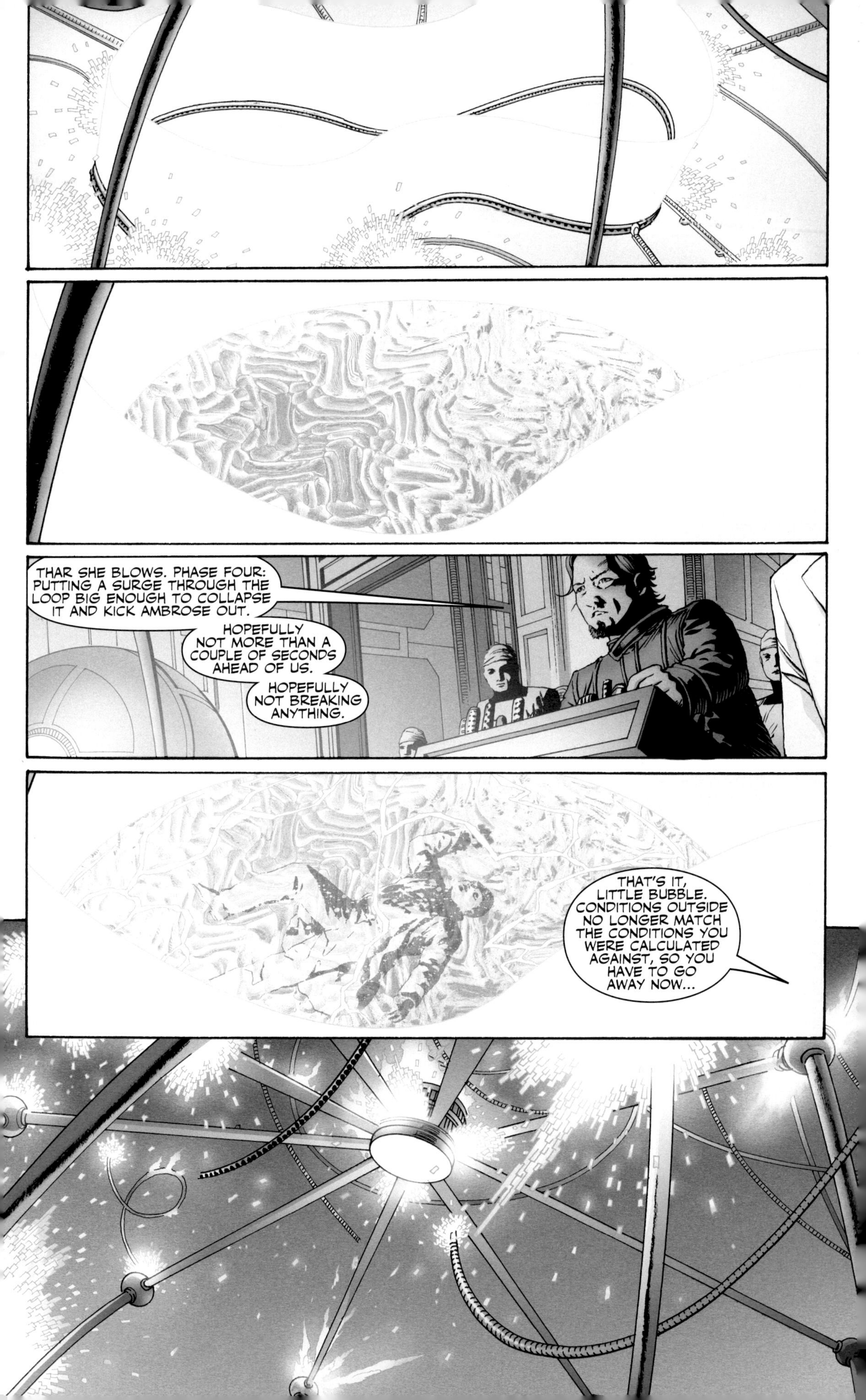
THAR SHE BLOWS. PHASE FOUR: PUTTING A SURGE THROUGH THE LOOP BIG ENOUGH TO COLLAPSE IT AND KICK AMBROSE OUT.
HOPEFULLY NOT MORE THAN A COUPLE OF SECONDS AHEAD OF US.
HOPEFULLY NOT BREAKING ANYTHING.
THAT'S IT, LITTLE BUBBLE. CONDITIONS OUTSIDE NO LONGER MATCH THE CONDITIONS YOU WERE CALCULATED AGAINST, SO YOU HAVE TO GO AWAY NOW...

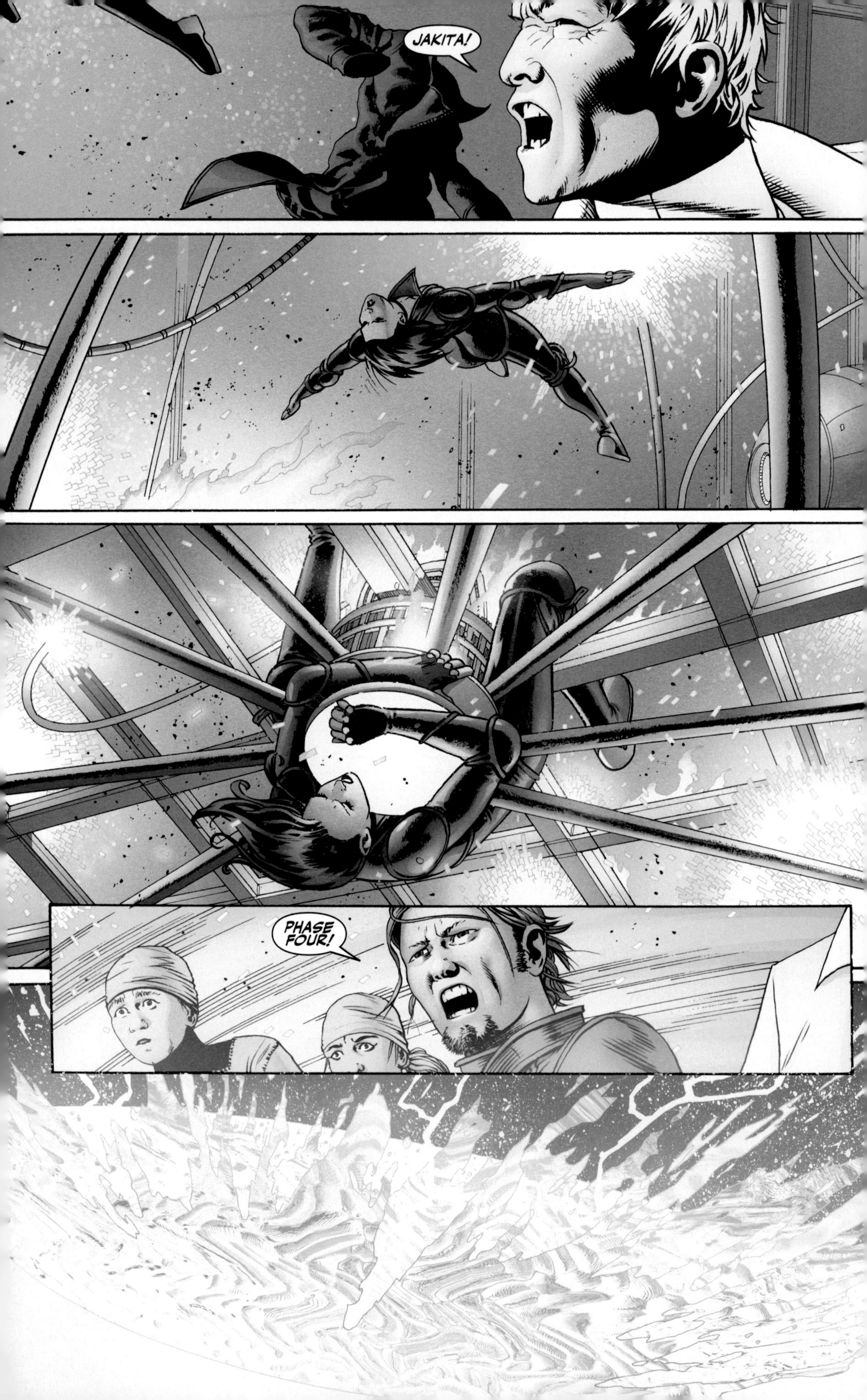
JAKITA!
PHASE FOUR!

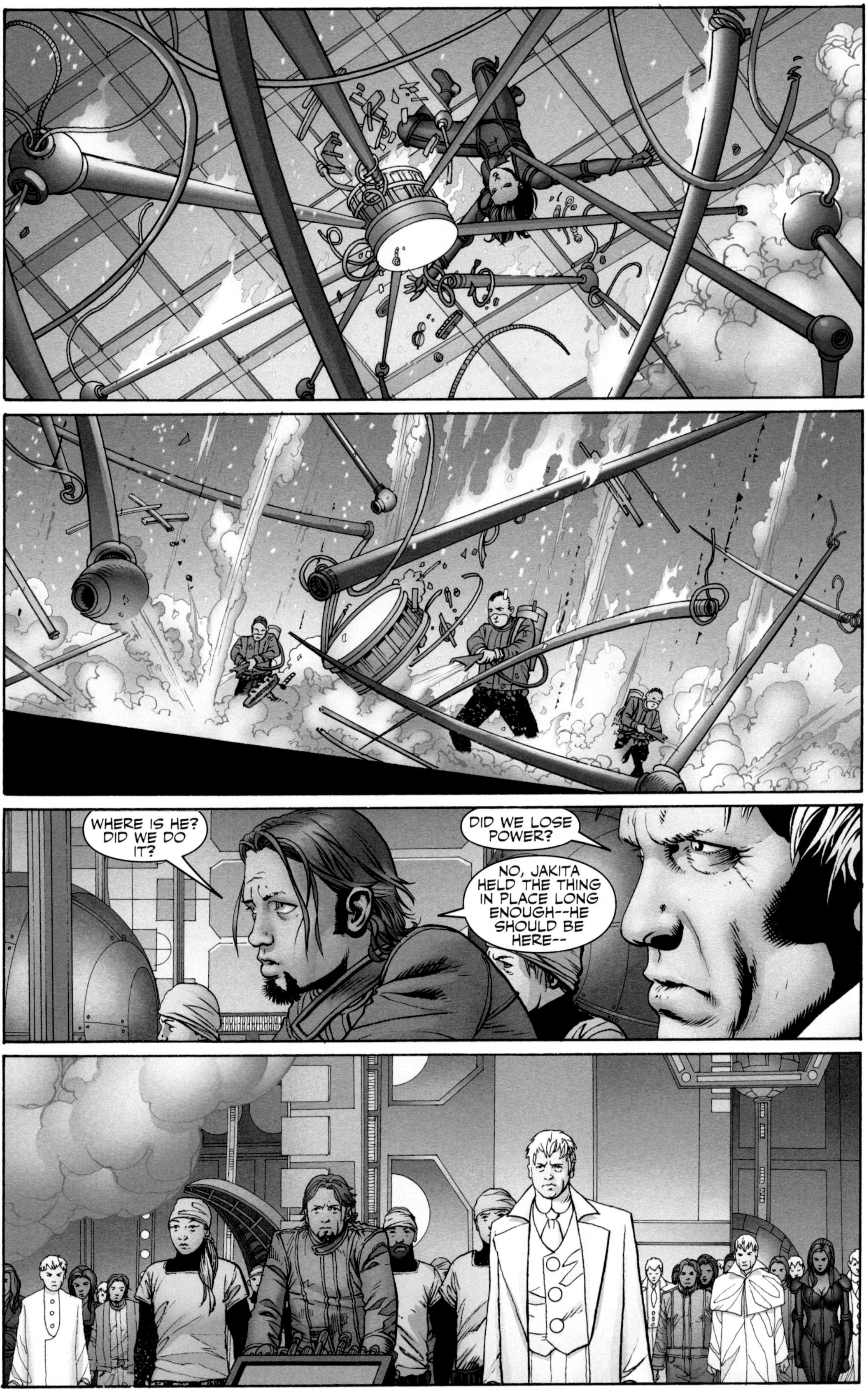
WHERE IS HE? DID WE DO IT?
DID WE LOSE POWER?
NO, JAKITA HELD THE THING IN PLACE LONG ENOUGH--HE SHOULD BE HERE--

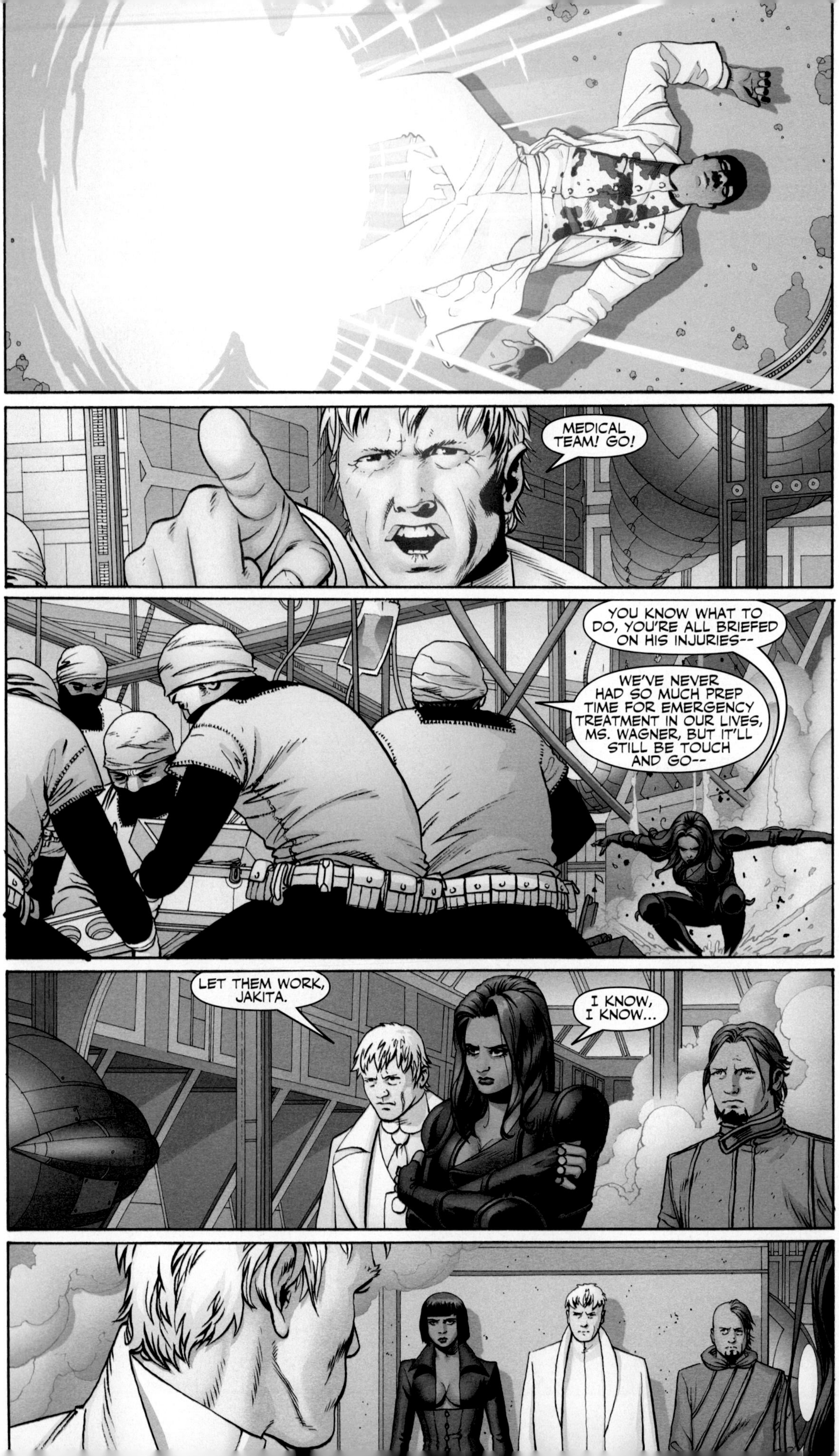
MEDICAL TEAM! GO!
YOU KNOW WHAT TO DO, YOU'RE ALL BRIEFED ON HIS INJURIES--
WE'VE NEVER HAD SO MUCH PREP TIME FOR EMERGENCY TREATMENT IN OUR LIVES, MS. WAGNER, BUT IT'LL STILL BE TOUCH AND GO--
LET THEM WORK, JAKITA.
I KNOW, I KNOW...

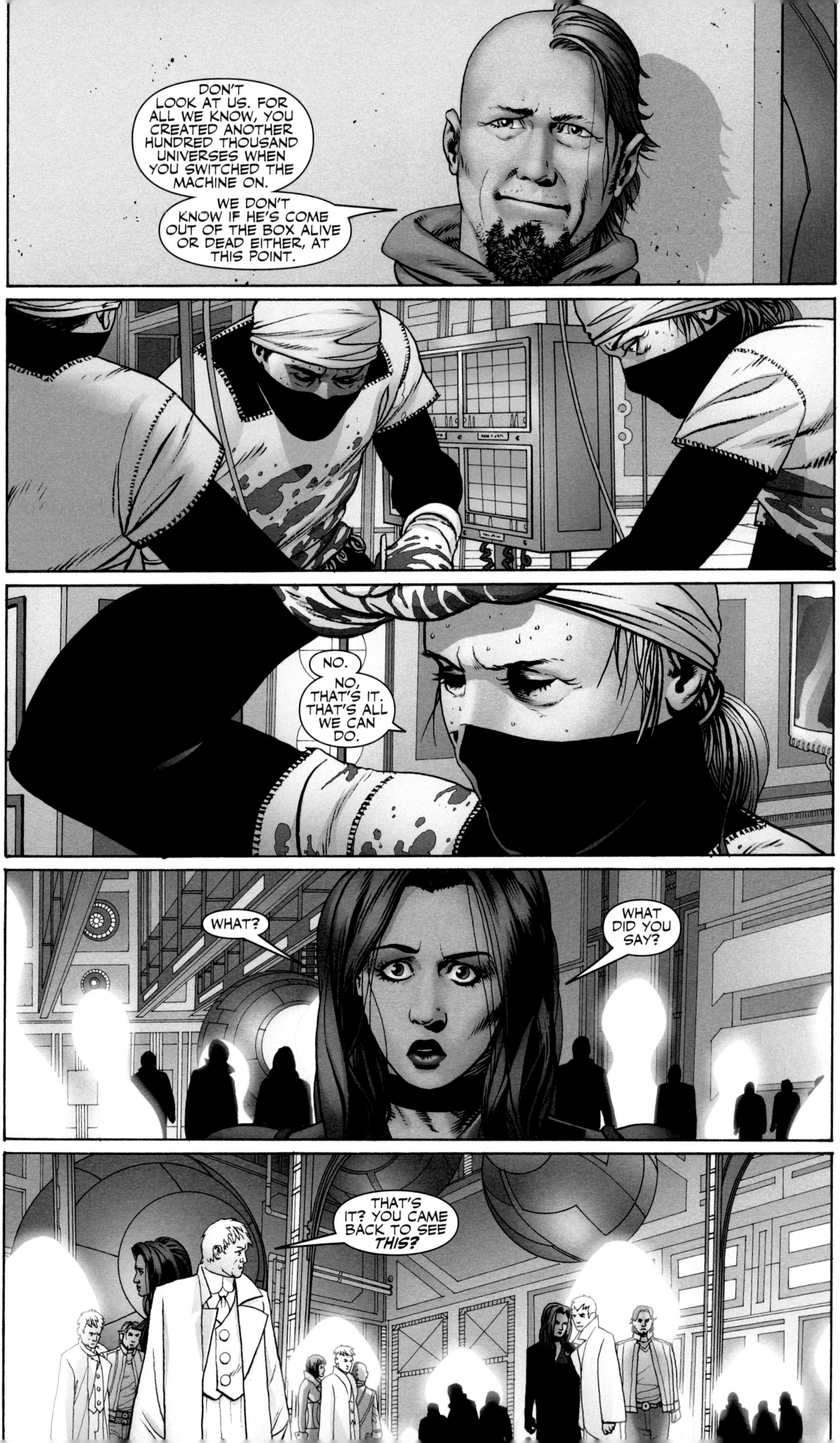
DON'T LOOK AT US. FOR ALL WE KNOW, YOU CREATED ANOTHER HUNDRED THOUSAND UNIVERSES WHEN YOU SWITCHED THE MACHINE ON.
WE DON'T KNOW IF HE'S COME OUT OF THE BOX ALIVE OR DEAD EITHER, AT THIS POINT.
NO.
NO, THAT'S IT. THAT'S ALL WE CAN DO.
WHAT?
WHAT DID YOU SAY?
THAT'S IT? YOU CAME BACK TO SEE *THIS?*

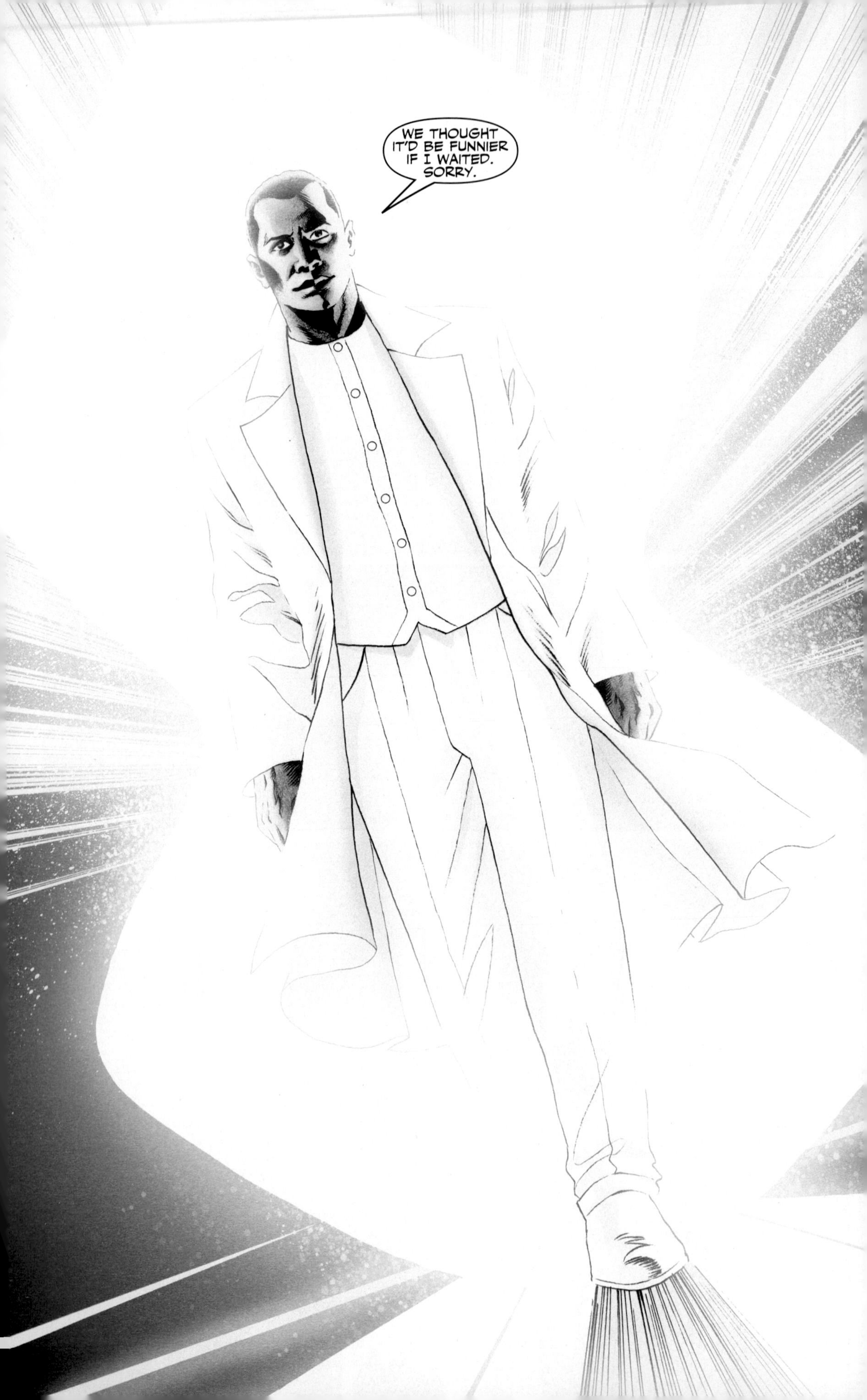
WE THOUGHT IT'D BE FUNNIER IF I WAITED. SORRY.

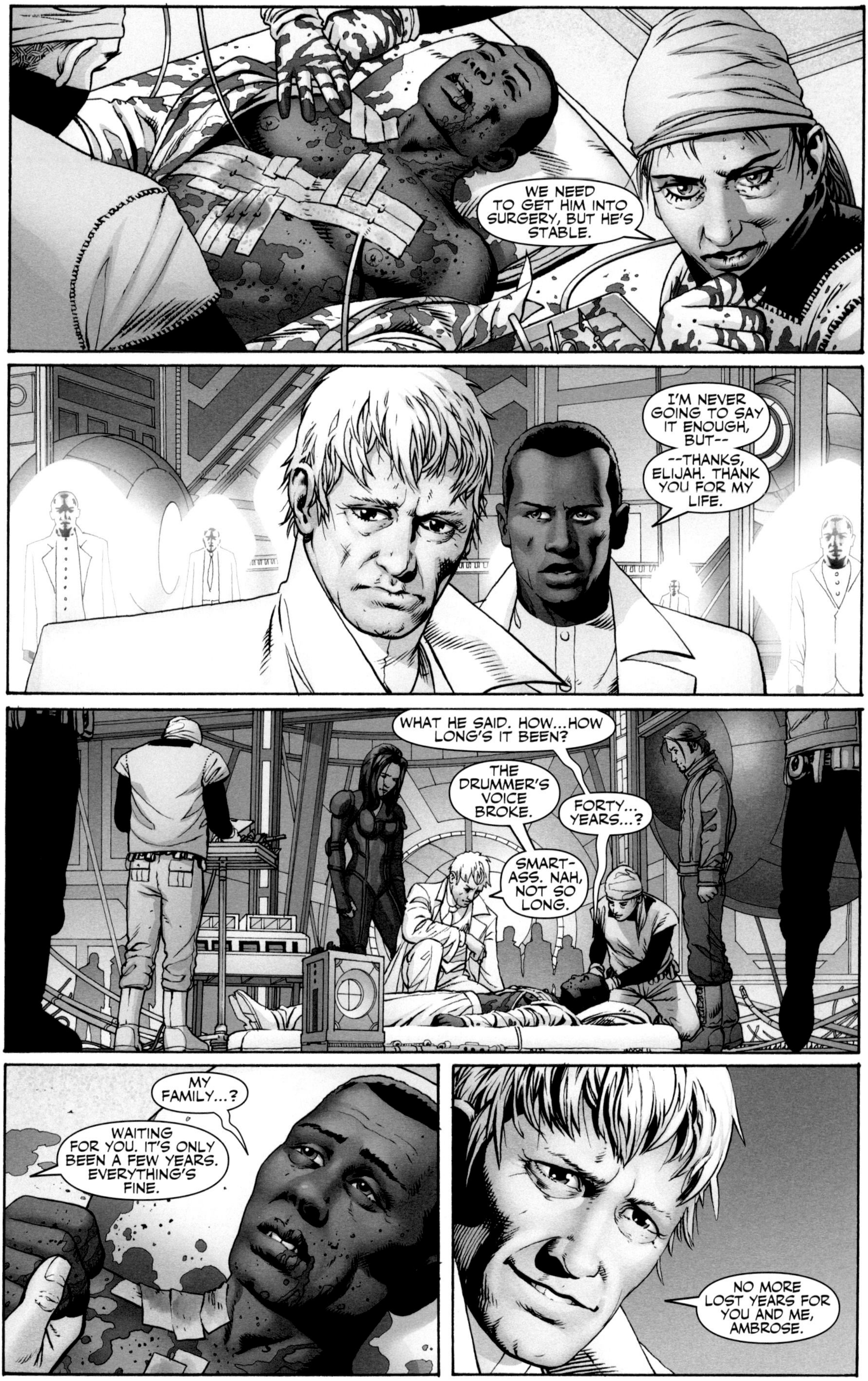
WE NEED TO GET HIM INTO SURGERY, BUT HE'S STABLE.
I'M NEVER GOING TO SAY IT ENOUGH, BUT--
--THANKS, ELIJAH. THANK YOU FOR MY LIFE.
WHAT HE SAID. HOW...HOW LONG'S IT BEEN?
THE DRUMMER'S VOICE BROKE.
FORTY... YEARS...?
SMART-ASS. NAH, NOT SO LONG.
MY FAMILY...?
WAITING FOR YOU. IT'S ONLY BEEN A FEW YEARS. EVERYTHING'S FINE.
NO MORE LOST YEARS FOR YOU AND ME, AMBROSE.

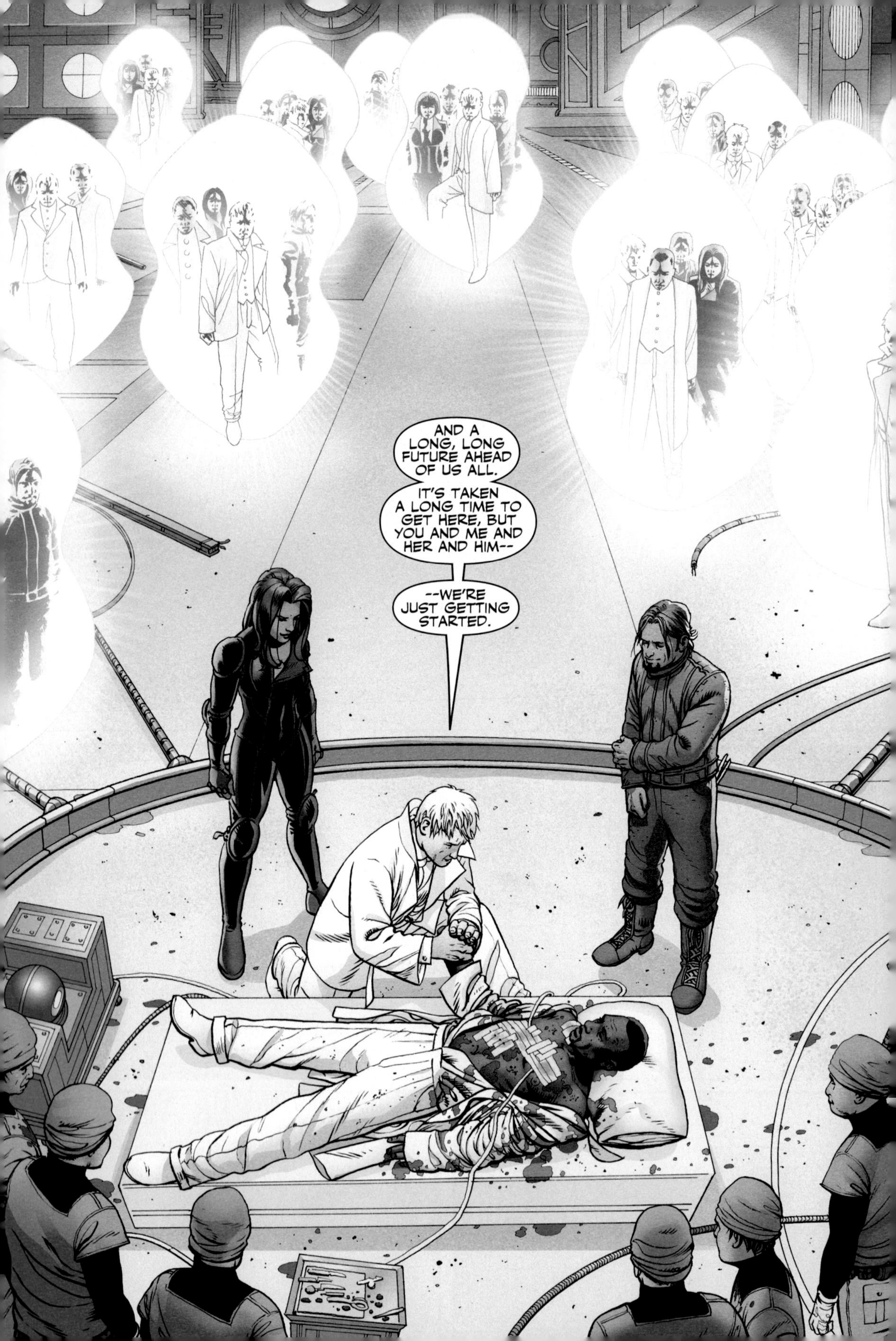
AND A LONG, LONG FUTURE AHEAD OF US ALL.
IT'S TAKEN A LONG TIME TO GET HERE, BUT YOU AND ME AND HER AND HIM--
--WE'RE JUST GETTING STARTED.

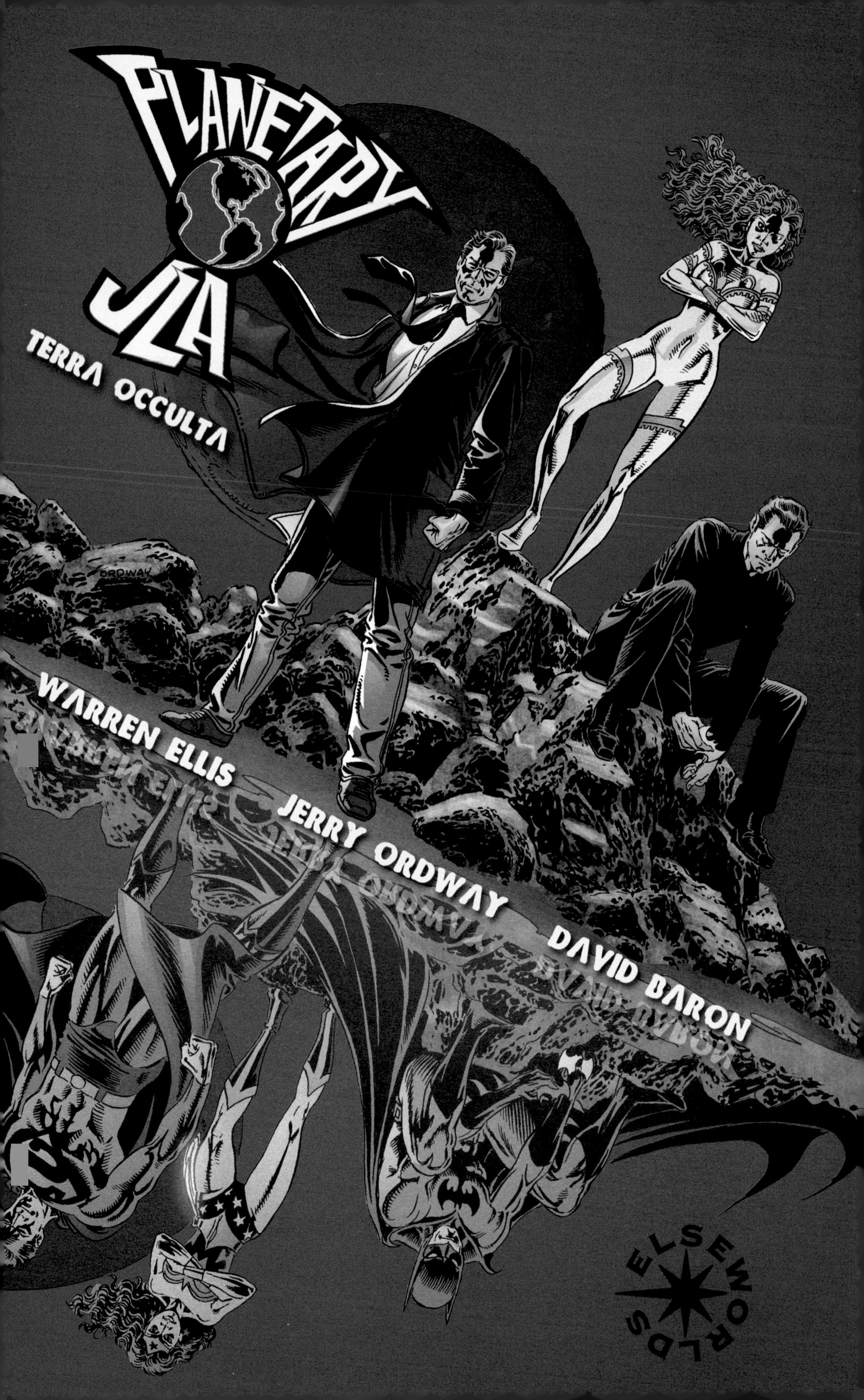
PLANETARY
JLA
TERRA OCCULTA
ORDWAY
WARREN ELLIS
JERRY ORDWAY
DAVID BARON
ELSEWORLDS

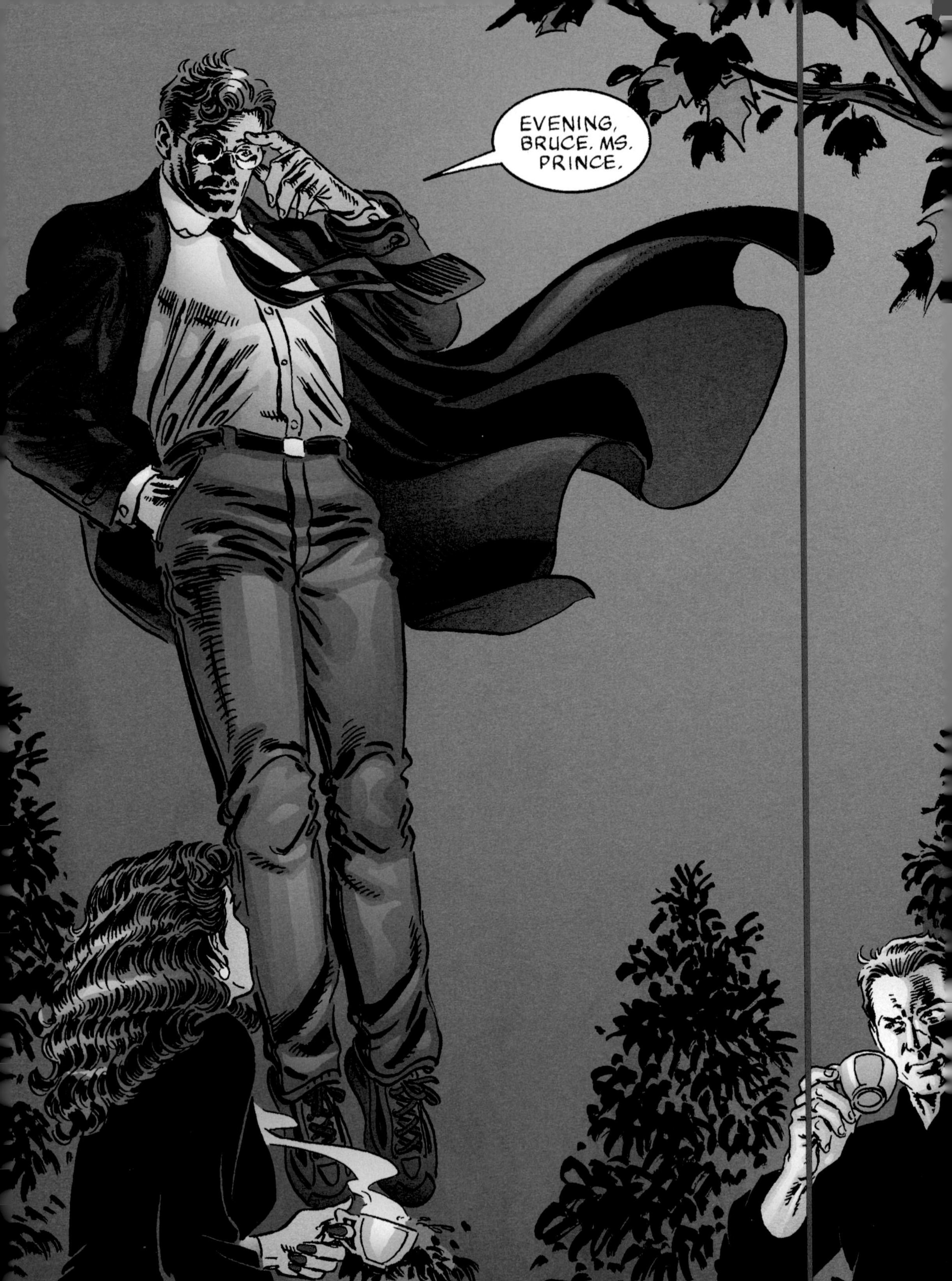
EVENING, BRUCE. MS. PRINCE.

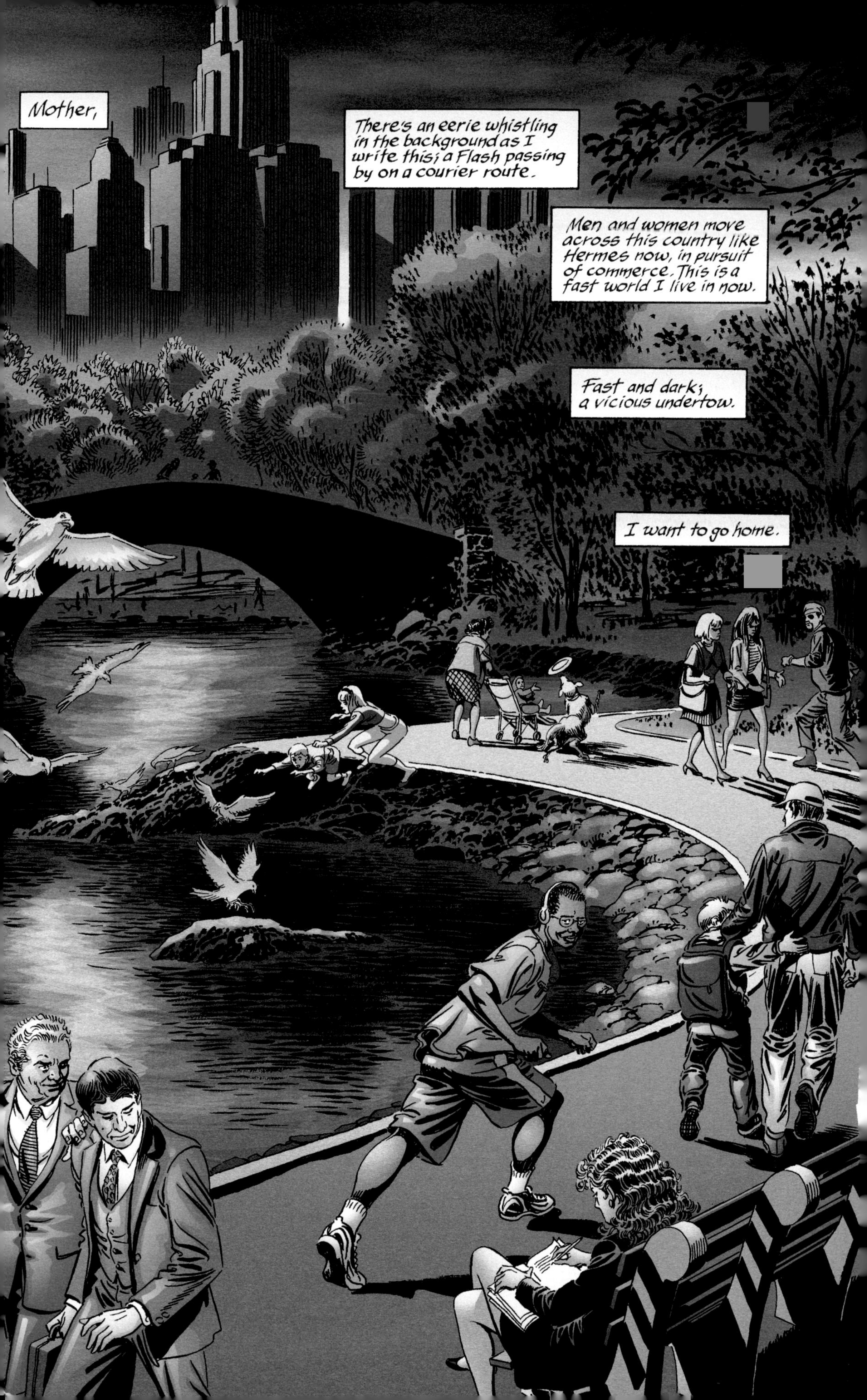
Mother,
There's an eerie whistling in the background as I write this; a Flash passing by on a courier route.
Men and women move across this country like Hermes now, in pursuit of commerce. This is a fast world I live in now.
Fast and dark; a vicious undertow.
I want to go home.

But I can't, of course. You know that as well as I do. Better than I do.

I am trapped here in Man's World, a civilization I learned of through viewscreens. Nothing prepared me for the way this place feels.

The VOICES. This is a city of voices, of constant chatter. There is no song here, Mother. Only the tinny riot of untrained voices from their radios, and the clatter of their talk.

I find myself longing for the days when their cars made noise.

GRAND CENTRAL STATION, PLEASE.

CUEROZ LIVERY

AIR GLIDE
$8.50 INITIAL CHARGE
$2.00 PER LOAD
$2.00 PER MIN.
$1.00 HOUR

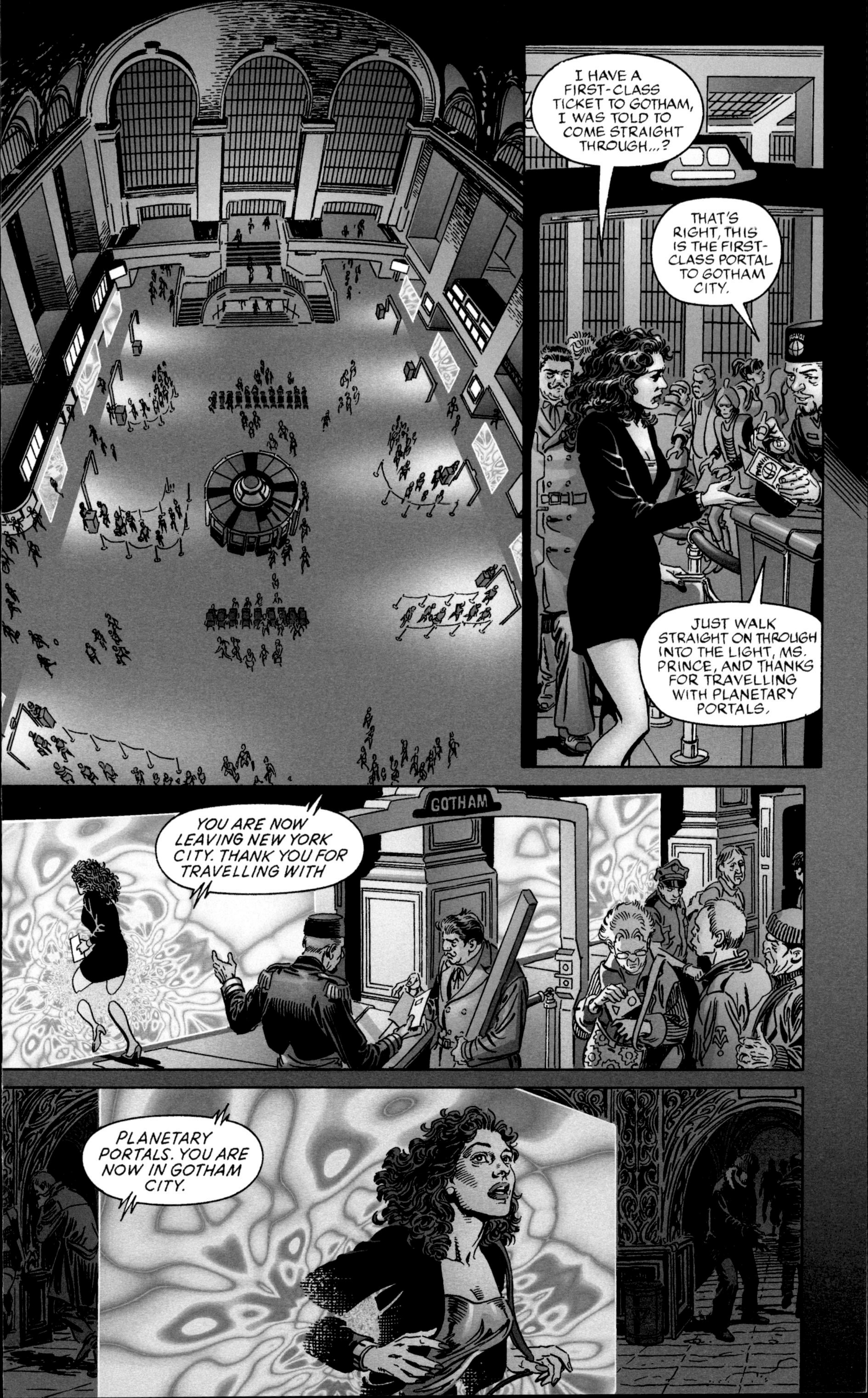
I HAVE A FIRST-CLASS TICKET TO GOTHAM, I WAS TOLD TO COME STRAIGHT THROUGH...?
THAT'S RIGHT, THIS IS THE FIRST-CLASS PORTAL TO GOTHAM CITY.
JUST WALK STRAIGHT ON THROUGH INTO THE LIGHT, MS. PRINCE, AND THANKS FOR TRAVELLING WITH PLANETARY PORTALS.
GOTHAM
YOU ARE NOW LEAVING NEW YORK CITY. THANK YOU FOR TRAVELLING WITH
PLANETARY PORTALS. YOU ARE NOW IN GOTHAM CITY.

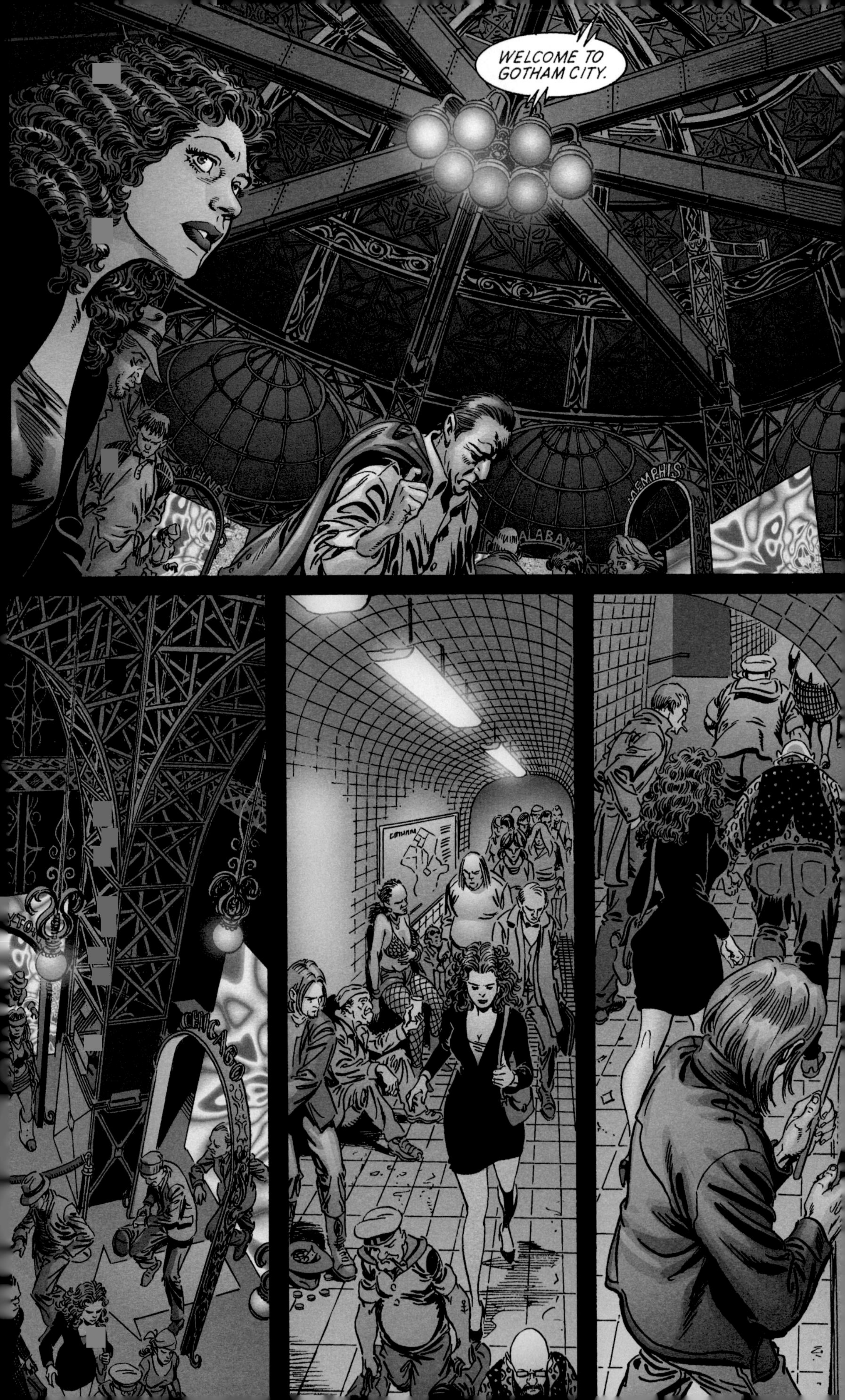
WELCOME TO GOTHAM CITY.
CHICAGO

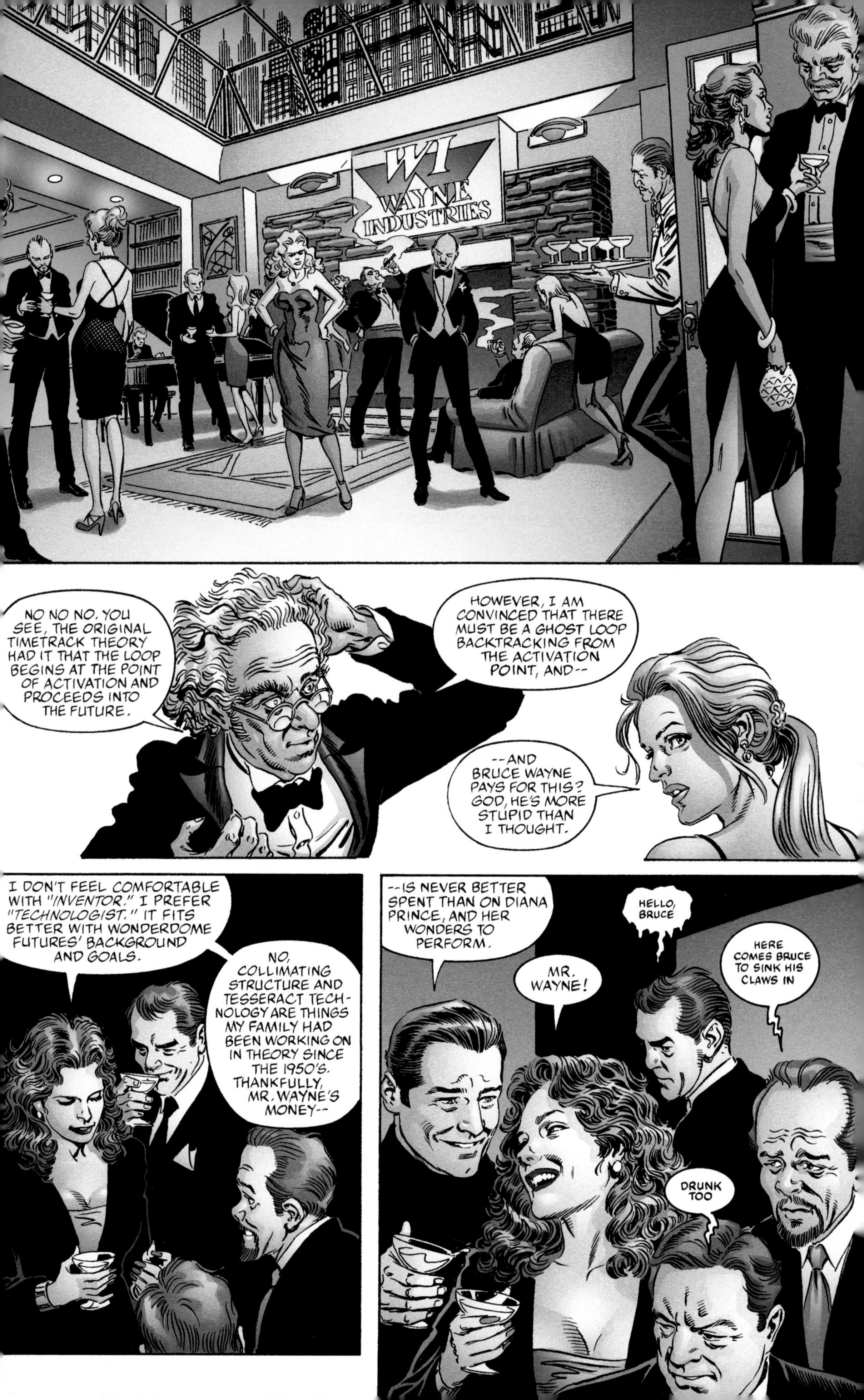
WI
WAYNE INDUSTRIES
NO NO NO. YOU SEE, THE ORIGINAL TIMETRACK THEORY HAD IT THAT THE LOOP BEGINS AT THE POINT OF ACTIVATION AND PROCEEDS INTO THE FUTURE.
HOWEVER, I AM CONVINCED THAT THERE MUST BE A GHOST LOOP BACKTRACKING FROM THE ACTIVATION POINT, AND--
--AND BRUCE WAYNE PAYS FOR THIS? GOD, HE'S MORE STUPID THAN I THOUGHT.
I DON'T FEEL COMFORTABLE WITH "INVENTOR." I PREFER "TECHNOLOGIST." IT FITS BETTER WITH WONDERDOME FUTURES' BACKGROUND AND GOALS.
NO, COLLIMATING STRUCTURE AND TESSERACT TECHNOLOGY ARE THINGS MY FAMILY HAD BEEN WORKING ON IN THEORY SINCE THE 1950'S. THANKFULLY, MR. WAYNE'S MONEY--
--IS NEVER BETTER SPENT THAN ON DIANA PRINCE, AND HER WONDERS TO PERFORM.
HELLO, BRUCE
MR. WAYNE!
HERE COMES BRUCE TO SINK HIS CLAWS IN
DRUNK TOO

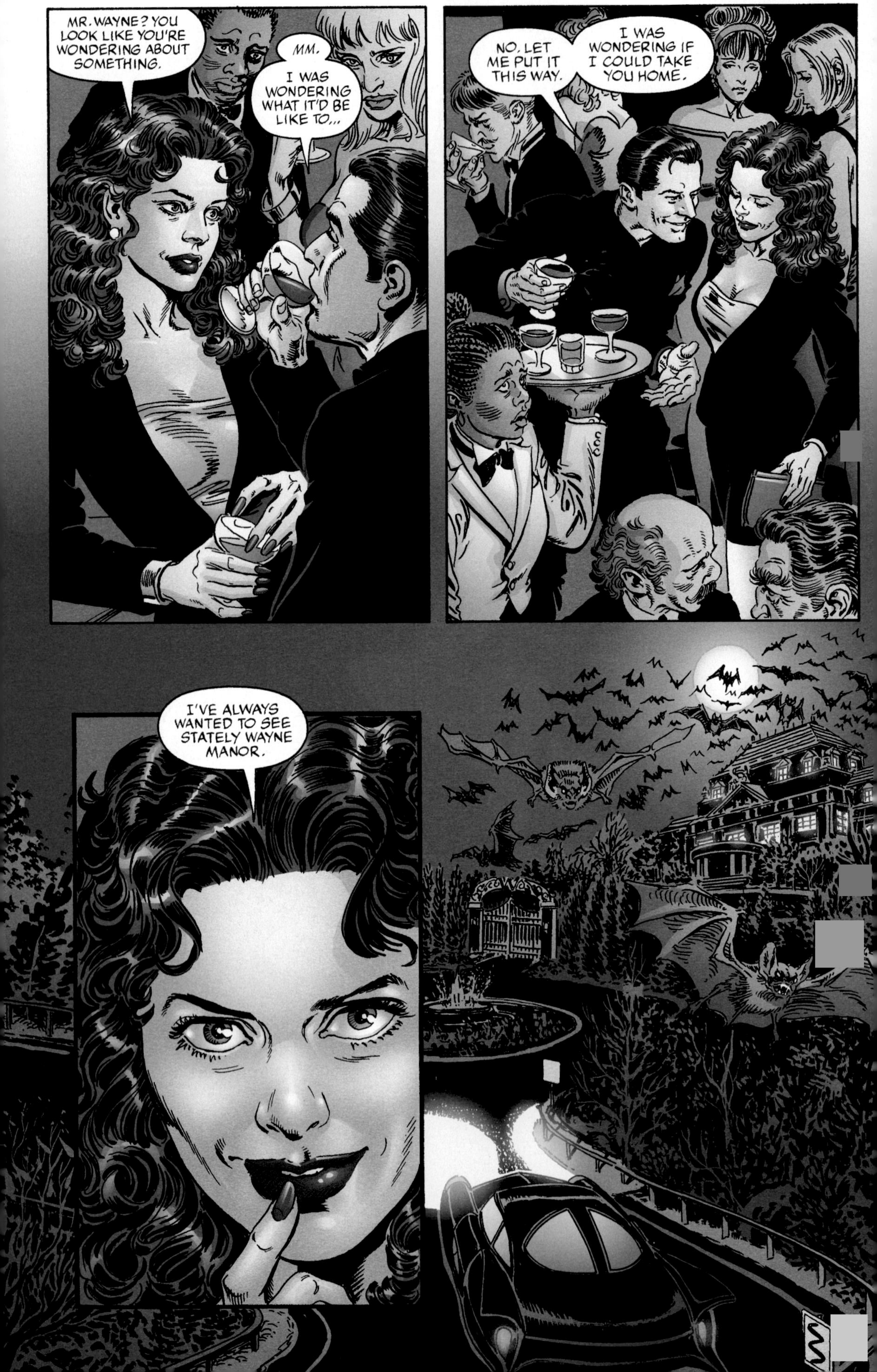
MR. WAYNE? YOU LOOK LIKE YOU'RE WONDERING ABOUT SOMETHING.
MM.
I WAS WONDERING WHAT IT'D BE LIKE TO...
NO. LET ME PUT IT THIS WAY.
I WAS WONDERING IF I COULD TAKE YOU HOME.
I'VE ALWAYS WANTED TO SEE STATELY WAYNE MANOR.

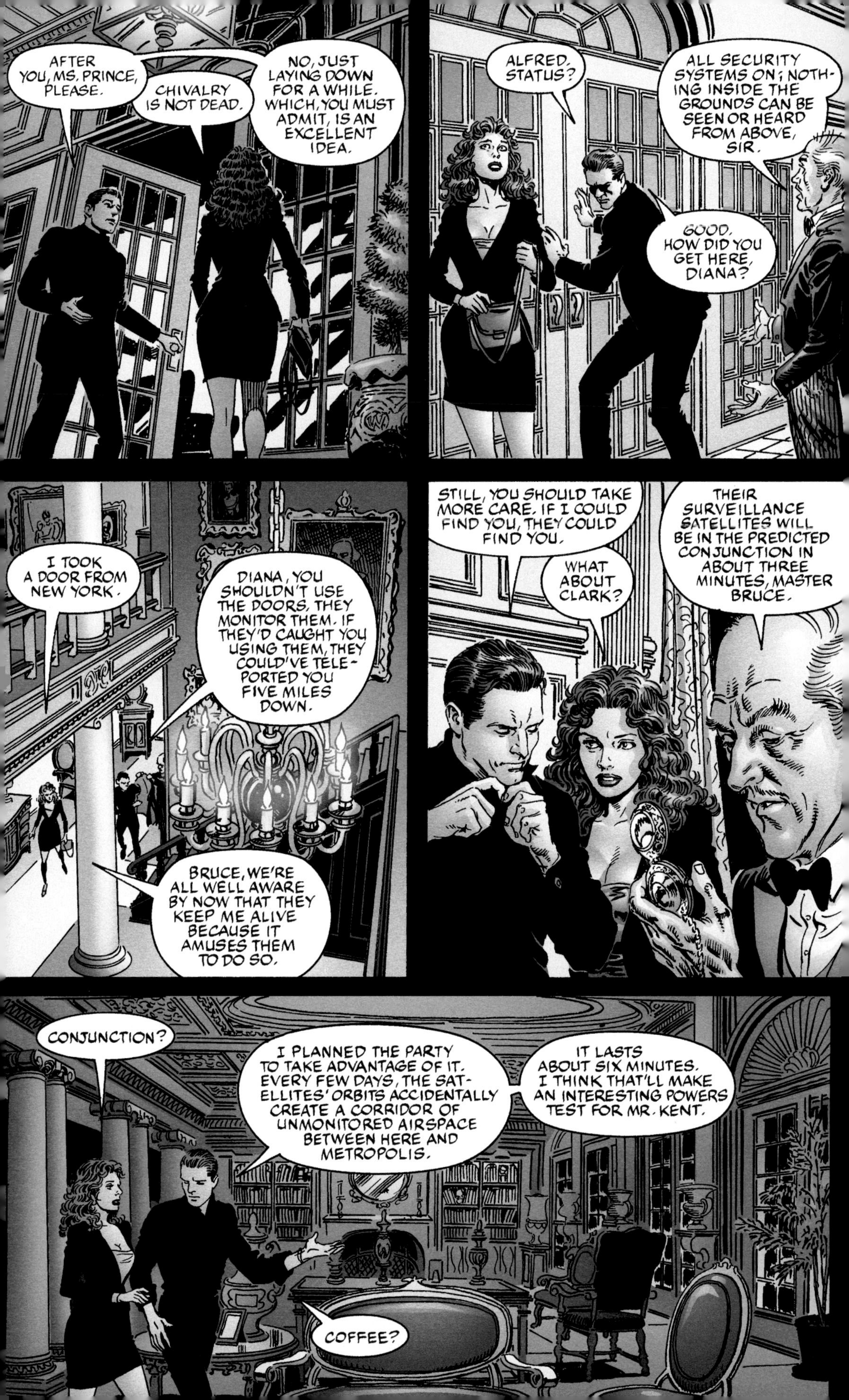
AFTER YOU, MS. PRINCE, PLEASE.
CHIVALRY IS NOT DEAD.
NO, JUST LAYING DOWN FOR A WHILE. WHICH, YOU MUST ADMIT, IS AN EXCELLENT IDEA.
ALFRED. STATUS?
ALL SECURITY SYSTEMS ON; NOTHING INSIDE THE GROUNDS CAN BE SEEN OR HEARD FROM ABOVE, SIR.
GOOD. HOW DID YOU GET HERE, DIANA?
I TOOK A DOOR FROM NEW YORK.
DIANA, YOU SHOULDN'T USE THE DOORS, THEY MONITOR THEM. IF THEY'D CAUGHT YOU USING THEM, THEY COULD'VE TELEPORTED YOU FIVE MILES DOWN.
BRUCE, WE'RE ALL WELL AWARE BY NOW THAT THEY KEEP ME ALIVE BECAUSE IT AMUSES THEM TO DO SO.
STILL, YOU SHOULD TAKE MORE CARE. IF I COULD FIND YOU, THEY COULD FIND YOU.
WHAT ABOUT CLARK?
THEIR SURVEILLANCE SATELLITES WILL BE IN THE PREDICTED CONJUNCTION IN ABOUT THREE MINUTES, MASTER BRUCE.
CONJUNCTION?
I PLANNED THE PARTY TO TAKE ADVANTAGE OF IT. EVERY FEW DAYS, THE SATELLITES' ORBITS ACCIDENTALLY CREATE A CORRIDOR OF UNMONITORED AIRSPACE BETWEEN HERE AND METROPOLIS.
IT LASTS ABOUT SIX MINUTES. I THINK THAT'LL MAKE AN INTERESTING POWERS TEST FOR MR. KENT.
COFFEE?

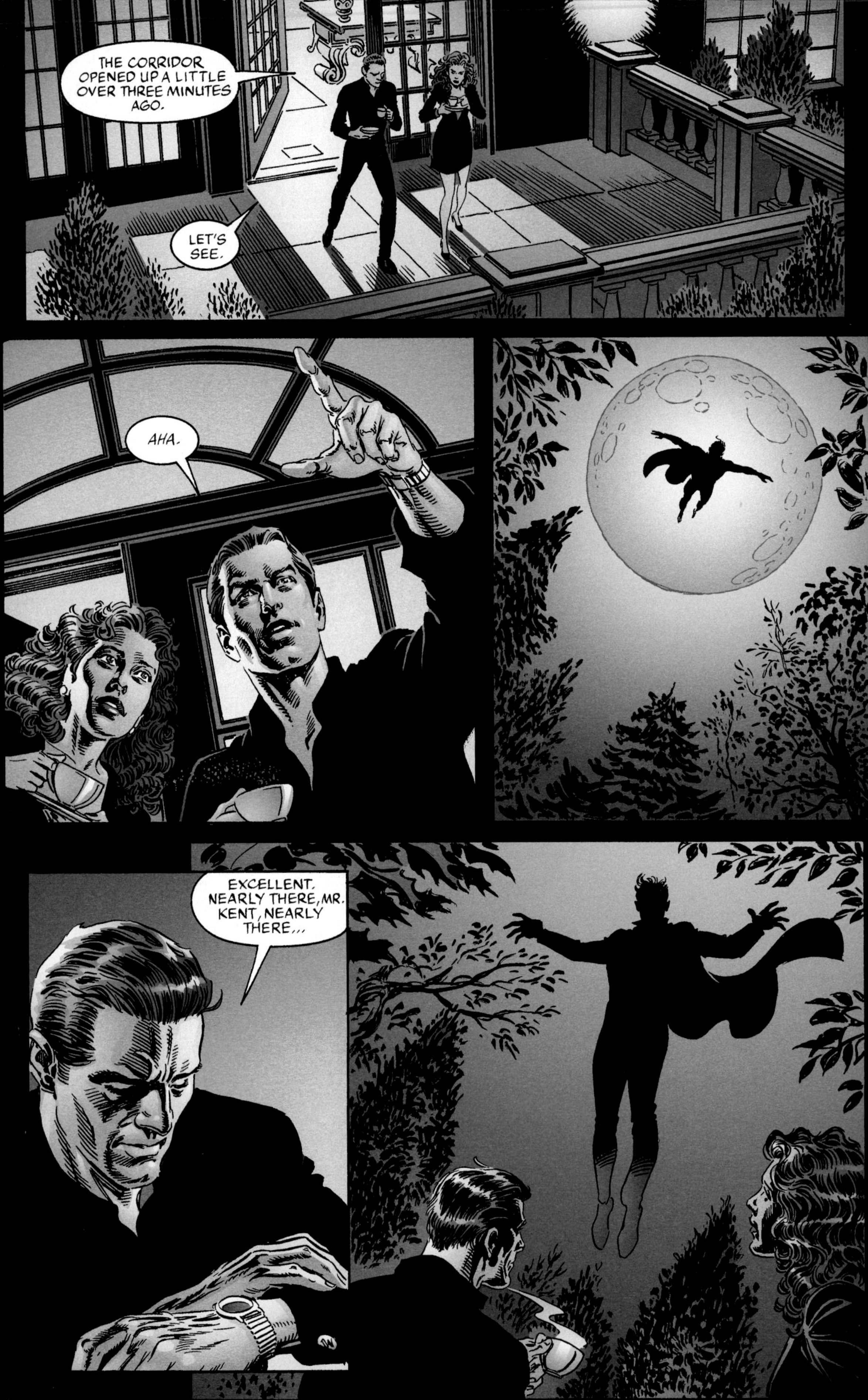
THE CORRIDOR OPENED UP A LITTLE OVER THREE MINUTES AGO.
LET'S SEE.
AHA.
EXCELLENT. NEARLY THERE, MR. KENT, NEARLY THERE...

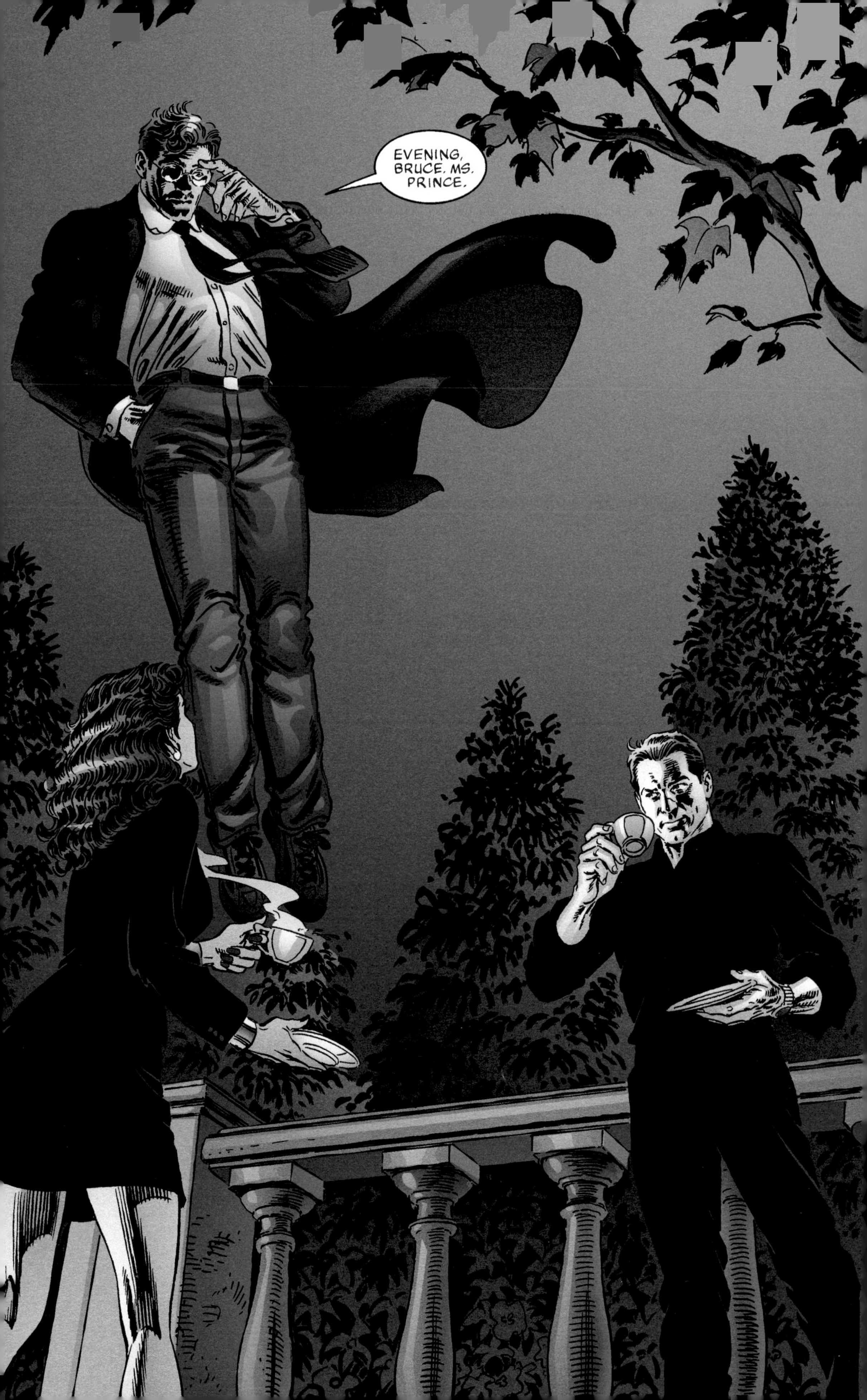
EVENING, BRUCE. MS. PRINCE.

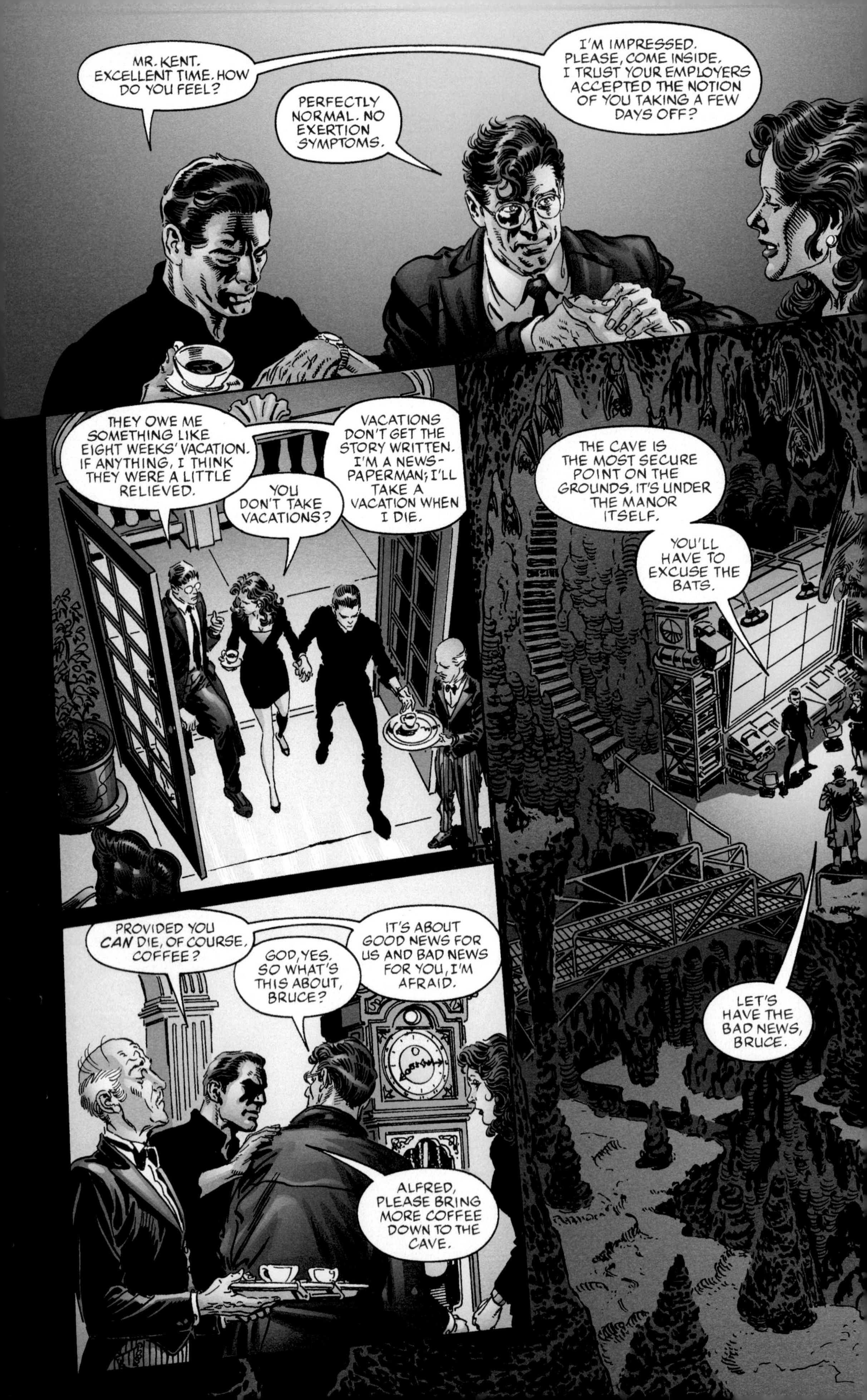
MR. KENT. EXCELLENT TIME. HOW DO YOU FEEL?
PERFECTLY NORMAL. NO EXERTION SYMPTOMS.
I'M IMPRESSED. PLEASE, COME INSIDE. I TRUST YOUR EMPLOYERS ACCEPTED THE NOTION OF YOU TAKING A FEW DAYS OFF?
THEY OWE ME SOMETHING LIKE EIGHT WEEKS' VACATION. IF ANYTHING, I THINK THEY WERE A LITTLE RELIEVED.
YOU DON'T TAKE VACATIONS?
VACATIONS DON'T GET THE STORY WRITTEN. I'M A NEWS-PAPERMAN; I'LL TAKE A VACATION WHEN I DIE.
PROVIDED YOU CAN DIE, OF COURSE. COFFEE?
GOD, YES. SO WHAT'S THIS ABOUT, BRUCE?
IT'S ABOUT GOOD NEWS FOR US AND BAD NEWS FOR YOU, I'M AFRAID.
ALFRED, PLEASE BRING MORE COFFEE DOWN TO THE CAVE.
THE CAVE IS THE MOST SECURE POINT ON THE GROUNDS. IT'S UNDER THE MANOR ITSELF.
YOU'LL HAVE TO EXCUSE THE BATS.
LET'S HAVE THE BAD NEWS, BRUCE.

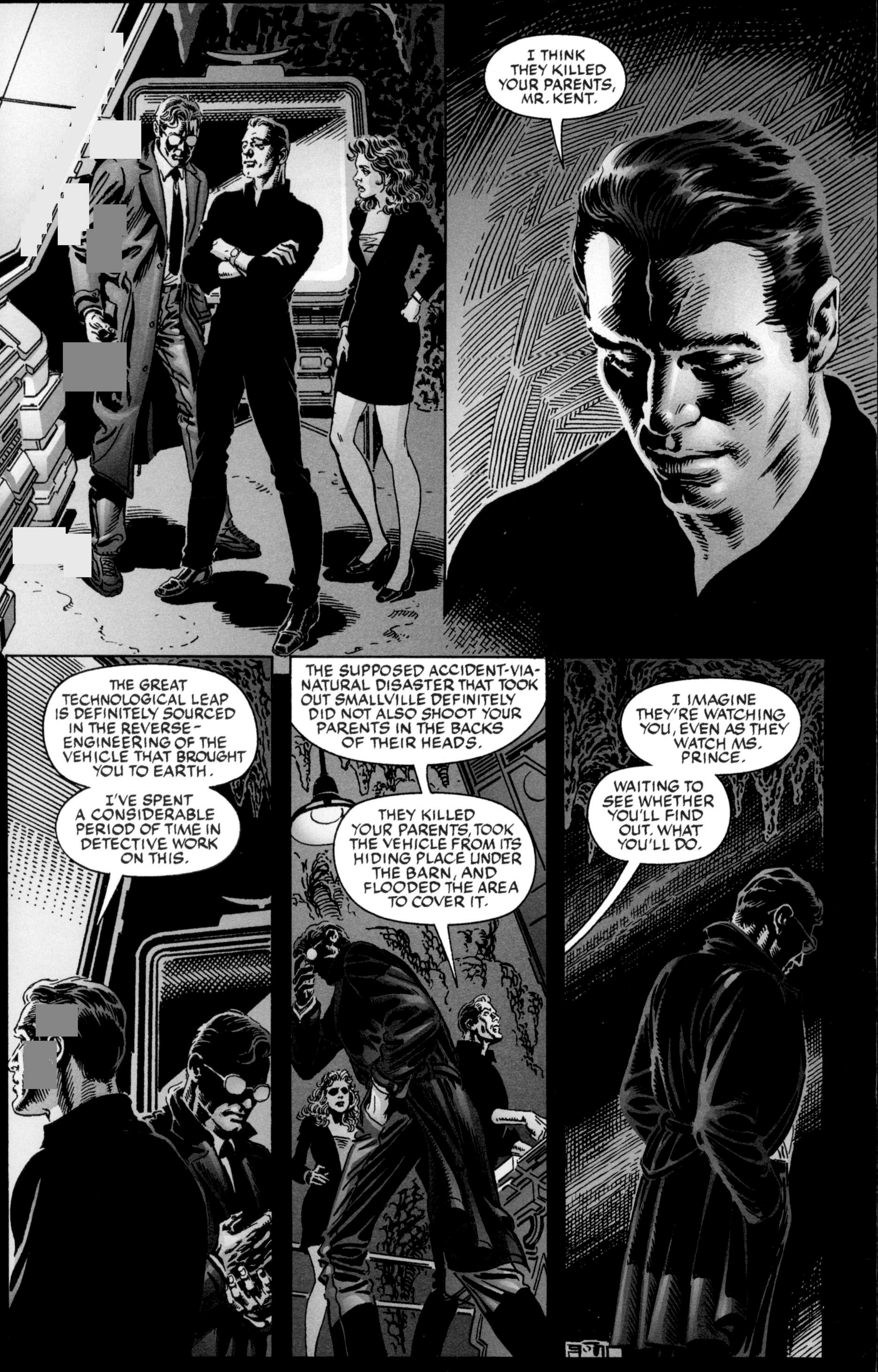
I THINK THEY KILLED YOUR PARENTS, MR. KENT.
THE GREAT TECHNOLOGICAL LEAP IS DEFINITELY SOURCED IN THE REVERSE-ENGINEERING OF THE VEHICLE THAT BROUGHT YOU TO EARTH.
I'VE SPENT A CONSIDERABLE PERIOD OF TIME IN DETECTIVE WORK ON THIS.
THE SUPPOSED ACCIDENT-VIA-NATURAL DISASTER THAT TOOK OUT SMALLVILLE DEFINITELY DID NOT ALSO SHOOT YOUR PARENTS IN THE BACKS OF THEIR HEADS.
THEY KILLED YOUR PARENTS, TOOK THE VEHICLE FROM ITS HIDING PLACE UNDER THE BARN, AND FLOODED THE AREA TO COVER IT.
I IMAGINE THEY'RE WATCHING YOU, EVEN AS THEY WATCH MS. PRINCE.
WAITING TO SEE WHETHER YOU'LL FIND OUT. WHAT YOU'LL DO.

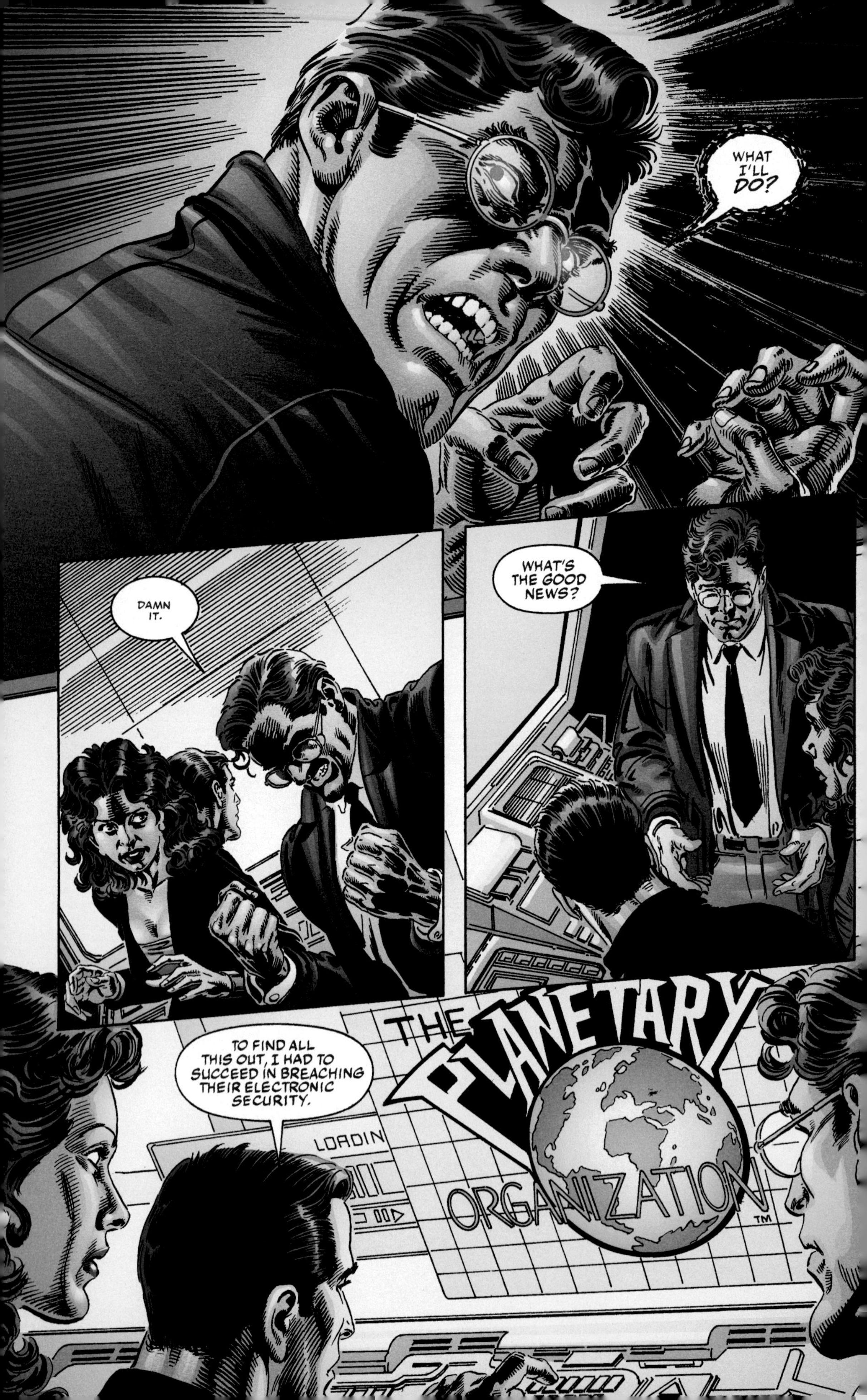
WHAT I'LL DO?
DAMN IT.
WHAT'S THE GOOD NEWS?
THE PLANETARY ORGANIZATION
TO FIND ALL THIS OUT, I HAD TO SUCCEED IN BREACHING THEIR ELECTRONIC SECURITY.
LOADIN

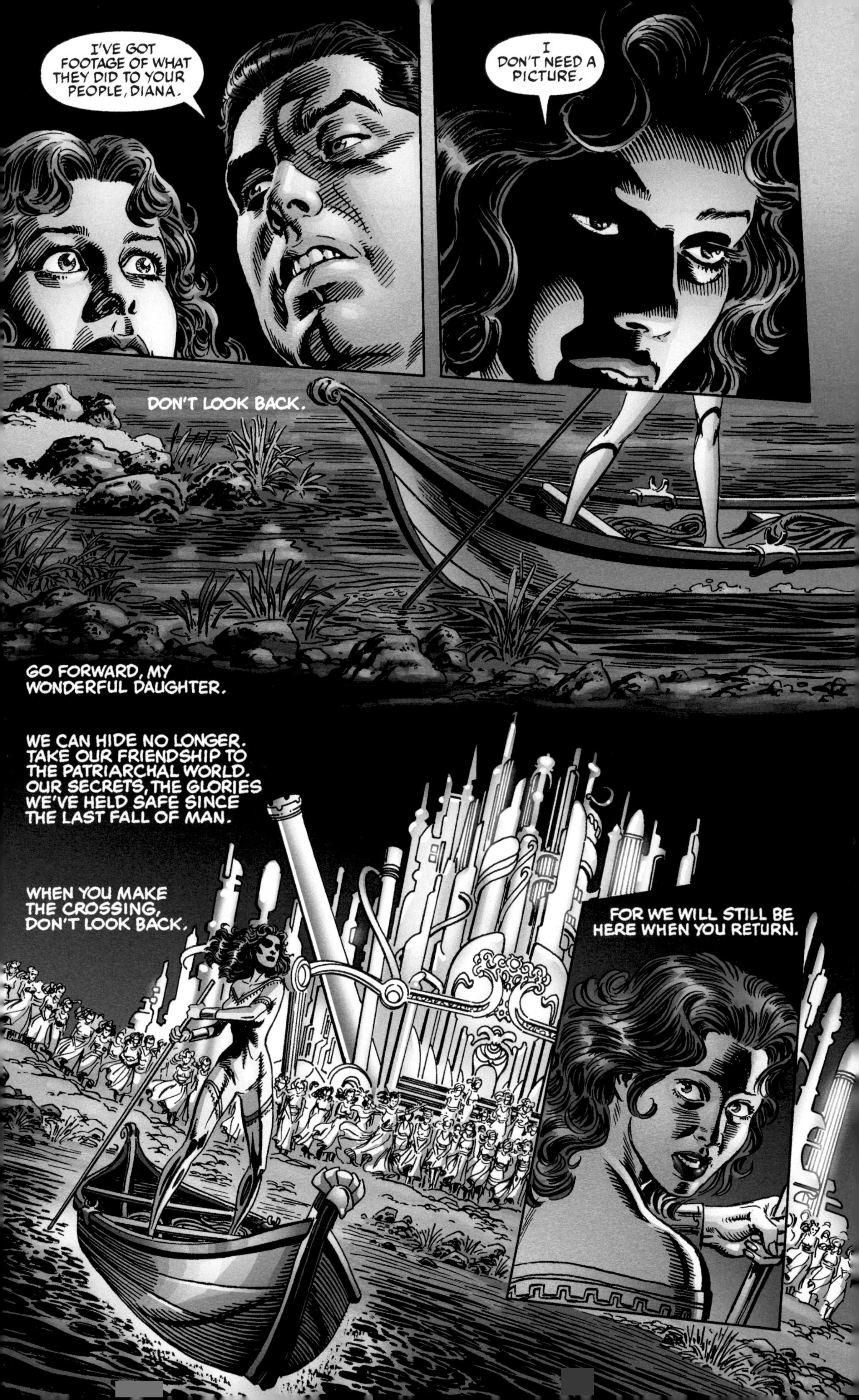

I'VE GOT FOOTAGE OF WHAT THEY DID TO YOUR PEOPLE, DIANA.
I DON'T NEED A PICTURE.
DON'T LOOK BACK.
GO FORWARD, MY WONDERFUL DAUGHTER.
WE CAN HIDE NO LONGER. TAKE OUR FRIENDSHIP TO THE PATRIARCHAL WORLD. OUR SECRETS, THE GLORIES WE'VE HELD SAFE SINCE THE LAST FALL OF MAN.
WHEN YOU MAKE THE CROSSING, DON'T LOOK BACK.
FOR WE WILL STILL BE HERE WHEN YOU RETURN.

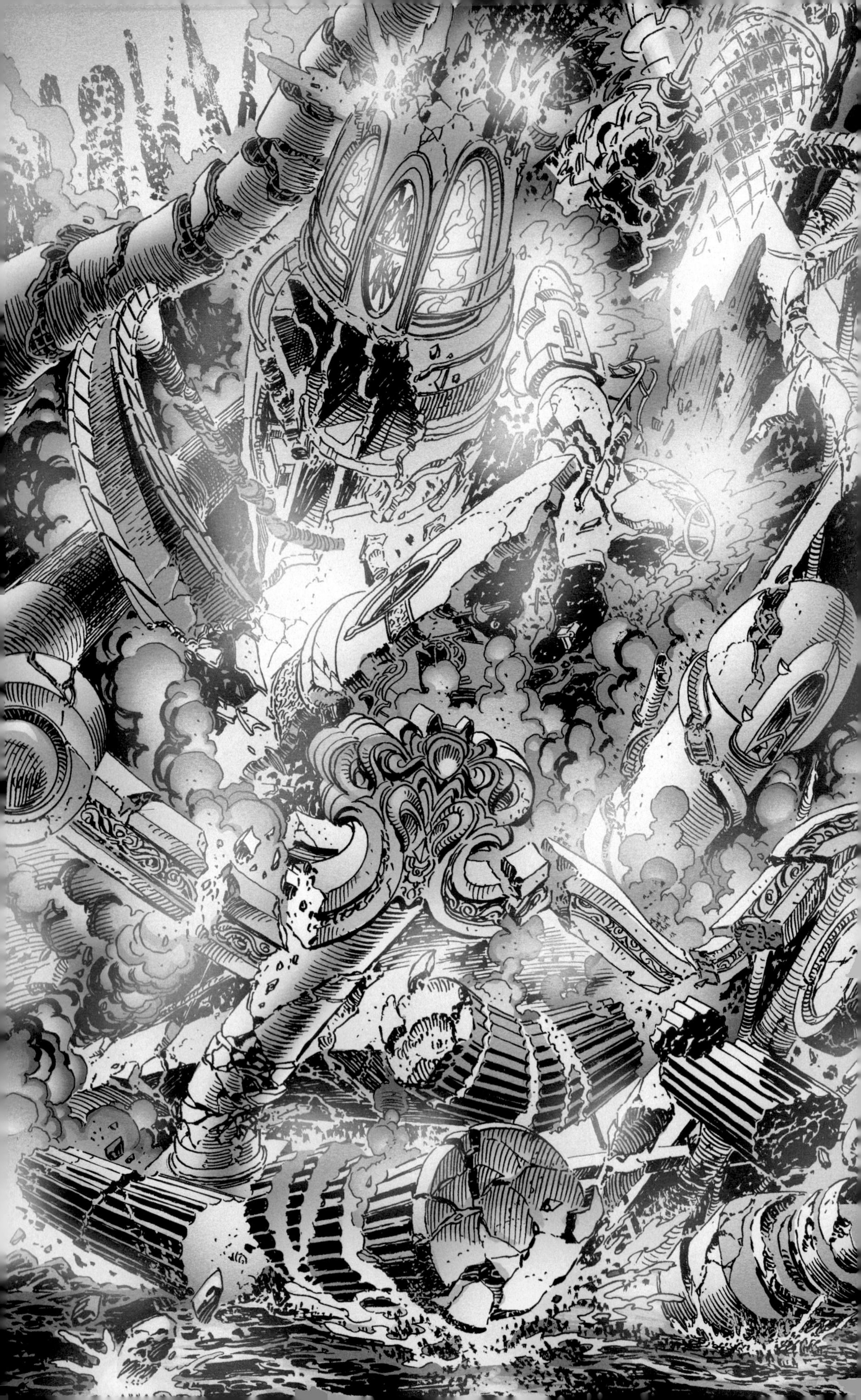

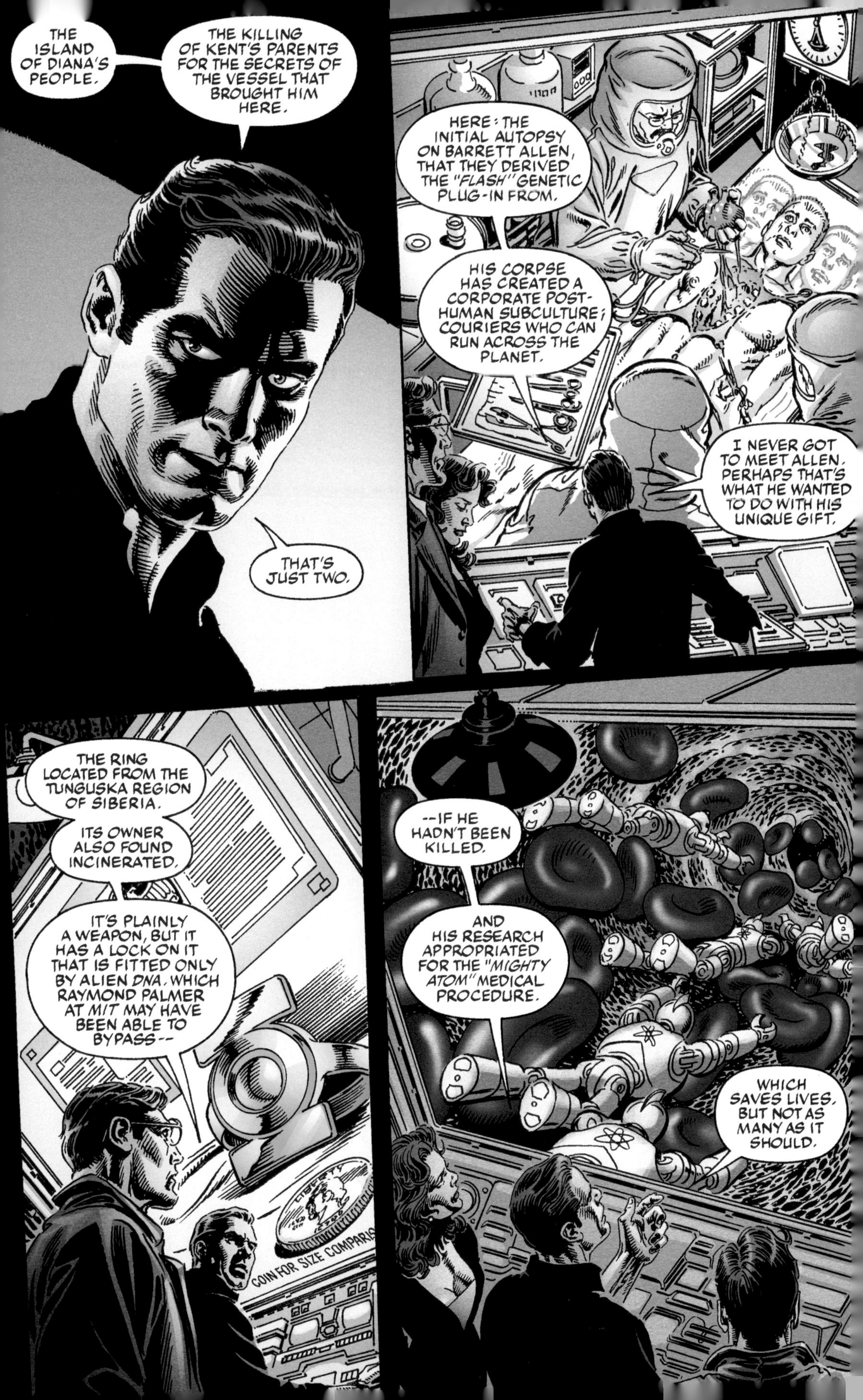
THE ISLAND OF DIANA'S PEOPLE.
THE KILLING OF KENT'S PARENTS FOR THE SECRETS OF THE VESSEL THAT BROUGHT HIM HERE.
THAT'S JUST TWO.
HERE: THE INITIAL AUTOPSY ON BARRETT ALLEN, THAT THEY DERIVED THE "*FLASH*" GENETIC PLUG-IN FROM.
HIS CORPSE HAS CREATED A CORPORATE POST-HUMAN *SUBCULTURE*; COURIERS WHO CAN RUN ACROSS THE PLANET.
I NEVER GOT TO MEET ALLEN. PERHAPS THAT'S WHAT HE WANTED TO DO WITH HIS UNIQUE GIFT.
THE RING LOCATED FROM THE TUNGUSKA REGION OF SIBERIA.
ITS OWNER ALSO FOUND INCINERATED.
IT'S PLAINLY A WEAPON, BUT IT HAS A LOCK ON IT THAT IS FITTED ONLY BY ALIEN *DNA*. WHICH RAYMOND PALMER AT *MIT* MAY HAVE BEEN ABLE TO BYPASS--
COIN FOR SIZE COMPARIS
--IF HE HADN'T BEEN KILLED.
AND HIS RESEARCH APPROPRIATED FOR THE "*MIGHTY ATOM*" MEDICAL PROCEDURE.
WHICH SAVES LIVES, BUT NOT AS MANY AS IT SHOULD.

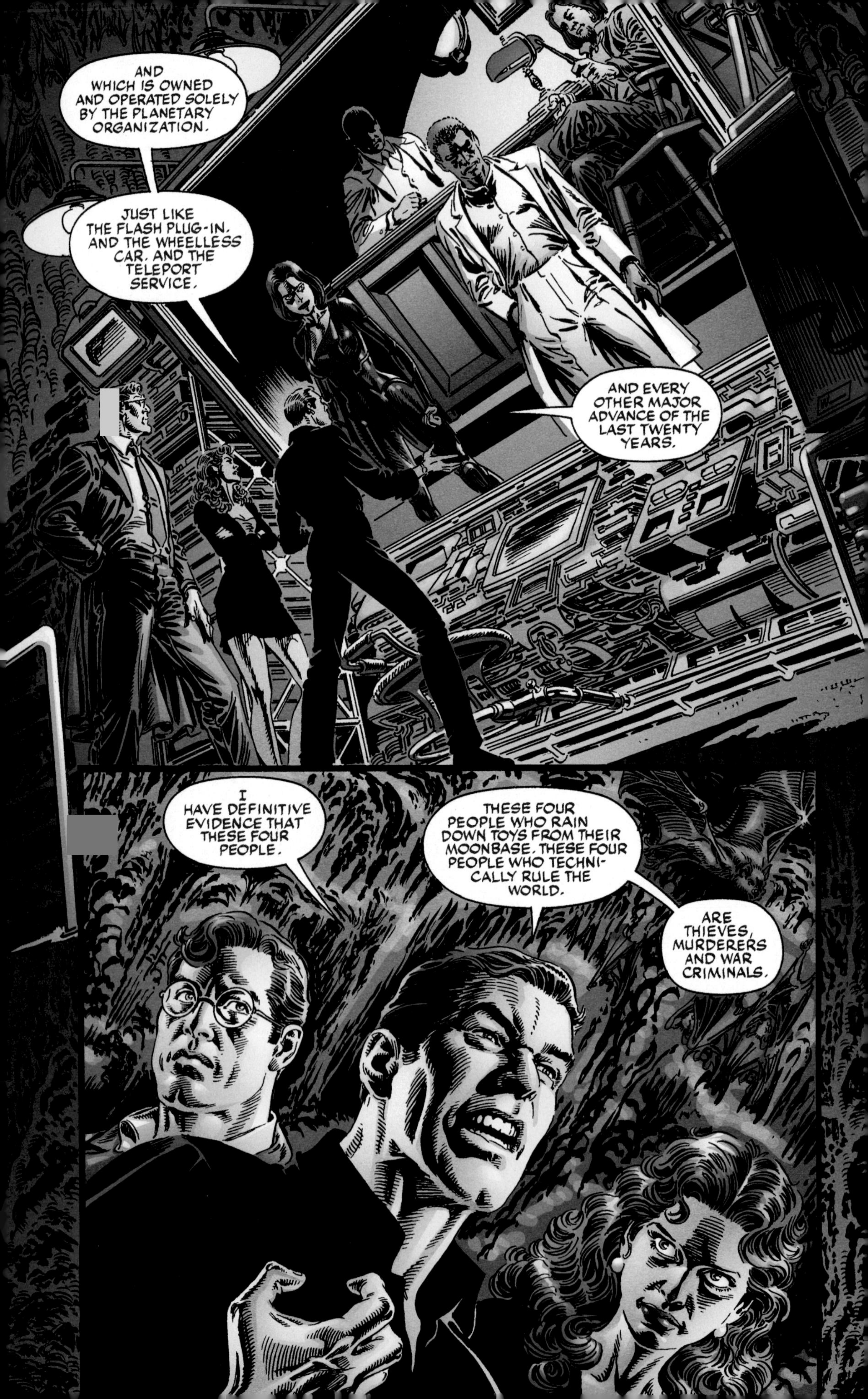
AND WHICH IS OWNED AND OPERATED SOLELY BY THE PLANETARY ORGANIZATION.
JUST LIKE THE FLASH PLUG-IN, AND THE WHEELLESS CAR, AND THE TELEPORT SERVICE.
AND EVERY OTHER MAJOR ADVANCE OF THE LAST TWENTY YEARS.
I HAVE DEFINITIVE EVIDENCE THAT THESE FOUR PEOPLE.
THESE FOUR PEOPLE WHO RAIN DOWN TOYS FROM THEIR MOONBASE, THESE FOUR PEOPLE WHO TECHNICALLY RULE THE WORLD.
ARE THIEVES, MURDERERS AND WAR CRIMINALS.

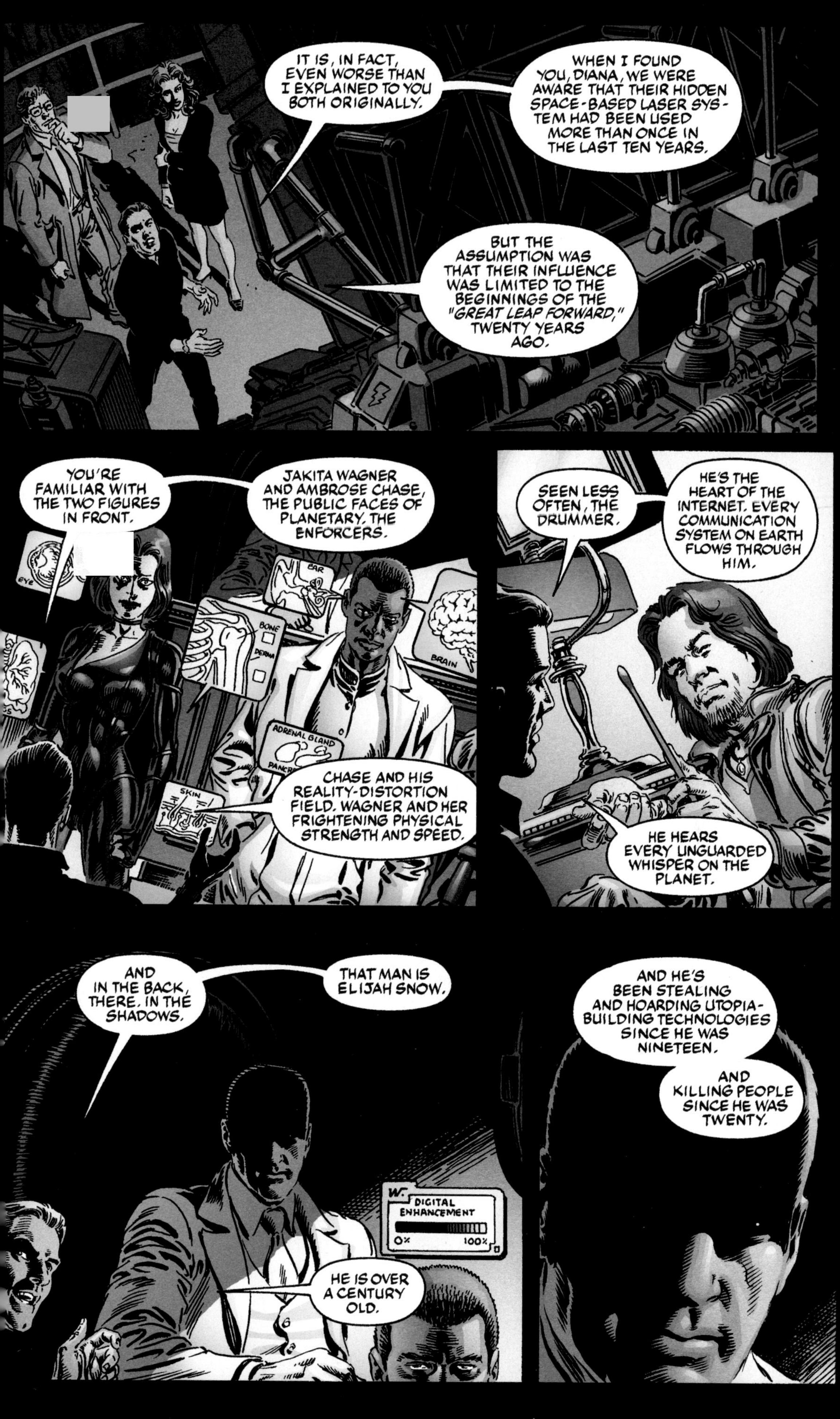
IT IS, IN FACT, EVEN WORSE THAN I EXPLAINED TO YOU BOTH ORIGINALLY.
WHEN I FOUND YOU, DIANA, WE WERE AWARE THAT THEIR HIDDEN SPACE-BASED LASER SYSTEM HAD BEEN USED MORE THAN ONCE IN THE LAST TEN YEARS.
BUT THE ASSUMPTION WAS THAT THEIR INFLUENCE WAS LIMITED TO THE BEGINNINGS OF THE *"GREAT LEAP FORWARD,"* TWENTY YEARS AGO.
YOU'RE FAMILIAR WITH THE TWO FIGURES IN FRONT.
JAKITA WAGNER AND AMBROSE CHASE, THE PUBLIC FACES OF PLANETARY. THE ENFORCERS.
EYE
EAR
BONE
DERMA
BRAIN
ADRENAL GLAND
SKIN
CHASE AND HIS REALITY-DISTORTION FIELD. WAGNER AND HER FRIGHTENING PHYSICAL STRENGTH AND SPEED.
SEEN LESS OFTEN, THE DRUMMER.
HE'S THE HEART OF THE INTERNET. EVERY COMMUNICATION SYSTEM ON EARTH FLOWS THROUGH HIM.
HE HEARS EVERY UNGUARDED WHISPER ON THE PLANET.
AND IN THE BACK, THERE, IN THE SHADOWS.
THAT MAN IS ELIJAH SNOW.
W.
DIGITAL ENHANCEMENT
0%
100%
HE IS OVER A CENTURY OLD.
AND HE'S BEEN STEALING AND HOARDING UTOPIA-BUILDING TECHNOLOGIES SINCE HE WAS NINETEEN.
AND KILLING PEOPLE SINCE HE WAS TWENTY.

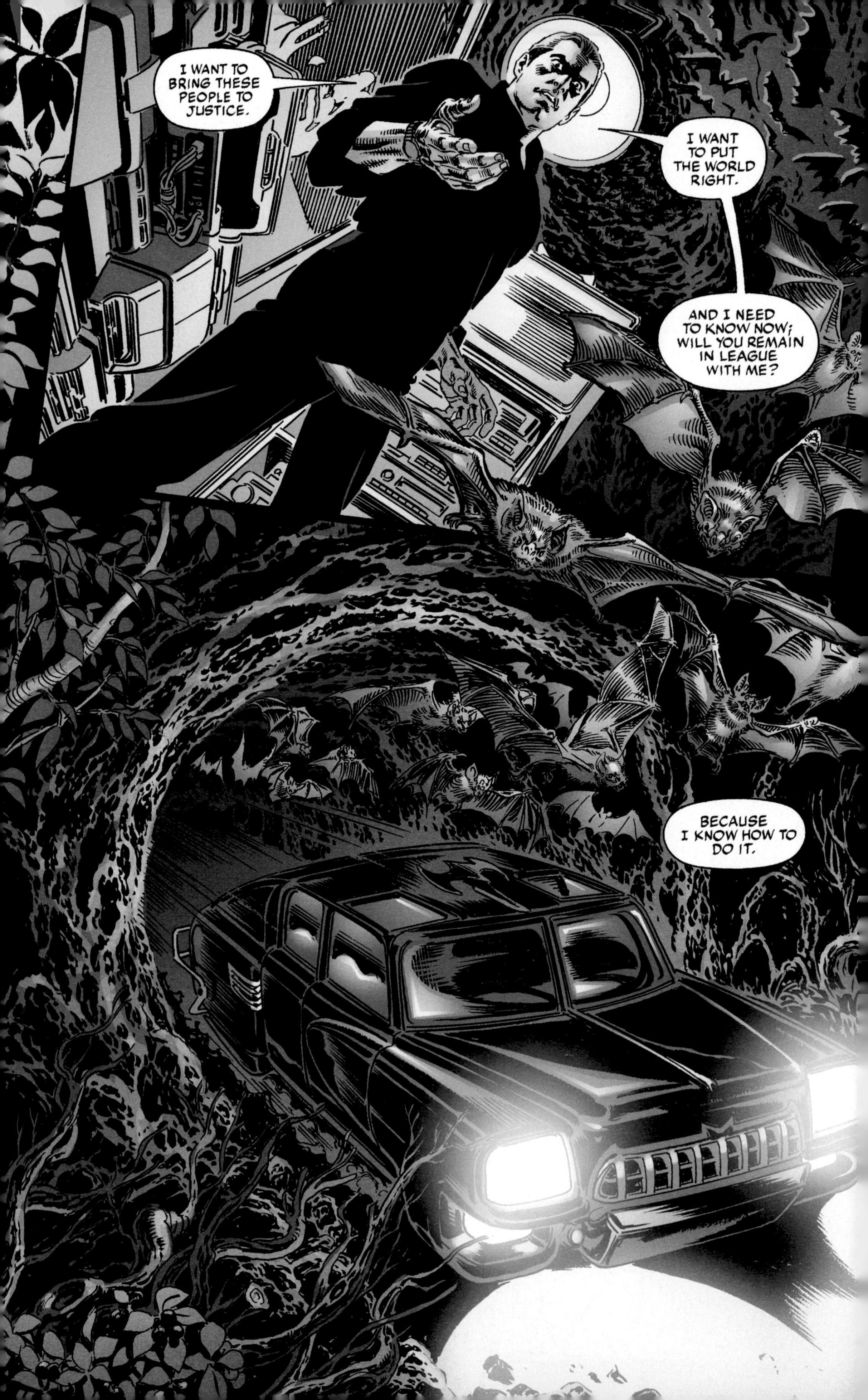
I WANT TO BRING THESE PEOPLE TO JUSTICE.
I WANT TO PUT THE WORLD RIGHT.
AND I NEED TO KNOW NOW; WILL YOU REMAIN IN LEAGUE WITH ME?
BECAUSE I KNOW HOW TO DO IT.

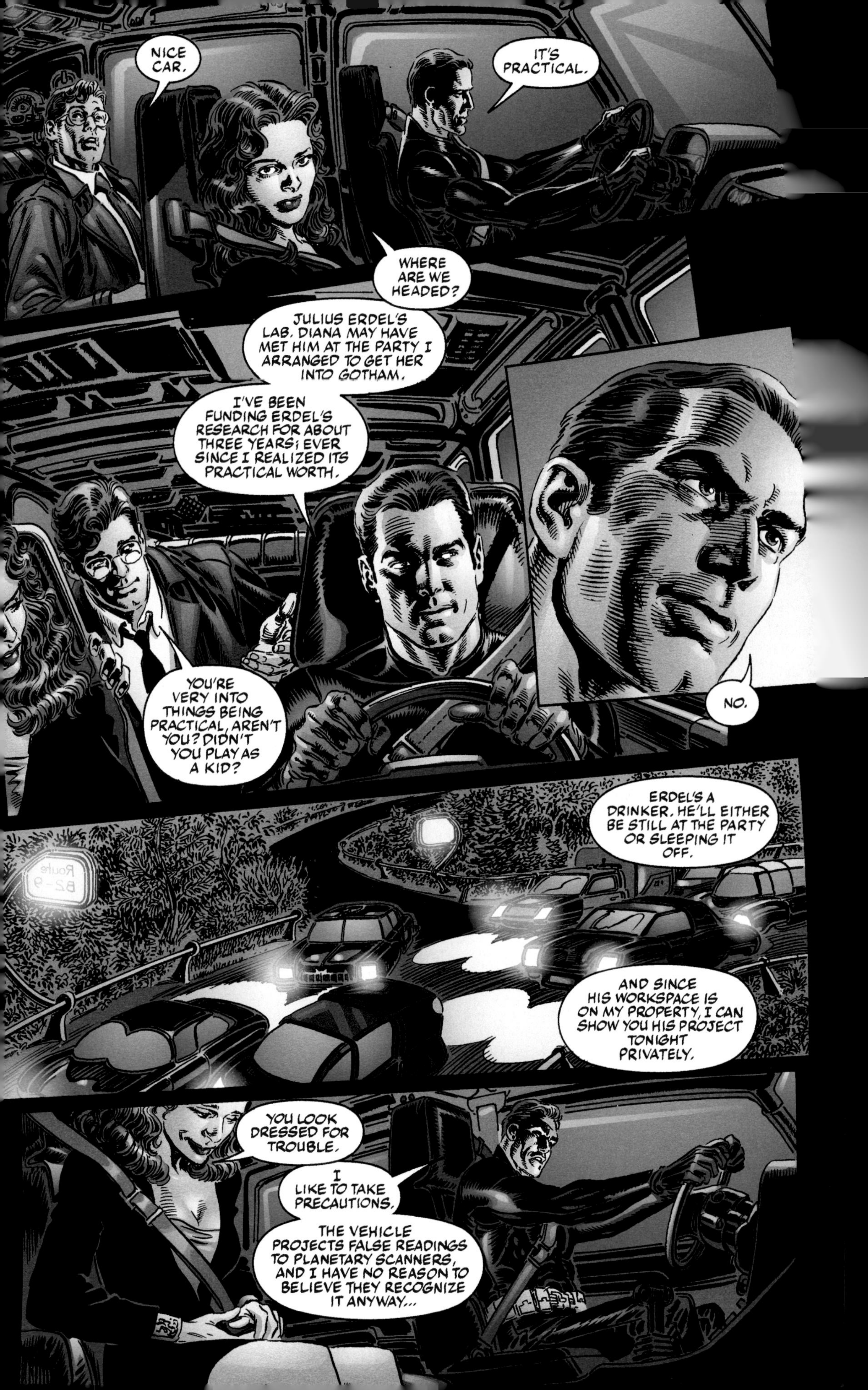
NICE CAR.
IT'S PRACTICAL.
WHERE ARE WE HEADED?
JULIUS ERDEL'S LAB. DIANA MAY HAVE MET HIM AT THE PARTY I ARRANGED TO GET HER INTO GOTHAM.
I'VE BEEN FUNDING ERDEL'S RESEARCH FOR ABOUT THREE YEARS; EVER SINCE I REALIZED ITS PRACTICAL WORTH.
YOU'RE VERY INTO THINGS BEING PRACTICAL, AREN'T YOU? DIDN'T YOU PLAY AS A KID?
NO.
Route BZ-9
ERDEL'S A DRINKER. HE'LL EITHER BE STILL AT THE PARTY OR SLEEPING IT OFF.
AND SINCE HIS WORKSPACE IS ON MY PROPERTY, I CAN SHOW YOU HIS PROJECT TONIGHT PRIVATELY.
YOU LOOK DRESSED FOR TROUBLE.
I LIKE TO TAKE PRECAUTIONS.
THE VEHICLE PROJECTS FALSE READINGS TO PLANETARY SCANNERS, AND I HAVE NO REASON TO BELIEVE THEY RECOGNIZE IT ANYWAY...

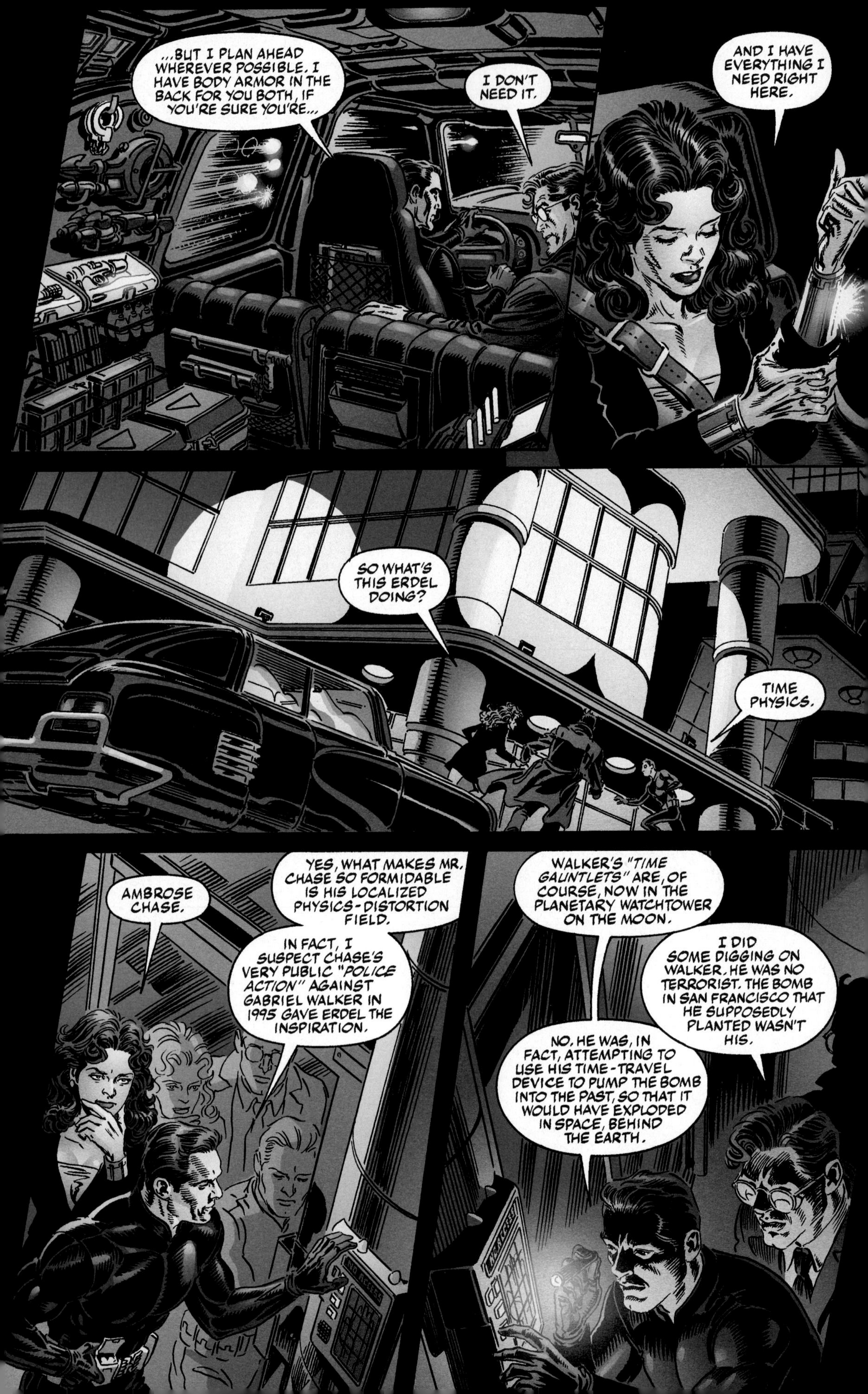
...BUT I PLAN AHEAD WHEREVER POSSIBLE. I HAVE BODY ARMOR IN THE BACK FOR YOU BOTH, IF YOU'RE SURE YOU'RE...
I DON'T NEED IT.
AND I HAVE EVERYTHING I NEED RIGHT HERE.
SO WHAT'S THIS ERDEL DOING?
TIME PHYSICS.
AMBROSE CHASE.
YES, WHAT MAKES MR. CHASE SO FORMIDABLE IS HIS LOCALIZED PHYSICS-DISTORTION FIELD.
IN FACT, I SUSPECT CHASE'S VERY PUBLIC "POLICE ACTION" AGAINST GABRIEL WALKER IN 1995 GAVE ERDEL THE INSPIRATION.
WALKER'S "TIME GAUNTLETS" ARE, OF COURSE, NOW IN THE PLANETARY WATCHTOWER ON THE MOON.
I DID SOME DIGGING ON WALKER. HE WAS NO TERRORIST. THE BOMB IN SAN FRANCISCO THAT HE SUPPOSEDLY PLANTED WASN'T HIS.
NO, HE WAS, IN FACT, ATTEMPTING TO USE HIS TIME-TRAVEL DEVICE TO PUMP THE BOMB INTO THE PAST, SO THAT IT WOULD HAVE EXPLODED IN SPACE, BEHIND THE EARTH.

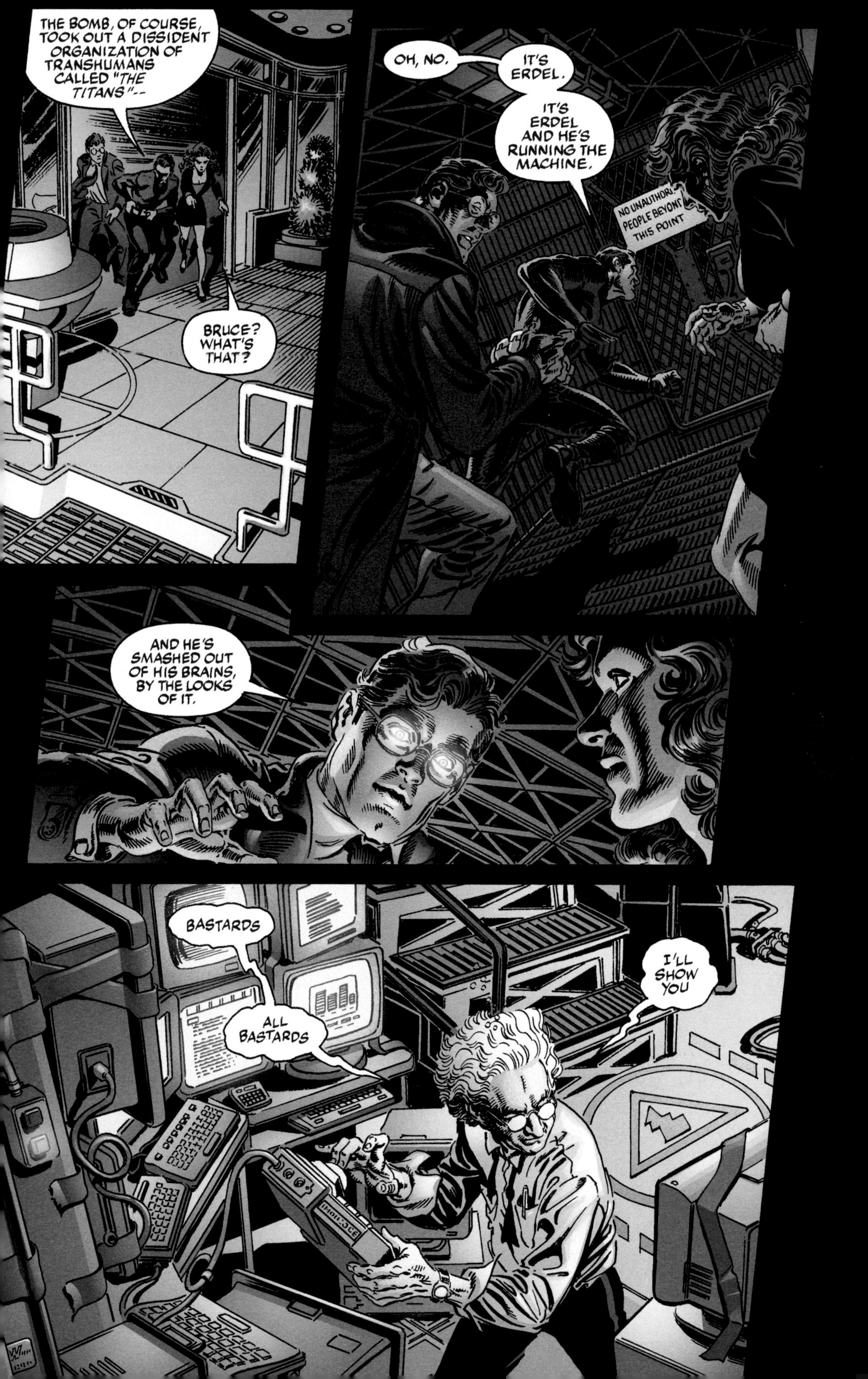
THE BOMB, OF COURSE, TOOK OUT A DISSIDENT ORGANIZATION OF TRANSHUMANS CALLED "THE TITANS"--
BRUCE? WHAT'S THAT?
OH, NO.
IT'S ERDEL.
IT'S ERDEL AND HE'S RUNNING THE MACHINE.
NO UNAUTHORI PEOPLE BEYOND THIS POINT
AND HE'S SMASHED OUT OF HIS BRAINS, BY THE LOOKS OF IT.
BASTARDS
ALL BASTARDS
I'LL SHOW YOU

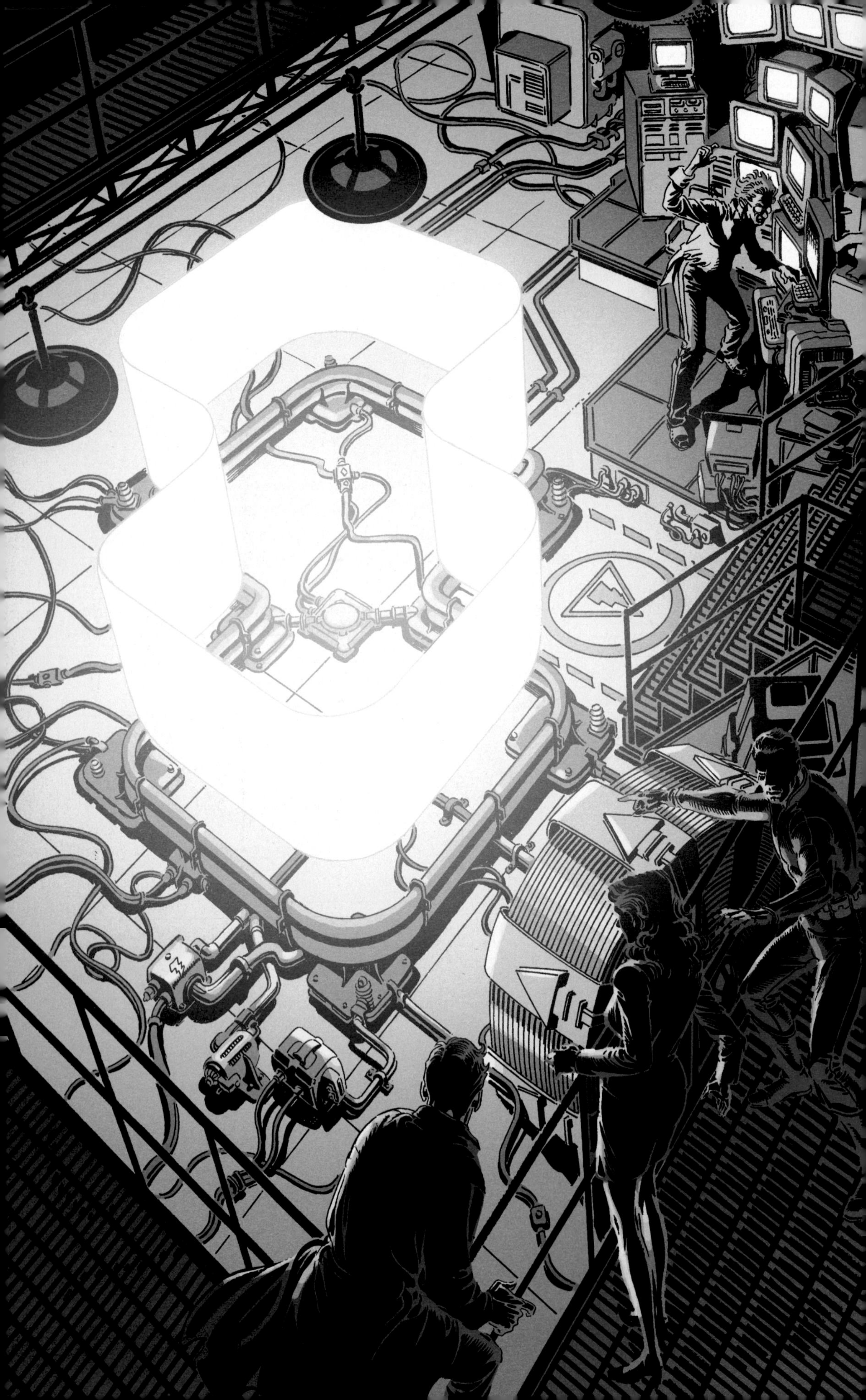

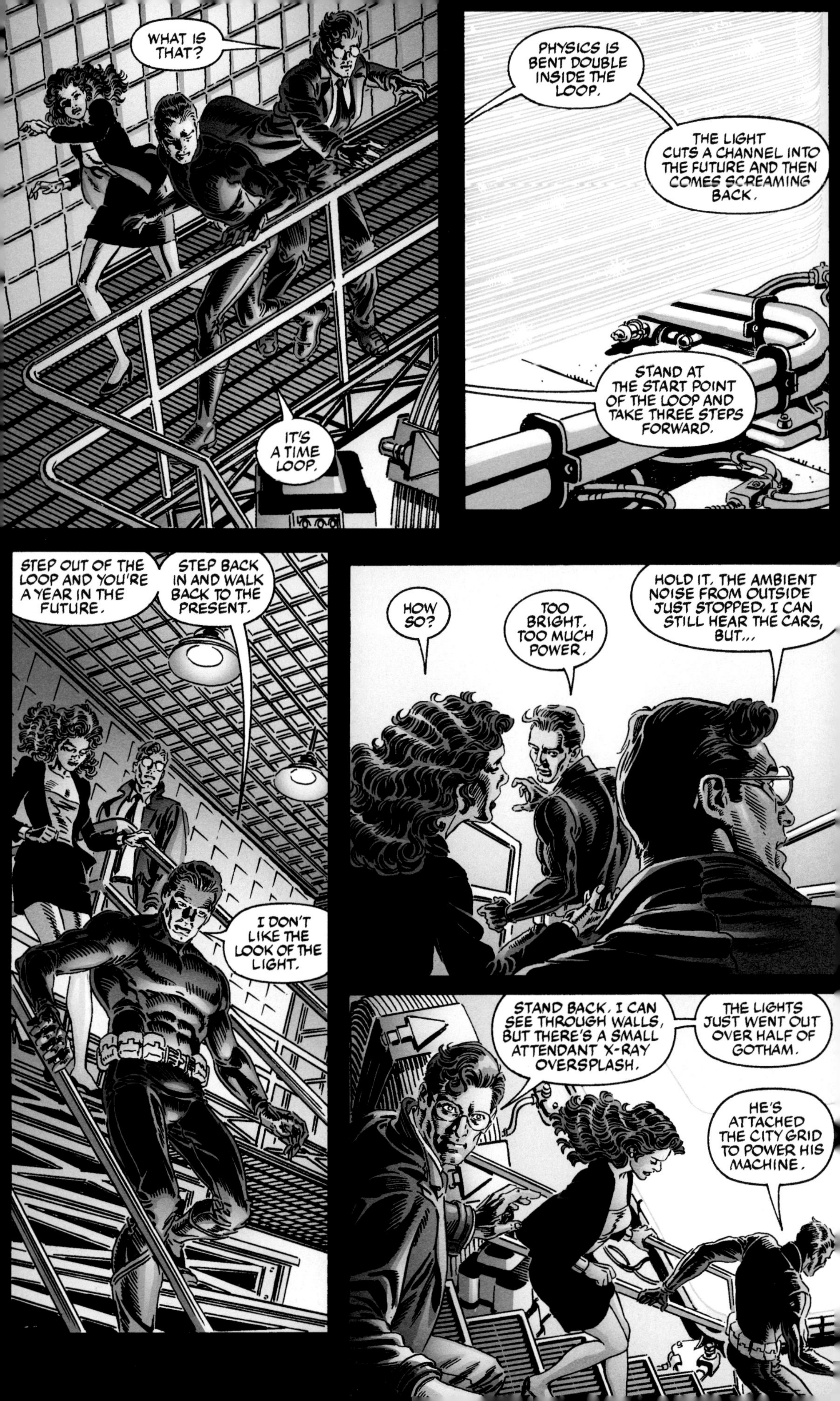
WHAT IS THAT?
IT'S A TIME LOOP.
PHYSICS IS BENT DOUBLE INSIDE THE LOOP.
THE LIGHT CUTS A CHANNEL INTO THE FUTURE AND THEN COMES SCREAMING BACK.
STAND AT THE START POINT OF THE LOOP AND TAKE THREE STEPS FORWARD.
STEP OUT OF THE LOOP AND YOU'RE A YEAR IN THE FUTURE.
STEP BACK IN AND WALK BACK TO THE PRESENT.
I DON'T LIKE THE LOOK OF THE LIGHT.
HOW SO?
TOO BRIGHT. TOO MUCH POWER.
HOLD IT. THE AMBIENT NOISE FROM OUTSIDE JUST STOPPED. I CAN STILL HEAR THE CARS, BUT...
STAND BACK. I CAN SEE THROUGH WALLS, BUT THERE'S A SMALL ATTENDANT X-RAY OVERSPLASH.
THE LIGHTS JUST WENT OUT OVER HALF OF GOTHAM.
HE'S ATTACHED THE CITY GRID TO POWER HIS MACHINE.

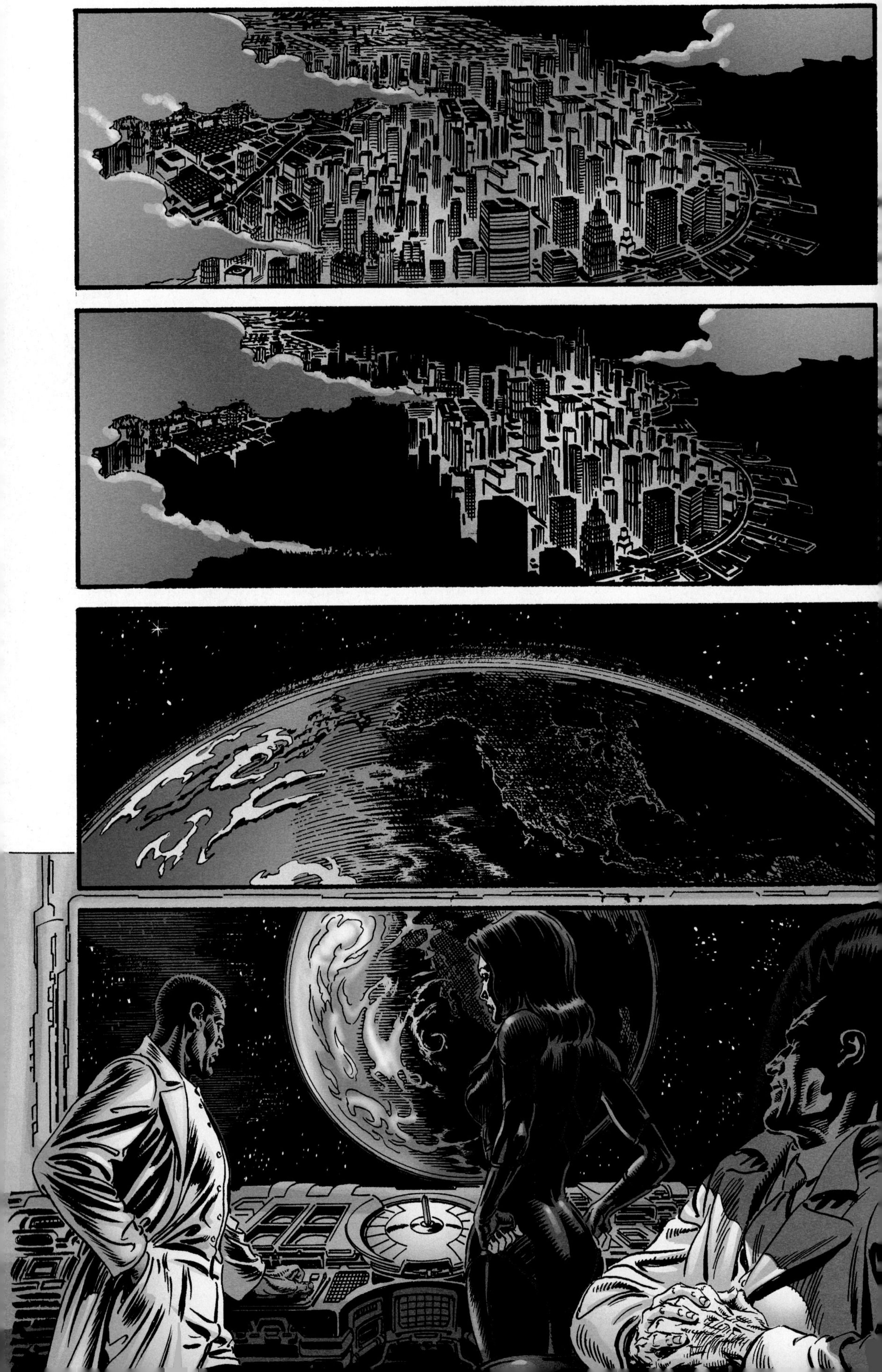

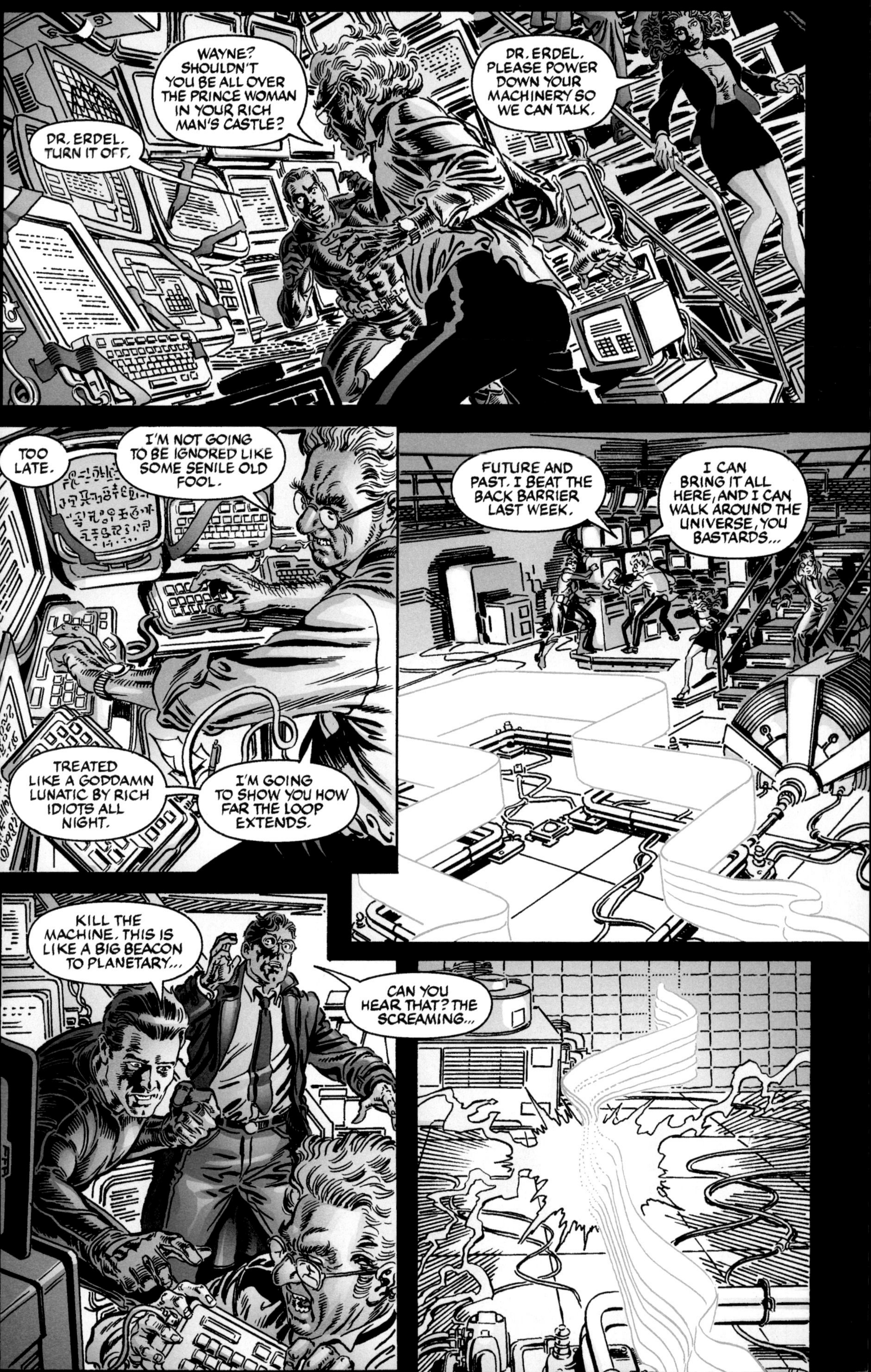
WAYNE? SHOULDN'T YOU BE ALL OVER THE PRINCE WOMAN IN YOUR RICH MAN'S CASTLE?
DR. ERDEL. PLEASE POWER DOWN YOUR MACHINERY SO WE CAN TALK.
DR. ERDEL. TURN IT OFF.
TOO LATE.
I'M NOT GOING TO BE IGNORED LIKE SOME SENILE OLD FOOL.
TREATED LIKE A GODDAMN LUNATIC BY RICH IDIOTS ALL NIGHT.
I'M GOING TO SHOW YOU HOW FAR THE LOOP EXTENDS.
FUTURE AND PAST. I BEAT THE BACK BARRIER LAST WEEK.
I CAN BRING IT ALL HERE, AND I CAN WALK AROUND THE UNIVERSE, YOU BASTARDS...
KILL THE MACHINE. THIS IS LIKE A BIG BEACON TO PLANETARY...
CAN YOU HEAR THAT? THE SCREAMING...

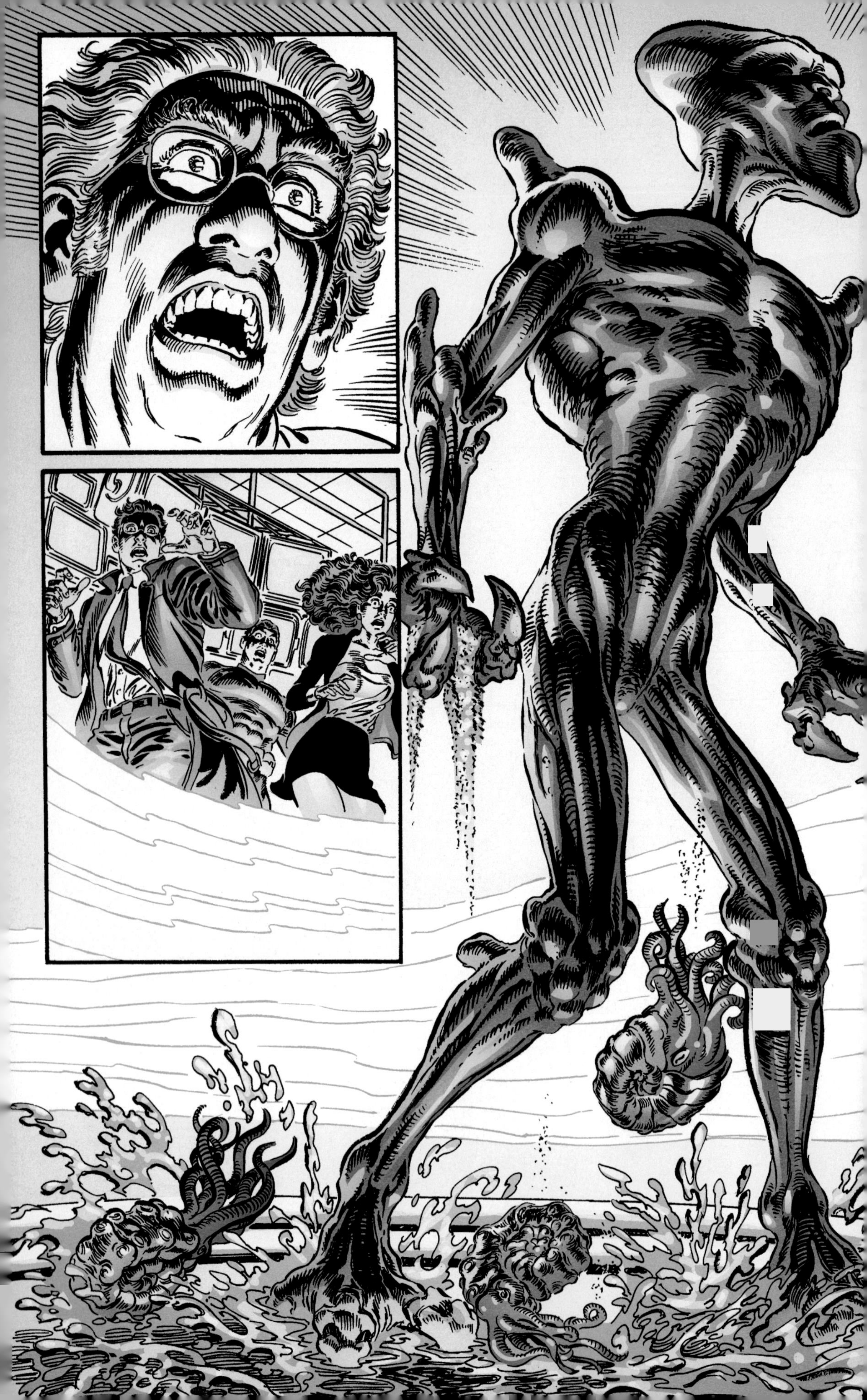

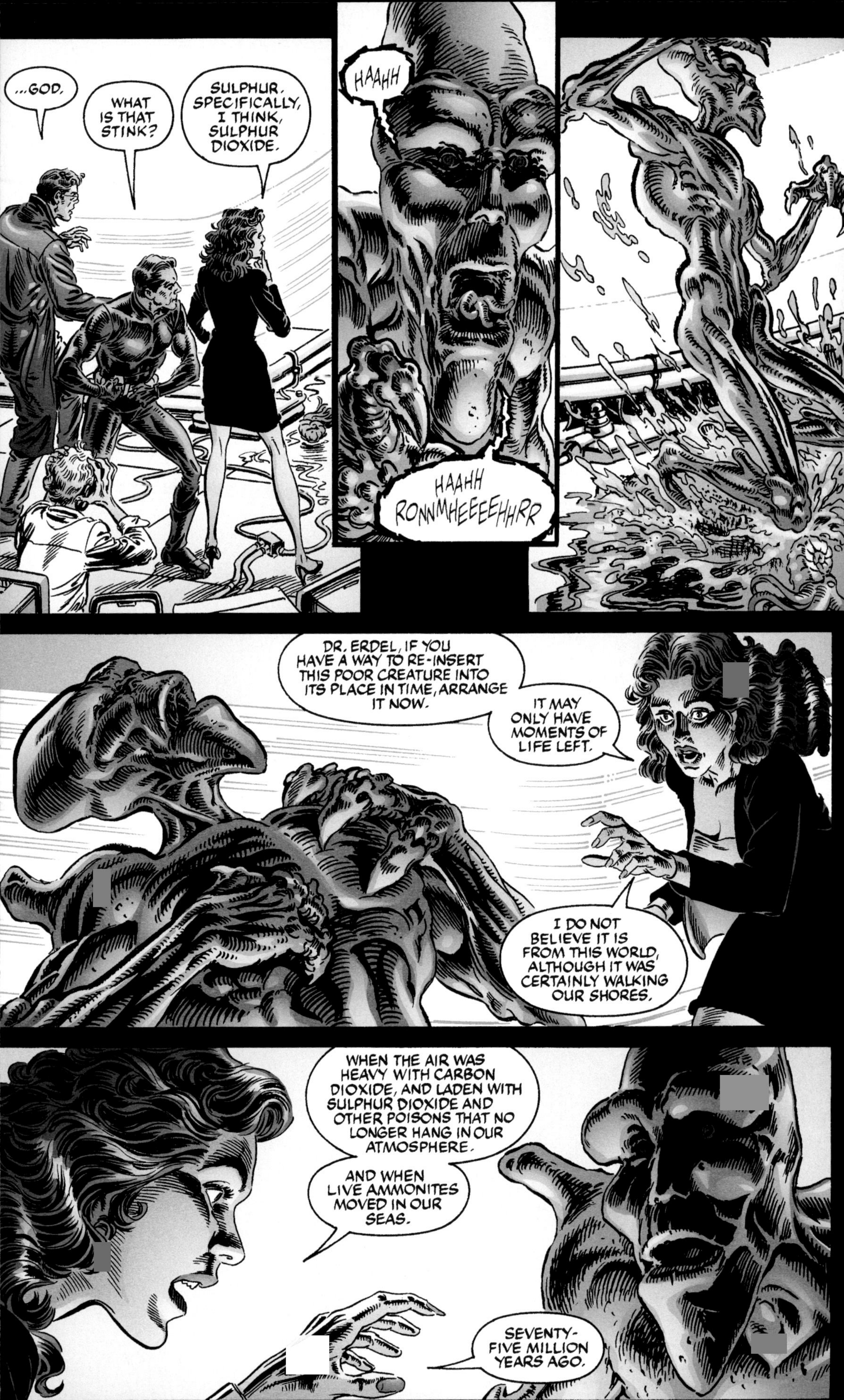
...GOD.
WHAT IS THAT STINK?
SULPHUR. SPECIFICALLY, I THINK, SULPHUR DIOXIDE.
HAAHH
HAAHH RONNMHEEEEHHRR
DR. ERDEL, IF YOU HAVE A WAY TO RE-INSERT THIS POOR CREATURE INTO ITS PLACE IN TIME, ARRANGE IT NOW.
IT MAY ONLY HAVE MOMENTS OF LIFE LEFT.
I DO NOT BELIEVE IT IS FROM THIS WORLD, ALTHOUGH IT WAS CERTAINLY WALKING OUR SHORES.
WHEN THE AIR WAS HEAVY WITH CARBON DIOXIDE, AND LADEN WITH SULPHUR DIOXIDE AND OTHER POISONS THAT NO LONGER HANG IN OUR ATMOSPHERE.
AND WHEN LIVE AMMONITES MOVED IN OUR SEAS.
SEVENTY-FIVE MILLION YEARS AGO.

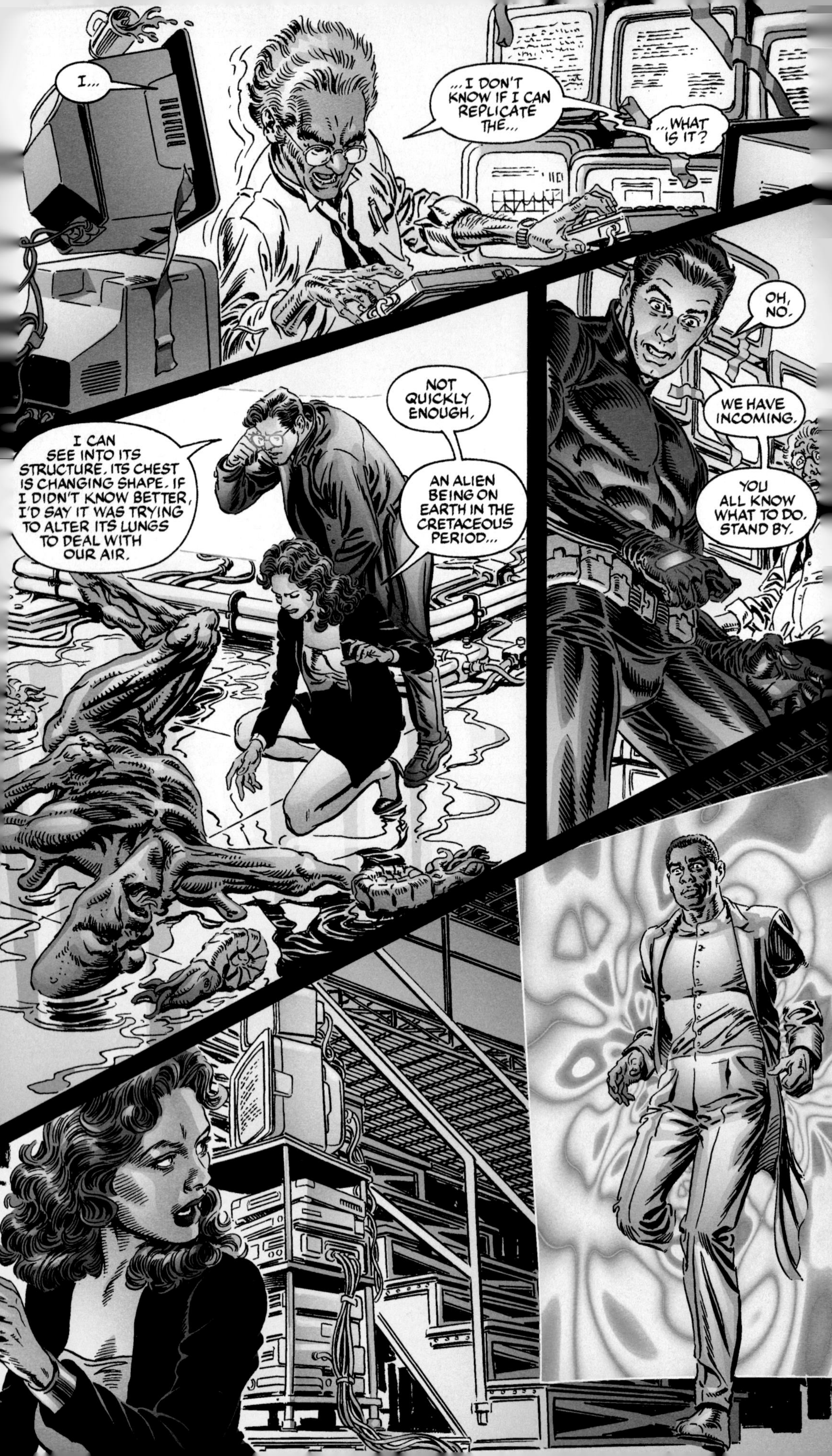
I...
...I DON'T KNOW IF I CAN REPLICATE THE...
...WHAT IS IT?
OH, NO.
WE HAVE INCOMING.
YOU ALL KNOW WHAT TO DO. STAND BY.
I CAN SEE INTO ITS STRUCTURE. ITS CHEST IS CHANGING SHAPE. IF I DIDN'T KNOW BETTER, I'D SAY IT WAS TRYING TO ALTER ITS LUNGS TO DEAL WITH OUR AIR.
NOT QUICKLY ENOUGH.
AN ALIEN BEING ON EARTH IN THE CRETACEOUS PERIOD...

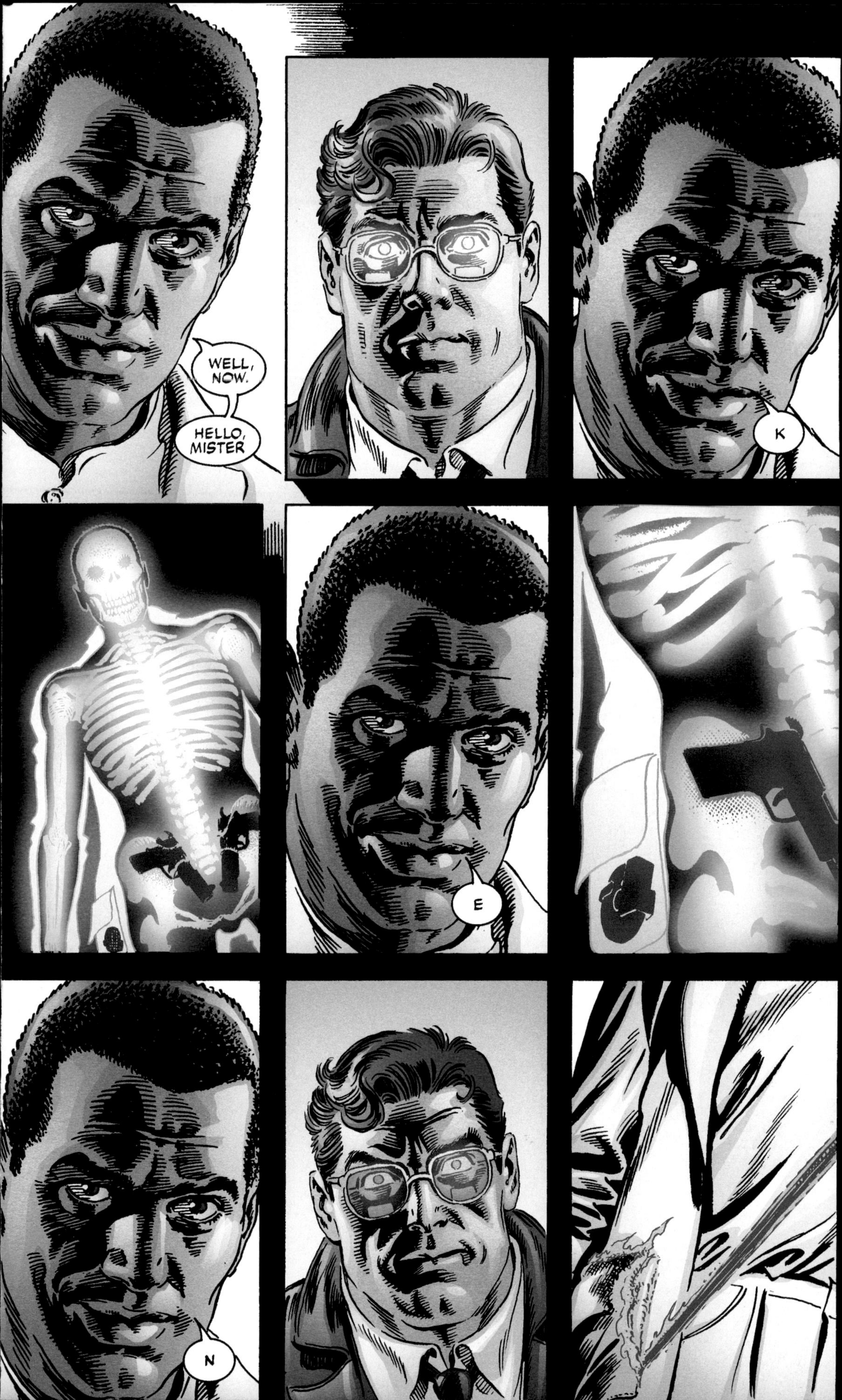
WELL, NOW.
HELLO, MISTER
K
E
N

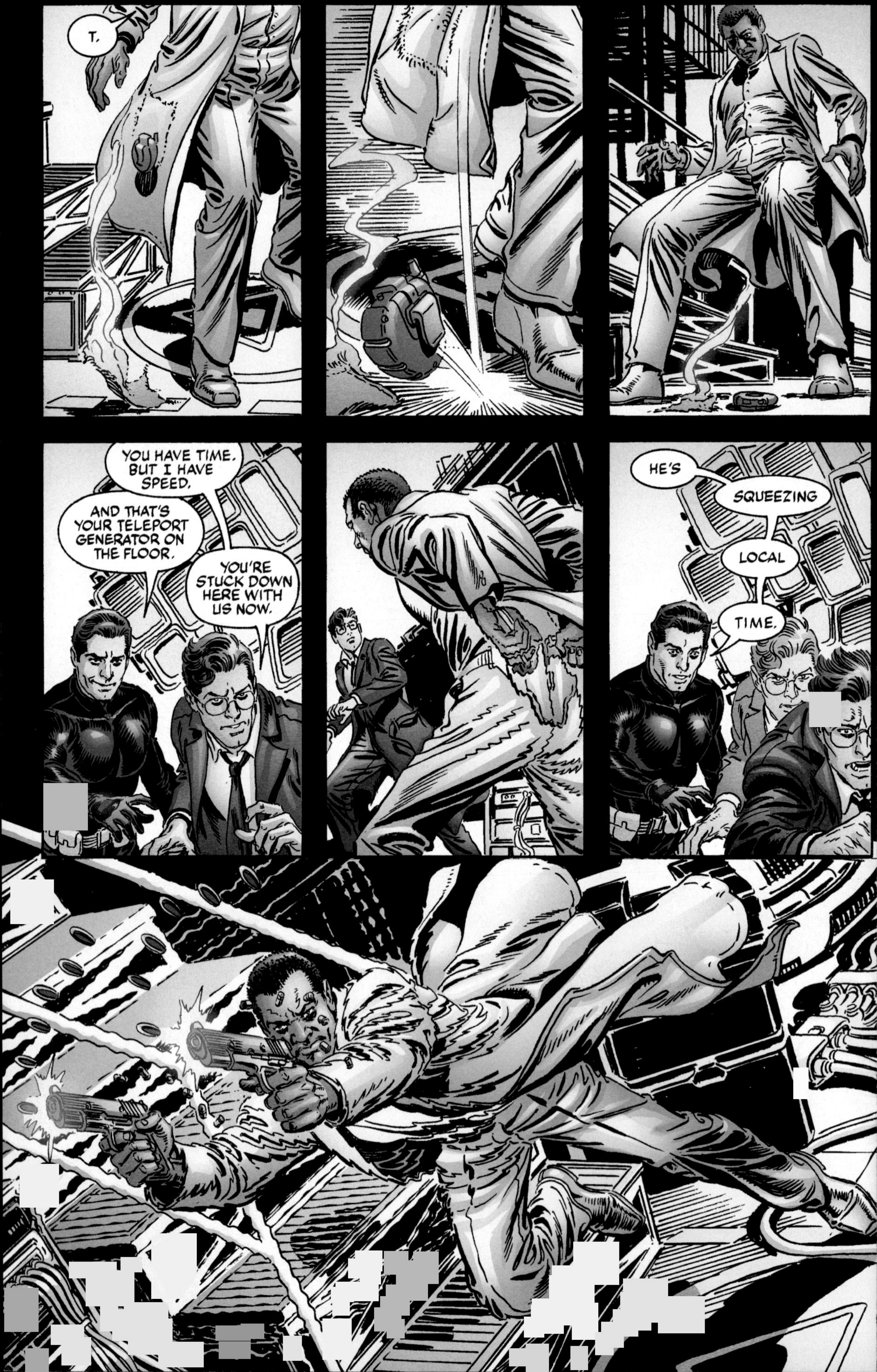
T.
YOU HAVE TIME. BUT I HAVE SPEED.
AND THAT'S YOUR TELEPORT GENERATOR ON THE FLOOR.
YOU'RE STUCK DOWN HERE WITH US NOW.
HE'S
SQUEEZING
LOCAL
TIME.

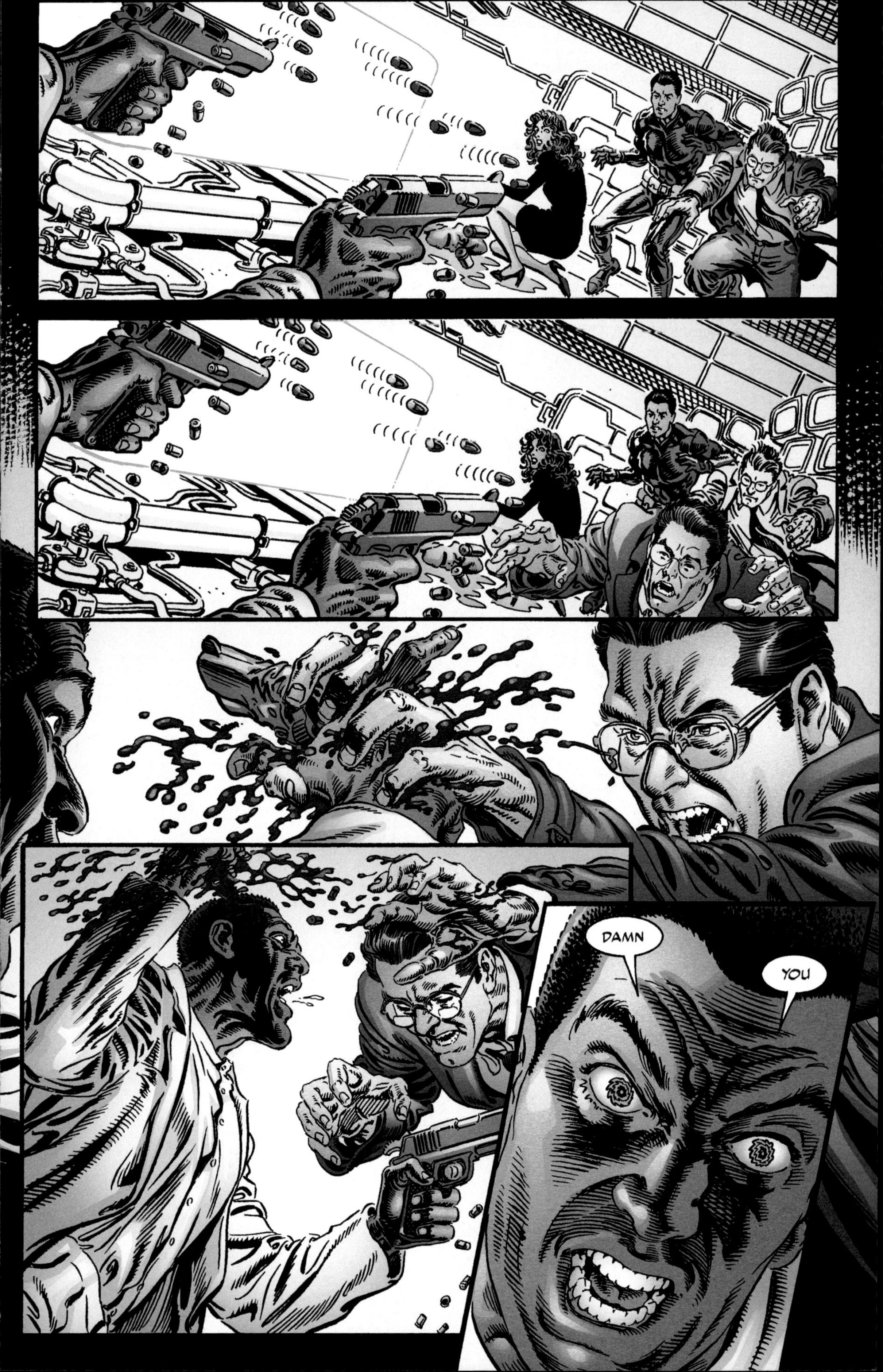
DAMN
YOU

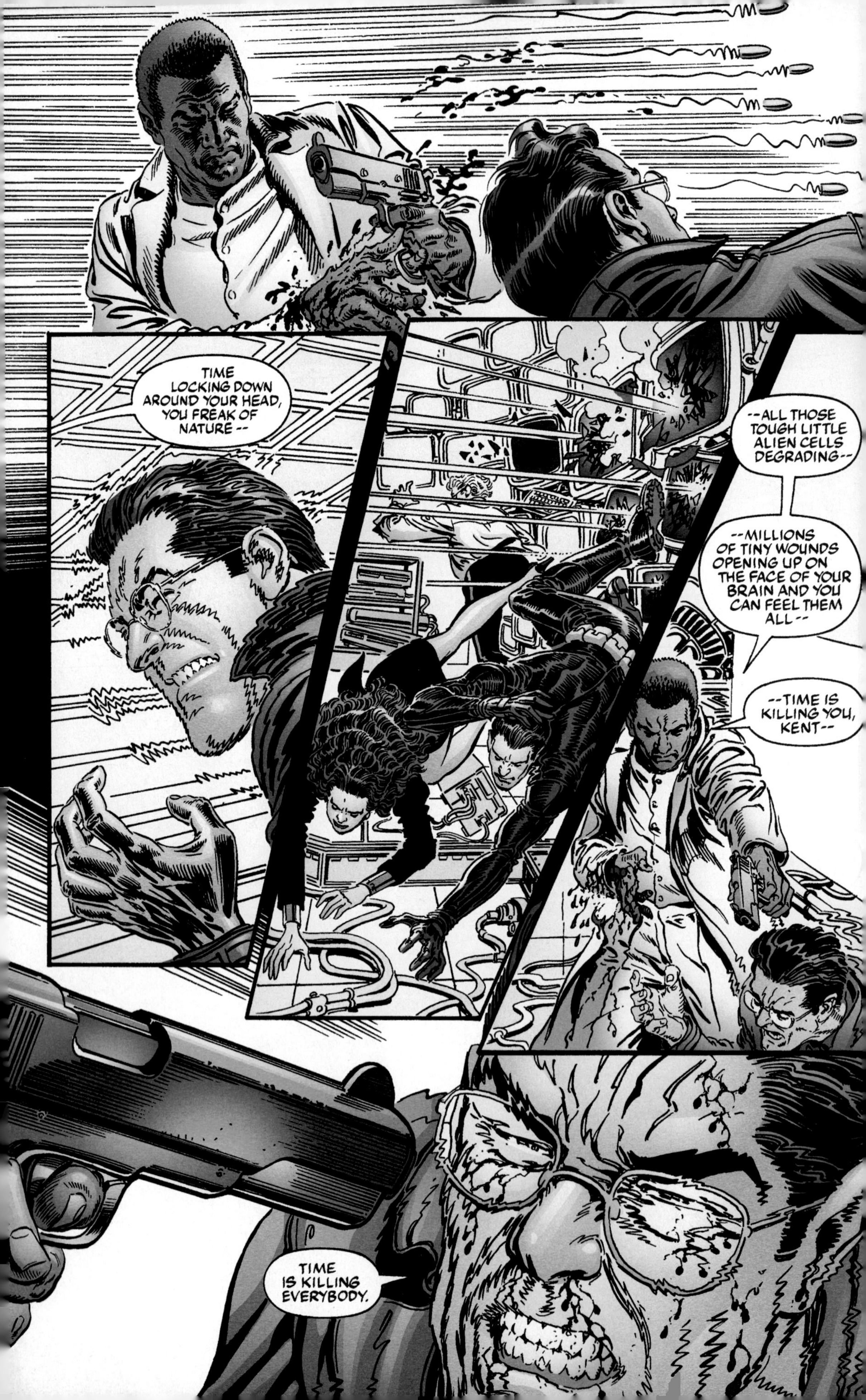

TIME LOCKING DOWN AROUND YOUR HEAD, YOU FREAK OF NATURE --
--ALL THOSE TOUGH LITTLE ALIEN CELLS DEGRADING--
--MILLIONS OF TINY WOUNDS OPENING UP ON THE FACE OF YOUR BRAIN AND YOU CAN FEEL THEM ALL--
--TIME IS KILLING YOU, KENT--
TIME IS KILLING EVERYBODY.

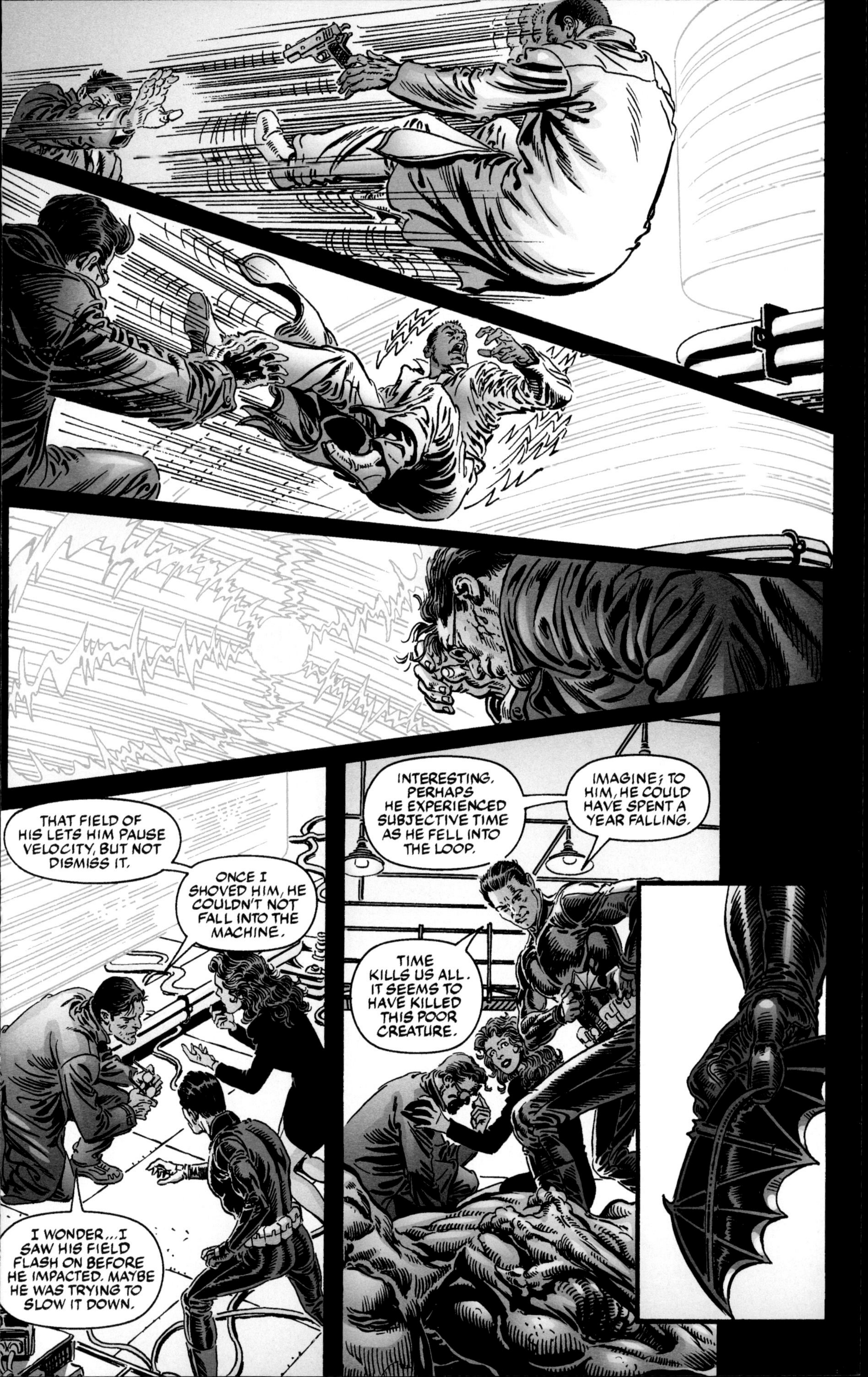
THAT FIELD OF HIS LETS HIM PAUSE VELOCITY, BUT NOT DISMISS IT.
ONCE I SHOVED HIM, HE COULDN'T NOT FALL INTO THE MACHINE.
I WONDER... I SAW HIS FIELD FLASH ON BEFORE HE IMPACTED. MAYBE HE WAS TRYING TO SLOW IT DOWN.
INTERESTING. PERHAPS HE EXPERIENCED SUBJECTIVE TIME AS HE FELL INTO THE LOOP.
IMAGINE; TO HIM, HE COULD HAVE SPENT A YEAR FALLING.
TIME KILLS US ALL. IT SEEMS TO HAVE KILLED THIS POOR CREATURE.

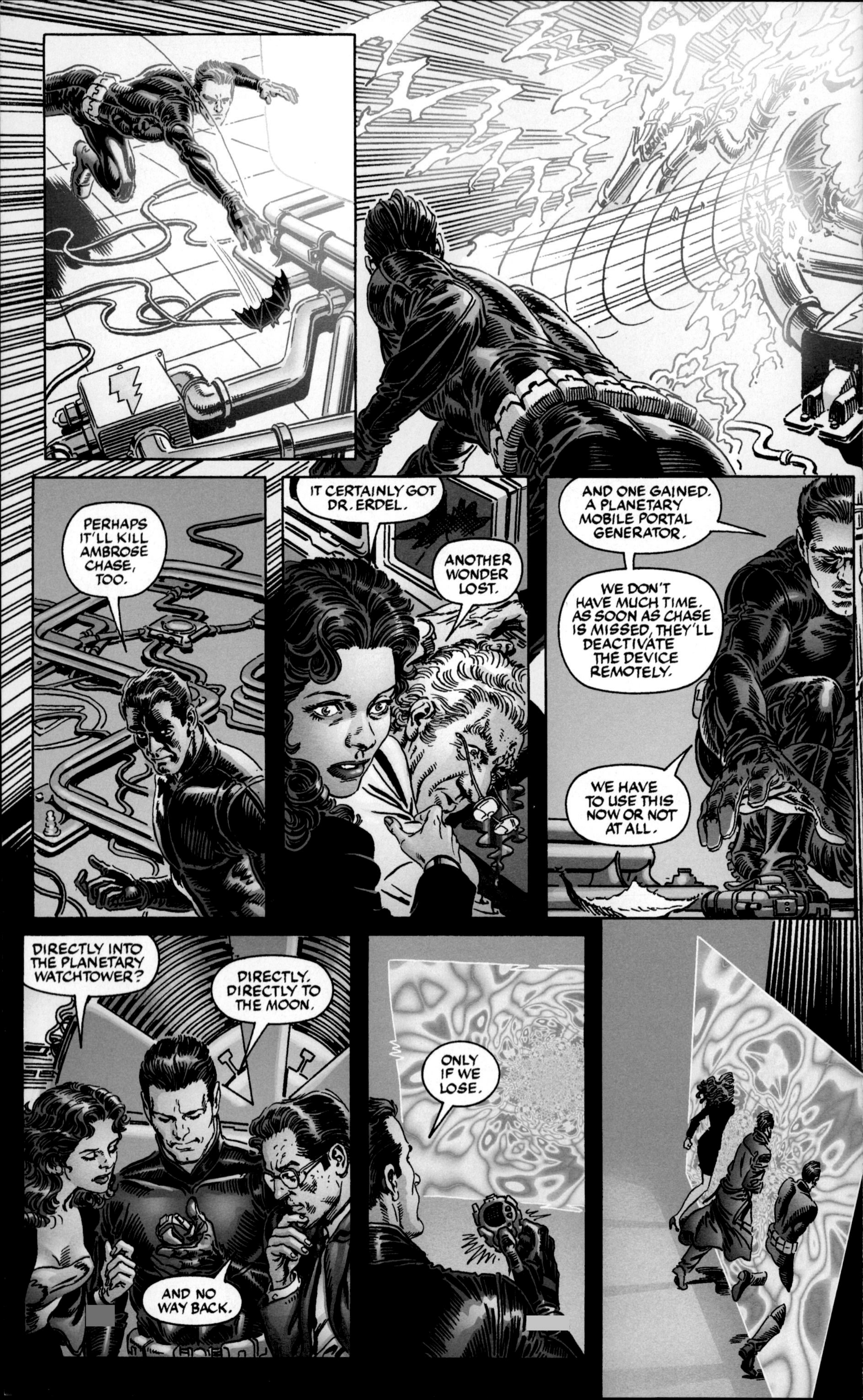
PERHAPS IT'LL KILL AMBROSE CHASE, TOO.
IT CERTAINLY GOT DR. ERDEL.
ANOTHER WONDER LOST.
AND ONE GAINED. A PLANETARY MOBILE PORTAL GENERATOR.
WE DON'T HAVE MUCH TIME. AS SOON AS CHASE IS MISSED, THEY'LL DEACTIVATE THE DEVICE REMOTELY.
WE HAVE TO USE THIS NOW OR NOT AT ALL.
DIRECTLY INTO THE PLANETARY WATCHTOWER?
DIRECTLY. DIRECTLY TO THE MOON.
AND NO WAY BACK.
ONLY IF WE LOSE.

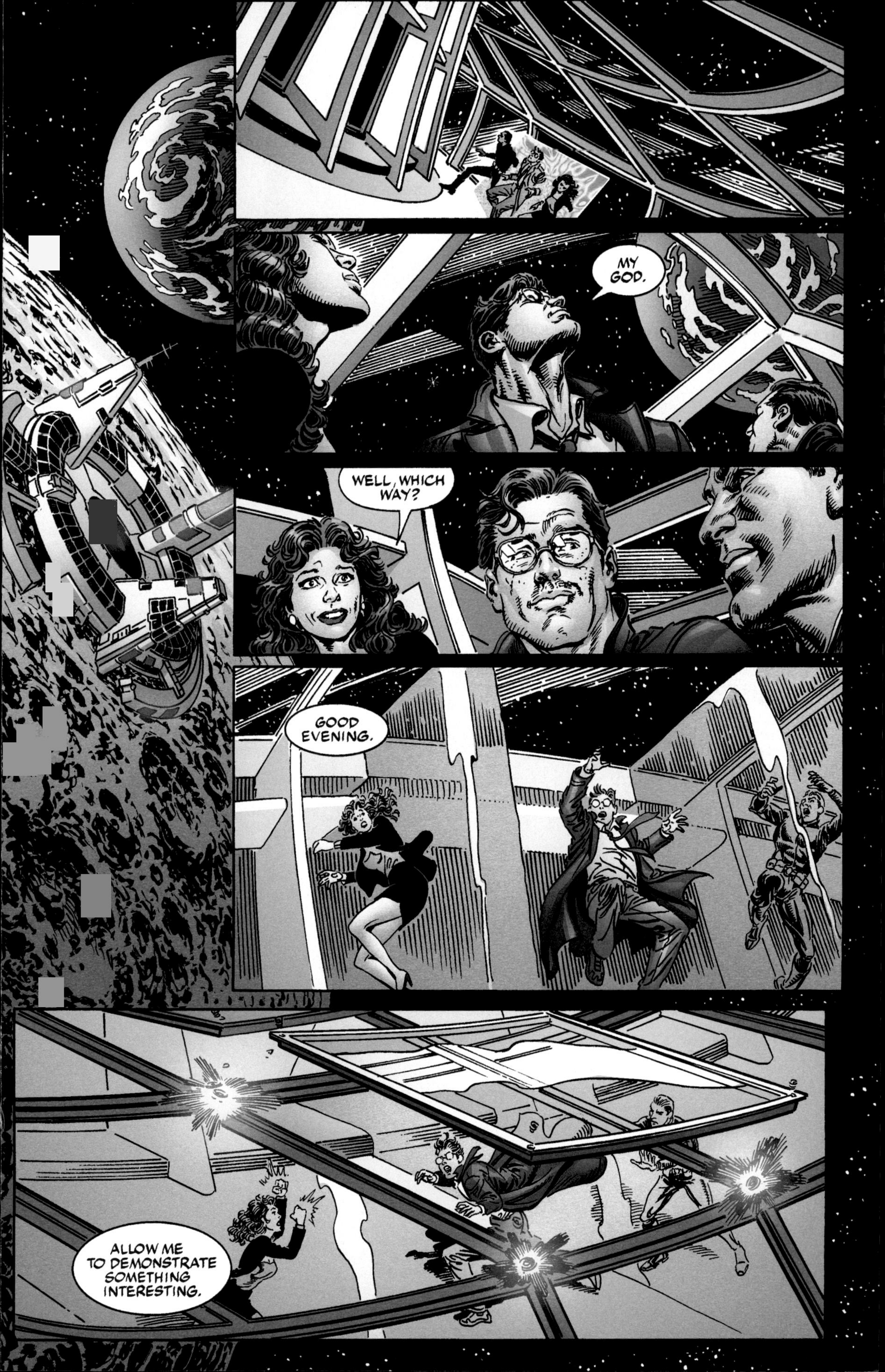
MY GOD.
WELL, WHICH WAY?
GOOD EVENING.
ALLOW ME TO DEMONSTRATE SOMETHING INTERESTING.

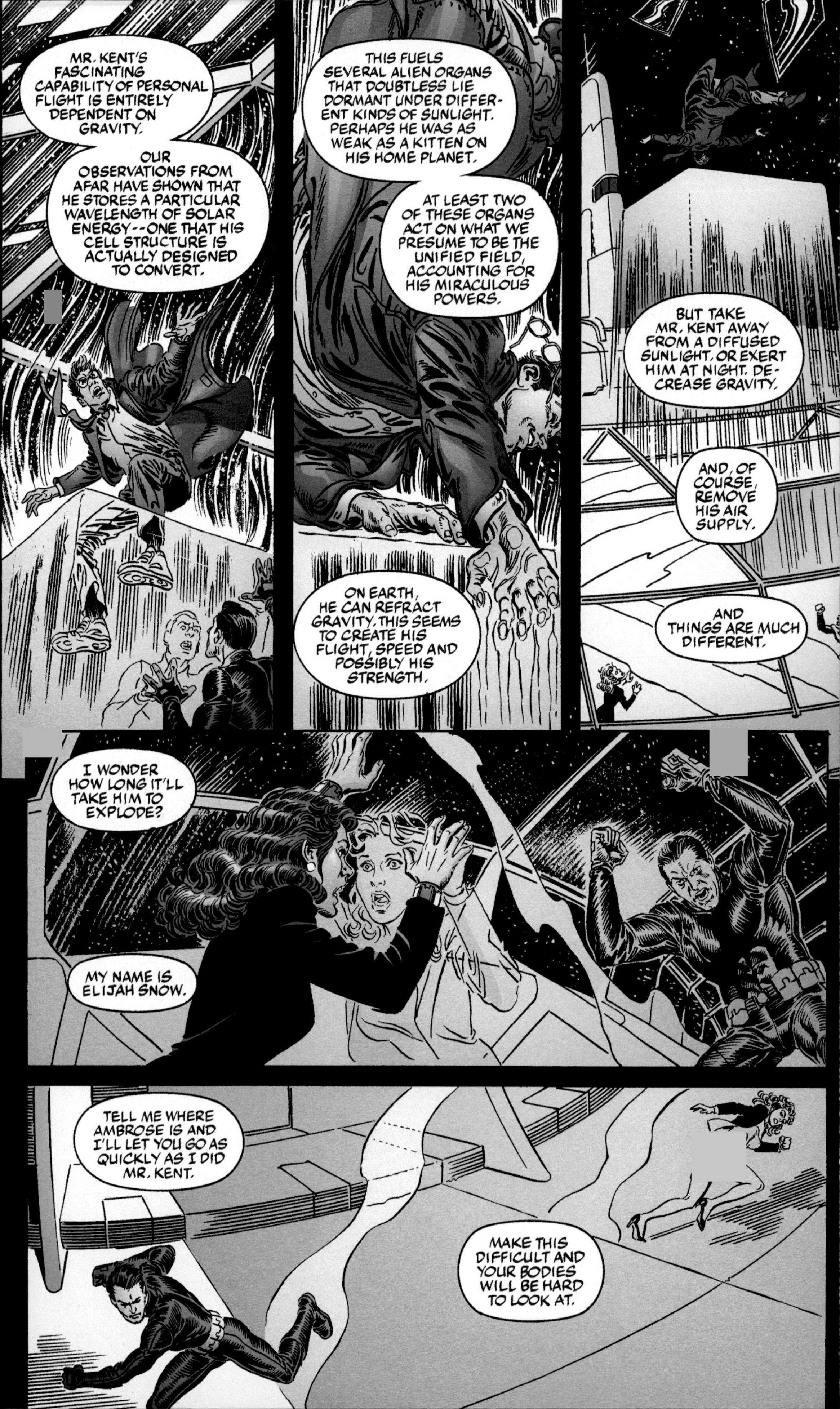
MR. KENT'S FASCINATING CAPABILITY OF PERSONAL FLIGHT IS ENTIRELY DEPENDENT ON GRAVITY.
OUR OBSERVATIONS FROM AFAR HAVE SHOWN THAT HE STORES A PARTICULAR WAVELENGTH OF SOLAR ENERGY--ONE THAT HIS CELL STRUCTURE IS ACTUALLY DESIGNED TO CONVERT.
THIS FUELS SEVERAL ALIEN ORGANS THAT DOUBTLESS LIE DORMANT UNDER DIFFERENT KINDS OF SUNLIGHT. PERHAPS HE WAS AS WEAK AS A KITTEN ON HIS HOME PLANET.
AT LEAST TWO OF THESE ORGANS ACT ON WHAT WE PRESUME TO BE THE UNIFIED FIELD, ACCOUNTING FOR HIS MIRACULOUS POWERS.
ON EARTH, HE CAN REFRACT GRAVITY. THIS SEEMS TO CREATE HIS FLIGHT, SPEED AND POSSIBLY HIS STRENGTH.
BUT TAKE MR. KENT AWAY FROM A DIFFUSED SUNLIGHT, OR EXERT HIM AT NIGHT. DECREASE GRAVITY.
AND, OF COURSE, REMOVE HIS AIR SUPPLY.
AND THINGS ARE MUCH DIFFERENT.
I WONDER HOW LONG IT'LL TAKE HIM TO EXPLODE?
MY NAME IS ELIJAH SNOW.
TELL ME WHERE AMBROSE IS AND I'LL LET YOU GO AS QUICKLY AS I DID MR. KENT.
MAKE THIS DIFFICULT AND YOUR BODIES WILL BE HARD TO LOOK AT.

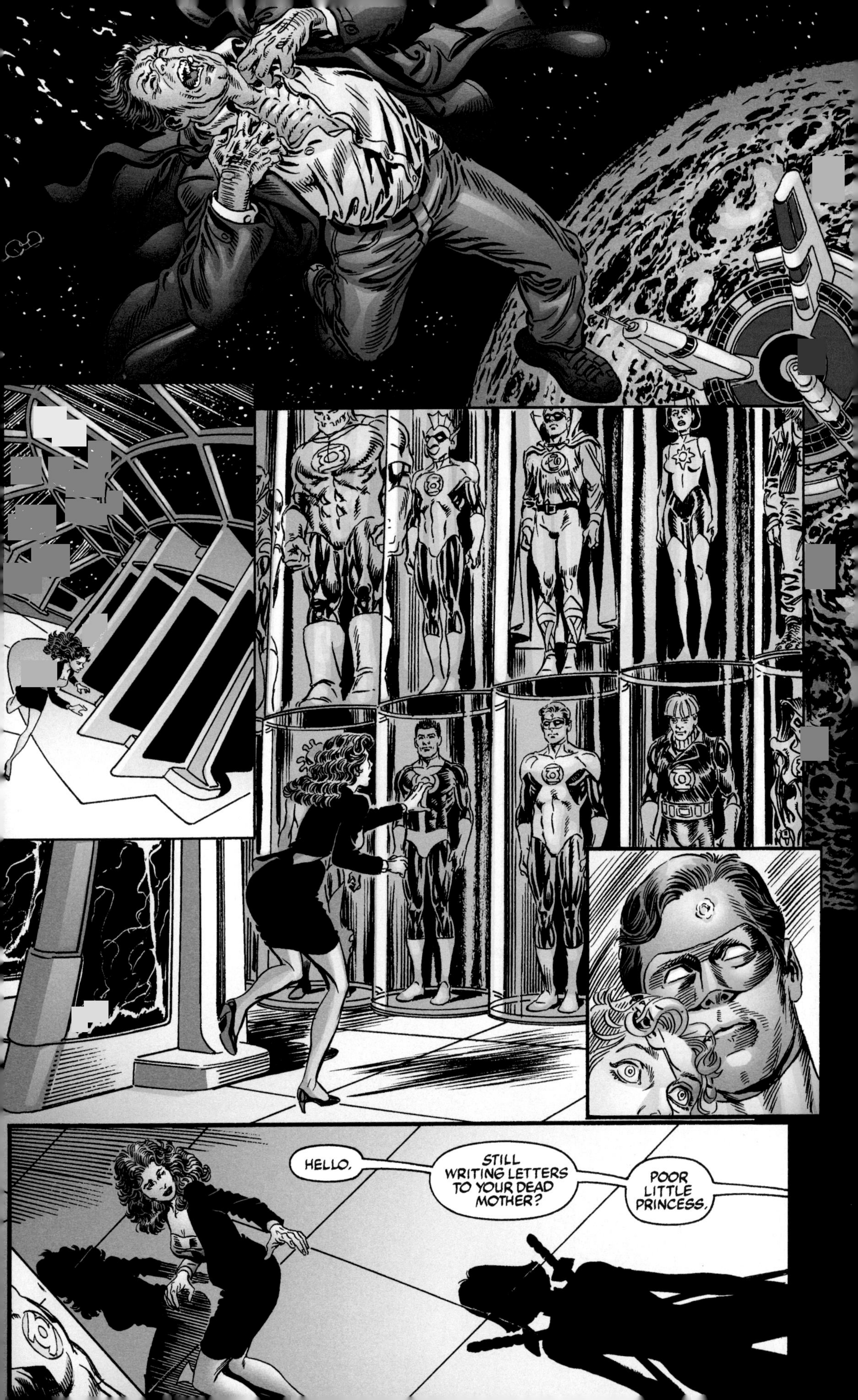
HELLO,
STILL WRITING LETTERS TO YOUR DEAD MOTHER?
POOR LITTLE PRINCESS.

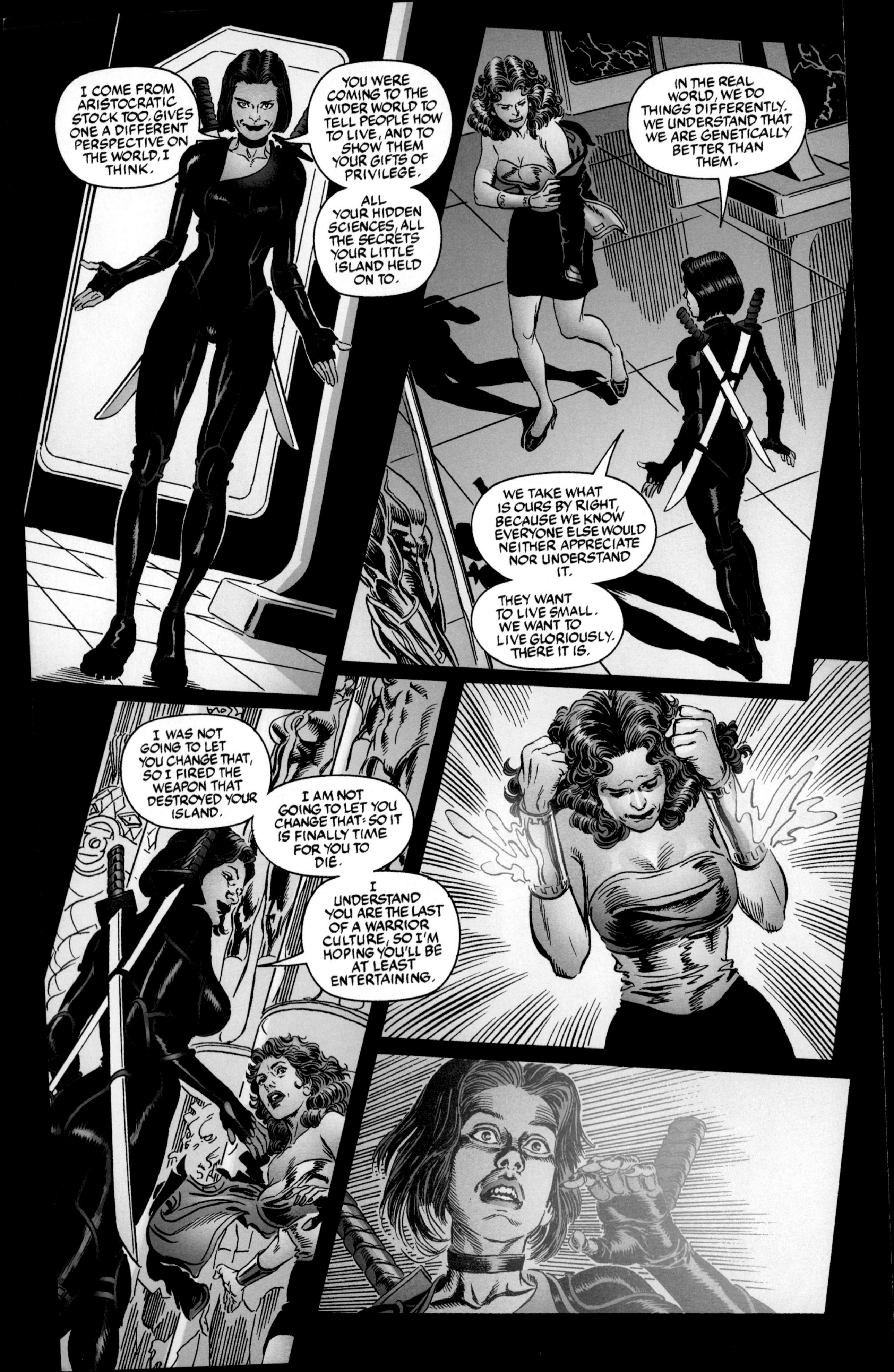
I COME FROM ARISTOCRATIC STOCK TOO. GIVES ONE A DIFFERENT PERSPECTIVE ON THE WORLD, I THINK.
YOU WERE COMING TO THE WIDER WORLD TO TELL PEOPLE HOW TO LIVE, AND TO SHOW THEM YOUR GIFTS OF PRIVILEGE.
ALL YOUR HIDDEN SCIENCES, ALL THE SECRETS YOUR LITTLE ISLAND HELD ON TO.
IN THE REAL WORLD, WE DO THINGS DIFFERENTLY. WE UNDERSTAND THAT WE ARE GENETICALLY BETTER THAN THEM.
WE TAKE WHAT IS OURS BY RIGHT, BECAUSE WE KNOW EVERYONE ELSE WOULD NEITHER APPRECIATE NOR UNDERSTAND IT.
THEY WANT TO LIVE SMALL. WE WANT TO LIVE GLORIOUSLY. THERE IT IS.
I WAS NOT GOING TO LET YOU CHANGE THAT, SO I FIRED THE WEAPON THAT DESTROYED YOUR ISLAND.
I AM NOT GOING TO LET YOU CHANGE THAT: SO IT IS FINALLY TIME FOR YOU TO DIE.
I UNDERSTAND YOU ARE THE LAST OF A WARRIOR CULTURE, SO I'M HOPING YOU'LL BE AT LEAST ENTERTAINING.

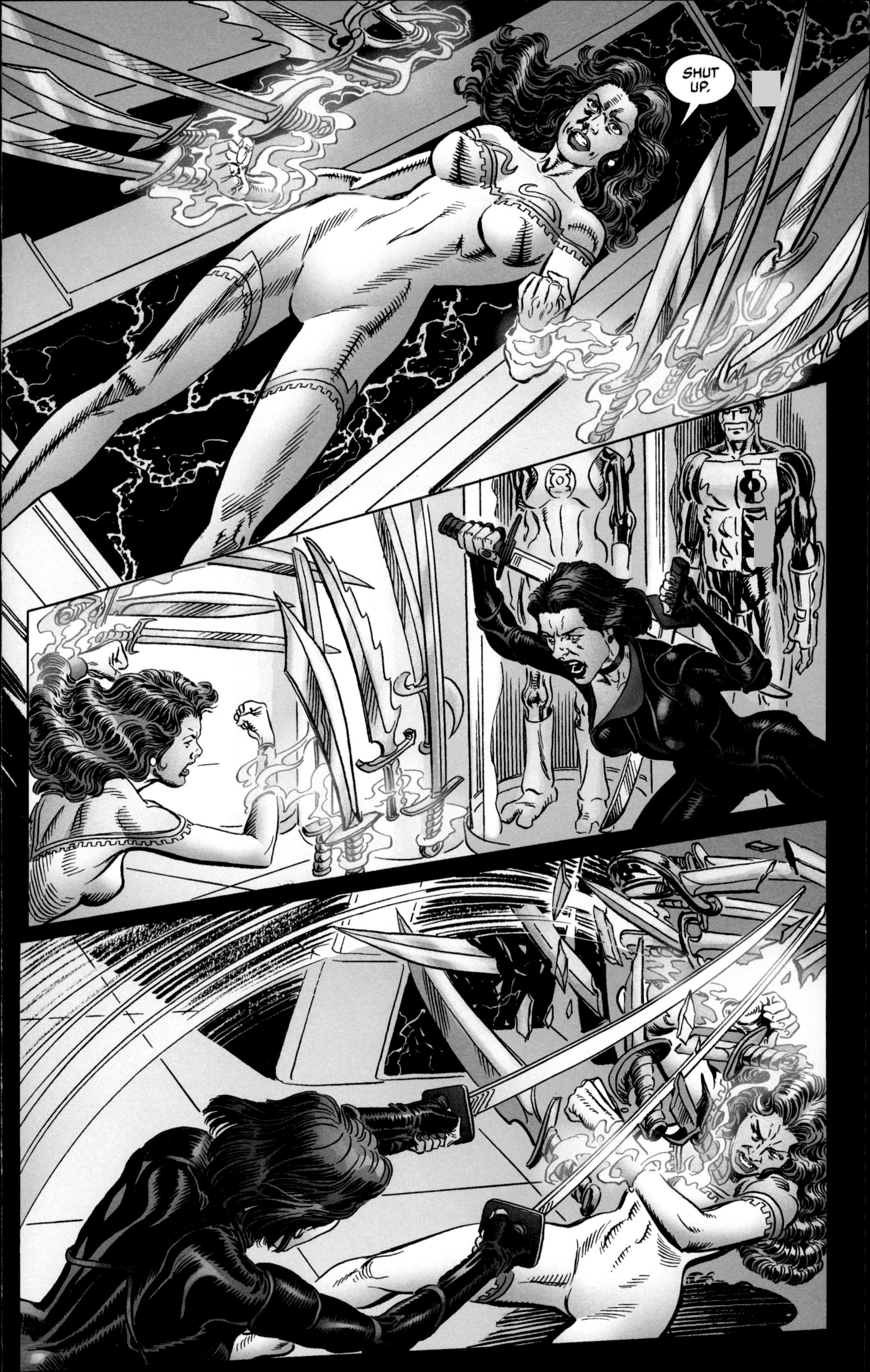
SHUT UP.

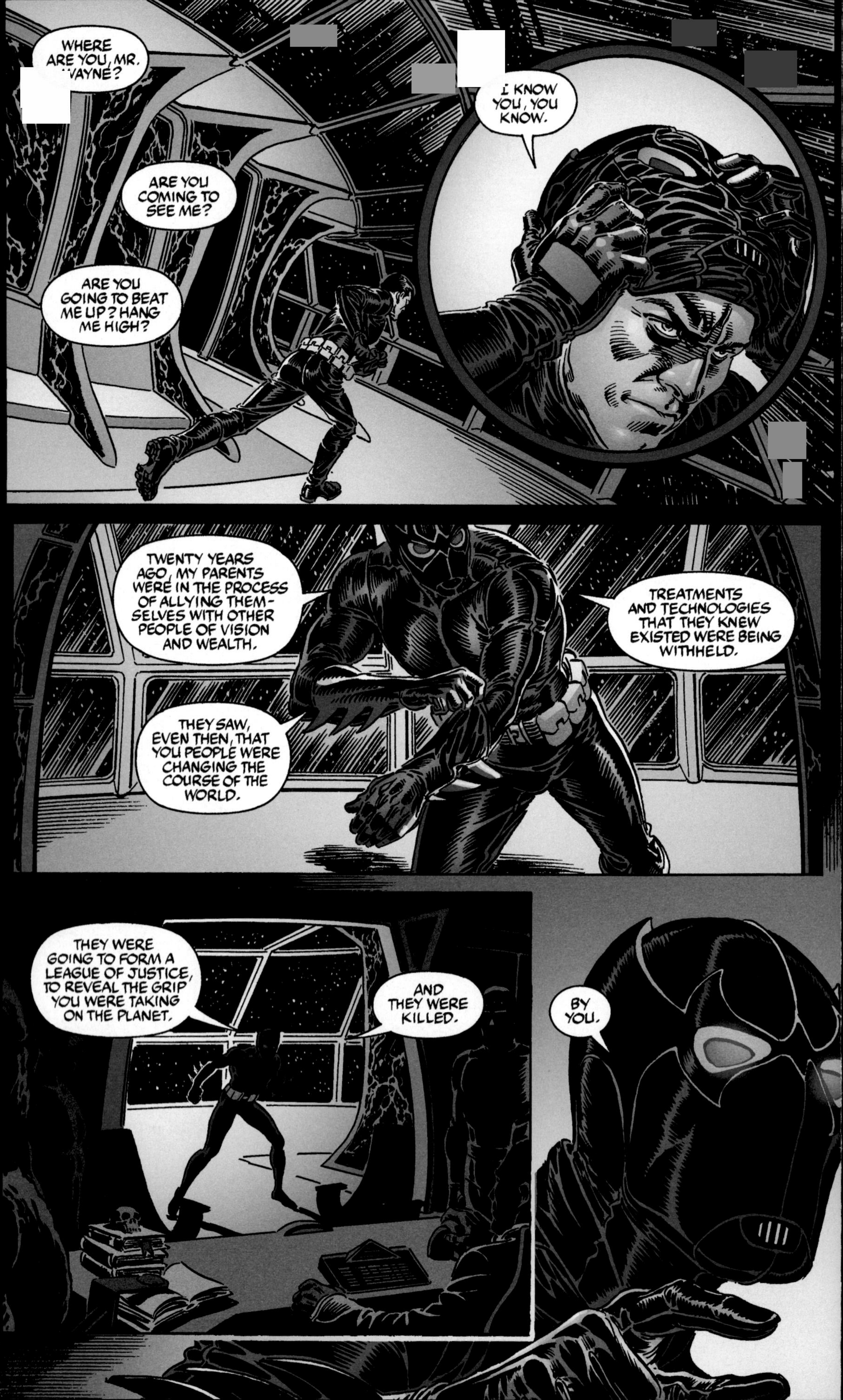
WHERE ARE YOU, MR. WAYNE?
ARE YOU COMING TO SEE ME?
ARE YOU GOING TO BEAT ME UP? HANG ME HIGH?
I KNOW YOU, YOU KNOW.
TWENTY YEARS AGO, MY PARENTS WERE IN THE PROCESS OF ALLYING THEM-SELVES WITH OTHER PEOPLE OF VISION AND WEALTH.
TREATMENTS AND TECHNOLOGIES THAT THEY KNEW EXISTED WERE BEING WITHHELD.
THEY SAW, EVEN THEN, THAT YOU PEOPLE WERE CHANGING THE COURSE OF THE WORLD.
THEY WERE GOING TO FORM A LEAGUE OF JUSTICE, TO REVEAL THE GRIP YOU WERE TAKING ON THE PLANET.
AND THEY WERE KILLED.
BY YOU.

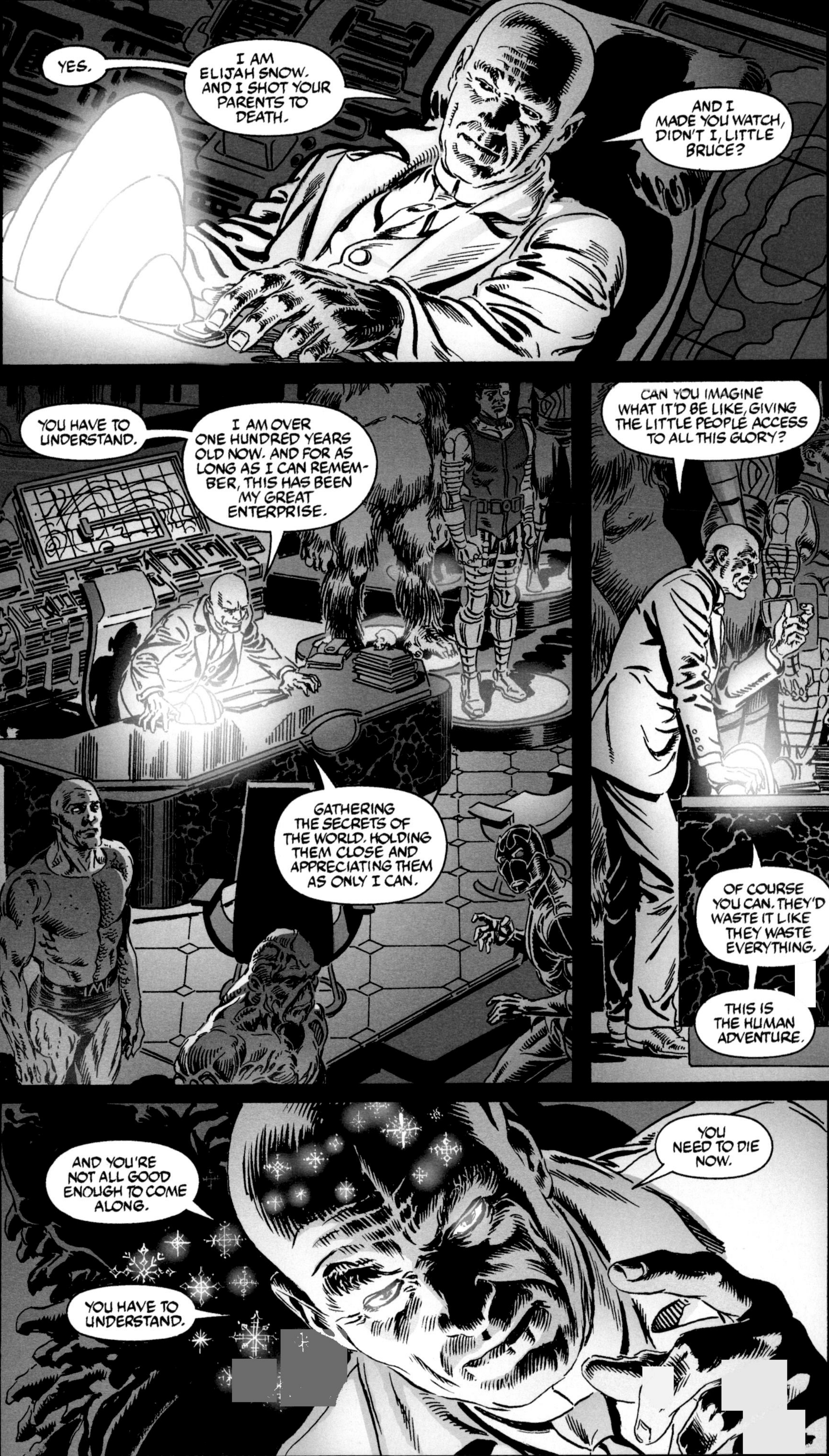
YES.
I AM ELIJAH SNOW. AND I SHOT YOUR PARENTS TO DEATH.
AND I MADE YOU WATCH, DIDN'T I, LITTLE BRUCE?
YOU HAVE TO UNDERSTAND.
I AM OVER ONE HUNDRED YEARS OLD NOW. AND FOR AS LONG AS I CAN REMEMBER, THIS HAS BEEN MY GREAT ENTERPRISE.
GATHERING THE SECRETS OF THE WORLD. HOLDING THEM CLOSE AND APPRECIATING THEM AS ONLY I CAN.
CAN YOU IMAGINE WHAT IT'D BE LIKE, GIVING THE LITTLE PEOPLE ACCESS TO ALL THIS GLORY?
OF COURSE YOU CAN. THEY'D WASTE IT LIKE THEY WASTE EVERYTHING.
THIS IS THE HUMAN ADVENTURE.
AND YOU'RE NOT ALL GOOD ENOUGH TO COME ALONG.
YOU HAVE TO UNDERSTAND.
YOU NEED TO DIE NOW.

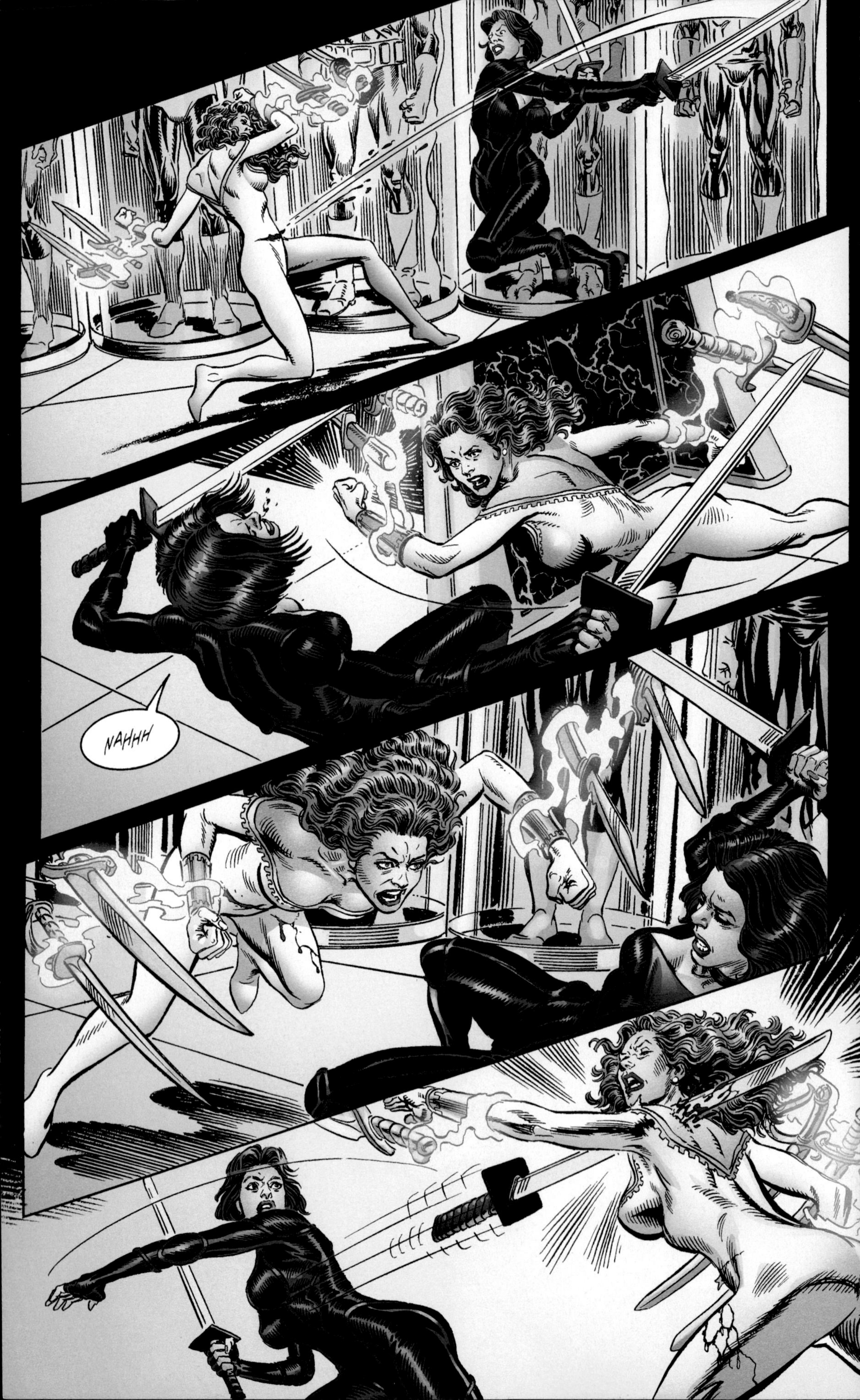
NAHHH

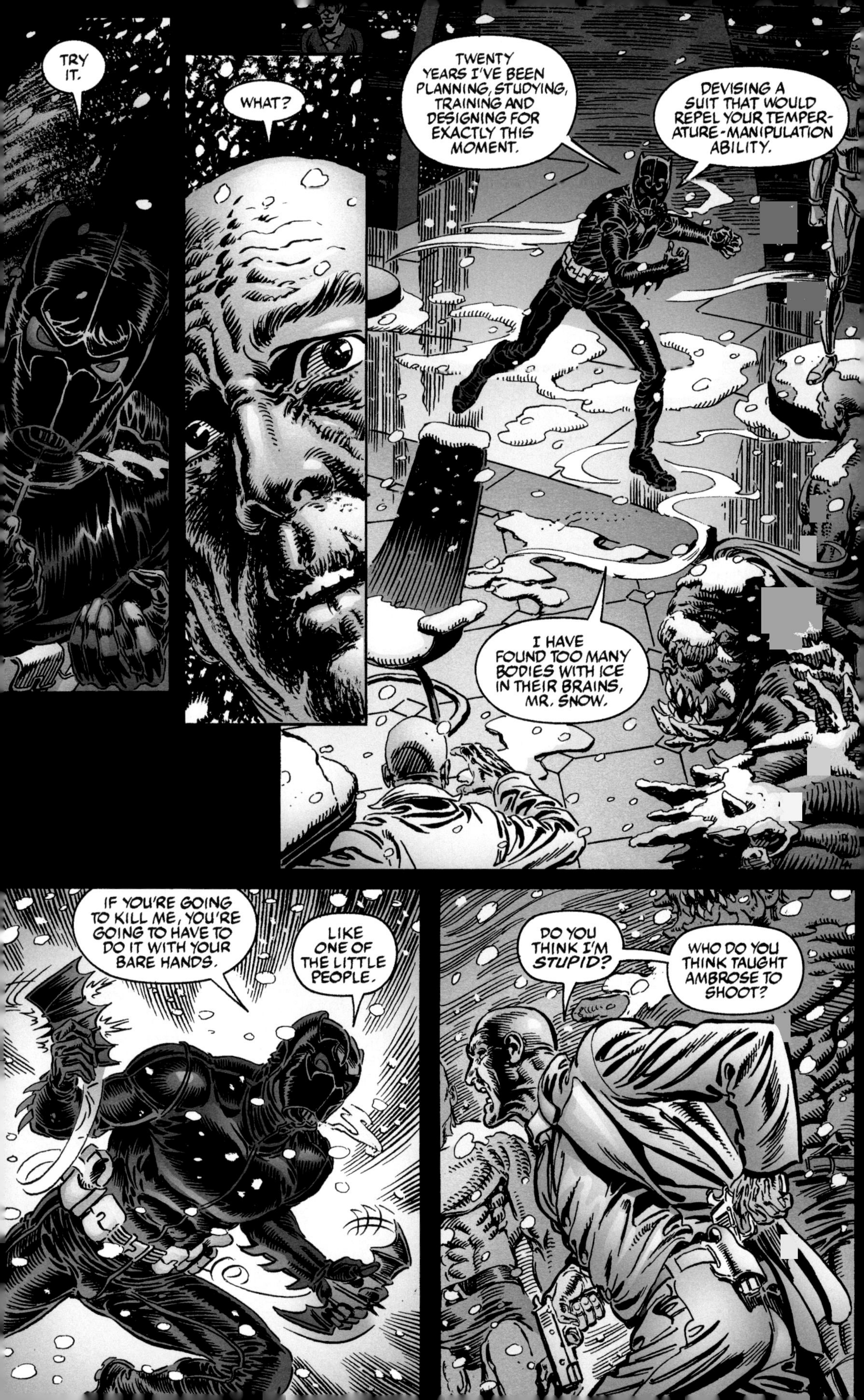
TRY IT.
WHAT?
TWENTY YEARS I'VE BEEN PLANNING, STUDYING, TRAINING AND DESIGNING FOR EXACTLY THIS MOMENT.
DEVISING A SUIT THAT WOULD REPEL YOUR TEMPERATURE-MANIPULATION ABILITY.
I HAVE FOUND TOO MANY BODIES WITH ICE IN THEIR BRAINS, MR. SNOW.
IF YOU'RE GOING TO KILL ME, YOU'RE GOING TO HAVE TO DO IT WITH YOUR BARE HANDS.
LIKE ONE OF THE LITTLE PEOPLE.
DO YOU THINK I'M *STUPID*?
WHO DO YOU THINK TAUGHT AMBROSE TO SHOOT?

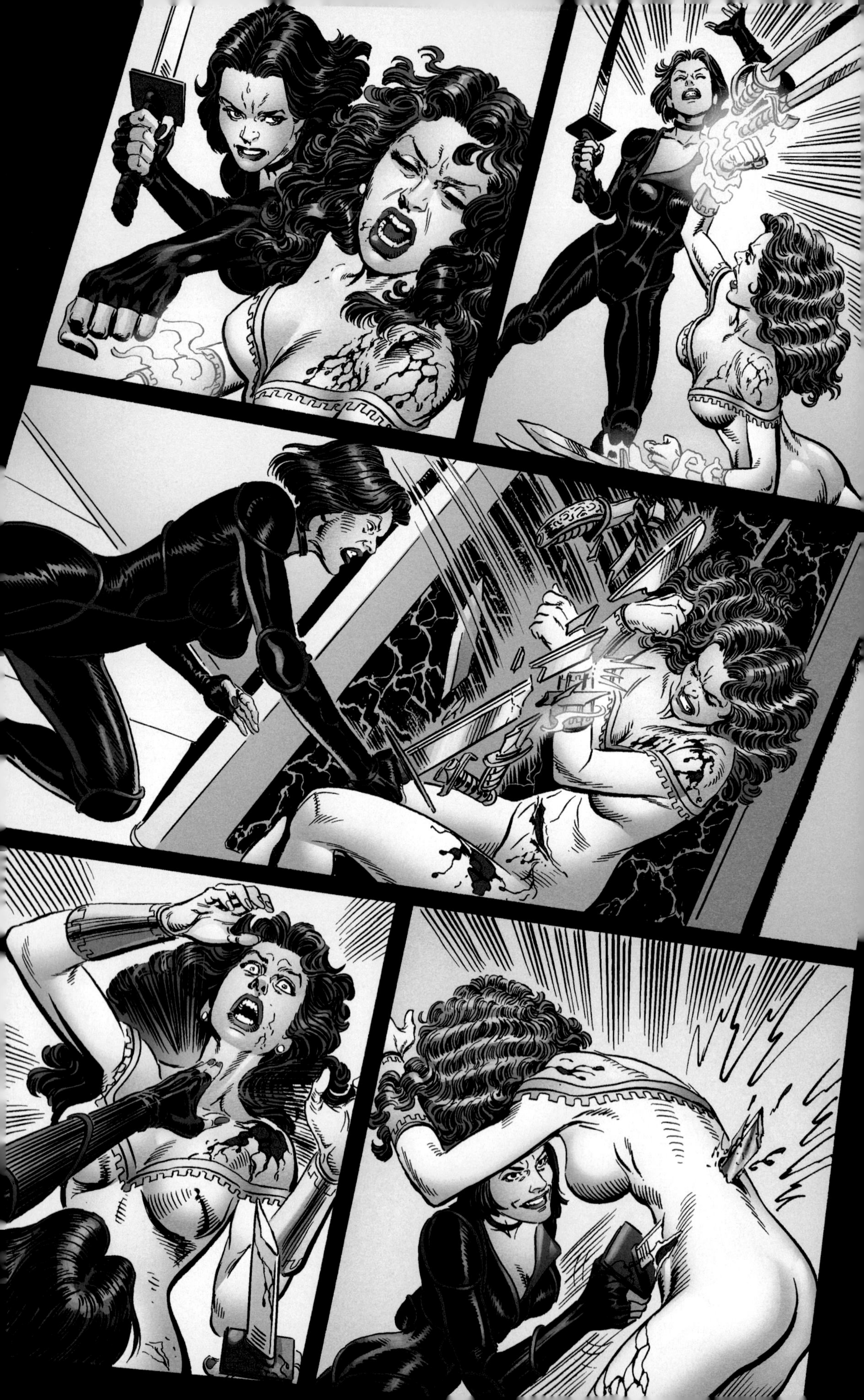

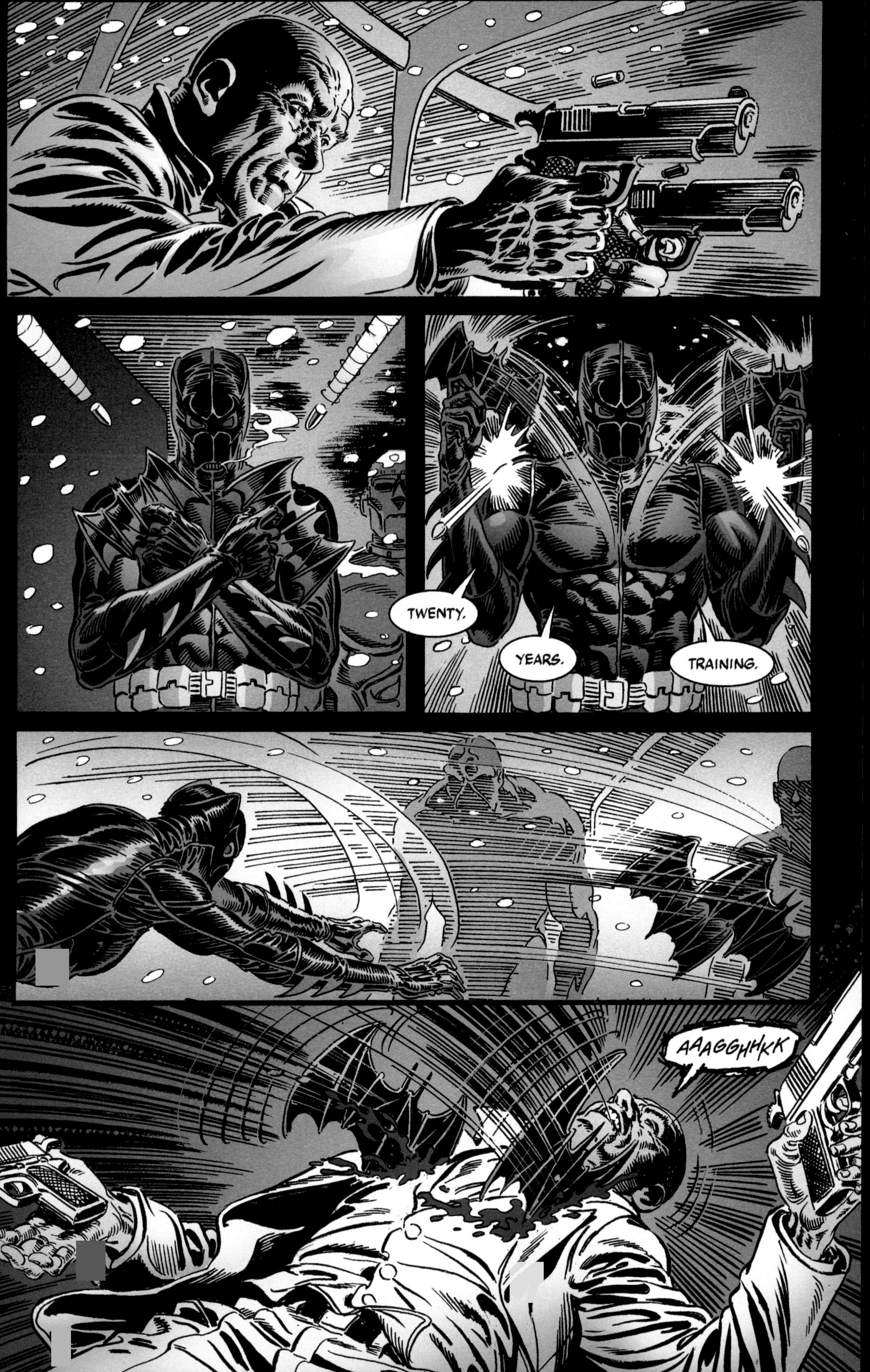
TWENTY.
YEARS.
TRAINING.
AAAGGHHKK

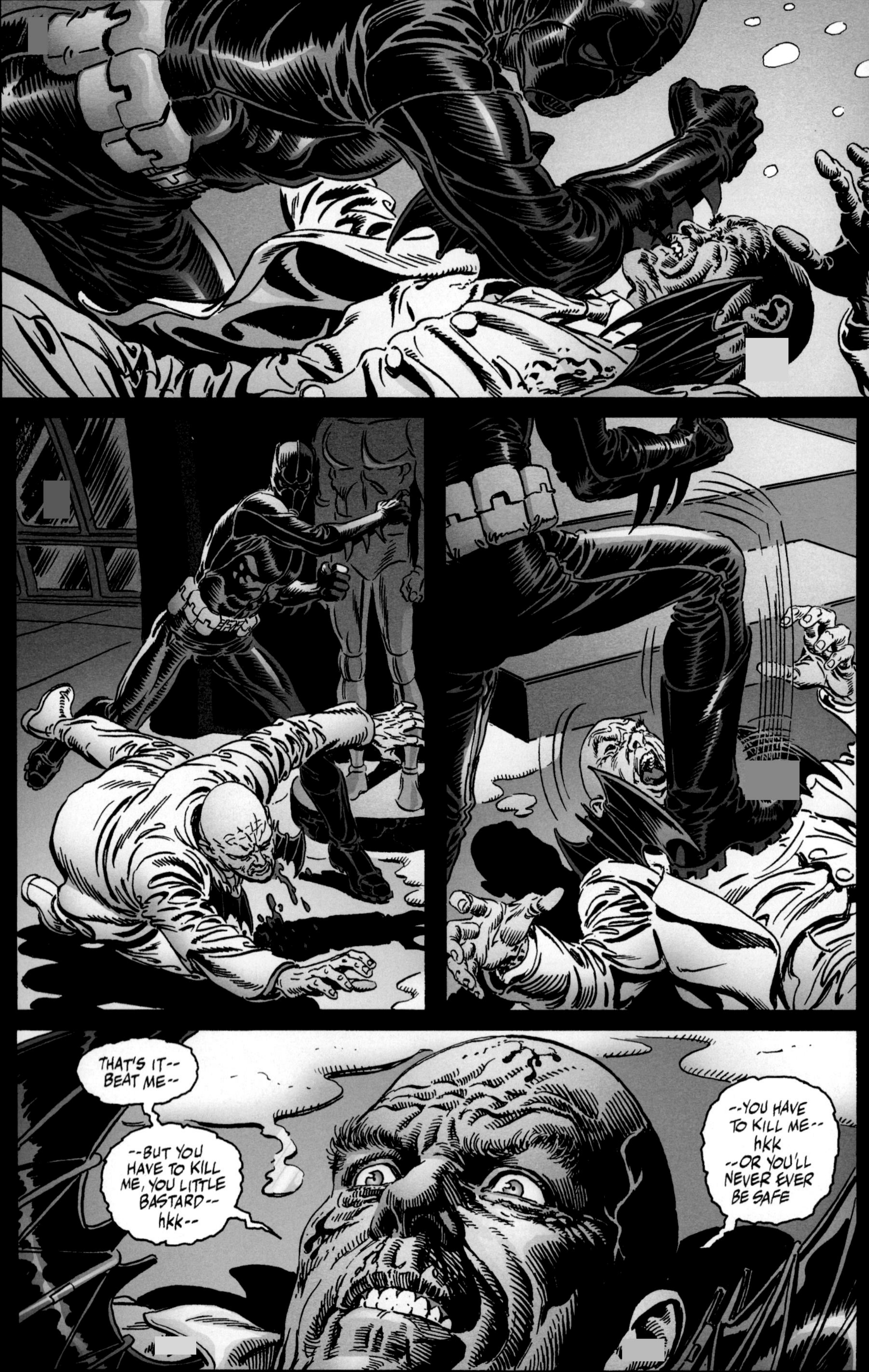
THAT'S IT-- BEAT ME--
--BUT YOU HAVE TO KILL ME, YOU LITTLE BASTARD-- hkk--
--YOU HAVE TO KILL ME-- hkk --OR YOU'LL NEVER EVER BE SAFE

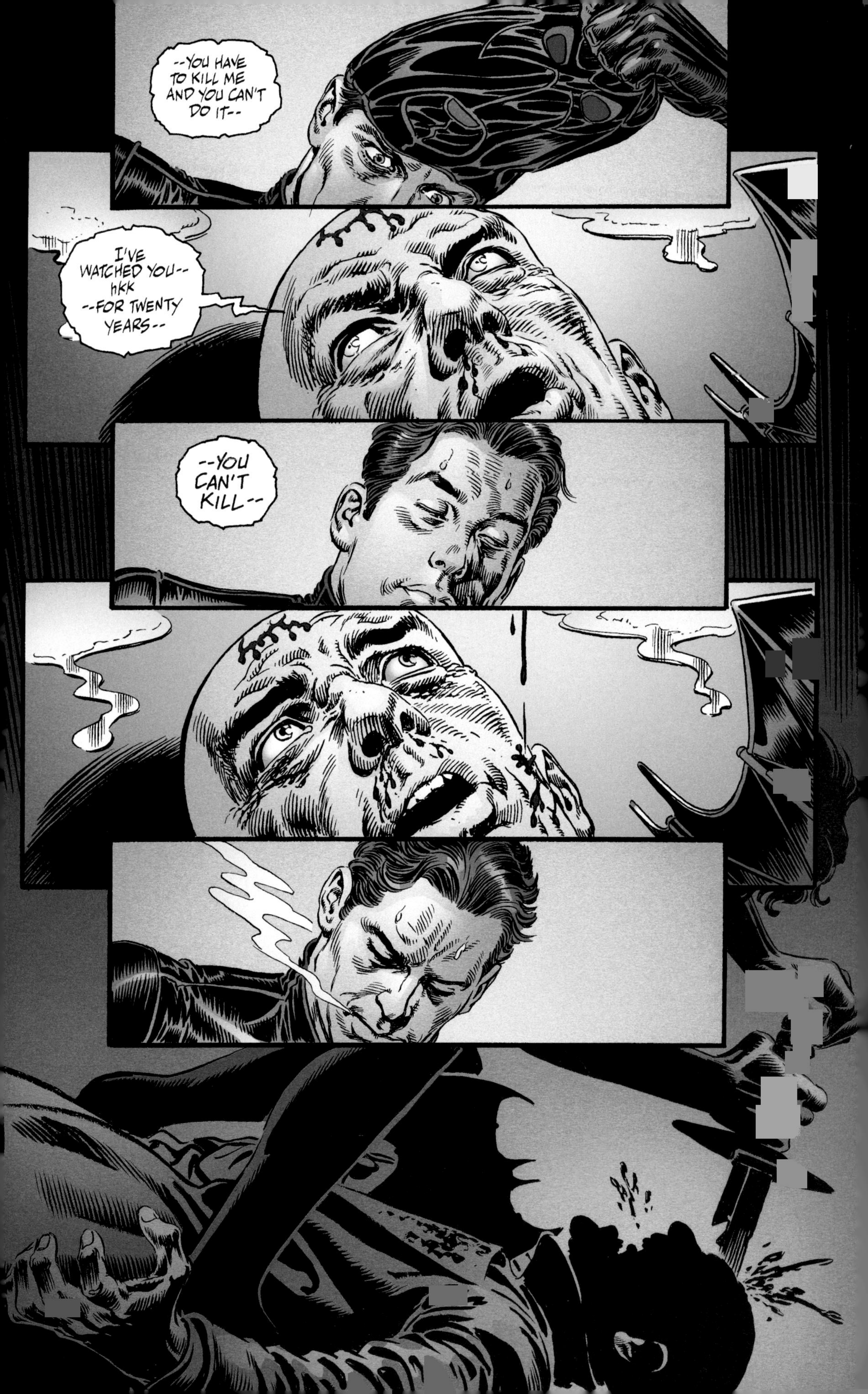
--YOU HAVE TO KILL ME AND YOU CAN'T DO IT--
I'VE WATCHED YOU-- hKK --FOR TWENTY YEARS--
--YOU CAN'T KILL--

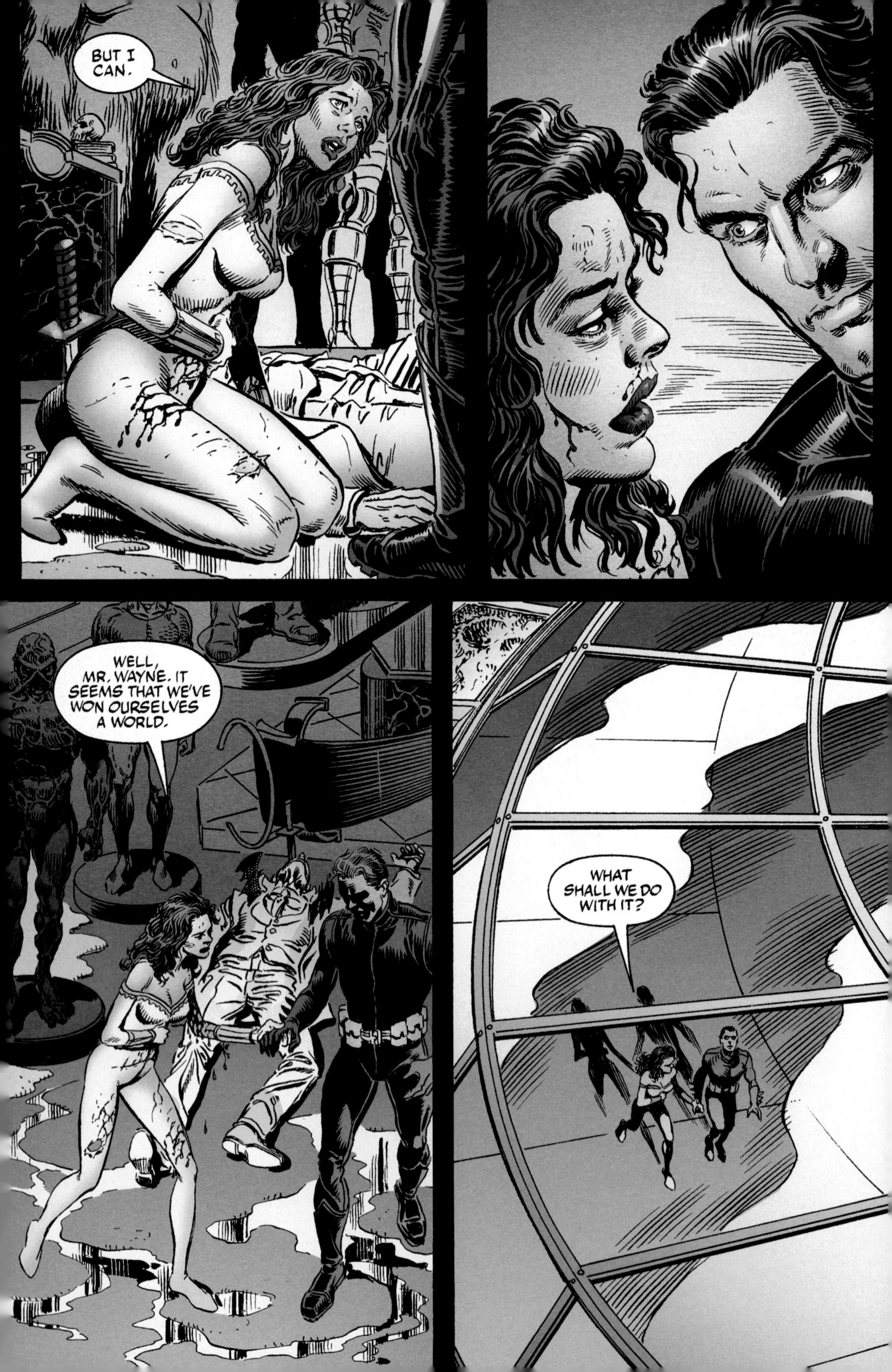
BUT I CAN.
WELL, MR. WAYNE. IT SEEMS THAT WE'VE WON OURSELVES A WORLD.
WHAT SHALL WE DO WITH IT?

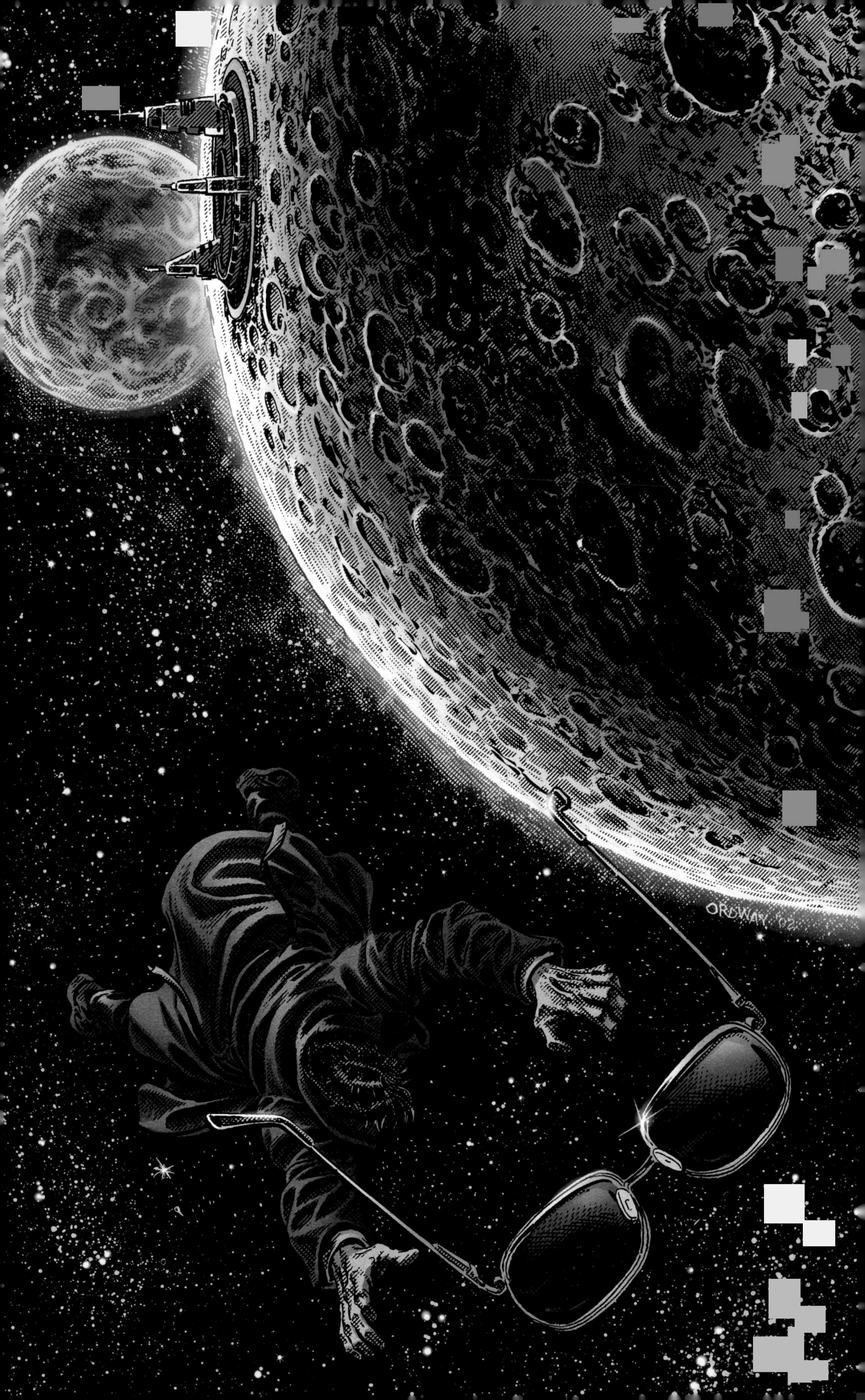
ORDWAY '02

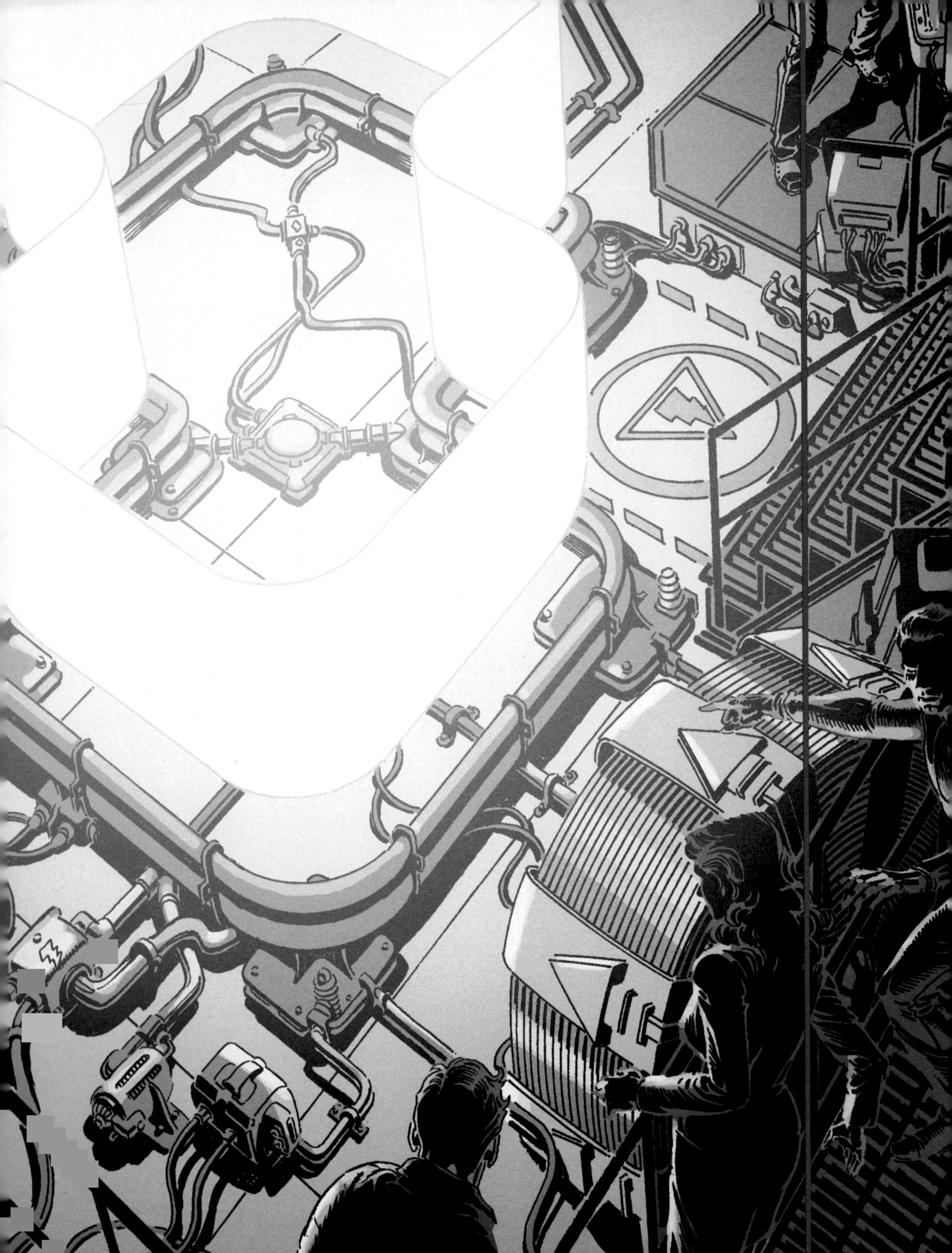

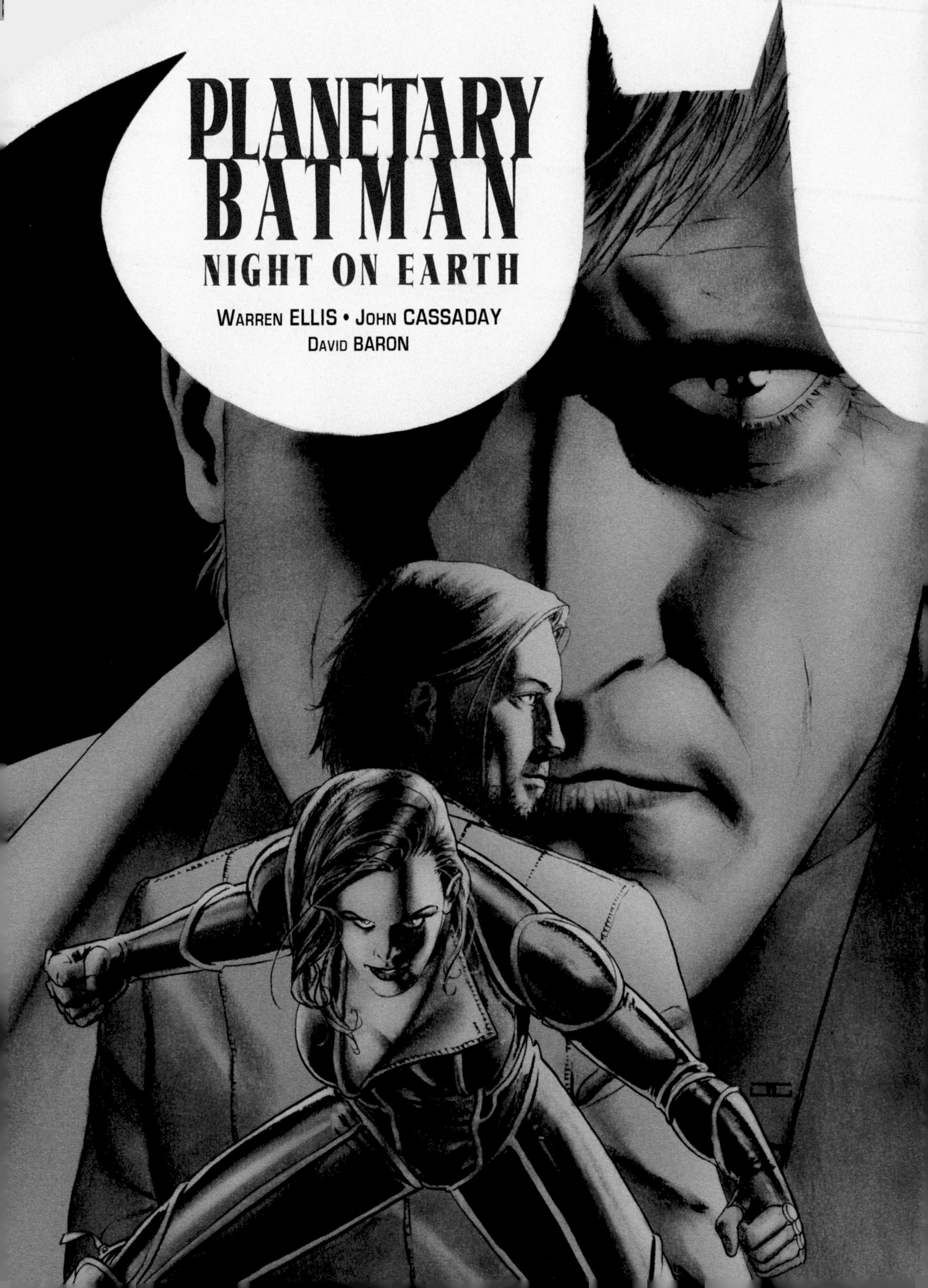
PLANETARY
BATMAN
NIGHT ON EARTH
WARREN ELLIS • JOHN CASSADAY
DAVID BARON

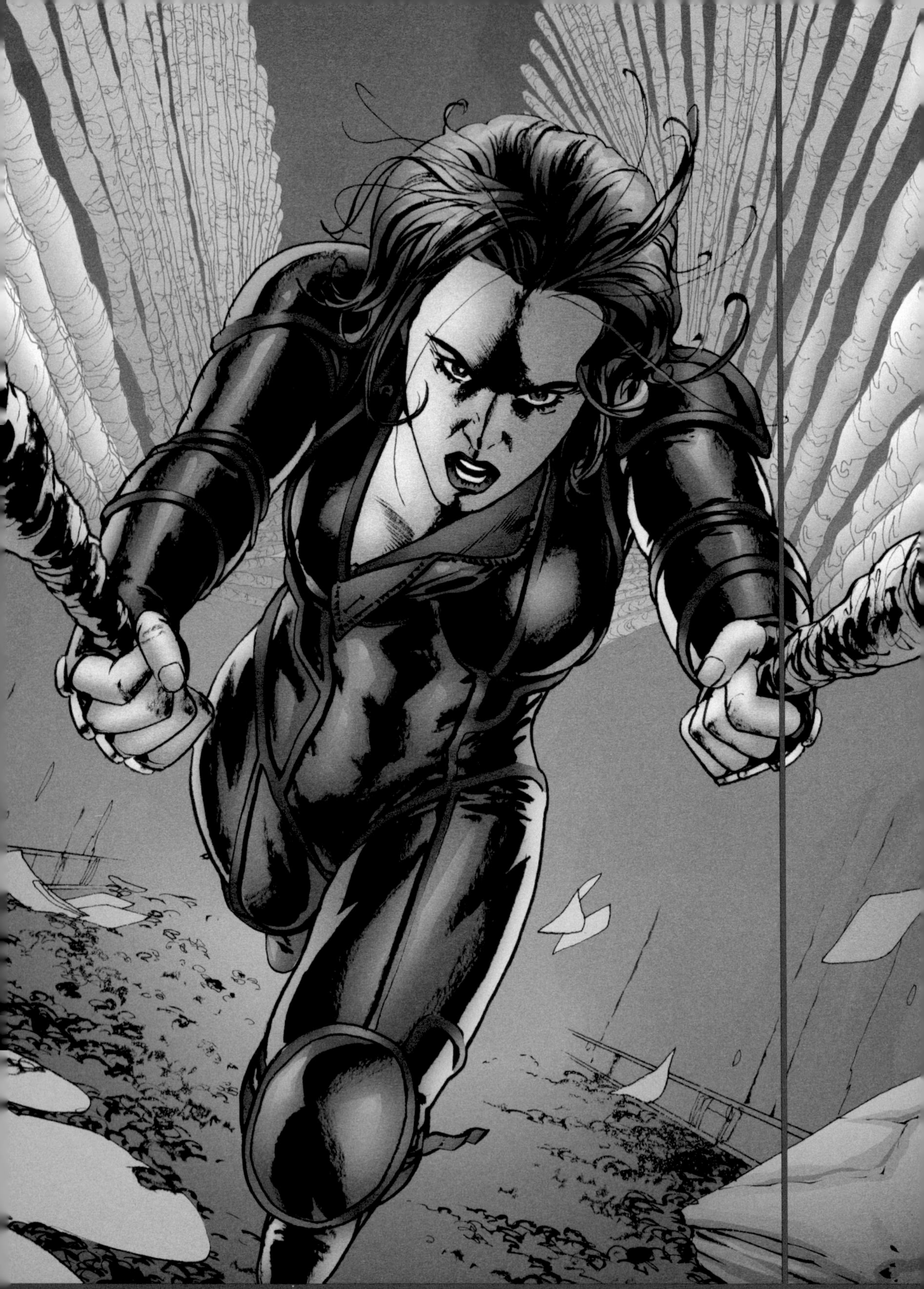

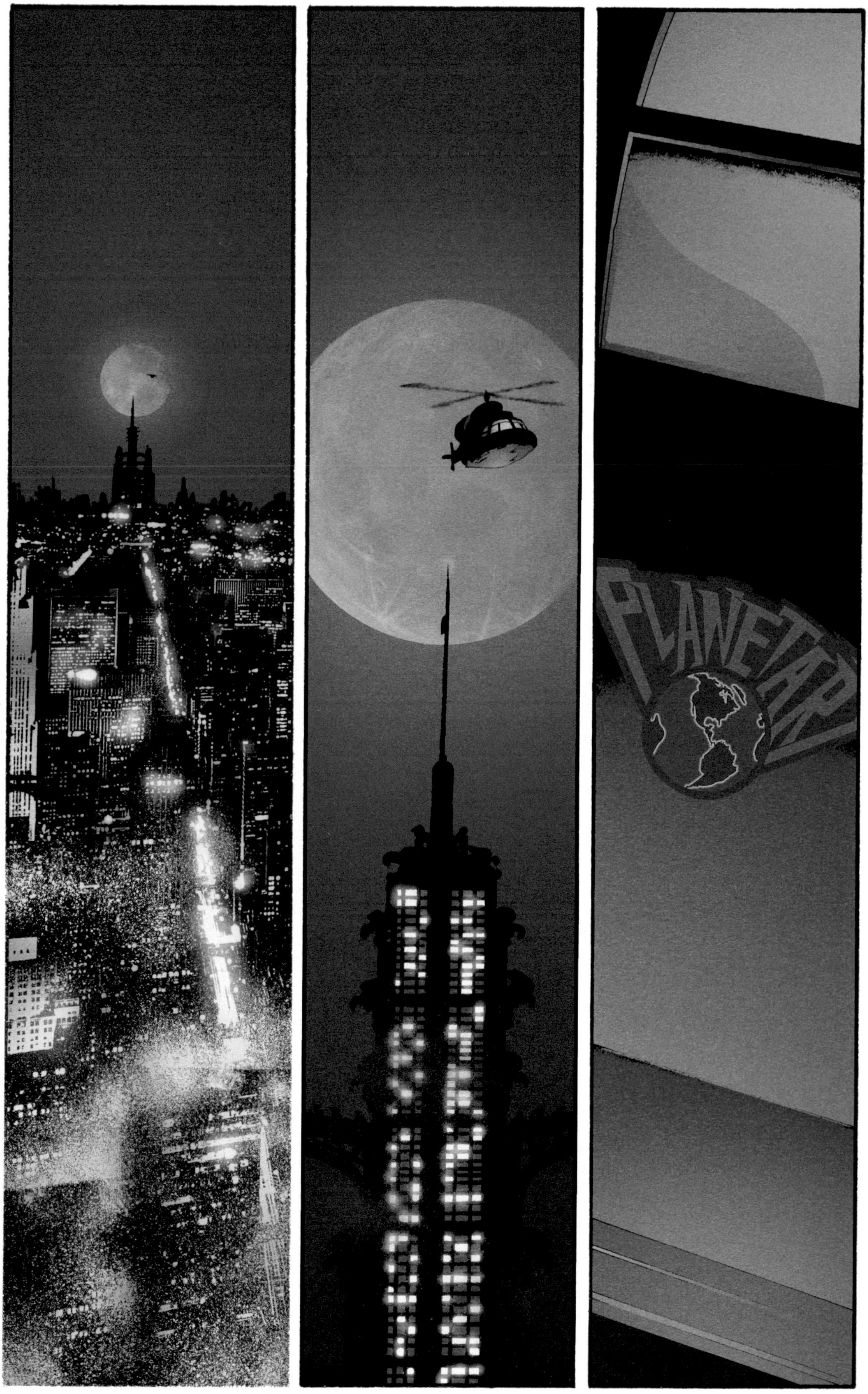

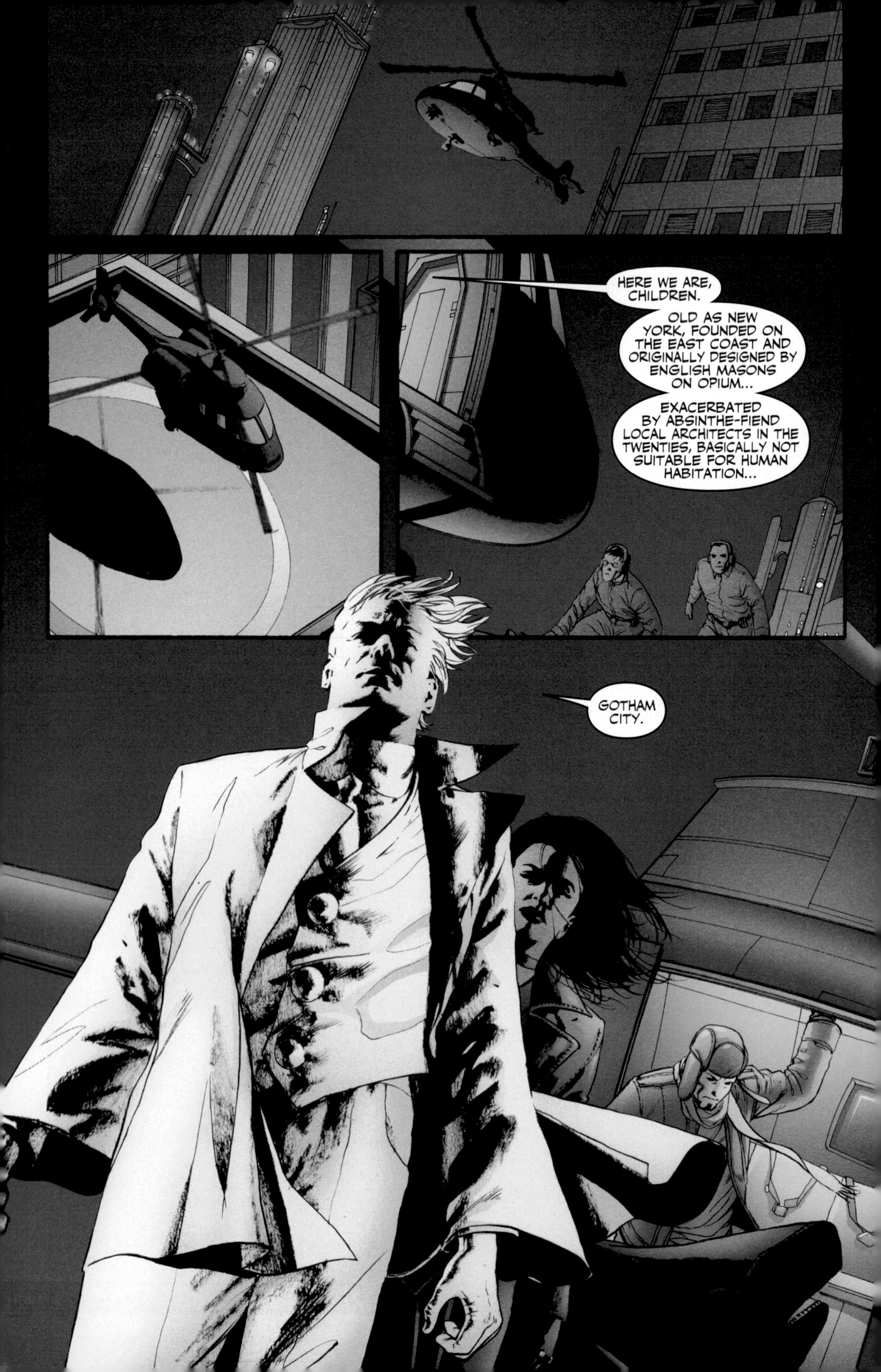
HERE WE ARE, CHILDREN.
OLD AS NEW YORK, FOUNDED ON THE EAST COAST AND ORIGINALLY DESIGNED BY ENGLISH MASONS ON OPIUM...
EXACERBATED BY ABSINTHE-FIEND LOCAL ARCHITECTS IN THE TWENTIES, BASICALLY NOT SUITABLE FOR HUMAN HABITATION...
GOTHAM CITY.

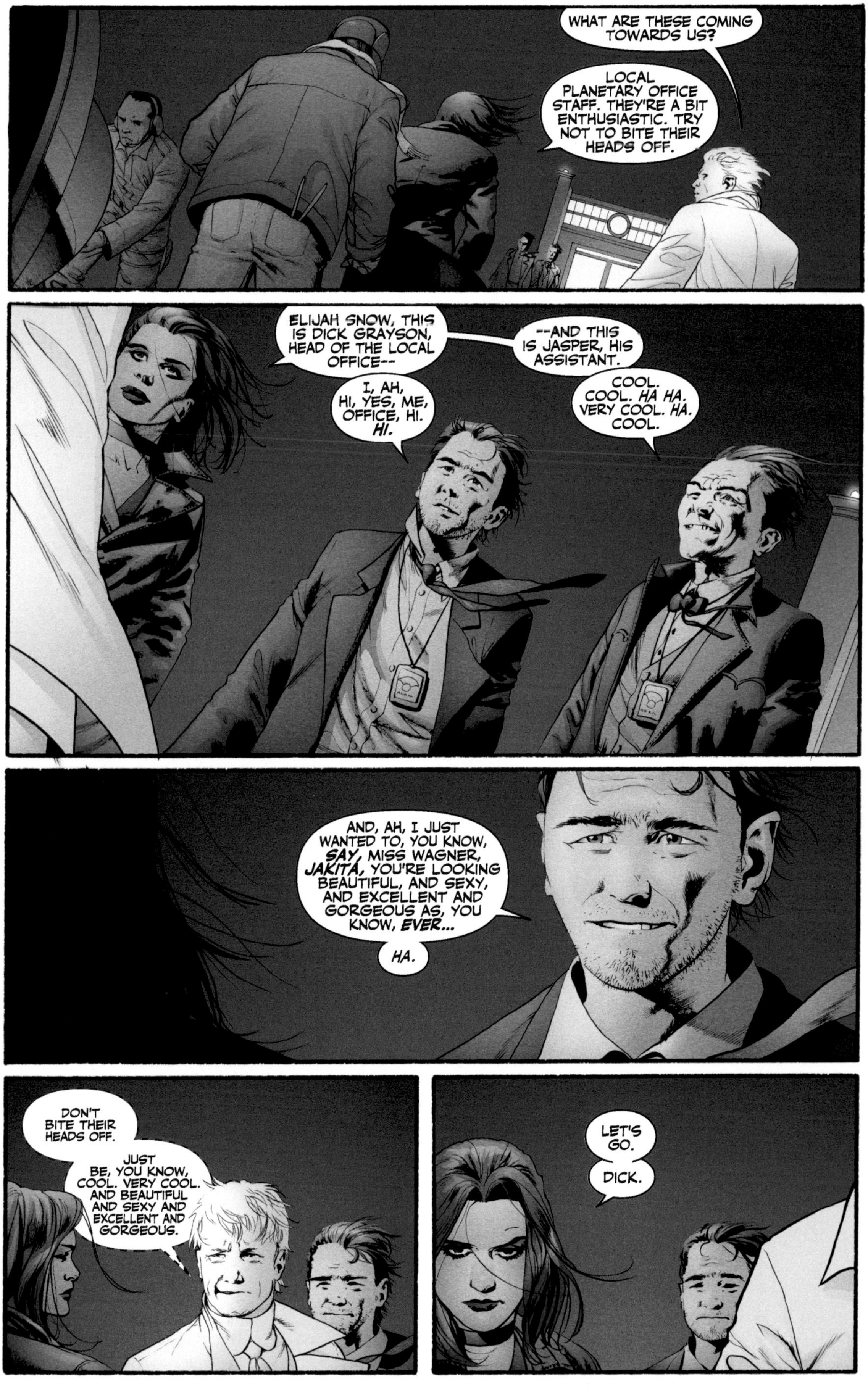
WHAT ARE THESE COMING TOWARDS US?
LOCAL PLANETARY OFFICE STAFF. THEY'RE A BIT ENTHUSIASTIC. TRY NOT TO BITE THEIR HEADS OFF.
ELIJAH SNOW, THIS IS DICK GRAYSON, HEAD OF THE LOCAL OFFICE--
--AND THIS IS JASPER, HIS ASSISTANT.
I, AH, HI, YES, ME, OFFICE, HI. *HI.*
COOL. COOL. *HA HA.* VERY COOL. *HA.* COOL.
AND, AH, I JUST WANTED TO, YOU KNOW, *SAY,* MISS WAGNER, *JAKITA,* YOU'RE LOOKING BEAUTIFUL, AND SEXY, AND EXCELLENT AND GORGEOUS AS, YOU KNOW, *EVER...*
HA.
DON'T BITE THEIR HEADS OFF.
JUST BE, YOU KNOW, COOL. VERY COOL. AND BEAUTIFUL AND SEXY AND EXCELLENT AND GORGEOUS.
LET'S GO.
DICK.

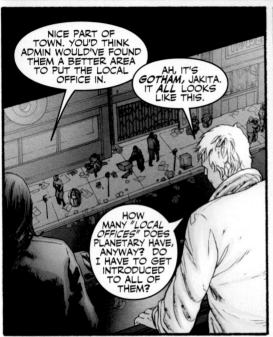

NICE PART OF TOWN. YOU'D THINK ADMIN WOULD'VE FOUND THEM A BETTER AREA TO PUT THE LOCAL OFFICE IN.

AH, IT'S *GOTHAM*, JAKITA. IT *ALL* LOOKS LIKE THIS.

HOW MANY *"LOCAL OFFICES"* DOES PLANETARY HAVE, ANYWAY? DO I HAVE TO GET INTRODUCED TO ALL OF THEM?

WELL, IT'S NOT CALLED PLANETARY BECAUSE WE ONLY HAVE OFFICES IN TWOBLONDES, ARIZONA.

IT'S A BIG JOB WE SET OURSELVES: UNCOVERING THE SECRET HISTORY OF THE WORLD.

SO WE'RE ALL OVER THE PLANET: DIGGING EVERYWHERE AT ONCE.

AH, MISS WAGNER...THE DRUMMER'S DOING SOMETHING TO MY TELEVISION SET AGAIN...

ZIP IT UP, DRUMS.

AND I'VE TOLD YOU BEFORE ABOUT MAKING INNOCENT PEOPLE'S TV SETS PICK UP SHOWS FROM OTHER PLANETS.

WASN'T DOIN' NOTHIN' WRONG

YOU WERE TUNING INTO THAT DAMN ALIEN PORN CHANNEL AGAIN AND YOU KNOW IT.

COME ON; LET'S GET THIS DONE AND GET BACK TO NEW YORK. THE LESS TIME I SPEND HERE, THE HAPPIER I'LL BE.

AND THE LESS LIKELY I'LL BE TO PAY ATTENTION TO YOUR NIGHT MANIPULATIONS.

JOHN BLACK. YOU HAVE VERIFIED SIGHTINGS OF HIM HERE IN GOTHAM. YOU KNOW WE WANT TO MEET HIM. YOU CALLED CENTRAL OFFICE LIKE GOOD BOYS.

SPEAK.

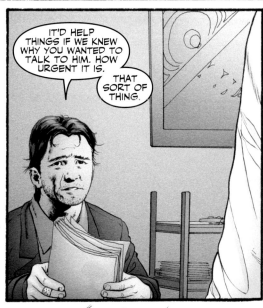

IT'D HELP THINGS IF WE KNEW WHY YOU WANTED TO TALK TO HIM. HOW URGENT IT IS.

THAT SORT OF THING.

WE'VE ASCERTAINED THAT HIS FATHER WAS ONE OF A HANDFUL OF SURVIVORS OF THE AMERICAN SECRET EXPERIMENTATION CAMP SCIENCE CITY ZERO.

WE'VE REASON TO BELIEVE THAT HIS FATHER'S ENHANCED GENETIC STRUCTURE WILL HAVE GIVEN JOHN SOME KIND OF SUPERHUMAN CAPABILITY.

WE WANT TO KNOW WHAT JOHN'S FATHER TOLD HIM ABOUT CITY ZERO, AND WE'D LIKE TO KNOW WHAT HE CAN DO.

KILL PEOPLE.

HE CAN KILL PEOPLE.

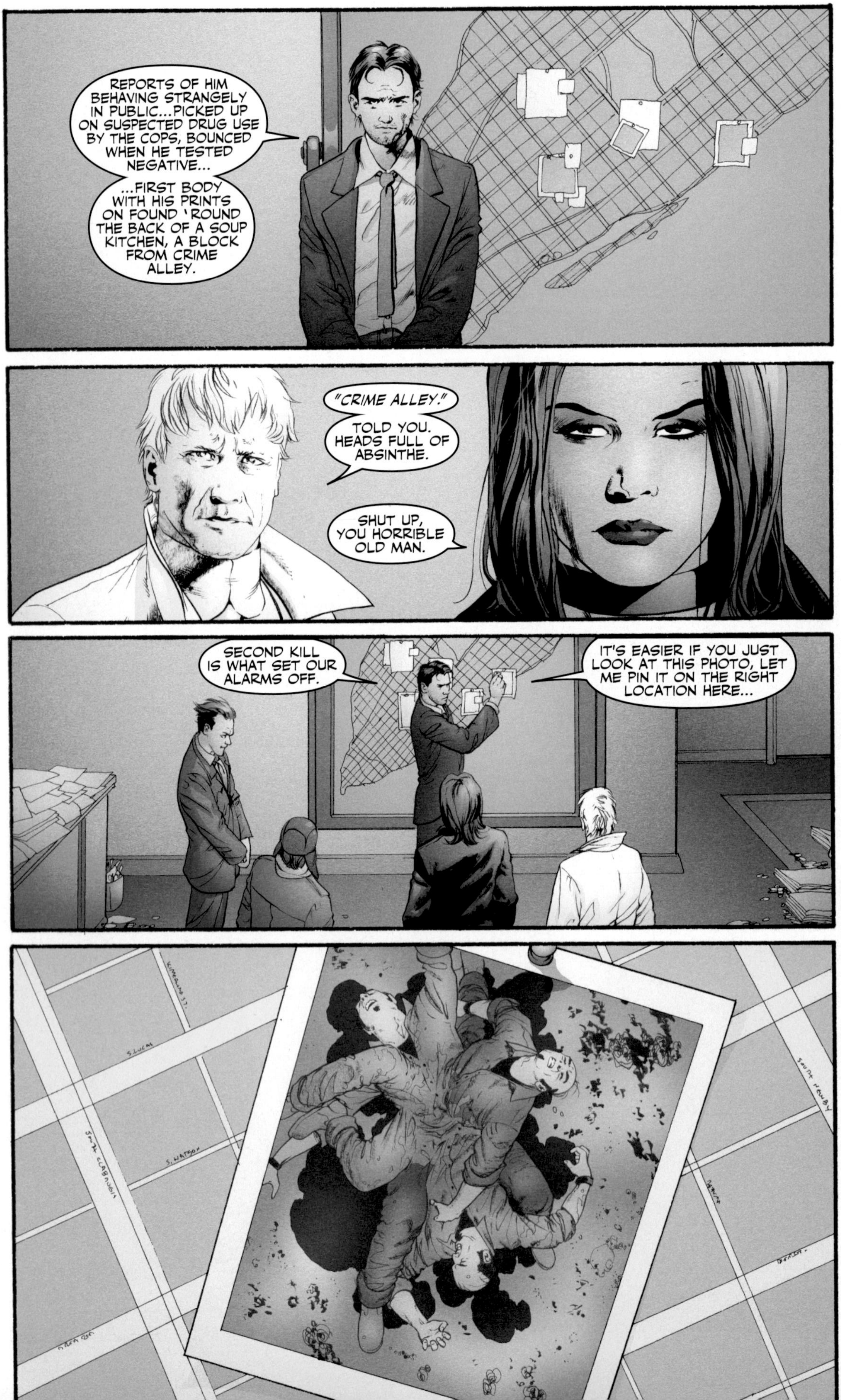
REPORTS OF HIM BEHAVING STRANGELY IN PUBLIC...PICKED UP ON SUSPECTED DRUG USE BY THE COPS, BOUNCED WHEN HE TESTED NEGATIVE...
...FIRST BODY WITH HIS PRINTS ON FOUND 'ROUND THE BACK OF A SOUP KITCHEN, A BLOCK FROM CRIME ALLEY.
"CRIME ALLEY."
TOLD YOU. HEADS FULL OF ABSINTHE.
SHUT UP, YOU HORRIBLE OLD MAN.
SECOND KILL IS WHAT SET OUR ALARMS OFF.
IT'S EASIER IF YOU JUST LOOK AT THIS PHOTO, LET ME PIN IT ON THE RIGHT LOCATION HERE...

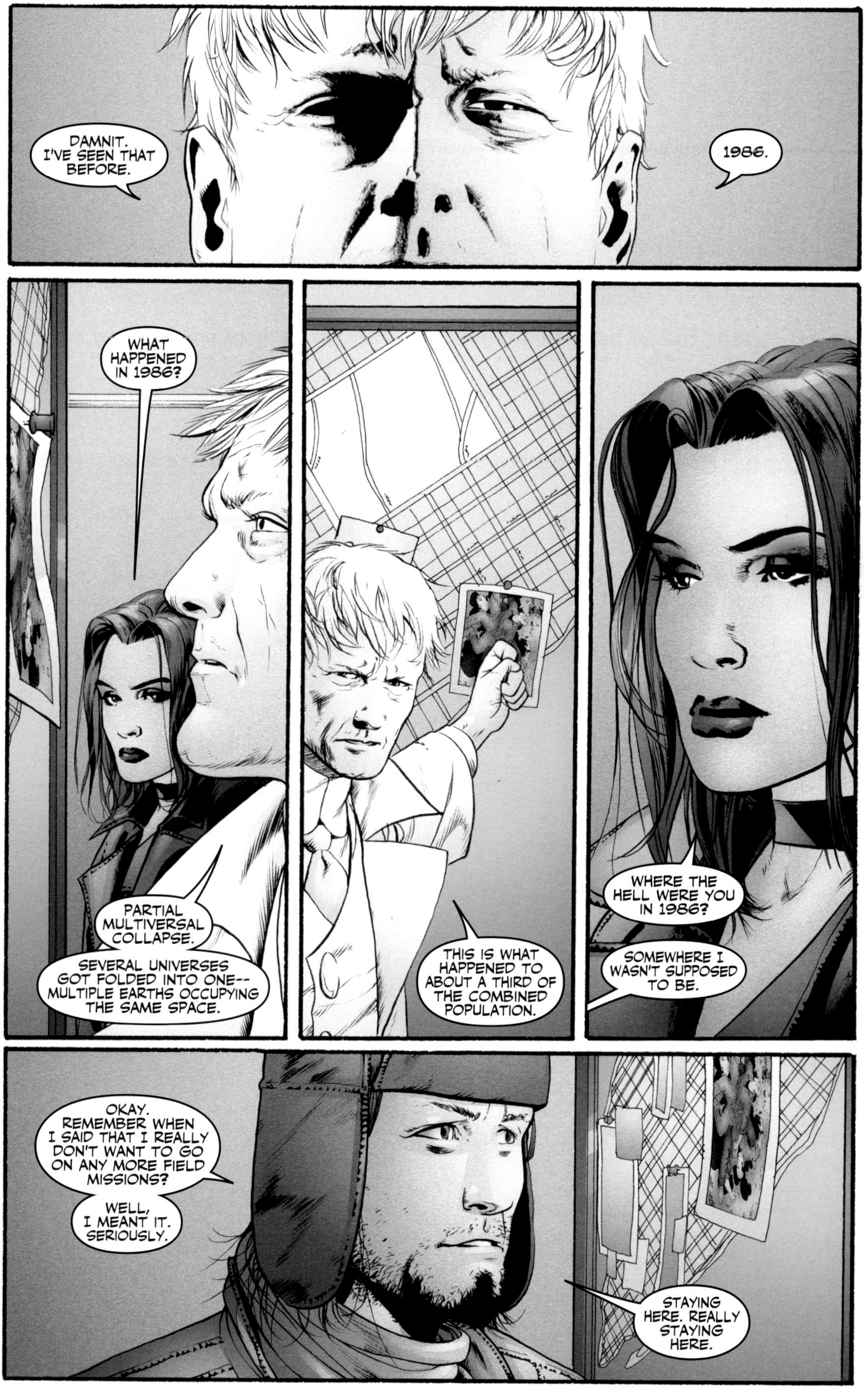
DAMNIT. I'VE SEEN THAT BEFORE.
1986.
WHAT HAPPENED IN 1986?
PARTIAL MULTIVERSAL COLLAPSE.
SEVERAL UNIVERSES GOT FOLDED INTO ONE-- MULTIPLE EARTHS OCCUPYING THE SAME SPACE.
THIS IS WHAT HAPPENED TO ABOUT A THIRD OF THE COMBINED POPULATION.
WHERE THE HELL WERE YOU IN 1986?
SOMEWHERE I WASN'T SUPPOSED TO BE.
OKAY. REMEMBER WHEN I SAID THAT I REALLY DON'T WANT TO GO ON ANY MORE FIELD MISSIONS?
WELL, I MEANT IT. SERIOUSLY.
STAYING HERE. REALLY STAYING HERE.

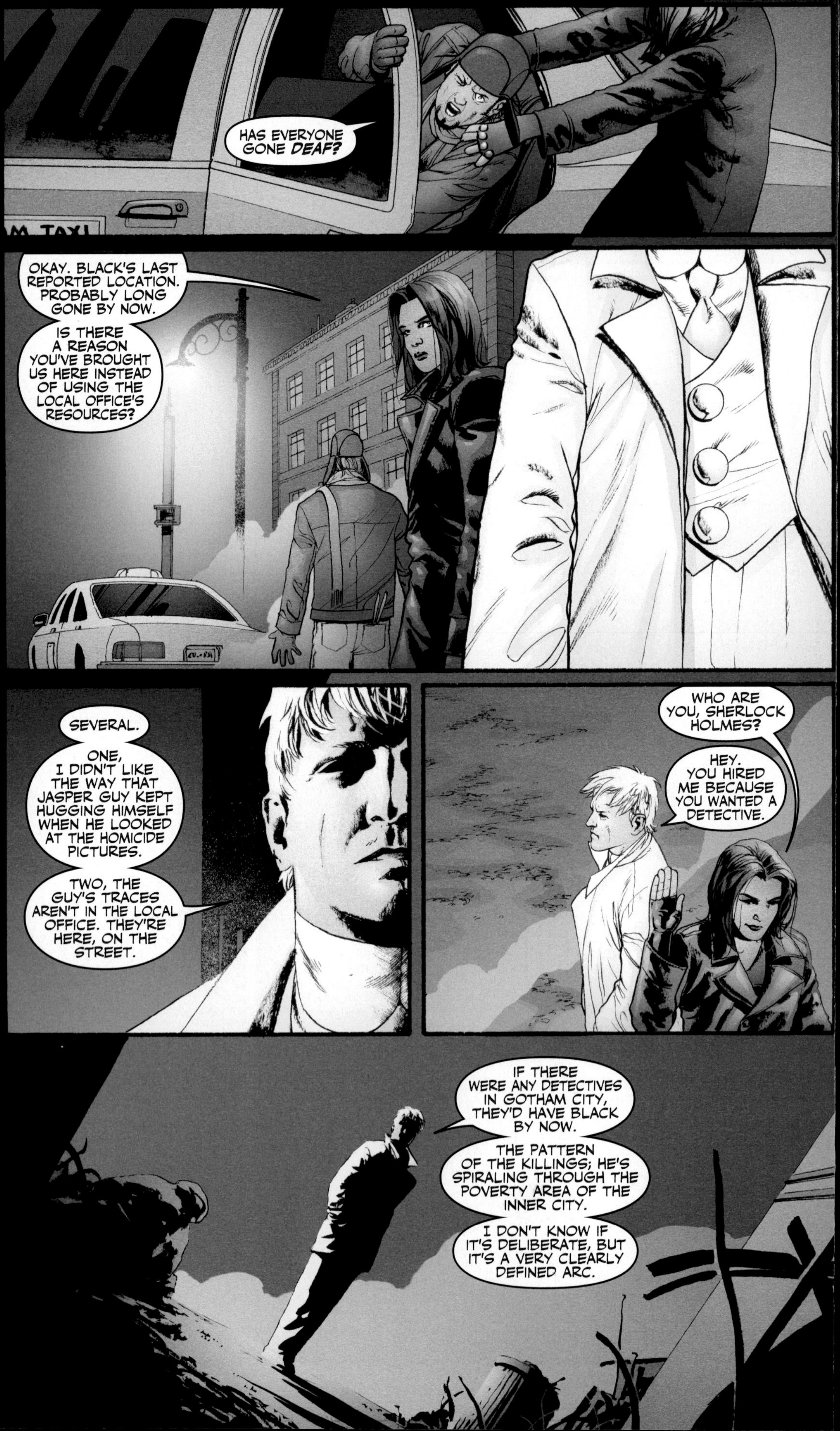
HAS EVERYONE GONE *DEAF?*
OKAY. BLACK'S LAST REPORTED LOCATION. PROBABLY LONG GONE BY NOW.
IS THERE A REASON YOU'VE BROUGHT US HERE INSTEAD OF USING THE LOCAL OFFICE'S RESOURCES?
SEVERAL.
ONE, I DIDN'T LIKE THE WAY THAT JASPER GUY KEPT HUGGING HIMSELF WHEN HE LOOKED AT THE HOMICIDE PICTURES.
TWO, THE GUY'S TRACES AREN'T IN THE LOCAL OFFICE. THEY'RE HERE, ON THE STREET.
WHO ARE YOU, SHERLOCK HOLMES?
HEY. YOU HIRED ME BECAUSE YOU WANTED A DETECTIVE.
IF THERE WERE ANY DETECTIVES IN GOTHAM CITY, THEY'D HAVE BLACK BY NOW.
THE PATTERN OF THE KILLINGS; HE'S SPIRALING THROUGH THE POVERTY AREA OF THE INNER CITY.
I DON'T KNOW IF IT'S DELIBERATE, BUT IT'S A VERY CLEARLY DEFINED ARC.

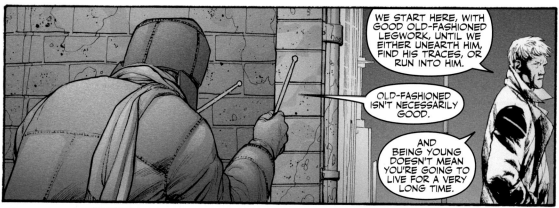

WE START HERE, WITH GOOD OLD-FASHIONED LEGWORK, UNTIL WE EITHER UNEARTH HIM, FIND HIS TRACES, OR RUN INTO HIM.

OLD-FASHIONED ISN'T NECESSARILY GOOD.

AND BEING YOUNG DOESN'T MEAN YOU'RE GOING TO LIVE FOR A VERY LONG TIME.

OH, GROW UP, THE PAIR OF YOU.

SO WHERE EXACTLY ARE WE?

FINGER STREET DISTRICT. THERE USED TO BE WHORES HERE, YOU KNOW.

HOW THE HELL DO YOU KNOW?

I BLEW THROUGH HERE WITH THE CONQUERORS OF THE UNCANNY BACK IN '59. FINGER STREET WAS A WILD PLACE, BACK THEN.

NOW LOOK AT IT. IT'S LIKE SOMEONE SHOT IT IN THE HEAD.

FORGIVE ME IF I DON'T USE THE PRESENCE OF INEXPENSIVE HOOKERS AS THE YARDSTICK OF A THRIVING DISTRICT.

LET'S WALK.

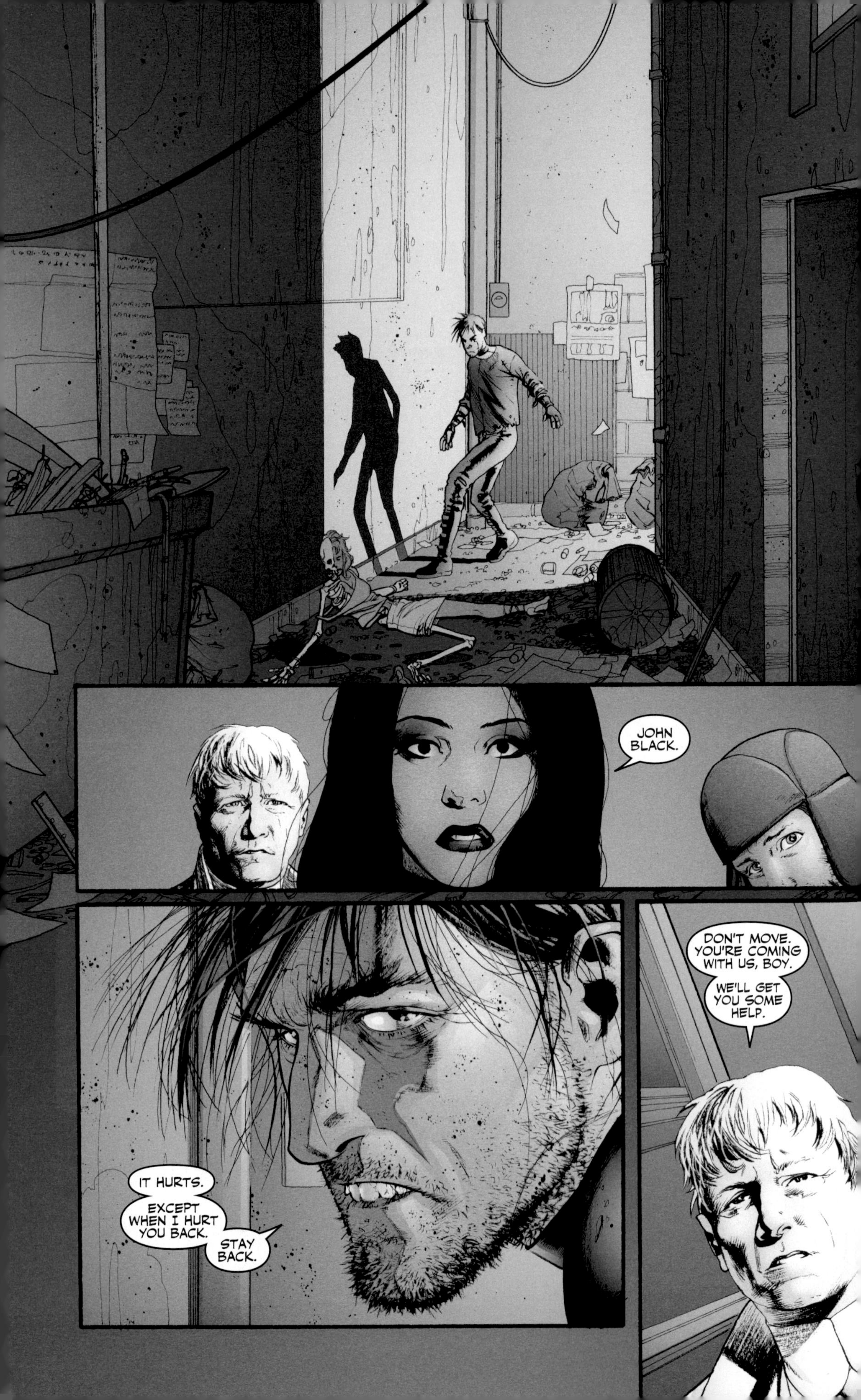
JOHN BLACK.
IT HURTS.
EXCEPT WHEN I HURT YOU BACK.
STAY BACK.
DON'T MOVE. YOU'RE COMING WITH US, BOY.
WE'LL GET YOU SOME HELP.

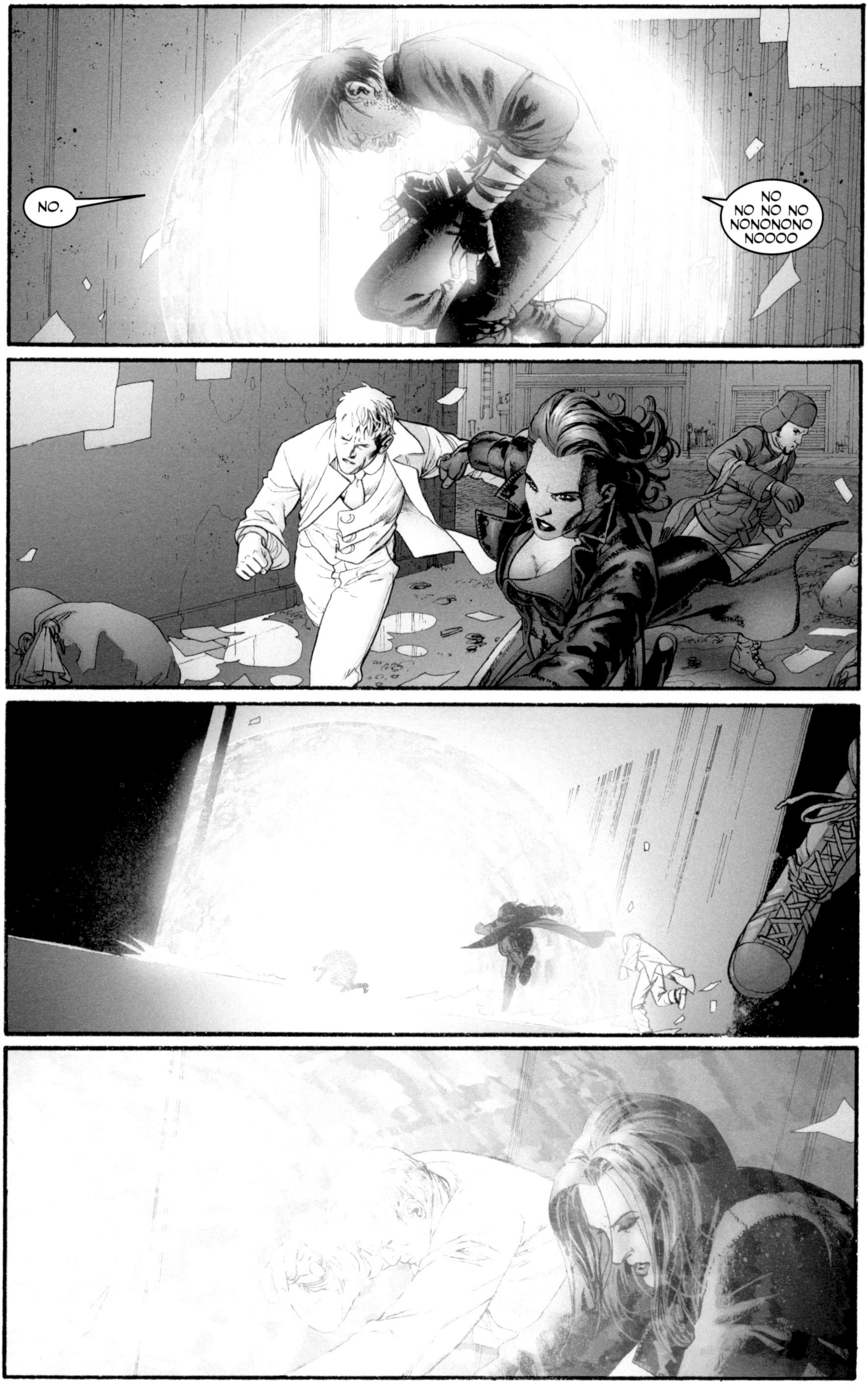
NO.
NO NO NO NO NONONONO NOOOO

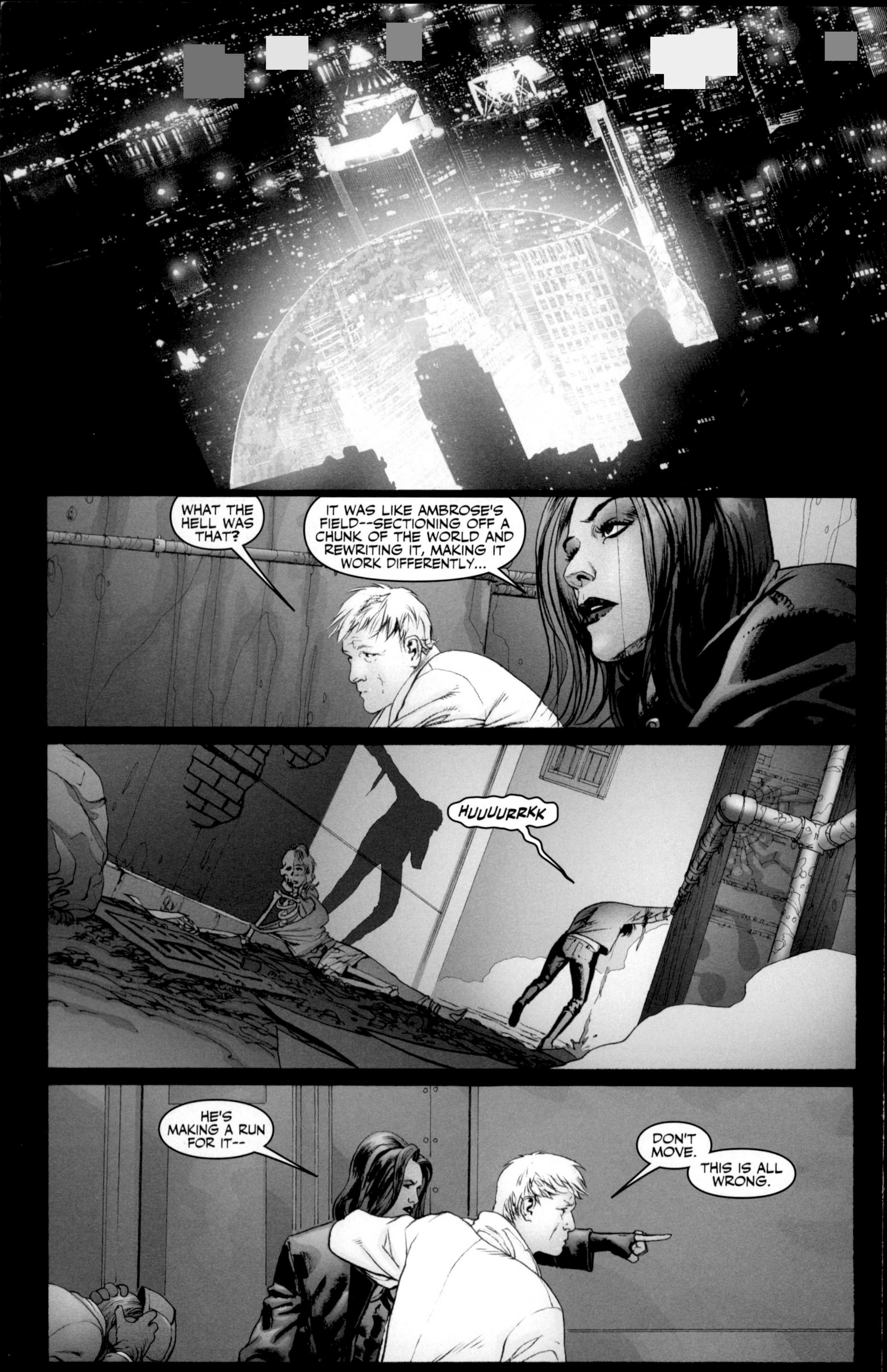
WHAT THE HELL WAS THAT?
IT WAS LIKE AMBROSE'S FIELD--SECTIONING OFF A CHUNK OF THE WORLD AND REWRITING IT, MAKING IT WORK DIFFERENTLY...
HUUUURRKK
HE'S MAKING A RUN FOR IT--
DON'T MOVE.
THIS IS ALL WRONG.

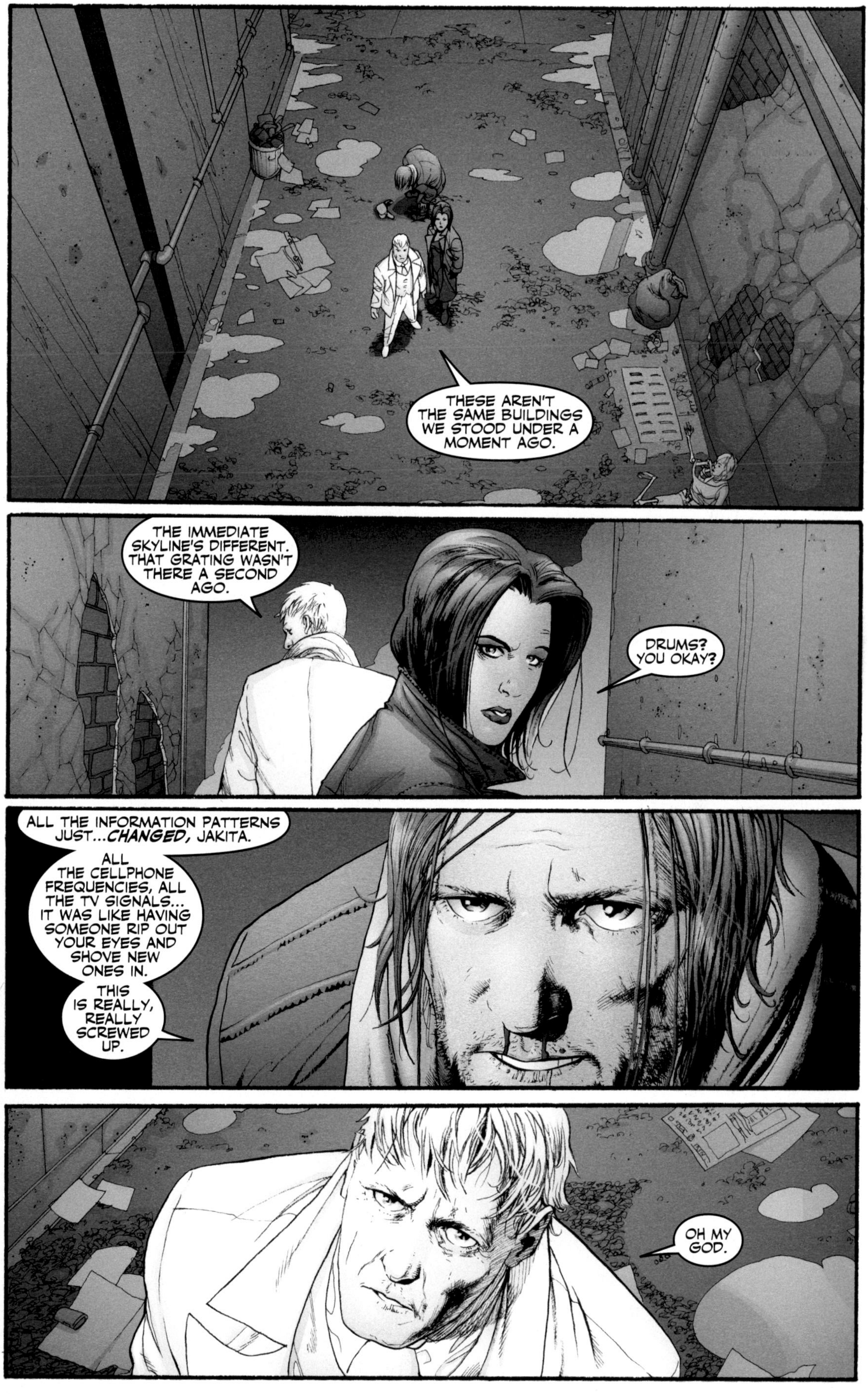
THESE AREN'T THE SAME BUILDINGS WE STOOD UNDER A MOMENT AGO.
THE IMMEDIATE SKYLINE'S DIFFERENT. THAT GRATING WASN'T THERE A SECOND AGO.
DRUMS? YOU OKAY?
ALL THE INFORMATION PATTERNS JUST...CHANGED, JAKITA.
ALL THE CELLPHONE FREQUENCIES, ALL THE TV SIGNALS... IT WAS LIKE HAVING SOMEONE RIP OUT YOUR EYES AND SHOVE NEW ONES IN.
THIS IS REALLY, REALLY SCREWED UP.
OH MY GOD.

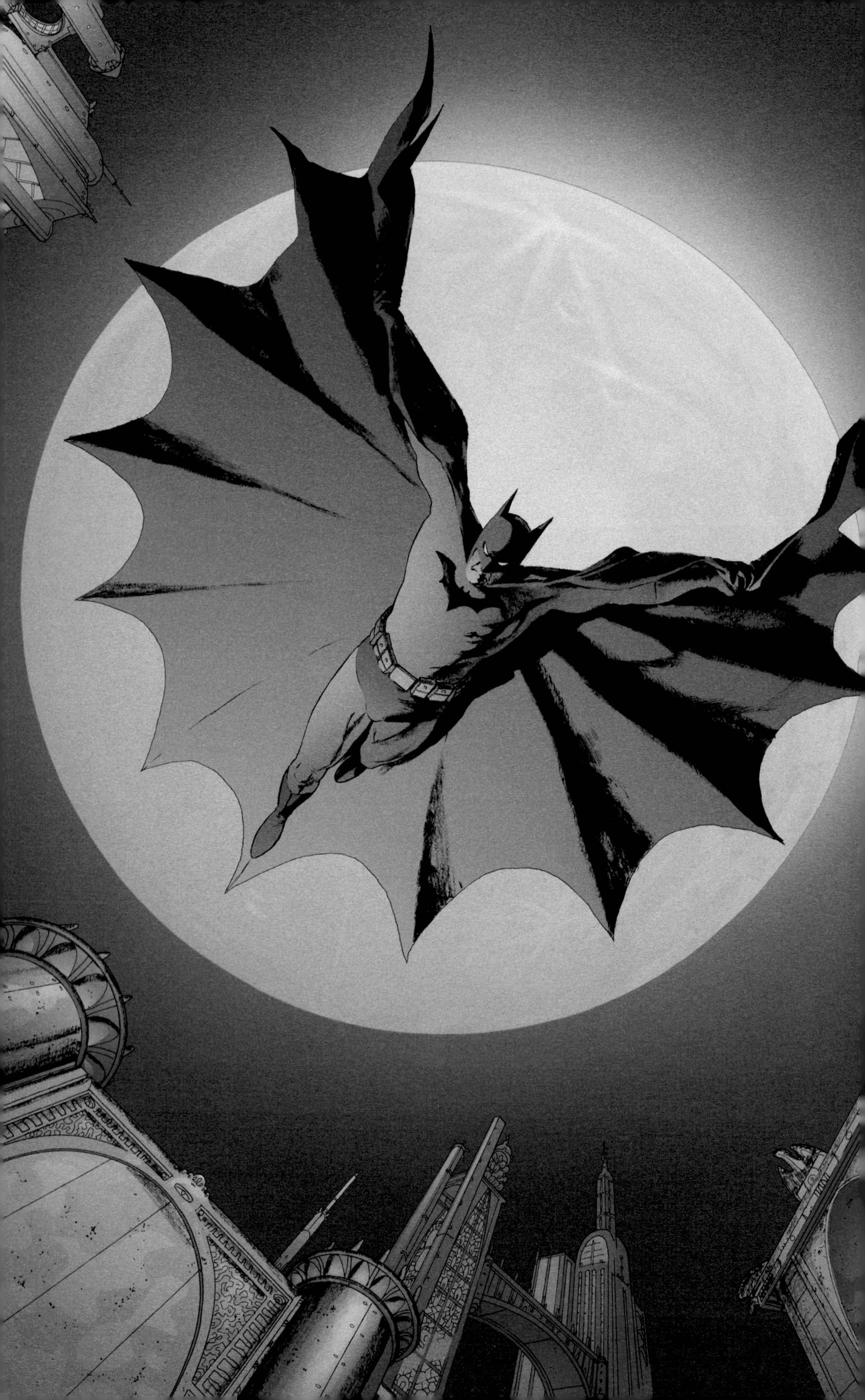

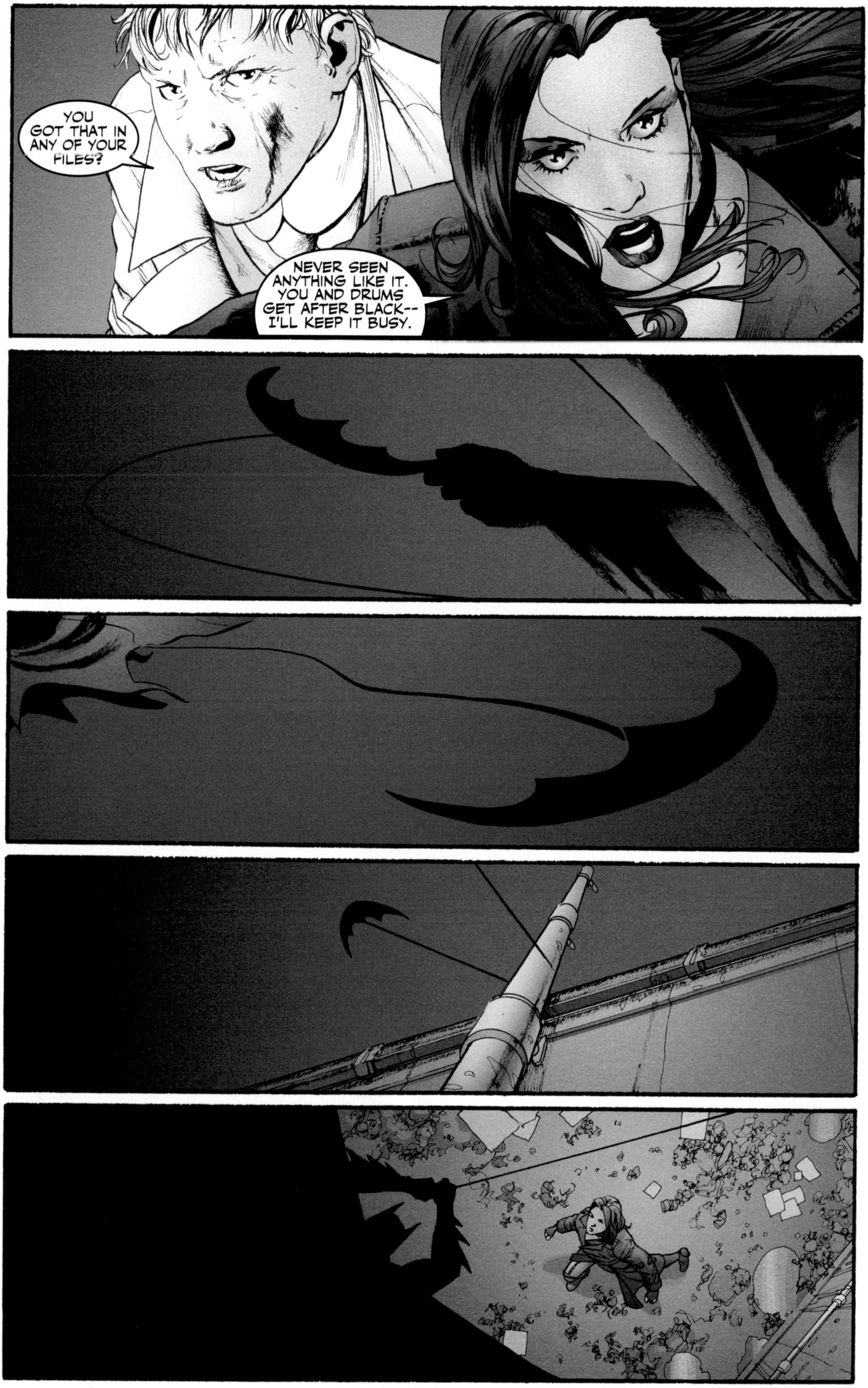
YOU GOT THAT IN ANY OF YOUR FILES?
NEVER SEEN ANYTHING LIKE IT. YOU AND DRUMS GET AFTER BLACK-- I'LL KEEP IT BUSY.

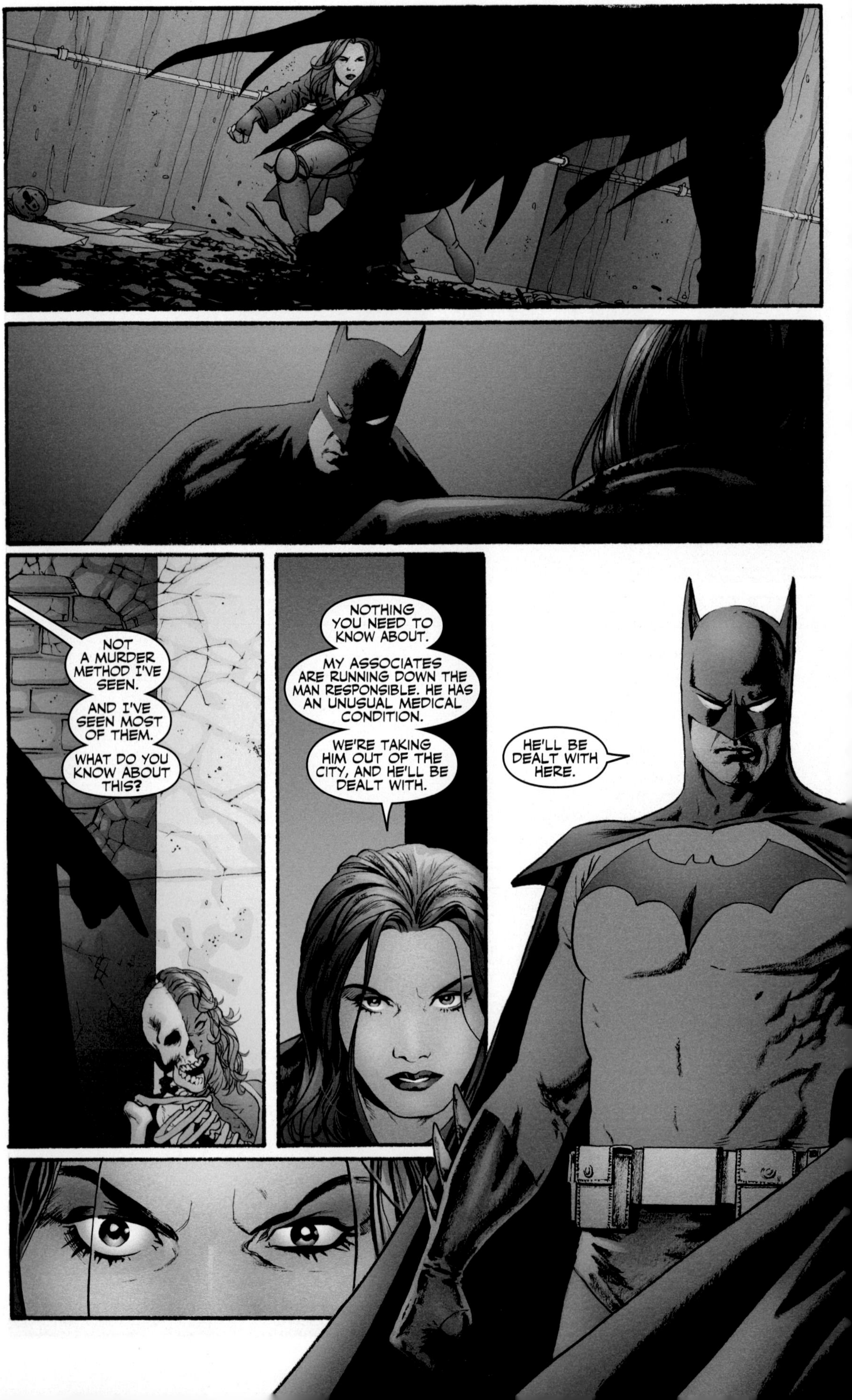
NOT A MURDER METHOD I'VE SEEN.
AND I'VE SEEN MOST OF THEM.
WHAT DO YOU KNOW ABOUT THIS?
NOTHING YOU NEED TO KNOW ABOUT.
MY ASSOCIATES ARE RUNNING DOWN THE MAN RESPONSIBLE. HE HAS AN UNUSUAL MEDICAL CONDITION.
WE'RE TAKING HIM OUT OF THE CITY, AND HE'LL BE DEALT WITH.
HE'LL BE DEALT WITH HERE.

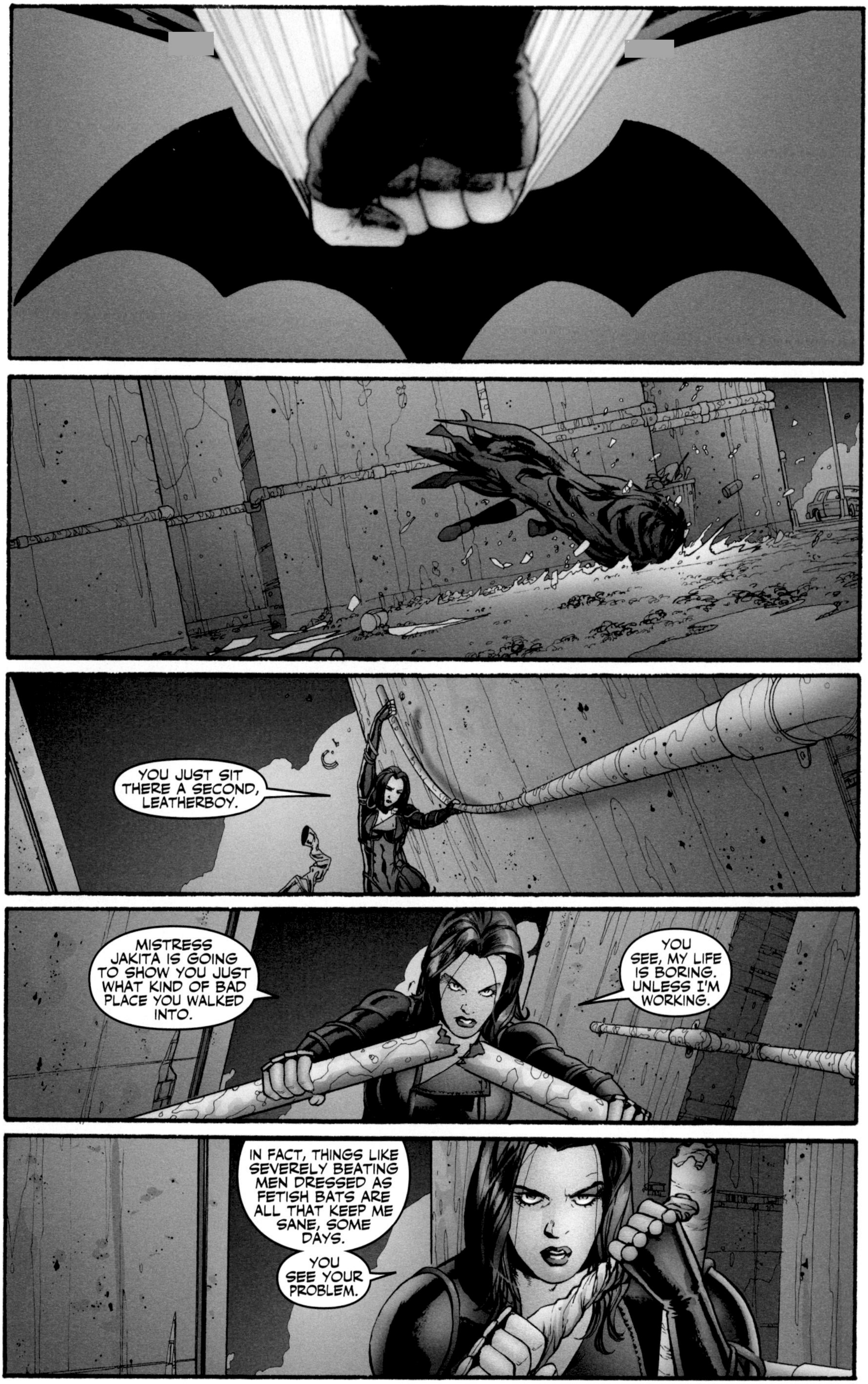
YOU JUST SIT THERE A SECOND, LEATHERBOY.
MISTRESS JAKITA IS GOING TO SHOW YOU JUST WHAT KIND OF BAD PLACE YOU WALKED INTO.
YOU SEE, MY LIFE IS BORING. UNLESS I'M WORKING.
IN FACT, THINGS LIKE SEVERELY BEATING MEN DRESSED AS FETISH BATS ARE ALL THAT KEEP ME SANE, SOME DAYS.
YOU SEE YOUR PROBLEM.

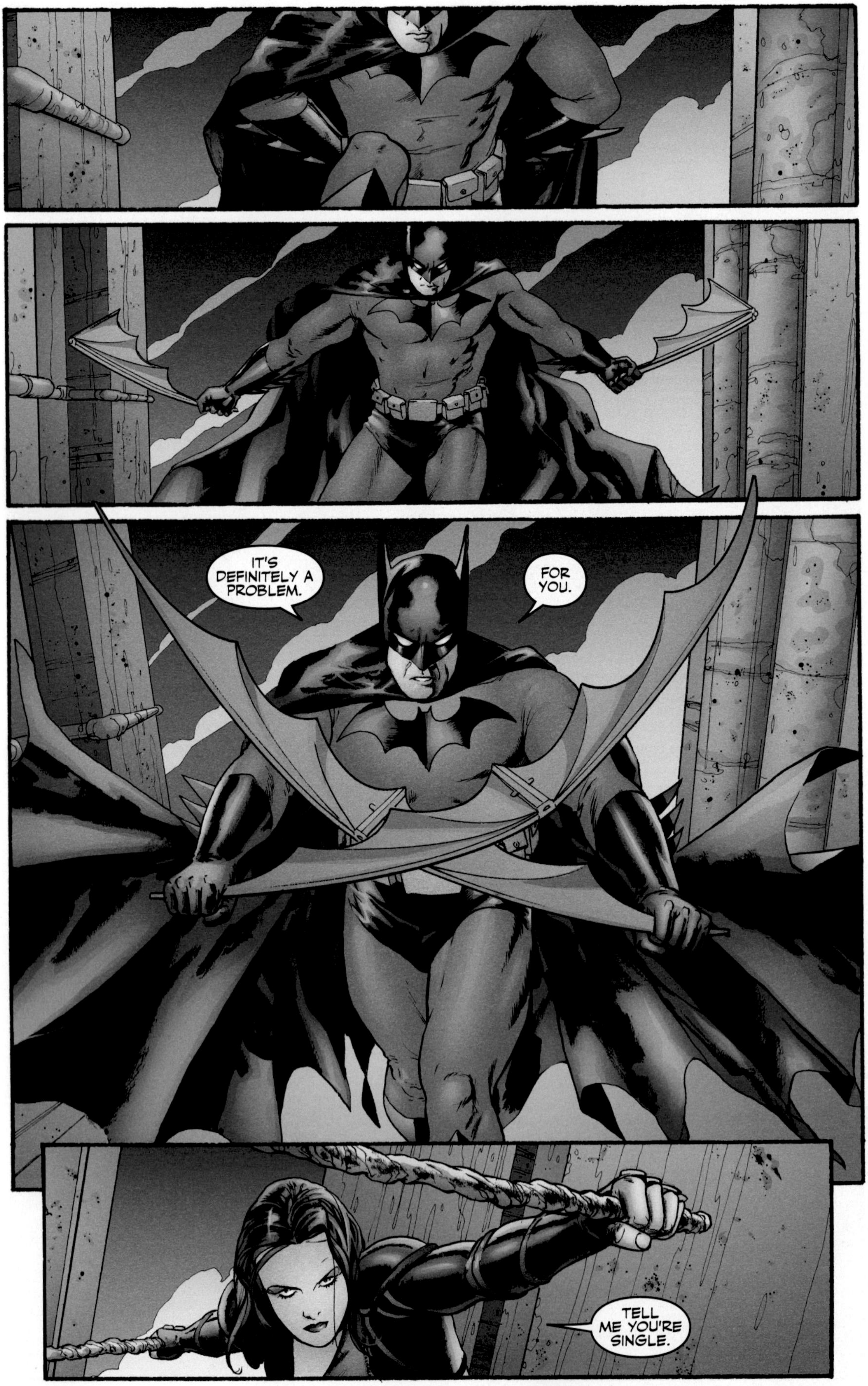
IT'S DEFINITELY A PROBLEM.
FOR YOU.
TELL ME YOU'RE SINGLE.

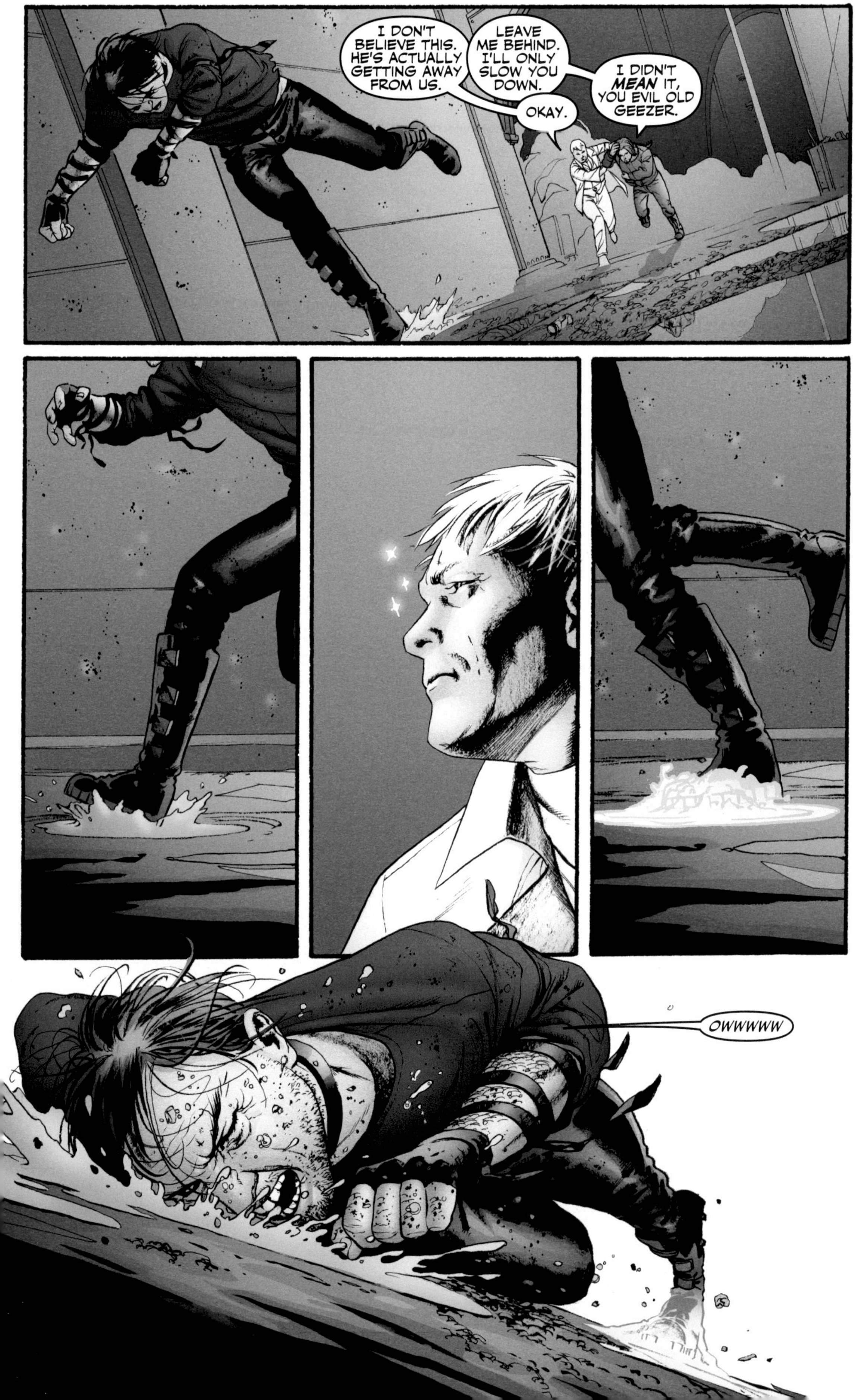
I DON'T BELIEVE THIS. HE'S ACTUALLY GETTING AWAY FROM US.
LEAVE ME BEHIND. I'LL ONLY SLOW YOU DOWN.
OKAY.
I DIDN'T MEAN IT, YOU EVIL OLD GEEZER.
OWWWWW

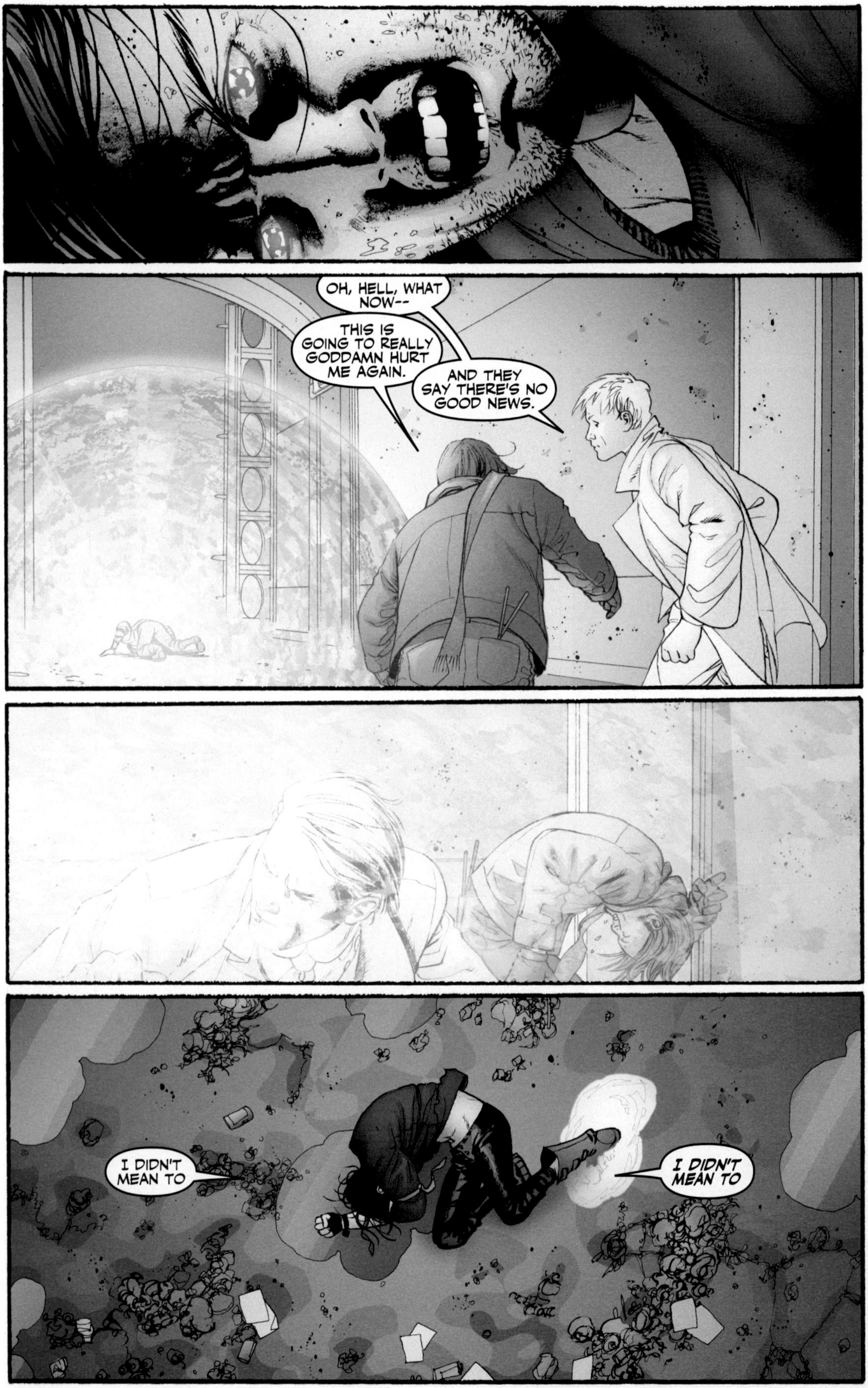
OH, HELL, WHAT NOW--
THIS IS GOING TO REALLY GODDAMN HURT ME AGAIN.
AND THEY SAY THERE'S NO GOOD NEWS.
I DIDN'T MEAN TO
I DIDN'T MEAN TO

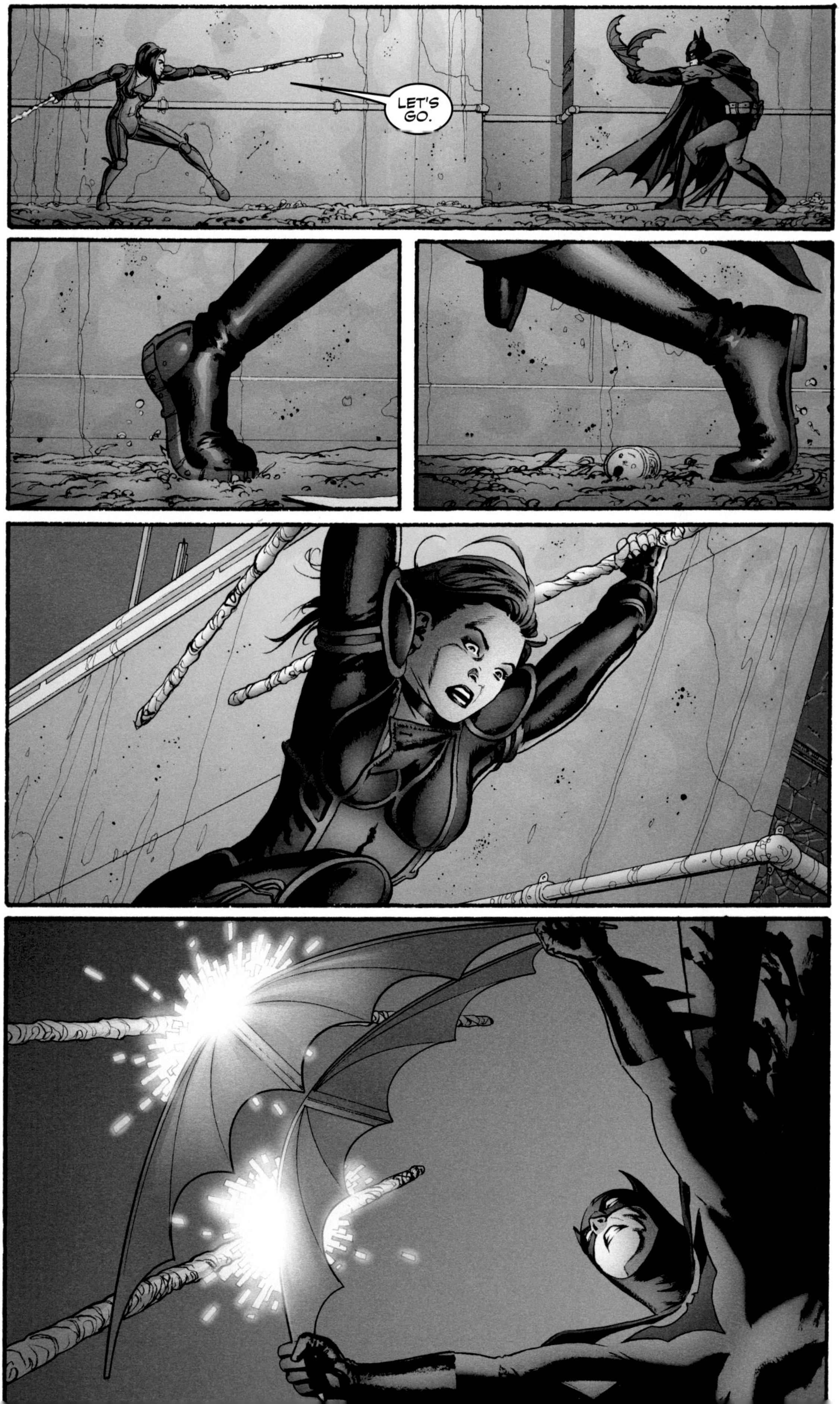
LET'S GO.

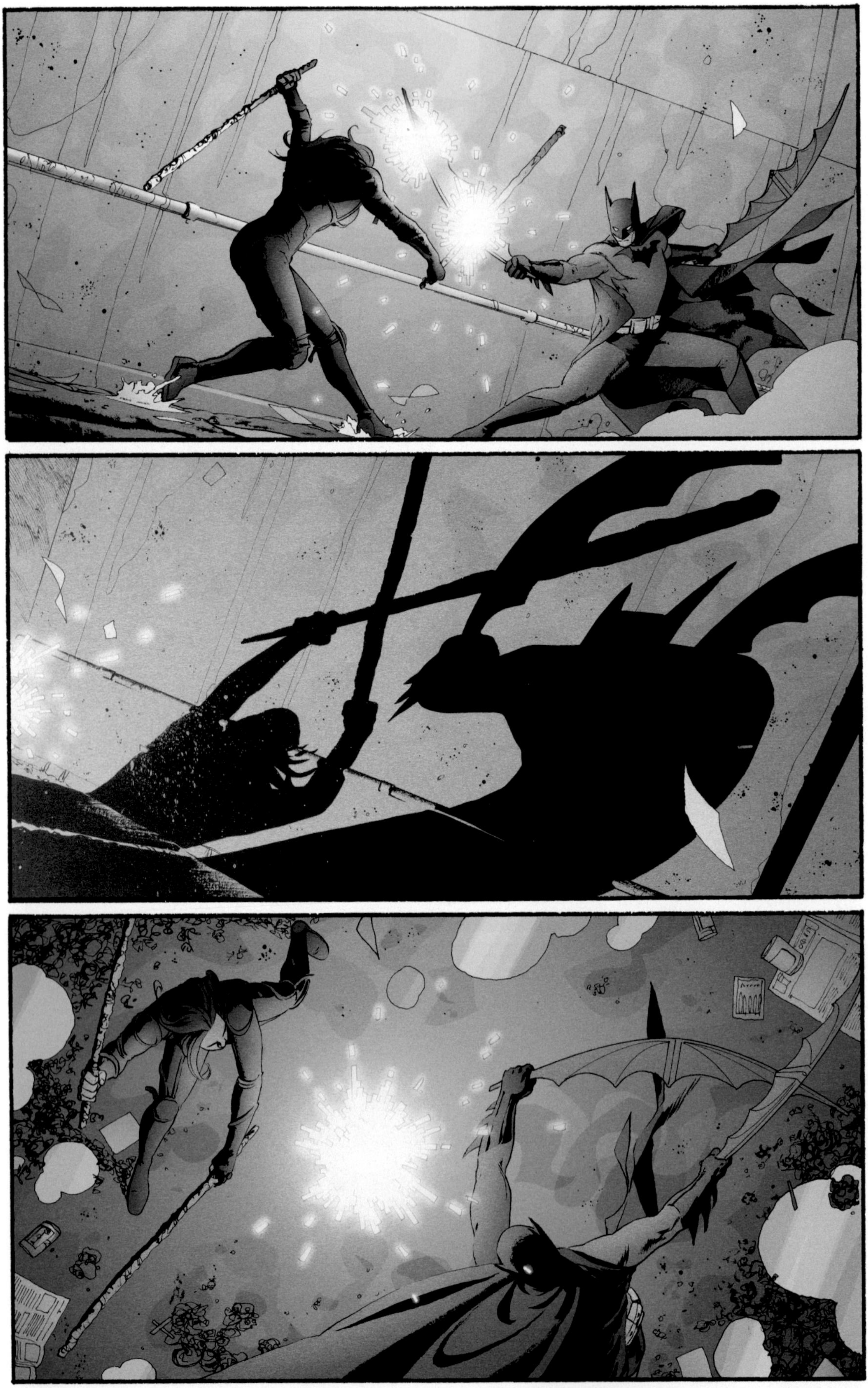

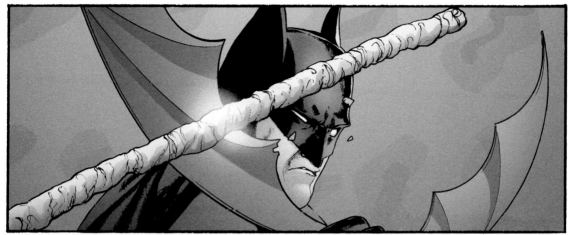

AAAAOWWW!

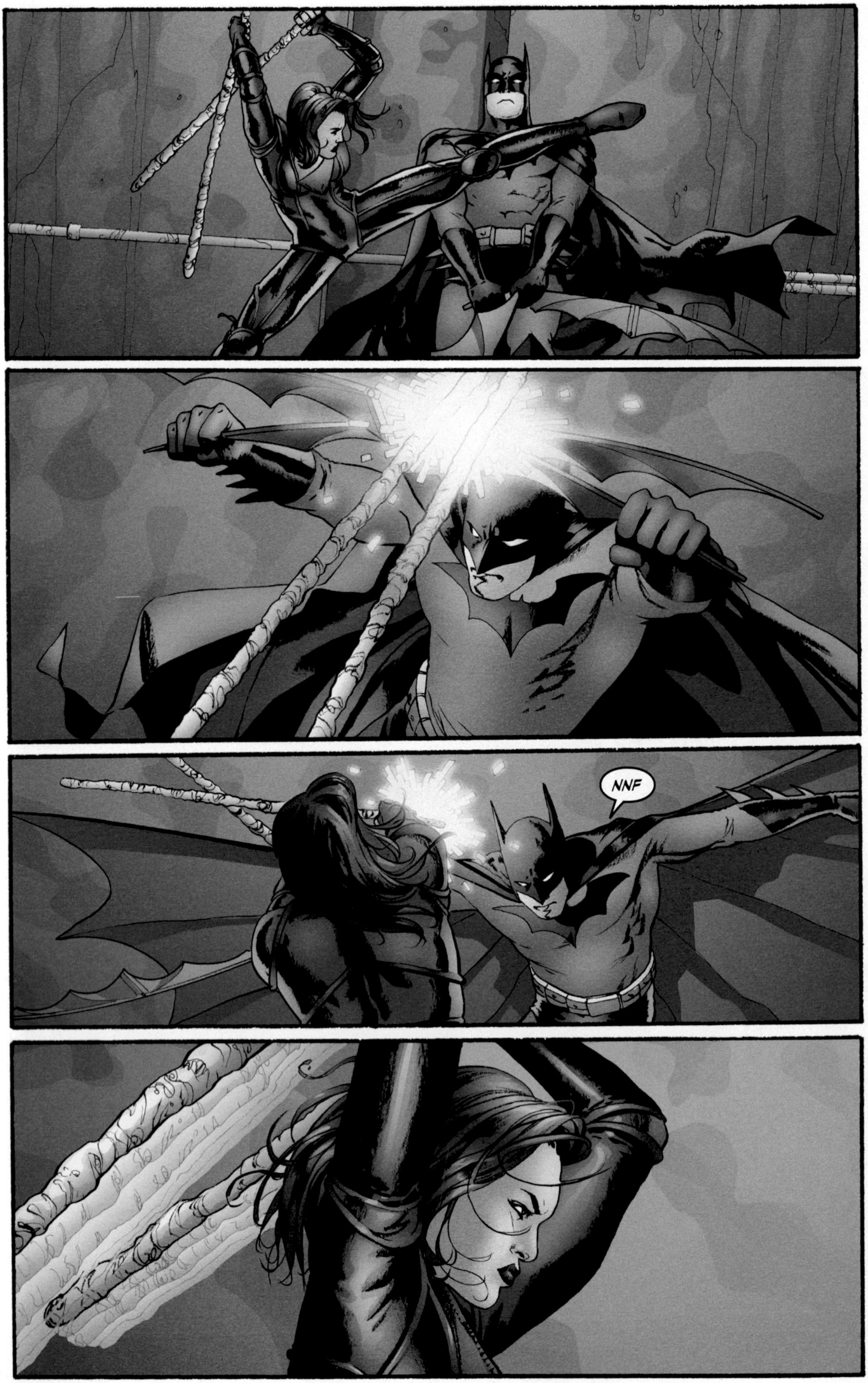
NNF

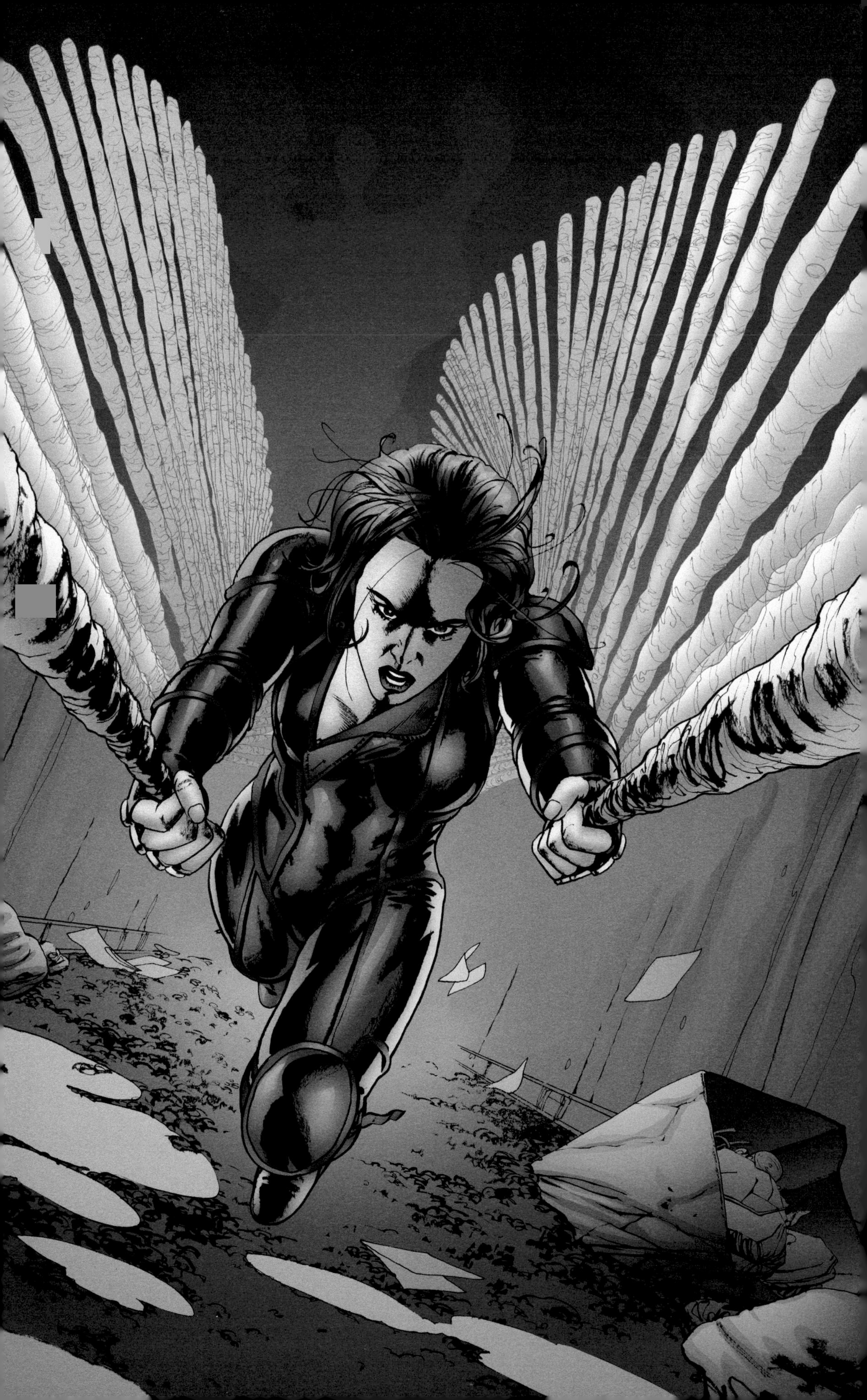

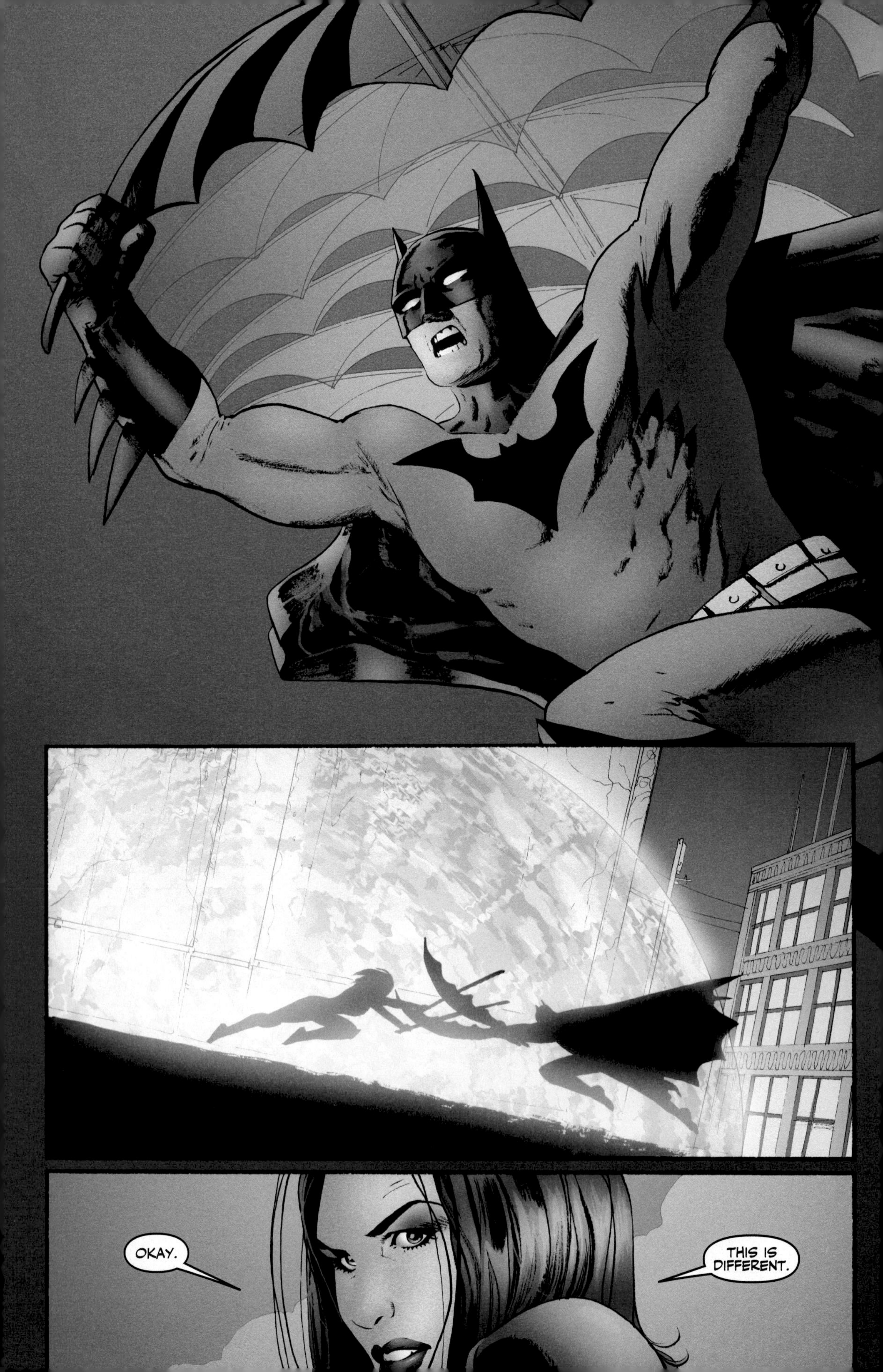
OKAY.
THIS IS DIFFERENT.

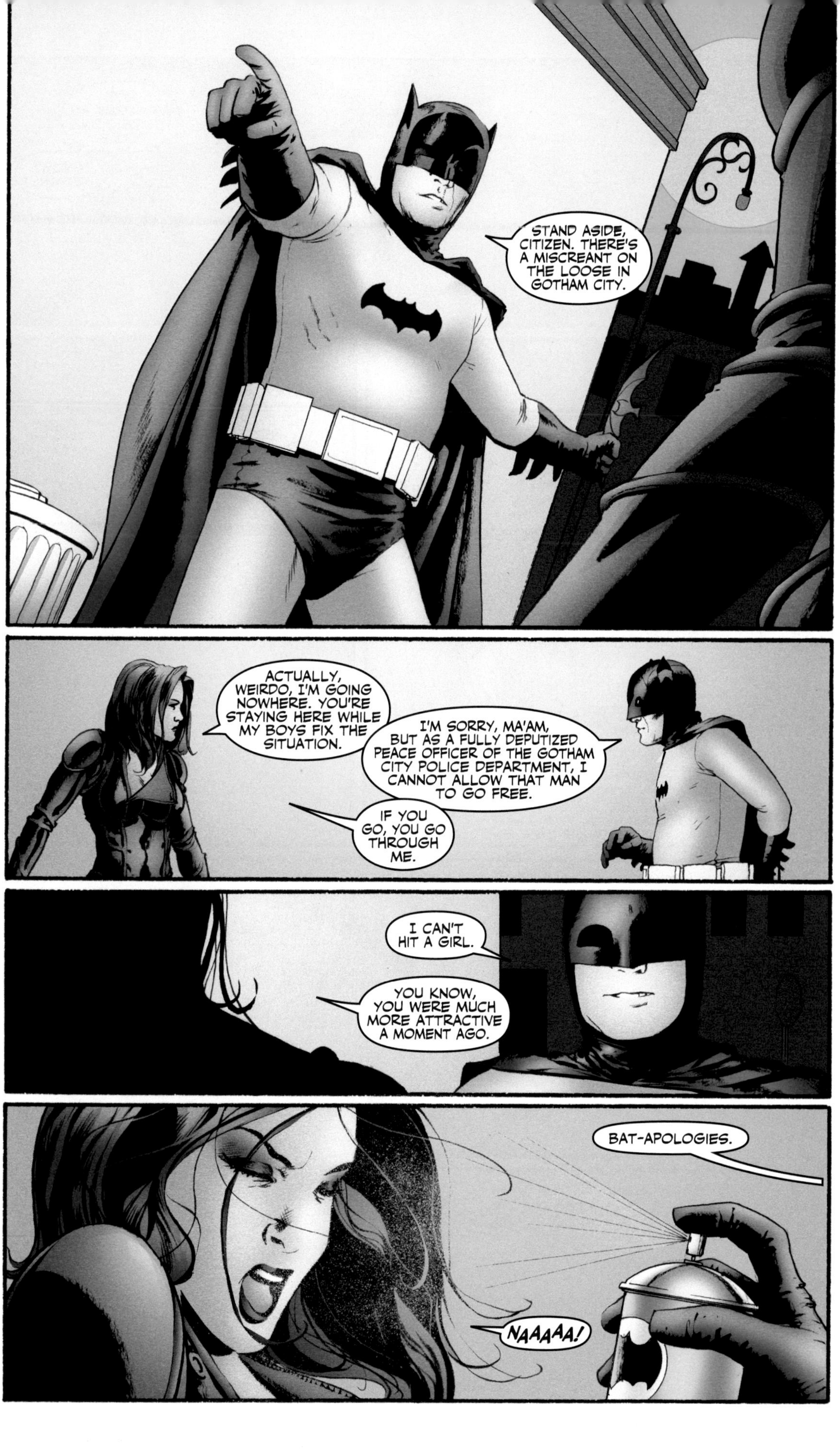
STAND ASIDE, CITIZEN. THERE'S A MISCREANT ON THE LOOSE IN GOTHAM CITY.
ACTUALLY, WEIRDO, I'M GOING NOWHERE. YOU'RE STAYING HERE WHILE MY BOYS FIX THE SITUATION.
I'M SORRY, MA'AM, BUT AS A FULLY DEPUTIZED PEACE OFFICER OF THE GOTHAM CITY POLICE DEPARTMENT, I CANNOT ALLOW THAT MAN TO GO FREE.
IF YOU GO, YOU GO THROUGH ME.
I CAN'T HIT A GIRL.
YOU KNOW, YOU WERE MUCH MORE ATTRACTIVE A MOMENT AGO.
BAT-APOLOGIES.
NAAAAA!

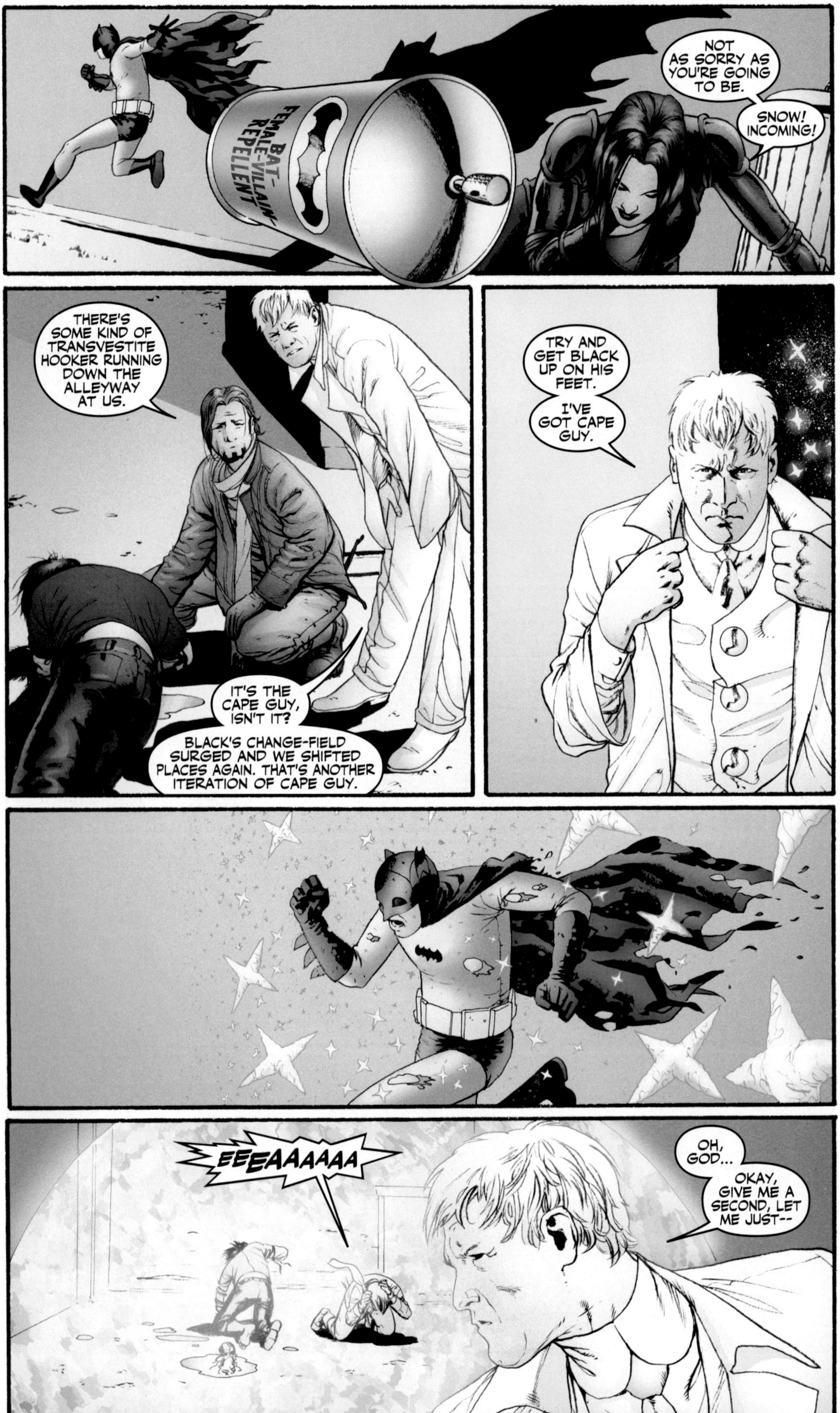

BAT-
FEMALE-VILLAIN-
REPELLENT
NOT AS SORRY AS YOU'RE GOING TO BE.
SNOW! INCOMING!
THERE'S SOME KIND OF TRANSVESTITE HOOKER RUNNING DOWN THE ALLEYWAY AT US.
IT'S THE CAPE GUY, ISN'T IT?
BLACK'S CHANGE-FIELD SURGED AND WE SHIFTED PLACES AGAIN. THAT'S ANOTHER ITERATION OF CAPE GUY.
TRY AND GET BLACK UP ON HIS FEET.
I'VE GOT CAPE GUY.
EEEAAAAAAA
OH, GOD...
OKAY, GIVE ME A SECOND, LET ME JUST--

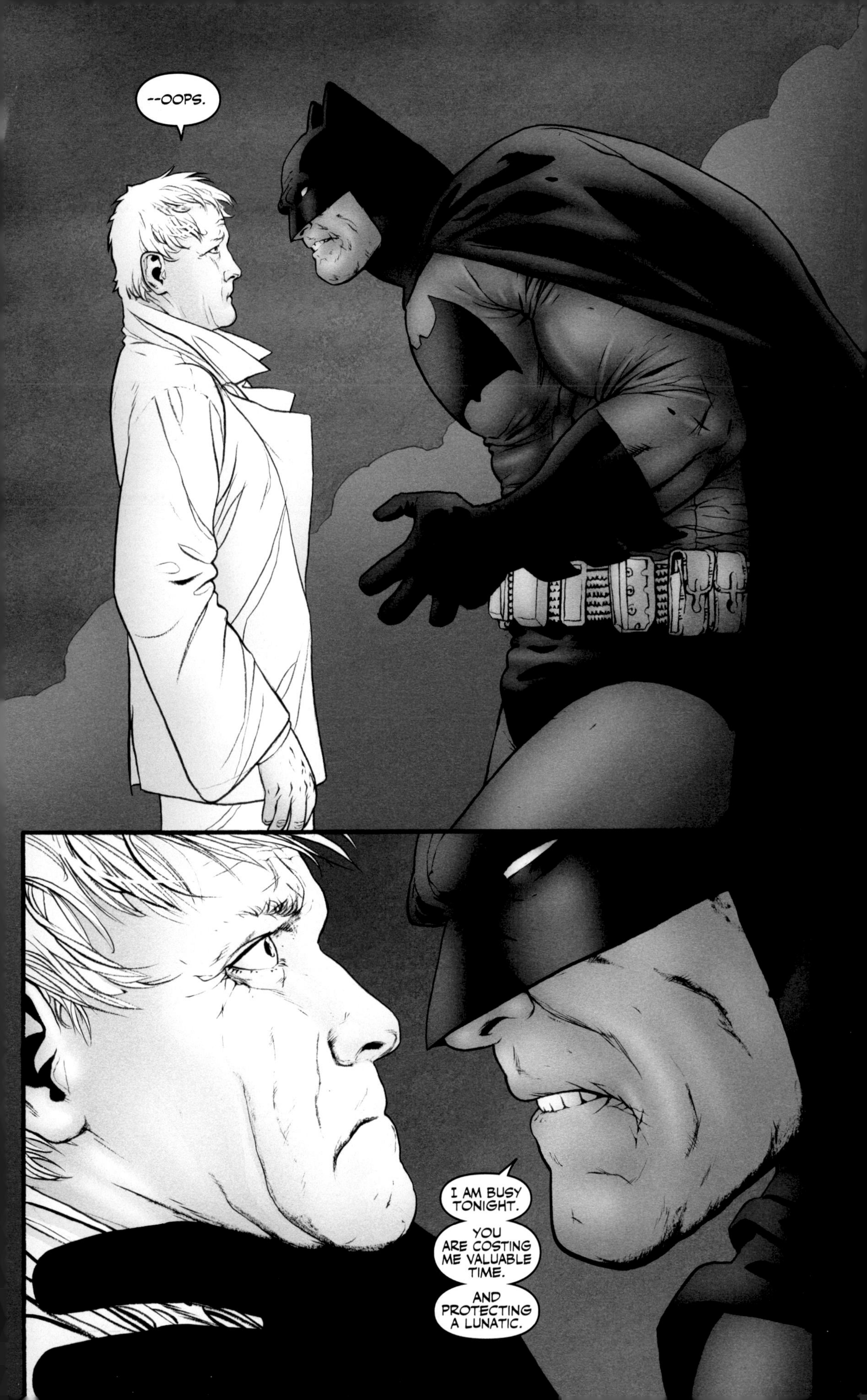
--OOPS.
I AM BUSY TONIGHT.
YOU ARE COSTING ME VALUABLE TIME.
AND PROTECTING A LUNATIC.

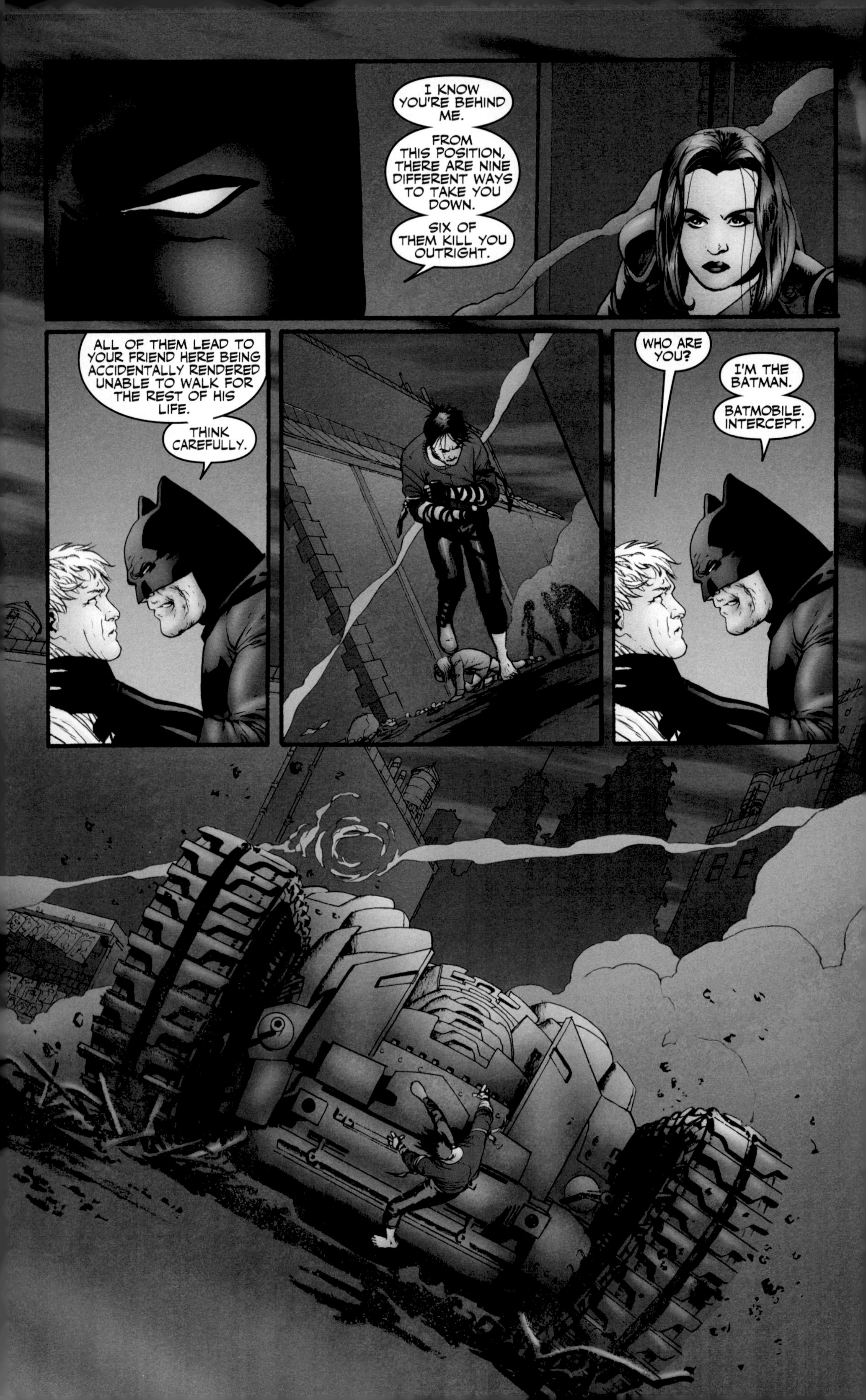
I KNOW YOU'RE BEHIND ME.
FROM THIS POSITION, THERE ARE NINE DIFFERENT WAYS TO TAKE YOU DOWN.
SIX OF THEM KILL YOU OUTRIGHT.
ALL OF THEM LEAD TO YOUR FRIEND HERE BEING ACCIDENTALLY RENDERED UNABLE TO WALK FOR THE REST OF HIS LIFE.
THINK CAREFULLY.
WHO ARE YOU?
I'M THE BATMAN.
BATMOBILE. INTERCEPT.

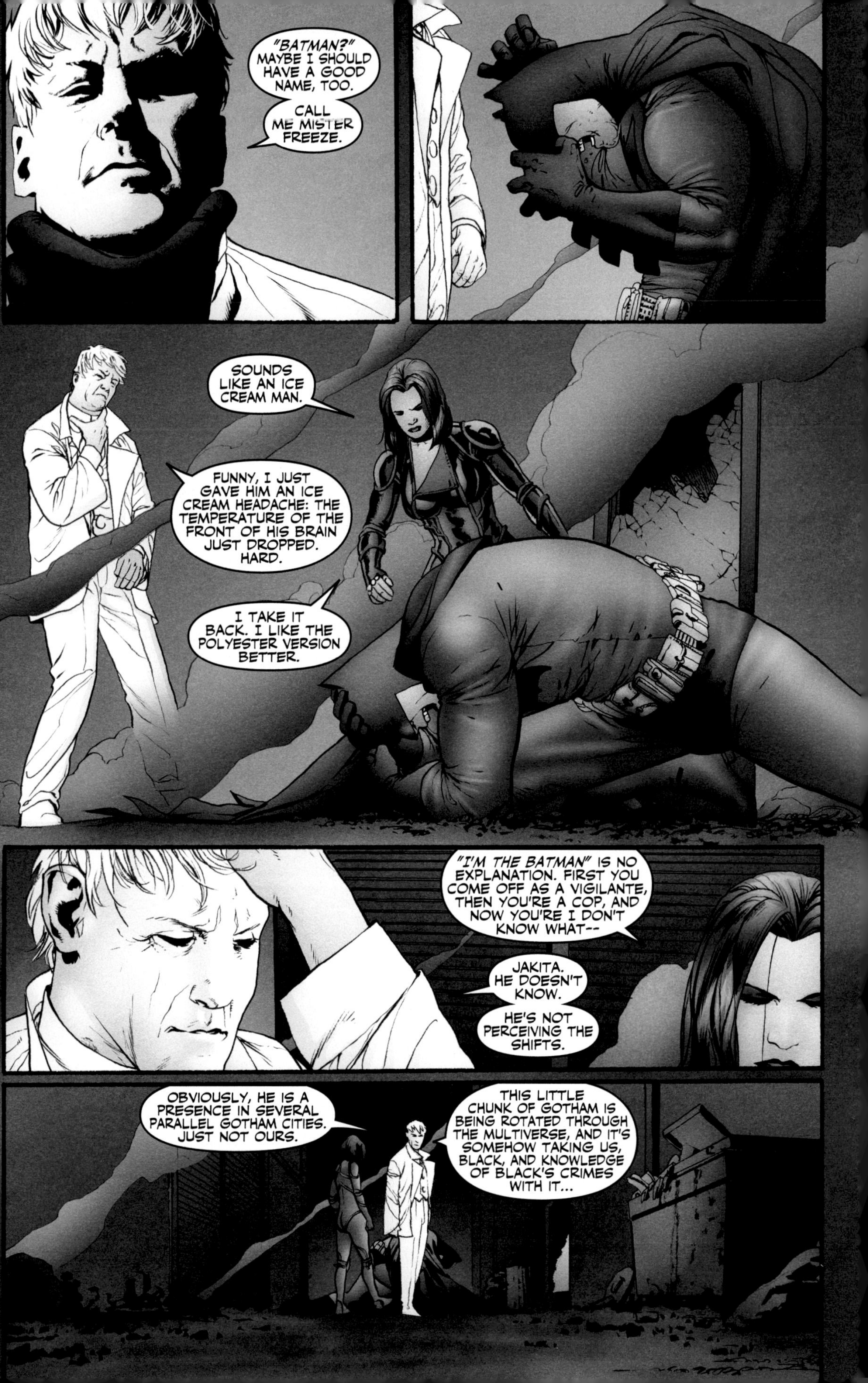
"BATMAN?" MAYBE I SHOULD HAVE A GOOD NAME, TOO.
CALL ME MISTER FREEZE.
SOUNDS LIKE AN ICE CREAM MAN.
FUNNY, I JUST GAVE HIM AN ICE CREAM HEADACHE: THE TEMPERATURE OF THE FRONT OF HIS BRAIN JUST DROPPED. HARD.
I TAKE IT BACK. I LIKE THE POLYESTER VERSION BETTER.
"I'M THE BATMAN" IS NO EXPLANATION. FIRST YOU COME OFF AS A VIGILANTE, THEN YOU'RE A COP, AND NOW YOU'RE I DON'T KNOW WHAT--
JAKITA. HE DOESN'T KNOW.
HE'S NOT PERCEIVING THE SHIFTS.
OBVIOUSLY, HE IS A PRESENCE IN SEVERAL PARALLEL GOTHAM CITIES. JUST NOT OURS.
THIS LITTLE CHUNK OF GOTHAM IS BEING ROTATED THROUGH THE MULTIVERSE, AND IT'S SOMEHOW TAKING US, BLACK, AND KNOWLEDGE OF BLACK'S CRIMES WITH IT...

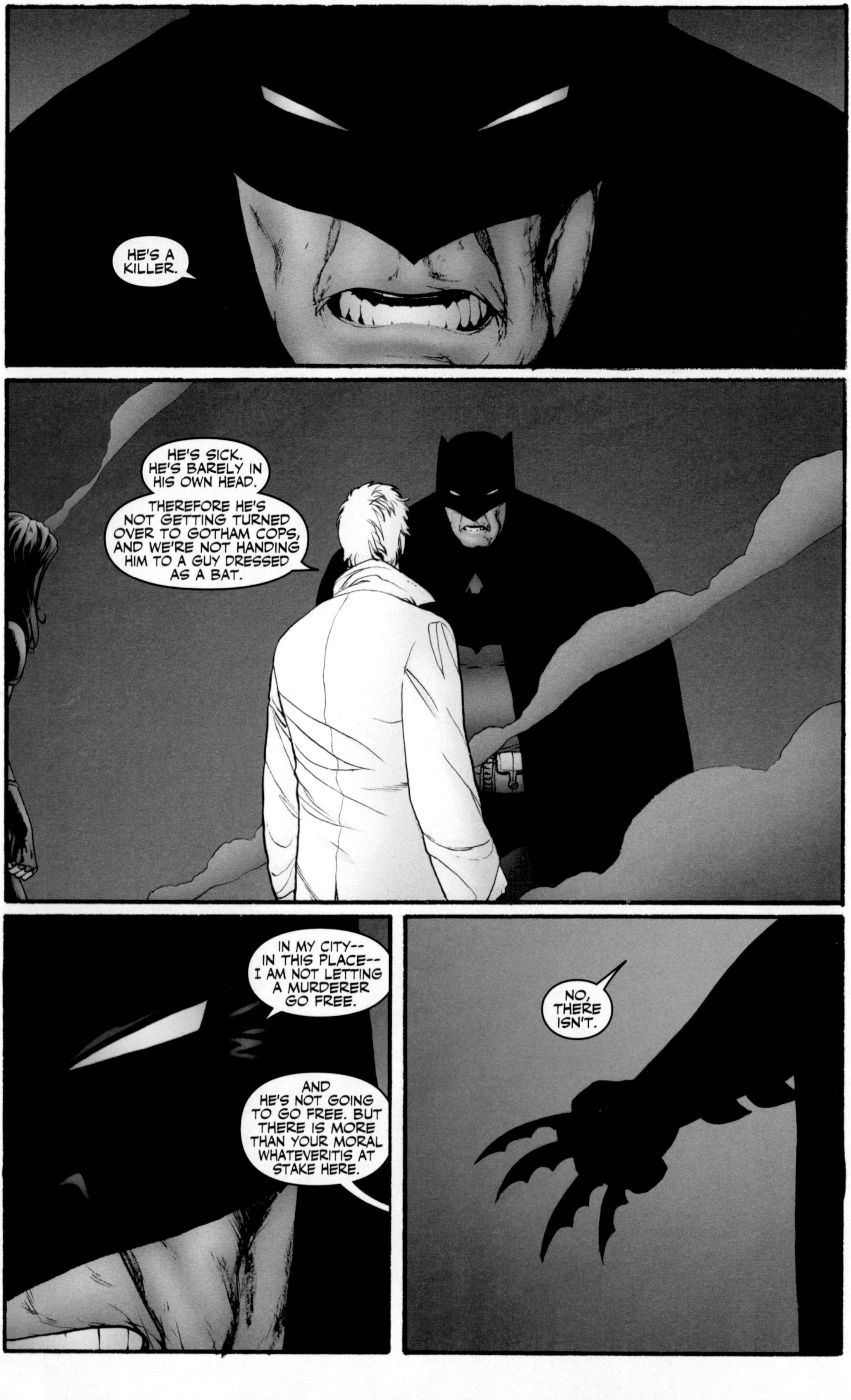
HE'S A KILLER.
HE'S SICK. HE'S BARELY IN HIS OWN HEAD.
THEREFORE HE'S NOT GETTING TURNED OVER TO GOTHAM COPS, AND WE'RE NOT HANDING HIM TO A GUY DRESSED AS A BAT.
IN MY CITY-- IN THIS PLACE-- I AM NOT LETTING A MURDERER GO FREE.
AND HE'S NOT GOING TO GO FREE. BUT THERE IS MORE THAN YOUR MORAL WHATEVERITIS AT STAKE HERE.
NO, THERE ISN'T.

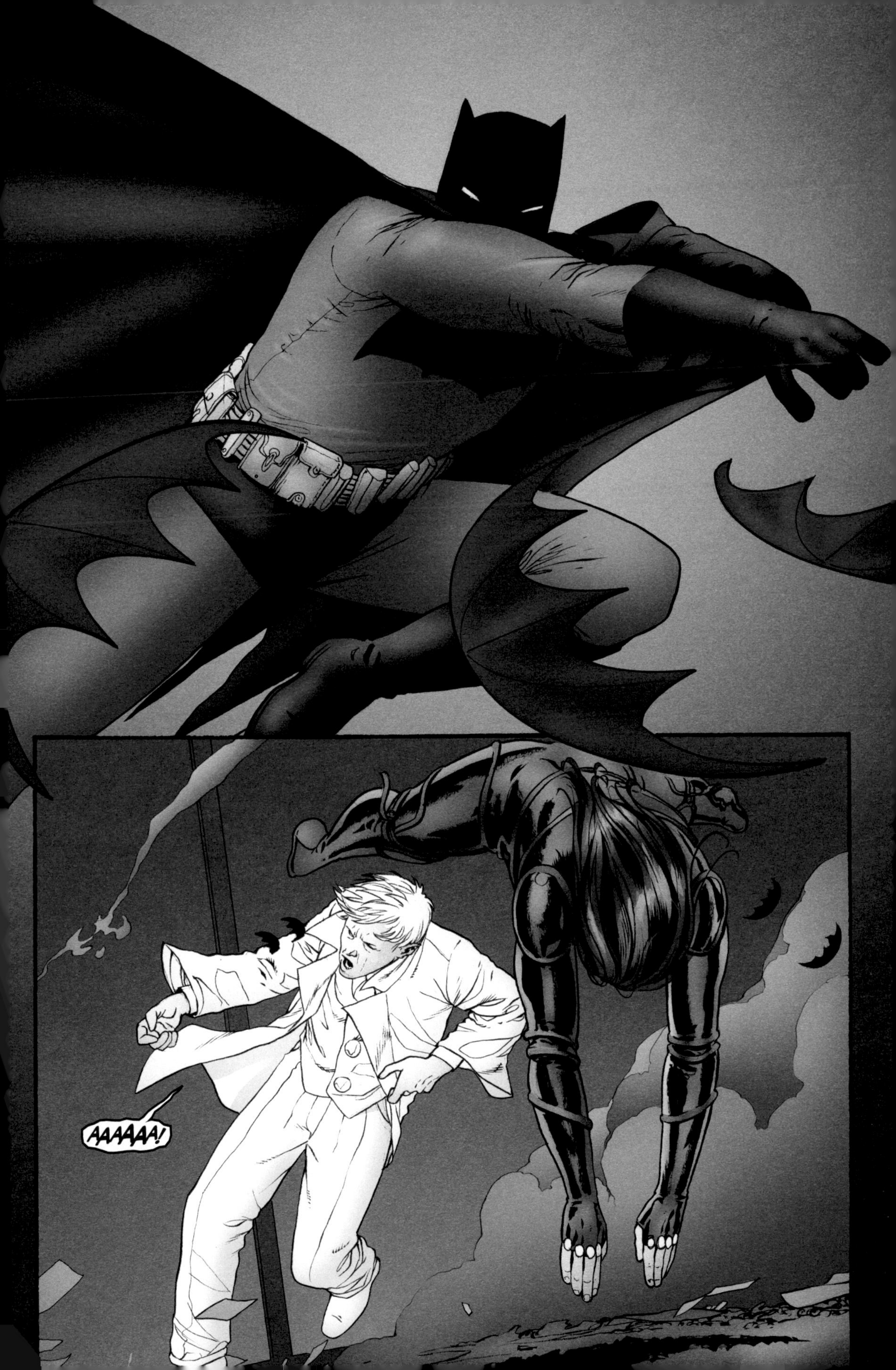
AAAAAA!

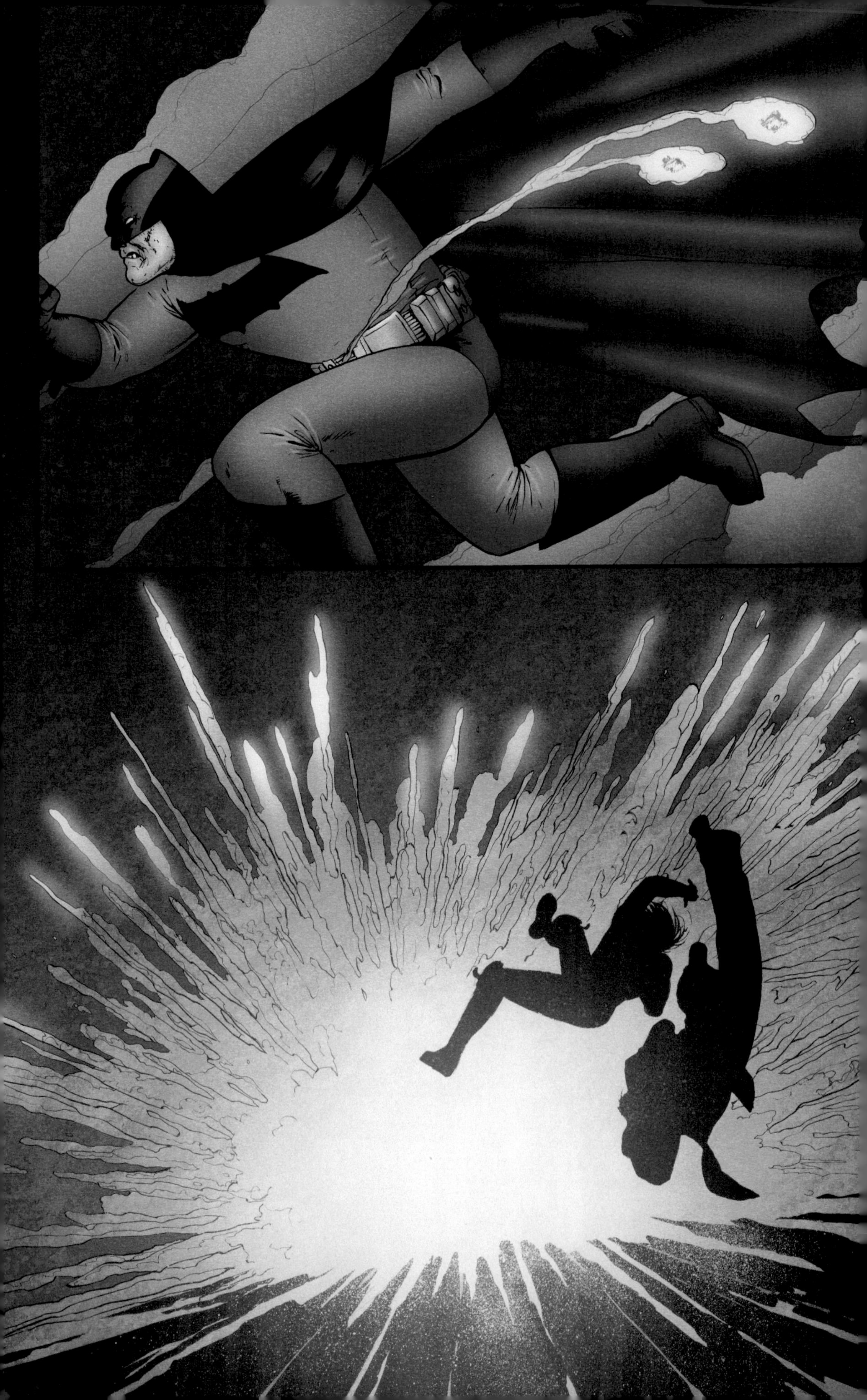

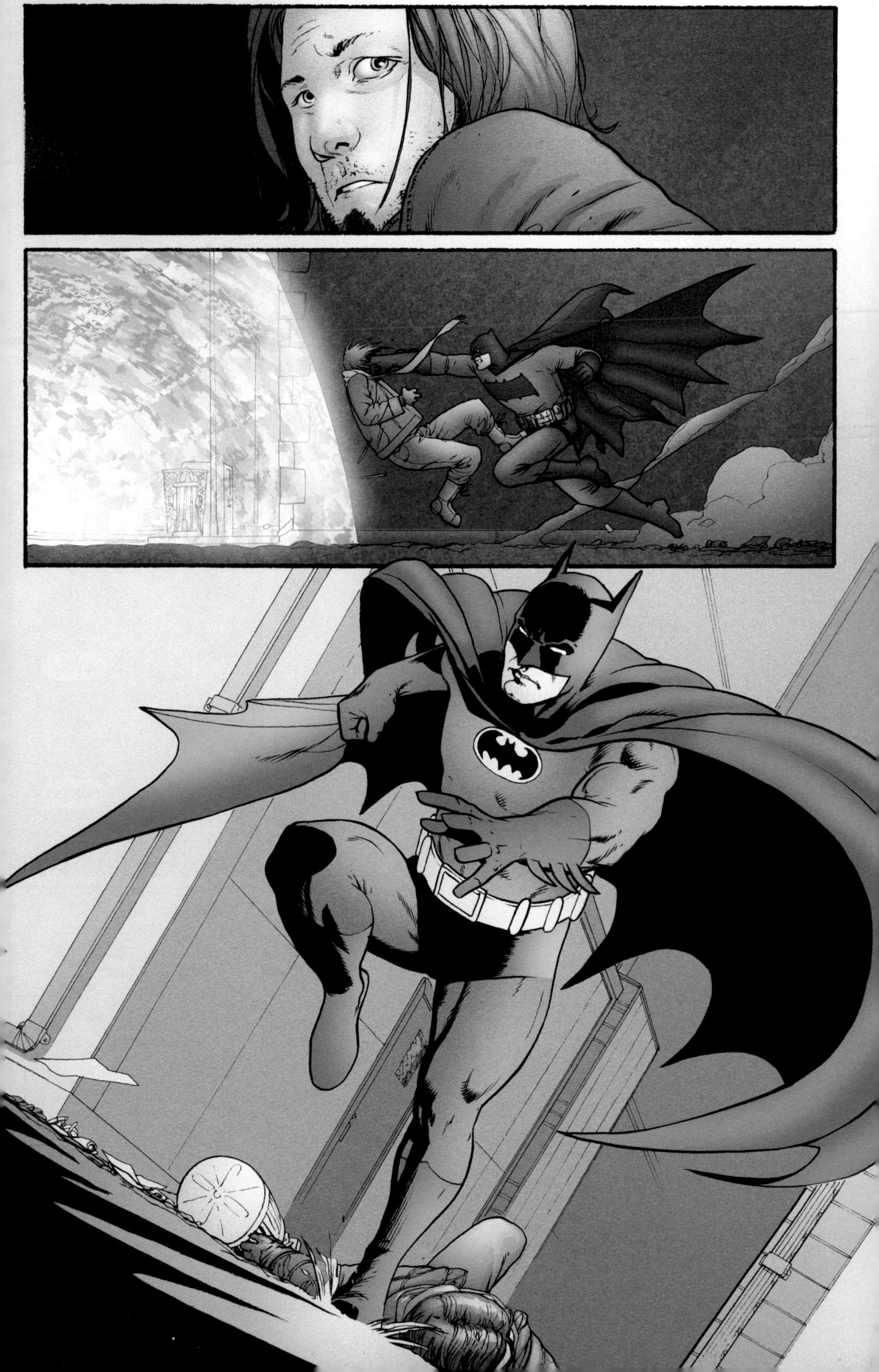

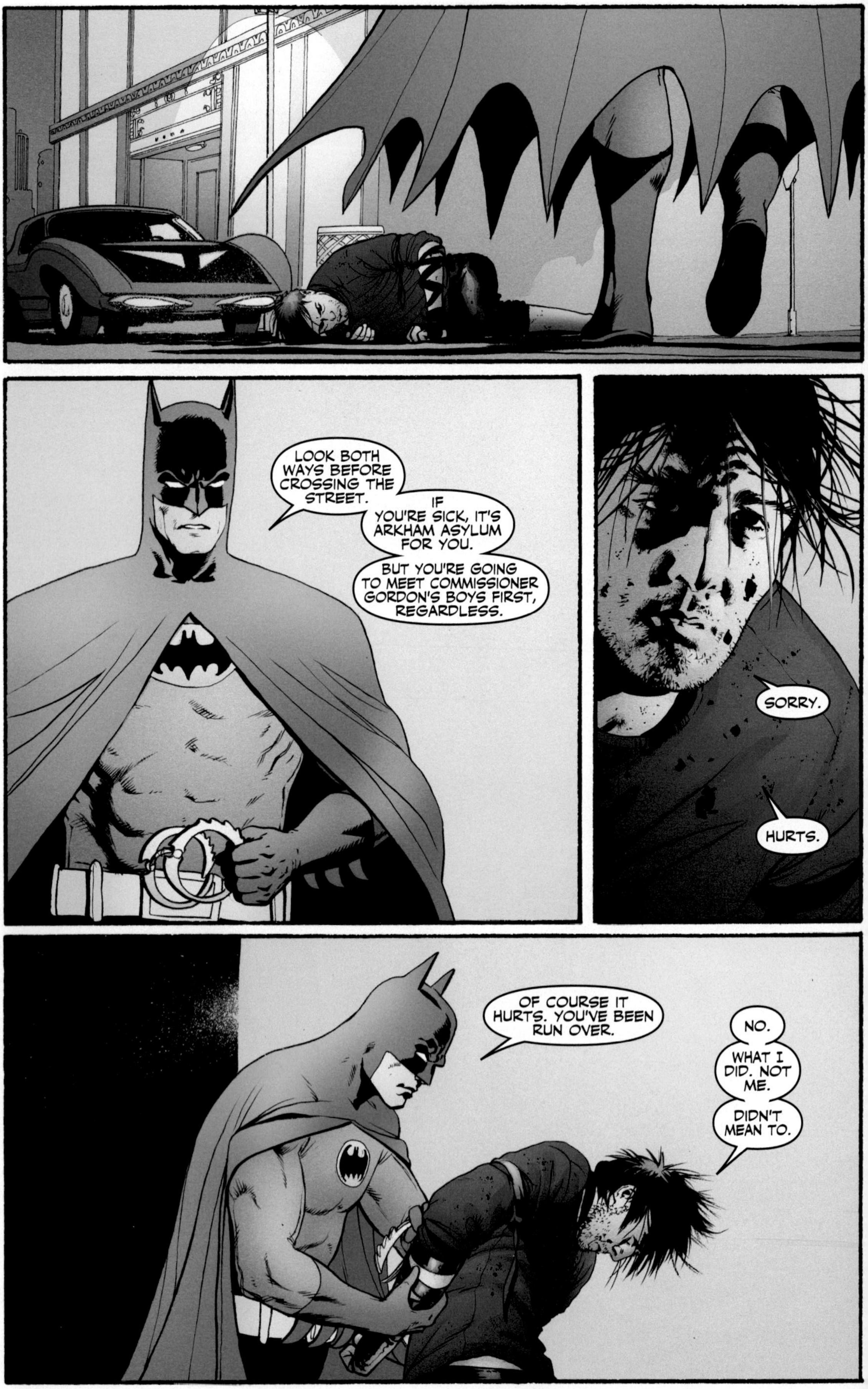
LOOK BOTH WAYS BEFORE CROSSING THE STREET.
IF YOU'RE SICK, IT'S ARKHAM ASYLUM FOR YOU.
BUT YOU'RE GOING TO MEET COMMISSIONER GORDON'S BOYS FIRST, REGARDLESS.
SORRY.
HURTS.
OF COURSE IT HURTS. YOU'VE BEEN RUN OVER.
NO.
WHAT I DID. NOT ME.
DIDN'T MEAN TO.

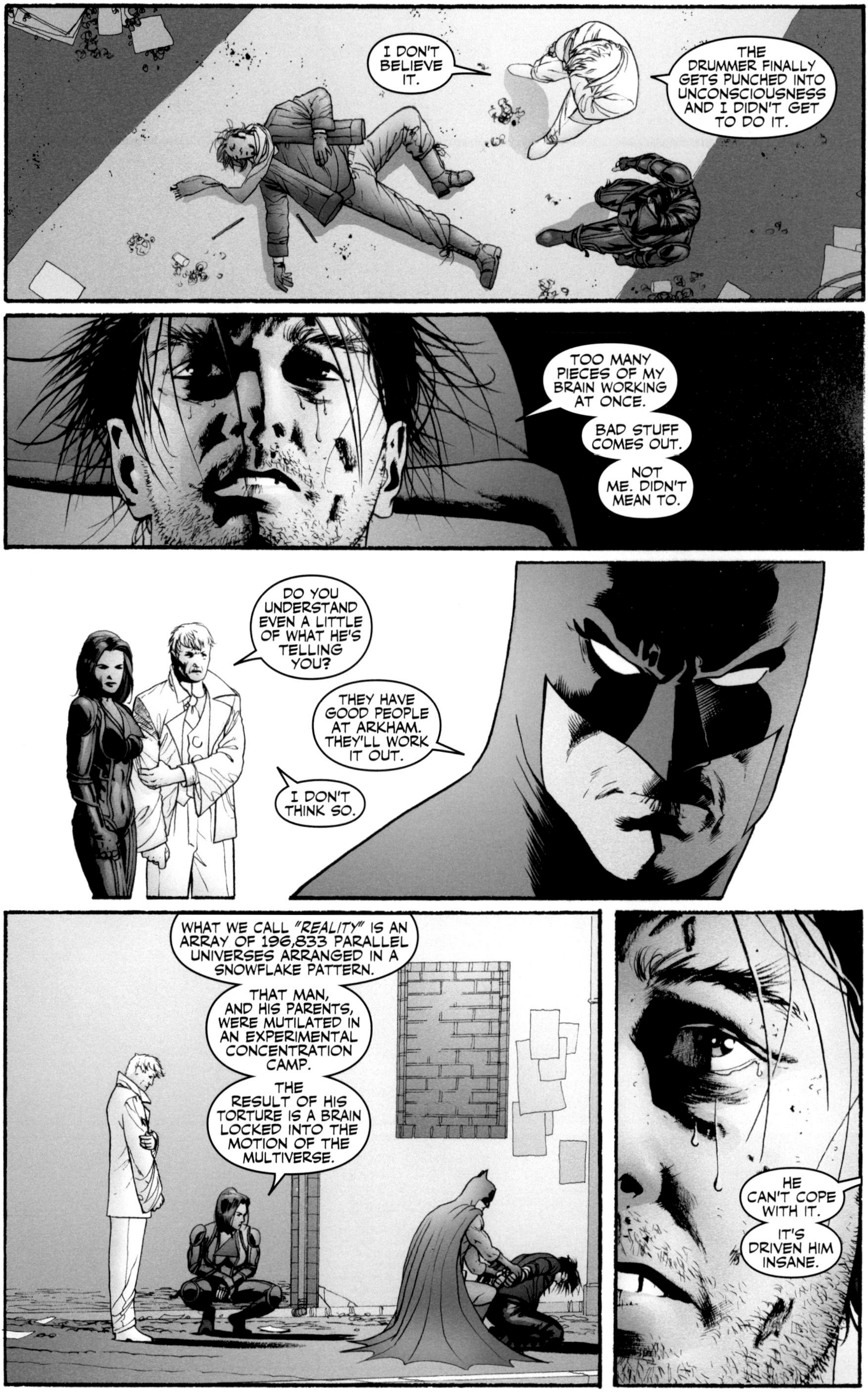
I DON'T BELIEVE IT.
THE DRUMMER FINALLY GETS PUNCHED INTO UNCONSCIOUSNESS AND I DIDN'T GET TO DO IT.
TOO MANY PIECES OF MY BRAIN WORKING AT ONCE.
BAD STUFF COMES OUT.
NOT ME. DIDN'T MEAN TO.
DO YOU UNDERSTAND EVEN A LITTLE OF WHAT HE'S TELLING YOU?
THEY HAVE GOOD PEOPLE AT ARKHAM. THEY'LL WORK IT OUT.
I DON'T THINK SO.
WHAT WE CALL "REALITY" IS AN ARRAY OF 196,833 PARALLEL UNIVERSES ARRANGED IN A SNOWFLAKE PATTERN.
THAT MAN, AND HIS PARENTS, WERE MUTILATED IN AN EXPERIMENTAL CONCENTRATION CAMP.
THE RESULT OF HIS TORTURE IS A BRAIN LOCKED INTO THE MOTION OF THE MULTIVERSE.
HE CAN'T COPE WITH IT.
IT'S DRIVEN HIM INSANE.

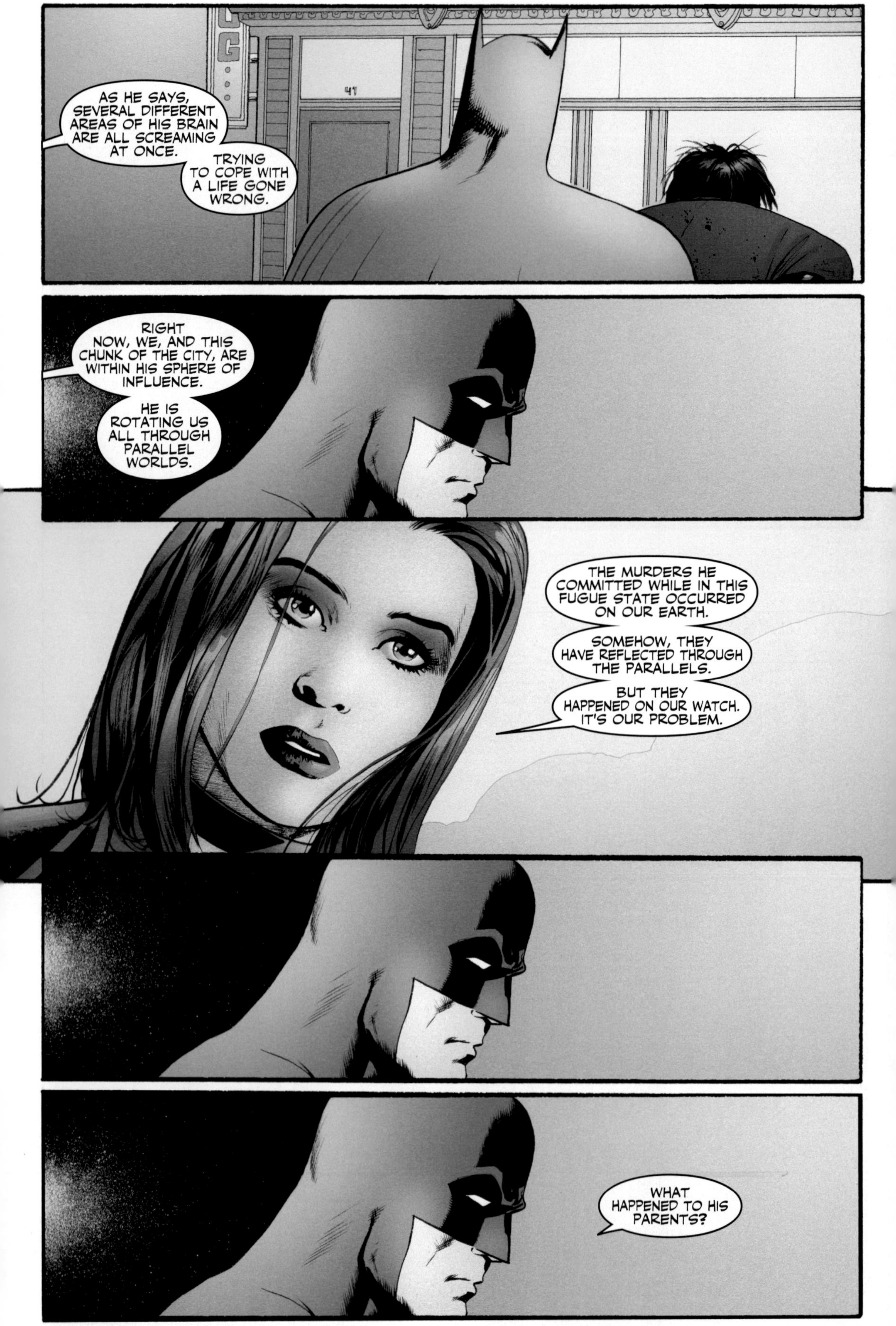
AS HE SAYS, SEVERAL DIFFERENT AREAS OF HIS BRAIN ARE ALL SCREAMING AT ONCE.
TRYING TO COPE WITH A LIFE GONE WRONG.
RIGHT NOW, WE, AND THIS CHUNK OF THE CITY, ARE WITHIN HIS SPHERE OF INFLUENCE.
HE IS ROTATING US ALL THROUGH PARALLEL WORLDS.
THE MURDERS HE COMMITTED WHILE IN THIS FUGUE STATE OCCURRED ON OUR EARTH.
SOMEHOW, THEY HAVE REFLECTED THROUGH THE PARALLELS.
BUT THEY HAPPENED ON OUR WATCH. IT'S OUR PROBLEM.
WHAT HAPPENED TO HIS PARENTS?

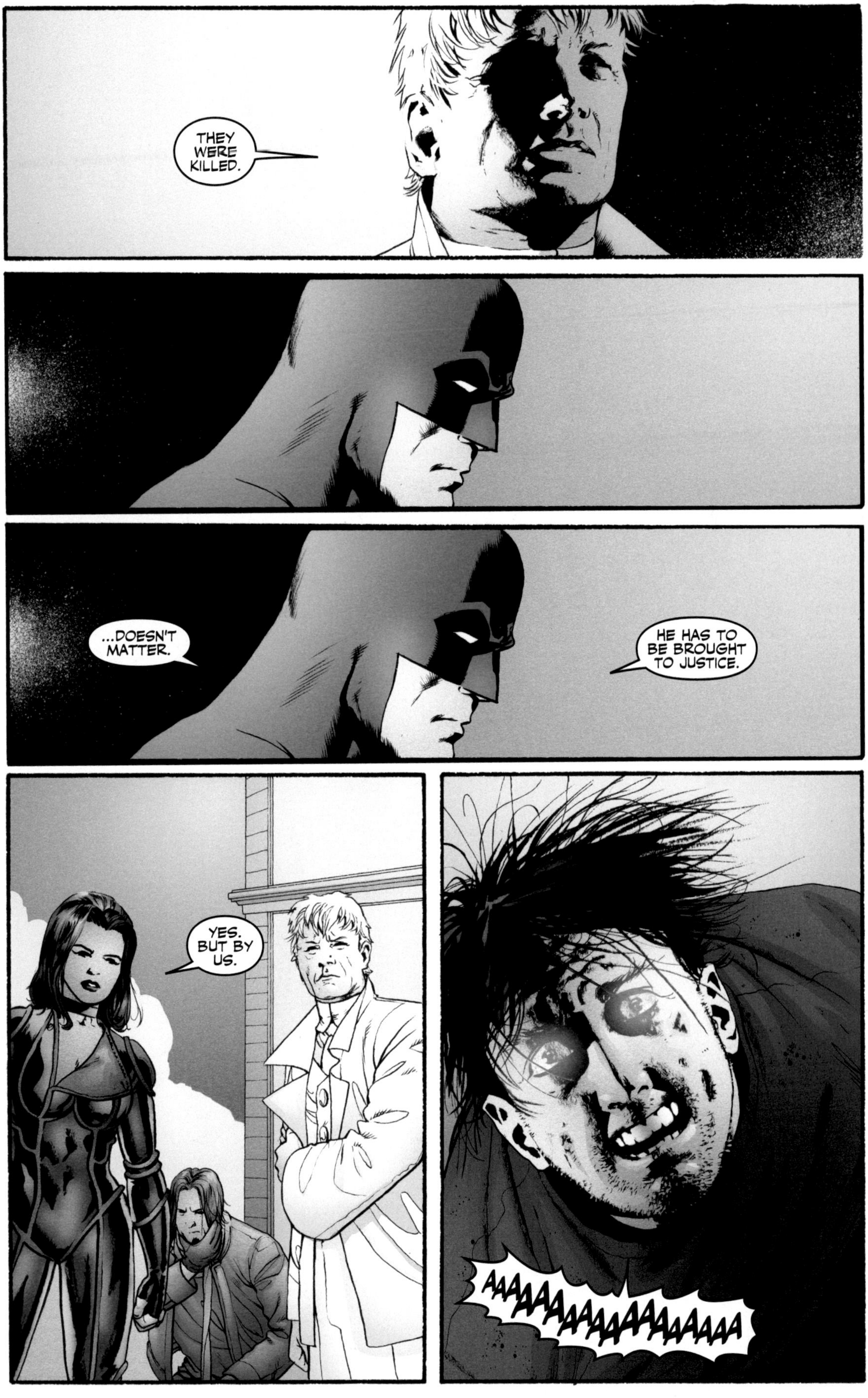
THEY WERE KILLED.
...DOESN'T MATTER.
HE HAS TO BE BROUGHT TO JUSTICE.
YES. BUT BY US.
AAAAAAAAAAAAAAAAAAAA

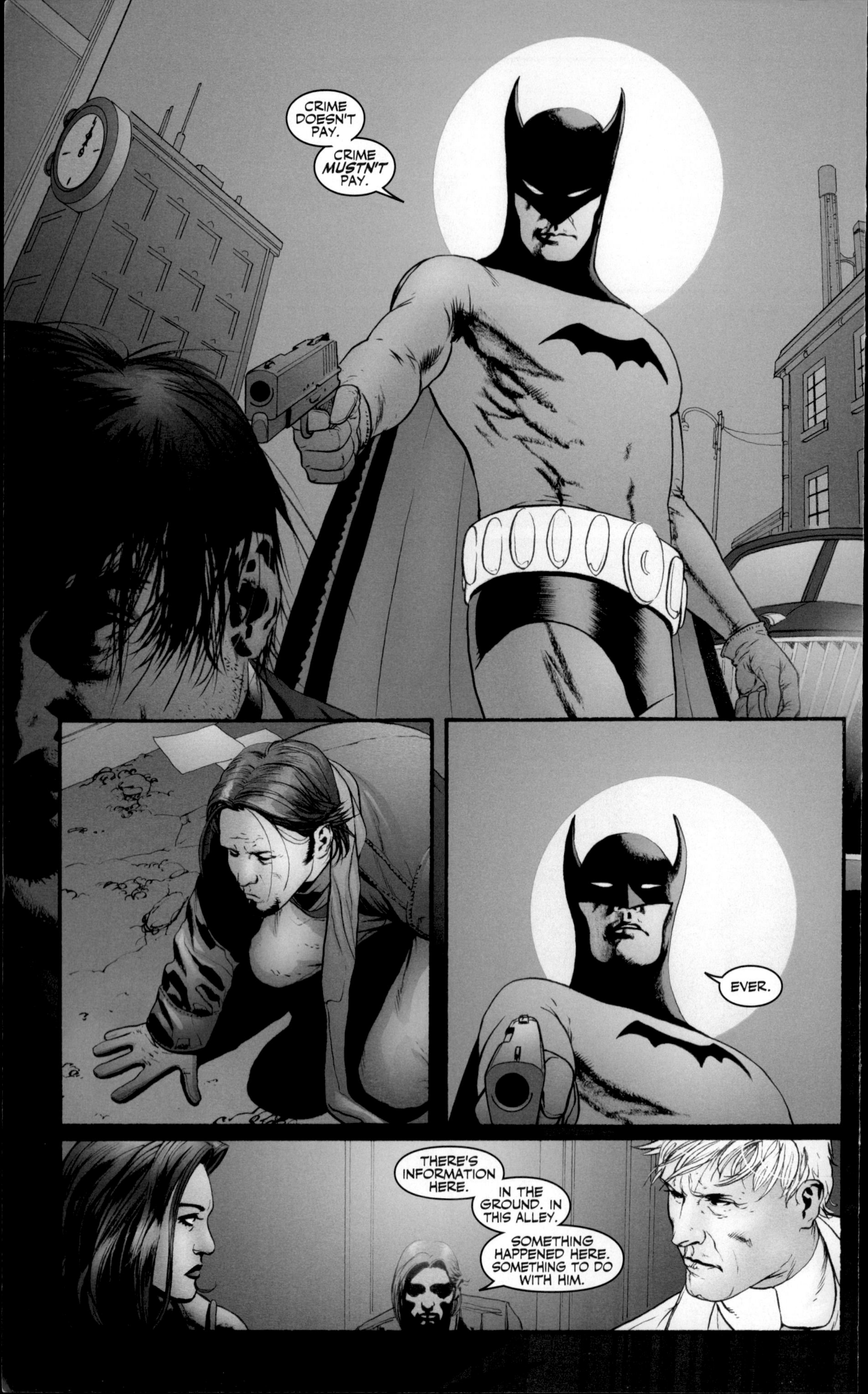
CRIME DOESN'T PAY.
CRIME *MUSTN'T* PAY.
EVER.
THERE'S INFORMATION HERE.
IN THE GROUND. IN THIS ALLEY.
SOMETHING HAPPENED HERE. SOMETHING TO DO WITH HIM.

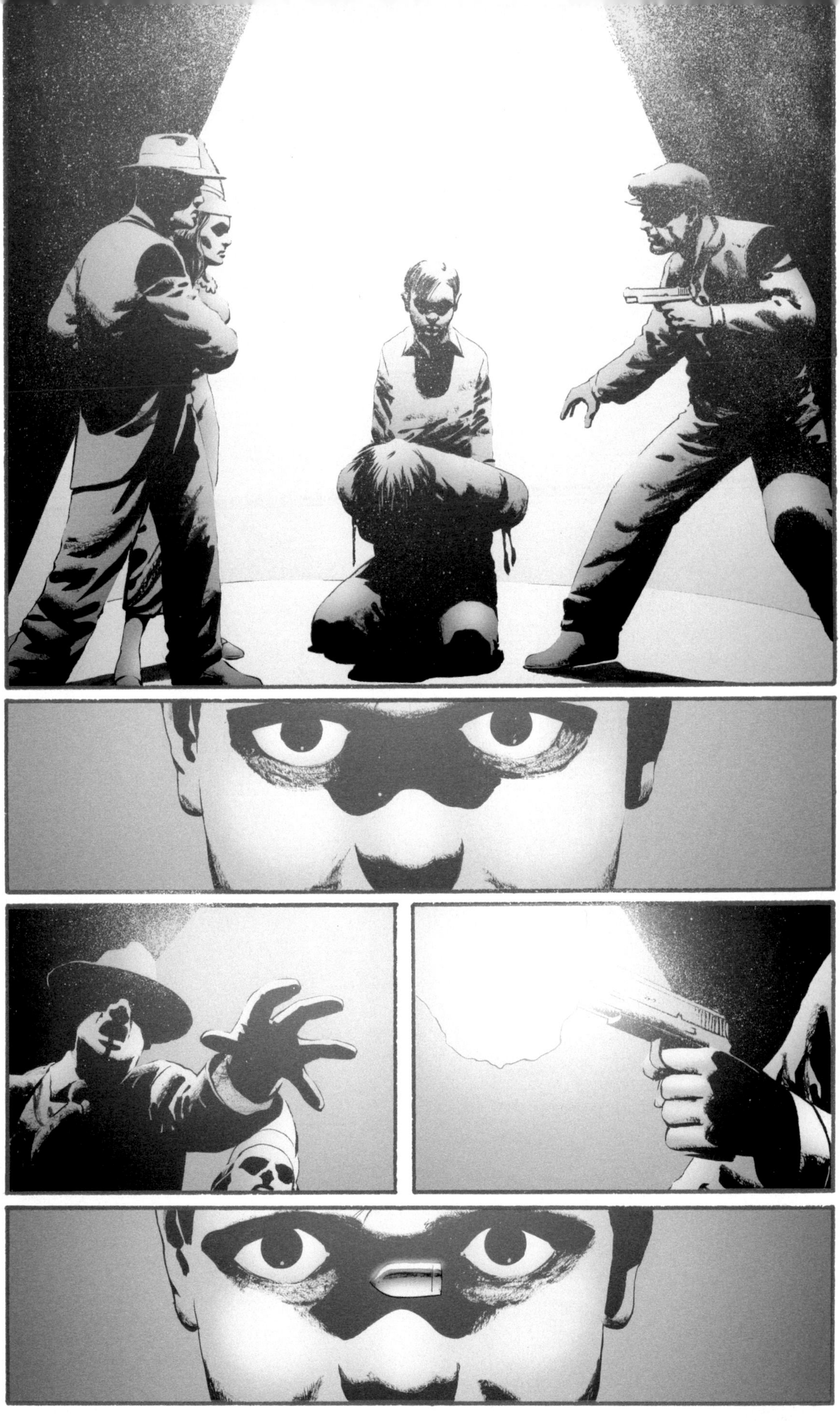

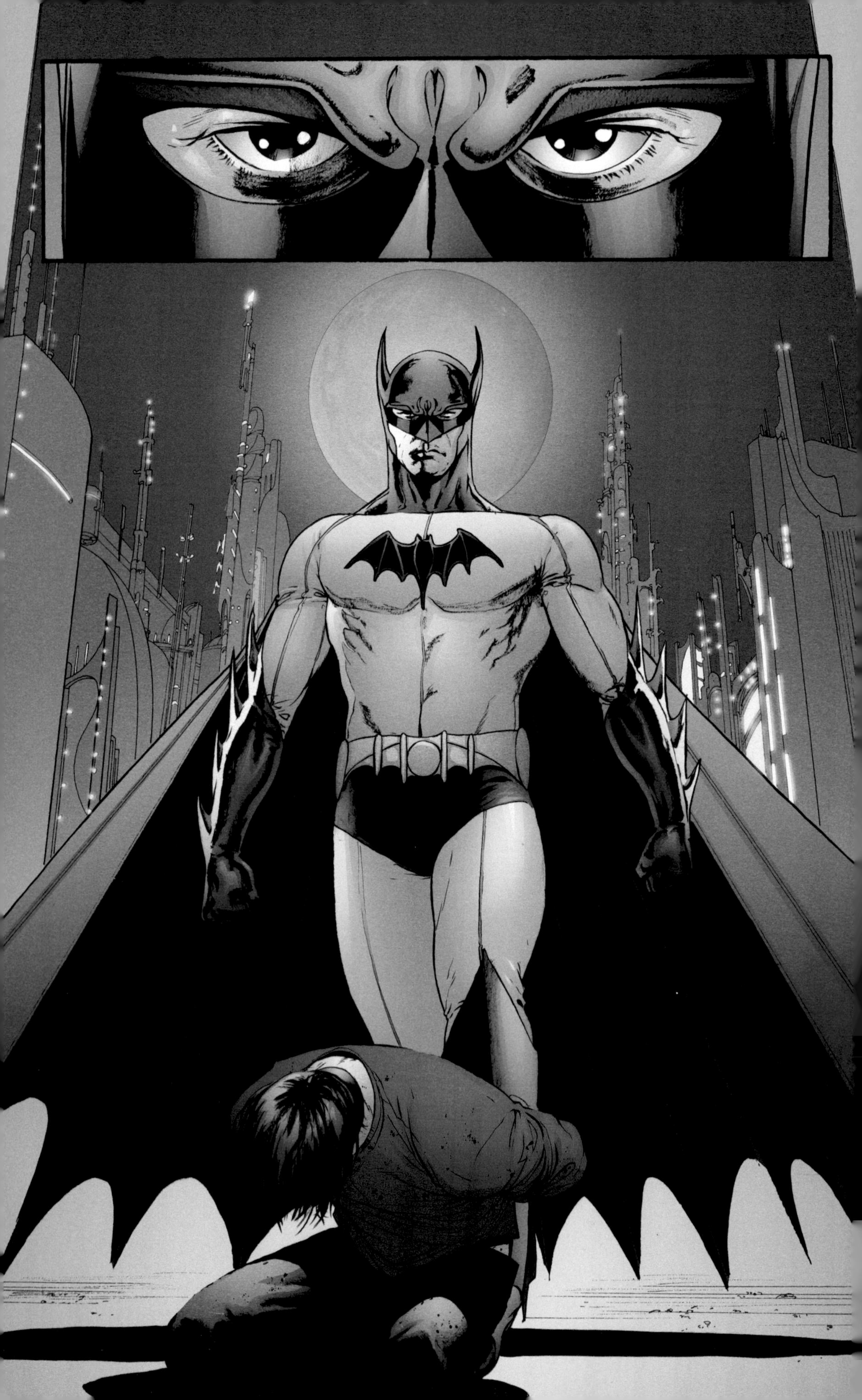

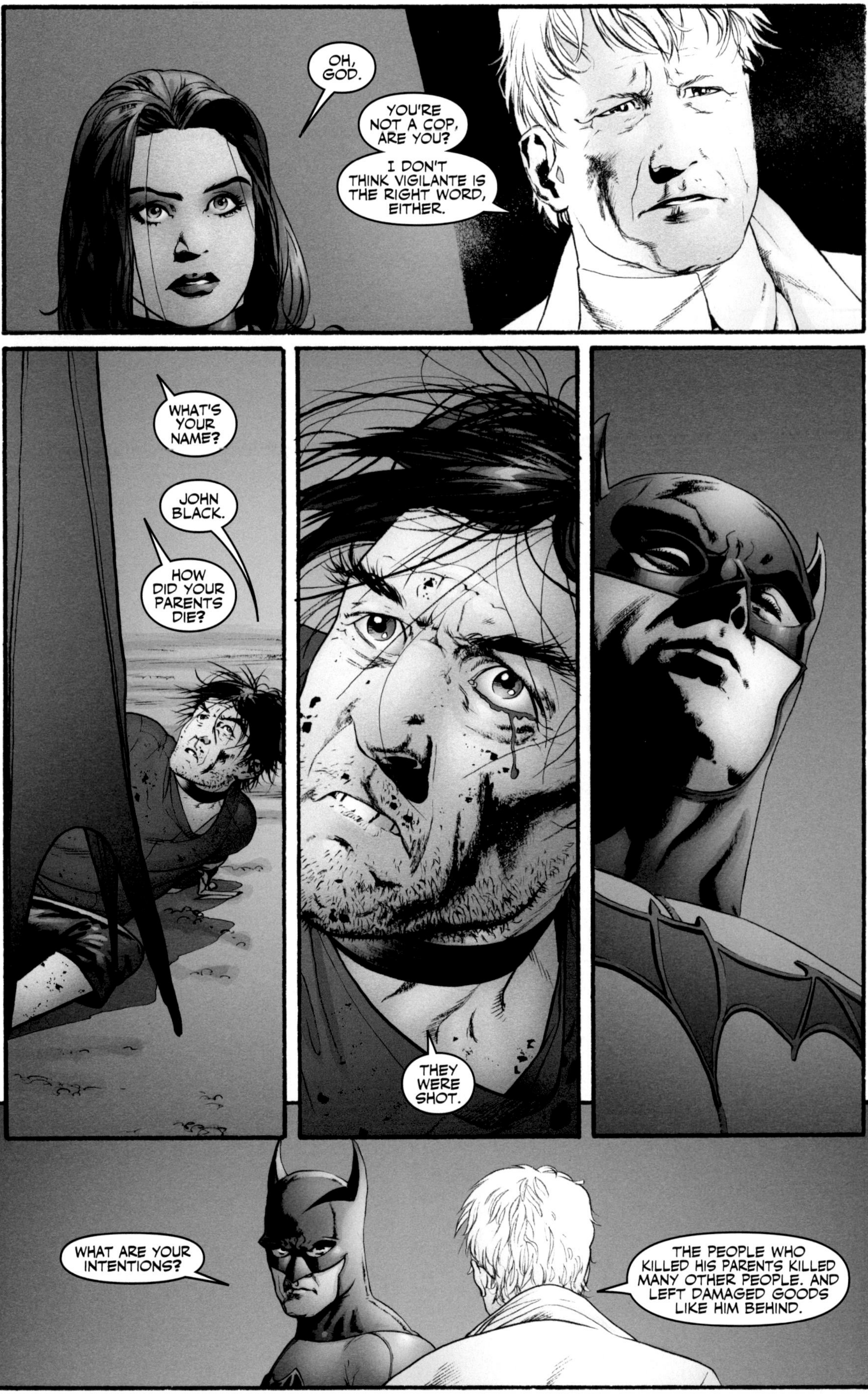
OH, GOD.
YOU'RE NOT A COP, ARE YOU?
I DON'T THINK VIGILANTE IS THE RIGHT WORD, EITHER.
WHAT'S YOUR NAME?
JOHN BLACK.
HOW DID YOUR PARENTS DIE?
THEY WERE SHOT.
WHAT ARE YOUR INTENTIONS?
THE PEOPLE WHO KILLED HIS PARENTS KILLED MANY OTHER PEOPLE. AND LEFT DAMAGED GOODS LIKE HIM BEHIND.

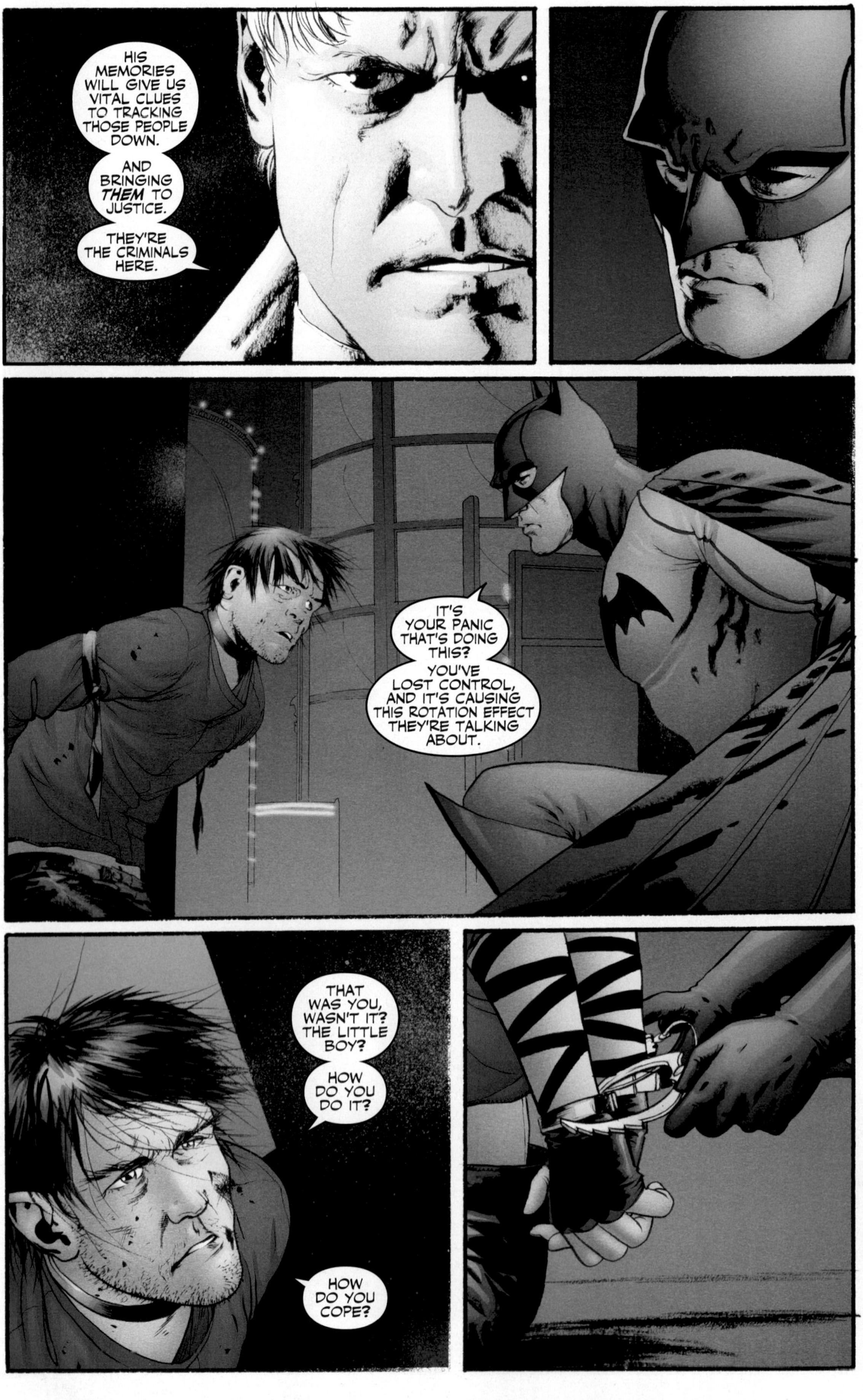
HIS MEMORIES WILL GIVE US VITAL CLUES TO TRACKING THOSE PEOPLE DOWN.
AND BRINGING *THEM* TO JUSTICE.
THEY'RE THE CRIMINALS HERE.
IT'S YOUR PANIC THAT'S DOING THIS?
YOU'VE LOST CONTROL, AND IT'S CAUSING THIS ROTATION EFFECT THEY'RE TALKING ABOUT.
THAT WAS YOU, WASN'T IT? THE LITTLE BOY?
HOW DO YOU DO IT?
HOW DO YOU COPE?

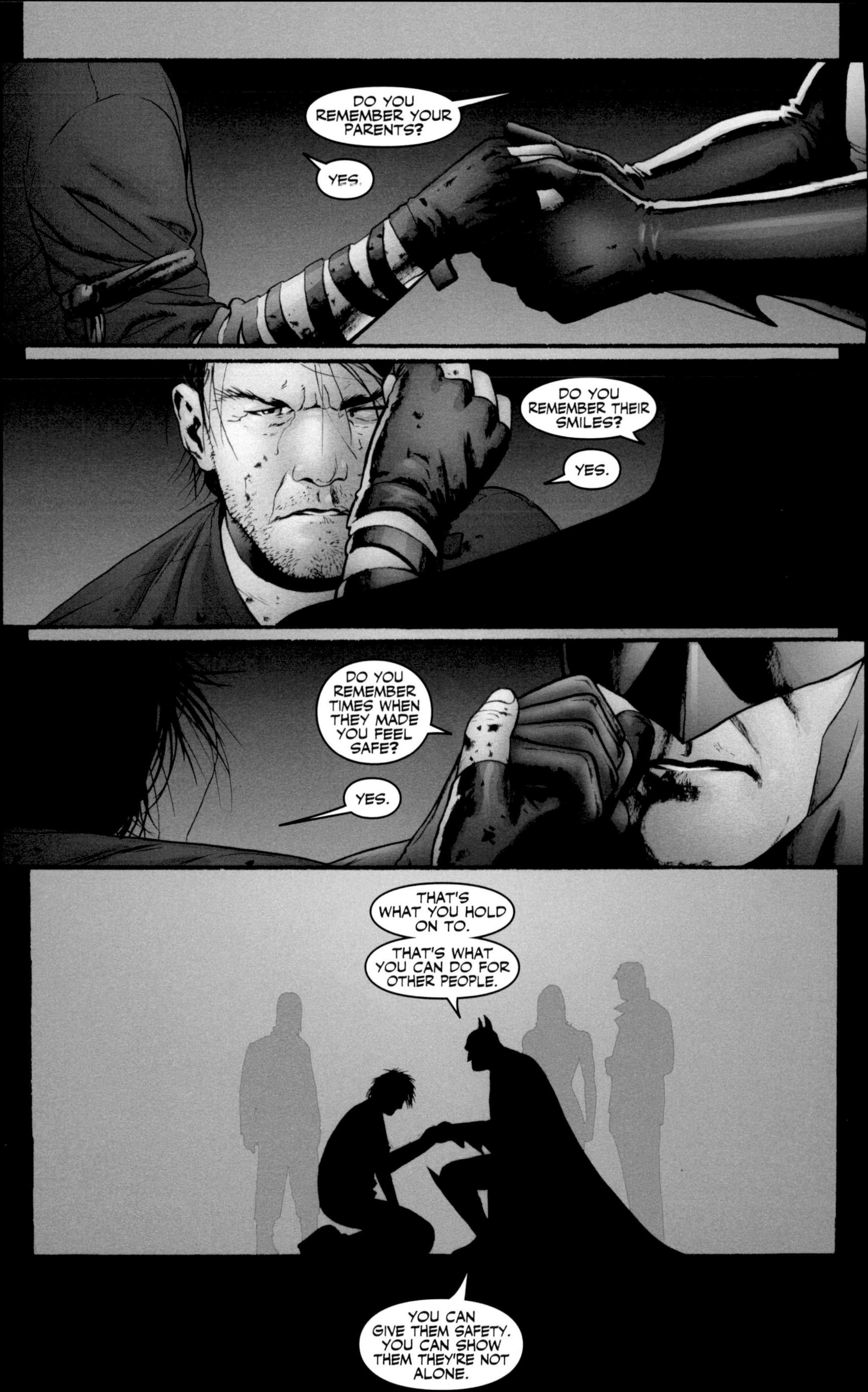
DO YOU REMEMBER YOUR PARENTS?
YES.
DO YOU REMEMBER THEIR SMILES?
YES.
DO YOU REMEMBER TIMES WHEN THEY MADE YOU FEEL SAFE?
YES.
THAT'S WHAT YOU HOLD ON TO.
THAT'S WHAT YOU CAN DO FOR OTHER PEOPLE.
YOU CAN GIVE THEM SAFETY. YOU CAN SHOW THEM THEY'RE NOT ALONE.

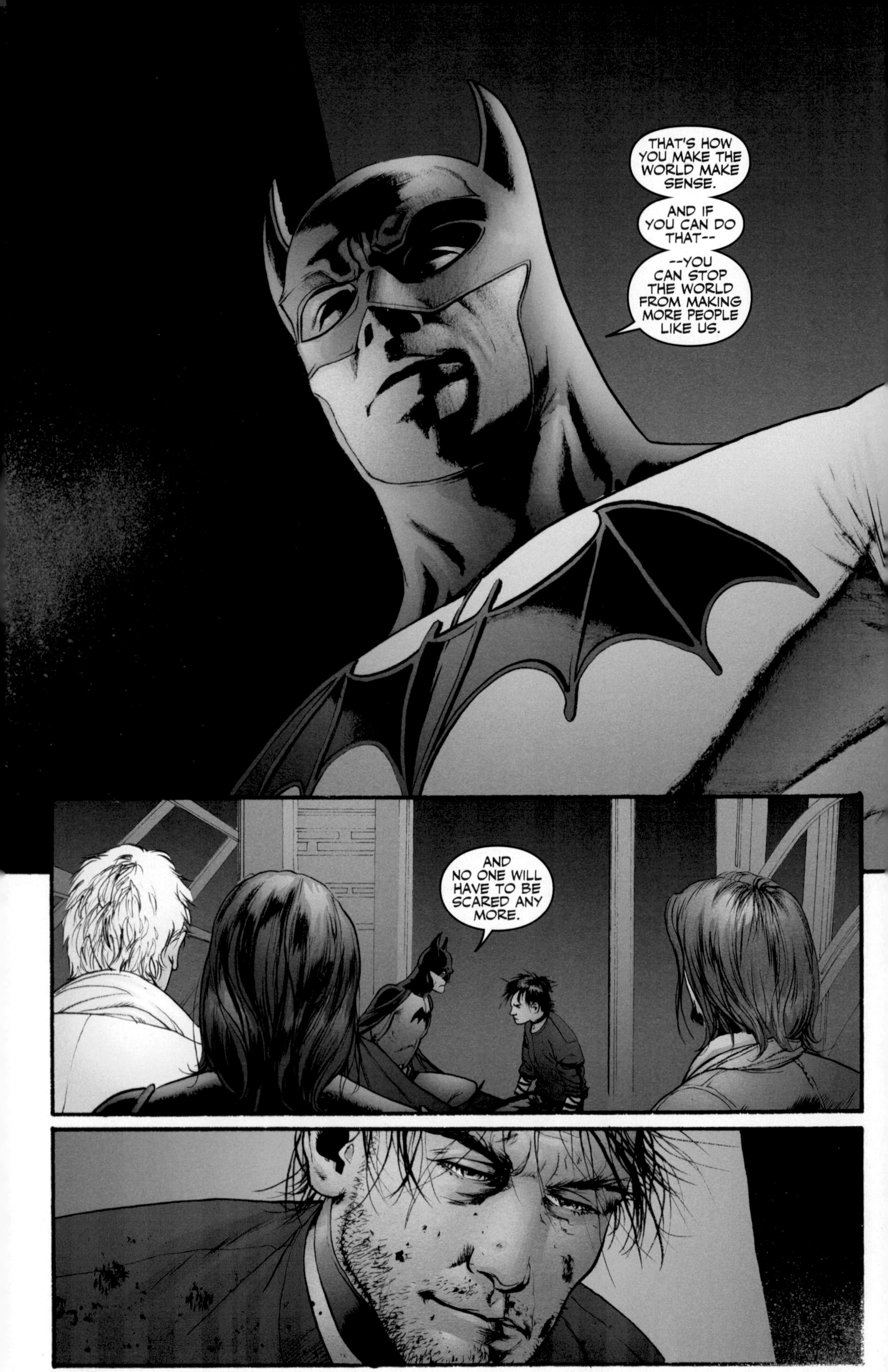
THAT'S HOW YOU MAKE THE WORLD MAKE SENSE.
AND IF YOU CAN DO THAT--
--YOU CAN STOP THE WORLD FROM MAKING MORE PEOPLE LIKE US.
AND NO ONE WILL HAVE TO BE SCARED ANY MORE.

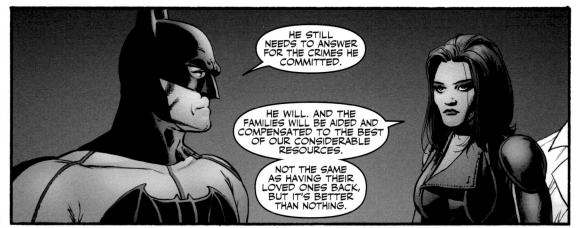

HE STILL NEEDS TO ANSWER FOR THE CRIMES HE COMMITTED.

HE WILL. AND THE FAMILIES WILL BE AIDED AND COMPENSATED TO THE BEST OF OUR CONSIDERABLE RESOURCES.

NOT THE SAME AS HAVING THEIR LOVED ONES BACK, BUT IT'S BETTER THAN NOTHING.

WE'RE ROTATING BACK. HE'S RELAXED.

I'M TRUSTING YOU TO DO THE RIGHT THING.

I DON'T CARE IF YOU'RE FROM MY "REALITY" OR NOT--THIS IS STILL MY CITY.

AND I'LL FIND YOU IF I HAVE TO.

I TOTALLY BEAT YOU UP, YOU KNOW.

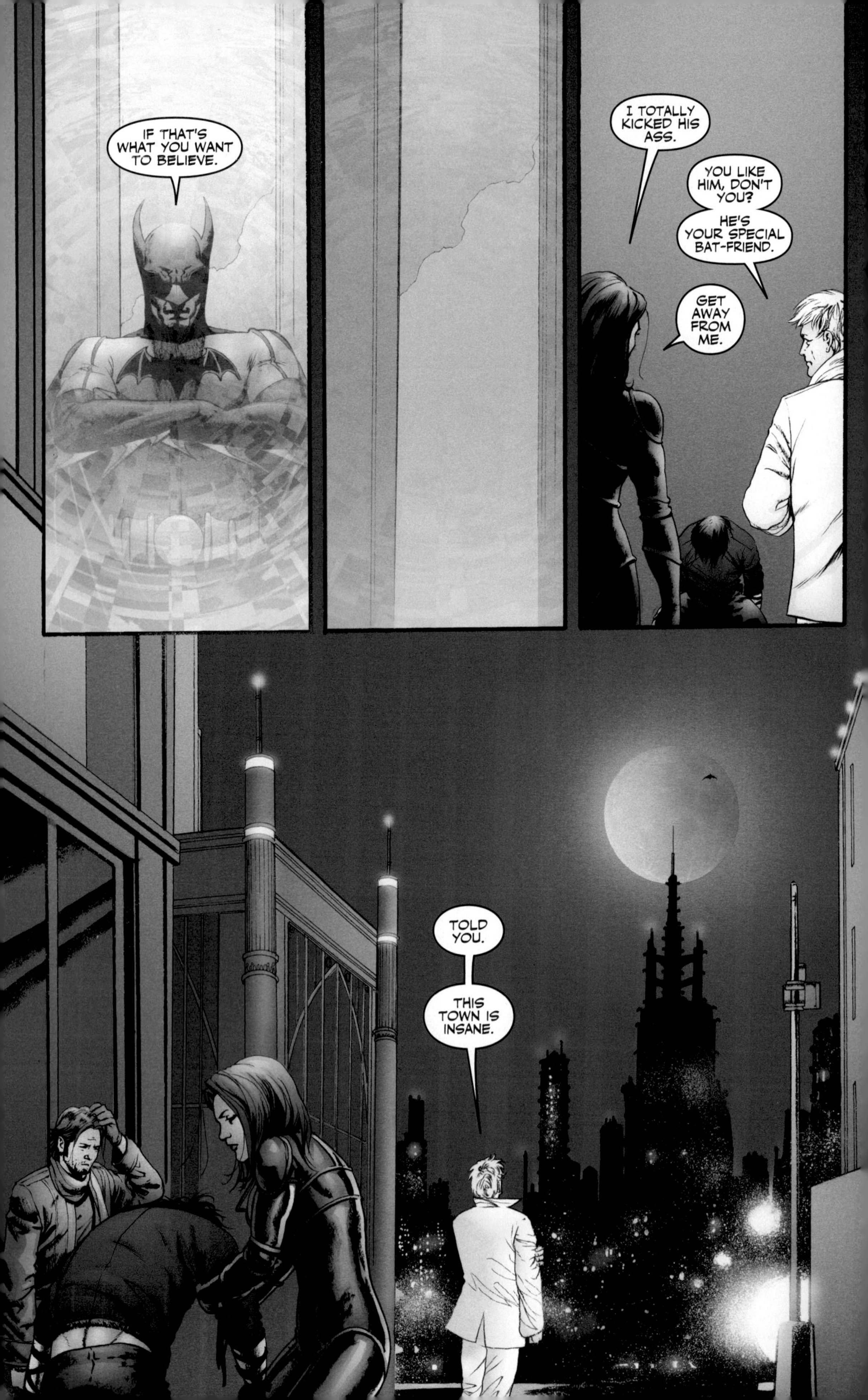
IF THAT'S WHAT YOU WANT TO BELIEVE.
I TOTALLY KICKED HIS ASS.
YOU LIKE HIM, DON'T YOU?
HE'S YOUR SPECIAL BAT-FRIEND.
GET AWAY FROM ME.
TOLD YOU.
THIS TOWN IS INSANE.

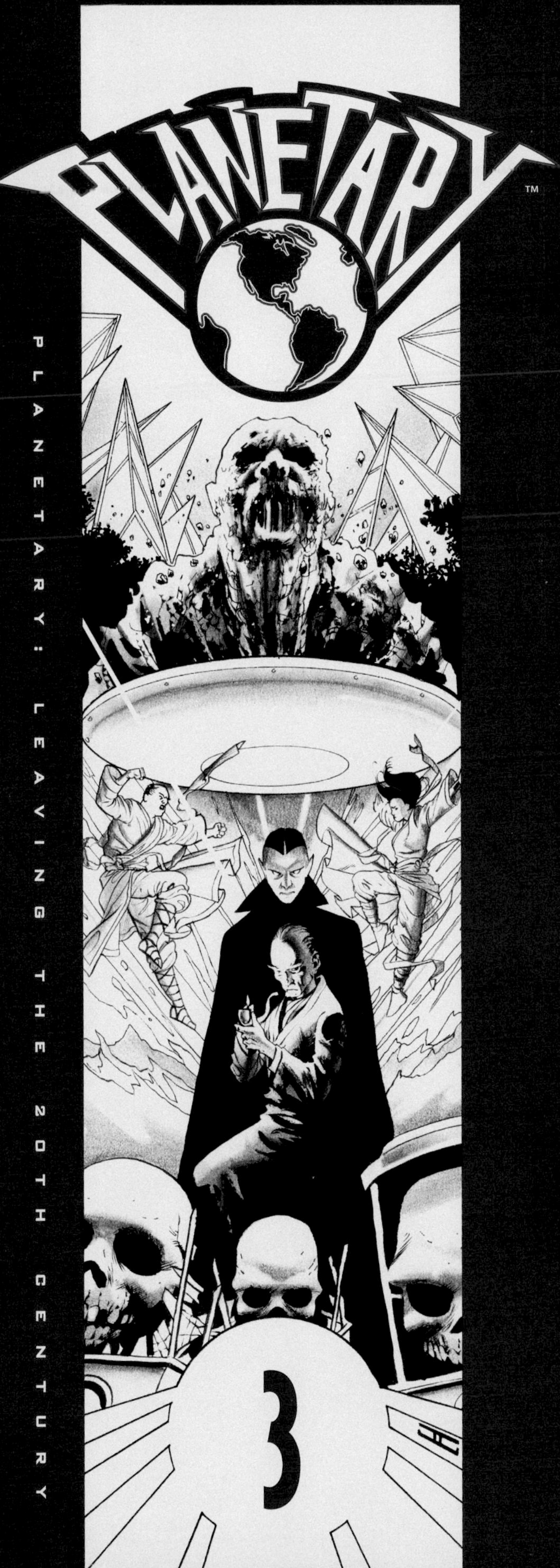
PLANETARY
3

PLANETARY: LEAVING THE 20TH CENTURY

PLANETARY VOL. 3: LEAVING THE 20TH CENTURY cover
By JOHN CASSADAY and LAURA MARTIN

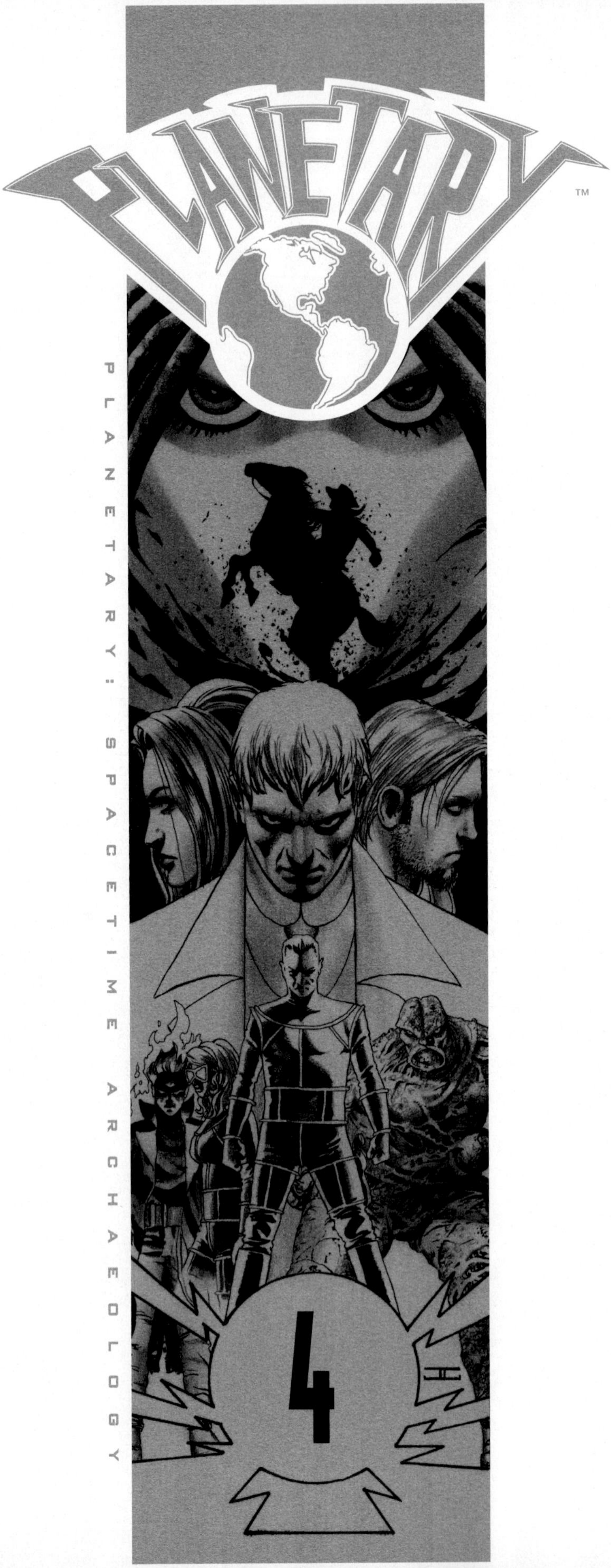
PLANETARY
PLANETARY: SPACETIME ARCHAEOLOGY
4

PLANETARY VOL. 4: SPACETIME ARCHAEOLOGY cover
By JOHN CASSADAY and LAURA MARTIN

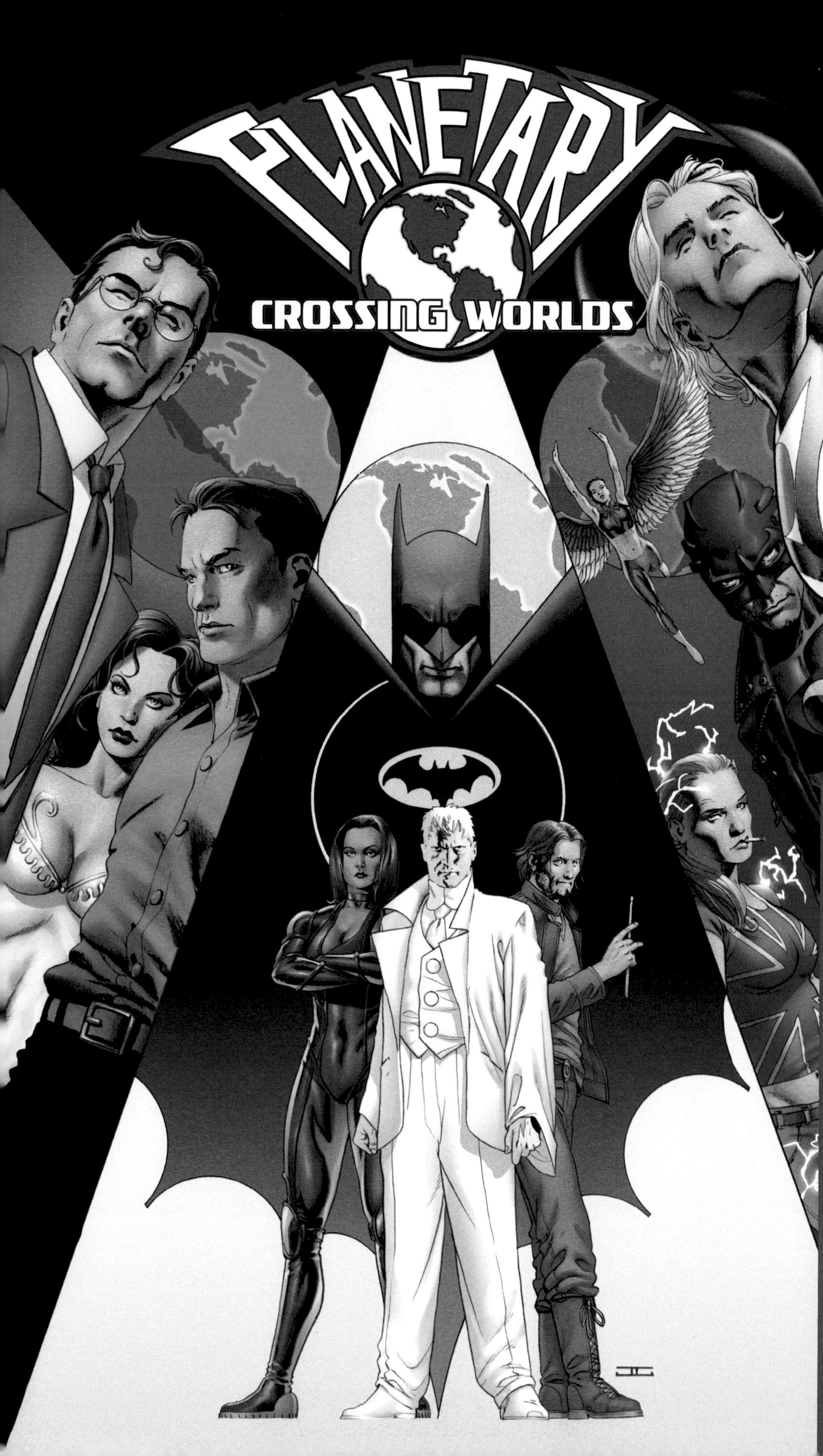
PLANETARY
CROSSING WORLDS

PLANETARY: CROSSING WORLDS cover
By JOHN CASSADAY and LAURA MARTIN

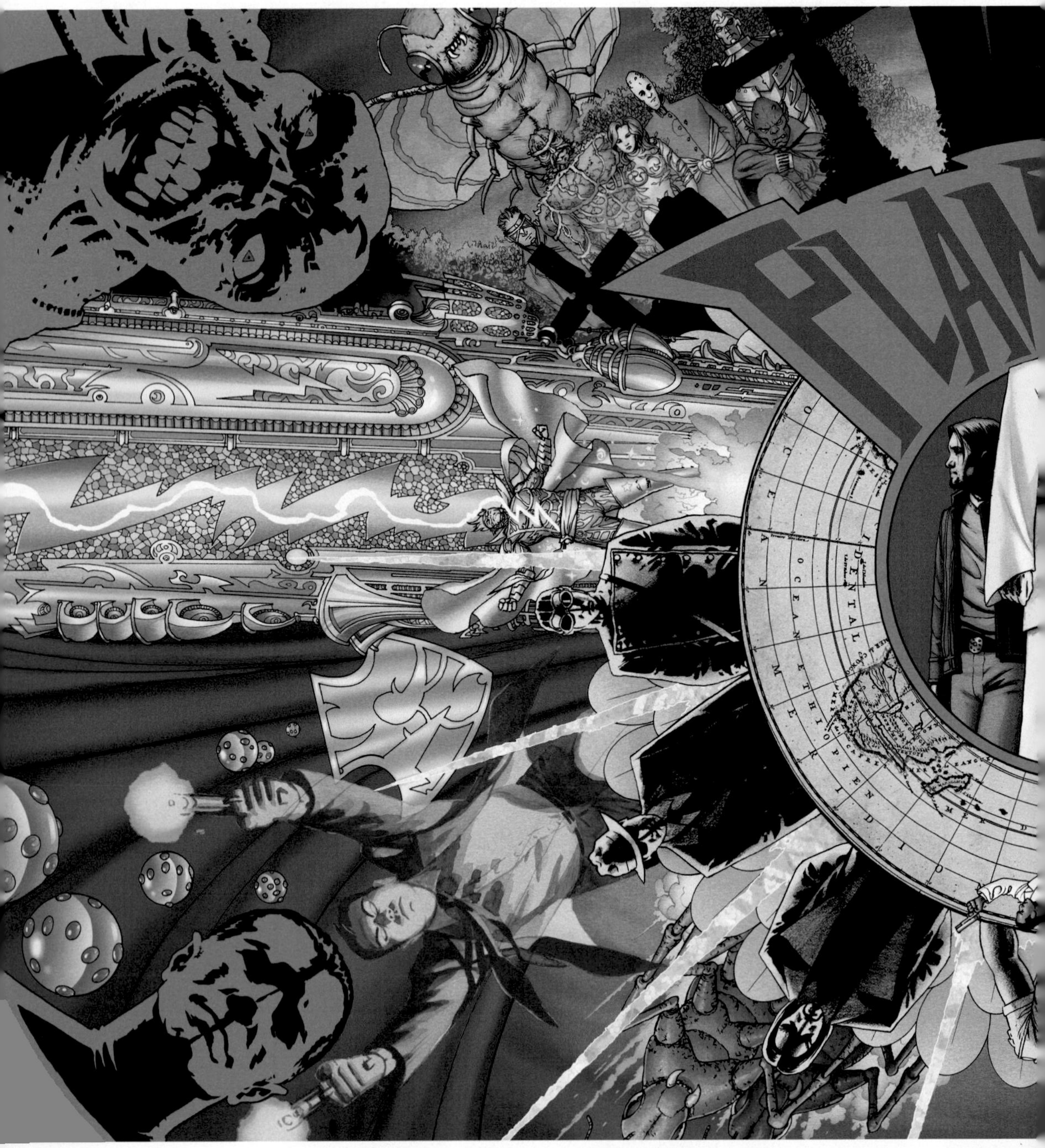

PLANETARY #27 cover
By JOHN CASSADAY and LAURA MARTIN

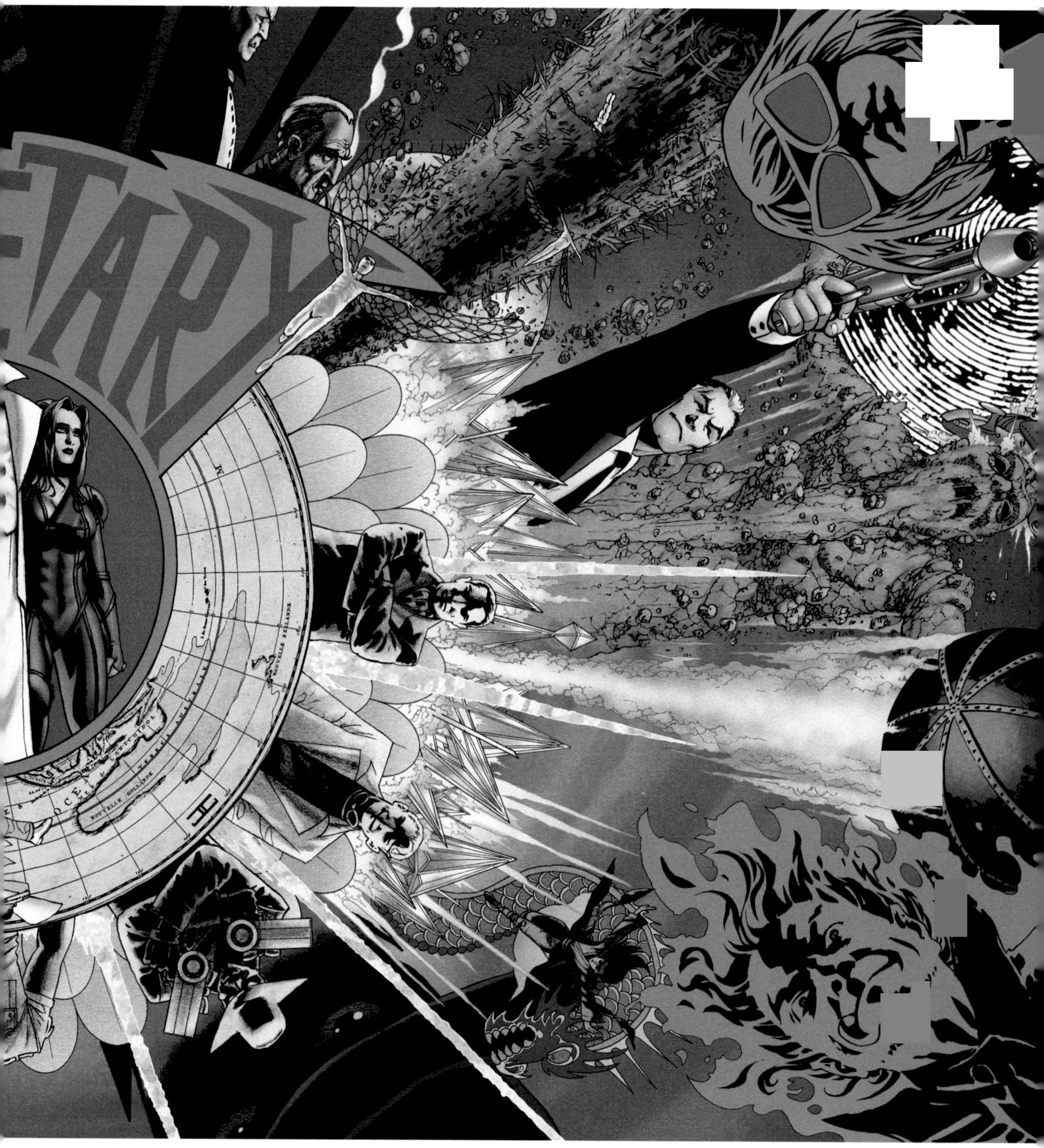

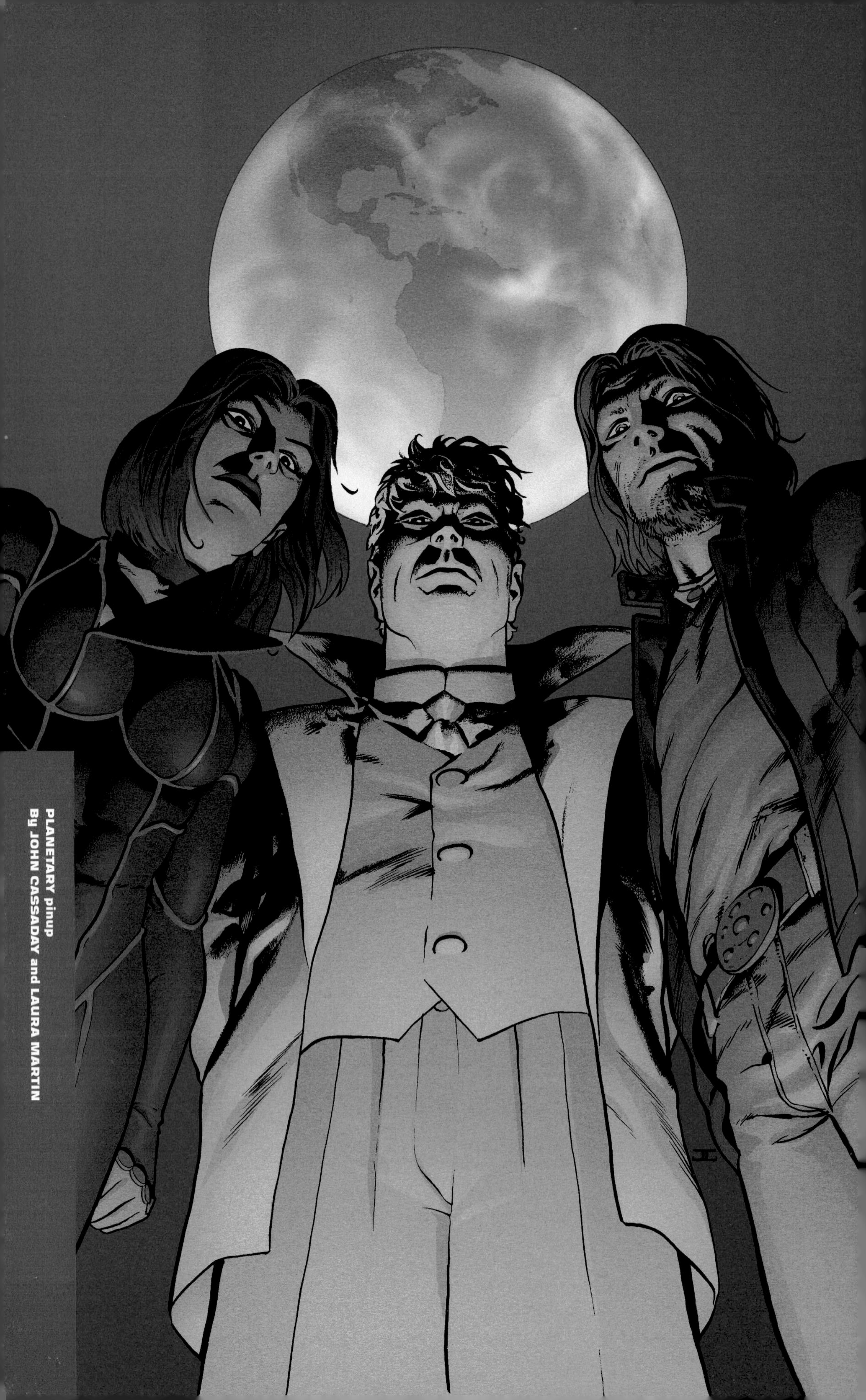

PLANETARY pinup
By JOHN CASSADAY and LAURA MARTIN

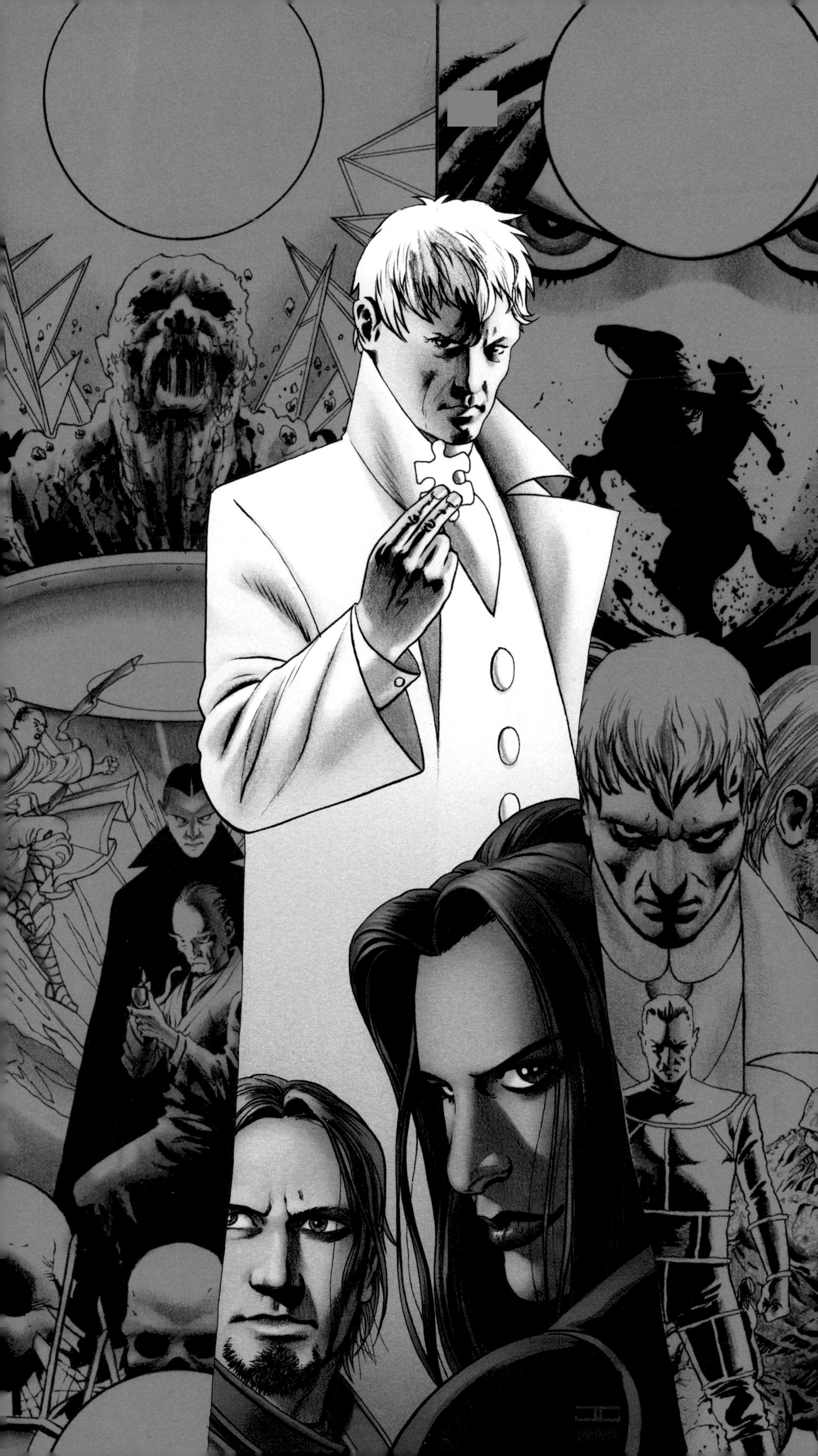

ABSOLUTE PLANETARY VOL. 2 cover
By JOHN CASSADAY and LAURA MARTIN

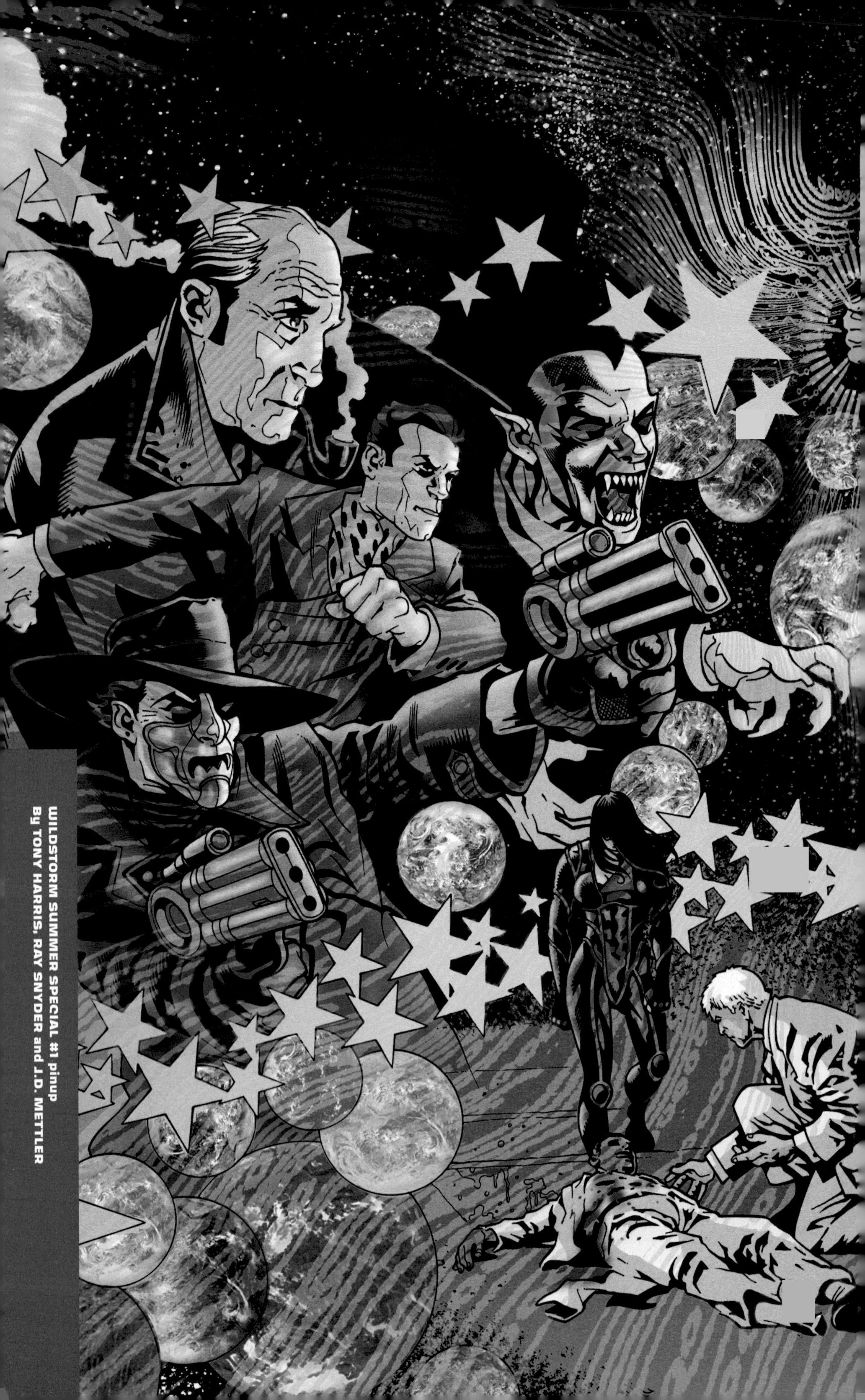

WILDSTORM SUMMER SPECIAL #1 pinup
By TONY HARRIS, RAY SNYDER and J.D. METTLER

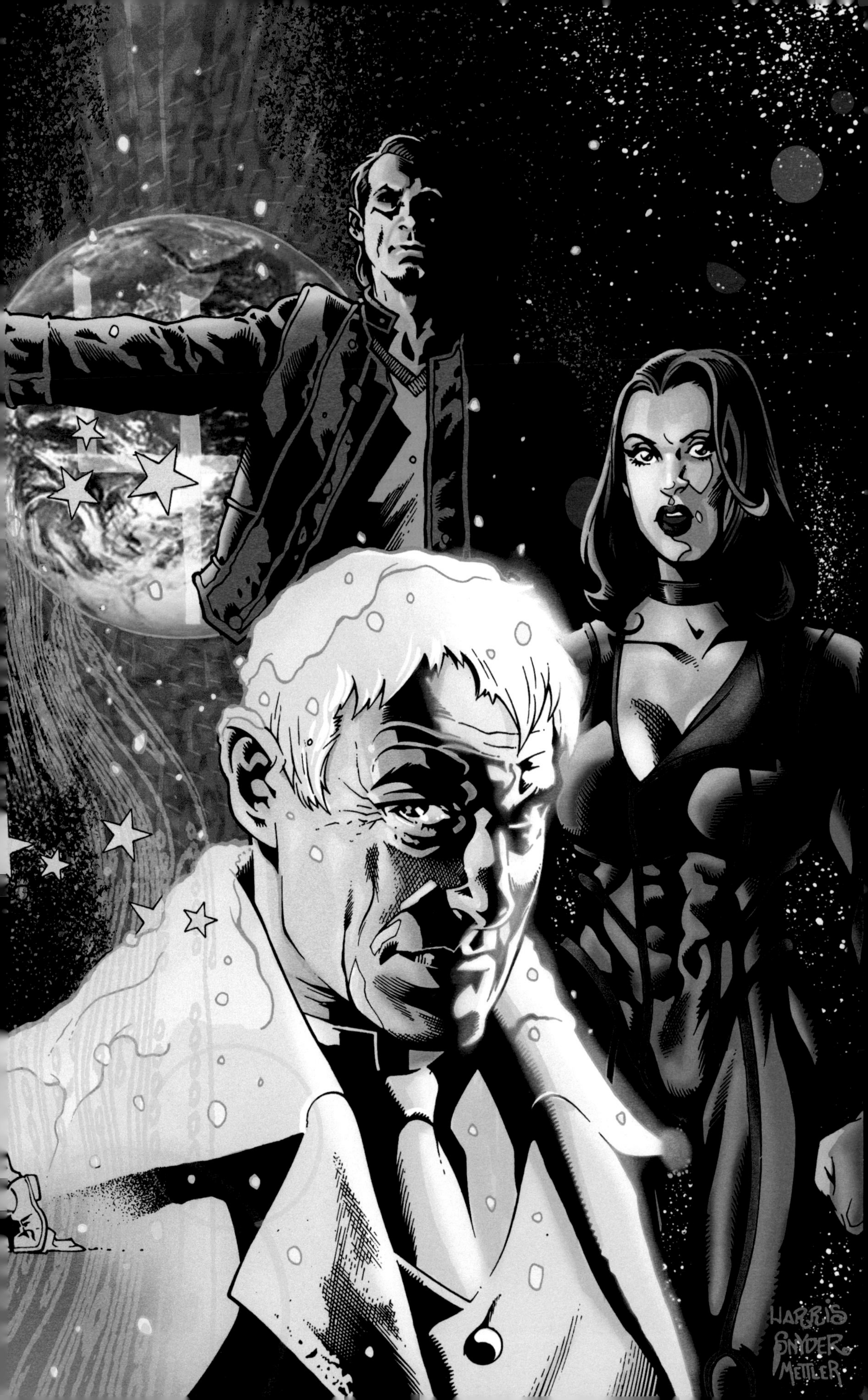
HARRIS
SNYDER
METTLER

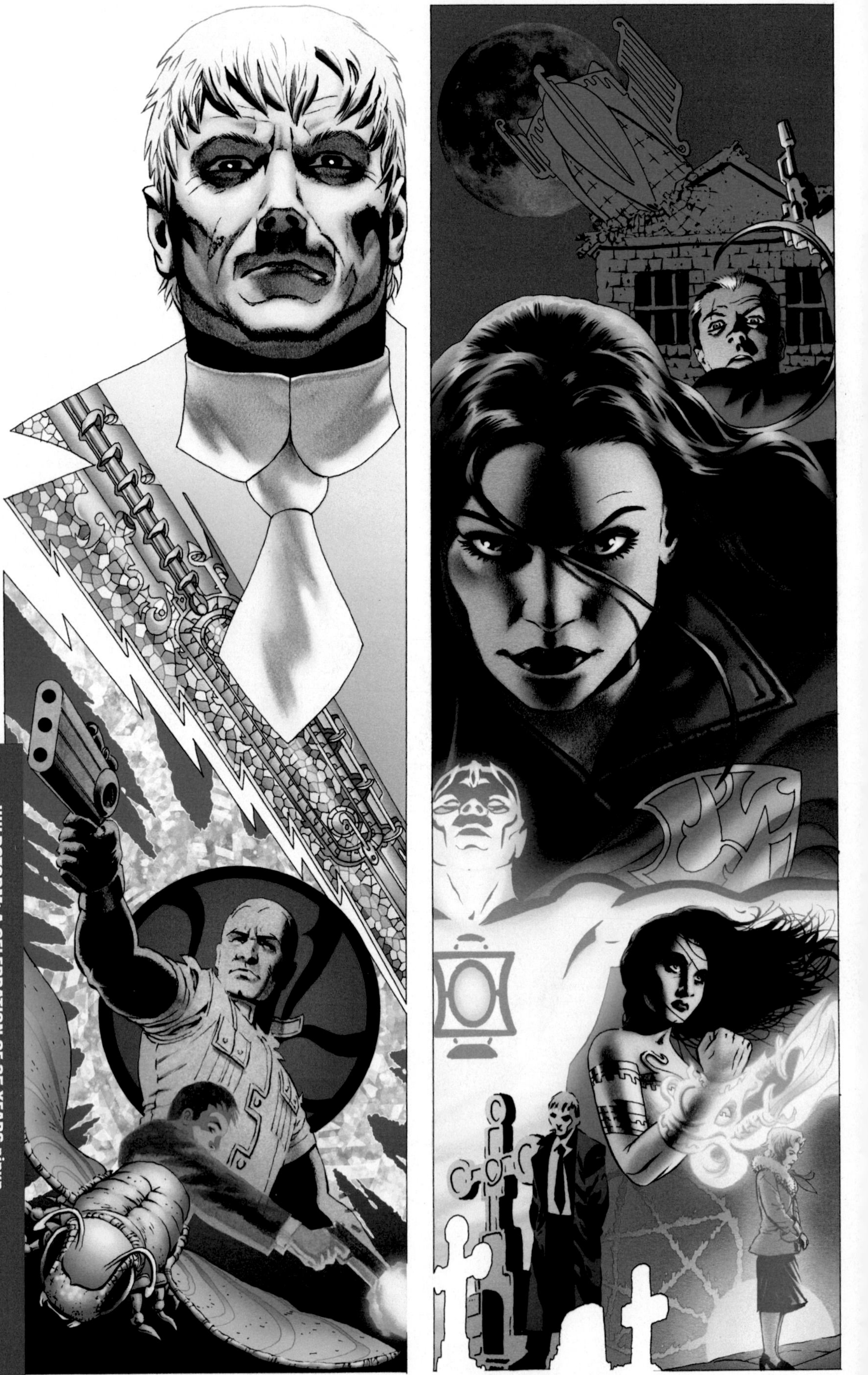

WILDSTORM: A CELEBRATION OF 25 YEARS pinup
By JOHN CASSADAY and LAURA MARTIN

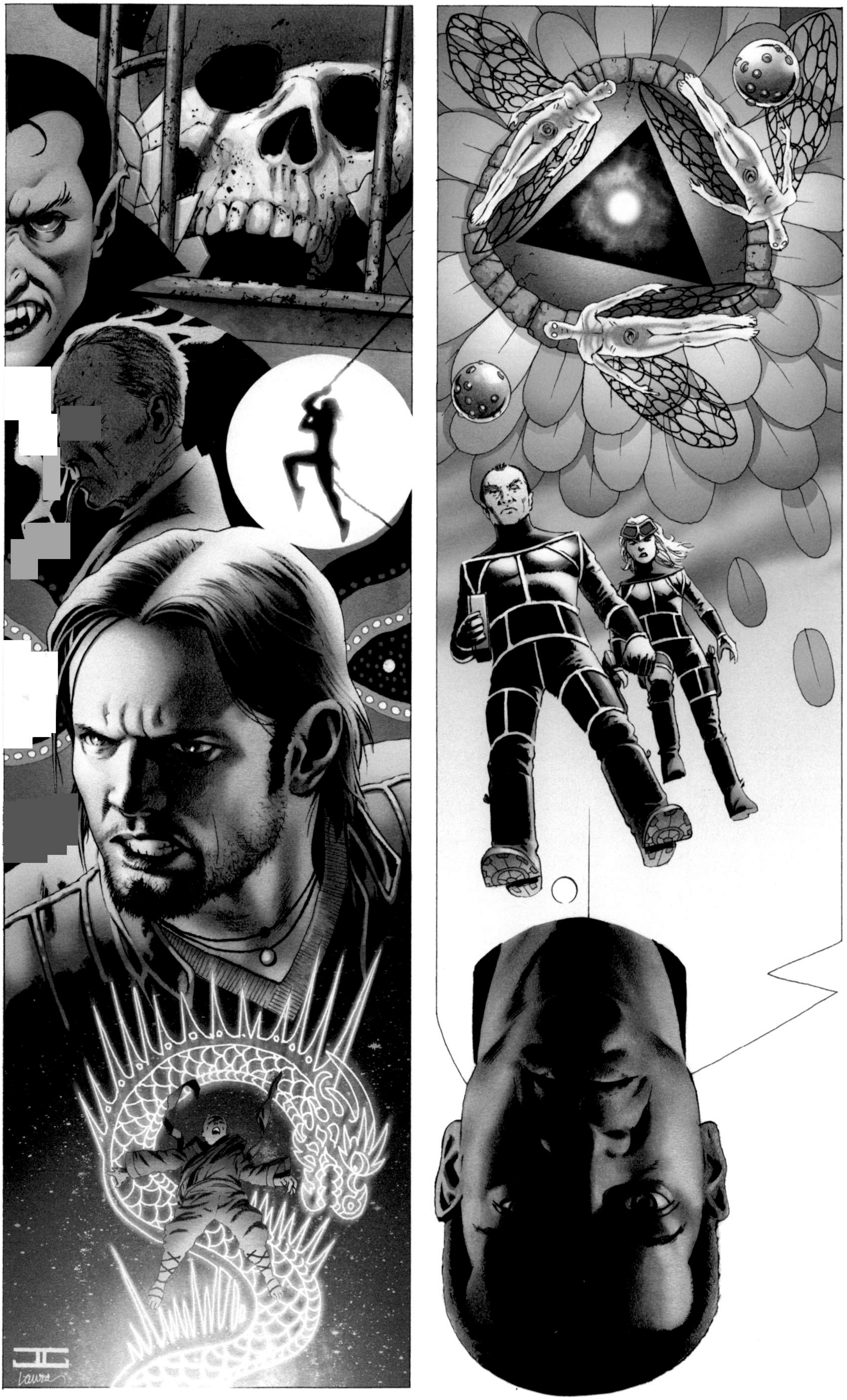

Biographies

WARREN ELLIS

Warren Ellis is the *New York Times* best-selling author of *Gun Machine* and *Normal*, and the award-winning graphic novelist of TRANSMETROPOLITAN, PLANETARY, *Injection*, and RED, which was adapted for a film starring Bruce Willis and Helen Mirren. He is the writer of the Netflix series *Castlevania*, and he has previously been a columnist for *Wired*, *Vice* and Reuters. A documentary about his work, *Captured Ghosts*, was released in 2012.

Recognitions include the NUIG Literary and Debating Society's President's Medal for service to freedom of speech, the Eagle Awards Roll of Honour for lifetime achievement in the field of comics and graphic novels, the Grand Prix de l'Imaginaire 2010, the Sidewise Award for Alternate History and the International Horror Guild Award for illustrated narrative. He is a Patron of the British Humanist Association, the literary editor of *Edict* magazine and a Visiting Professor at York St John University. He lives in south-east England.

JOHN CASSADAY

Born in Fort Worth, Texas, John Cassaday has called New York City home since 1997, the same year he broke into the comics and entertainment industry. In 1999 John co-created the highly acclaimed DC/Wildstorm series PLANETARY with Warren Ellis and in 2002 re-launched *Captain America* for Marvel Comics. Cassaday then collaborated with Joss Whedon (writer/director of *The Avengers*) on Marvel's best-selling A*stonishing X-Men*. John's work on PLANETARY and *Astonishing X-Men* garnered him an unprecedented three consecutive Eisner Awards for Best Artist. Cassaday's work has been exhibited in Hong Kong, New York City and the Smithsonian Institution in Washington, D.C. Aside from his comics projects, John has created designs for Ringling Bros. and Barnum & Bailey Circus, Levi's blue jeans and the film *Watchmen*. John made his directorial debut on Joss Whedon's FOX television series, *Dollhouse*. He is a member of the Society of Illustrators and the Director's Guild of America.